L8
LS 11/15
15 11/29
11 12/13

Regional Integration and the Global Trading System

Regional Integration and the Global Trading System

Edited by
Kym Anderson and Richard Blackhurst

St. Martin's Press   New York

First published in the United States of America in 1993

Printed in Great Britain

ISBN 0-312-10065-5

Library of Congress Cataloging-in-Publication Data applied for

Contents

Figures

Part 1

Part 2

Tables

Part 5

Appendix

Contributors

Kym Anderson is Professor of Economics and Foundation Director of the Centre for International Economic Studies at the University of Adelaide in Australia, and a Research Fellow of the London-based Centre for Economic Policy Research. At the time this volume was produced he was on extended leave at the Economic Research and Analysis Division of the GATT Secretariat in Geneva. He has written extensively in the areas of agricultural, development, environmental and international economics. Recent books include *The Political Economy of Agricultural Protection* with Yujiro Hayami, *Changing Comparative Advantages in China*, and *Disarray in World Food Markets* with Rod Tyers, plus edited volumes on *New Silk Roads: East Asia and World Textile Markets* and, with Richard Blackhurst, *The Greening of World Trade Issues*.

V. N. Balasubramanyam is Professor of Economics at the Management School of Lancaster University in England. He has written numerous articles on foreign direct investment and on the international transfer of technology. He is also the author of *International Transfer of Technology to India*, of *The Multinational Enterprise and the Third World* and of *The Economy of India*.

Robert E. Baldwin is Hilldale Professor of Economics at the University of Wisconsin-Madison in the United States and Director of the US Trade Relations Project of the National Bureau of Economic Research. He has written very extensively in leading journals on trade policy and economic development. Among his books are *Nontariff Distortions of International Trade*, *Foreign Trade Regimes and*

Economic Development: The Philippines and *The Political Economy of US Import Policy*, and he has a collection of his essays entitled *Trade Policy in a Changing World Economy*. He also has edited numerous books and has been on the editorial boards of several journals, including the *American Economic Review*, *Journal of International Economics* and *Review of Economics and Statistics*.

Richard Blackhurst is Director of Economic Research and Analysis at the GATT Secretariat and Professeur Associé at the Graduate Institute of International Studies in Geneva. His research interests embrace numerous aspects of trade policy in a growing and interdependent world. Among his publications are several GATT Studies in International Trade including *Trade Liberalization, Protectionism and Interdependence* and *Adjustment, Trade and Growth in Developed and Developing Countries*, both with Nicolas Marian and Jan Tumlir. He also is co-editor with Kym Anderson of the recent volume on *The Greening of World Trade Issues*.

Alice Enders is with the Economic Research and Analysis Division of the GATT Secretariat in Geneva. Her research interests include strategic aspects of international trade policy, an area in which she has published in journals, as well as the economics of problems posed by international cooperation.

Karl-Michael Finger is with the Economic Research and Analysis Division of the GATT Secretariat in Geneva. His principal research interests are in the compilation and analysis of trade and other international economic data, particularly for the GATT Secretariat's annual report, *International Trade*.

Hans Genberg is Professor of Economics at the Graduate Institute of International Studies and Director of Macroeconomic, Monetary and Banking Programs at the International Center for Monetary and Banking Studies in Geneva. He is the author of numerous articles in academic journals and conference proceedings volumes dealing with international monetary economics and macroeconomics.

David Greenaway is Professor of Economics, Foundation Director of the Centre for Research on Economic Development and International Trade, and Dean of the Faculty of Law and Social Sciences at the University of Nottingham in England. His research interests cover a wide area of international and development economics. He has authored or edited numerous books, including The *Economics of*

Intra-Industry Trade, Imperfect Competition and International Trade and *Economic Aspects of Regional Trading Arrangements*. He is presently an Associate Editor of the *Economic Journal* and Joint Managing Editor (with John Whalley) of *The World Economy*.

David Henderson was until recently Head of the Economics and Statistics Department of the OECD Secretariat. His earlier career was spent mainly as an academic (at the universities of Oxford and London), as a national civil servant in Britain (first in the Treasury, later in the Ministry of Aviation) and as an international civil servant at the World Bank. Among his many writings is his book *Innocence and Design: The Influence of Economic Ideas on Policy*.

Brian Hindley is Senior Lecturer in Economics at the London School of Economics in England. His primary research interest is in the economic analysis of the impact of national and international laws relating to international trade. He has published widely in the field of trade policy and is a consultant to several international organizations.

Bernard Hoekman is with the Economic Research and Analysis Division of the GATT Secretariat in Geneva and a Research Fellow of the London-based Centre for Economic Policy Research. His areas of research interest include the theory and practice of commercial policy, the economics of multilateral trade negotiations, and issues relating to international transactions in services. He has contributed numerous articles to conference volumes and academic journals in these and related areas.

Michael Leidy was with the Economic Research and Analysis Division of the GATT Secretariat in Geneva when he contributed to this volume, and has since moved to the Trade Policy Division of the International Monetary Fund in Washington, D.C. His research has focused on, among other things, the political economy of trade policy and firm behavior under alternative commercial policies. He has published in numerous books and academic journals on these topics.

John McMillan is Professor of Economics in the Graduate School of International Relations and Pacific Studies at the University of California, San Diego. A New Zealander, he has authored numerous journal articles on game theory, applied microeconomics and international trade. His recent books are *Incentives in Government Contracting, Game Theory in International Economics* and *Games, Strategies, and Managers*.

Edward D. Mansfield is an Assistant Professor of Political Science at Columbia University in New York. His primary research interests are international political economy and the causes of international conflict. He has published journal articles in *International Organisation, International Studies Quarterly, The Journal of Conflict Resolution* and *World Politics.*

Patrick A. Messerlin is Professor of Economics at the Institut d'Etudes Politiques de Paris in France and Director of the Research Unit on Factor Movements and International Trade at the Centre National de la Recherche Scientifique. His writings center on the theory and practice of commercial policy (in goods and services) and on competition and industrial policies. He has published papers on these topics in various books, academic journals and trade journals.

Francisco de Asis Nadal De Simone was with the Economic Research and Analysis Division of the GATT Secretariat when he contributed to this volume, and has since moved to the Department of Economics and Statistics at the National University of Singapore. His areas of research interest include monetary theory and exchange rate and interest rate determination. His recent publications in academic journals are in the field of currency area formation and the transformation of former socialist economies.

Hege Norheim was a graduate student intern in the Economic Research and Analysis Division of the GATT Secretariat when she contributed to this volume, on leave from her doctoral studies at the Norwegian School of Economics in Bergen. She is now with the PA Consulting Group in Oslo. In addition to regional economic integration, her research interests include trade and environment issues.

David Palmeter is a practicing attorney in Washington, D.C., and a partner in the law firm of Mudge Rose Guthrie Alexander and Ferdon. He also is Chairman of the Trade and Customs Law Subcommittee of the International Bar Association. He has published extensively in academic journals and conference proceedings volumes on international trade law and policy topics, particularly on anti-dumping, subsidies and countervailing duties, and rules of origin.

Frieder Roessler is Director of the Legal Affairs Division of the GATT Secretariat in Geneva. He worked for the World Bank before joining the GATT. He has taught international economic law and the law of the European Communities at various universities, presently as

Professeur Associé at the Jean Moulin University in Lyon, France. He has published numerous articles in the field of international economic law.

Murray Smith is Director of the Centre for Trade Policy and Law which is associated with both Carleton University and the University of Ottawa in Canada. Previously he was Director of the International Economics Program of the Institute for Research on Public Policy (1987–90) and before that was with the C. D. Howe Institute. During the Tokyo Round he was Director of International Economic Relations in the provincial government of British Columbia. He currently serves on the roster of panelists for disputes under Chapter 18 of the Canada–US Free Trade Agreement. He is author or co-author of several books and numerous articles on international economic issues.

Richard H. Snape is Professor of Economics in the Department of Economics at Monash University in Melbourne, Australia. He has written extensively on a wide variety of trade policy topics. As well as being author of *International Trade and the Australian Economy*, he has edited a volume of *Studies in International Economics* (with Ian McDougall) and *Issues in World Trade Policy*, and has spent periods as editor of *The World Bank Economic Review*, *The World Bank Research Observer* and (with Peter Lloyd) *The Economic Record*. Recently he has completed two reports for the Australian government on regional trade agreements, their implications and options for Australia.

T. N. Srinivasan is Professor of Economics at Yale University in New Haven in the United States. He is author of a large number of journal articles on many subjects in the areas of international trade and economic development. Among his books are *Lectures on International Trade* (with Jagdish Bhagwati) and a volume edited with John Whalley on *General Equilibrium Trade Policy Modelling*.

John Whalley is Professor of Economics and Foundation Director of the Centre for the Study of International Economic Relations at the University of Western Ontario in London, Canada. In addition to many journal articles on trade policy and general equilibrium analysis he has published numerous books including *Trade Liberalization Among Major World Trading Areas* and a volume edited with T. N. Srinivasan on *General Equilibrium Trade Policy Modelling*. He has recently coordinated a Ford Foundation project on Developing Countries and the Uruguay Round, and taken on the task of Joint Managing Editor (with David Greenaway) of the trade policy journal *The World Economy*.

L. Alan Winters is Professor and Head of the Department of Economics at the University of Birmingham in England and Co-Director (with Richard Baldwin) of the International Trade Programme of the London-based Centre for Economic Policy Research (CEPR). He has published widely in applied areas of econometrics and trade policy, is author of the textbook *International Economics*, and has edited a number of conference proceedings volumes for the CEPR, including *European Integration, Primary Commodity Prices, Open Economies, New Issues in the Uruguay Round* and *Trade Flows and Trade Policy After '1992'*. He is also an Associate Editor of *The Economic Journal*.

Ian Wooton is Associate Professor of Economics and Deputy Director of the Centre for the Study of International Economic Relations at the University of Western Ontario in London, Canada. His research interests lie in the area of international trade theory and policy. He has published extensively in journals, particularly on customs union theory, international factor migration and economic integration.

Soogil Young is a Senior Fellow and Director of the Trade and Industry Department of the Korea Development Institute in Seoul, South Korea. He has written many articles and reports on Korea's development strategy, on industrial and trade policy issues and on external cooperation, including *The Role of Industrial Policy and the Reform of Korea's Industrial Incentives* and *Korea's Trade Policy Problems and the Uruguay Round*.

Abbreviations

ACP	African, Caribbean and Pacific developing countries that are signatories with the EC to the Lomé Convention, initially signed in 1975 and revised in 1979, 1984 and 1989
AD	Anti-dumping (duty)
AFTA	ASEAN Free Trade Agreement
ANIEs	Asian newly industrialized economies
ANZCERTA	See CER below
APEC	Asian-Pacific Economic Cooperation, a forum involving North American, East Asian and Australian economies, with a small secretariat in Singapore since late 1992
ASEAN	Association of South East Asian Nations, formed in 1967
CACM	Central American Common Market, formed in 1961
CAP	Common Agricultural Policy of the EC, introduced in 1962
CARICOM	Caribbean Community, a customs union formed in 1973
CCC	Customs Cooperation Council of the United States
CER	Closer Economic Relations trade agreement of 1983 (and broadened in 1988) between Australia and New Zealand – also known as ANZCERTA
CET	Common external tariff of a customs union (introduced by the EEC in 1968)
CHP	Czechoslovakia, Hungary and Poland
CIS	Commonwealth of Independent States
CIT	Court of International Trade of the US
CITT	Canadian International Trade Tribunal

CM	Common market
CMEA	Council for Mutual Economic Assistance, formed among communist countries and disbanded in 1991 (usually referred to in the West as Comecon)
Comecon	See CMEA
CRS	Constant returns to scale
CTH	Change in tariff heading (a rule of origin for a FTA)
CU	Customs union
CUSFTA	Canada–United States Free Trade Agreement of 1988
CVD	Counterveiling duty
DEA	Developing East Asia
DSP	Dispute-settlement procedures
EACM	East African Common Market
ECSC	European Coal and Steel Community, as embodied in the 1951 Paris Treaty
EEA	European Economic Area agreement of 1991 between the EC and EFTA
EEC	European Economic Community, as embodied in the 1957 Treaty of Rome and the 1986 Single European Act and involving six countries until 1972, nine until 1981, ten until 1986 and twelve since then
EC	European Communities, involving not only the EEC but also the ECSC and the European Atomic Energy Community; EC also refers to the member states as a group
EFTA	European Free Trade Association (of non-EC countries of Western Europe), created in 1960 and modified in 1972
EMS	European Monetary System, operating within the EEC since 1979
EMU	Economic and monetary union, as envisaged for the EC at Maastricht in 1992
EU	Economic union (the EC's draft Treaty on Economic Union was signed at Maastricht in 1992)
FDI	Foreign direct investment
FTA	Free trade area (or agreement)
GATS	General Agreement on Trade in Services as proposed in the 1991 Draft Final Act of the Uruguay Round and subsequently revised
GATT	General Agreement on Tariffs and Trade
GDP	Gross domestic product
GNP	Gross National product
GSP	Generalized system of trade preferences for developing countries

IMF	International Monetary Fund
IRS	Increasing returns to scale
ISIC	International Standard Industrial Classification
ITO	International Trade Organization, as proposed in 1947 but not created; instead an Interim Committee of the ITO was formed (ICITO), which is another name for the GATT Secretariat
LAFTA	Latin American Free Trade Association, formed in 1960 and replaced by LAIA in 1980
LAIA	Latin American Integration Association, formed in 1980 from LAFTA
Mercosur	The 1991 agreement between Argentina, Brazil, Paraguay and Uruguay to form a Common Market by 1995–6
MFA	Multifiber Arrangement
MFN	Most-favored-nation
MNE	Multinational enterprise
MTN	Multilateral trade negotiations
MTO	Multilateral Trade Organization, as proposed in the December 1991 Draft Final Act of the Uruguay Round and subsequently revised
NAFTA	North American Free Trade Agreement, initialed in October 1992
NATO	North Atlantic Treaty Organisation
NIEs	Newly industrializing economies of East Asia
NTBs	Non-tariff barriers to imports
NTMs	Non-tariff measures distorting trade (including NTBs)
OECD	Organisation for Economic Co-operation and Development
OEEC	Organisation for European Economic Co-operation
OPEC	Organisation of Petroleum Exporting Countries
PTA	Preferential trade agreement (or area or arrangement)
QRs	Quantitative restrictions on trade
RIA	Regional integration agreement
ROW	Rest of World
SEA	Single European Act of the EC, approved in 1986 and enacted in 1987 (the launch of the EC's '1992' initiative)
SEM	Single European Market (resulting from the SEA's implementation)
TRIMS	Trade-related investment measures
TRQ	Tariff rate quota
UK	United Kingdom of Great Britain and Northern Ireland
UN	United Nations

UNCTAD	United Nations Conference on Trade and Development
US	United States of America
USITC	United States International Trade Commission
VER	Voluntary export restraint

Foreword

Stimulated by the European Communities' Single Market Programme, the draft North American Free Trade Agreement and initiatives in Latin America, Asia and the Pacific, regional integration agreements and their implications for the global trading system have figured prominently in recent trade policy discussions. Some commentators see regionalism and multilateralism as competing alternatives, and argue that the future of the GATT is in the balance if the number of regional groupings continues to increase. Others counter that not only is there no inherent contradiction between regionalism and multilateralism, but that they have been – and will continue to be – mutually reinforcing in a liberalizing direction.

The provisions of the GATT lend more weight to the latter view. In Article XXIV the drafters of the General Agreement recognized the desirability of allowing countries to increase the freedom of their mutual trade through customs unions and free-trade areas, subject to certain conditions, including the requirement that barriers to trade with non-members are not raised. Furthermore, the history of postwar trade liberalization under the GATT suggests that regional and multilateral initiatives have indeed tended to reinforce each other. The results of GATT rounds have often been taken over into regional agreements, just as regional liberalization measures have subsequently been generalized at the multilateral level.

It is worth considering, however, whether we can be confident that regional integration agreements and the GATT will continue to interact beneficially in the future. Both the growing relevance of GATT's rules to conditions of competition in global markets, and GATT's expanding membership, point to the continued strength of the multilateral system. But questions have been raised about the ability of GATT's existing rules and procedures to ensure that future regional integration agreements will have a liberal, outward orientation. Complacency about future trends could be very risky.

It is clear that the issues are more complex than in the past. The decline in border protection through successive GATT rounds has given greater prominence to domestic measures that affect the conditions of international competition. Services, and trade in this sector, are contributing more and more to growth, development and employment. Locational investment incentives and the protection of intellectual property are also issues of concern. Such developments take the analysis of regional and multilateral integration well beyond its previous focus on the effects of removing tariffs on intra-regional trade.

In view of the importance of the issue, the Secretariat invited trade policy experts and practitioners to reflect on the implications of regional integration agreements for the multilateral trading system and the global integration process. The contents of the papers in this volume, which form part of the background material for the Secretariat's forthcoming special study on regionalism, reflect the personal views of the authors. This holds not only for the outside experts who graciously agreed to participate in the project, but also for the members of the GATT staff whose papers appear in this volume. These papers have been written in the spirit of intellectual liberty needed to ensure a frank and informed examination of the interaction between regionalism and multilateralism. I am confident that they will make a significant contribution to advancing discussion on this most important subject.

Geneva   *Arthur Dunkel*
March 1993   *Director General of GATT*

Preface

This volume arose out of papers prepared as background material for the special topic in the GATT Secretariat's recent annual report on world trade. The papers were initially discussed at a conference in Geneva in September 1992, before being revised for publication.

The editors and contributors are grateful to all the conference participants (including Richard Baldwin, Victoria Curzon Price, Slobodan Djajic, Carsten Kowalczyk, Ernst-Ulrich Petersmann, Wouter de Ploey, Richard Pomfret and Per Magnus Wjikman) whose constructive comments facilitated the revision process; to Jagdish Bhagwati for his counsel at the outset of the project; to Lidia Silvetti, Sinead Deevy and Aishah Collautti, who as always managed with great care all the administrative details and word processing for the project under tight deadlines; and to Mark Allin, Kaylie Smith and Christopher Glennie of Harvester Wheatsheaf for making rapid publication of the volume possible.

The contributors also wish to acknowledge with thanks the support of their employing institutions, without implicating them of course. The opinions expressed in the volume are the responsibility of the authors alone, and in particular are in no way intended to represent the views of the GATT Secretariat or GATT contracting parties.

Geneva
October 1992

Kym Anderson and
Richard Blackhurst

1

Introduction and summary

Kym Anderson and Richard Blackhurst

Regional economic integration – the process of reducing the economic significance of national political boundaries within a geographic area[1] – has become a topical policy issue once again. It was popular in Europe beginning in the 1950s with the 1951 Paris Treaty on coal and steel, the signing by six countries in 1957 of the Treaty of Rome to create the EEC, the formation in 1960 of the European Free Trade Association (EFTA) among the other West European countries and, in the East, the creation of the Council for Mutual Economic Assistance (CMEA, or Comecon). Stimulated in part by these developments, interest spread in the 1960s to developing countries, particularly in Latin America and Africa (Machlup, 1976, 1977). But little came of the regional agreements signed then by developing countries, and effective regional integration efforts in the 1970s and early 1980s were confined mainly to Europe (where the motivation remained as much political and strategic as economic, or more so). Meanwhile, tariff reductions following the Kennedy and Tokyo Rounds of multilateral trade negotiations had reduced the purely economic incentive to enter into preferential trade agreements.

Why, then, has regionalism become popular again in recent years? Many factors have been at work but two events – one on either side of the Atlantic – coincided in the 1980s and explain much of the increased interest in integration initiatives. The conclusion in the mid-1980s of negotiations to expand the European Communities (EC) to include Portugal and Spain coincided with the laying of plans for completing the move to a Single European Market for goods, services, capital and labor. This led to concerns in much of the rest of the world that the EC might become (1) less open to trade with outsiders (a 'Fortress Europe') and (2) less interested in pursuing multilateral trade liberalization with other

1

contracting parties to the General Agreement on Tariffs and Trade (GATT). Subsequent developments calmed those concerns somewhat but they remained important factors in the minds of many people responsible for determining the response of other countries to what was occurring in the EC.

Fearful of finding themselves with less-advantageous access to the markets of their key trading partners, the response from several non-EC countries in Western Europe was a series of requests to become EC members. The EC's reaction was to suggest to the members of EFTA that they join with the EC to form the European Economic Area (EEA), which would add to the existing EC–EFTA free trade agreements many of the features of the Single Market. This the EFTA countries agreed in 1991 to pursue. But, since the EEA will give the EFTA countries little say in EC policy making, it is not surprising that several of them continue to seek full EC membership and see the EEA merely as a stepping stone to that status.

During the same period the Berlin Wall came down and Germany was united, Central and Eastern Europe began the transformation from plan to market, and both the Soviet Union and Comecon dissolved. The latter developments represented a move away from regionalism, but were immediately followed by calls from many East European countries for association agreements with the EC and with EFTA countries. This contributed to concerns outside Europe that the continent would shift to a more inward focus and that the EC would place a lower priority on multilateral issues, including further multilateral trade liberalization.

Meanwhile, efforts to re-create a free trade area joining Canada and the United States finally succeeded.[2] This was a possibility that had engaged one or both countries for decades and had produced along the way the 1965 pact that liberalized trade in automobiles and parts. Although the Canada–US Free Trade Agreement (CUSFTA), brought into force in January 1989, was primarily seen as a way of strengthening the two economies, it was hoped that it would also encourage other traders to help bring about a successful conclusion to the Uruguay Round negotiations.

Seen in their respective historical perspectives, it can be argued that these two developments, one in Europe and one in North America, occurred largely independently of one another and of policy trends in the rest of the world. In particular, both have roots that go back well before the failure in December 1990 to conclude the Uruguay Round on schedule.[3]

The same cannot be said of the renewed interest in regional integration agreements in the rest of the world. There the response was heavily conditioned by the experience of witnessing increased regional integration in the world's two largest trading entities, coupled with the continued difficulty of successfully concluding the Uruguay Round of multilateral trade negotiations.

Not long after the signing of the CUSFTA Mexico proposed to the United States that the two countries negotiate a free trade agreement. When the United States government responded favorably, the Canadian government indicated its desire to join the negotiations. In late 1992 the North American Free Trade Agreement (NAFTA) between Canada, Mexico and the Unites States was signed, and currently is awaiting ratification by the three legislatures. Again the motivation involved several factors, including the desire to strengthen the competitiveness of the three economies, to 'cement in' the recent economic and political reforms in Mexico, to increase the predictability of access to one another's markets and – by demonstrating the practical reality of a major regional integration agreement (RIA) outside Europe – to increase the incentive for other countries to help strengthen the multilateral system by coming to a Uruguay Round agreement.[4]

The developments in Europe and North America and the uncertain outlook for the Uruguay Round were particularly worrisome for the major traders in East Asia, with their heavy involvement in world markets and their outward-oriented development strategies. While continuing to voice strong support for the multilateral trading system, many countries in the region began exploring options for increased regional cooperation and integration in Asia. From a trade point of view, the most tangible result of this effort to date is the agreement among the ASEAN countries in October 1992 on a schedule of tariff cuts, over a 15-year period beginning in January 1993, that will create the ASEAN Free Trade Arrangement (AFTA).

The bringing of Mexico into a NAFTA and the middle-income Southern European economies into the EC is significant in that it creates RIAs involving countries at widely different levels of industrialization.[5] Understandably, given the importance of the major OECD markets as outlets for their exports, many other middle- and lower-income countries are now clamoring for some form of membership of one of these regional agreements. They see several virtues in membership: greater and preferential access to large markets; a lower probability of being denied such access by gray-area protectionist measures such as VERs or by anti-dumping duties; and, for governments of countries undergoing unilateral economic reforms, a means of reducing the risk that political pressures from interventionists at home will in the future cause a reversal of that reform process. This last motivation today also contrasts markedly with that of the 1960s: then, the governments of many Latin American and African countries viewed RIAs simply as a means of extending their national, inward-looking import-substitution policies to the regional level.

The fact that a key motivation of excluded countries to join an existing RIA or form a new one is their desire to safeguard their ability to pursue outward-oriented development policies suggests that RIAs can make a positive contribution to the liberalization of global trade. An important empirical question is whether that contribution is more or less than offset by possible negative effects of regionalism. The latter could take the form not only of higher external barriers to trade with third countries, but also of less multilateral liberalization on a global scale because the attention of governments is focused more on regional issues or because firms within the RIA are less interested in further liberalization because they now have access to the expanded internal market.

It is this latter, systemic effect of regionalism that is the primary focus of the present study. That is, are RIAs useful stepping stones toward freer global trade, or are they more likely to be stumbling blocks or at least to slow the global trade liberalization process? Since the economics profession in the early 1990s is spread along a spectrum that includes affirmative answers to both questions, it is evident that there is a need for further study. Hence the present volume.

Specifically, the chapters to follow address six sets of issues. First, to what extent, if at all, has world trade become more regionalized during this century and how has this affected global economic welfare? Second, what has been the nature and extent of regional economic integration in the three major trading areas of North America, Europe and East Asia? Third, how has regional integration affected − and been affected by − foreign direct investment and macroeconomic developments in the member states? Fourth, what roles have international and domestic political forces played in shaping regional integration agreements as compared with the rules of the multilateral GATT system? Fifth, what institutional and legal issues arise from the coexistence of RIAs and the GATT-based global trading system? And finally, how might RIAs and the GATT be adapted to better serve the cause of improving global welfare through trade liberalization?

Before turning to a summary of the studies addressing each of these questions, a few words on nomenclature are necessary. A wide variety of names has been given to regional integration agreements: free trade areas, preferential trade arrangements, trading blocs, regional trade associations, customs or economic unions, and other combinations of those or similar words. Theorists of economic integration typically rank them as follows: *preferential trade agreements*, or arrangements or areas (PTAs, in which signatories impose lower tariffs on each other's imports than on imports from third countries); *free trade areas*, or agreements

(FTAs, involving not just lower but zero tariffs between member states, although typically not on all goods and services); *customs unions* (CUs, which are FTAs but with the same external trade measures for all member states); *common markets* (CMs, which allow free movement of factors as well as products between member states); and *economic unions* (EU, involving not only common factor markets and trade policies but also harmonization of other micro- and macroeconomic policies).[6] The term *regional integration agreement* (RIA) covers all of these arrangements. Their common denominator is the reciprocal nature of the preferential treatment which the participants accord to one another, as distinct from, for example, the one-way preferences involved in the generalized system of trade preferences (GSP) given to developing countries. The general term RIA is used throughout this volume, except in situations in which an author wants to refer specifically to an arrangement of more limited scope or to a RIA involving countries which are not all from the same geographic region.

1.1   The extent of regionalization of world trade

What evidence is there that world trade has become more regionalized? To begin to answer this question the GATT Secretariat's economists have put together a time series of matrices of intra- and extra-regional trade flows. Those data (which are presented in detail in the Appendix and are analyzed in Chapter 2) show that for the hundred years from 1830, Europe (which accounted for nearly two-thirds of world trade throughout that period) became ever-more integrated with the rest of the world. This occurred not in the sense that the share of non-Europeans in its total trade rose: in fact that share remained steady at about two-thirds. Rather, integration occurred as the share of Europe's GDP that was traded with the rest of the world grew — indeed it trebled over that hundred-year period. For the period since 1928 data are presented for Eastern and Western Europe separately, as well as for five other geographic regions which together make up the world. On average the share of those regions' GDP that was traded extra-regionally fell in the 1930s, remained at that lower level until the 1970s, then began rising and by the 1980s was back to its peak of 1928. This is not to deny the rise (from an average of a third to a half during the post-war years) in the share of each region's trade that is intra-regional; it is simply to say that alongside that tendency to trade more with neighbors has been a tendency also to trade an increasing share of national production with other regions.

It is not possible to say from these data alone whether post-war RIAs have reduced the growth in the propensity for regions to trade extra-regionally, or whether they lowered economic welfare for insiders or outsiders. But since all that is required for welfare to increase for insiders (outsiders) is that the volume of intra- (extra-)regional trade be raised above what it otherwise would have been (Kemp and Wan, 1976), and since both those trade volumes have grown rapidly and certainly much faster than output since the 1940s, there is little reason to presume that RIAs have slowed welfare growth. Moreover, Chapter 2 points out that much of the post-war growth in the intra-regional share of Western Europe's trade is a result of removing former imperial trade preferences, the dismantling of which may itself have improved welfare.

To obtain a clearer idea of the trade and welfare effects of RIAs requires formal modeling of the global economy, Chapter 3 provides a survey of a large number of such studies. It concludes that there is near-unanimity that net trade creation occurred in Western Europe, although what proportion of that can be attributed directly to the RIAs remains an unanswered question. The evidence for net trade creation resulting from RIAs in other regions so far appears to be scant. As to the welfare effects of RIAs, that survey concludes they probably have been positive but not necessarily very large.

In short, some regionalization of global trade has been occurring since World War II but this has not precluded ongoing integration of the global economy, nor does it appear to have been welfare reducing. But whether welfare would have grown faster without the formation of RIAs, and – more importantly – whether the RIAs being formed and/or extended in the 1990s will lead to less beneficial outcomes than was the case in earlier decades, continue to be the subject of lively debate.

1.2   Regional integration in the major trading areas

The economic importance of different geographic regions, in addition to the political alliances within and between them, change significantly over time. But it is clear from Table 1.1 that the world's three major producing and trading regions are Western Europe, North America and East Asia. Together they account for more than 80 per cent of world GDP and trade, and have done so throughout most of this century. North America, the largest producing region until recently, includes what in effect was for a long time the most significant RIA, namely the United States. While North America's share of the world's international trade shrunk when the union was formed and as states were added (since

Table 1.1 Regional shares of world output and trade, 1928, 1958 and 1990

	Share of world GDP (%)			Share of world merchandise exports plus imports (%)		
	1928	1958	1990	1928	1958	1990
Western Europe	34	26	34	47	40	46
Eastern Europe (incl. SU)	4	8	4	5	9	5
TOTAL, Europe	38	34	38	52	49	51
North America plus Mexico	42	46	30	18	20	18
Latin America less Mexico	4	5	4	8	8	3
TOTAL, America	46	51	34	26	28	21
Asia	14	11	25	18	14	21
Japan	2	3	14	3	3	8
Australasia	2	2	2	3	2	1
Developing Asia	10	7	9	12	9	12
Africa	2	3	2	4	6	3
Middle East	..[a]	1	2	..[a]	3	3
TOTAL, WORLD	100	100	100	100	100	100

Note: [a] Less than 0.5
Sources: See the Appendix to this volume.

inter-state trade was no longer counted as world trade), it still represents one-sixth of global trade. And it may well grow further with the formation of NAFTA (and its possible extension to other Latin American countries in addition to Mexico). According to the author of Chapter 4, NAFTA will, on balance, be trade-liberalizing despite some clearly restrictive or discriminatory measures, including a number of Byzantine rules of origin. It will be even more liberalizing if the Uruguay Round concludes successfully, because that would reduce the preferential margin for trade within NAFTA through lowering most-favoured-nation (MFN) trade barriers.

The assessment in Chapter 5 of the recent and prospective integration initiatives in Europe is somewhat more guarded. 'Managed liberalization' is how the author describes EC preferences, not least because the reductions in intra-European trade barriers are scheduled to exclude some politically sensitive sectors (notwithstanding GATT's Article XXIV), particularly in the case of agreements with non-EC members. Regional liberalization there is seen as a poor substitute for genuine MFN liberalization because Western Europe's RIAs attenuate competition in precisely those sectors which are most in need of the improvements in efficiency that greater competition from abroad would stimulate.

East Asia is different from Western Europe and North America in not having any significant RIAs during the past four decades, yet the share of its trade that is intra-regional is growing. In Chapter 6 this is attributed simply to the growth in the region's importance in world trade. Thus East Asia provides an important case study in 'open regionalism' – a market-induced phenomenon, rather than one induced by preferential trade policies. A continuation of the East Asian success story – and its spread to other parts of the developing world – is heavily contingent on continued access to the major industrial country markets, however. The author of Chapter 6 believes that East Asia will and should continue to promote open regionalism, and that it would be far preferable for East Asia to continue to promote the GATT-based multilateral trading system than to form an East Asian RIA or to attempt to join NAFTA.

1.3 Regionalism, foreign investment, and the macroeconomy

Two indirect aspects of RIAs are important to keep in mind, namely that they affect – and are affected by – foreign direct investment and the macroeconomy generally. There was a surge in investment by US firms in the EC in the 1960s which led some to claim that this was evidence of a 'Fortress Europe' in the making. The implementation of the EC's Single Market initiative in recent years has similarly been followed by a surge in foreign direct investment (FDI), this time from East Asia and especially Japan. Again the question arises as to whether this is evidence of a rise in actual or expected external trade barriers. Or is it simply a response to the expected growth in the size of the EC internal market that can best be captured by producing locally?

If the FDI is motivated by a desire to jump actual or anticipated import barriers, it would amplify any trade diversion resulting from the formation/extension of the RIA and might reduce global welfare, whereas if it is a response to natural market growth prospects it is likely to be welfare-enhancing. Chapter 7 seeks to clarify which of these motivations has dominated in practice. It concludes in the case of the EC that a considerable share of its inward FDI has simply been a response to expanding market opportunities. Much of this FDI has been directed to the services sector, a large subset of which would be complementary to rather than a substitute for trade.[7] However, some of the FDI in industry appears to have been motivated by a desire either to ward off increases in import barriers that might have occurred had employment within the EC not been boosted by that FDI, or simply to locate behind the potential 'Fortress' wall.

Turning to the interaction between RIAs and the macroeconomy, Chapter 8 addresses the question of how, if at all, macroeconomic policy influences the success of RIAs. Drawing on economic theory and the experiences of several RIAs, the authors find that the greater the degree of economic integration that is sought, the more the need for coordination of monetary and fiscal policies among RIA economies increases. Greater coordination is necessary to avoid situations in which external imbalances jeopardize the process of liberalization within the RIA.[8] In RIAs involving economies of different sizes, the dominant economy (or economies) has or have no choice but to assume the main responsibility for macroeconomic discipline, but in so doing the RIA may help the governments of smaller economies become more disciplined in their monetary and fiscal policies. Insofar as that discipline contributes to economic growth, this becomes an additional contribution of RIAs to boosting global welfare. And its contribution is likely to become more significant as more RIAs involving advanced industrial economies welcome membership from developing countries instead of only from advanced economies.

1.4   Political economy of integration agreements

A general theory of the political economy of economic integration has yet to be developed, but some of the elements for such a theory are provided in Chapters 9 to 11. Chapter 9 focuses on the roles of hegemony and of international alliances on the incentives of countries to support the global trading system or to form preferential trading areas. Drawing on historical evidence, the author argues that with just one hegemon (e.g., the UK until the inter-war period and then the US until recently), a liberal global trading system is more likely to be pursued than if, as today, world power is spread more thinly among several nation states. But as well there is more incentive to form protectionist trading blocs in a period involving adversarial tension than in more peaceful times. With the Cold War coming to an end this would give reason to expect less-inward-looking RIAs to form in the 1990s, thereby more or less offsetting the effect on RIAs of hegemonic decline. It is thus difficult to conclude from this political science branch of the political economy literature whether these forces will cause future RIAs to be stepping stones or stumbling blocks to freer global trade.

The focus of the political economy analyses in Chapters 10 and 11 is, in contrast to Chapter 9's, on the impact of domestic interest-group pressures on trade-policy formation. Drawing on the economic theory of public choice, the authors question the validity of assuming that forming a RIA leads to freer intra-regional trade than would result from pursuing liberalization via the multilateral trading system. After examining numerous RIAs in Chapter 10 they conclude that little has been achieved by RIAs over and above what is provided for in mutilaterally negotiated commitments. This is not to deny, however, that regionally negotiated reforms are sometimes reflected in concurrent or subsequent efforts to achieve similar progress at the multilateral level, in which case the RIA could be viewed as a contributor to freer trade beyond as well as within the region in question. Indeed, it is because this is the case that the differences in rules and principles between major RIAs and the GATT have tended to be relatively minor.

The analysis in Chapter 10 also asks whether some types of RIAs will be less liberalizing than others. The authors give free-rider reasons to expect fewer demands for increasing protection if countries form a traditional FTA rather than a customs union or common market. On the other hand, because FTAs necessarily require rules of origin (as they – unlike customs unions or common markets – do not have a common external tariff), they can lead to greater protection even when each country's external tariffs are unchanged.[9] But the authors also point out that a hub-and-spoke system (effectively a set of bilateral FTAs centered on one 'hub' country) is likely to result in the least liberalization of all the RIA options, mainly because a larger number of 'sensitive' sectors will seek to prevent reform when there are several bilateral rather than just one multilateral FTA under negotiation. This conclusion is worrying given that many of the potential RIAs currently under discussion are of the hub-and-spoke type (notably with the US, the EC or Russia as the hub).

Chapter 11 turns to a more formal analysis of the political economy of international trade policy negotiations. It explicitly incorporates the possibility that vested interest groups attempt to influence the outcome of such negotiations, and shows how easily that can reduce the welfare gains from (minilateral and multilateral) trade liberalization. The authors stress that attention needs to be focused not just on the agreements as signed but also on their implementation over time. The greater the degree of administrative discretion given to the implementing authorities, the greater the incentive for vested interests to plead their special cause at the implementation stage. It is not possible to determine a priori whether the scope for lobbying is greater under a RIA than under a system involving multilateral negotiations, but what the authors are able to show is the difficulty involved in obtaining liberalization under either mode.

1.5 Institutional and legal issues

What institutional and legal issues arise from the coexistence of a growing number of significant RIAs and the GATT-based global trading system? Chapters 12 to 17 address several aspects of that question. In Chapter 12 a brief history of the GATT's handling of RIAs via its Article XXIV is provided. There it is argued that providing an exceptions clause to the unconditional most-favored-nation clause of Article I, in the form of Article XXIV which allows for FTAs and CUs, was necessary to attract and retain some parties that might not have otherwise joined or remained members of the GATT club. But in the hope of limiting the proliferation of FTAs and CUs among members, Article XXIV requires (1) that such preferential agreements involve free trade within the bloc in 'substantially' all products, and (2) that external trade barriers not be raised against excluded parties – two conditions that are based on political economy rather than purely economic considerations.

Indeed, as Chapter 13 points out, from the standpoint of economic theory there is a more appropriate criterion for GATT admissibility of RIAs than the requirement that barriers to trade with excluded economies not be raised. It is simply that the volume of the RIA's trade with excluded countries must not fall. However, as Chapter 14 notes, there would be two practical difficulties in applying this test. One is agreeing on what the trade volume would have been without the RIA. But some rules of thumb are suggested in Chapter 13 that, while rough, might still be superior in efficiency terms to the rules used at present. A more serious limitation is the difficulty of introducing a criterion that would require, in certain cases, *ex post* adjustments in one or more sections of an already established and operating FTA or CU. Chapters 14 and 19 each detail reasons why such *ex post* adjustments are very unlikely to be accepted by GATT's member countries.

Chapter 14 also responds to other criticisms of the GATT in relation to RIAs. The author underscores the practical value mentioned in Chapter 12 of the 'substantially-all-trade' clause in Article XXIV, and suggests that the concern that RIAs violate the MFN principle is overdone – not least because of the very substantial decline in border protection in recent decades. Rather, attention should be directed to two other issues. One concerns the pressure for harmonization of domestic regulations and coordination of domestic policies that impact on international competitiveness, which is much more evident within the major RIAs than at the multilateral level. The author argues that discriminatory elimination (within RIAs but not more broadly) of differences in these policies may prove to be a much bigger threat to international economic relations from RIAs than their adding of preferential market access rights, insofar as it increases the gap between multilateral commitments (which to date are few) and regional practices. A more positive view might be that some of the effort to harmonize and coordinate domestic policies at the regional level could spread to the broader multilateral level, just as has happened with trade policies.

The other issue in the relationship between RIAs and the GATT which merits attention has to do with dispute settlement procedures. Apart from the EC no RIA has a legal dispute settlement procedure nearly as comprehensive as the GATT's, and this will be even more so once the Uruguay Round is concluded. It is therefore very much in the interests of members of RIAs to retain their rights under the GATT legal system, including their rights to GATT dispute settlement. The experience of Canada and the US since the CUSFTA came into force, discussed in Chapter 16, underscores the importance of this point, especially for the smaller members of a RIA. That experience also demonstrates how regional and multilateral procedures – far from duplicating each other – can in fact strongly complement and reinforce each other.

Two further areas where the increasing importance of RIAs raises important issues for the GATT are rules of origin and contingent protection. Chapter 15 focuses on the former. It demonstrates that rules of origin in traditional FTAs can be such as to make them more like hub-and-spoke FTAs, thereby limiting the extent of liberalization that can occur within them and increasing the prospect that they lead to more trade diversion than trade creation. Harmonizing rules of origin would reduce this tendency, and it is argued in Chapter 15 that the process of harmonizing those rules would be less vulnerable to 'capture' by protectionist lobbies if they were negotiated and adopted multilaterally rather than in a regional context.

One of the driving forces behind the spread of regionalism, according to the authors of Chapter 17, is the erosion of guarantees of market access in the major industrial countries. Especially frustrating for traders are contingent protection measures such as anti-dumping and countervailing duties, for in practice they often appear (some would say by design) to be applicable whenever a government wishes them to be. Article VI of the GATT and the GATT's anti-dumping code are aimed at preventing arbitrary use of anti-dumping action, but they are only partially able to do so. Hence countries have sought – not always successfully[10] – to improve the security of access to their major markets through seeking to form or join a RIA with their main trading partner(s). Insofar as RIAs are able to provide this form of 'insurance' – the EC is the only current RIA that rules out contingent protection among participants – their spread is both understandable and also worrying. It is worrying because the increased use of contingent protection not only undermines liberal trade, but can divert countries' attention from multilateral liberalization to bilateral efforts to protect *existing* market access. The conclusion in Chapter 17 therefore is that if the expanding use of contingent protection measures can be reversed (for example, via a strong Uruguay Round agreement), at least one of the motivations for countries forming or joining RIAs will dissipate.

1.6   Looking to the future

In looking for alternative means of improving the global trading system, Chapter 18 raises the possibility of forming a GATT-Plus club involving the major trading countries which would agree to apply trading rules which are stricter and more extensive than those incorporated in the GATT. This club – which the author advocates even if the Uruguay Round is successfully completed – would be open to all countries willing to abide by those stricter rules, in return for which they would receive the greater benefits of membership (for example, greater access to the markets of signatories and better safeguards against unilateral retaliation). That is, the GATT-Plus club would offer much of what is currently being sought by countries trying to form or join existing RIAs, but with the additional advantages that (1) membership is not regionally based and thus not limited by geography, and (2) there would be no limit on the number of countries joining.

Among the issues raised by this proposal is the question of whether it underestimates the difficulty of getting the US, the EC and Japan – countries whose cooperative leadership the author recognizes would be essential to the club's success – to agree on reforms which would go beyond those in the Dunkel Draft of the Uruguay Round agreement. The negotiating history since Brussels in December 1990 suggests that it does. That is, if there is a Uruguay Round agreement, it seems unlikely that the three major traders would agree to go further prior to the next multilateral round, while if the Uruguay Round is not successfully concluded in the near future, the prospects for a GATT-Plus club based on US/EC/Japanese cooperation are dim indeed.

In concluding the volume the final chapter draws in part on earlier chapters in seeking to answer the question of how far RIAs contribute to global economic integration or, in other words, how far RIAs further the cause of liberalizing economic exchange globally. The authors first note that trade liberalization in a geographic region that includes several countries is, in principle, no different from the elimination of barriers to trade between the states or provinces within a country, and therefore cannot be considered an *inherent* threat to global economic integration.

Regarding the post-war experience with RIAs among OECD countries, including those currently under development, the authors' view is that they have made a positive net contribution to world-wide economic integration.

It cannot be automatically assumed that this will be true in the future, however. Whether any particular RIA is liberal or illiberal depends on its detailed contents and the ways in which the agreement is interpreted and administered. This means there is an important role for multilateral rules and surveillance in shaping the drafting and implementation of regional agreements. The authors argue that while the GATT-based trading principles and rules have been playing this role to a greater extent than is commonly assumed, there is room to improve on those rules and procedures. Further efforts at improvement are likely to be necessary not only to ensure that RIAs in the 1990s and beyond continue to be a stepping stone to welfare-enhancing trade liberalization, but also because if the GATT loses credibility in this area – in particular, because of perceived shortcomings in countries' compliance with RIA-related rules and procedures – there is a danger that its credibility generally will be undermined.

One way to increase the prospect of RIAs being welfare-enhancing is to examine periodically their compliance with GATT principles and rules in the same way that national trade policies are reviewed, namely, via GATT's existing trade policy review mechanism. The very existence of an ongoing review process would ensure (1) that negotiators of RIAs would make more effort to conform *ex ante* with the multilateral rules, and (2) that the *ex post* interpretation and administration of the agreements would conform more closely to GATT's rules and principles.

Notes

Helpful comments by John Croome and Bernard Hoekman are gratefully acknowledge.
1. Henderson (1992) points out that international economic integration can be the result of technical change (for example, the relative decline of international transport and communication costs) and/or of changes in policies affecting trade; and that the latter could be unilateral, minilateral (as with bilateral or regional trade agreements) or multilateral (involving, as with the GATT, a much larger group of countries). Our concern here is primarily with policy changes at the regional and multilateral levels.
2. From 1854 to 1866, trade between Canada and the United States was governed by a free trade agreement. See, for example, Winham (1988).
3. So too did the signing of the Israel–US Free Trade Agreement which, while not regional, contributed to concerns that preferential trading agreements were on the rise.

4. Although not always openly stated, a further motivation for the United States is to slow its rate of (often illegal) immigration from Mexico. A similar concern about migration from Eastern to Western Europe is part of the latter's motivation to sign association accords with East European countries.

5. Apart from imperial preferences, the only major agreements between developed and developing countries involve the generalized system of trade preferences (GSP) and the EC's association agreements with African, Caribbean and Pacific countries under the Lomé Convention. These provide selective, non-reciprocal tariff preferences.

6. On the economics of these different types of agreements, see, for example, Balassa (1962) and Robson (1987).

7. Hoekman (1992, Table 5) notes that a quarter of US, a third of Canadian, and almost half the stock of Japanese outward FDI to other industrial countries is in service sectors. And in the 1984−8 period the flow of inward investment in the EC averaged 60 per cent, both from other EC countries and from non-EC countries (UNCTC, 1991, Table 8).

8. The lack of such coordination is believed to be one of the reasons why many RIAs among developing countries failed in the 1960s and 1970s.

9. This can occur, for example, when a partner's tariff on an input is high and yet the country has to import the input from that partner rather than from a lower-cost foreign source in order to satisfy the rules-of-origin criterion for exporting the final product to that FTA partner. Krueger (1992) also makes this point.

10. Both the CUSFTA and the NAFTA continue to allow anti-dumping and countervailing duties on intra-North American trade, for example.

References

Balassa, B. (1962), *The Theory of Economic Integration*, London: Allen and Unwin.

Henderson, D. (1992), 'International Economic Integration: Progress, Prospects and Implications', *International Affairs* **68**: 633−55.

Hoekman B. (1992), 'Regional versus Multilateral Liberalization of Trade in Services', presented to a conference on Services Productivity and the Quality Challenge, University of Pennsylvania, 23−4 October.

Kemp, M. and H. Wan (1976), 'An Elementary Proposition Concerning the Formation of Customs Unions', *Journal of International Economics* **6**: 95−7.

Krueger, A. O. (1992), 'Free Trade Agreements as Protectionist Devices: Rules of Origin', mimeo, Duke University, September.

Machlup, F. (ed.) (1976), *Economic Integration: Worldwide, Regional, Sectoral*, London: Macmillan for the International Economic Association.

Machlup, F. (1977), *A History of Thought on Economic Integration*, London: Macmillan.

Robson, P. (1987), *The Economics of International Integration*, 3rd edition, London: Allen and Unwin.

UNCTC (United Nations Centre on Transnational Corporations) (1991), *World Investment Report 1991*, New York: United Nations.

Winham, G. (1988), *Trading With Canada: The Canadian−US Free Trade Agreement*, New York: Priority Press.

PART 1

Extent of regionalization of world trade

2

History, geography and regional economic integration

Kym Anderson and Hege Norheim

The recent proliferation of regional integration arrangements and proposals, and the difficulty of concluding the Uruguay Round, have fueled fears that international trade is becoming more of a regional affair in ways that will reduce global welfare. Outside Europe the concern is that the '1992' Single Market program of the European Community (EC) and its European Economic Area initiative, and the possible expansion later this decade in the number of full or associate members of the EC, will lead to a more exclusive 'Fortress Europe'. The response in North America has been to negotiate a free trade area there (NAFTA), which is adding to the concerns of third countries and causing them also to propose new, or seek membership of existing, regional integration agreements.

What evidence might be sought to test whether a welfare-reducing regionalization of world trade is occurring? A measure of changes in the average external tariff of free trade areas (FTAs) and customs unions (CUs) will not do, even though it is the criterion enshrined in Article XXIV of the GATT concerning the admissibility of FTAs and CUs. It would not do even if it captured the tariff-equivalent of non-tariff trade-distorting measures, for it misses the trade reductions caused by the *threat* of protection that gray-area protectionist measures such as anti-dumping legislation create. For that reason analysts have examined intra-regional trade shares. They point to the increase in the shares of industrial countries' trade that is intra-regional. During the past five decades, for example, Western Europe's intra-trade share rose from a half to almost three-quarters, while that of North America (including Mexico) rose from a quarter to two-fifths.

But the strengthening of regional integration agreements (RIAs) within Europe is only one of several possible contributors to that trend.

The demise of colonialism, the changing importance of different regions in world trade and other contributors to the geographic redistribution of trade ensure that changes in the share of a region's international trade that is intra-regional do not necessarily indicate a net increase in discriminatory, welfare-reducing trade practices. Moreover, as McMillan points out in Chapter 13 of this volume, we know from the analysis by Kemp and Wan (1976) that a new RIA will not worsen welfare in the rest of the world's economies so long as the *volume* (not necessarily the share) of its trade with the RIA countries does not fall, *ceteris paribus*. But, to be welfare-improving for the economies *within* the RIA, the volume of intra-RIA trade must increase following the RIA's formation. Thus it is quite conceivable for *both* trade volumes to rise, improving welfare for insiders and outsiders, but for the latter volume to rise faster than the former − in which case the intra-RIA trade share rises and the extra-regional share falls. Despite this insight from received economic theory, levels of protection and extra-regional trade shares continue to be used to make claims about the welfare effects of RIAs, pending the development of alternative simple-to-calculate indicators.

After pointing out how history, geography and even non-preferential trade policies can affect the geographic distribution of a country or region's trade, we provide in Section 2.1 of this chapter a simple method for disaggregating the change in the geographic distribution of a region's trade into component parts. In the process we define indexes of intensity and propensity to trade intra- or extra-regionally. The traditional intensity index overcomes several problems associated with using trade shares as indicators of trade bias. It is defined in the case of extra-regional trade as (roughly) the share of a region's trade with the rest of the world relative to the rest of the world's share of global trade. But even this indicator ignores the possibility that the region may be trading more or less with the rest of the world because of external trade policy changes. So we define an index of propensity to trade intra- or extra-regionally, which combines the effects of geographic bias (as measured by the trade intensity index) and overall 'openness' to trade (as measured by the trade-to-GDP ratio). These indexes, which have the virtue of being simple to calculate, are used in Section 2.2 to examine changes in Europe's external merchandise[1] trade pattern since 1830 and that of various other regions since 1928.

The findings are that the index of the propensity to trade extra-regionally increased for Europe throughout the hundred years to 1928; that it fell for all regions in the 1930s; and that it has increased for virtually all regions (though least so for Europe) since then. The rise is mainly because the proportion of GDP that is traded internationally has risen substantially. That is, the tendency to trade more of one's GDP with one's own region has been accompanied by the tendency to trade more with the rest of the world as well.

The chapter then focuses in Section 2.3 on the effect on regionalization of world trade of the dismantling of imperial trade preferences. During the nineteenth and early twentieth centuries the two major trading powers were Britain and France. The post-war growth in intensity of their trade with other European countries is shown to have been very much at the expense of trade with their former dependencies. And the recent reforms in the former communist countries and the collapse of Comecon are now leading to a further regionalization of Europe's trade via East–West trade expansion. This greater trade between the natural trading partners within Western Europe and between East and West Europe could be welfare-improving insofar as there are global gains from dismantling imperial preferences – gains that may exceed any global losses from their replacement in Europe of trade-diversionary regional preferences.

The chapter concludes in Section 2.4 by pointing out that the pertinent issue from the viewpoint of global welfare is thus not whether the world's trade is becoming more or less regionally focused, for there are numerous reasons apart from the growth of RIAs as to why regionalization may be occurring – and in any case such RIAs may be welfare-improving even for outsiders and even if extra-regional trade shares fall. [2] Rather, the key issue is simply whether overall world trade is becoming more or less liberal and predictable (and thereby more or less conducive to global investment and employment growth).

2.1 Components of regionalization in international trade[3]

Both history and geography, in addition to government policies, play fundamental roles in shaping the pattern of world trade. The very definition of national boundaries is the result of political events in history, events that are still ongoing as the recent unification of Germany and breakup of the Soviet Union and Yugoslavia testify. Through influencing the size of nations, history also thereby influences the share of GDP traded internationally, because large economies tend to trade a smaller proportion of their GDP.[4] Historical events also influence national factor endowment ratios and thereby comparative advantages, and hence the commodity composition of countries' international trade. And they of course also determine national languages, customs and legal systems, which in turn affect transactions costs of doing business with other nations as compared with domestically.

Geography influences all four of those determinants of the pattern of an economy's international trade as well (its GDP, share of GDP traded, commodity composition of trade, and relative transactions costs of doing business with different countries). The output and real income of a nation can be affected directly by proximity to a more affluent economy, as shown so dramatically in the 1980s by the reductions in trade barriers between southeast China and Hong Kong. Also, a nation's trade-to-GDP ratio is lower the lower the cost of transacting business domestically compared with internationally, and this is determined by transport and communication costs. These costs, which are affected by relative language difficulties and distance, vary across trading partners as well and change over time. They thereby influence the direction of a country's trade not only directly but also indirectly through altering its inter-sectoral and intra-industry commodity composition (Krugman, 1991).

And of course government policies also alter these four determinants of the pattern of international trade (Clarida and Findlay, 1992). Even a uniform international trade tax for all commodities is inherently discriminatory, in at least two respects. First, it discriminates between domestic and international trades and so is likely to lower both GDP (especially for small economies) and the nation's international trade-to-GDP ratio below their free trade levels. And second, it alters domestic producer incentives among tradable industries because a given change in goods prices translates to differential changes in value added, especially when the value-added share of output varies by industry and elasticities of substitution in production and consumption differ across commodities. In the usual case in which a government's trade taxes (and other policies) do differ across industries, these differences add to the distortions to domestic production and hence lower GDP further. But as well such differences tend to reduce trade more for those trading partners whose trade with the taxing country is concentrated in the goods taxed most. Moreover, these changes to goods trade will be accentuated if the country's trade policy allows international factor flows. Thus even if a country's policies were to contain no overtly discriminatory or preferential trade arrangements such as trade embargoes, VERs, free trade agreements, imperial trade preferences and the like, they nonetheless would have an impact on the geographic distribution of the country's trade.

For all these reasons the share of intra-regional trade in a region's total trade is a very inadequate indicator of preferential policy-induced regional trade bias. But there are two other reasons as well, based simply on arithmetic, as to why the intra-regional trade share can be misleading. They have to do with the (necessarily somewhat arbitrary) definition of a 'region'. One is that the share is affected by the number of countries in a region. To see this, consider a free trade world of five countries and two regions (three countries in one region and two in the other), each country with the same value of trade and each trading the same amount with the other four countries. Despite the absence (by assumption) of any geographic trade bias, the intra-regional trade share of the first region is a half while that of the second region is a quarter. More generally, the larger the number of countries in a region, the larger the region's intra-regional trade share, *ceteris paribus*.

To overcome this problem, one might be tempted to suggest defining regions to include a similar number of countries. But that raises a second and related problem, namely, that the value of countries' total trade matters. This can be seen by again considering a two-region world, this time of four countries (two per region), with three of the countries trading identical amounts and the fourth trading twice as much as the other three. If each country's trade with the other three is directly proportional to each of the others' share of world trade, this would imply no geographic trade bias. Yet in that case the intra-regional trade shares would differ: for the region without the large trader that share is a quarter, while for the other region it is two-fifths.

These two problems can be avoided, and determinants of the share of one country's trade that goes to another country or country group can be identified formally, by making use of the definition of I_{ij}, the index of intensity of country i's export trade with country (or country group) j:[5]

$$I_{ij} = x_{ij}/m_j$$
$$= x_{ij}/(q_j \cdot r_j) \tag{2.1}$$

where

x_{ij} = the share of country i's exports going to country j,

m_j = the share of country j in world imports (net of country i's imports since i cannot export to itself),[6]

q_j = the share of country j in world (net of country i's) GDP, and

r_j = the 'relative openness' of country j,[7] defined as j's import-to-GDP ratio divided by the world's (net of country i's) import-to-GDP ratio.

This index (and its counterpart for import trade) has the property that if trade is not geographically biased in the sense that the share of i's trade going to j equals j's importance in world trade, then it will have a value of unity for all j. And with slight modification,[8] equation (2.1) also can provide an index of intensity of trade when 'country' i is a regional group, thereby avoiding the two above-mentioned arithmetic problems (associated with the number or size of countries in the regions) that the trade share suffers in indicating regional bias in trade.

The intensity index does, however, still combine the effects of differences in bilateral trade complementarities and in relative transactions costs of trading with different countries. To separate them, Drysdale (1988, p. 87) suggests subdividing the intensity index into the product of a trade-complementarity index and a residual trade-bias index. An appropriate complementarity index (C_{ij}), derived using the 'revealed comparative advantage' index of trade specialization suggested by Balassa (1965), is:

$$C_{ij} = \sum_k [(x_i^k/t_w^k) \cdot (m_j^k/t_w^k) \cdot t_w^k]$$

$$= \sum_k [x_i^k \cdot m_j^k/t_w^k] \tag{2.2}$$

where

x_i^k = the share of commodity k in country i's exports,
m_j^k = the share of commodity k in country j's imports, and
t_w^k = the share of commodity k in world trade.

That is, C_{ij} is the weighted average of the product of i's export specialization index and j's import specialization index, the weights being the shares of the commodities in world trade. A transactions cost-driven index of residual bias in i's exports to j (B_{ij}) can then be defined such that $I_{ij} = B_{ij} \cdot C_{ij}$. Drysdale (1988) shows that B_{ij} is a weighted average of the intensity index for each commodity in i's exports to j, the weights being the proportional contribution of each commodity to complementarity in i's total exports to j.

By substituting $B_{ij} \cdot C_{ij}$ for I_{ij} in equation (2.1) and rearranging, the share of i's exports going to j can be partitioned as follows:

$$x_{ij} = q_j \cdot r_j \cdot B_{ij} \cdot C_{ij} \tag{2.3}$$

And swopping x and m in the above formulae provides a similar set of relationships for i's imports from j.

Equation (2.3) thus identifies the four components of the geographic pattern of trade mentioned at the outset: the relative size and 'relative openness' of different trading partners' economies, the transactions costs involved in i trading with them as compared with others, and the extent to which the commodity composition of their trade complements i's. One or more of these four may be able to provide a crude idea from trade data of the trade effects of preferential trade policies, but care is needed in their interpretation. Specifically, changes in B_{ij} in the absence of changes in transport and other transactions cost differences between trading partners may be attributable to changes in preferential trade policies. If, however, there have been changes in C_{ij} and they also are due to changes in preferential trade policies,[9] I_{ij} is a better indicator of the trade effects of those preference changes than B_{ij}. Moreover, calculating B_{ij} is very laborious, because it requires matrices of bilateral trade by commodity – unlike the intensity of trade index ($I_{ij} = B_{ij} \cdot C_{ij}$) which only requires bilateral trade totals. The intensity index thus provides at a much lower cost the same information as B_{ij} if C_{ij} has not changed over the period under consideration, or superior information to B_{ij} if C_{ij} has been affected by changes in preference policies. For these reasons, reliance will be placed in what follows on I_{ij} rather than B_{ij} to identify changes in intra- and extra-regional trade biases.

There is one further indicator that is useful in addition to I_{ij}. It is claimed by supporters (critics) of regional integration agreements that such agreements often are accompanied by general trade-policy changes which raise (lower) a country's trade-to-GDP ratio. Thus the establishment of a RIA may result in so much net trade creation that, even though the index of intensity of i's trade with other regions falls, there is a rise in its propensity to trade outside its own region because of an increase in the value of its trade with other regions as a proportion of i's GDP (rather than of i's total trade). To capture the combined effect of these two changes – in 'openness' and in extra-regional trade intensity – we define the index of the propensity to export extra-regionally (P_{ij}) as follows:

$$P_{ij} = t_{ij}/m_j$$
$$= t_i \cdot I_{ij} \tag{2.4}$$

where

$t_{ij} =$ i's exports to j divided by i's GDP, and
$t_i =$ the ratio of i's total exports to i's GDP;

and similarly for i's imports from j. The aggregate index of the propensity to trade extra-regionally – used in the next section – can then be defined as the average of the export and import intensity indexes multiplied by the ratio of exports plus imports to GDP (and similarly for the aggregate index of the propensity to trade intra-regionally).

P_{ij} is an especially useful summary index for across-time comparisons for i's trade with j when t_i has been changing because of the same policy changes that have affected I_{ij}. But it needs to be kept in mind that, unlike

I_{ij}, P_{ij} does not have a weighted average across all j of unity. Nor should it be used for comparing across different-sized countries or regions at a point in time because, as mentioned in note 4, t_i is necessarily dependent on the size of economy i, *ceteris paribus*.

2.2   Regionalization of international trade since 1830

Global economic integration through extra-regional trade has been going on for centuries, of course (Tracy, 1991). But with the rapid decline in the cost of ocean transport in the later nineteenth century, as iron and then steel replaced wood in ship construction and steam substituted for sails, intercontinental trade became much less costly (North, 1958). That, in the presence of strong imperial-colonial ties, often stronger trade complementarities between European and less-industrialized countries than among European countries, and intermittent animosities among European countries, ensured that for a hundred or so years from 1830 there was faster growth in inter- rather than intra-continental trade. Moreover, this extra-regional trade bias was reinforced by imperial preference policies that were strengthened in the early 1930s. It was only after the post-World War II reconstruction period that those preferences began to be dismantled – only to be replaced by regional preferences first in Europe and now in North America. Simultaneously, the volume of intra-industry trade among high-income industrial economies in sophisticated merchandise has become more important over time than those economies' inter-sectoral trade with exporters of primary products.

What has been the net effect of these forces, together with economic growth and the influences of other policies, on the pattern of intra-versus extra-regional trade of different regions? This depends of course on how we define 'regions'. While there is no ideal definition, pragmatism would suggest basing the definition on the major continents and subdividing them somewhat according to a combination of cultural, language, religious and stage-of-development criteria. We begin with Europe (East plus West), which for centuries has accounted for more than half of world trade and for which pertinent data are available from 1830.

2.2.1   Europe

According to the data compiled by Bairoch (1974, 1976a) for Europe as a whole, the share of Europe's trade that was intra-regional varied little from its average of two-thirds during the seven decades to 1900. It

Table 2.1 Trade shares and the intensity and propensity of regionalization in Europe's merchandise trade, 1830 to 1990

	1830	1840	1850	1860	1870	1880	1890	1900	1910	1928	1938	1948	1958	1968	1979	1990
Share (%) of trade[a] that is intra-European	67	67	65	64	69	68	67	66	64	61	61	52	61	71	72	76
Share (%) of world trade[b]	64	62	63	65	68	64	63	60	58	52	51	42	49	53	51	51
Intensity-of-trade index:[c]																
intra-European	1.06	1.10	1.05	0.98	1.03	1.09	1.07	1.11	1.11	1.20	1.21	1.27	1.27	1.35	1.43	1.51
extra-European	0.90	0.85	0.92	1.04	0.93	0.85	0.88	0.84	0.85	0.79	0.79	0.81	0.75	0.62	0.56	0.49
Share (%) of GDP traded:[d]																
total	9	12	15	20	24	28	28	26	29	33	24	34	31	35	46	45
extra-European	3	4	5	7	7	9	9	9	11	13	10	16	12	10	13	11
Propensity-to-trade index:[c]																
intra-European	0.10	0.13	0.16	0.20	0.24	0.31	0.30	0.29	0.32	0.40	0.29	0.42	0.40	0.47	0.66	0.68
extra-European	0.08	0.10	0.14	0.21	0.22	0.24	0.25	0.21	0.25	0.26	0.19	0.27	0.24	0.21	0.26	0.22

Notes: Three year averages around the years shown prior to 1928.
[a] Throughout the table, 'trade' refers to the average of merchandise export and import shares or intensity indexes, except that the share of GDP traded and the propensity index refer to exports plus imports of merchandise. Both Western and Eastern Europe (including Russia/USSR) are included as part of Europe.
[b] Refers to share of world exports up to 1910, and so slightly underestimates the share of exports plus imports. The League of Nations (1945, p. 157ff) suggests that the latter shares for Europe were 65 per cent in 1876–80, 66 per cent in 1896–1900 and 62 per cent in 1913.
[c] The intensity-of-trade and propensity-to-trade indexes for regions are defined following equations (2.1) and (2.4) in the text, respectively.
[d] Refers to GNP up to 1911, and is measured at current prices.

Sources: Data for the period to 1910 are from Bairoch (1976a, pp. 18, 78, 84) and supplemented with some of his unpublished data. For subsequent years the data are from the Appendix in this volume.

dropped a little in the early 1900s and stayed around 60 per cent until the early 1960s (apart from a dip associated with the late 1940s post-war reconstruction period), but then it rose steadily and is now more than 75 per cent (first row of Table 2.1). Since Europe's share of world trade also was steady during the nineteenth century, at a little below two-thirds according to Bairoch, the index of intensity of intra-European trade hovered at very little above unity throughout that century (rows 2 and 3). That is, despite the relative proximity of European countries to each other, they traded virtually no more among themselves last century than one would expect if one knew nothing more than their importance in world trade. Since World War I, however, that intensity index has risen steadily, from 1.1 to 1.5, as the intra-regional share of Europe's trade moved up and Europe's share of world trade fell.

Correspondingly, the intensity of Europe's trade with the rest of the world has fallen gradually during the past fifty years, from around 0.8 (a little below the average level of 0.9 maintained during the eight decades to 1910) to just under 0.5 by 1990 (row 4 of Table 2.1).

Even so, this does not necessarily mean that Europe has reduced its propensity to trade with non-Europeans, because one also needs to consider changes in the extent to which European economies have been opening up to international trade. Consistent time series of data on Europe's GDP are not available for the nineteenth century, but GNP estimates are available in Bairoch (1976a, b). They and more recent GDP estimates suggest that the trade-to-output ratio for Europe rose almost continuously during the 100 years to 1928,[10] that it fell in the 1930s, but that it has since risen again to well above its previous peak and is now five times its 1830s level (row 5 of Table 2.1). The share of Europe's GDP traded with non-Europeans has shown no long-term upward or downward trend during the past 60 years, however (row 6).

As a consequence, the index of Europe's propensity to trade within its own region has continued to rise throughout this long period, apart from a dip in the 1930s (row 7), while the index of its propensity to trade with the rest of the world — which ceased to grow at the end of last century – has at least been maintained (row 8). That is, despite the sharp decline during the post-World War II period in the intensity of Europe's trade with the rest of the world, its effect on the European propensity to trade extra-regionally has been more or less offset by the increasing openness of Europe's economies.

For the 1928–90 period it makes sense to examine Western and Eastern Europe (including the former USSR) as separate regions, and to compare the regionalization of their trade with that of other regions. The relevant data are summarized in Table 2.2.[11] They show that the share of Western Europe's trade with itself averaged around 50 per cent until

Table 2.2 Trade shares and the intensity and propensity of regionalization in world merchandise trade, 1928 to 1990

	1928	1938	1948	1958	1968	1979	1990
1. *Intra-regional trade share (%)*[a]							
Western Europe	51	49	43	53	63	66	72
Eastern Europe	19	14	47	61	64	54	46
TOTAL, Europe	61	61	52	61	71	72	76
North America	25	23	29	32	37	30	31
Latin America	11	18	20	17	19	20	14
TOTAL, America	45	44	59	56	52	47	45
Asia	46	52	39	41	37	41	48
Japan[f]	63	68	60	36	32	31	35
Australasia[f]	16	16	14	25	31	49	51
Developing Asia[f]	47	55	44	47	45	48	56
Africa	10	9	8	8	9	6	6
Middle East	5	4	21	12	8	7	6
TOTAL, WORLD	39	37	33	40	47	46	52
2. *Share (%) of world trade*[a]							
Western Europe	47	45	36	40	43	44	46
Eastern Europe	5	6	5	9	10	8	5
TOTAL, Europe	52	51	42	49	53	51	51
North America	18	14	22	19	19	15	16
Latin America	9	8	12	9	5	6	4
TOTAL, America	26	22	34	28	24	21	21
Asia	18	19	15	13	13	15	21
Africa	4	5	7	6	5	5	3
Middle East	1	1	2	3	3	7	3
3. *Intensity of intra-regional trade index*[b]							
Western Europe	1.13	1.14	1.21	1.38	1.51	1.57	1.60
Eastern Europe	4.36	2.61	10.22	7.62	7.30	7.88	10.88
TOTAL, Europe	1.20	1.21	1.27	1.27	1.35	1.43	1.51
North America	2.59	2.91	2.39	3.07	3.57	3.63	3.50
Latin America	1.37	2.30	1.71	1.95	3.55	3.80	3.53
TOTAL, America	1.76	2.00	1.77	2.07	2.21	2.29	2.26
Asia	2.61	2.83	2.74	3.15	2.84	2.77	2.31
Japan[f]	4.17	4.65	4.29	3.28	3.81	3.08	2.33
Australasia[f]	0.97	0.93	1.08	2.00	2.47	3.32	2.47
Developing Asia[f]	2.66	2.96	3.10	3.56	3.37	3.17	2.64
Africa	2.37	1.73	1.27	1.38	1.91	1.24	2.48
Middle East	7.56	3.47	9.55	4.25	3.00	1.17	2.23
TOTAL, WORLD[c]	1.85	1.92	2.43	2.65	2.81	2.64	2.62

(continued)

Table 2.2 (*Continued*)

	1928	1938	1948	1958	1968	1979	1990
4. Intensity of extra-regional trade index[b]							
Western Europe	0.89	0.89	0.88	0.76	0.64	0.58	0.51
Eastern Europe	0.85	0.91	0.56	0.42	0.40	0.49	0.57
TOTAL, Europe	0.79	0.79	0.81	0.75	0.62	0.56	0.49
North America	0.83	0.84	0.80	0.76	0.70	0.76	0.75
Latin America	0.79	0.89	0.91	0.91	0.86	0.84	0.90
TOTAL, America	0.73	0.72	0.61	0.60	0.63	0.67	0.68
Asia	0.66	0.59	0.71	0.68	0.83	0.69	0.66
Japan[f]	0.41	0.34	0.44	0.68	0.73	0.73	0.70
Australasia[f]	1.01	1.02	0.99	0.86	0.79	0.60	0.62
Developing Asia[f]	0.64	0.56	0.65	0.61	0.64	0.62	0.56
Africa	0.94	0.96	0.98	0.98	0.95	0.99	0.96
Middle East	0.96	0.97	0.81	0.90	0.94	0.99	0.96
TOTAL, WORLD[c]	0.86	0.82	0.83	0.75	0.67	0.68	0.62
5. Share (%) of GDP traded[a]							
Western Europe	33	24	35	33	34	48	46
Eastern Europe	30[e]	25[e]	25[e]	25[e]	40[e]	40[e]	41
TOTAL, Europe	33	24	34	31	35	46	45
North America	10	8	11	9	10	19	19
Latin America	45[e]	30[e]	30[e]	30	21	27	28
TOTAL, America	14	10	14	12	11	21	20
Asia	32	27	25	26	21	27	29
Japan[f]	35	29	8	19	17	20	18
Australasia[f]	38	32	47	31	25	29	30
Developing Asia[f]	30[e]	25[e]	25[e]	29	26	37	47
Africa	60[e]	50[e]	50[e]	58	37	56	53
Middle East	60[e]	50[e]	50[e]	46	38	48	49
TOTAL, WORLD	24	19	22	22	22	35	34
6. Index of propensity to trade intra-regionally[d]							
Western Europe	0.38	0.27	0.90	0.46	0.50	0.75	0.73
Eastern Europe	1.31	0.65	2.56	1.90	2.92	3.15	4.52
TOTAL, Europe	0.40	0.29	0.42	0.40	0.47	0.66	0.68
North America	0.27	0.22	0.26	0.29	0.34	0.70	0.67
Latin America	0.62	0.69	0.51	0.58	0.76	1.01	0.97
TOTAL, America	0.25	0.20	0.25	0.24	0.24	0.48	0.46
Asia	0.83	0.76	0.67	0.83	0.60	0.76	0.67
Japan[f]	1.37	1.57	0.28	0.53	0.31	0.55	0.42
Australasia[f]	0.39	0.21	0.43	0.57	0.71	1.03	0.89
Developing Asia[f]	0.82	0.72	0.84	1.07	1.09	1.23	1.21
Africa	1.42	0.86	0.63	0.63	0.73	0.60	1.21
Middle East	4.53	1.74	4.77	2.47	1.12	0.66	1.19
TOTAL, WORLD	0.45	0.37	0.54	0.57	0.61	0.91	0.88

Table 2.2 (*Continued*)

	1928	1938	1948	1958	1968	1979	1990
7. Index of propensity to trade extra-regionally[d]							
Western Europe	0.30	0.21	0.31	0.26	0.21	0.28	0.23
Eastern Europe	0.25	0.23	0.14	0.11	0.16	0.20	0.24
TOTAL, Europe	0.26	0.19	0.27	0.24	0.21	0.26	0.22
North America	0.09	0.06	0.09	0.07	0.07	0.15	0.14
Latin America	0.43	0.27	0.27	0.27	0.18	0.22	0.25
TOTAL, America	0.10	0.07	0.08	0.07	0.07	0.14	0.14
Asia	0.21	0.16	0.18	0.18	0.15	0.19	0.19
Japan[f]	0.14	0.10	0.04	0.13	0.12	0.15	0.13
Australasia[f]	0.37	0.31	0.45	0.29	0.23	0.27	0.28
Developing Asia[f]	0.25	0.21	0.18	0.20	0.22	0.30	0.35
Africa	0.56	0.48	0.49	0.45	0.37	0.48	0.47
Middle East	0.57	0.49	0.41	0.52	0.35	0.56	0.51
TOTAL WORLD	0.21	0.16	0.19	0.16	0.15	0.23	0.21

Notes: [a] Throughout the table, 'trade' refers to the average of merchandise export and import shares or intensity indexes, except that the share of GDP traded and the propensity index refer to exports plus imports of merchandise. All values are measured in current US dollars. Eastern Europe includes the former Soviet Union as one country and the former German Democratic Republic from 1948 as another. Turkey and Yugoslavia are included in Western Europe. North America refers to Canada and the United States, and Australasia refers to Australia and New Zealand.
[b] The intensity-of-trade index for regions is defined following equation (2.1) of the text.
[c] The world total intensity index is the weighted average across the seven regions, using the regions' shares of world trade as weights.
[d] The propensity-to-trade index is defined following equation (2.4) in the text. The world total refers to the weighted average for the seven regions, using the region's shares of world GDP as weights.
[e] In the absence of reliable estimates of GDP in the inter-war period for developing countries and until 1989 for Eastern Europe, 'guesstimates' have been made of the trade-to-GDP ratio for those regions. Given their small weights in world trade, the aggregates for Europe, the Americas and the world nonetheless will be reasonably reliable. The ratio is estimated at current prices.
[f] The rows for Japan, Australasia and Developing Asia differ from the other rows in that they are treated not as regions themselves but as part of their sum which is the Asian region.

Sources: See the Appendix in this volume. Trade data are based on the current US dollar value of merchandise exports, from League of Nations (1942) for 1928 (adjusted to include trade between Japan, Korea and Taiwan), from United Nations (1964) for 1938, 1948 and 1958, and from GATT (1987, 1992) for subsequent years. GDP data are from the World Bank's *World Tables* from 1968 and from the United Nations' *Statistical Yearbook*, particularly the 1954 and 1969 issues (based on official exchange rates) for years prior to 1968.

the late 1950s. But, following the formation of the EC in 1958 and EFTA in 1960, and the associated dismantling of imperial trade preferences, the share of West European trade that is with other West European countries grew rapidly. By the early 1970s it had risen to two-thirds, and today it is almost three-quarters (first row of part 1 of Table 2.2).

Since the importance of the region in world trade in recent years is similar to what it was in the 1920s and 1930s (part 2 of Table 2.2), there has been a similarly rapid rate of growth in the index of intensity of West Europe's intra-regional trade, from 1.1 in the inter-war period to 1.6 by the 1980s (part 3 of Table 2.2).[12]

This necessarily means the West European index of intensity of extra-regional trade has declined. It has fallen from 0.9 in the inter-war years to less than 0.6 now (part 4 of Table 2.2). But, because the share of Western Europe's GDP that is internationally traded has doubled since the 1930s (part 5 of Table 2.2), the index of Western Europe's propensity to trade extra-regionally, as defined above in equation (2.4), has been more or less maintained since 1928. In particular, this propensity of Western Europe's GDP to be traded with the rest of the world, after netting out the effect of changes in the latter's importance in global trade, has declined very little since the formation of the EC and EFTA and is still above its 1938 level. And this has happened despite the considerable GDP growth in, and the introduction of preferential trading arrangements among, Western Europe's economies.[13] Only a small proportion of that increased propensity to trade outside Western Europe is accounted for by the increased intensity of the region's trade with neighbouring Eastern Europe: as Table 2.3 shows, despite a 50 per cent increase in that intensity index during the past three decades, the Eastern bloc's share of West European trade has been no more than 5 per cent.

Turning to Eastern Europe's own trade, half or more of the trade of European members of Comecon was with other European members of that communist trade bloc during the Cold-War period (compared with less than one-fifth in the previous hundred-plus years). But since those countries accounted for one-tenth or less of world trade during the cold war, the intensity of intra-East European/Soviet trade has been extremely high. As shown in part 3 of Table 2.2, their index of intra-regional trade intensity has been more than 7 since the 1950s, compared with an average of less than half that in the inter-war period.

Most of that change for Eastern Europe has been at the expense of its trade with Western Europe: the intensity of trade index with those neighbors fell by two-thirds between the inter-war period and the 1950s. While it has remained low since then, it has been nontheless creeping up slowly, from 0.4 in 1958 to 0.5 in the early 1970s, 0.6 in the early 1980s and almost 0.7 in 1990. And so too has the intensity of East European/Soviet trade with the rest of the world (final section of Table 2.3). Thus by 1990 this region's index of propensity to trade outside Eastern Europe was as high as that of Western Europe (part 7 of Table 2.2).

Table 2.3 Trade shares and the intensity of regionalization of the merchandise trade for Western Europe (WE) and of Eastern Europe and the former Soviet Union (EESU), 1928 to 1990

	1928	1938	1948	1958	1968	1979	1983	1990
Share (%) of WE trade[a] that is:								
intra-WE	51	49	43	53	63	66	65	72
with EESU	7	9	5	4	5	5	5	3
with rest of world	42	42	52	43	32	29	30	25
Share (%) of EESU trade[a] that is:								
intra-EESU	19	14	47	61	64	54	58	46
with Western Europe	67	63	34	17	20	26	22	32
with rest of world	14	23	19	22	16	20	20	22
Index of intensity of WE trade:[b]								
intra-WE	1.13	1.14	1.21	1.38	1.51	1.57	1.72	1.60
with EESU	1.39	1.37	0.92	0.41	0.45	0.57	0.56	0.66
with WE and EESU	1.13	1.14	1.14	1.16	1.27	1.38	1.46	1.47
with rest of world	0.84	9.83	0.88	0.83	0.68	0.58	0.57	0.49
Index of intensity of EESU trade:[b]								
intra-EESU	4.36	2.61	10.22	7.62	7.30	7.88	7.28	10.88
with Western Europe	1.42	1.39	0.94	0.42	0.45	0.58	0.56	0.68
with EESU and WE	1.66	1.51	1.96	1.60	1.56	1.55	1.66	1.51
with rest of world	0.29	0.46	0.33	0.43	0.35	0.41	0.38	0.46

Notes: [a] Average of merchandise export and import trade. Eastern Europe is defined here to include Bulgaria, Czechoslovakia, the former German Democratic Republic (except in 1928), Hungary, Poland, Romania and the former Soviet Union. Western Europe includes Turkey and Yugoslavia as well as member states of the EC and EFTA. Trade between republics of the former Soviet Union is not counted.
[b] The trade intensity index is defined in the text following equation (2.1). The numbers shown are the average of indexes for merchandise exports and imports.

Sources: See the Appendix in this volume.

2.2.2 The Americas

Trade between Canada and the United States has represented about a third of North America's international trade during the post-war period. While this is higher than the inter-war share of about a quarter, it has been lower in recent years than at its peak around 1970. But since North America's share of world trade declined somewhat from the late 1960s, the intensity of its intra-regional trade rose in the 1970s before falling slightly since then, and conversely for the extra-regional trade intensity index (parts 1–4 of Table 2.2). (When Mexico is included in the definition of North America, the intra-regional trade intensity indexes are a little lower but otherwise show a similar trend – see row 7 of Table 2.4).

However, the share of GDP that is internationally traded has grown even faster for North America than for Western Europe (part 5 of

Table 2.4 Trade shares and the intensity of regionalization of the merchandise trade for North America including Mexico (NA + M) and Latin America excluding Mexico (LA − M), 1928 to 1990

	1928	1938	1948	1958	1968	1979	1983	1990
Share (%) of NA + M trade[a] that is:								
intra-(NA + M)	29	25	37	38	40	35	36	40
with LA − M	15	15	16	18	10	10	9	5
with rest of world	56	60	47	44	50	55	55	55
Share (%) of LA − M trade[a] that is:								
intra-(LA − M)	11	19	38	18	20	22	19	16
with NA + M	36	32	32	41	41	32	35	31
with rest of world	53	49	30	41	39	46	46	53
Index of intensity of NA + M trade:[b]								
intra-(NA + M)	2.21	2.33	2.24	2.72	2.90	3.09	2.98	3.21
with LA − M	1.84	2.01	1.31	1.98	1.96	1.87	1.91	1.63
with all the Americas	2.07	2.20	1.84	2.43	2.65	2.71	2.68	2.90
with rest of world	0.73	0.75	0.68	0.59	0.64	0.68	0.68	0.67
Index of intensity of LA − M trade:[b]								
intra-(LA − M)	1.51	2.73	3.55	2.22	4.28	4.82	4.57	5.70
with NA + M	1.96	2.11	1.41	2.11	2.09	1.97	2.02	1.73
with all the Americas	1.83	2.13	2.11	2.14	2.51	2.59	2.53	2.26
with rest of world	0.71	0.67	0.43	0.57	0.52	0.58	0.58	0.67

Notes: [a] Average of merchandise export and import trade.
[b] The trade intensity index is defined in the text following equation (2.1). The numbers shown are the average of indexes for merchandise exports and imports.

Sources: See the Appendix in this volume.

Table 2.2). As a consequence, the index of propensity for North America to trade extra-regionally has steadily increased since the 1930s, from 0.06 in 1938 and 0.07 in 1958 and 1968 to 0.14 by 1990 (part 7 of Table 2.2). A small part of that growth is attributable to trade with Mexico, but the share and intensity of North America's trade with other Latin American economies have actually declined (rows 2 and 8 of Table 2.4).

Latin America's intra-regional trade share rose in the 1930s and 1940s as those countries adopted inward-looking trade policies, but it has steadily declined since then. The decline is not surprising given the dramatic fall in the region's share of global trade (parts 1 and 2 of Table 2.2) – itself a consequence of their adoption of more protectionist policies. In fact the intensity of the region's intra-regional trade has more than doubled during the post-war period (part 3 of Table 2.2). This was boosted in large part by the formation of various RIAs in the 1960s, which sought to extend those countries inward-looking, import-substituting industrialization strategies from the national to the regional level. But because the region is such a small contributor to global trade the indexes of intensity and propensity of its extra-regional trade are little different now than they were in the early post-war years (parts 4 and 7 of Table 2.2).

2.2.3   Asia (including the Southwest Pacific)

About half of Asia's trade is intra-regional at present, as was the case in the inter-war period. But in the third quarter of the century it was barely 40 per cent. To understand why requires first examining Japan's international trade. That trade was very heavily focused on its neighbours in the inter-war period: as much as two-thirds of Japanese trade was then with other Asian economies. However, following the collapse of the Japanese empire in the mid-1940s and the decline of barriers to Japan's trade with other industrial economies between the 1950s and 1970s, the share of its trade with other Asian economies dropped to half the inter-war level (part 1 of Table 2.2). Thus the index of intensity of Japan's trade outside Asia has grown steadily, rising from a low of less than 0.4 in the 1930s to more than double that from the 1960s (part 4 of Table 2.2).

Australia and New Zealand, by contrast, traded little with Asia before the late 1950s as most of their ties were with the UK. The latter ties gradually weakened as Commonwealth preferences eroded, as the EC's Common Agricultural Policy reduced European demand for Australasia's farm products (particularly after the UK joined the EC in 1972), as restrictions on trade with Japan were relaxed from the mid-1950s, and as industrialization boomed first in Japan and then in a growing number of East Asia's developing countries (Anderson *et al.*, 1985). The net effect of these developments (aided in a small way by the RIA formed between Australia and New Zealand in the 1980s) was a trebling in the share and intensity of Australasia's trade with Asia between 1950 and 1980 (parts 1 and 3 of Table 2.2).

The share of developing Asian economies' trade within Asia fell a little with the collapse of the Japanese empire in the 1940s, but increased again over the post-war years as the region's share of world trade grew. Throughout the period their intra-regional trade intensity has remained high (part 3 of Table 2.2), reflecting not only relative proximity in terms of distance and culture but also strong complementarity with the more advanced economies of the region, especially Japan. But with the dramatic growth in the share of their GDP that is traded, the index of their propensity to trade extra-regionally has doubled in the post-war period (part 7 of Table 2.2).

The aggregate effect of these changes has been for Asia's indexes of propensity to trade intra-regionally and extra-regionally to both fluctuate

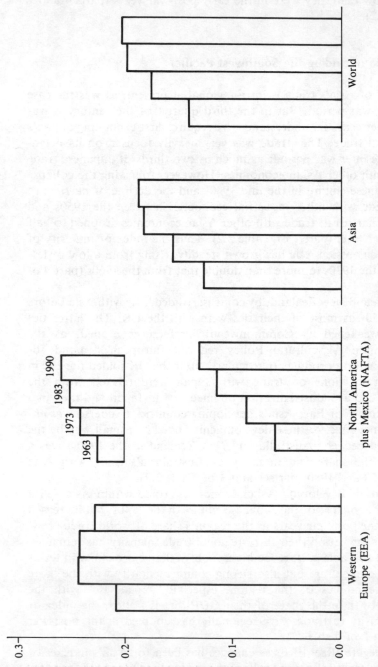

Figure 2.1 Index of propensity to trade extra-regionally,[a] various regions, 1963 to 1990.

Note: [a] The propensity to trade index is defined in equation (2.4) in the text. The numbers shown are based on the average of merchandise export and import trade intensities.

Sources: See the Appendix in this volume.

around a flat trend since 1928 (parts 6 and 7 of Table 2.2). But note that Asia's propensity to trade extra-regionally is significantly higher today than it was in the 1960s, and that this increase has occurred despite the deepening integration within Asia via market forces[14] – a phenomenon that has been described as 'open regionalism' (Drysdale and Garnaut, 1993).

2.2.4   Africa and the Middle East

The other developing countries, of Africa and the Middle East, in total account for less than one-tenth of world trade and so their impact on the extent of regionalization in global trade is necessarily minor. Even so, it is noteworthy that for each of these regions the share of their trade that is intra-regional has declined in recent decades. In the case of Africa this is not surprising because its share of world trade has been falling. In fact it has fallen faster than Africa's intra-regional trade share, causing its index of intensity of intra-regional trade to rise (part 3 of Table 2.2). But during the past decade or so a number of African economies have been increasing the share of their GDP that is traded. As a consequence, the indexes of their (and the Middle East's) propensity to trade extra-regionally have risen during the past two decades and are now about as high as they were in the 1930s (part 7 of Table 2.2).

In short, the world appears to have become more interdependent in recent decades, at least as measured by the indexes of the various geographic regions' propensities to trade extra-regionally. True, that index is no higher now than it was in 1928 for the world as a whole (as a weighted average for the seven regions shown in the last row of Table 2.2), but it is substantially higher than in the 1930s or 1950s. Figure 2.1 summarizes those indexes for the three major trading regions and globally for the past three decades. Even though several important intra-regional integration agreements have come into force during that period, Figure 2.1 shows that nonetheless the world has been opening up sufficiently rapidly for integration between regions to continue. Indeed, that index for the world has increased by almost 50 per cent since 1963 – and it has increased even for Western Europe.

2.3   The effects of dismantling imperial trade preferences[15]

A major contributor to the reduction in the share of Western Europe's trade with the rest of the world during the post-war years, apart from the

Table 2.5   Shares and intensities of the United Kingdom's merchandise trade with various country groups, 1854 to 1989

	Former British Empire[a]	EC-6[b]	Other Western Europe[c]	Rest of the world
Trade shares (%)[e]				
1854-9	28	23	46	
1870-9	26	28	46	
1890-9	28	26	46	
1913	35	31	10	24
1928	38	21	8	33
1938	48	15	11	25
1948	48	10	10	31
1958	39	14	15	32
1965	31	18	19	32
1971	23	21	21	36
1978	14	33 (40)[d]	22 (15)[d]	29
1984	11	38 (45)[d]	21 (15)[d]	30
1989	10	41 (51)[d]	20 (11)[d]	28
Trade intensity index[f]				
1913	2.44	0.87	0.93	0.57
1928	2.77	0.87	1.33	0.60
1938	3.49	0.71	1.48	0.46
1948	2.35	0.60	1.18	0.58
1958	2.56	0.58	0.50	0.62
1965	2.07	0.58	1.57	0.77
1971	1.65	0.63	1.77	0.86
1978	1.25	1.01 (1.17)[d]	1.94 (1.54)[d]	0.64
1984	0.83	1.43 (1.55)[d]	2.02 (1.72)[d]	0.60
1989	0.72	1.42 (1.50)[d]	1.63 (1.43)[d]	0.64

Notes: [a] The former British Empire is what GATT (1958) specifies as the Sterling Area plus Canada for the period up to 1957. Thereafter it is defined as the countries of the British Commonwealth plus Hong Kong, Pakistan and South Africa. Many of the 49 Commonwealth members are tiny traders for which data are difficult to obtain for all years. Hence only the largest 29 of those 49 are included, but they nonetheless account for 97 per cent of Commonwealth trade and 99 per cent of the population of the Commonwealth. The 29 countries by region are as follows: *Africa*: Ghana, Kenya, Malawi, Mauritius, Nigeria, Sierra Leone, Tanzania, Uganda, Zambia and Zimbabwe; *Asia* (including Southwest Pacific): Australia, Bangladesh, Brunei, Fiji, India, Malaysia, New Zealand, Papua New Guinea, Singapore and Sri Lanka; *Latin America*: Bahamas, Barbados, Guyana, Jamaica, and Trinidad and Tobago; *North America*: Canada; *Western Europe*: Cyprus, Malta and United Kingdom.
[b] Belgium, France, FR Germany, Italy, Luxembourg and the Netherlands.
[c] Austria, Denmark, Finland, Greece, Ireland, Norway, Portugal, Spain, Sweden, Switzerland and Turkey.
[d] The numbers in parentheses refer to the expanded membership of the EC and the corresponding reduction in the 'Other Western Europe' group of countries. In 1978 the EC included Denmark and Ireland (as well as the UK), in 1984 it included also Greece, and in 1989 Portugal and Spain.
[e] Average of merchandise export and import trade.
[f] The intensity of trade index is defined in the text in equation (2.1). The numbers shown are the average for merchandise exports and imports. It is not possible to calculate indexes prior to 1913 because of incomplete estimates of different regions' shares of world trade.

Sources: The data to 1913 are from the British Board of Trade (1903, 1930); the 1928, 1938 and 1948 data are from GATT (1958); subsequent data are from the International Monetary Fund, *Direction of Trade*, Washington, D.C., various years, as compiled by Garrand (1986) for 1958-84 and the authors for 1989.

building of regional trade preferences, has been the decline of imperial preferences. From the early 1800s until World War I the United Kingdom was the world's largest trading nation, and France was equal second, partly because both had large empires spread around the world.[16] The dismantling of those (and the Belgian, Dutch, Japanese and other) empires after World War II, and the gradual removal of their associated preferential trade agreements, may even have improved global welfare (as may the recent collapse of Comecon, the preferential trade arrangement among former centrally planned economies). One crude indicator of the reduction of those preferences is the decline, from very high levels, in the intensity of trade among members of former imperial blocs. We consider in turn the British and French colonial trade ties and then the communist bloc, before turning briefly to the experience in Asia with the building and then dismantling of the Japanese Empire during the first half of this century.

2.3.1 The British and French connections

From the mid-1800s until just prior to the Depression of the early 1930s, between 25 and 40 per cent of the UK's trade was with former British Empire economies (Table 2.5). There were some imperial tariff preferences in place prior to the 1930s, but they were perceived as being of only minor importance because the general level of British tariffs was so low (Benham, 1941). The Depression prompted radical tariff increases, however. Following the 1932 Ottawa Conference, British Commonwealth countries offered substantial preferential tariff rates on intra-Commonwealth trade. According to one set of estimates, the preferential margin on British exports to other Commonwealth countries doubled between 1929 and 1937 (from 5 percentage points), while that on Britain's imports from those countries increased four-fold (from about 3 percentage points – see MacDougall and Hutt, 1954, p. 237).

Other European powers also reoriented their trade more towards their former colonies from the late 1920s (Thorbecke, 1960; Pomfret, 1988). Most of the French colonies were brought into a free trade area with France in 1928 (Haight, 1941), by which time about one-sixth of France's trade was with those countries, and in the early 1930s France sought more imports from its overseas dependencies, etc., as a form of loan repayments (Table 2.6).

It is not surprising, therefore, to observe in column 1 of Tables 2.5 and 2.6 a jump in imperial trade shares in the 1930s. There was an increase of more than 10 percentage points in the shares of both the UK's and France's trade with their former colonies between 1928 and 1938. A

Table 2.6 Shares and intensities of France's merchandise trade with various country groups, 1881 to 1989

	Former French territories etc.[a]	EC-6[b]	Other Western Europe[c]	Rest of the world
Trade shares (%)[e]				
1881–90	10	24	66	
1891–1900	13	21	66	
1913	18	24	21	37
1928	16	15	17	52
1938	27	22	19	32
1955	27	22	17	34
1971	9	49	16	26
1980	7	41 (48)[d]	18 (11)[d]	34
1989	3	43 (59)[d]	24 (8)[d]	30
Trade intensity index[f]				
1928	6.23	1.67	1.15	1.07
1938	13.15	1.41	0.84	0.49
1955	9.66	1.28	0.80	0.57
1971	4.63	1.86	0.73	0.49
1980	4.09	1.72 (1.42)[d]	0.79 (0.84)[d]	0.63
1989	2.73	1.81 (1.72)[d]	0.96 (0.55)[d]	0.58

Notes: [a] The former French territories etc., include many tiny economies whose inclusion would make no difference to the data shown. The 33 included countries by region are as follows: *Africa*: Algeria, Benin, Burkina Faso, Cameroon, Central African Republic, Chad, Congo, Côte d'Ivoire, Djibouti, Equatorial Guinea, Gabon, Guinea, Madagascar, Mali, Mauritania, Morocco, Niger, Reunion, Senegal, Somalia, Togo, Tunisia, Upper Volta; *Asia* (including Southwest Pacific): Cambodia, French Polynesia, Laos, New Caledonia, Vanuatu, Viet Nam; *Latin America*: French Guiana, Guadeloupe, Haiti, Martinique.
[b] Belgium, Germany, Italy, Luxembourg and the Netherlands (plus France).
[c] Austria, Denmark, Finland, Greece, Ireland, Norway, Portugal, Spain, Sweden, Switzerland and Turkey and the United Kingdom.
[d] The numbers in parentheses refer to the expanded membership of the EC and the corresponding reduction in the 'Other Western Europe' group of countries. In 1980 the EC included Denmark, Ireland and the United Kingdom, in 1989 it included also Greece, Portugal and Spain.
[e] Average of merchandise exports and imports.
[f] The intensity of trade index is defined in the text in equation (2.1). The numbers shown are the average for merchandise exports and imports. It is not possible to calculate indexes prior to 1928 because of incomplete estimates of different regions' world trade shares.

Sources: INSEE (1947) for data to 1913; League of Nations (1941) for 1928 and 1938 data; thereafter from the IMF, *Direction of Trade*, Washington, DC, various years.

decade later those economies still accounted for much of the metropoles' trade, but since the early 1950s their shares have fallen steadily and now represent barely one-tenth of UK trade and less than one-twentieth of French trade.

Only a small part of the change in the share of Commonwealth countries in UK trade is due to changes in those former dependencies' shares of world trade. This can be seen by calculating the intensity of trade index (which is close to the ratio of those two shares – see equation (2.1) above). The lower half of Table 2.5 shows that in 1913 and 1928 the former British dependencies were 2.4 to 2.8 times as important to UK trade as were those economies to world trade; that by 1938 that ratio had increased to 3.5; but that thereafter it declined greatly and is now well below unity and barely one-fifth of its peak. It follows that almost none of the decline in these countries' share of UK trade is due to their declining importance in world trade.[17] The question is: how much of the rest is due to the gradual dismantling of Commonwealth preferences and the UK's switch from negative to positive discriminatory regional trade arrangements with continental Europe?

The UK joined the European Free Trade Association as a founding member in 1960. As a result, the share and intensity of its trade with those countries grew rapidly in the 1960s. The share of the UK's trade with the EC-6 also grew between 1958 and 1971, but not much faster than the EC's share of world trade, so the intensity of UK trade with the EC-6 grew only a little, and from a low base (see the middle two columns of Table 2.5). Once the UK left EFTA to join the EC in 1972, however, both its share and intensity of trade with other EC countries rose substantially. This occurred not so much at the expense of EFTA countries (which signed a free trade agreement with the EC in 1972 for most manufactured goods) but at the expense of Commonwealth countries and to a lesser extent the rest of the world.

The changes in the intensity of the UK's trade with these four groups of countries is clear from Figure 2.2: the index for the EC is now above that for other Western Europe for the first time (having been barely or less than half prior to the 1970s), and that for Commonwealth countries is now little higher than that for the rest of the world (having been four to seven times as high prior to the UK joining EFTA). While some of this change in recent years is attributable to the increased complementarity in intra-industry trade in manufactures as European incomes rose (Sapir, 1992), the change is far too great for that to be a major contributor.

Furthermore, the decline in the importance of Commonwealth countries in UK trade is not due to just a few countries. Anderson and Norheim (1992, Table 6) show that the intensity of the UK's export trade with Commonwealth countries has decreased for all geographic regions, though least so for Africa which continues to enjoy some preferential access to UK (and other EC) markets under the Lomé Convention. In turn, the intensities of those Commonwealth countries' exports not only to the UK but also to other Commonwealth countries have in most cases and certainly on average declined, as Commonwealth preferences have been dismantled. But the indexes of intra-regional trade intensity remain

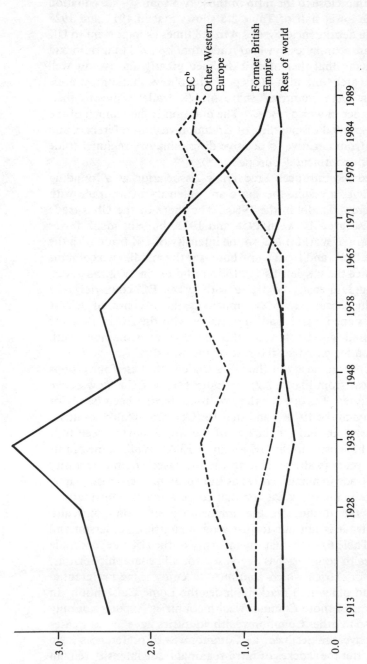

Figure 2.2 Index of intensity of the United Kingdom's merchandise trade with various country groups, [a] 1913 to 1989.

Note: [a] Average of the export and import trade intensity indexes reported in Table 2.5, where the definitions of the indexes and country groups are given.
[b] EC refers to EC-6 up to 1971, EC-9 in 1978, EC-10 in 1984 and EC-12 in 1989; other Western Europe refers to all but EC-6 up to 1971 but thereafter excludes also the new members of the EC (Denmark and Ireland from 1978; Greece also from 1984; Spain and Portugal also in 1989).

Source: Table 2.5 above.

well above those for extra-regional trade among those countries, testifying to the continuing importance of geography in addition to history and preferential trade policies.

For France the decline in the index of intensity of its trade with its former colonies, etc., was from an even greater height than was the case for the UK, from about 6 in 1928 and 13 in 1938 to less than 3 today (lower half of Table 2.6). Thus less than one-eighth of the decline in the share of France's trade with those economies is the result of the declining importance of the latter in world trade. Again the question is: how much of the residual can be explained by changes in trade preferences?

Many of France's former dependencies were not as badly affected as Britain's by the formation of the EC, because a much larger proportion of their trade retained preferential access to French markets via the Lomé Convention.[18] Thus the index of intensity of their trade with France still averages 2.7, compared with 0.7 for the trade of Commonwealth countries with the UK. The index of intensity of France's trade with other founding members of the EC-6 took a distinct jump after the EC's formation in 1958, from less than 1.3 to nearly 1.9 by the early 1970s, or 1.7 by the late 1980s when the more recent six EC entrants also are included. Meanwhile, France's trade intensity with the rest of Western Europe has declined considerably to less than 0.6, and the intensity of its trade with the rest of the world has remained at a similarly low level. In short, preferential trade policies would appear to have had a very substantial influence on the past pattern of France's trade, and their influence continues to be considerable.

2.3.2   The communist connection

The European members of the former Comecon, the trade grouping of centrally planned economies, have been relatively open. According to the (admittedly still poor) statistics recently compiled by the World Bank, their trade-to-GDP ratios in 1989 and 1990 averaged a little over 40 per cent. Even though those data ignore trade between the former Soviet republics, that ratio is almost as high as the West European average. But, as mentioned in the previous section, fully half of that trade was with other European members of Comecon at the time of its collapse. Since the economies in that region accounted for only 5 per cent of world trade at that time, this meant the index of intensity of their intra-regional trade was around 10, and appears to have been more than 7 throughout the post-war period (Table 2.3).

Nor has the rest of East Europe's post-war trade been dominated by neighbouring Western Europe, despite strong historical ties based on both proximity and complementarity. Animosity between East and West and separate regional integration agreements in both regions ensured that in 1958 the index of intensity of East Europe's trade with West Europe was only as high as that for its trade with non-European countries (0.4). The former index increased somewhat by the 1970s, was static until the mid-1980s, but has since increased substantially and is now 50 per cent above that for the rest of the world (Table 2.3). That trend is likely to continue for some time, given the current dismantling of preferences among former Comecon members and the establishment of new association accords and cooperation agreements between the economies of East and West. This development is thus providing another example of increased (Europe-wide) regionalization, due to the dismantling of imperial preferences, that is likely to be welfare-improving. Whether the recent and prospective RIAs between East and West Europe and among East European and CIS economies turn out to provide a net improvement in economic welfare is a moot point, however, just as the net benefits of RIAs among West European economies are still being debated.[19]

2.3.3   The Japanese connection

In Japan's case, imperial trade ties with Korea and Taiwan grew to be extremely strong during the inter-war period. The index of intensity of Japan's trade with those two former colonies averaged 12 in 1928 and 16 in 1938 – higher even than France's imperial trade intensity. Most of the increase in Japan's trade share with Asia in the 1910–38 period was due to trade within its empire (which included Kwantung Province and Manchuria). The share of those colonies and China in Japan Proper's trade rose steadily from 28 to 36 per cent between 1910 and 1928 and then jumped to 53 per cent by 1938 (Yamazawa and Yamamoto, 1979). The trade policy of the empire had significant trade-diversionary elements, not least for farm products where the objective was imperial self-sufficiency in food (Anderson and Tyers, 1992).

Those preferences ended with the collapse of the empire at the end of World War II, which is reflected in the big drops, shown in Table 2.2, in the share and intensity of Japan's trade with Asia in the 1950s. By 1990 the index of Japan's trade intensity with Korea and Taiwan averaged about 2.7 – still well above unity although not unreasonably so given their proximity, cultural connections and the strong complementarity in the commodity compositions of their trades, but only one-sixth of its peak in the 1930s.

Japan's trade share with other Asian countries since the 1950s has been boosted by the gradual removal of discriminatory policies of other Asian/Pacific countries against Japan following the war. In Australia's case this − together with the UK's switch from imperial to regional preferences − contributed substantially to the regionalization of its trade: the intensity of Australia's export trade with Japan rose from 3.0 to 4.9 between 1951−5 and 1975−80, and that of its import trade from 1.2 to 2.7 (Anderson *et al.*, 1985). Thus the contribution of discriminatory and preferential trade policies to the regionalization of Asia's trade has been mixed, with some changes lowering intra-regional trade shares and others boosting them. But the net effect of those and other changes has been for Asia as a whole to increase both its intensity and propensity to trade with other regions.

2.4   Conclusions

Several conclusions can be drawn from the above analysis. The first is that in the absence of a computable general equilibrium (CGE) model of world trade and estimates of policy distortions to prices, it is nonetheless possible to get some idea from trade data of the trade effects of discriminatory policies. It is true that the indexes used show the combined effect of natural and policy-induced determinants of the geographic distribution of world trade. But if further research were to show that the natural determinants have not changed much over time, it would not be unreasonable to suspect that the above index trends are due in large part to changes in discriminatory policies.

Second, the trade data suggest that despite increases in the shares and even the indexes of intensity of the major regions' trade that are intra-regional, the propensity of regions to trade a portion of their GDP with other regions has been rising for all the major geographic regions in recent decades. That is, countries have become sufficiently more 'open' over time so that even if RIAs have caused some trade diversion, integration between regions − at least as measured by merchandise trade − has continued for the world as a whole (as depicted in Figure 2.1). We suspect that, if the bilateral trade data were available, the same result would emerge for services trade and factor (or at least investment) flows.[20]

And third, much of Europe's intra-regional economic integration since the mid-1940s has resulted from the dismantling of imperial trade preferences, the global welfare effects of which need not have been negative.

In short, global integration has progressed despite the formation and enlargement of regional integration agreements, and despite the gradual disappearance of imperial preferences that had previously artificially encouraged North–South trade. Some of the former may have at times reduced global welfare through diverting trade, but the latter may have had the opposite effect.[21]

This is not to deny that the world might be a better place without regional integration agreements, of course. (As Bhagwati (1992) has argued forcefully, greater liberalization of global trade might well have occurred if no new RIAs had formed in the post-war years.) Rather, the point is simply that (1) such agreements are not the sole reason – and may not even be a major reason – for the growth in intra-regional trade shares and intensities, and (2) the latter have been accompanied by a general liberalization of trade globally, at least as measured by the trend in the shares of GDP traded internationally and by the decline in the previously extremely high trade intensities within former imperial blocs.

The issue for the 1990s and beyond is whether the recent and prospective proliferation of regional integration agreements will be accompanied by a continuation or reversal of this trend toward a more liberal and more integrated trading world. While both the West Europeans and the North Americans claim they are not and will not be raising external trade barriers, the increased frequency of use of gray-area protection measures in recent years has given cause for concern for excluded economies – to the point that many are lining up to join one or other of those major RIAs or are discussing ways to form another one, such as in the Asian region (Anderson, 1992).

This raises the question of whether an international agency should be monitoring RIAs to determine whether they are harmful to outsiders and, if so, how. One possibility, suggested recently by the GATT's Director General, is that the GATT's Trade Policy Review Division (which currently restricts itself to reviewing national trade policies) be given the task. As McMillan argues in Chapter 13 below, however, a better and more precise criterion would need to be found for determining the GATT admissibility of a RIA than is currently provided in Article XXIV of the GATT. McMillan suggests simply asking whether the volume of a RIA's trade with the rest of the world has increased: as we know from Kemp and Wan (1976), that would ensure excluded economies were better off.

By way of conclusion, it is noteworthy that by that standard the index of propensity to trade extra-regionally used above is a very conservative test of admissibility. It is conservative because it is based on shares of a growing volume of trade and output, rather than just on the volume of trade itself. This adds further strength to the conclusion drawn above that, despite the proliferation of RIAs, trade has continued to contribute to welfare-enhancing integration of the world economy in the past.

Closer monitoring of the external trade effects of RIAs could help to ensure that this continues in the future.

Notes

Thanks are due to Karl-Michael Finger, Paul Bairoch and Ippie Yamazawa for help with sources of data, and to Slobodan Djajic and other conference participants for constructive comments.

1. Only merchandise trade is included because comprehensive data on the direction of international trade in services are not available, even for recent years (despite the fact that services account for about a fifth of world trade in goods and services).
2. Although see the cautionary comments in, for example, Bhagwati (1992) and in Chapter 10 in this volume, by Hoekman and Leidy.
3. This and the next section draw on Anderson and Norheim (1993).
4. The negative relationship between size of economies and their trade-to-GDP ratios has been amply demonstrated empirically (Perkins and Syrquin, 1989). In 1989, for example, the coefficient of correlation between exports plus imports as a percentage of GDP, and the logarithms of area, population and GDP, are respectively -0.48, -0.42 and -0.19, based on a sample of 126 countries for which there are data in GATT (1992, Appendix Tables 4 and 5). There are several reasons for the negative correlation. One is that physically larger countries tend to have a more diverse stock of natural resources and so are better able to match domestic demand and supply, assuming that the structure of demand is not correlated with country size. Another is that transport costs of doing business are likely to favor domestic producers over their foreign competitors for a wider range of products in large countries than in small countries. And when size is measured by GDP, there is a tautological reason that is best illustrated by considering a two-country world with balanced trade: their ratios of trade to GDP will necessarily be inversely proportional to their shares of world GDP. Alternatively, imagine three countries with the same GDPs and trade-to-GDP ratios: if two of them were to merge, the trade ratio in the now large economy would be half that of the small one.
5. The trade intensity index was first popularized by Brown (1949). For a detailed discussion of its use in bilateral trade analysis, see Drysdale and Garnaut (1982).
6. If j is a country group and country i is part of country group j, it is necessary to subtract country i's imports from j's imports not only in the denominator but also in the numerator of the m_j ratio, and likewise to subtract country i's GDP from j's GDP in the numerator of the q_j ratio.
7. The term 'relative openness' is in quotes because the trade-to-GDP ratio should not be interpreted as a measure of the extent to which an economy is subject to trade restrictions, not least because that ratio is affected by the relative size of the economy, as pointed out in note 4 above. For more discussion of measures of openness, see Leamer (1988) and the references therein.
8. An adjustment is necessary because when i is a region there can be international trade between the countries in the region. If all countries in the

region have the same total trade, the required adjustment to the intra-regional trade intensity index involves (1) subtracting not all of 'country' i's imports or GDP from the world but instead only one n-th of that amount in the denominator of the m_j, q_j and r_j ratios, where n is the number of countries in the region, and (2) also subtracting one n-th of 'country' i's imports or GDP from 'country' j's imports or GDP in the numerator of the m_j, q_j and r_j ratios (where j is in fact i in this case). For the extra-regional trade-intensity index, only the first of these two adjustments is needed. Normally of course the total trade values differ between countries of the region, but even then these adjustments will provide close approximations in the sense that if there were no regional trade bias the calculated index values would be close to unity (and more so the smaller the differences in national trade totals within the region).

9. For example, the formation or expansion of a regional customs union could induce foreign direct investment (FDI) or immigration from other regions, thereby altering different regions' comparative advantages.

10. Details of the liberalizations involved can be found in Bairoch (1989), Kindleberger (1975) and the references in the latter. It should be kept in mind that the GNP estimates for this period have even wider confidence bands than the estimates of trade values.

11. For data availability reasons we have adopted the same seven geographic regions as used by GATT statisticians. As well as Western and Eastern Europe, these are North and Latin America, Asia including the Southwest Pacific islands, Africa, and the Middle East. For details, see the Appendix in this volume.

12. By way of comparison, the index of intra-regional trade intensity in 1990 was 3.5 in both North and Latin America and 2.3 in Asia. Caution is needed in comparing these index values, however, for at least two reasons. First, as equations (2.2) and (2.3) above make clear, the index will be lower the less complementary are the commodity compositions of neighbors' trades within regions. And second, the larger a region's share of world trade, the closer its index of intra-regional trade intensity will be to unity, *ceteris paribus*. Since Western Europe's share of world trade is more than twice that of North America or Asia, this alone gives reason to expect the index to be somewhat lower for Europe than for North America or Asia.

13. Western Europe's relatively rapid income growth, particularly in per capita terms, is significant partly because larger economies tend to trade less (note 4 above) but also because more affluent economies tend to engage more in intra-industry trade in differentiated products among themselves (Linder, 1961).

14. According to regression analyses by Frankel (1992), the increase in intra-Asian trade is explainable by normal market developments, leaving no bias left to be explained by discriminatory policies or practices within Asia. See also Leamer (1988) and Petri (1992).

15. This section draws on Anderson and Norheim (1992).

16. In the latter half of the nineteenth century the UK accounted for between 20 and 25 per cent of world trade and its colonies and dominions contributed a further 10 per cent. The next largest traders, France, Germany and the United States, each contributed around 10 per cent during that period (Kuznets, 1966, Table 6.3).

17. Nor was it due in the 1960s and 1970s to a major decline in complementarity

in trade between the UK and Commonwealth countries. See, for example, the estimates reported in Garrand (1986, Table 2.6) of C_{ij}, the index of trade complementarity defined above in equation (2.2).

18. About the same proporton (almost half) of both the British and the French colonies listed in note [a] of Tables 2.5 and 2.6 became ACP countries under the Lomé Convention and thereby have been able to enjoy preferential access to EC markets. But the favored half of those with British connections represented in 1990 only one-twentieth of the trade and GDP of all those listed countries with British connections, whereas the favored half of those with French connections represented a third of the trade and GDP of the former French dependencies.

19. Winters (1992), for example, argues that the EC's economic growth performance has been lackluster, and not least because of the numerous protective aspects of its external trade policy. Sapir (1992), on the other hand, offers a more positive assessment. The truth depends on whether one views a cup as half full or half empty: Western Europe's economies have not performed as well as East Asia's, but they have certainly out-performed North America's and the rest of the world's. Between 1958 and 1990 (and hence after the post-war reconstruction boom), for example, the shares of global GDP changed as follows: increases from 26 to 34 per cent for Western Europe and from 11 to 25 per cent for Asia, compared with decreases from 45 to 29 per cent for North America and from 18 to 12 per cent for the rest of the world (see Table A8 in the Appendix in this volume).

20. It needs to be kept in mind, though, that not all of the increased 'openness' of economies is due to policy reform; some of the increase in the trade-to-GDP ratios is the result of (1) declines in natural barriers to trade such as international transport and communication costs, and (2) the increased importance of intra-industry trade as specialization in producing intermediate inputs grows and as customer preferences for product variety intensify.

21. There is still no clear consensus on even the direction of the actual welfare effects of RIAs on excluded countries and hence on global welfare (Lloyd, 1992; and the following chapter in this volume, by Srinivasan, Whalley and Wooton). Indeed Hoekman and Leidy argue in Chapter 10 below that, given the loopholes that allow contingent protection (anti-dumping, countervailing the safeguards provisions) under current trade agreements, it is impossible to estimate all their effects.

References

Anderson, K. (1992), 'Regional Integration Agreements, Excluded Economies, and the Global Trading System', presented at a conference on NAFTA, the Pacific and Australia/New Zealand, Austin, Texas, 1–2 October.

Anderson, K. *et al.* (1985), 'Pacific Economic Growth and Prospects for Australian Trade', Pacific Economic Papers No. 122, Canberra: Australia–Japan Research Centre, May.

Anderson, K. and H. Norheim (1992), 'From Imperial to Regional Trade Preferences: Its Effects on Europe's Intra- and Extra-regional Trade', mimeo, GATT Secretariat, Geneva, July (forthcoming in *Weltwirtschaftliches Archiv*, 1993).

Anderson, K. and H. Norheim (1993), 'Is World Trade Becoming More regionalized?', *Review of International Economics* **1** (forthcoming June).

Anderson, K. and R. Tyers (1992), 'Japanese Rice Policy in the Inter-War Period: Some Consequences of Imperial Self Sufficiency', *Japan and the World Economy* **4**: 103–27.

Bairoch, P. (1974), 'Geographical Structure and Trade Balance of European Foreign Trade From 1800 to 1970', *Journal of European Economic History* **3**: 557–608.

Bairoch, P. (1976a), *Commerce exterieur et developpement economique de l'Europe au XIXe siecle*, Paris: Mouton.

Bairoch, P. (1976b), 'Europe's Gross National Product 1800–1975', *Journal of European Economic History* **5**: 273–340.

Bairoch, P. (1989), 'European Trade Policy, 1815–1914', in *The Cambridge Economic History of Europe, Vol. VIII: The Industrial Economies*, edited by P. Mathias and S. Pollard, Cambridge: Cambridge University Press.

Balassa, B. (1965), 'Trade Liberalization and "Revealed" Comparative Advantage', *Manchester School of Economic and Social Studies* **33**: 90–124.

Benham, F. (1941), *Great Britain Under Protection*, London: Macmillan.

Bhagwati, J. N. (1992), 'Regionalism and Multilateralism: An Overview', presented to the World Bank/Centre for Economic Policy Research Conference on New Dimensions in Regional Integration, Washington, DC, 2–3 April.

British Board of Trade (1903, 1930), *Statistical Tables Relating to British and Foreign Trade and Industry*, London: HMSO.

Brown, A. J. (1949), *Applied Economics: Aspects of the World Economy in War and Peace*, London: George Allen and Unwin.

Clarida, R. H. and R. Findlay (1992), 'Government, Trade, and Comparative Advantage', *American Economic Review* **82**: 122–7.

Drysdale, P. (1988), *International Economic Pluralism: Economic Policy in East Asia and the Pacific*, New York: Columbia University Press.

Drysdale, P. and R. Garnaut (1982), 'Trade Intensities and the Analysis of Bilateral Trade Flows in a Many-Country World', *Hitotsubashi Journal of Economics* **22**: 62–84.

Drysdale, P. and R. Garnaut (1993), 'The Pacific: An Application of a General Theory of Economic Integration', in *Pacific Dynamism and the International Economic System*, edited by M. Noland, Washington, DC: Institute for International Economics.

Frankel, J. A. (1992), 'Is Japan Creating a Yen Bloc in East Asia and the Pacific?', mimeo, University of California, Berkeley, April.

Garrand, R. (1986), 'The Changing Pattern of Commonwealth Trade: An Analysis of biases in Trade', unpublished honours thesis, Flinders University, Adelaide, Australia.

GATT (1958), *Trends in International Trade: A Report by a Panel of Experts*, Geneva: General Agreement on Tariffs and Trade.

GATT (1987), *International Trade 1986–87*, Geneva: General Agreement on Tariffs and Trade.

GATT (1992), *International Trade 1990–91, Vol. II*, Geneva: General Agreement on Tariffs and Trade.

Haight, F. A. (1941), *A History of French Commercial Policy*, New York: Macmillan.

INSEE (1947), *Annuaire Statistique, 1946: Resumé Retrospectif*, Paris: Imprimerie Nationale.

Kemp, M. C. and H. Wan (1976), 'An Elementary Proposition Concerning the Formation of Customs Unions', *Journal of International Economics* 6: 95–7.

Kindleberger, C. P. (1975), 'The Rise of Free Trade in Western Europe, 1820–1875', *Journal of Economic History* 35: 20–55.

Krugman, P. (1991), *Geography and Trade*, Cambridge, MA: MIT Press.

Kuznets, S. S. (1966), *Modern Economic Growth: Rate, Structure and Spread*, New Haven: Yale University Press.

League of Nations (1941), *Europe's Trade: A Study of the Trade of European Countries With Each Other and With the Rest of the World*, Geneva: League of Nations.

League of Nations (1942), *The Network of World Trade*, Geneva: League of Nations.

League of Nations (1945), *Industrialisation and Foreign Trade*, Geneva: League of Nations.

Leamer, E. E. (1988), 'Measures of Openness', in *Trade Policy Issues and Empirical Analysis*, edited by R. E. Baldwin, Chicago: University of Chicago Press.

Linder, S. B. (1961), *An Essay on Trade and Transformation*, New York: Wiley.

Lloyd, P. J. (1992), 'Regionalization and World Trade', *OECD Economic Studies* 18: 7–34.

MacDougall, D. and R. Hutt (1954), 'Imperial Preferences: A Quantitative Analysis', *Economic Journal* 64: 233–57.

North, D. C. (1958), 'Ocean Freight Rates and Economic Development, 1750–1913', *Journal of Economic History* 18: 537–55.

Perkins, D. H. and M. Syrquin (1989), 'Large Countries: The Influence of Size', in *Handbook of Development Economics, Vol. 2*, edited by H. Chenery and T. N. Srinivasan, Amsterdam: North-Holland.

Petri, P. (1992), 'The East Asian Trading Bloc: An Analytical History', Working Paper No. 315, Brandeis University, Waltham, MA, March.

Pomfret, R. W. T. (1988), *Unequal Trade: The Economics of Discriminatory International Trade Policies*, Oxford: Basil Blackwell.

Sapir, A. (1992), 'Regional Integration in Europe', *Economic Journal* 102: 1491–506.

Thorbecke, E. (1960), *The Tendency Towards Regionalization in International Trade, 1928–1956*, The Hague: Martinus Nijhoff.

Tracy, J. (ed.) (1991), *The Rise of Merchant Empires*, Cambridge: Cambridge University Press.

United Nations (1964), *Yearbook of International Trade Statistics*, New York: United Nations.

Winters, L. A. (1992), 'European Integration: A Case of Successful Integration?', presented at a World Bank/Centre for Economic Policy Research conference on New Dimensions in Regional Integration, Washington, DC, 2–3 April.

Yamazawa, I. and Y. Yamamoto (1979), *Estimates of Long Term Economic Statistics of Japan Since 1868, Vol. 14: Foreign Trade and the Balance of Payments*, Tokyo: Toyo Keizai Shimposha.

3

Measuring the effects of regionalism on trade and welfare

T. N. Srinivasan, John Whalley and Ian Wooton

The post-war years have seen a steady growth in regional integration agreements in the global economy.[1] The period from the late 1950s through to the mid-1970s saw the formation of the EC and EFTA, the Canada–US Auto Pact, and integration agreements in East Africa, Latin America and elsewhere. Recent years have seen a second wave of regionalism with the Canada–US Free Trade Agreement (CUSFTA), negotiations on a North American Free Trade Agreement (NAFTA), Europe '1992', the Australia–New Zealand Closer Economic Relations Trade Agreement (ANZCERTA) and commitments to an ASEAN Free Trade Arrangement (AFTA).[2]

This chapter assesses the effects of these regional integration agreements (RIAs) on trade and welfare. We draw on theoretical and empirical literatures and examine both time-series trade data for various regional groupings and *ex ante* and *ex post* studies of RIAs. We then draw general lessons as to the possible trade and welfare implications of both older and more recent RIAs, as well as the regionalism that may follow in the 1990s.

We make three main points in the paper concerning the quantitative effects of RIAs. First, the data we examine show that, despite a long and ever-growing list of post-war RIAs, the share of global trade which takes place within regions seems to have changed little over the post-war years. With the exception of the EC between 1960 and 1970, RIAs seem to have had relatively little long-term impact on trading patterns, suggesting that concerns over the impacts of new regionalism on the global economy in the 1990s could be somewhat overblown.

Second, model-based and other studies as to the trade and welfare effects of such agreements are somewhat inconclusive. Older studies show small welfare effects from RIAs. Newer studies capturing scale economy and market structure effects generally show larger welfare effects, but with high variance in results. These effects also enter analyses in ad hoc ways. Both sets of studies generally show larger trade than welfare effects. Other studies of shifts in trade patterns following regional integration are not based on meaningful microeconomic foundations, do not yield results on welfare effects, and face numerous econometric problems. In light of these inconsistencies we suggest, somewhat tentatively, that the picture from these studies is murky, although the mid-point in results may not be that far from the conclusions from our trade data analyses reported above.

We emphasize additional reasons as to why, in our view, the new regionalism will likely do little to significantly further change regional trade patterns in the global economy. One reason is that, in contrast to the earlier wave of post-war regionalism, new RIAs are more defensive than integrationist in nature, with smaller countries seeking 'safe-haven' trade agreements[3] with larger countries. A second reason is that they tend to focus on smaller trade linkages than the older regional schemes that preceded them. And third, the extent to which there is genuine new liberalization in these agreements is in doubt.

Finally, it is worth emphasizing that much of the literature on measuring the effects of RIAs on trade and welfare uses a classical Vinerian trade-creation/trade-diversion framework which, we argue, is not well suited to the study and quantification of more recent regional integration.[4] The *new regionalism* reflects, in part, efforts by smaller countries to achieve safe-haven agreements with larger countries. It also indicates a movement toward regional trading blocs and weakened multilateral disciplines, with threats of global trade wars and impaired economic performance for excluded smaller countries. Neither of these concerns is addressed by available studies. Also, regionalism and multilateralism do not represent exclusive choices, having coexisted in the trading system since 1947, and the central current issue is the potential effects of a more pronounced tilt toward regional agreements rather than the effects of RIAs themselves.

3.1   Theoretical issues

Theoretical literature on RIAs has tended to focus on geographically discriminatory tariff-based arrangements of the customs union type, rather than the range of discriminatory arrangements actually used in RIAs around the world.[5] Discussion of the welfare and trade effects of customs unions has been one of the staples of trade theorists over the post-war years, from Viner (1950), through Meade (1955) and Lipsey (1957), to Berglas (1979), Wonnacott and Wonnacott (1981), and Wooton (1986).

In a competitive world, a global Pareto-optimal allocation is achieved when there is free trade between countries. While a move away from a tariff-free world will reduce aggregate world product, country welfare will increase for a non-small open economy if it imposes a small tariff.[6] But as Scitovsky (1941) and Johnson (1953) showed, such beggar-thy-neighbor policies may induce retaliation by the country's trading partners, resulting in a world economy characterized by distortions and inefficient production.

While a multilateral agreement achieving complete trade liberalization in all countries would restore the world economy to a Pareto optimum, it may not be possible to achieve this for a number of reasons. The costs of negotiating with other countries may be too high, or an individual country may simply be better off in the tariff-ridden equilibrium compared to global free trade. While that country may be induced to join a multilateral agreement through transfers from other countries, it is typically difficult to reach agreement as to the appropriate level of compensation to be paid and which countries should pay it.

The question then arises as to whether a subset of countries would benefit from an alternative RIA. If there are relatively few countries involved, it may be easier to reach agreement. But does a regional free trade agreement have the potential to yield benefits to the participating countries? Because comparisons between second-best situations are involved, in general it is not possible to make a policy-ranking across the various potential trade agreements available. Although a RIA is not first-best for the world, as trade impediments between the region and the rest of the world remain, it may still be optimal policy for the countries in the region.

What then does theory have to suggest about the benefits of and effects from regional, rather than multilateral, trade liberalization? The seminal contribution to the literature on the effects of RIAs is that of Viner (1950). He distinguishes between two effects, one in which trade between partner countries expands in accordance with international comparative advantage (and would have occurred under multilateral liberalization as well), and the other in which trade between countries expands as a result of the preferential treatment given to imports from within the region as compared to those from the rest of the world. The former effect he named 'trade creation', the substitution of imports of lower-cost goods produced by a country's partner for its own domestic products, and the latter he called 'trade diversion', the shift in imports from the least-cost exporter to the more expensive product from the nation's partners.

But while this categorization is a useful *description* of the effects of customs-union formation, it is inappropriate as a basis for *measuring* the welfare effects of a RIA. From a global standpoint, trade diversion represents a shift in the trade pattern counter to comparative advantage; but the importing country may benefit from trade diversion as domestic prices of goods fall. This may offset any losses in tariff revenues from the switch in the trade pattern. Thus the induced changes in the pattern of trade are not reliable predictors of the welfare consequences of regional free trade from the point of view of individual countries participating in such schemes.

But why do countries seek international trading agreements, rather than unilaterally liberalizing their trade? For a country to enter a RIA, it must be the case that the effects of its partners removing their trade barriers to its exports are sufficiently large to offset any loss from the concessions that it makes to them (Wonnacott and Wonnacott, 1981; Kowalczyk, 1992). As in multilateral trade liberalization this cannot generally be guaranteed, but, as fewer countries are involved in the agreement, it may be easier for them to come to some agreement as to the international transfers that are made to ensure that all of the partners in the RIA do indeed benefit. With such a transfer mechanism in place, it is possible for any arbitrary grouping of countries to benefit from establishing a regional accord. Kemp and Wan (1976) demonstrated that, while maintaining the same volume of trade with the rest of the world, any group of countries could benefit from trade liberalization within the group.[7] Consequently, aggregate world welfare *can* rise from increased intra-regional trade. Thus countries can gain from forming preferential trading agreements, and such benefits need not be at the expense of the rest of the world.

What has not yet been addressed is the optimal design of the RIA with respect to the rest of the world and the best countries to have as partners. We examine the first of these questions in terms of Wooton's (1986) model of preferential trading agreements.[8] Wooton considers a three-country, *n*-good model of the world trading system, where the countries are labelled A, B and C. Countries A and B form a regional integration agreement, each changing its respective tariff structure to give preference to imports from its new partner. The national income-expenditure relation for country A is initially:

$$e^a(p^a, u^a) = r^a(p^a) + t^a \cdot m^a \tag{3.1}$$

where $e^a(\cdot)$ is the expenditure necessary at A's domestic prices, p^a, to achieve a level of welfare equal to u^a; $r^a(\cdot)$ is the income from domestic production; while the last term is the total tariff revenue earned on imports of m^a, subject to specific (non-negative) import taxes at rates t^a. A similar expression holds for country B.

Let A and B now adjust their tariff structures marginally.[9] The impact on national welfare is:

$$e_u^a \ du^a = -m^a \cdot dp^e + t^a \cdot dm^a + m^{ab} \cdot dT \tag{3.2}$$

where the marginal utility of money income e_u^a is a positive term, dp^e is the change in world prices, m^{ab} is the volume of trade A conducts with partner country B ($m^a = m^{ab} + m^{ac}$), and dT is a measure of the change in regional prices from world prices. Thus a country's welfare is affected by shifts in its international terms of trade, changes in its tariff revenues, and adjustments in the prices at which it trades with its partner.

How does a country gain from a regional trading agreement? First, consider the Kemp and Wan case where the rest of the world is insulated from the effects of forming the RIA. In these circumstances, world prices will not change and the first term on the right-hand side of equation (3.2) is zero. Note also that $m^{ab} = -m^{ba}$, and hence any gains from intra-regional price effects made by one country will be at the expense of its partner. A measure of the aggregate change in welfare in the region can be found by adding up equation (3.2) and the equivalent expression for country B:

$$e_u^a \ du^a + e_u^b \ du^b = t^a \cdot dm^{ab} + t^b \cdot dm^{ba} \tag{3.3}$$

Thus intra-regional welfare can only increase if intra-regional trade rises.

What effect do RIAs have on world trade as a whole? As has been argued above, a RIA will benefit its members only if the volume of intra-regional trade increases. Thus, if trade with the rest of the world were held constant (as in the Kemp and Wan case), a Pareto-improving RIA area would involve an increase in intra-regional trade relative to inter-regional trade. Consequently, an observation that world trade was becoming relatively more 'regional' need not, in itself, indicate any harm (in a welfare sense) to the global economy.

Of more concern is the case when the level of trade between the region and the rest of the world falls. Consequently, gains for the region are at the expense of other regions. This may be purely the result of liberalization of intra-regional trade, whereby trade is diverted by the discriminatory nature of tariffs. It may also be a reflection of the increased shared market power of the countries in the region. These terms-of-trade effects are stronger the larger the size and number of countries participating in the RIA. They may choose to exploit this monopoly power in trade by increasing their external trade barriers relative to those that they had imposed unilaterally.

Which country is the most desirable partner for a RIA? There is no simple answer to this question, as several (sometimes conflicting) economic, as well as non-economic, forces apply.[10] An argument can be made for a country joining its principal trading partner[11] in a free trade agreement, as this reinforces the pattern of comparative advantage and provides a 'safe haven' in the face of a potential tide of protectionism. But countries with similar production and export characteristics (for example, both countries having exports concentrated in a particular commodity) might also choose a trading agreement in order to operate as an international cartel. Yet another possibility is that countries with similar import preferences might join forces in order to increase their joint monopsony power with respect to the rest of the world. Theory is thus unable to provide any simple rules as to the suitability on welfare grounds of particular countries as partners in a RIA.

3.2 Post-war regionalism: the record

Despite the inability of the theoretical literature to resolve fully whether or not RIAs can be welfare-improving, it remains the case that such preferential arrangements have been present in the global trading system since GATT's formation in 1947. Indeed they have a long history, being part of the colonial trading systems and the large-power dominated trading systems of the late nineteenth century that continued through into the first part of the twentieth century.

The key RIAs that have entered the global trading system over the post-war years include the formation of the European Economic Community in 1957, the subsequent formation in 1960 of the European Free Trade Association (EFTA), bilateral arrangements between the United States and Canada under the Auto Pact of 1965 and the 1988 Canada–US Free Trade Agreement, and more recently other initiatives including EC enlargement, an EC/EFTA negotiation to form the EEA, Canada–US–Mexico negotiations to form NAFTA, and others.

A large number of RIAs between other countries besides the US and the EC have also emerged. They include the Latin American Free Trade Association (LAFTA) of 1960, the Central American Common Market (CACM) of 1961, and the East African Common Market (EACM) of the same period. More recent examples are the Chile–Mexico Bilateral Trade Agreement concluded in 1991, and the 1992 Chile–Venezuela bilateral arrangement. In UNCTAD a negotiation on trade preferences among developing countries, the global system of trade preferences (GSTP), continues.[12] These have attracted less attention than the large-power arrangements because the trade covered by them has been relatively small.

While many (or most) of these smaller-country agreements have subsequently broken down, they serve to emphasize the point that, despite the GATT, post-war RIAs have been a central feature in the development and evolution of the global trading system, rather than an exception. Indeed, Japan remains the only major industrialized country that is not currently a participant in some form of explicit RIA. And even Japan now has an informal investment and trade arrangement with the ASEAN countries, and may be poised to move further in a regional direction in the 1990s.

Despite this growth in RIAs, post-war global trade growth has been strong. Hamilton and Whalley (1992) report indexes and growth rates for exports of OECD countries in volume terms (that is, removing the effects of inflation on the value of trade) over the period 1960 to 1988. World trade growth in real (volume) terms averages 6.4 per cent per year over this period. Annual trade growth was 8.5 per cent from 1960 to 1970; in the 1970s it grew at 6.4 per cent; and between 1985 and 1988 it grew at 5.7 per cent. Strong growth in global trade is also evident in the late 1980s, following the recession of 1981–2. Thus, overall, the post-war period shows strong growth in world trade, and at rates significantly above the inter-war and pre-World War I periods.

But growth in global trade has also been non-uniform, with trade involving different regions and particular product categories growing at varying rates in different decades. This uneven pattern, in part, is a result of the rapidly growing economies (Japan, Korea, Taiwan) quickly penetrating industrial country markets in particular product categories, and in a short period of time generating product-specific trade surges of substantial orders of magnitude.

As can be seen in Table 3.1, initial post-war trade growth, especially in Europe and Japan, was exceptionally strong. Japanese trade growth continues at high levels over the whole period, with a slowing trend through the 1970s and 1980s, while growth in external EC trade slowed and then closely tracked that of the US. While there have been times during which growth rates for trade between large regions and neighboring smaller trading partners had been higher, these far from dominate the overall picture. In the late 1980s, growth in trade between Japan and other Pacific Rim countries significantly exceeded the growth of Japan's total trade, while this was not so in the early 1980s. Growth in internal EC trade sharply exceeded that of external EC trade in the 1960s, but not in the 1970s and the early 1980s. And there is a higher growth rate for US–Canada/Mexico trade than for other US trade in the 1960s and early 1980s (if by a less pronounced margin), but not in the late 1970s and mid- to late 1980s.

Table 3.1 Trade growth by region (average real growth rates, per cent per year).

	1955–60	1960–5	1965–70	1970–5	1975–80	1980–5	1985–88
Exports by major regions to the rest of the world:							
United States	6.3	5.0	7.1	5.4[a]	5.4[a]	2.3	3.9
EC[b]	n.a.	4.6	8.3	6.6	5.3	2.2	3.3
Japan	3.8	16.0	14.7	15.4	8.5	8.3	9.5
Exports by major regions to neighboring countries.							
US to Canada and Mexico	n.a.	7.4	7.5	5.4	3.4	7.0	3.2
EC to EFTA[c]	n.a.	15.9	15.1	n.a.	7.2	−0.3	9.1
Internal EC trade	n.a.	12.2	11.6	6.5	8.4	1.4	9.9
Japan to other Pacific Rim	n.a.	15.2	16.1	8.7	9.0	6.5	12.7

Notes: [a] 1970 to 1980.
[b] External EC trade only.
[c] Data in this row are affected by changes in the membership of EFTA, most notably in the mid-1970s when Denmark, Ireland and the UK joined the EC.

Sources: Hamilton and Whalley (1992), who use data for UNCTAD (1979, 1987 and 1990, Tables 1.1 and 2.3), and the IMF, *Direction of Trade,* Washington, DC, various issues.

It thus seems questionable, outside of the initial surge of intra-West European trade in the 1960s, whether regional trade has been one of the more dynamic elements of world trade.[13] It is true that regional partners now frequently provide the largest sources of trade for each of the three major traders in the global system; EFTA for the EC,[14] and Canada for the US (with Mexico its third-largest partner).[15] But these trade links have traditionally been large, and other non-regional trade links are growing. For instance, US trade with the four Asian NIEs (Hong Kong, Korea, Singapore and Taiwan) and with the other five ASEAN countries (Brunei, Indonesia, Malaysia, Philippines and Thailand) has recently been growing rapidly.[16]

Indeed, despite the long list of RIAs introduced into the global economy in the post-war years, intra-regional trade has not grown nearly as quickly as is often supposed. The last column of Table 3.2 reports the shares of intra-regional trade conducted by various formal and informal regional trade groupings. The share of intra-regional trade in world trade (that is, that taking place within the regional groupings identified) is roughly the same now as in the late 1960s: there was a rise in the 1960s, a fall in the 1970s and early 1980s, and another rise in the latter 1980s.[17] A similar picture emerges from the data in Table 3.2 for individual regions.[18] For industrial countries, data for a variety of trade groups are listed: the current EC-12, the original EC-6, EFTA, and North America excluding Mexico. In the case of Western Europe there is a clear shift toward more intra-regional trade between 1960 and 1970, but such a shift is less prominent in North America and Asia.

Table 3.2 also suggests that where there have been attempts at forming RIAs among developing countries, such as in East Africa, in Central and South America and elsewhere, these schemes are initially accompanied by a surge in intra-regional trade. This is an indication of initial trade-diversion effects of these RIAs. But when they subsequently begin to break down, there is typically regression to more traditional trade patterns with reduced intra-regional trade.

Thus, looking at the global economy over the post-war years the data indicate that, despite a surge in formal RIAs, the proportion of intra-regional trade in world trade has not changed greatly except in Europe, which seems to have been an aberration relative to experiences elsewhere. The present fear that new RIAs might be accompanied by marked growth in intra-regional trade relative to overall global trade may thus be unwarranted, especially since so many of the RIAs likely to be at issue focus on trade flows which are relatively small as a proportion of world trade.

Table 3.2 Shares of intra-regional trade (per cent) in total trade, by region, 1960 to 1990

	Western Europe			North America	Asia			Africa	Central and Latin America		World[c]
	EC-12	EC-6	EFTA[a]	US/Canada	ASEAN	East Asia[b]	ANZCERTA	EACM	CACM	LAFTA	
1960	40	34	11	30	27	28	5	1	7	9	28
1970	52	49	17	35	17	29	6	16	25	11	40
1980	52	43	14	27	18	33	6	6	21	12	35
1985	52	41	14	33	19	37	7	5	14	11	34
1990	59	45	14	30	17	40	7	4	12	12	40

Notes: [a] EFTA is defined here to be Finland, Iceland, Norway, Sweden and Switzerland.
[b] East Asia is defined here to be ASEAN, China, Japan, South Korea, Hong Kong and Taiwan.
[c] World intra-regional trade is defined to be all trade taking place within these regional integration agreements: EC, EFTA, US/Canada, ASEAN, ANZCERTA, EACM, CACM and LAFTA.

Sources: IMF, *Direction of Trade Statistics*, Washington, DC, various issues: Department of Statistics, *Monthly Statistics of Exports and Imports*, Taipei, various issues.

3.3   Studies of impacts of regional agreements

A large number of studies have been conducted over the years as to the effects of particular RIAs. These go substantially beyond statistical analyses of data showing time trends in regional and global trade patterns, such as presented above and in the preceding chapter by Anderson and Norheim. In this section we review some of the more prominent studies, identifying the themes that emerge from each and indicating the features of methodology or model structure which underlie them. The studies differ both in their methodological approaches and the particular results that they generate. They all involve key assumptions, implicit structures, or representations of economies which in part predetermine their results. In some cases they use relatively little underlying theoretical structure. In turn, the difficulties of obtaining reliable parameter values, as with all such analyses, are intimidating.

We have classified the available studies into three broad groupings for the purpose of synthesizing the main themes emerging from results. The first, following de la Torre and Kelly (1992), we call *ex post* studies. These are typically studies of RIAs made after the formation of any given regional grouping, and use various kinds of econometric and other data analyses to identify the contribution of the particular RIA to the trading patterns which occurred after the agreement was signed. These studies mainly concentrate on the EC and were in vogue in the latter 1960s. As far as we can determine no such studies have been executed since the early 1970s.

The second and third sets of studies cover model-based counterfactual analyses of RIAs. The second set are counterfactual analyses assuming competitive markets and constant-returns-to-scale technology. The third set of studies has the added features of market structure and scale economies incorporated in a variety of ways. We refer to these as imperfectly competitive counterfactual analyses. This latter group of studies has been much in vogue since the mid-1980s, and generally shows larger welfare and trade effects of RIAs than the earlier studies which do not incorporate market-structure and scale-economy effects. Not all the effects this set shows, however, relate to barrier removal alone; various integration effects not involving barrier reductions also are considered. There is also much larger variance in the results of the imperfectly competitive counterfactual analyses, with both large positive, as well as small and even negative, effects on welfare (depending upon the model treatment of market structure and pricing behavior). Both of these sets of studies involve either partial or general equilibrium modeling, and are designed to be consistent with widely used trade theories and to capture patterns of trade implied by comparative advantage. Parameter values

Table 3.3 *Ex post* studies of regional integration agreements

Study	Approach	Data	Main conclusions
Balassa (1967)	A partial equilibrium study primarily focusing on the determination of income elasticities of import demand before and after formation of the EC.	The pre-formation period are 1953–9 and the post-formation period is 1959–65. The data used is broken down into seven major commodity groups.	The results show trade creation for manufactures, no trade diversion for raw materials, and trade diversion for foodstuffs due to the formation of the EC. The gain to the EC was estimated to be an increase in the real GNP growth rate of 0.1 per cent per year.
Aitken and Lowry (1972)	A partial equilibrium cross-sectional econometric study of trade flows for the LAFTA and CACM regions. The study attempts to measure the increase in trade among member countries.	The data used are from 1955–67. For each of these years a set of trade flow equations is estimated.	Neither CACM nor LAFTA had significant trade-diverting effects, but they did have significant trade-creating effects.
Truman (1975)	A partial equilibrium econometric study of trade shares for the EC-6 and EFTA before and after the formation of these RIAs. Hypothetical import shares are calculated after integration and compared to the actual import shares. Two methods are used: the first attempts to adjust for country-specific cyclical effects, whereas the second does not.	The pre-formation period is 1953–60. The year of comparison between hypothetical and actual import shares is 1968. Eleven manufacturing industries are examined.	Using the first method, in 37 per cent of the commodity cases, trade shares decrease for non-member countries, 43 per cent of the cases see trade shares increase for non-member countries, and in 20 per cent of the cases trade shares fall for both member and non-member countries. The first method gives an $11b trade increase, of which the extra-regional trade increase is $2b. The second method gives a $1b trade increase, including an extra-regional trade fall of $2.3b.

Table 3.4 Competitive counterfactual analyses of regional integration agreements

Study	Approach	Regional scenarios	Main conclusions
Verdoorn (1954)	A static partial equilibrium study. Assumes consumption elasticities of substitution between imports and domestic production of -0.5 and between different country's exports of -2.	Tariffs between 10 OEEC countries are eliminated on manufactures. A common tariff is then imposed by all countries after formation of the RIA.	Assuming unchanged exchange rates, total world exports increase by $400m (or 2.6 per cent of 1952 total world exports). Intra-bloc exports increases by $1b (or 19 per cent of 1952 intra-bloc exports), of which $600m (or 6 per cent of 1952 intra-ROW exports) is diverted from the rest of the world.
Johnson (1958)	A static partial equilibrium calculation. Calculates maximal potential welfare gains to the UK through the impact of lower tariffs or prices received by UK exporters and paid by UK importers.	Tariffs between the UK and EC are eliminated on manufactures. A common tariff is imposed after the formation of the RIA.	Trade gains accrue to the UK of between £62m and £192m (or 0.8 per cent and 2.4 per cent) on the export side and £31m (or 0.3 per cent) on the import side. The minimum of these welfare gains is roughly 1 per cent of GNP for the UK in 1970.
Scitovsky (1958)	A static partial equilibrium study. Assumes that the difference in marginal costs between countries in an industry is due to the import tariff of the importing country. The gains from the integration are thus the resource gains from equalization of marginal costs.	Uses trade data from Verdoorn (1954), assuming that exchange rates appreciate to get the same trade balance as before the customs union, to calculate welfare effects of West European integration.	Europe gains $74m, the amount lost by the rest of the world. This is a gain from increased specialization and represents less than 0.05 per cent of European GNP. Europe gains $465m from a favorable terms-of-trade improvement.
Miller and Spencer (1977)	A static general equilibrium model. Uses an Armington structure with two final goods per country, constant returns to scale and perfect competition.	There are two scenarios for the UK joining the EC, both involving the abolition of mutual tariffs and the imposition by the UK of the EC's common tariff. The first involves the UK transferring 90 per cent of its tariff revenue to the EC, while the second does not.	The UK gains from a small terms-of-trade gain on entry. This is more than offset by the transfer to the European budget on entry. The price of agricultural goods rises by 22 per cent compared to manufactured goods rises by 22 per cent for the UK. Under the no-transfer scenario, the UK increases its manufactured exports and imports to the EC by 50 per cent in both cases. Also the UK increases its agricultural imports from the EC by 72 per cent and decreases its imports from the Commonwealth by 0.8 per cent.

Hamilton and Whalley (1985)	A static general equilibrium model, with 8 world blocs and 6 goods per country, 5 of which are tradable. The Armington assumption is used. There are constant returns to scale and perfect competition.	The first scenario looks at RIAs between the US and each of the other 7 blocs. Then 3 RIAs involving EC and Japan, the industrial countries and the developing countries are examined. Finally a more-intensive examination of a RIA between the US and the EC is made.	Industrial countries always gain from a RIA with the US, but the developing countries lose. The second scenario sees the first two RIAs increasing all of the members' welfare but the NIEs losing in the third RIA. Only the RIA of the US and the EC is examined in detail, with US exports rising by 9.7 per cent to the EC, and EC exports rising by 5.8 per cent to the US. The US exports less to, and imports more from, other areas whereas the reverse is true for the EC. These effects are small.
Harrison, Rutherford and Wooton (1989)	A static general equilibrium model. There are 11 regions and 6 goods, all of which are tradable. The Armington assumption is used. There are constant returns to scale and perfect competition. There are non-tariff barriers (as well as tariffs, subsidies, etc.) of 40 per cent between non-EC countries and 20 per cent between EC members.	1. Eight cases of various countries leaving the EC (with CAP remaining in place). 2. Eight cases of each country leaving the EC (no CAP).	In both scenarios, all EC countries would have welfare reductions on leaving the EC. The US would have a small welfare gain in all cases. The highest loss is for Ireland (8 per cent of GDP) and the smallest for France and Italy (0.9 per cent of GDP).

for production, preferences and trade barriers are introduced into these systems, and counterfactual analyses performed to show the potential impact of the RIA. The majority of these studies have been executed in advance of the formation of particular RIAs, with an associated model projection generated to see what the effect of the RIA might be. A small number of studies have conducted their analyses the other way around, taking data on trade, production and consumption in the presence of an established RIA in the base period, and performing a counterfactual analysis to see what the constructed model (using the observed data) would show to be the trade and other patterns in the absence of the RIA. [19]

3.3.1   Ex post studies

In Table 3.3 we identify some of the more prominent *ex post* studies of RIAs, namely, those by Balassa (1967), Aitken and Lowry (1972), and Truman (1975). These studies generally involve simple econometric analyses of data on intra- and extra-regional trade patterns. No welfare analyses are possible with such studies because the underlying theoretical structures are not specified in terms of microeconomic underpinnings. There are many econometric problems with these studies such as specification bias, parameter value instability, and simultaneity bias. Even so, one can summarize the conclusion from these studies as being that in the West European case there is evidence of a limited amount of trade creation in the 1960s. Although this is not particularly large, it nonetheless shows up in the studies. In the Balassa study, trade-creation and trade-diversion effects yield an estimated impact on real GDP growth rates of 0.1 per cent per year. The Aitken and Lowry study – the one that we refer to as a non-European case of integration – investigates the effects of two regional integration schemes in Latin America, neither of which is shown to have any significant trade-diverting effects, although some trade-creation effects follow from the lowering of barriers associated with the liberalization schemes.

3.3.2   Competitive counterfactual analyses

In Table 3.4 we report on model-based competitive counterfactual analyses. The well-known Verdoorn (1954) study is an early example and provided a static partial equilibrium calculation of the effects of an intra-OEEC trade arrangement (effectively, among the current OECD countries). This showed an increase in intra-bloc trade of 19 per cent among OEEC countries. Johnson (1958), a later partial equilibrium study, calculated the potential benefits associated with the UK's entry into the EC, showing a welfare gain of approximately 1 per cent of GNP. Scitovsky's (1958) partial equilibrium study of the formation of the EC, relying heavily on the trade results from the earlier Verdoorn study, produced even smaller numbers in estimating that Europe-wide welfare gains would be no more than 0.05 per cent of GNP.

Miller and Spencer (1977) provide the first full, numerical, general equilibrium analysis of a RIA. They use an Armington structure[20] with four regions identified: the UK, the EC, Commonwealth countries (primarily Australia and New Zealand), and the United States and the rest of the world. They look at the effects of UK entry into the EC, involving not only lower trade barriers with the EC-6 but also the elimination of Commonwealth trade preferences by the UK. Interestingly, their results show that the welfare effects associated with entry would be small, but from a UK point of view were dominated by UK contributions to the European budget. (At that time, the UK was a large net importer of agricultural products and, through the Common Agriculture Policy, was poised on entry to become a significant contributor to the budget.)

Large price effects also show up in their model results, particularly a price rise in the UK in agricultural products, as might be expected. Associated with this were significant trade effects, particularly between the UK and EC, and the UK and the Commonwealth. For instance, in the case without transfers through the European budget, the UK increased its exports to, and imports from, the EC by 50 per cent in manufactured goods. The UK increased its agricultural imports from the EC by 72 per cent but, somewhat surprisingly, decreased its imports from the Commonwealth by only 0.8 per cent.

A later competitive counterfactual study by Hamilton and Whalley (1985) uses a multi-country global general equilibrium model, somewhat similar to that of Miller and Spencer but with larger dimensionality, to look at a variety of potential pair-wise RIAs. It examines regional arrangements between the US and other regional blocs identified in their model, as well as possible regional arrangements between the EC and Japan, the OECD countries and developing countries. Their results generally show that the welfare effects of RIAs are relatively small but, as in other studies, trade effects are somewhat larger. Their results also show significant terms-of-trade effects associated with all these RIAs.

Harrison, Rutherford and Wooton (1989) use a somewhat similar structure to look at the effects that might be expected if member countries left the EC. The model covers six tradable goods and eleven countries/regions, and uses the Armington assumption. They show that any country leaving the EC would suffer a welfare loss, with the highest

Table 3.5 Imperfectly competitive counterfactual analyses of regional integration agreements

Study	Approach	Regional scenarios	Main conclusions
Harris and Cox (1984), and Harris (1985)	A static general equilibrium model is used to study various regional trade regimes involving Canada. Assumes 9 constant-returns-to-scale (CRS) perfectly competitive industries and 20 increasing-returns-to-scale (IRS) non-competitive industries. The IRS firms have constant per-unit variable costs as well as fixed costs. Canada takes import prices as given, but it can affect export prices. The Armington assumption is used. There is a representative agent who maximizes utility.	Unilateral free trade (UFT) where Canada sets all of its tariffs to zero; multilateral free trade (MFT) where Canada and the rest of the world set their tariffs to zero; selective tariff cuts in 12 of the 20 IRS industries; bilateral free trade (BFT) with the US; and sectoral free trade (SFT) with the US in textiles, steel, agricultural machinery, urban transport equipment and chemicals.	Canada receives welfare gains of 4, 9, 9 and 1.5 per cent of GDP under scenarios UFT, MFT, BFT and SFT. Canada's trade volumes with the world increase by 55, 90, 88 and 15 per cent with UFT, MFT, BFT and SFT respectively. Canada's trade volume increases by 99 and 14 per cent with the US under BFT and SFT. Real wages in Canada rise by 10, 25, 28 and 6 per cent under UFT, MFT, BFT and SFT.
Smith and Venables (1988)	A static partial equilibrium model is used to study the effects of lower non-tariff barriers on various sectors in the EC. Ten sectors are considered, each of which has firms which use IRS technology. The firms each produce a differentiated product and the Armington assumption is used. The rest of the economy is modeled as a perfectly competitive industry with CRS technology in each case. All products are tradable. The trading regions considered are France, Germany, Italy, the UK, the rest of the EC and the rest of the world. The home country consumer has a preference for domestic goods over foreign goods.	Sector-by-sector trade barrier reductions of the order of 2.5 per cent of the base value of intra-EC trade are analyzed in eight different cases. Segmented and integrated markets when barriers are removed are studied with Cournot conjectures and constant and variable numbers of firms, and Bertrand conjectures and constant and variable numbers of firms.	Under Cournot conjectures, welfare effects for segmented markets and barrier removal range from −0.01 per cent of consumption for cement, lime and plaster to 1.3 per cent for office machinery. Under integrated markets, increases under barrier removal range from 0.2 per cent in cement, lime and plaster to 5.6 per cent in artificial and synthetic fibers. Under Bertrand conjectures, the segmented markets' welfare results change insignificantly, whereas integrated markets increase the range from 0.04 to 1.2 per cent in the respective industries. Trade changes under Cournot range from a 78 per cent decrease for cement, lime and plaster under integrated markets to an increase of 164 per cent in the same industry under segmented markets. Bertrand conjectures result in considerably smaller absolute changes.

| Baldwin (1992) | A small dynamic general equilibrium model of the dynamic gains of trade for the EC. Single infinitely lived representative consumer and IRS technology for firms in each country. Discount rate, inter-temporal elasticity of substitution and capital share of income are assumed to be 0.05, 0.1 and 0.3. Divergence of social and private returns on capital due to IRS is the key assumption. | Integration of EC markets is assumed to lower non-tariff trade barriers, and static gains calculated by Cecchini, Catinat and Jacquemin (1988) are assumed. These are then dynamized. | Dynamic welfare effects from trade liberalization increase welfare from between 15 and 90 per cent of the static gains |
| Smith, Venables and Gasiorek (1992) | General equilibrium study of gains from lowering non-tariffs trade barriers and the integration of segmented markets in the EC in the spirit of earlier Smith and Venables (1988) work. There are 14 IRS and 1 CRS sectors. Factors of production include four types of labor, capital and intermediate goods. There is a single representative consumer. For each country and industry, firms are symmetric. | Markets are either segmented or integrated. Firms use Cournot conjectures. There is a short run with a fixed number of firms and a long run with a variable number of firms. | Welfare increases range from 0.2 per cent of GDP for Germany in the short run, to 1.4 per cent for the EC South in the long run under segmented markets. For integrated markets, the range is 0.2 per cent increase for Germany in the short run, to 2.9 per cent for the EC South in the long run. Under segmented markets, changes in exports by the EC to the ROW range from a decrease of 0.4 per cent in banking and finance in the short run, to an 8.3 per cent increase in transport equipment in the long run. Import decreases range from −0.8 per cent for banking and finance in the long run, to −20.2 per cent for transport equipment in the long run. Under integrated markets, the absolute value of these effects is increased by roughly a factor of two. |

(continued)

Table 3.5 (*Continued*)

Study	Approach	Regional scenarios	Main conclusions
Mercenier (1992)	Both partial and general equilibrium analyses are used to study the integration of segmented EC markets in 1992. There are 4 CRS and 5 IRS sectors. The Armington assumption is imposed for the CRS sectors. There is a single representative consumer who maximizes utility. Capital and labor are only domestically mobile in the short run but capital is internationally mobile in the long run.	Both Bertrand and Cournot conjectures are used. Sector-by-sector integration is analyzed as is complete EC integration. The short run fixes the number of firms while the long run allows the number of firms to vary.	For partial integration, there are small welfare increases for EC countries, with mixed results for the rest of the OECD. Output generally rises and the number of firms and average costs of firms fall. For complete integration, there are also small welfare gains for the EC countries, with the rest of the OECD experiencing virtually no change. The terms of trade generally increase for all of the EC countries and fall for the rest of the OECD. No trade effects are reported.
Haaland and Norman (1992)	General equilibrium study of effects of EC integration on EC, EFTA, Japan and US. Model is similar to Smith, Venables and Gasiorek (1992). There are 11 IRS and 1 CRS tradable goods and 1 CRS non-tradable good for each region. Factors of production are skilled and unskilled labor, capital and intermediate goods. There is a single representative agent in each region. EC and EFTA each consist of 6 separate, but identical, countries and submarkets. Firms are assumed to be symmetric in each industry within a region.	Four scenarios: (1) trade costs between segmented EC markets are reduced by 2.5 per cent of the initial value of EC trade, with initial trade costs assumed to be 10 per cent within EC and EFTA and 20 per cent between Europe, Japan and the US; (2) trade costs are reduced and EC markets are integrated; (3) trade costs in Europe (including EFTA) are reduced, as in first scenario; and (4) same as scenario 2, except now for all Western Europe.	For scenario (1), EC gains a 1 per cent increase in welfare. EFTA, US and Japan have declines in welfare of 0.3, 0.02 and 0.02 per cent respectively. For scenario (2), EC experiences welfare gains of 1.9 per cent but there are falls in EFTA, US and Japan by 0.4, 0.4 and 0.6 per cent respectively. For scenarios (3) and (4), EFTA experiences positive welfare gains while the EC gains in welfare are smaller than in scenarios (1) and (2). The welfare losses for Japan and the US are smaller.

loss being for Ireland (8 per cent of GDP) and the lowest for France and Italy (0.9 per cent of GDP).

3.3.3 Imperfectly competitive counterfactual analyses

More recent model-based counterfactual analyses of RIAs incorporate non-competitive market structure and scale economies, reported in Table 3.5. One of the earliest, the Harris and Cox (1984) study, is an analysis of the effects of Canada–US trade integration, although in their trade scenarios they also look at multilateral and unilateral free trade, as well as bilateral and sectoral free trade. In their model there is an implicit assumption of collusive behavior by producers around a focal point of the world price gross of the tariff in the Canadian market.[21] Fixed costs at plant level are modeled for Canadian firms, but these fixed costs are not sunk costs, and hence a significant reduction in the number of domestic firms tends to produce large welfare gains as fixed costs are spread over a smaller number of firms.[22]

In their results, trade liberalization shows much larger welfare gains than in the earlier models referred to in Table 3.4. In the cases of bilateral or multilateral free trade, these gains for Canada (the smaller country) are as large as 8 to 10 per cent of GDP,[23] with even larger effects on Canada's trade volume (as high as 90 per cent in some cases).[24] Some of the larger welfare and trade effects in results from the early versions of the Harris/Cox model were substantially reduced in later versions of the model used by the Canadian Department of Finance (1988) in generating their own economic assessment of the bilateral agreement between Canada and the US. This was due, in part, to a downward revision in the trade barrier estimates used earlier by Harris and Cox, and to revisions in other parameter values. In some cases, estimated welfare fell by as much as a factor of four. Also, because Canada is considerably smaller than the US, global welfare gains and welfare effects in the US are considerably smaller as a fraction of world and US GDP, as are the effects on corresponding trade flows.

A later attempt at imperfectly competitive counterfactual analysis is Smith and Venables (1988), one of a series[25] of papers which look at various scenarios for European integration as part of the '1992' exercise undertaken to complete the EC's internal market. The counterfactual analyses in Smith and Venables are largely done on a partial equilibrium basis,[26] and involve scenarios that do not necessarily fully correspond to formal changes in trade barriers. Their analyses involve an initial assumption of market segmentation, and the central counterfactual which they analyze is a full market-integration case, which does not necessarily correspond to cases where only trade barriers change. Indeed, in some of their model analyses where trade barrier changes alone are considered, some of the projected impacts are extremely small. They use different market structure assumptions and different assumptions on conjectures by firms of both the Cournot and Bertrand types, and their welfare and trade results depend crucially upon the scenarios which they consider. In the case of full market integration, welfare effects are always positive but vary widely in magnitude, with ambiguous results for effects on trade. Where trade barrier changes alone are identified these welfare effects are somewhat smaller and trade effects larger for Cournot conjectures, with no significant differences from using Bertrand conjectures.

A final and recent paper, by Baldwin (1992), using increasing returns also obtains strong effects of trade liberalization. This piece does not explicitly consider regional arrangements, but instead uses the estimates of potential static welfare gains from the 1992 EC program due to Cecchini, Catinat and Jacquemin (1988), which he then dynamizes using a simple inter-temporal model. He shows that if, due to scale economies, private and social rates of return on capital differ, then the exploitation of these scale economies can yield additional dynamic gains from trade liberalization. Using estimates from Caballero and Lyons (1989), he demonstrates that these dynamic gains can be large. No trade or other impacts are reported; and if these gains are indeed achievable, they could also be generated by other policy interventions (such as tax policy).

It is difficult to generalize over the results of all of these three groups of studies because their individual characteristics are so varied, as are the results. While some studies provide detailed analyses of the trade impacts, their analysis of welfare impacts may be more limited. Also, some of the model-based studies, while providing analyses of trade and welfare impacts, do not provide results in a form which makes it easy to disentangle the various influences on trade and welfare.

We, therefore, see these studies as shedding somewhat incomplete and at times conflicting light on the effects of post-war RIAs on trade and welfare, to say nothing of what might be the likely future effects of prospective RIAs. There seems to be near unanimity that trade creation occurred in Europe, but its size and the precise contribution of the RIAs relative to other factors is unclear. Nor is it clear that significant trade creation from RIAs has occurred elsewhere. The associated welfare effects of the barrier changes involved seem relatively small from a number of studies, although the Harris/Cox study suggests larger orders of magnitude in the Canada–US case and Baldwin's recent calculations, though not of a regional agreement per se, are even more in this direction. On the whole, if the variance in results across scenarios is removed, perhaps one can argue that they are not inconsistent with the picture which we project from the trade data analysis in the previous section; but their incompleteness and inconsistencies leave many unanswered questions as to the precise contribution that RIAs have made to trade and welfare during the post-war years.

3.4   The possible impacts of the new regionalism

How marked the recent acceleration in RIAs has been compared to the earlier post-war period, and whether the 1990s will see a further sharp growth in intra-regional trade along with the associated welfare effects involved, have emerged as among the key questions for global trade policy makers in the early 1990s.

It is, in our view, important to emphasize that the formation of these new RIAs has been driven by a number of factors which are not captured in currently available quantitative analyses of existing RIAs. A key one is the search for safe-haven trade agreements by smaller countries, which now, more than ever before, wish to secure access to the markets of large neighboring trading partners because of their fear of higher trade barriers in the future (the insurance value of secure access to a larger market). A second is the frustration felt by larger countries with progress toward new multilateral liberalization and their belief that their threatening to negotiate (or actually negotiating) regional agreements may force otherwise reluctant larger powers to make concessions multilaterally. A third is that RIAs are now viewed positively in some circles as facilitating growth in world trade. A fourth is the desire of developing countries to lock in domestic policy reforms by signing international agreements; and regional arrangements, if easier to negotiate than multilateral arrangements, have been seen as attractive for such purposes.[27] Drawing on the studies cited above to yield insights into these dimensions of the new regionalism is clearly difficult. But these have been powerful arguments, and the result has been that earlier RIAs already in the trading system have broadened and expanded in coverage over the last five or so years, generating lively debate.

The fear that the global trading system is becoming more regionalized is a fear of the intensification of existing RIAs as much as a fear of proliferation of more regional agreements. Along with this comes the fear of more-exclusionary RIAs. Hence, concerns over regionalism in the 1990s reflect increases in the coverage of countries in existing regional schemes; in product and area coverage such as services and investment provisions; and in coverage of other instruments of trade protection such as rules of origin.

In our view, the desirability or otherwise from a global efficiency viewpoint of large-power regionalism in the global trading system depends on how it is conducted. If RIAs are pursued to put pressure on other large powers to negotiate multilaterally, or to indicate loss of interest in the multilateral process, then they are more aggressive in intent. If, instead, they are pursued as vehicles to generate new growth in trade flows, provide new disciplines in areas not covered by GATT which could subsequently be multilateralized, and perhaps accompany a trilateral trade-management framework, then they are more complementary to present system objectives. Clearly, recent accelerating regional trends in the system reflect both of these elements, as well as some degree of frustration with the multilateral GATT process. That the recent acceleration in regionalism has occurred during an ongoing GATT Round is unusual; since in the past negotiating Rounds have restrained GATT Contracting Parties from moving too strongly in non-multilateral directions.

New RIAs which concentrate on further liberalizing components of trade can be both trade- and welfare-promoting if they focus on the dynamic and more rapidly growing portions of the world economy. But if, with a perceived failure of the multilateral process in light of the difficulties in coming to a Uruguay Round agreement, small countries want the relative safety of a safe-haven agreement with their largest trade partners, then seeing other smaller countries potentially moving in the same direction may cause them to rush forward to beat the queue. Large countries see a line-up of smaller countries wanting to negotiate with them, and view the prospect of successful bilateral negotiation as a way of pressuring other larger powers multilaterally. And as more exclusionary agreements begin to be negotiated, the rush to be in at least one of these becomes a stampede, and surprisingly quickly the global trading system can experience further fragmentation along regional lines.

Regionalism in the trading system in the 1990s is likely to continue to generate a wide range of reactions for some time, from the hostility of committed multilateralists to the passionate embrace of regionalists. Our view is that all such reactions are based on some degree of overstatement as to the likely quantitative impacts on performance of the global economy. Indeed, as Hamilton and Whalley (1992) suggest, the 1990s may reveal a trading system which progressively devolves toward two separate sets of disciplines: multilateral disciplines dominated by large-power negotiations between American, European and Pacific groupings led by the US, the EC and Japan; and a second tier of regional agreements which apply to trade between dominant and smaller powers whose trade is largely with one of the former. These may also show great variety due to the differences in pair-wise country and institutional structures.

Irrespective of the outcome, the challenge for global economic performance will be to harness the trade-liberalizing elements, and weaken the trade-exclusionary and erosion-accelerating features, in whatever agreements result. One approach would seem to be to encourage regionalism for the reasons we state above: liberalizing the dynamic component of global trade, frustration with the multilateral process, and the chance that bilateral negotiation will reignite multilateral negotiations. The other is to resist it on the argument that regional negotiations will lead to a weaker set of multilateral trade institutions and will produce exclusionary and inefficient RIAs. The key will probably be to balance these two and, if our reading of the trade data and studies is correct, even to downplay the issue from its current profile on the grounds that the quantitative impacts involved may not be very large.

Notes

We are grateful to Richard Baldwin, Carsten Kowalczyk and other participants in the GATT conference for their comments. Philip Gunby provided excellent research support.

1. The word 'region' has a geographical connotation, but there have also been preferential trading agreements (e.g. GSP, former Commonwealth preferences) which are not regional, as well as agreements that apply to specific commodities (multifiber) and countries (VER on autos by Japan). We do not cover all restrictions and preferences that violate the multilateral MFN principle, only the subset of geographically focused preferential trade agreements.

2. The implications of this new regionalism for trade and factor flows in the global economy are now the subject of major debate. Bhagwati (1990), for instance, has argued that the growing profusion of regional arrangments has eroded the multilateral system, has undermined non-discrimination and is inefficient. He also sees these arrangements as weakening the position of smaller countries, which can now be selectively discriminated against, and as increasing the possibility that there may eventually be a reversion to a 1930s-style global trade retaliatory episode. In contrast, Krugman (1991) has suggested that trade between neighboring states is the most rapidly growing portion of global trade and that, if faced with a choice between newly liberalizing regionalism and stagnant multilateralism, the former should be chosen.

3. That is, trade agreements which provide security of access as much as they do improved access.

4. The terms 'trade-creation' and 'trade-diversion' are used in this chapter in a descriptive sense, indicating changes in the pattern and volume of trade, and not in any normative sense. This distinction is discussed more fully in the following section.

5. A central issue neglected in the theoretical literature is what exactly is meant by a RIA. These run in practice from integration schemes going beyond trade, as in the EC, to barter trade as used to occur between India and the former Soviet Union, to currency-clearing house arrangements as in some RIAs between developing countries. In the theoretical literature, analysis of RIAs is usually limited to preferential tariff schemes.
6. Strictly speaking, with internal lump-sum transfers, an allocation that Pareto-dominates the free trade allocation for the residents of the country can be achieved with a tariff.
7. The Kemp—Wan result also implies that moving from a union of n countries to a union of $n + 1$ countries could be made Pareto-improving.
8. Full details of the model can be found in Wooton (1986).
9. Of course, the formation of any RIA will involve non-marginal adjustments in tariffs. The question of how this may be reconciled with the approach set out here is addressed in Harrison, Rutherford and Wooton (1992).
10. For a discussion of the traditional economic arguments, see Lloyd (1982).
11. Although in a multi-country world a country that is a large trading partner on the export side need not be a large partner on the import side.
12. But see the cautionary discussion of the GSP scheme by Hudec (1989), who argues that negotiating preferences in a regime of unbound tariffs (as most developing-country tariffs are) is virtually doomed to failure. More details on the GSP scheme can be found in UNCTAD (1988).
13. The interpretation of these data also enters other recent discussions of whether the trading system is moving towards regional trading blocs. Nierop and De Vos (1988) emphasize movement toward regional integration between 1950 and 1980 and identify the dominant countries in each trading sphere as being the United States, Japan and Western Europe. See also Zerby (1990) and Pomfret (1988). But GATT (1990) data show a large amount of inter-regional trade for the period 1979—89 especially between North America and Asia and between Western Europe and Asia. GATT also asserts the movement to regional blocs is not as quick as some suggest. According to data in GATT (1990, p. 27), inter-regional trade, especially merchandise trade between North America and Asia and between Western Europe and Asia, was especially dynamic in the 1980s, growing faster than intra-regional trade.
14. See GATT (1989, Table A.3).
15. In 1989, the United States exported $78 billion to Canada, $45 billion to Japan and $25 billion to Mexico (IMF, 1990).
16. From $38 billion of exports in 1986 to $69 billion of exports in 1990 (IMF, 1990). This compares with 1990 Japanese exports to the US of $94 billion.
17. These data reflect a grouping of countries currently involved in formal RIAs, rather than an exhaustive categorization of all countries in the world. Alternative calculations could be made on such a basis, and are for a longer time period in the Appendix to this volume.
18. The data shown in Table 3.2 are similar to, but go further than, the data analysis presented in de la Torre and Kelly (1992).
19. See Harrison, Rutherford and Wooton (1989) as an example of this.
20. The Armington treatment involves assuming that products produced in different countries are imperfect substitutes one for another (e.g. Japanese, European and US cars). Its now-widespread use in numerical general equilibrium modeling reflects a number of concerns: to rule out complete

specialization; to avoid the need to net out trade flows in seemingly similar products (cross-hauling) and sharply reduce the size of trade; and to facilitate model calibration to estimated trade elasticities. See Shoven and Whalley (1984) for more discussion of these points.

21. This is what they refer to as Eastman–Stykolt (1967) pricing. This differs from Negishi (1961) monopolistic pricing, which they also incorporate in their model, with equal weighting on this and Eastman–Stykolt pricing.

22. For some of their trade scenarios, Harris and Cox show reductions in the number of firms in Canada of nearly 50 per cent (Harris, 1985, p. 173).

23. These estimates are of a similar order of magnitude to those obtained by Wonnacott and Wonnacott (1967), who made the strong assumptions that, under free trade with the US, Canadian wage rates would equate with US wages and the exchange rate would move to parity. These imply a large once-and-for-all productivity gain for Canada in their treatment, accounting for the 10 per cent gain with which they have since been associated. No formal model underlies their calculation.

24. In the autos and parts sector, Harris and Cox's initial results from multilateral free trade showed a 250 per cent increase in trade, despite the fact that bilateral free trade already effectively applied under the Canada–US Auto Pact (Harris, 1985, pp. 162–3).

25. See also Cecchini, Catinat and Jacquemin (1988), Haaland and Norman (1992), Smith, Venables and Gasiorek (1992), and Mercenier (1992).

26. The most recent Smith, Venables and Gasiorek paper (1992) involves a general equilibrium analysis of their earlier partial equilibrium formulations using only Cournot behavior by firms; somewhat similar to the approach followed by Mercenier (1992). Both of these papers project somewhat similar, if slightly smaller, results compared to the earlier Smith/Venables work.

27. This factor has been especially important in Mexico's desire to negotiate a NAFTA.

References

Aitken, N. and W. Lowry (1972), 'A Cross Sectional Study of the Effects of LAFTA and CACM on Latin American Trade', *Journal of Common Market Studies* 11: 326–36.

Balassa, B. (1967), 'Trade Creation and Trade Diversion in the European Common Market', *Economic Journal* 77: 1–21.

Baldwin, R. (1992), 'Measurable Dynamic Gains from Trade', *Journal of Political Economy* 100: 162–74.

Berglas, E. (1979), 'Preferential Trading Theory: The n Commodity Case', *Journal of Political Economy* 87: 315–31.

Bhagwati, J. (1990), 'Multilateralism at Risk: The GATT is Dead, Long Live GATT', *The World Economy* 13: 149–69.

Caballero, R. and R. Lyons (1989), 'Increasing Returns and Imperfect Competition in European Industry', mimeo, Columbia University, New York.

Canadian Department of Finance (1988), *The Canada–US Free Trade Agreement: An Economic Assessment*, Ottawa: Department of Finance.
Cecchini, P., M. Catinat and A. Jacquemin (1988), *The European Challenge, 1992: The Benefits of a Single Market*, Aldershot: Wildwood House.
de la Torre, A. and M. Kelly (1992), *Regional Trade Arrangements*, IMF Occasional Paper No. 93, Washington, DC: International Monetary Fund.
Eastman, H. and S. Stykolt (1967), *The Tariff and Competition in Canada*, Toronto: Macmillan.
GATT (1989), *International Trade 88–89, Vol. II*, Geneva: GATT Secretariat.
GATT (1990), *International Trade 89–90, Vol. II*, Geneva: GATT Secretariat.
Haaland, J. and V. Norman (1992), 'Global Production Effects of European Integration', in *Trade Flows and Trade Policy After '1992'*, edited by L. A. Winters, Cambridge: Cambridge University Press.
Hamilton, C. and J. Whalley (1992), *The Future of the World Trading System*, Washington, DC: Institute for International Economics.
Hamilton, R. and J. Whalley (1985), 'Geographically Discriminatory Trade Arrangements', *Review of Economics and Statistics* 67: 446–55.
Harris, R. (1985), 'Summary of a Project on the General Equilibrium Evaluation of Canadian Trade Policy', in *Canada–United States Free Trade*, edited by J. Whalley, Toronto: University of Toronto Press.
Harris, R. G. and D. Cox (1984), *Trade, Industrial Policy, and Canadian Manufacturing*, Toronto: Ontario Economic Council Research Study.
Harrison, G., T. Rutherford and I. Wooton (1989), 'The Economic Impact of the EC', *American Economic Review* 79: 288–94.
Harrison, G., T. Rutherford and I. Wooton (1992), 'An Alternative Welfare Decomposition for Customs Unions', mimeo, University of Western Ontario, London, Canada.
Hudec, R. (1989), 'The Structure of South–South Trade Preferences in the 1988 GSTP Agreement: Learning to Say MFMFN', in *Developing Countries and the Global Trading System, Vol. 1*, edited by J. Whalley, London: Macmillan.
IMF (1990), *World Economic Outlook*, Washington, DC: International Monetary Fund.
Johnson, H. (1953), 'Optimum Tariffs and Retaliation', *Review of Economic Studies* 21: 142–53.
Johnson, H. (1958), 'The Gains from Freer Trade with Europe: An Estimate', *Manchester School* 26: 247–55.
Kemp, M. and H. Wan (1976), 'An Elementary Proposition Concerning the Formation of Customs Unions', *Journal of International Economics* 6: 95–7.
Kowalczyk, C. (1992), 'Welfare and Customs Unions', NBER Working Paper No. 3476, Dartmouth College, Hanover.
Krugman, P. (1991), 'Is Bilateralism Bad?', in *International Trade and Trade Policy*, edited by E. Helpman and A. Razin, Cambridge, MA: MIT Press.
Lipsey, R. (1957), 'The Theory of Customs Unions: Trade Diversion and Welfare', *Economica* 24: 40–6.
Lloyd, P. J. (1982), '3 × 3 Theory of Customs Unions', *Journal of International Economics* 12: 41–63.
Meade, J. (1955), *The Theory of Customs Unions*, Amsterdam: North-Holland.
Mercenier, J. (1992), 'Completing the European Internal Market: A General Equilibrium Evaluation Under Alternative Market Structure Assumptions', Working Paper No. 0892, Centre de Recherche et Développement en Economique, Université de Montréal.

Miller, M. and J. Spencer (1977), 'The Static Economic Effects of the UK Joining the EEC: A General Equilibrium Approach', *Review of Economic Studies* **44**: 71–93.

Negishi, T. (1961), 'Monopolistic Competition and General Equilibrium', *Review of Economic Studies* **28**: 196–201.

Nierop, T. and S. De Vos (1988), 'Of Shining Empires and Changing Roles: World of Trade Patterns in the Post-War Period', *Tijdschrift voor Economische en Sociale Geografie* **79**: 343–64.

Pomfret, R. (1988), *Unequal Trade: The Economics of Discriminatory International Trade Policies*, Oxford: Basil Blackwell.

Scitovsky, T. (1941), 'A Note on Welfare Propositions in Economics', *Review of Economic Studies* **8**: 77–88.

Scitovsky, T. (1958), *Economic Theory and Western European Integration*, London: Allen and Unwin.

Shoven, J. and J. Whalley (1984), 'Applied General Economic Models of Taxation and International Trade: An Introduction and Survey', *Journal of Economic Literature* **22**: 1007–51.

Smith, A. and A. Venables (1988), 'Completing the Internal Market in the European Community: Some Industry Simulations', *European Economic Review* **32**: 1501–25.

Smith, A., A. Venables and M. Gasiorek (1992), '1992: Trade and Welfare – A General Equilibrium Model', in *Trade Flows and Trade Policy After '1992'*, edited by L. A. Winters, Cambridge: Cambridge University Press.

Truman, E. (1975), 'The Effects of European Economic Integration on the Production and Trade of Manufactured Products', in *European Economic Integration*, edited by B. Balassa, Amsterdam: North-Holland.

UNCTAD (1979), *Handbook of International Trade and Development Statistics, 1979*, Supplement, New York: United Nations.

UNCTAD (1987), *Handbook of International Trade and Development Statistics, 1987*, Supplement, New York: United Nations.

UNCTAD (1988), *Handbook of International Trade and Development Statistics, 1988*, Supplement, New York: United Nations.

UNCTAD (1990), *Handbook of International Trade and Development Statistics, 1990*, Supplement, New York: United Nations.

Verdoorn, P. (1954), 'A Customs Union for Western Europe: Advantages and Feasibility', *World Politics* **6**: 482–506.

Viner, J. (1950), *The Customs Union Issue*, New York: Carnegie Endowment for International Peace.

Wonnacott, R. and P. Wonnacott (1967), *Free Trade Between the US and Canada*, Cambridge, MA: Harvard University Press.

Wonnacott, P. and R. Wonnacott (1981), 'Is Unilateral Tariff Reduction Preferable to a Customs Union? The Curious Case of the Missing Foreign Tariffs', *American Economic Review* **71**: 704–13.

Wooton, I. (1986), 'Preferential Trading Arrangements: An Investigation', *Journal of International Economics* **21**: 81–97.

Zerby, J. (1990), *Prospects for Trading Blocs in the Asia-Pacific Region*, Montreal: Centre for International Business Studies, University of Montreal.

PART 2

Regional integration in the major trading areas

4

The North American Free Trade Agreement: global impacts

Murray Smith

The prospect of a North American Free Trade Agreement (NAFTA) has raised concerns that there will be a 'Fortress North America' and that there will be significant trade and investment diversion. Many in the Caribbean, Latin-American and Asia-Pacific regions are concerned that their present trade links with North America will be weakened, while protectionist interests in the United States are concerned that investment from outside North America will use Mexico as a backdoor export platform to the United States. The validity of these concerns will depend upon how one assesses the structure of a NAFTA (assuming it is implemented on the basis of the text of the agreement initialed on October 7, 1992), what is the outcome of the Uruguay Round of multilateral trade negotiations, what will be the behavior of the three NAFTA parties in subsequent multilateral negotiations, and what will be the dynamics of possible accession of other countries to the NAFTA.

This chapter first discusses the alternative approaches that might have been pursued to the negotiation of NAFTA, examines the relationship between NAFTA and the Canada–US Free Trade Agreement (CUSFTA), and considers the emerging architecture of the NAFTA approach to regional integration. The chapter then turns to the linkage between the trilateral arrangements and the Uruguay Round. Third, some of the key elements of NAFTA are reviewed and a few observations made about a very preliminary qualitative assessment of the trade-creation and trade-diversion effects. Fourth, the broader repercussions for the global trading system and the potential issues raised by any extension of NAFTA to other countries are discussed and some suggestions are made on how multilateral review of regional integration agreements (RIAs) might be clarified and strengthened. Finally, some conclusions are registered.

4.1   The emerging architecture

The overall architecture of the proposed NAFTA can be evaluated on the basis of three broad options which could have been pursued to achieve a trilateral free trade agreement:

1. *Trilateralization of the CUSFTA.* Mexico could have acceded to the existing CUSFTA with only minor adjustments to that. In essence this option would have involved one common North American free trade agreement (FTA) built directly from that agreement. The principal obstacles to this approach were that it was difficult to accommodate Mexican sensitivities in areas such as energy trade and investment without a full renegotiation of CUSFTA.

2. *A common core FTA.* An alternative approach to full trilateralization, which permits more flexibility for bilateral differentiation in the obligations, involves a core or umbrella free trade agreement encompassing Canada, Mexico and the US, but with two or possibly three separate bilateral agreements to accommodate some distinctive bilateral issues and sensitivities.[1] The essential feature of this approach would be a common FTA with common rules of origin for trade in goods among the three economies. Compliance with rules of origin is costly and the maintenance of two separate rules of origin for Canada–US–Mexico and Canada–US trade would inhibit the longer-term expansion of trade and investment within North America.[2] The other principal feature of this approach would be to develop a common institutional framework for the North American FTAs. The dispute settlement mechanism could be generalized to include third countries fairly readily and trilateralization might serve to depoliticize some issues, but other issues could be the subject of bilateral protocols.

3. *A generic FTA with country protocols.* A different way of accommodating national sensitivities involves a generic FTA, which provides common rules for trade in goods and services, investment and protection of intellectual property and a common framework of dispute settlement procedures, while each country has a protocol of exceptions and derogations.

Although these alternative possible approaches to the architecture of NAFTA may seem to be mere differences in form, they have substantive implications for the substance of the intra-North American arrangements both immediately and in shaping their future evolution. Moreover, these alternative approaches have different implications for trade and investment relations with third countries and the possibility of future accession of new partners.

Among the options outlined, or along this spectrum, the outcome is a hybrid involving a blend of all three options. The NAFTA provides common rules of origin for the elimination of border measures according to an agreed schedule (but there are bilateral tariff schedules because the tariffs between Canada and the US are already substantially eliminated, while tariff reductions with Mexico will begin January 1, 1994), common rules for trade in goods, services, investment and intellectual property, and common dispute settlement procedures. However, energy trade and investment, trade in agricultural products, and cultural trade and investment are highly asymmetric or bilateral in their application. Although NAFTA will replace the Canada–US FTA, residual elements of CUSFTA will continue to apply or will be incorporated into NAFTA. In addition, each country has a schedule of reservations or derogations for chapters such as investment and services. Compared to CUSFTA, the NAFTA has evolved a long way toward a generic free trade area – indeed to a free trade area plus. Although potential accession by non-members will have to be negotiated on a case-by-case basis, the extension of NAFTA will not require extensive renegotiation among the partners, in contrast to the situation involved in adapting CUSFTA to incorporate Mexico.

One striking feature of NAFTA is that it is a regional integration agreement encompassing countries with significant differences in per capita incomes. Although Mexico has special national sensitivities which are reflected in NAFTA, such as the constitutional restrictions on foreign investment in the energy sector, Canada and the US also have their own national sensitivities, which are reflected in derogations from the general NAFTA provisions. There is no special and differential treatment for Mexico as a developing country. Thus Mexican participation in NAFTA is another major step in the dramatic liberalization of the Mexican economy since the mid-1980s. At the same time, although the differences in income levels raise anxieties and concerns about the labor-adjustment implications in the US and Canada, the NAFTA negotiations have moved on a very fast timetable and Mexico will be relatively quickly integrated into the rest of the North American economy. In contrast to the European Community approach of establishing a full common market and fiscal transfers, the NAFTA approach, of a conventional free trade area supplemented by investment, services and carefully delimited temporary entry provisions (instead of full labor mobility), could prove more flexible in facilitating regional economic integration when countries have different income levels.

At the same time the implications of the NAFTA architecture cannot be assessed fully at this point. Some important issues were not resolved in NAFTA pending the outcome of the Uruguay Round negotiations, and the success or failure of the Round will have significant implications for the evolution of NAFTA within North America and its potential extension to other countries. It is noteworthy that NAFTA goes beyond CUSFTA and anticipates the outcome of the Uruguay Round in incorporating an intellectual property chapter based on the Dunkel Draft Final Act of December 1991. In addition, NAFTA contains a number of new provisions about the environment. Moreover, environmental issues and human rights issues will attract considerable interest in the US Congress as the NAFTA implementation process proceeds.

4.2   Linkages to the Uruguay Round and the multilateral trading system

The uncertainties about the outcome of the Uruguay Round after the impasse at the 1990 Brussels Ministerial and the failure to break this impasse at the July 1992 Munich Summit complicate the intra-North American arrangements, as well as creating potential problems for fourth countries in their trade and investment relations with NAFTA members. From the very beginning of the NAFTA negotiations it appeared that there was a vague consensus among the three countries that it would be very convenient if the most difficult issues – textiles trade restrictions, agricultural subsidies and trade barriers, trade rules for subsidies and for countervailing and anti-dumping duties, government procurement practices, and rules for intellectual property – were resolved through the multilateral process. Although an impasse in the multilateral negotiations has reinforced interest in RIAs, the failure to deal with these more difficult issues, as well as more prosaic ones such as multilateral tariff reductions, made the substantive negotiations among the US, Mexico and Canada more difficult. And a continuing impasse will complicate the evolution of NAFTA as well as making its impact on the multilateral system more problematic.

The outcome of the Uruguay Round could significantly affect the trade diversion consequences of NAFTA. It is evident that the potential for trade diversion in a FTA involving Mexico, the US and Canada is significant because Mexico is a lower-wage, complementary economy. Much of the potential for trade diversion derives from Canadian and US trade barriers. For example, Mexico is not a major supplier of textiles and apparel products to Canada, and Canada does not have bilateral restrictions on Mexican exports under the Multifiber Arrangement (MFA), but, because Canada imposes high tariffs and bilateral restraints on low-cost suppliers under the MFA, Mexico might expand substantially its exports of these products once it is exempted from Canadian tariffs. At present, the US applies both MFA restraints and high tariffs on Mexican exports, and the issue is how trade patterns will change as these barriers are reduced on imports from Mexico. The domestic textile and apparel industries in Canada and the US are concerned that increased Mexican exports of these products will increase significantly the share of imports in domestic consumption, but if external trade barriers remain high then the result could be trade diversion, with Mexican exports displacing exports from other developing countries. If, however, significant liberalization of tariff and non-tariff barriers to textiles and apparel trade can be achieved in the Uruguay Round, then the potential for trade diversion will be reduced.

Agricultural trade and subsidy issues illustrate some of the difficulties for the NAFTA negotiations arising from the impasse in the Uruguay Round. Much of Mexico's remaining import licenses and most of the import quotas of Canada and the US are concentrated in the agricultural sector. The delays in achieving a meaningful outcome to the Uruguay Round negotiations on agricultural subsidies and trade barriers have set the parameters for the trilateral negotiations. This is not a new problem. Neither the US nor Canada was prepared to reduce domestic agricultural subsidies in the CUSFTA negotiations, and the FTA does not impose any meaningful restriction on the use of export subsidies for sales to offshore markets (because of concerns about the impact of EC and Japanese agricultural policies). For its part, Mexico was reluctant to dismantle its restrictions on imports of corn, grains and lentils, because millions of small farmers depend upon these products, and Mexican reluctance was intensified since the US and Canada retain substantial agricultural subsidies.

Closing the NAFTA deal before the conclusion of the Uruguay Round posed an especially serious problem for Canada on agriculture, because Canada remains politically committed to its Uruguay Round position (aligning it with other noted agricultural importers such as Japan and Korea) of seeking to preserve and to extend import quotas for supply-managed products under Article XI of GATT. Thus, Canada was preoccupied with preserving the exceptions for these import quotas contained in the CUSFTA. As a result, the agricultural arrangements in NAFTA consist of three bilateral agreements.

The Mexico–US bilateral provides for replacement of import quotas and licenses with tariff rate quotas (TRQs) and the tariffs are eliminated over a 10- or 15-year time frame. Mexico has corn and dry beans and the US has sugar and orange juice on a 15-year phase-out. The Canada–Mexico chapter is analogous, except that dairy, poultry and eggs are excluded. Thus, apart from Canada's idiosyncrasies, the market access elements of NAFTA on agricultural products are remarkably comprehensive. However, the obligations on domestic support and export subsidies are merely hortatory, except to incorporate the GATT obligations which are to be part of the conclusion of the Uruguay Round. In this respect, the agricultural chapter of the FTA which remains in force between Canada and the United States contains stronger disciplines because of the prohibition of export subsidies on a bilateral basis.

The situation on subsidies and countervailing duties in NAFTA is analogous to that on agricultural subsidies. NAFTA proposes to implement the relevant parts of the Dunkel Draft on subsidies and countervailing duties at the conclusion of the Uruguay Round and abandon the effort to develop subsidy and countervailing duty rules, which was mandated in the CUSFTA. Certainly the Dunkel text on subsidies and countervailing duties offers a useful basis for introducing subsidy disciplines, both in the form of prohibitions and/or as giving some effect to the serious prejudice obligations under the GATT. Politically a Uruguay Round deal involving Europe and Japan has the potential muscle to get changes in countervailing duty laws through the Congress, while NAFTA does not.

However, it is curious that the NAFTA countries do not contemplate the possibility that they might wish to improve or refine the rules for subsidies and countervailing duties among themselves either at the end of the Uruguay Round or subsequently. An unusual aspect of the Dunkel text on subsidies is that it imposes tighter disciplines on the use of subsidies by subnational governments than on national governments.[3] As three federal nations, the NAFTA countries might find it in their interests to modify this provision among themselves. Perhaps the NAFTA negotiators are being shrewd and anticipate that the provision of the Dunkel subsidies text, which imposes greater discipline on subnational governments (there in the text as a result of EC insistence), will be modified now that the Maastricht Treaty faces some obstacles to implementation.

Government procurement is another example of where the Uruguay Round could go further than NAFTA, because of the attraction of the opening of the European and Japanese markets. There is a substantial procurement package in NAFTA, however, that will go further than that under CUSFTA and the present GATT procurement code. In addition to coverage of the entities covered under the GATT procurement code, the US is willing to include the purchases of entities such as the Army Corps of Engineers, the Rural Electrification Administration and regional power authorities, and Canada will cover the purchases of departments such as Transportation and Fisheries and crown corporations such as the Canadian National Railway Company. The reason that the US and Canada are prepared to participate in a more substantial opening of government procurement is because Mexico is covering procurement of major state enterprises including Pemex (the state oil company), the Federal Electricity Commission and National Railways of Mexico (Ferronales) as well as a wide range of direct government purchases. By opening procurement of Pemex and other utilities to bidding by NAFTA partners, Mexico is offsetting some of the trade effects of preserving Pemex's statutory monopoly and exempting the energy sector from key obligations under NAFTA.

The interaction between NAFTA and the Uruguay Round with respect to intellectual property rules is intriguing. In essence the three countries have adopted the Dunkel text on intellectual property, but the rights and obligations will apply only among the three countries unless the Uruguay Round is also implemented by January 1994. Thus, the discriminatory aspects of Section 337 of the Tariff Act of 1930 will be modified in conformity with the GATT panel report, but this might apply only to NAFTA partners unless the Uruguay Round is implemented at the same time.

4.3   A brief review of NAFTA: managed trade or free trade?

The *Wall Street Journal* has described NAFTA as managed trade, not free trade. This section reviews selected key elements of NAFTA and considers the broad question of whether it promotes managed trade or freer trade, as well as the more conventional question of whether NAFTA is trade-creating or trade-diverting.

4.3.1   Rules of origin and border measures

The proposed NAFTA will eventually eliminate tariffs and export duties among the three economies. In this respect NAFTA would parallel CUSFTA, but the timetable for tariff reductions between Mexico and the US and Mexico and Canada lags behind the present schedule of tariff reductions between Canada and the US under the FTA. The rules of origin for NAFTA differ from those of CUSFTA most notably in the textiles and apparel sector, automotive products and a few others.

Rules of origin are an essential element of any FTA (see Chapter 15 below, by Palmeter). The valid purpose of rules of origin is to prevent trade and investment diversion when there are high and differentiated external trade barriers. However, restrictive rules of origin can frustrate the benefits of the removal of trade barriers.

The pressure for restrictive rules of origin is greater in industries characterized by significant non-tariff barriers to trade. Moreover, rules of origin in themselves can become significant non-tariff barriers to trade. Considerable effort was expended in order that the trilateral NAFTA have clear and transparent rules of origin, with the objective that compliance costs and administrative discretion be minimized. The existing CUSFTA utilizes primarily a change of tariff classification criteria to determine substantial transformation. However, assembly activities have a 50 per cent direct-cost-of-manufacturing requirement which may be subject to some degree of ambiguity in measurement and administration. Under NAFTA more products have a rule of origin defined by change of tariff headings, which makes the determination of origin more predictable.

Many misgivings by other countries about the NAFTA negotiations were prompted by US proposals for more restrictive rules of origin in sectors such as textiles and apparel, automobiles and computers. Protectionist groups in the US sought to manipulate the rules of origin to restrict competition from Mexico and in some cases sought to claw back benefits under CUSFTA as well as to limit the opening of trade under NAFTA. In the end, some of the more extreme proposals were discarded. In the case of computers, US multinationals appear to have belatedly realized that the proposed restrictive and cumbersome rules would be damaging to their US operations in a technologically dynamic and globalized industry. Part of the solution to this issue was to agree to implement a low common MFN tariff in the computer sector. The mercantilists inside and outside the US government lost this particular battle, but it appears there will be residual effects in the form of restrictive rules of origin for cathode ray tubes, televisions and certain other electronic equipment.

The differences between the proposed NAFTA arrangements and those of the existing CUSFTA can be illustrated by reference to a particular industrial sector which was a central focus of concern during the trilateral negotiations, namely the automotive sector. The US pressed for a restrictive rule of origin for trade in automotive products under the trilateral free trade agreement. From a trade policy perspective it is puzzling why the US, with a tariff of 2.5 per cent on automotive products currently and a MFN tariff that could be even lower after completion of the Uruguay Round, would care very much about the rules of origin for automotive products, because the potential incentives for trade diversion or trade deflection are extremely limited with such a low MFN tariff. (Of course the situation is somewhat different with light trucks, which have a 25 per cent tariff as a result of the US–EC chicken war.) However, the economic impact and political clout of the automotive sector is such that the rules for this sector will receive great scrutiny in the Congress.

The NAFTA negotiations over automotive rules of origin were influenced by trade disputes between Canada and the US. Bilateral disputes over whether certain vehicle manufacturers are meeting the rules of origin under the FTA have important implications for the companies involved and will influence the perceptions of fourth-country investors. Complicated technical issues are involved in the current disputes over whether vehicles manufactured by the GM–Suzuki joint venture and the Honda subsidiary meet the rules of origin under the FTA. The key issue in each case is whether there is sufficient value-added occurring in Canada and the US for the vehicles to qualify for duty-free trade under the FTA. Customs administration and legal interpretation of customs law are arcane issues, as was illustrated by a sudden ruling in the late 1970s that light trucks assembled in the US were not transformed sufficiently to avoid paying the 25 per cent US duty.

Rules of origin became a lightning rod for protectionism under CUSFTA as well as in the NAFTA negotiations. These protectionist pressures were stimulated by the lingering recession in the US economy. There have been a number of bilateral disputes between Canada and the United States over the interpretation of the rules of origin in the FTA. For example, the controversial audit of Honda by the US Customs Service of the Treasury raises complicated issues. One of the issues involves the administration of 'roll-up' or 'roll-down'. Under this approach, if major components such as the engine are deemed to meet the FTA rule of origin then all of the value of the engine counts toward the required 50 per cent direct cost of manufacturing the engine is 'rolled-up'. On the other hand, if the engine is deemed not to meet the FTA rule of origin then it is 'rolled-down' and only a small proportion of the value of the engine is counted toward the direct cost of manufacturing. Roll-up or roll-down is a key issue in the Honda dispute. Since engines machined and assembled by Honda in Ohio are not deemed to meet the FTA rules of origin then the Honda Civics assembled in Alliston, Ontario, are not qualified for duty-free entry from Canada to the US. As an illustration of the technical complexity, one of the issues is the non-arm's-length relationship between the Honda subsidiaries in the US and Canada and the interpretation of the FTA by US Customs. The NAFTA seeks to resolve these technical problems for automobiles through more detailed rules of origin, but the quid pro quo was tracing of the content and changes in the rules of origin requirements.

Some of the technical issues involved in automotive rules of origin were the subject of an arbitration panel under CUSFTA. The binational panel under Chapter 18 ruled unanimously that Canada's interpretation permitting the deductibility of different types of interest charges was correct. However, many of the technical problems in the FTA rules of origin were addressed in the NAFTA negotiations. For example, in the NAFTA, alternatives to the controversial roll-up process are proposed which, it is claimed, would be more easily administered by the governments. In addition, the NAFTA arrangements propose a new mechanism to develop common interpretations of rules of origin, which is aimed at limiting the scope for unilateral interpretation of the rules of origin by the national customs authorities. This appears to be a useful innovation, but it remains to be seen whether this mechanism and the proposed new definitions of rules of origin can stand the rigors of legalistic deconstructionism which dominates the US conduct of trade relations at the present time.

Mexico and Canada resisted restrictive rules of origin in the automotive sector, in part because of concerns about the impact on existing Japanese assembly plants on new automotive investment by offshore firms. This issue and related issues about the Mexican automotive decree and duty drawback were among the most contentious in the negotiations.

The clarification of rules of origin to a net cost basis apparently offsets a higher content number than the 50 per cent direct cost of manufacturing in the CUSFTA, but the equivalent percentage is debatable. Under NAFTA the content requirement will stay at 50 per cent for four years, rise to 56 per cent for four years and then be 62.5 per cent. The latter number is more restrictive than the existing requirements under CUSFTA, notwithstanding the redefinition of rules of origin for automotive products. In order to cushion the impact on new investment, new automotive production facilities qualify for 50 per cent content level for five years.

It is customary in RIAs to eliminate duty drawbacks for exports qualifying for preferred access to the markets of FTA partners. Thus duty drawbacks were scheduled to be eliminated by January 1, 1994, in the CUSFTA. For Canada, full duty drawback was extended for two years in NAFTA. Mexico obtained a seven-year transition period, before full duty drawback – known as *maquiladora* in Mexico – disappears in a NAFTA. What is retained permanently is a device to eliminate double taxation; the lesser of the import duty and the drawback of the duty on imported inputs will be permitted to be remitted. Thus goods not meeting the NAFTA rules of origin will continue to receive drawback, which removes a potential anomaly under CUSFTA.

In addition to the rules of origin for preferential tariff access, the other key issue for border measures under NAFTA will be the coverage of quotas and import licenses. In principle, all such quantitative restrictions should be eliminated, but there will be pressures to retain, at least for a considerable period, many of them. For example, Mexico is phasing out its import-licensing and trade-balancing requirements for the automotive sector over 10 years, but the phase-out favors the five existing automobile manufacturers in Mexico – the Big US Three, Nissan and Volkswagen.

The issue of restrictive rules of origin and the retention of quantitative restrictions on imports often are closely linked. Both Canada and the United States maintain extensive restraints on imports of textiles and clothing from low-cost countries (Smith and Bence, 1989). As a result of concerns, especially on the US side, about the potential for trade diversion involving apparel made from offshore fabrics, special, more restrictive rules of origin for apparel were included in CUSFTA. Under CUSFTA, there was a double transformation test for apparel to qualify under the FTA – the fabric had to be woven and the garment manufactured in Canada or the US to qualify for FTA treatment. Canadian apparel manufacturers, who utilized fabrics from offshore sources, complained and obtained substantial temporary TRQs for exports of garments to the US that were manufactured with offshore fabric.

The situation in NAFTA is analogous, but even more complicated. Canada does not impose MFA restraints on Mexico, presumably because competitive pressures are not intense, but the US does impose extensive restraints on Mexican apparel exports. Responding to intense political pressures from textile and apparel producers concerned about lower-wage competition from Mexico, the United States proposed and NAFTA contains triple transformation 'yarn forward' and even quadruple transformation 'fiber forward' rules of origin for textiles and apparel.[4]

These even more restrictive rules of origin for textiles and apparel in NAFTA created anxiety for Canadian textile and apparel manufacturers. Since the United States does not apply MFA restrictions to Canada, since the FTA rules of origin were less restrictive, and since Canada already had temporary TRQs for apparel manufactured with offshore fabric, the arrangement that was negotiated was a series of TRQs with growth factors for Canadian exports of textiles and apparel. The Canadian textiles industry seems to be satisfied with this result but the apparel industry has claimed catastrophe, although the grounds for their claim seem dubious.

The highly restrictive rules of origin in textiles and apparel are motivated by protectionist pressures in the US, but they may inadvertently serve the valid purpose of limiting trade diversion at least in the short term. Longer term, investment diversion could become more of an issue as the restructuring of the textile and apparel industry within the North American market proceeds under the new regime. Liberalization of textiles and apparel trade on a multilateral basis may increase short-term concerns about adjustment to import competition in the US and Canada, but it could also ease pressures for restrictive rules of origin for trilateral trade in this sector. Thus, these rules of origin in textiles and apparel ought to be revisited in the future, especially if the MFA is phased out as planned in the Uruguay Round.

The existing CUSFTA influenced the negotiations of rules of origin significantly. Canadian exporters, and hence the Canadian government, resisted the negotiation of NAFTA rules of origin that were more restrictive than those under the CUSFTA, and in many product areas this proved an important check on proposals for restrictive and discriminatory rules of origin. At the same time, fixing some of the problems with the CUSFTA rules of origin was a major preoccupation of NAFTA rules of origin negotiations.

Several summary points can be made about the rules of origin in NAFTA and the potential for trade and investment diversion. First, the rules of origin are not as restrictive as some lobby groups would have wished and the restrictive rules of origin appear to be confined to textiles and apparel, automotive, and selected agri-food sectors such as sugar-containing products. Second, the NAFTA was negotiated in the context of a prolonged recession and there may be opportunities to amend the rules of origin in a more buoyant economy as the agreement is implemented. Third, if the products in question are subject to low-bound MFN tariffs in all three NAFTA partners, then the primary effect of a restrictive rule of origin is to limit the effective coverage of the NAFTA in the opening of trade among the partners. Fourth, if the external barriers are high tariffs and/or import quotas, then a restrictive rule of origin may serve to limit trade diversion at least in the short term. Fifth, at the same time, with high and differentiated external barriers, a restrictive rule of origin may stimulate investment diversion. Thus the key to limiting the amount of trade and investment diversion is the elimination of import quotas by all three NAFTA partners and the reduction of MFN tariffs. Completion of the Uruguay Round is an obvious critical first step that would do much to limit the potential trade and investment diversion resulting from the NAFTA.

4.3.2 Internal measures and the trade laws

The negotiation of import quotas and trade laws is often linked to internal measures including subsidies, procurement preferences and environmental regulations. Yet the asymmetries in the size and level of development of the three North American economies make it difficult to negotiate any restraints on domestic policies. Mexicans and also Canadians have often been extremely concerned about the threat to their sovereignty which could arise from US dominance. For its part the

United States is likely to resist any restraints on its ability to take unilateral actions. The issues are as follows:

1. *Subsidies*. It proved impossible to agree on disciplines on either agricultural or non-agricultural subsidies in the CUSFTA negotiations, and it is evidently more difficult to develop effective rules limiting the use of domestic subsidies when an economy like Mexico's, which has much lower income levels and greater infrastructure needs, is added to the negotiations. As a result the subsidy issues, both agricultural and non-agricultural, are referred to the Uruguay Round for resolution. As noted above, it is curious that the NAFTA countries do not contemplate the possibility of refining these subsidy rules among themselves.

2. *Anti-dumping laws and competition policies*. As with the countervailing duty laws, national anti-dumping laws are retained by each of the NAFTA partners. As was noted above, Mexico will amend its trade laws and procedures to make them similar to those of the US and Canada. There is a chapter in NAFTA dealing with monopolies and restrictive business practices. A working group is proposed to examine the anti-dumping laws and competition policies, but there is no deadline. Although the proposal of replacing anti-dumping laws with competition law remedies is virulently opposed by some business interests in the US today, the prospects for negotiation of this approach could be much better five or ten years hence as implementation of the NAFTA proceeds. The lack of any substantial progress on the trade laws, apart from elaboration of the FTA restraints upon the use of safeguards or emergency import measures on trade with NAFTA partners, will be perceived as a shortcoming of NAFTA by many. However, this minimalist approach has one significant virtue. At least the three countries have avoided the route of common external anti-dumping and countervailing duty laws, such as is the case with the European Community. Common external trade laws would increase the risk of managed trade substantially.

3. *Environmental measures*. Although at the outset the governments stated that environmental issues were being dealt with outside the trilateral free trade negotiations, the agreement contains a number of environmental-related provisions. The preamble makes an explicit reference to sustainable development. There are proposals to include environmental experts in panels and to make certain environmental evidence is presented to panels. Responding to concerns about environmental issues, there is a proposed obligation that derogation of environmental standards should not be used as an investment

inducement or to defer plant closure. This provision does not impose mandatory contractual obligations, since the only requirement is for intergovernmental consultation. However, this provision offers a vehicle for the proposed trilateral environment ministers council and the trilateral trade commission to address concerns about investment-inducement effects of relaxation of environmental measures, and the effects on competitiveness of differences in environmental regulations. Since the NAFTA retains the FTA provision permitting the parties to either take bilateral disputes to the GATT or handle them under the FTA, there may be implications for GATT dispute-settlement mechanisms and especially for cases involving environmental issues. The NAFTA gives precedence to international environmental agreements, including the Convention on International Trade in Endangered Species of Wild Fauna and Flora (CITES), the Montreal Protocol on Substances that Deplete the Ozone Layer, the Basel Convention on the Control of Transboundary Movements of Hazardous Wastes, and some bilateral environmental agreements. This approach raises some interesting questions about the relationship between international environmental agreements and trade agreements, and the process of resolving trade disputes involving environmental factors.

4.3.3   Services, investment and temporary entry

In addition to a free trade area for trade in goods, the NAFTA contains chapters covering cross-border trade in services, temporary entry for business and professional people, and investment. The services chapter follows a negative-list approach by covering all services with obligations for national treatment, for MFN treatment, and governing regulatory requirements for establishment, licensing and certification, unless the service is explicitly excluded or specific derogations for particular policy measures are registered in country annexes. Services such as land transportation and specialty air transportation, which were not covered by the CUSFTA, are covered by NAFTA. There are separate chapters governing telecommunications and financial services.

The investment chapter follows an approach analogous to the services chapter by requiring derogations to be registered in country schedules or annexes. In contrast to the CUSFTA, which grandfathered all existing derogations from services and investment obligations, the requirement to list derogations provides more transparency and predictability for firms operating within NAFTA. One of the innovative and intriguing aspects of NAFTA is an investor-state private arbitral mechanism, which provides firms operating in NAFTA the opportunity to obtain financial compensation through international arbitration if a government contravenes either the investment obligations or obligations about the conduct of monopolies and state enterprises.

The temporary entry chapter covers business visitors, traders and investors, intra-company management transfers, and professionals. The chapter builds on a similar chapter in CUSFTA, but the US imposes a quantitative limit on the number of Mexican professionals who may gain temporary visas.

4.3.4 Dispute settlement

The general dispute settlement mechanism under Chapter 18 of the CUSFTA could be adapted to the NAFTA in a relatively straightforward fashion, but the special binational appeal mechanism for anti-dumping and countervailing duty cases under Chapter 19 of the CUSFTA raised some special issues for trilateralization, because of differences between Mexico's legal system and the legal systems of Canada and the United States.

Under the CUSFTA, Chapter 19 sets up a binational appeal mechanism, which can replace existing judicial review by the domestic courts of final decisions by the national administering agencies, as well as a review mechanism to monitor changes in anti-dumping and countervailing duty laws as they apply to the partner country. The objective of these dispute-settlement procedures is to provide a more timely appeal mechanism than is available through the courts and to provide joint scrutiny of the decisions taken by the administrative authorities in both countries (Steger, 1988; Coffield, 1988; Dearden, 1988; Horlick and Valentine, 1988). Although the softwood lumber dispute influenced the negotiations and the resulting agreement, the understanding on softwood lumber negotiated between Canada and the US in late 1986 after the preliminary determination by the Department of Commerce was not affected by the CUSFTA. Thus, the issue of stumpage subsidies remained to be resolved either through the future negotiations on subsidies or through the dispute settlement processes under the CUSFTA. Now that Canada has terminated the softwood lumber memorandum of understanding and the United States has initiated a countervailing duty case against softwood lumber, the application of the dispute settlement processes to this difficult set of issues will be tested.

The CUSFTA negotiations were, however, able to resolve some contentious subsidy issues in other sectors. In the automotive sector, the issue of Canada's export-based duty remission mechanism was resolved in a way which served both Canadian and US objectives, while avoiding a potential US countervailing action which would have been very disruptive to bilateral trade.[5]

The influence of US protectionist pressures was evident in the softwood lumber dispute between Canada and the US. Although various congressional bills directed against softwood lumber imports did not become law, a change in the interpretation of US countervailing duty law by the US Commerce Department in the 1986 *Softwood Lumber Case* resulted in a negotiated settlement where Canada imposed a 15 per cent export tax on lumber shipped to the United States (Percy and Yoder, 1987). The bitter conflict over softwood lumber shaped official attitudes on both sides during the negotiations and influenced the agreement that emerged. In effect the CUSFTA seeks to prevent the recurrence of a softwood lumber situation where the administrative interpretation of the trade laws was perceived by Canadians as being altered in response to protectionist pressures. Just as the 1986 softwood lumber dispute shaped Canadian attitudes to the CUSFTA negotiations, so the outcome of the 1991–2 softwood lumber countervailing duty case will influence Canadian and also US attitudes to the dispute settlement processes for the trade laws in the NAFTA. Furthermore, the outcome of the 1991–2 case could influence the implementation of NAFTA.

There are difficulties in generalizing the review mechanisms governing the trade laws under Chapter 19. Although there are technical differences, Canadian and US trade laws are remarkably similar. It is more difficult to apply the CUSFTA review mechanism for decisions involving anti-dumping and countervailing duties to a third country like Mexico whose domestic trade laws and administrative procedures differ substantially from those of the US and Canada. To respond to this concern Mexico has agreed to implement trade laws and procedures similar to those of the US and Canada. In addition, it is difficult to involve Mexico in this type of judicial review because the Mexican legal system does not have the same basic concepts of administrative law and judicial review (which are common to the Canadian and US legal systems). The proposed NAFTA arrangement does extend the Chapter 19 mechanism to Mexico, but it introduces a new Special Committee process which can be triggered if a country fails to initiate a binational panel or to implement panel results.

4.4 Impact on the global trading system

This section considers a much broader set of issues. There is a debate between those who take the view that there is a constructive and creative

tension between regional economic integration and multilateral liberalization, and those who take the opposite view that regional integration
efforts can be corrosive and even cancerous to the multilateral system.
This is an issue on which economists, who broadly share a consensus
about the benefits of trade liberalization, have divergent views. There
was considerable debate in the 1940s and 1950s about the fundamental
concepts of trade creation and trade diversion in the economics of RIAs.
The basic conclusion reached was that if there is sufficient trade creation,
then, indeed, removing barriers among a group of countries can be
beneficial, not only to the partners but to other countries as well.

There is a simple per se rule incorporated in Article XXIV of the
General Agreement on Tariffs and Trade which provides a rough
approximation to the economic analysis. Article XXIV stipulates that the
countries forming a customs union or free trade area must remove all
duties and other restrictive regulations of commerce among the partner
countries. It likewise requires that there should be no increase in external
barriers to trade with third countries after a transaction period. I would
argue that in applying this test even the European Community (EC) has
been trade-creating. This resulted both initially at the time of its
establishment and following the liberalization of its multilateral trade
barriers after the Kennedy and Tokyo Rounds of GATT negotiations.

Of course, countries such as Argentina, Australia, Brazil, and Canada
and other members of the Cairns Group may be skeptical about the
proposition that the EC has been trade-creating, because of the singular
exception to one of these conditions in EC trade policy, namely, the
Common Agricultural Policy (CAP). In the case of the CAP, the
external tariff barriers of the EC were largely unbound since there were
few GATT-tariff bindings on farm products. Moreover, there has been
a subsequent proliferation of internal farm subsidies. There has thus
been trade diversion on a very substantial scale in the agricultural sector
because barriers to trade with third countries have increased, and this has
posed particular problems to the global trading system.

But there are also considerations of size. As Long (1985, p. 19)
observes:

> Those who drafted the article (Article XXIV) certainly did not have in
> mind a structure of the size and importance of the European Economic
> Community (EEC), but rather arrangements between two or three
> countries, such as Benelux for instance. They did not envisage the
> conclusion by the EEC of preferential arrangements with developing
> countries with whom member countries of the EEC had been linked in the
> past by special relationships. Neither did they foresee that many
> developing countries would seek, through regional integration, the
> promotion of their economic development and that, in so doing, they

would adopt the model of a customs union or free-trade area despite lacking the economic resources necessary fully to meet the strict criteria of Article XXIV.

The NAFTA will create another large trading bloc and it cannot but add to the repercussions for the global trading system that the EC has caused.

Concluding NAFTA could stimulate trade liberalization either through progress in resolving the outstanding issues in the Uruguay Round, through competitive regionalism in Europe or Asia, or through more countries acceding to NAFTA. The complicated and customized structure of NAFTA means that fourth-country accession will not necessarily be straightforward. Although NAFTA has an accession clause, it appears that each accession will have to be negotiated on a case-by-case basis. The concept of an 'Enterprise of the Americas' led to a proposal that Western Hemisphere countries should be given the opportunity to accede to NAFTA, on the terms contained in the original agreement, without having to go through the same Congressional approval procedure. However, this proposal was rejected and the accession clause requires approval by the legislatures of the parties to NAFTA, and there is no geographic limitation on the accession to NAFTA.

4.5   Conclusion

The broad answer to the question of whether NAFTA will represent more managed trade or freer trade is that it will, on balance, mean freer trade. Some of the rules of origin are Byzantine in their complexity, and some are clearly restrictive or discriminatory. The rules of origin in textiles and apparel are very restrictive, but this is more an issue among the NAFTA partners than for other countries. The restrictive rules of origin in this sector actually may serve to limit trade diversion. The complicated arrangements in the automotive sector do not lend themselves to a summary assessment, but the issue is more a matter of investment diversion or restriction than of trade diversion. Moreover, the automotive provisions are most problematic after 2002 when the 62.5 per cent content rule is triggered. Much could happen before then.

A successful outcome to the Uruguay Round will enhance the prospects for achieving deeper liberalization of trade within NAFTA and reduce the potential for trade and investment diversion. The key to limiting the amount of trade and investment diversion resulting from NAFTA is the elimination of import quotas by all three NAFTA partners and the reduction of MFN tariffs. Completion of the Uruguay Round is an obvious critical first step that would do much to limit the potential trade and investment diversion resulting from the NAFTA. It is in the interests of all three North American economies to avoid any tendency to form a 'Fortress North America'. An open and outward-looking NAFTA could serve to stimulate trade and investment flows across the Pacific and globally.

The NAFTA avoids any serious shift to managed trade and is on balance trade-creating because it reduces trade barriers among the partners without raising barriers against trade with other countries. According to conventional criteria under GATT's Article XXIV, such an arrangement is usually considered to be trade-creating. But NAFTA is likely to receive rigorous scrutiny by GATT members and it could prompt tighter review of RIAs under GATT or its successor organization after the Uruguay Round. Clarification of some of the criteria for RIAs under Article XXIV, such as requiring the elimination of duty drawback when the agreement is fully implemented, will help ensure that smaller economies joining a large trading zone like NAFTA have additional incentives to continue the reduction of their MFN trade barriers. Beyond the issue of trade creation/trade diversion a critical question is how the NAFTA partners behave in subsequent multilateral negotiations.

Other countries may accede to NAFTA in the future, but accession will have to be negotiated on a case-by-case basis. Hopefully, concluding the NAFTA deal and the prospect of more countries acceding to the arrangement will build pressure to break the impasse in the Uruguay Round. Beyond the Uruguay Round, NAFTA raises some important issues about the linkage of trade, environment, investment and competition policies that will need to be on the agenda for subsequent multilateral trade negotiations.

Notes

1. This general approach was suggested in Lipsey and Smith (1989). The application of this approach to Mexico's free trade initiative is examined by Lipsey (1990).
2. This is a different point than Wonnacott's incisive analysis of hub-and-spoke bilaterals, since this involves overlapping FTAs. See Wonnacott (1990).
3. The Dunkel text not only imposes a de facto specificity test in the definition of actionable subsidies, which in itself imposes a stricter standard on subnational governments (Smith, 1990), but goes further in defining as actionable all subsidies by subnational governments (Article 2.2). The provision is carefully drafted to refer to 'countries' instead of 'contracting parties' so that it applies to federal nations like Canada, Mexico and the United

States, but apparently does not apply to the European Community, which is the contracting party to the existing Subsidies Code. The rationale for this provision is that if countries have floating exchange rates, any competitive advantage from a generally available subsidy (such as government assistance for worker training or health programs) will be offset by exchange rate adjustment along the lines of the border tax adjustment, but within countries this exchange rate adjustment mechanism does not operate to offset competitive advantage. Yet the logic of this argument suggests that if France and Germany each has a different labor assistance program and is part of the European Monetary System, then these subsidies will be actionable under countervailing duties and the strengthened serious prejudice provisions of the proposed new Subsidies Code. Clearly the logic of this argument would be strengthened with European currency union.

4.   Recall that cotton is protected by Section 22 import restrictions in the United States, which helped trigger the short- and long-term agreements for cotton textiles in the 1960s.

5.   For an analysis of the implications of the automotive provisions of the FTA, see Wonnacott (1988).

References

Coffield, S. A. (1988), 'Dispute Settlement Provisions on Antidumping and Countervailing Duty Cases in the Canada—U.S. Free Trade Agreement', pp. 73–84 in *Understanding the Free Trade Agreement*, edited by D. McRae and D. Steger, Halifax: Institute for Research on Public Policy.

Dearden, R. G. (1988), 'Antidumping and Countervailing Duty Provisions: Judicial Review by Binational Panels', in *Understanding the Free Trade Agreement*, edited by D. McRae and D. Steger, Halifax: Institute for Research on Public Policy.

Horlick, G. N. and D. A. Valentine (1988), 'Improvements in Trade Remedy Law and Procedures Under the Canada—U.S. Free Trade Agreement', in *Understanding the Free Trade Agreement*, edited by D. McRae and D. Steger, Halifax: Institute for Research on Public Policy.

Lipsey, R. (1990), *Canada at the U.S.—Mexico Free Trade Dance: Wallflower or Partner?*, Toronto: C. D. Howe Institute.

Lipsey, R. and M. G. Smith (1989), 'The Canada—U.S. Free Trade Agreement: Special Case or Wave of the Future?', in *Free Trade Areas and U.S. Trade Policy*, edited by J. J. Schott, Washington, DC: Institute for International Economics.

Long, O. (1985), *Law and its Limitations in the GATT Multilateral Trade System*, Dordrecht: Martinus Nijhoff.

Percy, M. and C. Yoder (1987), *The Softwood Lumber Dispute and Canada—U.S. Trade in Natural Resources*, Halifax: Institute for Research on Public Policy.

Smith, M. G. (1990), 'Overview of Provincial and State Subsidies: Their Implications for Canada—U.S. Trade', in *International Economic Issues*, Halifax: Institute for Research on Public Policy.

Smith, M. G. and J.-F. Bence (1989), 'Tariff Equivalents for Bilateral Export Restraints on Canada's Textile and Apparel Trade: Analytical Issues,

Measurement Methodologies, and Selected Estimates', mimeo, Institute for Research on Public Policy, Ottawa.

Steger, D. P. (1988), 'Dispute Settlement Mechanisms of the Canada–U.S. Free Trade Agreement: Comparison with the Existing System', in *Understanding the Free Trade Agreement*, edited by D. McRae and D. Steger, Halifax: Institute for Research on Public Policy.

Wonnacott, P. (1988), 'The Auto Sector', in *The Canada–United States Free Trade Agreement: The Global Impact*, edited by J. J. Schott and M. G. Smith, Washington, DC: Institute for International Economics, and Halifax: Institute for Research on Public Policy.

Wonnacott, R. (1990), *Canada and the U.S.–Mexico Free Trade Negotiations*, Commentary No. 21, Toronto: C. D. Howe Institute.

5

Expanding EC membership and association accords: recent experience and future prospects

L. Alan Winters

The EC has been unique among regional integration agreements in the way in which it has progressively extended its influence geographically. This chapter considers this process and explores the pressures for and, briefly, the consequences of such extension. It defines extension to include not only enlargement – the accession of new members – but also the preferential trading arrangements and Association Agreements concluded by the EC with EFTA, various Mediterranean countries, and the African, Caribbean and Pacific (ACP) countries.

Two sets of events lend this exploration considerable current relevance. First, EC–EFTA relations were extended in the early 1990s from mere industrial free trade to the wide-ranging European Economic Area (EEA) agreement, and to discussions about full membership of the EC for several EFTA countries (Wijkman, 1992a). Writing in August 1992, there seems little doubt that any EFTA countries seeking membership will be admitted quickly, and so their case is treated below as one of accession. Second, the more advanced Central European economies – Czechoslovakia, Hungary and Poland – have signed deep and wide preference and cooperation agreements with the EC (the so-called Europe Agreements – see Winters, 1992c). These agreements allude to eventual EC membership, and will soon place these countries at the top of the EC's pyramid of preferences. Accession is not assured, however, and the present chapter will use past experience to assess when and how EC accession for them might be achieved.

The first section of the chapter argues that political factors – such as bolstering new democracies – play an important role in the EC's motives for extension, as do positive economic forces such as seeking to open markets. However, these stimuli are frequently constrained, sometimes wholly captured by, negative economic pressures and pressure groups. Hence enlargement – its timing and to a small extent its conditions – and preferences are managed in such a way as to reduce the adjustment pressure on existing members' economies. This is particularly so for the more sensitive EC sectors, such as agriculture, iron and steel, and textiles, but is detectable for all sectors in the way in which EC environmental and social protection standards have to be adopted by partners.

Section 5.2 examines four cases of enlargement. The first enlargement – the addition of the United Kingdom, Ireland and Denmark in 1973 – was essentially economic on both sides, driven strongly by concerns about lost markets. It also offered the UK not the 'cold shower' of competition that unilateral free trade would have done, but a moderate and manageable supply shock. The second enlargement – the addition of Greece, Portugal and Spain – was essentially political, but was hedged around with very long transitional periods in critical sectors. It also increased the EC's financial commitment to cohesion. The next enlargement I examine involves the current EFTA countries. This seems highly likely to occur and reflects economic as much as political factors. The EFTA countries offer the EC budgetary contributions and markets and, on their side, are concerned about being left behind in the '1992' great leap forward. I also consider the possible enlargement to include Turkey. This has been firmly rejected by the EC, revealing several concerns: about the cost of allowing in poorer agricultural members, about the dilution of the EC's deepening objectives by allowing in members that could not undertake all its requirements and, above all, about immigration. Section 5.2 concludes with a brief discussion of the lessons of EC enlargement for other integration schemes. It notes the importance of budgetary transfers, the role of integration in making changes in policy regimes credible, and the attractions of evading arbitrary trade policy by getting inside the trading club. It also notes that while the formation of the EC probably reduced protectionism, such an outcome was far from inevitable.

Section 5.3 considers the EC's other preferential trading arrangements. These reflect a desire to consolidate a sphere of influence but also, for the Mediterranean countries, to reduce the pressures for immigration. Section 5.4 continues the theme, examining the recent Europe Agreements with Czechoslovakia, Hungary and Poland. The discussion of enlargement suggests that those former socialist countries will not accede in the next two decades, and so these Europe Agreements are critical to the transition and development of those economies. Unfortunately, because of a number of features of those economies they may be given rather restricted market access to EC markets. This illustrates well the role of EC pressure groups from the sensitive sectors of agriculture, clothing and, effectively, iron and steel.

5.1   The motives for EC extension

EC enlargement and preferential extension have arisen from a variety of (sometimes conflicting) motives, the relative importance or even presence of which varies from instance to instance. Political aspects have been very important, especially in enlargement: they include the desire to reinforce market democracy, the wish to maintain a European sphere of influence, and a vision of pan-Europeanism. Economic motivations also have been significant, however, especially for preferences. Examples include a desire to discourage immigration, a mercantilist desire to open up other markets (if possible preferentially), and a wish to divert criticism of the limits on market access in existing integration arrangements. Other economic factors have constrained or even deflected the basic political thrust toward enlargement, such as a desire to protect EC agriculture and maintain other traditional sectors. I argue that extension through preferences, and even to some extent enlargement, is a partial substitute for genuine openness to world commerce; it is a poor one, however, because it encourages a degree of discretionary economic management.

Turning to the EC's partners, the motives for them joining and associating with the EC include the attraction of gaining markets or preventing their loss,[1] the possibility that accession allows them to manage liberalization more closely than unilateral schemes, and the credibility that making commitments to Brussels lends to their national political structures and economic reform programs.

5.2   Enlargement

Enlargement – the accession of new members – has been a major feature of the EC from its inception. Article 237 provides the legal framework for it – unanimous agreement among existing members – and convention has dictated that, although accession is preceded by extended negotiation, the EC makes no compromises on the application of its fundamental policies. Accedants must accept fully the *acquis communautaire* – loosely, the EC's legislation, institutional structure and modes of behavior – and now also the *finalité politique* – the EC's ultimate objective of political union. The process is very much one of joining an existing club rather than the creation of a new customs union.

Negotiation concerns issues such as the period of transition, political representation, financial contributions and transfers, and, in the case of the first enlargement, the position of the accedents' ex-colonies.

From a political point of view the refusal to reconsider the Community's fundamental structures has the obvious attractions of identifying genuine aspirants for membership and of constraining the field of negotiation. Economically it makes sense if one is confident that the EC has the correct set of policies initially and that the enlargement does not alter them significantly. Even if one does not accept the latter point, it might be argued that changes can be introduced later when the accedant has attained full membership. This view, however, ignores the political difficulties of reopening issues which have been previously and publicly agreed − difficulties both with partner countries and with internal interest groups. Interest groups that have gained from accession will be reluctant to risk losing their gains, while the government will be reluctant to revive the interest and fortunes of those which have lost in the sense that they have had to be bought off or suppressed in the accession debate. Thus, for example, neither the UK nor the southern enlargements have had much impact on the Common Agricultural Policy's (CAP) excessive support for the temperate products produced most intensively by the original six members of the EC.

5.2.1 The first enlargement

The first approaches for accession came soon after the birth of the EC − in 1961−2, from Denmark, Ireland, Norway and the UK. The UK, which initiated the application, was concerned at the potential market losses of being left out of a dynamic and potentially powerful economic bloc, while for the others the trade diversion that would result from UK accession, especially in agriculture, was the major consideration. France rejected these applications promptly, legitimately doubting the UK's commitment to the *acquis communautaire*; the British had, after all, sought to renegotiate several aspects of the Treaty of Rome including reductions in industrial tariffs, guarantees over access for Commonwealth suppliers, and such long transitional periods in agriculture that they amounted to rejecting the CAP. France also had political objections to UK accession − for instance, the UK's links with the US and the dilution of French influence in the EC − but this episode illustrates two important economic aspects of enlargement: the pressure of market access on the potential accedents, and the EC's wish to maintain the preferences and protection it had created.

The British tried again during the mid-1960s and, after one further rebuff, eventually succeeded in joining the EC in 1973. The political commitment was extremely high on this occasion – led by the then Prime Minister, Edward Heath – and the economic case for joining had become overwhelming. As a result the accession was very largely on Brussels' terms. Britain sought access to its large dynamic neighbors and also said that it desired the stimulating effects of increased industrial competition. It could, of course, have obtained the latter through unilateral free trade, but that might have involved too much of a good thing and would perhaps, for that reason, not have been an entirely credible threat to inefficient British producers. Although the Conservative government of the early 1970s was liberal by the standards of the day, there was still a widespread belief in the virtues of intervention. The EC provided an attractive half-way house: its competition policy and internal free trade appeared to preclude major backsliding, but its pragmatism in the application of these policies, its tradition of managing internal trade frictions, and its secure outer frontier of protection all appeared to provide a welcome safety net.

The effects of the enlargement are difficult to identify with any confidence: *anti-mondes* are speculative at any time, but the 1970s saw a number of economic shocks which could conceal the effects of enlargement in relatively short time series. We may be confident, however, that accession to the EC reduced the UK's average industrial tariffs (Han and Liesner, 1971) and that it also caused considerable trade creation in manufactures (Winters, 1984, 1985, 1987; Grinols, 1984). Grinols concludes, however, that the benefits from manufacturing were more than offset by trade diversion in agriculture and net budgetary contributions.

Denmark and Ireland were almost certainly beneficiaries from accession, but arguably for less than satisfactory reasons. As agricultural exporters they gained from high internal EC prices. Ireland was also a strong net recipient of budgetary transfers and of inflows of foreign direct investment (FDI) looking for a platform from which to serve the whole EC. Both agriculture and FDI, however, involve issues of trade diversion: the rest of the EC is obliged to purchase higher-cost Danish and Irish produce rather than cheaper world supplies, and any rents that this generates accrue to the new members. Contrary to the perception in popular debate – and even in the minds of many policy makers, with their mercantilist outlooks – the additional gross flow to Denmark and Ireland is clearly not all rent, because by the very nature of protection much of it is wasted in excess real costs.

There are parallels to the British caution about excessive liberalism in the Scandinavian countries' present discussions about accession (Norman, 1991). Norway and Sweden have rather liberal trade policies in industrial goods, but not in services and agriculture.[2] Accession to the EC would impose and underpin a mild liberalization in both of the latter sectors, but in a much more manageable fashion than entirely free trade.

5.2.2 The southern enlargement

The second, or southern, enlargement had different origins from the first. Greece, Portugal and Spain were all relatively poor countries with newly established democracies. Accession offered them a means of securing these political gains by increasing the costs of defection, by introducing an external authority which could take some of the 'heat' for unpopular policies, and from the enhanced credibility that commitment to the EC lent their proposed changes in economic regime. They were also attracted by the possibility of transfers from EC institutions, especially the enlargement of the European Regional Development Fund (which was negotiated as part of the Iberian accession – the so-called integrated Mediterranean policy) and the European Social Fund. Finally, of course, the EC offered an attractive market for many of their labor-intensive and agricultural exports, especially if they could maintain EC external protection. Winters (1992b) shows the market gains for these countries in footwear, while Greece's initial opposition to Iberian accession and Iberia's current hostility to liberalizing the MFA and to the Europe Agreements with Czechoslovakia, Hungary and Poland illustrate the latter issue.[3]

The attractions of the southern accession to the EC – by then the EC-9 – were essentially political. Securing democracy was desired by the southern countries for both altruistic and pragmatic reasons, the latter having to do with stability along their borders and in their sphere of influence. The potential market gains for the EC, such as disposing of grains in Spain and Portugal, were positive but probably not very significant. It is also possible that the EC felt that its international legitimacy would suffer if it excluded aspiring neighboring economies, especially if this caused them apparent losses of export sales.

The southern enlargement has also apparently influenced trade patterns (see, for example, Bliss and Braga de Macedo, 1990), although it is rather early to tell in some cases. In part this reflects the long transitional periods negotiated in sensitive sectors. For example, it took until 1992 to permit the free movement of labor between Iberia and the rest of the EC; there were quotas on iron and steel sales until 1993; and it will be 1996 before Spanish fruit, vegetables and vegetable fats have complete access to EC markets.

5.2.3   The EFTA countries[4]

The aspirants to membership over the last decade fall into two groups: the EFTA countries and the Mediterranean ones. Among the former, Austria, Finland, Sweden and Switzerland have applied for membership, and Norway seems fairly likely to follow. Their accession seems to pose few serious difficulties for the EC. The political issues of their neutrality and of the Soviet Union's objections to Austria and Finland joining a Western bloc have been dissolved, and the potential economic differences over fisheries and regional policies look resolvable. Hence it seems sensible to explore their cases as studies of actual integration.

The two most important negotiating issues for EFTAn accession are probably the social dimension of the EFTAns' agricultural policies, and fisheries. With the recent exception of Sweden the EFTA countries maintain higher levels of agricultural protection than the EC (OECD, 1992), but provide a larger share of it in terms of direct payments to farmers in inhospitable regions. This reflects conscious decisions – or at least explicitly articulated excuses – to maintain populations in either the Alpine or the far northern areas of the respective countries. This approach to agricultural policy differs from the EC's CAP, the formal aim of which is to raise productivity in poor agricultural regions or, if this proves impossible, to ease the sector's decline. The EFTAn regions are far too affluent to benefit from the regional justification for offering state aids (Article 92.3 of the Treaty of Rome), and in any case the CAP could not support such large and widespread direct payments. The recent MacSharry reforms' proposed direct payments are explicitly in compensation for declining prices and are based on historical yields and areas. Hence although the EFTAn governments undoubtedly welcome the external discipline that Brussels will provide on farm spending(!), a compromise permitting them to offer their own 'inhospitable area' payments – like the CAP's existing hill-farm subsidies – seems likely to emerge during negotiation.

Concern over fisheries has already led Iceland to decide against a membership application and may yet do the same for Norway. Here the EC has appeared to be rather rigidly concerned that the accedants' resources must be opened to all EC residents. However, as Gylfason (1991) shows, this need not entail a loss of income if fishing rights are sold by the owning country. This, after all, is what happens to land-based resources or to drilling rights for oil in the North Sea.

The attractions to the current EC membership of extending membership to the EFTAn countries are considerable. These economies are similar to the richer EC members' and thus pose few cultural problems and make no demands for transfers. Their accession offers the EC significant markets in agriculture and services, areas which are currently constrained. There will also be small gains from greater integration in industrial products and through labor mobility and direct investment, but, given the existing free trade arrangements between EFTA and the EC and the small size of EFTA relative to the EC, these are not likely to be great. The most important attraction lies in the EFTAn accedants' potential budget contributions. EFTA will increase the EC's GDP by about 14 per cent. With higher than average GDP per head, EFTA will contribute disproportionately to the GDP-based component of Brussels' own-resources. Because they are about as open to non-EC imports as existing EC members, their customs tariffs and levies under the common policies will roughly parallel their GDP share, as will their VAT (Value Added Tax) contributions. Hence overall EC gross revenue will be increased by around 14 per cent when the EFTAns join, and since they will make relatively low demands for agricultural support and structural fund transfers, there will be a significant net contribution.[5]

Finally, on politics, EFTAn accession offers a relatively painless way of proving that the EC is open and of satisfying the EC notion of Europe's vocation to unify (Luyten, 1989). It also offers the EC a little more scope for active commercial diplomacy. The GATT requirement for non-discrimination means that policies aimed at East Asia and, to a lesser extent, the United States must, as things are now, formally also be applied to EFTA. Since EFTA and the EC enjoy very harmonious relations, this constrains the EC to moderate its policies and/or to suffer the political costs of making them discriminatory. Bringing EFTA into the club removes that constraint and allows the consolidation of a genuinely pan-European (or at least West European) bloc.

The advantages to the EFTAns of deeper integration with the EC are also considerable. I have already mentioned the liberalization of services and agriculture, and this is supplemented by the fear that investment will be diverted from EFTA to the EC, and by their potential loss of sales in the EC (a major market for them) as the 1992 Single Market initiative boosts EC competitiveness. On the former, the evidence is already strong: between 1986 and 1990 the EC's share of EFTA inflows of foreign direct investment fell from 47 to 36 per cent while its share of EFTAn outflows increased from 30 to 63 per cent. In value terms the flow of direct investment from EFTA to the EC increased from US$2.4 billion to $16.7 billion (CEPR, 1992).

Turning to trade flows, EFTA countries are very nearly as integrated with the EC as are EC member countries themselves: their shares of exports and imports with the EC are at about the same levels, as is their degree of intra-industry trade. The EC accounts for between 50 and 70 per cent of EFTAn international trade, or 15 to 20 per cent of their GDP.

Hence reducing the costs of that trade, and maintaining some influence over the terms on which it is conducted, are important elements of EFTAn economic policy.

Perhaps the clearest illustration of the strategic disadvantage that EFTA suffers from falling outside the EC Single Market comes from Haaland and Norman's (1992) general equilibrium simulations. Recognizing the importance of imperfect competition, Haaland and Norman suggest that the '1992' Single Market initiative could reduce EFTA's real income by almost one-half of 1 per cent of their expenditure on tradable goods. The integration of EC markets has its greatest beneficial effects on EC skill-intensive and imperfectly competitive sectors – those in which significant rents can be earned. As EC output expands and prices fall in these sectors, EFTAn producers, who are already relatively efficient but who receive no *added stimulus* from '1992', lose sales and rents. If, on the other hand, EFTA joins and becomes fully integrated with the EC, in the sense that neither EC nor EFTA firms can price-discriminate between EC and EFTA markets and that EFTA adopts all the EC's pro-competitive '1992' policies, then EFTA's real incomes rise by about 3 per cent of tradables expenditure. The latter figure reflects not only the direct benefits of reducing trade costs, but also the strong pro-competitive effects of accession on EFTAn markets. As relatively small – albeit relatively open – markets, EFTA countries suffer a degree of imperfect competition which is swept away by the unfettered access that integration offers to EC firms. Moreover, Haaland and Norman consider only tradable manufactures. If we could add into the calculation the pro-competitive effects of liberalizing services (see Norman and Stradenes (1992) for the example of airlines), the effects would be enhanced.

Many of the economic advantages of membership are available under the European Economic Area (EEA) agreements, which offer the EFTAns the economics of '1992' without the commitment to the EC's political deepening. The main exceptions are that the EEA excuses them from the Common Agricultural Policy, the common external tariff, some elements of competition policy and most of the budgetary contributions. The first three factors probably make full membership more attractive than the EEA, but the last certainly does not. It is offset, however, by the additional credibility and permanence that membership appears to offer. Particularly for investment flows, but possibly also for the retention of highly skilled labor, any suggestion that the EEA could be unpicked in future would be highly deleterious. Even more important, however, is the fact that the EEA requires the EFTA countries to accept all EC legislation affecting the EEA with no formal power to affect its formulation. They must be consulted, to be sure, but they have no powers to influence the drafting of new legislation. Moreover, once the

EC adopts a new piece of legislation, either the EFTAns accept it, or the relevant part of the EEA is suspended; that is, EFTA can never choose the maintenance of the status quo (the EEA with the 'old' legislation). It might all work out for the best, but the dangers are obvious, and most EFTA countries are consequently pursuing full membership.

5.2.4   Mediterranean candidates

The EC has three outstanding applications for membership from the Mediterranean: Turkey, Cyprus and Malta. All have preferential trading agreements with the EC, but desire a deeper relationship. Malta and Cyprus are so small as hardly to matter to the EC economically, but they would pose political problems: internally, whether they would have commissioners and take the presidency, and externally, the precedent they would create for other Mediterranean enlargement; an additional problem for Cyprus is the conflict between the Greek and Turkish communities. The same issue, of course, afflicts the Turkish application itself, and was possibly sufficient to ensure that it failed. That episode, however, is also interesting for the other terms in which it was rejected in the Commission's 'Opinion'.

The Commission of the European Communities (1989) begins by noting the greater demands that accession puts on future members now compared with twenty years ago, arising from the EC's own ambitious plans for deeper integration as well as the time necessary for the EC's constitutional changes and for the completion of the internal market. It also notes the large size of Turkey geographically and in terms of population, and its patchy record on human rights. The implication was not only that Turkey would receive no compromises on accession, but that the introduction of a major member which differed fundamentally from the EC average would not be allowed to threaten the deepening process on which the EC was launched.

The principal economic issues identified by the Commission concerned Turkey's poverty – its GDP per head (in terms of purchasing power parity) is one-third the average level for the EC; its rapid population growth – with resulting low labor productivity; its highly agricultural workforce – over 50 per cent of employment is agricultural; its macroeconomic imbalances, including high unemployment; its high levels of protection from import competition; and its lack of social legislation. The combination of these concerns raises two explicit fears in the minds of the Commission: the burden of cohesion spending, and immigration. The proferred consolation prize of an enhanced

Association Agreement, with both political and economic components, promised trade benefits without these threats.

The attractions to Turkey of acceding on the normal terms of cohesion and agricultural support plus the chance of influencing future EC policy are obvious enough. The EC response is also clear: it is not prepared to risk either immigration, or heavy expense in terms of cohesion spending, or the dilution of the *acquis* or *finalité politique*. This is not necessarily an unreasonable position to adopt, but it has implications for future eastwards enlargement.

5.2.5   The preconditions for enlargement

The agenda for enlargement negotiations has evolved through time, with the preconditions for membership becoming tougher as EC ambitions and self-confidence have grown, and perhaps also as the EC's growing economic weight has increased the incentives for new members to accede. Nevertheless, certain themes do reoccur and may be presumed to continue into the future. First, accedants have to accept existing policy – the *acquis communautaire* – unconditionally, even though existing members may be exempt from parts of it. Existing members surrender nothing of what they have already agreed. This determination to proceed regardless is also evident in the EEA in which, formally at least, the EC decides what it wants and the EFTA countries take it or leave it.

Second, given its essentially political origins – to prevent future Franco-German conflict – the EC's commitment to fostering market democracy in Europe is very strong. Thus Greece was brought in as soon as, or possibly before, it was ready, and Spain and Portugal were admitted fairly quickly too. The parallels for Central Europe – Czechoslovakia, Hungary and Poland – are plain.

Third, the commitment to cohesion – narrowing the differences in income per head between different parts of the EC – is strong, if backed by relatively few resources, and this constrains the admission of poorer countries. Turkey is the obvious example, but again parallels for Czechoslovakia, Hungary and Poland are unavoidable. The same factors acting in reverse have smoothed the paths of the United Kingdom's, and potentially EFTA's, accession: net contributors to the budget are more welcome, especially to the poorer existing members – witness Spanish enthusiasm for EFTAn accession.

Fourth, migration is a remaining worry, and on both sides. The EFTAns are nervous about the potential inflows from EC countries and the EC has been explicit in its fears about migration associated with southern and Mediterranean enlargement.

Fifth, transition periods have been used to delay the effects of enlargement on sensitive sectors. For example, the full integration of labor and agricultural markets have been delayed by up to ten years. Given that full integration is the ultimate destination, this might be just political pragmatism, but given too the scope for regimes to change over ten years – especially in agriculture – it might also reflect a means of managing the integration in a way that spares existing interest groups some of its pressures.

5.2.6   General lessons for EC enlargement

What lessons does EC enlargement have for other regional integration schemes? First, it suggests the unrealism of the proposal that the GATT should require integration schemes to be freely open to any country that is prepared to abide by their rules. Corden (1987) and Bhagwati (1991) suggest this as a condition for the approval of free trade areas, but in schemes as far-ranging as the EC, an open door is frankly inconceivable. Existing members are affected by accession not only through their trade, but also via factors such as budgetary transfers and shifts in the balance of political power.

Second, the willingness of the EC-9 to make budgetary transfers to the southern accedants clearly smoothed their entry path. Whether it was essential, however, is difficult to tell, for the transfers were not the only perceived long-term benefit to the new members. It is reasonable to argue, however, that the transfer mechanism – small as it is compared with those in federal and unitary states – has been essential to the running of the EC once the southern accession had occurred. Distribution is a major factor in EC decision making, but the existence of institutions to address it prevents it from becoming an impassable barrier to progress. It also reduces the scope for distributional issues to confuse and frustrate efficiency decisions.

Third, the need for accedants to adopt the common external tariff and other EC external policies affects the aggregate level of protection. The impact effect of Iberian accession was to lower the accedants' external protection almost across the board. The impact of the first enlargement was less clear cut, however: while UK average manufactured tariffs fell, agriculture became much more restricted. Similarly, if Sweden and Norway accede they will be obliged to become more restrictive in many industrial products as they adopt current and future EC gray-area measures and anti-dumping policy. Thus while EC enlargement has probably reduced the average degree of trade distortion among member countries, there is nothing inevitable in the notion that enlargement reduces protectionism. Moreover, enlargement influences the process of trade policy making – one policy for one large group rather than *n* for *n* small ones – and could easily do so in a restrictive direction.

Winters (1993) notes several possible reasons why combining into blocs could increase trade restrictions. First, the optimum tariff for one large group generally exceeds that of its component parts acting individually. Second, partners might act more aggressively toward a large group than toward several smaller countries. For example, the US export enhancement scheme for grains would almost certainly be different if instead of the EC's CAP there were twelve individual national agricultural policies. Third, the committee decision-making mechanisms of the EC encourage universalism (Shepsle and Weingast, 1981), whereby it is easier for Britain, for example, to seek protection for its favored sectors as part of a trade policy or agricultural policy package than to resist the package itself. Moreover, all the protection that is agreed is spread across the whole EC: thus Denmark has to restrict imports of Japanese cars and Germany its imports of Korean footwear, which they would almost certainly not do to the same extent under national policies. Fourth, the need for near unanimity to change anything, coupled with the absence of an exit mechanism, makes it difficult to change the status quo. This frustrates liberalization – witness the difficulty over the EC's positions in the Uruguay Round – especially on agriculture.[6]

A fourth general lesson is that accession offers the new members more credible steps towards liberal policies than would unilateral action. The latter is a more extreme policy that is less easily controlled by governments without undermining their credibility. Accession, on the other hand, offers security in that major problems are negotiated and bargained over, and although the resultant erosions of liberalism are frequent, they are finite and controlled largely by external agents (Brussels). Hence major shocks can be ameliorated without suggesting a complete reversal of the accedant's liberalizing policy. If other means of establishing credibility were available, accession would lose some of its charm.

Fifth, accession guarantees fairer treatment for the accedant's exports to the EC. In particular, they become subject to competition rather than dumping policy: both constrain predatory behavior but the latter is open to huge abuse. Similarly, accession offers some influence over standards, regulations and so on. Where the existing union is a major market – as the EC is for EFTA, for example – these factors can be important. The quid pro quo for these concessions by the union is the need for the accedant to adopt common policies, which often will constrain their competitiveness and comparative advantage.

5.3 Trade preferences

The EC is also unusual in the extent and complexity of its preferential trading agreements. It is a confirmed advocate of such agreements, seeing them as a legitimate tool of policy, especially for relations with neighboring countries (Luyten, 1989). At present the EC maintains five broad sets of preferences (see Table 5.1), although within the groups there are several subdivisions (World Bank, 1987, Box 9.2). In most cases the preferences form part of wider-ranging association agreements, but it is probably true to say that they are the major components of those agreements.

5.3.1 The EC's association agreements

The origins of the various preference schemes reflect combinations of the factors identified in Section 5.1 but with somewhat different emphases than in the cases of enlargement. The GSP is available to most developing countries and parallels policies in other industrial countries. It is best viewed as part of a global rather than a specifically EC system (see Langhammer and Sapir (1989) for its basic principles).

The arrangements with the African, Caribbean and Pacific (ACP) states are essentially ex-colonial links; their continuation is partly altruistic (the beneficiary countries are mostly very poor), but also partly designed to boost markets and to maintain a sphere of influence. The Lomé Convention offers unilateral trade preferences to the ACP countries, although the other elements of the Convention, such as the aid flows and commodity stabilization finance, help to maintain EC exports

Table 5.1 The EC's principal preferential trading agreements

Country/area	Extent of trading preferences
General system of preferences (GSP)	Limited tariff-free access for most industrial goods; few agricultural concessions; active safeguards.
EFTA (pre-1993)	Free trade in industrial goods; many cooperation agreements.
Africa, Caribbean and Pacific (ACP) countries	Lomé Convention: free access to EC in industrial goods, some preferences for agricultural goods; exemption from MFA restrictions on textiles and clothing.
Mediterranean countries	Duty-free access for industrial goods, but several non-tariff import barriers; a few agricultural preferences; but most subject to ceilings.
Eastern Europe (post-1992)	Free access for industrial goods to be phased in over six years; agricultural preferences; considerable harmonization of laws; rights of establishment.

Source: GATT (1991, pp. 61–74).

at significantly greater levels than would otherwise be expected (Wang, 1992).

Both the GSP and Lomé tariff preferences are subject to quantitative limits: nearly all involve tariff quotas rather than unlimited preferences. The permitted limits are usually tight for sensitive products, and some very sensitive products are excluded altogether. It is fine that a relatively small proportion of categories and supplying countries are constrained by the quota limits, but these are the potentially important ones, and the fact that rapidly growing trade flows could be, and have been, constrained greatly by these quotas reduces the incentive for suppliers to establish effective export channels to the EC.

The EFTA agreements arose from the need to reduce market losses in industrial goods when the UK acceded in 1973.[7] The UK had industrial free trade with these countries by virtue of its membership of EFTA, and provided a major market for their exports; the sudden application of the common external tariff would have damaged EFTA economically and the EC politically.

The similarities between the EFTA and EC economies have made relations between them very harmonious over the twenty years of industrial free trade. Neither, for example, was interested in agricultural free trade. Also, EFTA countries have been favored in a number of ways in industrial trade: for instance, EFTA is the EC's major supplier of steel, and in return for self-restraint and adherence to the so-called 'triple clause' – EFTAn exports to the EC are to be spread relatively evenly over time, space and commodities – EFTA countries are subject to much less formal monitoring and policing than, say, Eastern Europe. Similarly, EFTA suppliers have been subject to very few anti-dumping actions. As a result the integration of the EC and EFTA industrial economies is already substantial. Observe, however, that the harmony, and indeed to some extent the integration, arise from a common view about what needs to be managed: the high degree of intra-industry trade in manufactures does not raise too many problems but, as I noted above, full integration would increase adjustment pressures and political friction if it were extended to areas such as agriculture, fisheries or banking. Also as noted above, the evolution of EFTA–EC relations toward the European Economic Area or to full membership arises principally from EFTAn fears that the existing level of integration will be undermined by the '1992' Single Market initiative itself and/or by subsequent developments in EC trade policy.

The twelve Mediterranean agreements are rather heterogeneous: all offer concessionary access to EC markets, most include technical assistance and aid clauses, but only those with the more developed partners require any reciprocal market access concessions. In some cases the agreements reflect historical factors, such as those stemming from French links with Morocco and Algeria. But in the main they reflect a desire to bind the Mediterranean region into the EC sphere of influence, while simultaneously managing its trade and controlling the pressure for heavy immigration. The agreements also help to defuse criticism over market access – especially in agriculture, in which some EC concessions are made. Mediterranean products are generally less favored by the CAP than temperate ones, however, so these concessions are easier to make than some others. Moreover, southern accession has increased internal opposition to such concessions (Musto, 1987).

5.3.2 The role of preferences

Trade preferences and association agreements fulfil several objectives for the EC. First, they can constitute a sort of waiting room for potential members – as was the case, for example, with Greece prior to accession. Second, they can be a dark closet into which unwelcome callers are pushed: when Turkey's application was rejected in 1989 (Commission of the European Communities, 1989), for example, the Commission promised deeper association and trade links. Third, they offer a means of binding neighbors and former colonies into a sphere of influence without greatly disrupting the EC's sensitive sectors. Fourth, they are clearly intended in some cases to reduce the pressure for immigration – a very sensitive issue among existing members.

The preferential agreements differ in four major respects from genuine enlargement. First, they exclude migration. The EC has a profound desire to avoid major immigration. By offering selected market access it attempts to relieve the pressure of immigration, while avoiding the worst adjustment pressures on industry through the careful selection of sectors and the maintenance of safeguards and anti-dumping policies. Second, although the association agreements often involve transfers to the non-EC partners, these are unilateral ex gratia payments with limits well below the levels of transfers to poorer member states. Third, trade policy: enlargement entails reciprocal trade policy changes, usually entailing tariff reductions by accedants on their imports from both EC and non-EC countries. Preferences, on the other hand, entail no changes in tariffs on extra-EC trade and, for developing countries, none on imports from the EC. Thus enlargement has been a stronger liberalizing force than preferences. Fourth, preferences rely on restrictions against imports from the rest of the world for their effectiveness. This may discourage further liberalization on both sides. The disappointments in the EC's positions in the Uruguay Round, and the recent raising of tariffs in Poland, could both be interpreted in this light.

5.4   Eastern Europe

The various pressures toward preferential trade and eventual full enlargement are well illustrated by the EC's recent negotiations with Czechoslovakia, Hungary and Poland, which resulted in the Europe Agreements of 1992. The EC had a strong political concern about stability on its borders, especially given that migration, more than anything, had determined the precipitous speed of German unification. It also clearly felt a strong duty and desire to succour its neighbors and to preserve their fragile democracies. Both EC officials and the newly formed governments in the East saw close association with the EC as the means to this end. The EC also saw Eastern Europe as an issue on which it could legitimately expect to exercise leadership on a world scale (in the Group of 24), which further encouraged active EC involvement.

Czechoslovakia, Hungary and Poland have all apparently been very keen to assume full membership of the EC as soon as possible. This position is, one suspects, partly based on a misunderstanding of – or at least undue optimism about – the degree of economic restructuring that will be required. It also, however, reflects their wholehearted commitment to market democracy. The EC, on the other hand, is much less keen on accession, largely for the reasons that led it to reject the Turkish application. Because of the much greater sensitivity and the political commitment to these countries' aspirations, these have not been formally articulated. However, it is plain that with low per capita incomes (perhaps one-third of Spain's), large agricultural workforces, and, for Poland, large populations, the cost of accession to existing members in terms of cohesion payments would be very high. The House of Lords (1992) estimates that current budgetary and cohesion policies would entail annual net transfers of ECU 6.3 billion to Poland, ECU 2.0 billion to Hungary and ECU 1.6 billion to Czechoslovakia, while CEPR (1992) suggests figures of ECU 5.2, 1.4 and 1.2 billion respectively.

Given that the EC is likely to strengthen rather than weaken its commitment to cohesion, these figures suggest that Czechoslovakia, Hungary and Poland need to undertake a large degree of catch-up before accession is realistic. But all the available evidence suggests that this will be a long process. Hamilton and Winters (1992), for example, suggest that at least thirty years is necessary to make up half the difference between current Eastern incomes and the *current* EC average. Moreover, very substantial institutional, policy and structural changes will be required before those economies can cope with full integration. Hence, I suspect that their accession is not a realistic possibility inside twenty years.

Given this distant horizon for accession, the transitional arrangements are very important. It is easy to imagine that events could evolve down either of two paths, the only difference between which is initial expectations (CEPR, 1992). Under an optimistic scenario, residents of these Central European countries would anticipate eventual accession and prosperity: they would invest their savings and skilled labor would remain at home, and the productivity and hence wages of less skilled workers would rise, generating greater demand and savings. Under a pessimistic scenario, a supposedly poor outlook would undermine investment, encourage a brain-drain and lead to a low-level equilibrium. What distinguishes these scenarios? Partly animal spirits, but these in turn will be based on the commitment to eventual accession and on the immediate ability to sell the produce of current investment. The latter essentially means the openness of the EC market: their own domestic markets are too small and weak to provide take-off by themselves, and for geographical and cultural reasons the EC will remain their largest export market.

For these reasons the political goodwill that the EC has towards its eastern neighbors must realistically be manifest in association agreements – the so-called Europe Agreements – rather than accession negotiations.

Unfortunately, however, the EC's good intentions have been moderated, arguably entirely captured, by entrenched economic interests in the EC. The Europe Agreements are the deepest and widest of the EC's association agreements but, even so, the market opening they provide for has been delayed and is subject to a number of potential restrictions. Indeed, one of the acid tests of the EC's commitment to liberal policy and to its Eastern neighbors will be how it interprets and operates the Europe Agreements. As written, they provide the EC authorities with several opportunities to meddle with and restrict international commerce, but do not generally commit them to do so. An optimistic commentator would argue that such opportunities are inherent in the *Realpolitik* of trade agreements – consider, for example, the GATT – and that well-intentioned governments can generally avoid their exploitation. I am not so sure, and feel obliged to register a note of caution: at the minimum, the application of the Europe Agreements must be carefully monitored.[8]

Based on Winters (1992a), the principal components of the Europe Agreements are as follows:

- Czechoslovakia, Hungary and Poland (CHP) must open their markets within ten years to EC goods – implicitly preferentially, and in one clause explicitly so if CHP maintain any import restrictions.
- The EC will open its 'non-sensitive' markets virtually immediately, but for 'sensitive' industrial markets the abolition of tariffs and quantitative restrictions on imports will take from four to six years.
- The EC will offer concessions, but nothing like free trade, on agriculture.
- CHP must adopt EC competition policy within three years, its intellectual property policy within five, and make best endeavors to approximate its other laws to EC standards. Environmental protection – an agreed priority between CHP and the EC – is to converge to EC standards.
- Despite the adoption of EC competition policy, CHP goods will still be subject to the EC's anti-dumping policy, although on the basis of 'market economy' rather than 'state trading economy' dumping rules.
- There are no special provisions for the mobility of ordinary workers, although de facto the mobility of highly skilled workers is likely to occur.
- There are strong provisions to encourage and protect EC direct investment in CHP – for example, commitments over the flows of funds for repatriating profits and disinvestment, and rules of origin that require non-EC-owned firms in CHP to have 60 per cent local content before their exports to the EC qualify for trade concessions.

In summary, the Europe Agreements seem designed to promote EC sales and production facilities in CHP, to manage access to EC markets both directly and indirectly by imposing the EC commercial environment on CHP, and, above all, to avoid serious levels of migration. The Agreements foresee the possibility of eventual EC-membership for CHP, so many of the institutions they impose appear perfectly sensible over the long run, given the convention that accedants must adapt to the Community and not vice versa. But membership is a long way off and, in the meantime, it is difficult not to see in the Europe Agreements a degree of 'managed liberalization'.

5.5   Conclusion

'Managed liberalization' is perhaps the principal feature of EC preferences, and it is also present in genuine enlargement. The EC exploits the weakness of GATT Article XXIV's injunction that preferences must cover substantially all trade and foresees the abolition of intra-area tariffs to protect particular sectors from competition. On accession, it addresses non-members' worries about market shares by bringing partners into the club; but it does so on its own terms and in a fashion that mitigates at least some of the competitive pressures on existing members. Managed liberalization is a substitute for genuine liberalization, but a poor one because it typically attenuates competition in precisely those sectors which are most in need of improved efficiency.

Notes

The author is grateful to Carl Hamilton, the editors, and participants in the GATT conference for comments on the earlier draft, and Tina Attwell for typing.
1. Wherever external prices exceed marginal costs there are potential gains to increasing exports.
2. However, Sweden is currently attempting a unilateral agricultural reform.
3. The long transitional periods negotiated for Iberian accession have been argued to constrain the speed of liberalization with Eastern Europe, because it would be considered not right that the latter have more liberal access to other EC markets than the former, even temporarily. This is sometimes said to explain the Spanish position.
4. This section draws on conversations with Richard Baldwin, to whom I am grateful. See also CEPR (1992) and Wijkman (1992b).
5. In its opinions on Swedish and Austrian accession, the Commission has suggested somewhat smaller contributions, especially for the latter because Austrian exports to the EC will no longer pay import levies.
6. Winters (1993) also examines – somewhat skeptically – the argument that the creation of the EEC had a net liberalizing effect by stimulating the Dillon and Kennedy Rounds of multilateral trade negotiations. Even if true, it was akin to aggressive unilateralism – by threatening trade diversion the EEC brought its partners to the negotiating table.
7. Each EFTA country has a separate agreement with the EC, but they are all very similar.
8. I note for example, that, in August 1992 Germany was allowed to impose quantitative limits on imports of steel pipes from Czechoslovakia (Winters, 1992a).

References

Bhagwati, J. N. (1991), *The World Trading System at Risk*, London: Harvester Wheatsheaf.

Bliss, C. and J. Braga de Macedo (1990), *Unity with Diversity in the European Economy*, Cambridge: Cambridge University Press.

CEPR (Centre for Economic Policy Research) (1992), *Enlarging the European Community: How Far, How Fast?*, London: CEPR.

Commission of the European Communities (CEC) (1989), 'Opinion on Turkey's Request for Accession to the Communities', SEC(89) 2290 final/2, Brussels: CEC.

Corden, W. M. (1987), 'On Making Rules for the International Trading System', in *US Trade Policies in a Changing World Economy*, edited by R. M. Stern, Cambridge, MA: MIT Press.

GATT (1991), *Trade Policy Review: The European Communities, Vol. 1*, Geneva: GATT Secretariat.

Grinols, E. L. (1984), 'A Thorn in the Lion's Paw: Has Britain Paid Too Much for Common Market Membership?', *Journal of International Economics* 16: 271–93.

Gylfason, T. (1991), 'Iceland on the Outskirts of Europe: the Common Property Resource Problem', in *EFTA Countries in a Changing Europe*, Geneva: EFTA Secretariat, July.

Haaland, J. I. and V. D. Norman (1992), 'Global Production Effects of European Integration', in *Trade Flows and Trade Policy After '1992'*, edited by L. A. Winters, Cambridge: Cambridge University Press.

Hamilton, C. B. and L. A. Winters (1992), 'Trade with Eastern Europe', *Economic Policy* 14: 78–116.

Han, S. S. and H. H. Liesner (1971), *Britain and the Common Market: The Effect of Entry on the Pattern of Manufacturing Production*, Department of Applied Economics Occasional Paper No. 27, University of Cambridge.

House of Lords (1992), *Enlargement of the Community*, London: HMSO, June 9.

Langhammer, R. J. and A. Sapir (1989), *Economic Impact of Generalised Tariff Preferences*, Aldershot: Gower.

Luyten, P. (1989), 'Multilateralism vs Preferential Bilateralism: A European View', in *Free Trade Areas and US Trade Policy*, edited by J. Schott, Washington, DC: Institute for International Economics.

Musto, S. (1987), 'Southward Enlargement and Developing Countries: a Shift in the Community's Policy of Preferences?', in *Europe and the International Division of Labour: EEC and the Third World*, edited by C. Stevens and P. Verloren van Themat, London: Hodder and Stoughton.

Norman, V. D. (1989), 'EFTA and the Internal European Market', *Economic Policy* 9: 423–66.

Norman, V. D. (1991), '1992 and EFTA', in *European Integration: Trade and Industry*, edited by L. A. Winters and A. J. Venables, Cambridge: Cambridge University Press.

Norman, V. D. and S. P. Stradenes (1992), 'Deregulating Scandinavian Airlines: A Case Study of the Oslo–Stockholm Route', in *Empirical Studies in Strategic Trade Policy*, edited by A. Smith, Chicago: University of Chicago Press.

OECD (1992), *Agricultural Policies, Markets and Trade: Monitoring and Outlook 1992, Assistance to OECD Agriculture*, submitted to the OECD Committee for Agriculture meeting, Paris, April 27–9.

Shepsle, K. A. and B. R. Weingast (1981), 'Political Preferences for the Pork Barrel: A Generalisation', *American Journal of Political Science* 25: 96–111.

Wang, Z. K. (1992), 'Studies in Chinese Export Performance', unpublished PhD dissertation, University of Birmingham.

Wijkman, P. M. (1992a), 'The EEA Agreement – At Long Last', in *EFTA Trade 1992*, Geneva: EFTA Secretariat.

Wijkman, P. M. (1992b), 'The Existing Bloc Expanded? The European Community, EFTA, Eastern Europe and the CIS', presented at the Pacific Trade and Development Conference, Institute for International Economics, Washington, DC, September 10–12.

Winters, L. A. (1984), 'British Import of Manufactures and the Common Market', *Oxford Economic Papers* **36**: 103–18.

Winters, L. A. (1985), 'Separability and the Modelling of International Economic Integration', *European Economic Review* **27**: 335–53.

Winters, L. A. (1987), 'Britain in Europe: A Survey of Quantitative Trade Studies', *Journal of Common Market Studies* **25**: 315–35.

Winters, L. A. (ed.) (1992a), *Trade Flows and Trade Policy After '1992'*, Cambridge: Cambridge University Press.

Winters, L. A. (1992b), 'Integration, Trade Policy and the European Footwear Trade', in *Trade Flows and Trade Policy After '1992'*, edited by L. A. Winters, Cambridge: Cambridge University Press.

Winters, L. A. (1992c), 'The Europe Agreements: With a Little Help From Our Friends', mimeo, University of Birmingham.

Winters, L. A. (1993), 'The EC: A Case of Successful Integration', in *New Dimensions in Regional Integration*, edited by J. de Melo and A. Panagariya, Cambridge: Cambridge University Press (forthcoming).

World Bank (1987), *The World Development Report 1987*, Washington, DC: The World Bank.

6

East Asia as a regional force for globalism

Soogil Young

The 1980s saw the emergence of East Asia as a major centre of world production and trade. This has been associated with a rapid regionalization of economic relations, as evidenced by remarkable increases in interdependence among the East Asian economies through trade and investment. Toward its end, the decade also saw the revival of regionalism elsewhere in the world, especially in Western Europe and North America, in the form of programs for the deepening and widening of the European Community (EC) and the Canada–US Free Trade Agreement. More recently, it has been agreed that the latter will be expanded to include Mexico and become the North American Free Trade Agreement (NAFTA).[1]

To many observers, these developments seem to indicate the emergence of two giant trading blocs as well as the demise of the multilateral trading system, thereby posing a threat to the preservation of the trade-based dynamism of the East Asian economies. As a result, the notion that East Asia needs an institutional scheme of its own in response to the regionalist trends elsewhere is rapidly gaining popularity in the region. The idea is to respond to trading blocs in kind, with a counter-bloc in East Asia, which would derive its strength from the region's ongoing economic integration.

In fact, it seems to be this idea which motivated Malaysian Prime Minister Mahathir's proposal for an East Asian Economic Group in December 1990, right after the breakdown of the Brussels Ministerial on the Uruguay Round. The proposal received rather cool and even hostile responses from inside and outside East Asia, and so was modified later into that of an East Asian Economic Caucus. Still, an East Asian trade bloc remains an attractive option to many East Asians and, furthermore,

more favorable thoughts on the idea seem to have begun to emerge during 1991–2.

A danger with regionalism is that, depending on its formulation and implementation, it can serve as a self-fulfilling prophecy: an East Asian bloc which is conceived as a defense against fragmentation of the world economy is likely to contribute to such fragmentation. Despite such dangers in responding to regionalism in kind, the question remains for East Asia as to how best to compete in a world economy increasingly driven by what appears to be two large trade blocs. The purpose of this chapter is to discuss that question.

Section 6.1 examines the trade performance and pattern of regionalization in East Asia that has been associated with the economic success of the East Asian economies. Section 6.2 distinguishes regional integration from regionalization of trade and examines the pattern of integration and normative aspects of that regionalization. Then Section 6.3 analyzes East Asia's options in responding to the growth of regional integration agreements (RIAs) elsewhere. The chapter concludes by summarizing its major findings.

The term 'East Asia' will be used throughout to refer to Japan, the East Asian newly industrialized economies (ANIEs) of Hong Kong, the Republic of Korea, Singapore and Taiwan, and the four ASEAN economies (ASEAN 4) other than Singapore and Brunei, namely, Indonesia, Malaysia, the Philippines and Thailand. Those other than Japan are referred to jointly as developing East Asia (DEA). The term 'Australasia' refers to Australia and New Zealand, and 'South America' is used as shorthand for all Latin American countries except Mexico.

6.1   The changing pattern of East Asian trade

Since 1970, East Asia's trade growth has been 16 per cent per year in current dollar terms, outperforming every other region of the world. The ANIEs and China, in particular, have maintained rates of growth in their trade of almost 20 per cent per year, or half as much again as the global average. Because of this rapid growth of trade, East Asia has rapidly increased its share of world trade (Table 6.1). In 1970, East Asia accounted for 11 per cent of world trade, while North America accounted for nearly twice as much and the EC nearly four times the amount. By 1990, however, the shares of both North America and the EC had declined slightly while East Asia had almost doubled its share to 19 per cent. Thus by 1990, East Asia had a slightly larger trading volume than North America while the EC traded about twice that amount. The combined share of East Asia, Australasia and North America increased

Table 6.1 Regional shares of world trade (per cent), 1970 and 1990

	1970	1990
East Asia	10.8	19.4
Japan	5.9	7.7
ANIEs	2.5	7.0
ASEAN 4	1.8	2.7
China	0.6	2.0
Australasia	2.1	1.5
North America	20.7	18.1
United States	14.7	13.3
Canada	5.3	3.6
Mexico	0.8	1.2
South America	5.8	4.2
Western Europe	48.2	46.8
EC-12	40.8	40.0
EFTA	7.6	6.8
Rest of world	12.6	10.0

Source: International Monetary Fund, *Direction of Trade*, Washington, DC, various issues; International Economic Data Bank, Australian National University, *World Trade Tape*, Canberra, 1992.

from 34 per cent in 1970 to 39 per cent by 1990, nearly equalling the EC's share. South America's share of world trade, meanwhile, declined from 6 to 4 per cent between 1970 and 1990.

East Asia's increasing share of world trade is largely due to the dynamism of the developing economies in the region. The ANIEs, in particular, nearly tripled their combined trade share between 1970 and 1990, from 2.5 to 7.0 per cent. China also tripled its share, from 0.6 to 2.0 per cent. In addition, both Japan and the ASEAN 4 have realized substantial gains in their shares of world trade (Table 6.1).

The rapid growth of the East Asian economies' trade has been accompanied by deteriorations in the trade accounts of the United States and the EC vis-à-vis Japan and developing East Asia. That deterioration has posed a serious balance-of-payments problem for the United States especially, and raised trade frictions between the US and East Asia to crisis level during the second half of the 1980s. The exchange rate realignments that followed the Plaza Accord of 1985 reduced the US trade deficit considerably, but it remains substantial enough to call for continuing balance-of-payments adjustment efforts. The combined trade account of the EC economies also recorded large trade deficits during the early 1980s. Although the EC's overall trade account has improved considerably since then, its trade deficits with Japan and DEA have continued to grow (Table 6.2).

While the DEA's trade accounts have improved vis-à-vis the US and EC, they have deteriorated against Japan, contributing further to Japan's trade surplus. This reflects the so-called trilateral pattern of East Asia's trade (Park and Park, 1991). Under this pattern, the DEAs have developed production structures vertically integrated with Japan by importing raw materials, and intermediate goods as well as capital goods mostly from Japan, fabricating the raw materials and intermediate goods, and then exporting the finished goods to destinations outside the region.

Under this trilateral pattern of trading, the rapid growth of East Asia's exports has been creating serious adjustment problems for the rest of the world. For example, East Asia as a whole continues to penetrate the markets for manufactures in North America and Western Europe without (until recently) much reciprocal import of those goods. Consequently, East Asia has been a major source of adjustment pressure for the rest of the world during the past two decades, at both the industry and macroeconomic levels. This pressure has contributed to a rapid surge of trade frictions and the consequent weakening of the multilateral trading system.

Table 6.3 shows that, during the past two decades, East Asia and North America have provided the two largest markets for East Asian exports. The EC has provided the third largest, but a much smaller, outlet. The share of the intra-regional market in East Asia's exports has steadily increased over time, while North America's share has fluctuated, reaching a trough in the mid-1970s and a peak in the mid-1980s. During the second half of the 1980s, however, the US share shrank due to payment imbalances and trade frictions, causing a sharp increase in the share of the intra-regional market and of the EC in East Asia's exports.

Table 6.2 Overall and bilateral trade balances of Japan, the United States and the EC (current US$ billions), 1970, 1980 and 1990

| | 1970 Balance with | | | 1980 Balance with | | | 1990 Balance with | | |
	World	Japan	DEA	World	Japan	DEA	World	Japan	DEA
Japan	0		2	−11		3	52		23
US	1	−2	−1	−36	−12	−5	−124	−45	−42
EC-12	−8	−1	0	−81	−13	−8	−48	−32	−16

Source: International Monetary Fund, *Direction of Trade*, Washington, DC, various issues.

Table 6.3 Shares of various regions in the merchandise exports of East Asia, North America and the EC (per cent), 1970 to 1990

		East Asia	North America	South America	EC-12	EFTA	Rest of world
East Asia	1970	31	31	3	14	2	19
	1975	32	23	5	13	2	25
	1980	34	24	4	15	2	21
	1985	34	35	3	11	2	15
	1990	39	29	2	16	2	12
North America	1970	14	33	12	25	3	13
	1975	14	30	13	21	2	20
	1980	18	27	14	23	3	15
	1985	19	28	11	18	2	22
	1990	23	34	11	21	3	8
EC-12	1970	3	10	4	53	12	18
	1975	3	7	3	52	11	24
	1980	3	6	3	56	11	21
	1985	4	11	2	54	10	19
	1990	6	8	2	61	10	13

Sources: International Monetary Fund, *Direction of Trade*, Washington, D.C., various issues; International Economic Data Bank, Australian National University, *World Trade Tape*, Canberra, 1992.

In North America's case, too, its own region provides the largest market from its exports, and increasingly so over the 1980s. The EC had been North America's second largest market until the early 1980s, but it has since been eclipsed by East Asia. Indeed, South America was nearly as large as East Asia as an export market for North America during the early 1970s, but since then it has fallen to half that of East Asia.

Table 6.3 also shows that two-thirds of EC exports had gone to West European countries during most of the 1970s and 1980s, with a slight rise to 71 per cent in 1990. During the 1970s, the share of the East Asian market in the EC's exports was even smaller than that of South America. By 1990, however, that share had doubled to 6 per cent (but that was still only a quarter of the share of North America's exports going to East Asia).

Clearly, all three main regions of the world depend heavily on their respective intra-regional markets, but the degree of regional interdependence differs significantly between the regions: it is highest in the case of the EC at 61 per cent and lowest in the case of North America at 34 per cent, as of 1990. Notice that North America's market dependence is the most evenly distributed between East Asia, Western Europe and North America. But notice also that East Asia recorded a sharp increase in its dependence on the EC market during the second half of the 1980s. This demonstrates the ever-more global scope of East Asia's marketing efforts.

Table 6.4 Shares of various regions in the merchandise exports of Japan, ANIEs, ASEAN 4 and China (per cent), 1970 to 1990

		Japan	DEA	North America	Western Europe	Rest of world
Japan	1970		24	35	15	26
	1980		26	27	17	30
	1985		24	41	14	21
	1990		30	35	22	13
ANIEs	1970	12	18	35	18	17
	1980	10	21	27	18	24
	1985	10	23	38	13	16
	1990	11	29	30	17	13
ASEAN 4	1970	30	23	21	17	9
	1980	35	20	19	14	12
	1985	31	26	21	12	10
	1990	24	28	21	17	10
China	1970	14	47	1	22	16
	1980	22	31	6	15	26
	1985	22	36	10	9	23
	1990	14	46	12	11	17

Sources: International Monetary Fund, *Direction of Trade*, Washington, DC, various issues; International Economic Data Bank, Australian National University, *World Trade Tape*, Canberra, 1992.

A closer examination of the changes in East Asia's direction of exports by country group leads to the following observations (see Table 6.4). First, for both Japan and the ANIEs it is North America and developing East Asia (DEA) that have been their predominant markets, while Western Europe has been a distant third. In both cases, DEA is now rivalling North America as their largest market. For the ANIEs, Japan was barely one-third as important as either North America or DEA as an export market in 1990. Second, for the ASEAN 4 Japan was the largest market but its share fell rapidly during the 1980s. Its second largest market was North America during the 1970s and the ANIEs during the 1980s, while Western Europe remained less important than America. And third, by far the largest market for China has been the ANIEs, importantly, but not solely, because of Hong Kong's entrepôt role. Clearly, the region's developing economies have been a rapidly growing market for East Asian exports, to the point where they are now the major export outlet for virtually all economies in the region.

6.2 The pattern of economic integration in East Asia

The preceding discussion shows that during the past two decades there has been a steady regionalization of East Asian trade in terms of the increase in the share of the intra-regional market in East Asian trade. Regionalization of trade, however, is not the same thing as regional integration.

An increase in integration means a reduction or removal of resistances to trade. Resistances to trade may be classified into two groups. One is the group of institutional resistances, including trade restrictions at the border and incongruity of other policies between nations. The other is the group of natural resistances such as physical resistances which raise transport costs, and informational resistances which make it costly to gather information on firms, products and foreign countries as well as to process information on foreign markets and trading partners' policies.[2] Integration may be promoted on a regional basis or a global basis. Global integration will be accompanied by trade creation, whereas regional integration will be accompanied not only by trade creation but also by trade diversion. Trade may be diverted in the sense that, *ceteris paribus*, some trade with extra-regional partners is replaced by trade with intra-regional partners.

Integration may be promoted with liberalization and/or harmonization of trade policies, or by infrastructural investments which reduce physical, informational or cultural resistances to trade. Liberalization of trade removes the gap between private transactions costs (which include, for example, tariffs) and social transactions costs, by bringing down the former. While promotion of regional integration with preferential trade liberalization could be welfare-reducing, its promotion by other means will normally be welfare-improving (Drysdale and Garnaut, 1993).

Infrastructural investments in transportation and informational facilities, as well as cultural assimilation, may be made by private firms, which are always seeking to reduce marketing costs and find new markets. Thus, trading activities by themselves tend to generate market forces for further integration of national economies with others. But there also is a case for government promotion of these investments, since both economies of scale and externalities are common features of these investments (Drysdale and Garnaut, 1993).

Before turning, in the next section, to the question of whether countries should promote regional integration or global integration, it is useful to examine the effects of East Asia's past practices and policies for export promotion. A helpful indicator for this purpose is the index of trade intensity. The trade intensity index is defined for the j-th reporting country with respect to the i-th partner region as the ratio of the j-th region's share in the i-th country's total exports over the j-th region's share in the total world imports (see Chapter 2 above, by Anderson and Norheim). The intensity index eliminates from the actual size of a bilateral relationship the effect of the size of the partner region as an importer. We may analogously define the trade intensity index for the i-th reporting region with respect to the j-th partner region as the weighted sum of the value of the trade intensity index for each of the constituent economies in the i-th region calculated with respect to the j-th region.[3]

Table 6.5 shows the changing values of the intra- and extra-regional trade intensity indexes for the major regions of the world since 1970. The trade intensity index by far exceeds unity in all regions. In 1970 it was far higher for East Asia than for North America or the EC, but the difference has narrowed considerably during the past two decades. This decrease from a high level in the value of the intra-regional trade intensity index for East Asia is consistent with Petri's (1992) report that the intra-regional trade intensity index for East Asia was even higher during the first half of the twentieth century. Japan had a well-established trading network in East Asia but East Asia's trade with the rest of the world suffered from severely underdeveloped trading

Table 6.5 Indexes of intensity of intra- and extra-regional export trade,[a] 1970, 1980 and 1990

		East Asia	Australasia	North America	South America	EC-12	EFTA
East Asia	1970	3.1	1.6	1.8	0.6	0.4	0.3
	1980	2.6	2.0	1.7	0.6	0.4	0.3
	1990	2.3	1.6	1.6	0.5	0.4	0.3
Australasia	1970	3.0	5.6	1.0	0.2	0.7	0.1
	1980	2.8	7.8	0.9	0.2	0.5	0.1
	1990	2.6	7.5	0.7	0.4	0.4	0.3
North America	1970	1.4	1.2	1.9	2.1	0.7	0.4
	1980	1.4	1.4	1.8	2.4	0.6	0.4
	1990	1.3	1.4	1.9	2.8	0.5	0.4
South America	1970	0.5	0.1	2.1	3.0	0.8	0.4
	1980	0.4	0.2	2.4	3.5	0.6	0.4
	1990	0.5	0.3	2.2	3.9	0.6	0.4
EC-12	1970	0.3	0.9	0.6	0.7	1.4	1.6
	1980	0.2	0.6	0.4	0.5	1.5	1.6
	1990	0.3	0.6	0.4	0.5	1.5	1.6
EFTA	1970	0.3	0.5	0.5	0.6	1.4	2.5
	1980	0.3	0.6	0.4	0.5	1.5	2.3
	1990	0.4	0.6	0.5	0.4	1.5	2.1

Note: [a] See the text for the definition of the intensity of trade index.

Sources: International Monetary Fund, *Direction of Trade*, Washington, DC, various issues; International Economic Data Bank, Australian National University, *World Trade Tape*, Canberra, 1992.

infrastructures. The long-term downward trend in East Asia's intra-regional trade intensity since the 1960s, in turn, reflects the progress in the region's global integration efforts that has been due to the strong and steady export drive of the East Asian economies.

Table 6.5 also shows the changing patterns of inter-regional trade intensities. It reveals two relatively well-integrated regions in the world. One is the Asia-Pacific region consisting of East Asia, North America and Australasia. The other is Western Europe, consisting of the EC and EFTA. The Asian-Pacific region and Western Europe remain only weakly integrated with each other. South America has been closely integrated with North America but remains poorly integrated with the Asian-Pacific region as a whole insofar as its trading intensities with East Asia and Australasia are quite low.

A feature shared by both East Asia and North America is that there had been no significant preferential integration agreements in those regions until recently. ASEAN, the only regionalist body in East Asia, signed a Preferential Trade Agreement in 1977 but 'it fell into disrepute when it became clear that most of the items on the list were put there because they were so little traded.'[4] In February 1992, ASEAN decided to launch a program to establish an ASEAN Free Trade Area (AFTA) in 15 years, with the aim of reducing most tariffs within ASEAN to a maximum of 5 per cent during this period; but it is unlikely to have a major impact. And in 1989 in North America, the Canada–US Free Trade Agreement came into effect (see Chapter 4 above, by Smith).

The high degree of Asian-Pacific integration is explained by the previously globalist feature of the two component regions, while the lack of integration between the Asian-Pacific region and Western Europe may be explained by the discriminatory trade agreements of the EC and EFTA. The East Asian economies, in particular, have taken full advantage of the vast open market in the Asian-Pacific region by launching and sustaining rapid export-led growth and aggressively seeking markets both inside and outside East Asia.

6.3   East Asia's strategy for the future: regionalism or globalism?

Due to recent changes in the international environment, East Asia's globalist approach to economic integration appears to have run into a phase of diminishing returns. Two principal reasons for this may be cited. On the one hand, the multilateral trading system which has worked reasonably well for a long time has suffered from the emergence of the so-called new protectionism. In particular, the United States has begun to pursue aggressive unilateralism, with a consequent rise in trade tensions with East Asian economies and especially with Japan. During the second half of the 1980s, there was a revival of regionalism, with the launching of the Single Market program in the EC and what has now become NAFTA in North America.

On the other hand, the East Asian markets have accelerated their growth, and promise to maintain that momentum in the future, thereby raising the expected return to the pursuit of 'open' regional integration. For example, Southeast Asia and China have emerged with new industrial dynamism as a second tier of ANIEs. China's new dynamism became evident soon after the country's adoption of its open-door policy in 1978. The Southeast Asian economies also began to grow and industrialize rapidly from the mid-1980s. An important measure which helped these economies to take off was their opening up to foreign direct investment. The subsequent inflow of investment, especially from Japan and the ANIEs, has expanded substantially the stocks of capital and technology with which to industrialize.

Additionally, the East Asian economies have been opening their domestic markets unilaterally to foreign goods and services. This policy of unilateral trade liberalization was launched on a voluntary base for the purpose of enhancing domestic efficiency, although pressure from the US has been instrumental in expediting these efforts. Together with the exchange-rate realignments following the 1985 Plaza Accord, these measures have unleashed strong demand for the import of consumer goods, especially in Japan and the ANIEs.

These recent changes in the international environment, especially the latter development, seem to favor a regionalist approach to economic integration relative to the globalist approach. But, in order to determine the validity of this view, it is helpful to examine the implications of recent trade policy developments in some detail.

The future of the multilateral trading system will depend very much on the outcome of the Uruguay Round. It is true that even a highly successful Uruguay Round will not strengthen the multilateral system greatly. Rather, it may do no more than 'keep things more or less as they are' (Wolf, 1991). It will not undo many of the non-tariff barriers that have been the main feature of the new protectionism. Nor will a successful Uruguay Round have much impact on the abuse of contingency protection such as anti-dumping measures, or restrict the aggressive unilateralism of the United States. On the other hand, though, a successful Uruguay Round will still be very important because failure to reach an agreement would probably damage the multilateral trading system irreparably. Trade tensions would surge, and unilateralism, bilateralism and regionalism would become the main rules of the game.

What are the threats posed by the new regionalism as represented by recent European integration initiatives and NAFTA? Before discussing these threats, we should first note that the formation of these RIAs may very well be beneficial to East Asia, since the objective of each is to accelerate economic growth in the member countries. When economic growth accelerates, demand for imports will increase.

Still, European integration, the core of which is the internal market program, poses two challenges to East Asia. One is the protectionist challenge in the form of trade-diverting external policy. The other is the competitiveness challenge in the form of the improved competitiveness of industries which may lead to the loss of East Asia's share of world markets. The protectionist challenge arises from the possibility of strengthened discrimination against East Asian products.

Discrimination against developing East Asian economies is expected to increase in two ways.[5] First, the program will be accompanied by a new structure of trade preferences which may be highly discriminatory to the developing economies of East Asia. These trade preferences will favor the present member countries of EFTA, the Mediterranean countries of Turkey, Malta and Cyprus, the East European countries and the CIS countries in different manners. Developing East Asian economies compete with these countries over a broad range of products and, hence, will be hurt by the EC's trade preference system to be introduced on top of the current arrangements.

Second, competition among firms within the EC will intensify in many products in which the East Asian countries have strong export interests, and this will increase the demand for more protection against East Asian developing countries. Intra-EC competition will increase because of the extension of trade preferences to neighboring countries and also because of reductions in internal trade barriers. The EC Commission is unlikely to ignore such demands. It can increase protection against the East Asian exporters by pooling national quotas into the Community-wide restrictions; footwear, automobiles, electronic goods, textiles and clothing are the likely targets. And it can make more stringent use of anti-dumping duty provisions.

NAFTA does not pose the same degree of protectionist threat, and by itself it is unlikely to cause any serious trade diversion from the standpoint of East Asia.[6] Mexico is economically rather small, and tariffs on Mexican exports to the United States are already low at about 4 per cent. However, complications may arise because NAFTA may be followed by a series of other Latin American FTAs which may eventually lead to a Western Hemisphere FTA (Krause, 1992). The foundation for this scenario has already been provided in the form of US President Bush's Enterprise for the Americas Initiative, and so far the Latin American countries have responded to this proposal with enthusiasm. Such a Western Hemisphere FTA is likely to be more highly trade-diverting than NAFTA, and would pose a more serious challenge to East Asia.

As far as NAFTA itself is concerned, its main beneficiary will be Mexico, and the benefit will come in the form of higher economic growth resulting from increased investment in Mexico, induced by Mexico's stable and liberal trade and investment policy that is part of the NAFTA accord. While higher economic growth will increase its demand for imports, investment inflows will increase the competitiveness of Mexican industry. Since Mexico has comparative advantages over a broad range of labor-intensive products, NAFTA may pose a challenge to the competitiveness of Southeast Asia and China. At the same time, however, Japan and the ANIEs may benefit from Mexico's increased demand for intermediate inputs and capital goods.

Having identified the two challenges of the new regionalism, competitiveness and protectionism, we now ask what the East Asian economies can do to respond to these challenges. In order to cope with the former, it would be helpful for the East Asian economies to promote regional integration. To cope with the latter, the East Asian economies should strengthen their efforts to defend and improve the multilateral trading system. The East Asian economies should pursue these two objectives at the same time. It is important to note here that the two need not conflict with each other, for there can be two types of regionalism – closed and open – and the conflict with the multilateral system does not arise in the second case.

We have seen that regional integration can be promoted in a number of ways, such as preferential trade liberalization, harmonization of policies, and infrastructural investments. The first amounts to the formation of a trading bloc. However, it could involve serious welfare-reducing trade diversion and, more critically, it works against the multilateral trading system. For this reason, the proposal to form an East Asian Economic Caucus, if its aim is to create a counter-bloc in East Asia, should be rejected as lacking in economic wisdom.[7] For a similar reason, we may also question the wisdom of AFTA but take comfort in the fact that the aimed tariff-cut by the ASEAN participants is rather modest and that the economic weight of ASEAN is small.

In contrast, the other two types of integration efforts are unambiguously welfare-improving and entirely consistent with the multilateral trading system. It is in this sense that they represent open regionalism and define an area of actions the East Asian economies may take in response to the worsening of the international environment.[8]

The pursuit of open regionalism will have the additional benefit of easing the trilateral pattern of trading that has been a major source of pressure on the multilateral trading system. Still, special emphasis will have to be placed on the need to address this problem of trilateralism. The importance of fully opening the domestic markets of the East Asian economies to manufactured goods and services on unilateral bases, and in regard not only to the border measures but also to trade-restricting domestic practices and institutions, should be emphasized.

Open regionalism should be practiced alongside efforts to defend and strengthen the multilateral trading system. For this purpose, the East Asian economies should step up their efforts to bring the Uruguay Round to a successful conclusion. In these efforts, two critical players will be Japan and Korea, whose more forthcoming concessions on agriculture would be an essential contribution. Furthermore, whether the Uruguay Round is concluded with success or failure, they should continue their efforts to strengthen the multilateral trading system. At this stage, the so-called GATT-Plus suggests itself as a promising avenue (see Chapter 18 below by Baldwin, and Young (1993)). We have seen that the GATT system is in need of repair in some of its most fundamental aspects but, as Baldwin argues in Chapter 18, the chance of getting all members to agree on how to repair the system is remote. The failure of the Uruguay Round would only reinforce this point. On the other hand, it is clear from the current negotiations that a number of key countries agree on the need for significant changes in various negotiating areas. Accordingly, those like-minded members of the GATT may work out a new agreement on additional responsibilities and privileges which would apply only to those who accept the new one. Non-member countries will also be welcome to join the agreement at a later time. In other words, the most-favored-nation (MFN) principle would apply conditionally.

There are two possibilities as to how the GATT-Plus idea might evolve. Should the Uruguay Round be concluded successfully, the likely participants are most of the East Asian economies (including Japan and the ANIEs), the North American countries and the EC. Should the Uruguay Round be concluded unsuccessfully, the Asian-Pacific countries would be the main participants while the EC would not be one of them. However, the EC might join at a later time and, in fact, the main role of the conditional MFN principle would be to serve as a standing invitation to the EC.

For all these efforts, the East Asian countries will need other countries in the Asia-Pacific region, especially those in North America as well as Australia and New Zealand, as partners. This is so essentially because, as Tables 6.3–6.5 show, these countries share strong interdependence and many common interests. For this purpose, the Asian-Pacific Economic Cooperation (APEC) initiative will provide the most appropriate forum through which like-minded partners in the region could promote their joint efforts.

Should we not extend the above line of reasoning further and recommend the formation of a Pacific Free Trade Area (FTA)? This may come about, for example, as a result of the East Asian economies and Australasia joining NAFTA. The balance of considerations suggests a negative answer. We conclude the present section by discussing this point.

What would be the major implications of a Pacific FTA? Such an FTA would roughly rival that of Western Europe (the EEA) in terms of trading volume, and would overshadow it in terms of output.[9] Accordingly, it would involve a sizable amount of trade diversion, but trade creation is likely to be far larger. Trade creation is expected because the member economies of the Pacific FTA are highly complementary in terms of their economic structure. Much of this complementarity, however, has been suppressed with various trade restrictions. And given the large size of the Pacific FTA, the scale of trade creation would accordingly be large. This implies that the FTA could provide a strong stimulus not only to Asian-Pacific economies but also to non-members, including European economies.

A Pacific FTA also is likely to contribute to the liberalization of global trade. To the extent that its members are committed to outward-oriented development, the FTA would want to extend its membership to whomever would be willing to accept the obligations involved. Once such a FTA with the Asian-Pacific countries as its initial members got started and proved to be successful in terms of stimulating trade and economic growth, it would continue to attract new members. And while the Pacific FTA continued to expand its membership and liberalize its trade, the EC might be encouraged to seek negotiations for global trade liberalization and even want to join the FTA at some point.

But is a Pacific FTA a feasible idea to begin with? The answer is no, or at least not for now. The main problem is the high degree of complementarity that exists among the Asian-Pacific economies but remains suppressed by the current pattern of trade restrictions (see Anderson, 1991a): since the removal of these restrictions would trigger far-reaching inter-sectoral adjustments, the idea is likely to run into insurmountable political resistance in many member countries.

A Pacific FTA might also have other problems. For one thing, many would-be participants would seek derogations and exceptions to the provisions of the FTA (Drysdale and Garnaut, 1989): some developing countries would want to argue for infant-industry protection, and such countries as China and Vietnam would ask for special treatment because of the practical difficulties resulting from their economic systems. But if a 'clean' FTA is not available for the reasons mentioned above, no FTA may be better than having a porous and hence discriminatory one.

Also, once negotiations for a Pacific FTA got under way, they would divert much of the region's trade policy-making resources away from focusing on the rest of the world, so that economic and other relations with non-member countries would risk being neglected. In the meantime, the global trading environment might continue to deteriorate, sharpening the division between the European bloc, the Asian-Pacific bloc, and the rest of the world.

And a further problem would emerge between the East Asian countries and other industrial countries − and between Japan and the United States in particular − in the form of negotiating difficulties, which would arise from the difference in the nature of their policy regimes. In East Asia, governments are prone to market intervention, an approach to policies that tends to be informal and opaque. Consequently, a credibility gap exists between East Asian governments and those of other industrial countries. This credibility gap is a major problem underlying the current US−Japan trade dispute. The difference in the nature of the policy regime not only makes negotiation difficult but seems to have led people in Washington to believe that a FTA with Japan is simply not feasible.

6.4   Summary

The success of the East Asian developing economies' trade and growth during the last three decades has been associated with the rapid regionalization of trade in East Asia. East Asia's export success would not have been possible, however, without the availability of Asian-Pacific markets and especially the North American market. The availability of the European market has been rather limited and, as a result, two large integrated regions have emerged in the world, namely, Western Europe and the Asian-Pacific region. The emergence of the latter as an integrated region has been due to the globalist trade policies of both the East Asian and North American economies. That is, regionalization of East Asian trade should not be attributed to the promotion of regional integration in East Asia. To the contrary, the East Asian economies have been pursuing a rather aggressive globalist approach to international integration, and this has promoted economic integration with North America in particular. It is simply because of the rapid growth of the economies of East Asia that their intra-regional trade shares have grown.

In the meantime, the international trading environment has been worsening. The revival of regionalism, especially in Western Europe and

North America, has been the most fundamental threat to the efficacy of the globalist trade policies of the East Asian economies. What should be East Asia's response to this threat? East Asia should simultaneously pursue what may appear to be two conflicting courses of actions. One is the pursuit of open regionalism. This involves coordinating efforts to harmonize national policies, practices and institutions and investing in various infrastructures to reduce physical, communicational and cultural gaps among the regional economies. An East Asian RIA would not be a politically acceptable component of this course of action, however.

The other course of action is to try to strengthen the multilateral trading system. Every effort needs to be made to bring the Uruguay Round to a successful conclusion. Furthermore, efforts to launch a GATT-Plus agreement after the successful (or unsuccessful) conclusion of the Round could be contemplated. Core participants in any negotiations for such an agreement are likely to be the Asian-Pacific economies. But a Pacific Free Trade Area, despite its similarity to a GATT-Plus agreement with an Asian-Pacific focus, is unlikely to be feasible.

In order to practice open regionalism as well as globalism, the East Asian economies need other Asia-Pacific economies as partners. This point underlines the importance of the APEC process. APEC should be assigned the central role in any type of cooperative effort among the Asian-Pacific economies, and both NAFTA and AFTA should be made the supervisory responsibility of APEC.

Notes

The author would like to thank Kym Anderson for his valuable comments on an earlier version and Peter Drysdale for having made available the necessary trade data from the Australian National University. The author also expresses his gratitude to Seongyun Kang for his most able research assistance.
1. See de la Torre and Kelly (1992) for a comprehensive survey of the major regional integration agreements.
2. See Amelung (1990) for a transactions cost analysis of these resistances.
3. Strictly speaking, as Anderson and Norheim point out in Chapter 2 above, trade intensity should be regarded as the product of complementarity and bias in trade flows (see also Drysdale and Garnaut, 1993). Complementarity refers to the degree to which the export structure of one country matches the import structure of a partner country, whereas the index of residual bias in trade flows measures the degree to which the balance of resistances to trade favors bilateral trade relative to global trade. In the subsequent analysis on trade intensity, I simply assume that there was not much change in complementarity in the bilateral trade flows during the period of observation.

4. See the article 'Fortress Asia?' in the October 24, 1991, issue of *The Economist*.
5. The analysis here is based on Anderson (1991b) and Page (1992).
6. This present analysis of NAFTA is based on Krueger (1991) and Krause (1992).
7. An additional criticism of the proposal is that it lacks political wisdom insofar as an East Asian bloc would inevitably be dominated by Japan. See Anderson (1991a) and Young (1992).
8. See Elek (1992), who makes essentially the same point and lists a number of initiatives which the East Asian economies may undertake in cooperation with other countries in the Asia-Pacific region for this purpose.
9. According to Tables A3 and A8 of the Appendix to this volume, in 1990 Asia (including Australasia) and North America accounted for 39 per cent of world trade and 55 per cent of trade GDP, while Western Europe's shares were 46 and 34 per cent respectively.

References

Amelung, T. (1990), 'Explaining Regionalization of Trade in Asia Pacific: A Transaction Cost Approach', Working Paper No. 423, Institute of World Economics, Kiel.

Anderson, K. (1991a), 'Is an Asian-Pacific Trade Bloc Next?', *Journal of World Trade* 25: 27–40.

Anderson, K. (1991b), 'Europe 1992 and the Western Pacific Economics', *Economic Journal* 101: 1538–52.

de la Torre, A. and M. R. Kelly (1992), *Regional Trade Arrangements*, Occasional Paper No. 93, Washington, D.C.: International Monetary Fund.

Drysdale, P. and R. Garnaut (1989), 'A Pacific Free Trade Area?', in *Free Trade Areas and U.S. Trade Policy*, edited by J. J. Schott, Washington, DC: Institute for International Economics.

Drysdale, P. and R. Garnaut (1993), 'The Pacific: An Application of a General Theory of Economic Integration', in *Pacific Dynamism and the International Economic System*, edited by M. Noland, Washington, DC: Institute for International Economics.

Elek, A. (1992), 'Pacific Economic Co-operation: Policy Choices for the 1990s', *Asian-Pacific Economic Literature* 6: 1–15.

Krause, L. B. (1992), 'The North American Free Trade Area and Asia-Pacific Economic Cooperation', prepared for the Kyushu University International Symposium on Which Direction is the Asia-Pacific Region Moving?, Fukuoka, July 27–8.

Krueger, A. O. (1991), 'American Bilateral Trading Arrangements and East Asian Interests', prepared for the 2nd National Bureau of Economic Research (NBER)-East Asian Seminar on Economics, Taipei, June 19–21.

Page, S. (1992), 'Some Implications of Europe 1992 for Developing Countries', prepared for the Research Program on Globalization and Regionalization, OECD, Paris, March.

Park, Y. C. and W. A. Park (1991), 'Changing Japanese Trade Patterns and the East Asian NICs', in *Trade with Japan: Has the Door Opened Wider?*, edited by P. Krugman, Chicago: University of Chicago Press.

Petri, P. A. (1992), 'The East Asian Trading Bloc: An Analytical History', Working Paper No. 315, Brandeis University, Waltham, MA, March.

Young, S. (1992), 'Economic Development of East Asia: Its Impact on the Asia-Pacific Region', prepared for the Kyushu University International Symposium on Which Direction is the Asia-Pacific Region Moving?, Fukuoka, July 27–8.

Young, S. (1993), 'Globalism and Regionalism: Complements or Competitors?', in *Pacific Dynamism and the International Economic System*, edited by M. Noland, Washington, DC: Institute for International Economics.

Wolf, M. (1991), 'Pushing the Boulder Uphill: The Uruguay Round Crisis and the Future of the GATT', prepared for the Royal Institute of International Affairs Conference on Uruguay Round Negotiations: Crisis and Response, London, March 7–8.

PART 3

Regionalism, foreign investment and the macroeconomy

7

Regional integration agreements and foreign direct investment

V. N. Balasubramanyam and David Greenaway

The debate on the interrelationship between regionalism and foreign direct investment (FDI) dates back at least to the 1960s, when there was a surge of FDI from the United States into the newly formed European Economic Community (EC). The issue then was the nature of FDI in the EC: was it the tariff-jumping variety or was it attracted by the prospects for growth in incomes in an enlarged market? The consensus appears to be that it was market size and growth which attracted US firms rather than impediments to their exports to the EC. The debate has been revived in recent years in the context of enlargements of the EC and the '1992' Single Market initiative. This time it is not so much American FDI but the dramatic growth of FDI in the EC from the East Asian countries, principally Japan, that has revived interest in the interrelationship between regionalism and FDI. Is the surge of East Asian FDI a reflection of a 'Fortress Europe' syndrome, or is it fueled by the prospect of an enlarged Single Market? If the growth in FDI is of the tariff-jumping variety, it would contribute to any trade diversion resulting from the establishment of the Single Market. But if it is in response to growth prospects in an enlarged market, it could complement trade. The welfare implications of the two alternative reasons for FDI, both for the EC and for the rest of the world, therefore differ. The principal objective of this chapter is to analyze the factors responsible for the growth in FDI in recent years in the context of the spread of regionalism. As we shall see later, direct investment into the EC has increased from a number of sources, most notably Japan and other West European countries (the member states of EFTA). We focus our attention on Japan for the simple reason that FDI from Japan is the newer phenomenon.

The chapter is organized as follows. Section 7.1 focuses on trends and patterns in FDI, both global and regional. In Section 7.2 we review the determinants of FDI and the factors which influence the net benefits of a particular inward investment. Section 7.3 is concerned with policy toward investment. From an EC standpoint this involves both internal measures and measures vis-à-vis non-EC entities, and both incentives and disincentives for FDI. In Section 7.4 we consider how completion of the EC Single Market can be expected to impact on inward investment. This sets the agenda for Section 7.5 where the focus is policy coordination within the EC. Since EC trade and investment policies are set against the wider firmament of multilateral rules and disciplines, Section 7.6 concentrates on activity in the GATT and OECD. Finally Section 7.7 offers some concluding comments.

7.1   Trends in foreign direct investment

The post-war period has seen an extraordinary growth of world trade and a concomitant growth in foreign direct investment.[1] The EC, the US and Japan together accounted for 78 per cent of the total flow of $217 billion of FDI in 1990, about half of which was among those economies. Of the three, the growth in Japan's FDI has been the most dramatic. In terms of annual average outflows it increased from $10 billion during the period 1979–81 to $126 billion during 1988–90. From a situation where Japanese corporations held less than 1 per cent of the total stock in 1960, by 1990 they controlled more than 15 per cent of that stock. Even more dramatic is the growth of Japan's FDI in the EC and the US. In the case of the US it increased from $4 billion to $65 billion and in the case of the EC it rose from a mere $1 billion to $27 billion. Another significant development is the appearance of the newly industrializing East Asian economies on the FDI scene. Taiwan, the Republic of Korea, Singapore and Hong Kong have emerged as significant investors since the early 1980s but, until recently, much of their FDI was in other developing countries, mostly Asian ones.

The composition and characteristics of Japanese FDI in the EC has been examined elsewhere by the authors in Balasubramanyam and Greenaway (1992). The key features are that the investment is fairly concentrated geographically and sectorally. About 40 per cent of all FDI in the EC goes to the UK and around 30 per cent to the Netherlands. This seems to be driven by a number of factors: the long-standing openness of the UK to FDI; relatively low labor costs there; the importance of London as a financial center; and the role of the English language.

Financial services and commerce account for around 60 per cent of total FDI in the EC, the remainder finding its way into manufacturing.

7.2 International trade and capital flows: the analytical context

The links between international trade and capital flows, the forces driving FDI, the benefits and costs of FDI and the operation of multi-national enterprises (MNEs) have all been subjected to extensive analysis. Here we are concerned with a subset of these issues, namely, the determinants of FDI and the net benefits associated with it. We need to be so in order to understand what is driving the current upsurge in FDI to the EC, and its potential impact.

7.2.1 Determinants of FDI

Numerous economists have focused on the issue of what motivates firms to engage in FDI rather than arm's-length trade (for a review, see Cantwell, 1992). Dunning's (1988) 'eclectic paradigm' shows a way to summarize the factors which drive foreign investment. According to this, the decision to engage in local production and/or intra-firm trade, rather than to license or to engage in arm's-length trade, is driven by consider-ations of ownership, location and internalization (OLI). What this so-called OLI paradigm claims is that conditions under all of these headings must be met before FDI will occur.

Take a specific example of a firm which has a valuable proprietary asset such as a strong brand image or a reputation for financial prudence. The positive rate of return which this yields confers an ownership advan-tage. Now suppose there is a foreign market with no competing brand where this asset can yield a rate of return at least as high as on the home market. Production conditions/transportation costs may lead the firm to decide on a strategy of supplying locally rather than at arm's length. Why should it set up a production plant rather than license? One possi-bility is to ensure certain quality control conditions are met. Alter-natively the proprietary product may be produced by a proprietary technology, control of which the firm wishes to retain. Either way the result is the same: to fully exploit the ownership/locational advantages the firm has to internalize the transaction by setting up a production facility.[2]

Table 7.1 lists possible ownership, locational and internalization advantages. Associated with the former there may be advantages

Table 7.1 The OLI paradigm for explaining FDI

Ownership advantages
Size:
  Obtain inputs more cheaply or obtain exclusive access to inputs
  Better access to product markets
  Product or process diversification
  Economies of scale, at both the plant level and the firm level
Intangible assets:
  Proprietary knowledge, technology, trademarks, product management, marketing,
  research and development, human capital
Government policies:
  Favoring business in the home country

Location advantages
Inputs:
  Spatial distribution of inputs and markets
  Input prices, quality and productivity
Economies of scale:
  Extent to which plant-level economies of scale make for centralization of production
Government policies:
  Control of imports (tariffs, etc.), tax rates, incentives, investment climate, political
  stability
Other:
  Transport and communications costs
  Infrastructure (commercial, legal, transportation)
  Psychic distance (language, culture, business customs)

Internalization advantages
Market failure in market for final goods:
  Reduce costs associated with market transactions
  Compensate for absence of futures markets
Market failure in market for inputs:
  Avoid costs of enforcing property rights
  Buyer uncertainty about nature and value of inputs
  Control supplies and conditions of sale of inputs
Monopoly power:
  Where market does not permit price discrimination
  Control market outlets
  Engage in anti-competitive practises such as cross-subsidization and predatory pricing
Product differentiation:
  Need of seller to protect quality of product
Government policies:
  Avoid or exploit government intervention (quotas, tariffs, taxes, price controls)

Source: Adapted from Dunning (1988).

attached to size, intangible assets like reputation, or government policy. Where location is concerned, access to particular inputs, or economies of scale, or government policy, or infrastructural factors might be important. Internalization advantages might derive from failures or imperfections in input or output markets. Alternatively product differentiation or government policy can all play a role. The great advantage of this eclectic paradigm is that it provides a general hypothesis for explaining FDI which encompasses all other model-specific hypotheses.

7.2.2 Net benefits of FDI

Analysis of the welfare impact revolves around, *inter alia*: employment effects, externalities, trade balance effects, and income redistribution:

1. *Employment effects*. Opponents of FDI argue that it must be employment-reducing on the grounds that foreign firms replace local firms as suppliers of final goods, and typically the former rely on imported inputs to a greater extent than the latter. Moreover, it is sometimes also argued that those jobs which are created are low value-added/low human-capital intensity jobs. Evidence from the US does suggest that foreign MNEs in general and Japanese MNEs in particular are more import-intensive than indigenous firms (see for example Lipsey, 1991; and Graham and Krugman, 1991). However, this does not necessarily mean that they will be a source of net employment decline. As Graham and Krugman (1991) point out, aggregate employment has much more to do with supply-side conditions, in particular the occupational and geographical mobility of labor. The 'quality of employment' argument also is questionable. Critics argue that MNEs set up 'screwdriver' plants geared towards low-value-added, low-wage functions. However, longer-term evidence from US investment in Western Europe, and more recent evidence on Japanese investment in the US and in the UK, suggests that this is not in fact the case.

2. *Externalities*. It is possible to argue that FDI has positive spill-over effects through its impact on technology transfer. The contribution of modern endogenous growth theory has been to provide an explicit role for technology in the growth process. FDI is an obvious source of embodied technology, as cross-border investment is potentially a major stimulus to growth. There is evidence to suggest that in some sectors – automobiles in the UK being an excellent example – foreign firms install best-practice technology and management techniques and these tend to then be adopted by local producers as well.

3. *Trade balance effects*. Concern here derives from the allegedly high import dependence of foreign firms, combined with the allegedly low-value-added nature of the operations. This combination impacts adversely on the trade balance. As noted earlier, there is some evidence that Japanese firms tend to have a higher import dependence than local firms, but this may be just a temporary phenomenon: once the foreign firm becomes established it sets up local supply networks for sourcing inputs. Moreover, the initial investment itself often brings in its wake subsequent investments from downstream producers. Another response is that the goods

which are actually produced may replace imports rather than
domestically produced import substitutes. This has probably been
the case in consumer electronics and automobiles.

4. *Income redistribution.* Typically, because market imperfections
preclude a potential supplier from fully appropriating the returns
to firm-specific assets, FDI allows certain transactions to be
internalized. However, the existence of internal markets creates
opportunities for MNEs to engage in transfer pricing. Insofar as this
results in revenues that would otherwise accrue to the host government leaking overseas, it represents a welfare loss. There is evidence
from developing countries which shows that transfer pricing does
occur on a non-negligible scale. The same kind of evidence is not
available for the EC or US, but the practice is likely to be less
important there for three reasons: first, the range of controls and
restrictions which stimulate it are nothing like as pervasive as in
developing countries; second, double taxation agreements are more
common; and third, disclosure rules are tighter. The second of these
is likely to be especially important in the case of Japanese FDI in the
EC, since full credit for taxes paid in Europe is provided by the
Japanese government.

Thus FDI, like international trade, promotes specialization in production. As with international trade, one can identify static gains (through
resource reallocation) and dynamic gains (through exploitation of scale
economies, pro-competitive effects on local markets, and a stimulus to
growth), which are a corollary to the process. Clearly the net employment effects or trade balance effects will vary from one industry to
another, depending upon supply conditions, market structure and so on.
Overall, however, there is a strong presumption that FDI confers net
benefits to the host country.

7.3 Policies toward foreign direct investment

Since investment is a key determinant of economic growth, policy
makers strive to create an environment conducive to investment formation. The pervasiveness of investment codes in developing countries and
the diversity of investment incentives in industrialized countries is
testimony to this. Historically, investment measures have been regarded
as a non-border issue. When economies were relatively closed this was
a reasonable simplification. However, with the remarkable growth of
trade over the post-war period and the concomitant globalization of
production, the border/non-border distinction has become increasingly

meaningless. The fact that trade-related investment measures (TRIMs) are an agenda item in the Uruguay Round reflects this. From an EC standpoint this is a two-track issue involving internal measures and measures vis-à-vis non-EC entities. Both will be examined later in greater detail. For the moment we focus on the range of instruments which can be deployed.

7.3.1   Investment incentives

Many initiatives to encourage capital investment are economy-wide, regionally based or sectorally based, and some are targeted specifically at MNEs. Their rationale is based on three presumptions: first, that FDI supplements indigenous investment, and no crowding-out takes place; second, that there are net benefits to the host economy arising from FDI; and third, that the supply of FDI is responsive to incentives. Table 7.2 lists a range of instruments of investment policy, classified according to whether their initial impact is aimed at the input or output side, and their intended effects. Empirical evidence suggests these incentives tend to be (1) more prevalent in developing than industrialized countries, (2) geared toward input rather than output support, (3) targeted at encouraging investment in the export sectors of developing countries and in the high-tech sectors of industrialized countries, and (4) used as an instrument of regional or social policy. There is no evidence at present to link the prevalence, or absence, of these measures to RIAs. As we will argue later, however, the trend toward regionalism could mean that they become more widely deployed in the future.

Table 7.2   An inventory of investment incentives

Input incentives	
Instrument:	Intended effect:
Duty drawback	Subsidy on imported inputs
Tax exemptions on equipment	Input subsidy
Accelerated depreciation	Subsidy to capital equipment
Investment allowances	Subsidy to capital equipment
Training credits	Subsidy to human capital formation
Research and development support	Encouragement to technological innovations
Output incentives	
Instrument:	Intended effect:
Export subsidy	Boost exports
Tax holiday	Exempt profits from taxation for a specified period
Market reserve commitments	Local market monopoly conferred on investor
Export retention schemes	Allow MNE to retain foreign exchange earnings

7.3.2   Trade-related investment measures

The declaration which initiated the Uruguay Round drew specific attention to the need to examine the applicability of GATT articles to the
trade-restricting and trade-distorting effects of investment measures.
TRIMs are intended to accomplish three things: first, to influence the
location and pattern of economic activity; second, to ensure that the
likelihood of benefits which the host government wishes to secure is
greater than it otherwise would be; and third, to redistribute part of the
surpluses generated by FDI away from the MNE and toward residents
of the host country. These are discussed by Greenaway (1990) under the
headings of the resource allocation, insurance and rent-shifting targets
respectively. The last is especially important and explains the conjunction of investment incentives and/or protection and TRIMs. In general
TRIMs are second-best instruments and can be 'beggar-thy-neighbor'
policies with trade-distorting effects. As with investment incentives, there
is no evidence to link their usage to RIAs. Again, however, as we will
argue later with the proliferation of regional trading blocs, they could
become more widely used.

7.4   EC '1992' and Japanese inward investment

A number of studies have pointed to the positive association between
economic integration and FDI, particularly in the case of the EC
(Greenaway, 1987; Yannopolous, 1990; Balasubramanyam and
Greenaway, 1992; Shepley, 1992). This association is connected with the
opportunities which integration offers to exploit firm-specific ownership
advantages. Evidence also shows, as we saw earlier, that the EC '1992'
program has been associated with a growth in inward FDI. The growth
of Japanese FDI since the early 1980s has a number of explanations.
These can be broadly classified into three groups: finance and cost of
capital explanations; trade policy explanations (which have a '1992'
dimension); and other factors including EC market size, globalization
strategies of Japanese firms, ownership advantages enjoyed by Japanese
firms, and the response of Japanese firms to increased regionalization of
EC trade. We examine these in turn.

7.4.1   Finance and cost of capital

Finance-oriented explanations attribute the growth of Japanese FDI to
the sustained current account surpluses enjoyed by Japan and the

appreciation of the yen. In theory, a current account surplus translates into a capital outflow to preserve balance of payments equilibrium. Also, the appreciation of the yen lowers the cost of acquisition of assets valued in dollars and other foreign currencies. There is, however, no suggestion in this theoretical construct that the outflow of capital would necessarily take the form of FDI, particularly since portfolio options are widening with the liberalization of stock markets. These financial factors do pave the way for portfolio capital movements out of Japan, but FDI requires more than just access to finance. In the absence of some form of ownership advantages related to technology or management, an FDI operation owned and managed by the capital-exporting country cannot be mounted. It is not inconceivable for FDI to occur without a major outflow of capital from the investing country provided the investing firms possess ownership advantages which are not enjoyed by firms in the host countries. Access to relatively inexpensive sources of finance is neither necessary nor sufficient for FDI to occur. Having said that, however, macroeconomic factors are clearly relevant to explaining why much Japanese FDI is financed from Japan rather than in the host country. Japan's current account surplus may mean that the cost of capital in Tokyo is lower than in, say, London, providing an incentive to raise funds in the former. Moreover, as we have noted, a large proportion of total Japanese FDI is in financial services, a part of which may indeed be the recycling of current account surpluses.

7.4.2 Import restrictions and FDI

The second set of explanations center on the impact of import restrictions on inward FDI. Simply put, the argument is that, faced with restrictions, exporting firms choose to penetrate foreign markets through FDI. This proposition can be traced back to Mundell's (1957) demonstration that trade in goods and international movement of factors can be substitutes. This is a much-discussed phenomenon in the context of FDI in developing countries. Several countries that have pursued an import-substitution strategy, such as India and Indonesia, have attracted foreign firms into their protected industries. But as Bhagwati (1978) has argued, protection is one among many factors which influences the magnitude of FDI in a country and, with due adjustments for political stability and economic size, it is countries with relatively free foreign-trade regimes that attract a relatively high volume of FDI.[3] Evidence from studies on US investment in the EC during the 1960s also suggests that the prospects of growth and an enlarged market rather than restrictions on imports from non-member countries played a major role in the decision of US firms to invest in the EC.

Even so, it can be argued that Japanese FDI is 'different'. Both the nature and extent of restrictions on Japanese exports differ from those faced by American firms now or in the past. Japanese exports are subject to a number of source-specific restrictions including anti-dumping actions and voluntary export restraints (VERs), especially so in the case of electronic goods and transport equipment. Most VERs are negotiated by EC member states and these restrictions have induced Japanese firms to invest in the EC to circumvent them. Once producing within the EC these firms can also export to EC markets which are not subject to VERs. By contrast, in developing countries, import restrictions may have failed to induce substantial amounts of FDI because of the absence of a healthy investment climate and a wider regional market.

The logical conclusion of this line of reasoning is that Japanese FDI in the EC is of the tariff-jumping variety. This carries with it the implication that the natural method of foreign market penetration preferred by Japanese and other East Asian firms is exporting as opposed to FDI. It is only when they are deterred from exporting that they resort to FDI. If this were so, tariff-jumping FDI would be inferior to that which takes place spontaneously.

Although one can link some investments to the presence of particular restraints (as in the automobile sector), it is unlikely that Japanese FDI is undertaken by firms which possess little by way of ownership advantages. Otherwise, tariff-jumping FDI would occur in one burst immediately following the imposition of import restrictions (as may be occurring in some Eastern European countries), rather than expanding steadily over the years as it in fact has done. Moreover, evidence shows that managerial practices and technological superiority are the main ownership advantage most Japanese firms possess, and they have transferred such advantages to the host EC countries. Evidence based on surveys of Japanese firms in Europe, conducted by JETRO (1991), suggest that most of the firms surveyed assigned a relatively low rank to import restrictions as a reason for their decision to invest. The group which cited this most frequently was the manufacturers of components for the transport equipment industry. While most other groups cited import restrictions as a factor, they assigned them much less weight compared with other factors such as globalization of Japanese business to meet the needs of European consumers, and the need to supply components to other Japanese manufacturers in Europe.

Bhagwati (1985, 1987) has proposed another novel trade-oriented explanation for FDI from Japan. Grounded in the political economy of protection, it is that FDI takes place not to circumvent tariffs but to defuse the threat of protection. This is quite distinct from the tariff-jumping explanation. In the latter, FDI occurs *after* the imposition of protection; in the former, it occurs *in anticipation of* its imposition, in which case FDI which transfers technology and promotes employment is in the nature of a bribe paid to the host country in return for allowing free access to the investor country's exports. Hence Bhagwati's coining of the term 'quid pro quo FDI'. The investment undertaken in the first period in anticipation of the threat of tariffs in the second period may not be profitable but, to the extent that it paves the way for exports in the second period, it is in the interest of the investor country. The lobbyists for the exporting countries can cite the benefits from FDI to soften protectionist demands from protectionist lobbies in the host countries. Bhagwati cites several examples of such quid pro quo FDI from Japan in the US including joint ventures between Japanese and US firms, especially in automobiles.

Quid pro quo FDI may serve to preserve liberalized trade regimes and could be a major force in damping protectionist pressures. While there is some evidence in support of quid pro quo FDI in the context of Japanese FDI in the US, its incidence in the EC cannot be established with certainty. The bargaining process in the EC is more complicated, because an investor may be seeking to appease both member-state lobbies and EC lobbies. The enthusiasm with which relatively depressed regions in the EC are embracing Japanese FDI may be one sign of the growth of the quid pro quo variety of FDI, but it could also be consistent with other explanations, in particular the provision of investment incentives.

There is a widespread belief that one of the principal factors in the surge of East Asian FDI in the EC is the concern that the Single Market would be heavily protected. The existing structure of protection with national quotas would give way to EC-wide quotas and a tighter trade regime. Most surveys and interviews with Japanese businessmen indicate that fear of 'Fortress Europe' is one factor in their decision to invest. Is it likely that FDI undertaken in response to perceived threats of protection will succeed in warding off protection, or is it merely a case of getting inside the fortress before the drawbridge is removed? Japanese firms inside the EC may have a better chance of limiting if not eliminating protection than firms outside. For one thing, increased production by Japanese firms inside the EC would reduce the need to impose tariffs and quotas to the extent that such FDI displaces imports. For another the visible contribution of Japanese firms to employment and investment in the EC would dilute the case of the lobbies for protection and create counter-forces – the role of the UK government in attempting to resist tight European VERs on Japanese autos is a good example. Moreover, the EC with resident Japanese firms would be a strong contender for export markets elesewhere in the world, including Japan. For these reasons a proportion of Japanese FDI in the EC could qualify as quid pro quo FDI.

7.4.3 Market growth and FDI

The prospects of a vast unified market within the EC involving 330 million people (360 million with EFTA included) is a major attraction to inward investors. Although opinion is divided on the issue, the formation of the Single Market is expected to add 5 per cent to the growth rate of the GDP of the EC over the next five years, to create two million extra jobs, and to provide economies of scale and scope and thereby reduce manufacturing costs substantially. Available evidence suggests that these benefits of integration are a major factor in the decision of Japanese firms to invest in the EC. Most Japanese firms in the EC surveyed by JETRO (1991) assign the objective of serving consumers in the EC as a major factor in their decision to invest.

Dynamic effects of integration as opposed to the static trade creation and trade diversion effects have been widely noted in the literature on integration. While increased FDI in response to existing levels of protection or perceived threats of protection would be in the nature of investment diversion, FDI which takes place in response to potential dynamic benefits of integration could be regarded as investment creation. Protection or even threats of protection which induce investment in the EC would displace imports financed by domestic investment. Whether or not it results in domestic production within the EC comparable in price and quality with that of the imports it displaces is arguable. If such domestic production is expensive relative to imports, import-displacing FDI could be regarded as investment diversion analogous to trade diversion.

Investment-creating FDI would create trade and be complementary to it rather than a substitute for it. Quid pro quo FDI which does not displace trade would also belong to this category. A characteristic of such FDI would be the exploitation of ownership advantages and the transfer of skills and know-how to which it gives rise. This would promote intra-industry trade within the EC, building on the opportunities for scale and scope economies which integration affords. Recent trends in FDI and trade in the Asian region show that both intra-Asian trade and intra-Asian FDI have increased substantially with FDI. This is also likely to be the case in the Single Market, with both East Asian and American FDI promoting intra-European trade. We noted earlier the proposition advanced by Mundcll (1957) that trade in goods and factor movements are substitutes. Agmon (1979) showed that where intra-industry trade is concerned, trade and factor movements are more likely to be complements. In fact Markusen (1983) shows that the Mundellian case may indeed be a special one. Thus, there are sound theoretical reasons for expecting trade in goods and FDI to grow together.

7.5   Policy coordination within regions

The EC has a common commercial policy vis-à-vis third countries, including a common external tariff. Moreover, variations in the level of the tariff, and exceptions to it, are negotiated at the Community level. In recent years, however, this common policy has been eroded by national measures, most notably source-specific restraints such as VERs. This seems to be part of a wider process often referred to as instrument substitution. Together with a wide range of other non-tariff measures, these have served to fragment the EC market in some sectors (for example, automobiles and textiles). The '1992' program aims to sweep these away. Harmonization of a range of policies, together with the abolition of Article 115 provisions, will result in a truly common commercial policy. This reduces the scope for independent action on the part of individual member states.

In the past, measures like VERs have proved attractive as a palliative to adjustment problems. Once that degree of freedom is foreclosed, there is a possibility that in the same way that VERs substituted for tariffs, investment policy could be substituted for VERs. The extent to which this occurs will be fashioned by adjustment pressures, and the degree to which state aid and regional support policies are harmonized. The Cecchini Report and other analyses have forecast adjustment pressures in the form of transitional unemployment. From an economic stand-point, this is neither a surprise nor necessarily a problem. After all, adjustment is the price we pay for growth-enhancing change. However, from a political economy standpoint, adjustment pressures can be troublesome, particularly when they are non-randomly distributed. It is not easy to forecast exactly which sectors/regions will be most affected. Two points can, however, be made. First, some recent research suggests that the marked increase in intra-industry specialization may have recently tailed off, and possibly even reversed (Greenaway and Hine, 1991). The importance of this is that adjustment to trade expansion may be smoother in a setting of intra- as opposed to inter-industry expansion. The second point is that the EC already has a 'regional problem' in that a number of areas, largely on the periphery, are relatively underdeveloped and have relatively low incomes per head and relatively high unemployment. These sectors could be more exposed in the adjustment to market completion.

For these reasons governments could come under pressure to provide adjustment assistance of some form. As already noted, source-specific restraints have proved popular in the past, and some alternative such as state aids to encourage investment could prove popular in the future. From the Community's standpoint there are dangers associated with uncoordinated action. First, some of the benefits of a common commercial policy could be eroded if member states make greater independent use of regional investment incentives to attract FDI. Second, conflicts over investment policy could spill over to other issues, thereby threatening consensus. Third, from the standpoint of the Community as a whole, competition between member states to attract inward FDI redistributes some of the potential gains from FDI away from the host country and toward the investing corporation.

The discussion in the previous section implied that alternative policies can substitute for each other. The basic theory of trade policy confirms that this is so. Recent research has revealed important interconnections between trade policy, investment policy, competition policy and regulation in the services sector. Therefore, in addition to harmonization of investment measures, there is also an issue of the compatibility of investment and other measures. The problem of policy compatibility arises for three reasons. First, as we have already stressed, increasing openness means that investment policy can no longer be thought of simply as a non-border measure. Many instruments of investment policy have trade effects. Second, and related to the foregoing, different instruments of policy can have equivalent effects. And third, investment policy might have multiple objectives, both macroeconomic and microeconomic. This potentially gives rise to two problems: feedback between policy instruments, and porosity across instruments.

Feedback can be positive or negative, reinforcing or counteracting the effects of other policies. An example of positive feedback is where tax allowances encourage investment in a particular region, where other government investments such as in central services are in place. An example of negative feedback is where state aids to encourage investment in a particular sector run counter to the objectives of competition policy. Clearly in the latter case policy conflict arises. Not only can this lead to conflict between agencies; it can also stimulate further feedback effects.

The latter is related to the problem of porosity. Because different policy instruments can have equivalent effects, regulation in one area can lead to increased use of unregulated instruments. If, for example, investment grants are tightly regulated, more flexible arrangements on reporting, or intellectual property protection, could be offered to attract a MNE. This is important from both a regional and a multilateral stand-point. If there are perceived to be net benefits from FDI, and if governments compete to secure such investment, the by-product distortions of intervention are minimized with compatible policies. With further integration, this becomes increasingly important.

There is also a global dimension to this. One of the major priorities for the Uruguay Round negotiations is to ensure that agreements on TRIMs, subsidies, services and IPRs are compatible. Beyond the Uruguay Round, a key issue for any new Multilateral Trade Organization is the compatibility of regulation in these areas with competition policy. These are issues to which we now turn.

7.6   Multilateral policy coordination

From the above discussion two points stand out. First, MNEs are key actors, and increasingly so, in the process of international specialization and exchange, a process which is shaped in part by regionalism. Second, a wide range of policy instruments is available to influence the locational decisions of MNEs. By definition MNEs are internationally mobile. Their ability to arbitrage regulatory regimes or support measures can be a source of policy convergence, but also potentially a source of policy competition and policy conflict. The fact that MNEs can 'vote with their feet' can put pressure on governments to minimize disincentives to invest. One could argue that this is a natural source of self-regulation. On the other hand, however, the footloose nature of multinationals provides a source of pressure to governments to compete in the provision of distortionary incentives. This may require regulation.

The growing influence of MNEs has resulted in a great deal of inter-national negotiation and cooperation to set standards regarding the treatment which they face in host countries and, to a lesser extent, to regulate their behavior.

As noted in Section 7.2, investment policy has historically been regarded by host governments as a non-border instrument. This being so, it is hardly surprising that bilateral investment treaties should have proliferated, with close to three hundred in existence. Their function is largely as a signaling mechanism – host governments commit themselves to certain standards of treatment relating to nationalization, compensation, most-favored-nation (MFN) treatment, dispute settlement and so on. As such they can offer insurance of sorts to inward investors. As with bilateral trade agreements, however, the resulting patchwork may be a less-efficient, less-transparent solution than a multilateral regime.

There have been a large number of regional and multilateral investment agreements since the early 1960s, but especially of regional arrangements (UNCTC, 1990). Mostly they are directed at setting standards relating to, *inter alia*, treatment of investors, investment climate, entry conditions, ownership, conditions of employment, transfer of technology, consumer protection, jurisdiction, and dispute settlement. The most active multilateral forum has been the OECD, followed by the World Bank. Since, however, GATT is becoming involved, it could become the lead institution.

TRIMs were explicitly included as an agenda item in the Uruguay Round. At the time of writing, no draft agreement has proved acceptable to all parties. Developing countries in particular have resisted multilateral disciplines on the grounds that many TRIMs do not have direct trade-distorting effects, and even those that do are investment measures rather than border measures. The submissions of most industrial countries are equally adamant that some TRIMs (most notably local content and minimum export requirements) have trade-distorting effects, and their use needs to be disciplined. The principle of a waiver for the least-developed countries has been accepted, albeit on a time-constrained basis. Since local content requirements have been found by a GATT panel to be contrary to Article III in at least one important case (against the Canadian FIRA), it is probable that greater discipline can be brought to bear on TRIMs through existing mechanisms. This, together with the (surprising) degree of consensus on the part of industrial countries regarding the principle of disciplining trade-distorting TRIMs, makes an eventual agreement likely.

As we saw in Section 7.2, investment incentives are also a fairly heterogeneous mix of instruments. The most-commonly used are some form of direct subsidy (typically operating through a cash grant), accelerated depreciation or development subvention. Several GATT articles pertain to subsidies, including Articles VI, XVI and XXIII. The first of these sanctions recourse to countervailing duties (CVDs), if material injury to domestic producers can be associated with a foreign subsidy. Article XVI places an obligation on contracting parties to notify any trade-relevant subsidies, while Article XXIII provides dispute-settlement procedures. The Code on Subsidies agreed in the Tokyo Round supplements and clarifies these obligations but has not worked well. Thus, subsidies too are an agenda item in the Uruguay Round. Some convergence has occurred on the part of contracting parties around the so-called traffic-light approach (see Balasubramanyam and Greenaway, 1992). The sticking point to an agreement here relates not to the traffic-light principle but to the components of the various categories. As with TRIMs, if an agreement is reached it should bring greater discipline to the use of investment incentives.

The final issue to consider on multilateral issues is how disciplines could evolve under the auspices of GATT. This is not to assert that the GATT is the only forum in which agreement could be reached; both the UN and the OECD have been active in this respect. However, if significant progress is to be made, the GATT is the key institution as it is in a position to nest any codes in the wider framework of trade rules. This is especially important since investment rules are part of a much bigger picture. As borders shift back with increasing openness, and the role of conventional trade instruments (most notably tariffs) declines, issues that were formerly regarded as non-border measures – investment policies, regulation of services, protection of intellectual property, competition policy – are increasingly becoming the subject of trade friction within and between regions. The inclusion of services, intellectual property rights and TRIMs on the Uruguay Round agenda is an acknowledgement of this. Circumstances in the world economy and world trading system have changed profoundly since the GATT's inception, and the need for a more rules-based system which can accommodate investment, as well as other issues, is paramount.

This of course begs the question of exactly how investment can be accommodated under GATT disciplines. This question is addressed by Greenaway and Sapir (1992) in an assessment of progress on all the new issues. It is argued there that GATT disciplines as they apply to merchandise trade could not be transposed to the new issues. Complete harmonization is not necessarily desirable because differences in regulatory regimes arise for historical reasons, and it is not always clear that one regulatory regime is necessarily more efficient than another. Efforts at complete harmonization would quickly run up against the buffer of national sovereignty. However, existing principles can be extended to the new issues in general, and investment in particular. Specifically, national treatment, mutual recognition and MFN are all transferable. In the case of investment the first two are especially important. For the Uruguay Round this means identifying those TRIMs which have significant trade-distorting effects and affirming the applicability of appropriate GATT articles. As argued above, however, TRIMs are only part of the picture and, in the longer term, a code covering direct investment is required embracing rights of establishment, home- and host-country obligations, and dispute-settlement mechanisms.

7.7   Concluding comments

We began by reviewing the growth in FDI in general and Japanese FDI in the EC in particular. Our interest in this stems from the observed association between regional integration and FDI. A number of possible explanations of the growth in FDI were reviewed. The range of policy instruments which can be deployed were discussed and the possible evolution of regulatory regimes both within and between regions were evaluated.

Japanese FDI into the EC has grown dramatically. A priori theorizing and empirical evidence suggests that this is partly due to the potential growth of the EC's Single Market but may also be of a quid pro quo nature. Its location may have been influenced by the willingness of Member States to provide support and incentives. FDI promotes international specialization and, when it is of a quid pro quo nature, may also help defuse protectionist threats. In this respect, the upsurge of investment in Europe may help to reduce the likelihood of a 'Fortress Europe' emerging. However, there are employment and other benefits which derive from FDI and which encourage governments to compete in their efforts to attract it. This competition occurs both within and between regions. As we saw, there are some dangers of spill-over to other areas of policy. At present, multilateral disciplines on the use of investment incentives and disincentives are relatively weak and need to be strengthened. With the inclusion of TRIMs on the Uruguay Round agenda, investment measures are, for the first time, being explicitly embraced by GATT. A MTO agreement would pave the way for more comprehensive disciplines.

Notes

The authors gratefully acknowledge research assistance from Mohammed Salisu, and helpful comments on the first draft from participants at the GATT conference, in particular Wouter de Ploey, John Whalley, Richard Snape and Murray Smith, and useful advice and support from the editors.
1. Following the IMF, foreign direct investment is defined as investment operating in an economy other than that of the investor, the purpose being to have an effective voice in the management of the enterprise. The data on FDI in this paragraph are from the UN Centre on Transnational Corporations and JETRO (1992).
2. Shepley (1992) has recently criticized this framework as being too static. For purposes of specifying a model which explains a particular investment, this may be so. However, the framework is still useful as a means of commenting on the range of influences that may be relevant. Moreover, it is possible to integrate dynamic considerations into the framework. For example, technological competence can be thought as an ownership advantage.
3. For empirical support for this argument, see Balasubramanyam and Salisu (1991) and the references therein.

References

Agmon, T. (1979), 'Direct Investment and Intra-Industry Trade: Substitutes or Complements?', in *On the Economics of Intra-Industry Trade*, edited by H. Giersch, Tübingen: J. C. B. Mohr.

Balasubramanyam, V. N. and D. Greenaway (1992), 'Economic Integration and FDI: Japanese Investment in the EC', *Journal of Common Market Studies* **30**: 175–94.

Balasubramanyam, V. N. and M. Salisu (1991), 'EP, IS and Direct Foreign Investment in LDCs', in *International Trade and Global Development: Essays in Honour of Jagdish Bhagwati*, edited by A. Koekkoek and L. B. M. Mennes, London: Routledge.

Bhagwati, J. N. (1978), *Foreign Exchange Regimes and Economic Development: Anatomy and Consequences of Exchange Control Regimes*, Cambridge: Ballinger for the National Bureau of Economic Research (NBER).

Bhagwati, J. N. (1985), 'Investing Abroad', Esmee Fairbain Lecture delivered at the University of Lancaster.

Bhagwati, J. N. (1987), 'VERs, quid pro quo DFI and VIEs: Political-Economy-Theoretic Analysis', *International Economic Journal* **1**: 1–4.

Cantwell, J. (1992), 'International Production and International Trade', in *Surveys in International Trade*, edited by D. Greenaway and L. A. Winters, Oxford: Basil Blackwell.

Dunning, J. (1988), *Explaining International Production*, London: Unwin Hyman.

Graham, E. and P. R. Krugman (1991), *Foreign Direct Investment in the United States*, Washington, DC: Institute for International Economics.

Greenaway, D. (1987), 'Intra-Industry Trade, Intra-Firm Trade and European Integration', *Journal of Common Market Studies* **26**: 153–72.

Greenaway , D. (1990), 'Trade-Related Investment Measures: Political Economy Aspects and Issues for GATT', *The World Economy* **13**: 367–86.

Greenaway, D. and R. C. Hine (1991), 'Intra-Industrial Specialisation, Trade Expansion and Adjustment in the European Economic Space', *Journal of Common Market Studies* **25**: 603–22.

Greenaway, D. and A. Sapir (1992), 'New Issues in the Uruguay Round: Services, TRIMs and TRIPs', *European Economic Review* **36**: 509–18.

JETRO (Japan External Trade Organization) (1991), *Survey of European Operations of Japanese Companies in the Manufacturing Sector*, 7th Survey Report, London: JETRO.

JETRO (Japan External Trade Organization) (1992), *White Paper on Foreign Direct Investment*, London: JETRO.

Lipsey, R. (1991), 'Foreign Direct Investment in the US and US Trade', National Bureau of Economic Research (NBER) Working Paper No. 3623, Cambridge, MA: NBER.

Markusen, J. (1983), 'Factor Movements and Commodity Trade as Complements', *Journal of International Economics* **14**: 341–56.

Mundell, R. A. (1957), 'International Trade and Factor Mobility', *American Economic Review* **48**: 321–35.

Shepley, S. (1992), 'FDI in the Context of European Economic Integration', mimeo, European Commission, Brussels.

UNCTC (United Nations Centre on Transnational Corporations) (1990), *Regional Economic Integration and the Transnational Corporations in the 1990s*, New York: UNCTC.

Yannopolous, G. (1990), 'Foreign Direct Investment and European Integration: The Evidence from the Formative Years of the European Community', *Journal of Common Market Studies* **28**: 235–59.

8

Regional integration agreements and macroeconomic discipline

Hans Genberg and Francisco Nadal De Simone

The question we address in this chapter is whether macroeconomic policy can be important for the success or failure of regional integration arrangements and, if so, whether it is possible to make an inventory of the macroeconomic preconditions that facilitate such integration. Even though the answer depends in part on the degree of economic integration pursued, it is possible to say in general that market integration and interdependence among a group of economies produce the need for some coordination of their macroeconomic policies. But coordination, although necessary, is not sufficient for reaping all the benefits from integration. Macroeconomic policy *discipline* also is required for the integration process to take place and be beneficial.

The discussion of the links between market integration and macroeconomic policy is made particularly difficult by the lack of a sufficiently general theory of economic integration. Earlier work on the topic discerned at least five stages in the process of abolishing policy-designed discrimination between domestic and foreign goods, services and factors of production. Balassa (1962) distinguished between: a free trade area (FTA); a customs union (CU); a common market (CM); an economic union (EU); and total economic integration. In the first three levels of economic integration, governments are assumed to interfere in the economy only at the border and with commercial policy (Pelkmans, 1980). Economic policy more generally is assumed to be exogenous. In the last two levels, governments are assumed to perform a much larger role in the economy as they are involved in monetary, fiscal and exchange rate policies, and as they are also assumed to work together within an institutional framework that allows other member states to influence national policy decisions.

In the context of examining whether and, if so, why there is a relation between market integration on the one hand and macroeconomic performance and policies on the other, two specific questions are examined: (1) what degree of macroeconomic policy coordination and discipline is necessary for economic integration agreements to have their desired effects, and (2) whether increased market integration affects the incentives of policy makers to surrender part of their policy autonomy and to submit to a certain degree of discipline that they otherwise would not have observed.

The first section of the chapter presents some stylized facts about macroeconomic policies in three areas which have pursued economic integration, the EC in Europe, and the CACM and the LAFTA/LAIA in Latin America. The experiences of these areas raise a number of issues concerning the extent to which the relative success of European integration has been due to macroeconomic policy convergence, and the extent to which large real exchange rate fluctuations have been detrimental to the Latin American processes.

To analyze the question of policy integration, Section 8.2 reviews the mechanisms through which macroeconomic disturbances are transmitted between countries. The influence of various forms of economic integration on these transmission mechanisms is investigated in some detail, and it is shown that market integration increases the cross-border effects of macroeconomic policies and decreases the domestic effects. Market integration thus increases macroeconomic interdependence, which in turn increases the need for policy integration.[1] However, policy integration must be accompanied by policy discipline in order to be beneficial. The issue of how the process of economic integration influences the behavior (discipline) of policy makers is addressed in Section 8.3. That section also discusses the need for special institutional arrangements to support the process of macroeconomic policy integration.

The final section summarizes the main points and draws some conclusions from the analysis for the likely success of current integration processes such as the NAFTA, those between Central and Eastern European countries and the EC, and Mercosur.

8.1   Macroeconomic developments and regional integration: some lessons from the EC, CACM and LAIA

Three regional integration agreements (RIAs), one among industrial countries – the European Communities (EC) – and two among developing countries – the Central American Common Market (CACM) and the Latin American Integration Association (LAIA, formerly the Latin

Table 8.1 Targets, means and achievements of selected regional integration agreements

Regional group	Target	Means	Achievements
European Community (EC). Treaty of Rome of 1957; Single European Act of 1987.	Free movement of goods, services, factors of production.	Free trade in goods and a common external tariff. Exchange rate arrangements to reduce exchange rate variability. Harmonization of rules affecting mobility of goods, services and factors of production. A very restrictive agricultural policy.	Removal of tariffs by 1968; removal of QRs ahead of schedule; common external tariff ahead of schedule. Members acted on schedule. 1992 program is on schedule so far.
Central American Common Market (CACM). Signed in 1960 and effective in 1961.	Customs union for processed goods originating in member countries and industrial planning. Removal of foreign exchange constraints in intra-CACM trade.	Common external tariff and clearing-house arrangement.	After a promising start in the 1960s, deteriorated in the 1970s because of political and economic difficulties. Revitalization is underway, but the integration level achieved in the late 1960s has not yet been regained. Common external tariff is not effective in all members.
Latin American Integration Association (LAFTA/LAIA). Signed in 1960 and effective in 1961 as LAFTA, and in 1980 as LAIA.	Free trade association and industrial planning. Facilitation of bilateral cooperation.	Regional tariff preferences, additional bilateral preferences, industrial cooperation, clearing and credit schemes.	Partial implementation in the 1960s. Intra-regional trade expanded mostly for manufacturers. In 1987, about 40 per cent of intra-LAIA imports were eligible for preferences, with variations by country in product coverage. Tariff cuts in specific industries between congenial partners (e.g., Argentina and Brazil) are disproportionate.

American Free Trade Association or LAFTA) – will be briefly discussed with the aim of identifying the role of macroeconomic factors in their respective developments. As background, Table 8.1 provides a summary of the targets pursued, the means used, and the achievements of these integration agreements.

In the literature, the preconditions normally identified for the success of a RIA refer to the structural characteristics of the member countries that make market integration optimal, *inter alia*, large intra-regional trade before the creation of the RIA, a low common external tariff, or similar production and price structures.[2] While we agree that these characteristics are of paramount importance, in keeping with the focus of the chapter we emphasize here only the macroeconomic factors that influence the success or failure of RIAs in achieving their integration objectives.

The Treaty of Rome of 1957 stated that the objective of the EC was the creation of a CM. However, until the Single European Act was put into effect from 1987, only the free mobility of goods and a common commercial policy vis-à-vis the rest of the world were implemented. All tariffs on goods were removed by 1968 and quantitative restrictions were eliminated ahead of schedule. The setting of a common external tariff also took place ahead of schedule in 1970.[3] The share of intra-regional exports in total exports of the EC grew from less than 35 per cent in 1960 to nearly 49 per cent in 1970 before leveling off in the 1970s (de la Torre and Kelly, 1992). In the 1980s, the share of EC intra-regional trade increased again to reach about 60 per cent in 1990. After the Single European Act was signed, the EC resumed moving toward the full implementation of the Treaty of Rome and the creation of an EU. By June 1991, about 70 per cent of the nearly 300 proposals submitted by the EC Commission concerning the creation of the Single Market had been approved by the EC Council, and about 70 per cent of them had been implemented at the national level. In the area of money and finance, integration has gone particularly far. Capital movements have already been almost completely liberalized, and at the time of writing only Greece did not participate in the exchange rate mechanism of the EMS, and, with the exception of Ireland and Portugal, exchange controls have been lifted. In December 1991, the EC member countries agreed to establish a single currency and a common central bank by 1999. Convergence of inflation rates, as measured by changes in the GDP deflator, has increased since 1987 when compared with the period 1979–86 (Table 8.2). Remaining areas where full agreement has yet to be achieved include the free movement of people, the harmonization of indirect taxation, and imports affecting politically sensitive sectors.

Table 8.2 GDP deflators, EC, LAIA and CACM economies (average percentage change), 1960 to 1991[a]

A. *EC*

	1960–78			1979–86			1987–90		
	Av.	Max.	Min.	Av.	Max.	Min.	Av.	Max.	Min.
Belgium	6	13	1	5	7	4	2	5	2
Denmark	8	13	5	6	11	4	2	5	2
France	7	13	3	8	12	5	2	3	3
Germany	5	8	2	3	5	2	2	3	2
Greece	7	21	1	17	25	18	12	20	13
Ireland	9	24	− 1	9	17	5	2	5	− 1
Italy	9	20	2	12	20	8	5	8	6
Luxembourg	5	17	− 4	5	11	2	3	6	2
Netherlands	7	15	1	3	6	1	2	3	− 1
Portugal	9	26	1	26	72	19	10	14	11
Spain	11	23	0	10	17	10	5	7	6
United Kingdom	8	27	1	7	20	4	5	7	5

B. *LAFTA/LAIA*

	1960–82			1983–90		
	Av.	Max.	Min.	Av.	Max.	Min.
Argentina	67	432	− 9	351	3300	78
Bolivia	18	179	1	223	13641	12
Brazil	42	105	− 5	365	2564	141
Chile	74	692	− 5	18	33	14
Colombia	17	29	7	22	29	20
Ecuador	9	40	− 10	37	75	21
Mexico	13	61	0	56	139	25
Paraguay	9	24	− 1	25	36	14
Peru	24	100	2	365	6328	75
Uruguay	49	118	11	62	101	53
Venezuela	7	45	− 3	27	84	3

C. *CACM*

	1960–75			1976–91		
	Av.	Max.	Min.	Av.	Max.	Min.
Costa Rica	7	25	− 1	21	84	8
El Salvador	3	11	− 6	14	37	1
Guatemala	3	16	− 2	14	42	4
Honduras	4	12	1	8	28	2
Nicaragua	5	23	− 1	299	13243	5

Note: [a] Calculations for Belgium, Denmark, Portugal, Costa Rica and Nicaragua start in 1961. Data for Brazil start only in 1964. Data for 1990 are not available for Argentina. Average annual percentage changes are calculated using the geometric mean.

Sources: International Monetary Fund, *International Financial Statistics*, Washington, D.C., various years. Data for Portugal are from the OECD, *National Accounts*, Paris, various years. Data for Mexico (years 1987 to 1989) are from Banco de México, *Indicadores Económicos*, March 1992.

The EC integration agreement has been conspicuously more successful than agreements among developing countries. Within Latin American countries, however, there is a wide spectrum of relative failure and success. Two cases will be used as illustrations here, the CACM and LAFTA/LAIA.

As stated by Langhammer and Hiemenz (1991), Latin American countries adopted regional integration to surmount the limits of import substitution in narrow domestic markets and to increase their competitiveness before opening to the world market. However, they did not have a high level of institutional integration. The CACM between El Salvador, Guatemala, Honduras and Nicaragua was signed in 1960 and became effective in 1961. Costa Rica became a member in 1962. The objective of the agreement was the creation of a CM and the promotion of region-wide industrial planning. It was the developing world's most ambitious RIA, as it included a regional payments system and the removal of foreign exchange constraints on intra-CACM trade. It also provided for the harmonization of fiscal policies. During the first decade, the CACM achieved greater success in trade liberalization than in industrial planning. In 1966, more than 94 per cent of the items of the CACM tariff classification were subject to free trade and a common external tariff (Edwards and Savastano, 1989). By 1970, it had reached CU status. Intra-regional trade shares climbed from 6 per cent in 1960 for imports and 7 per cent for exports to about 24 and 27 per cent respectively in 1970. Some of the traded products also penetrated other markets. However, problems appeared due to asymmetries in the system reflected in balance-of-payments imbalances, especially for the poorer members (Honduras and Nicaragua). These problems contributed to the gradual decline of the arrangement. Falling prices of primary commodities by the end of the 1960s made countries incur serious foreign exchange losses. The conflict between Honduras and El Salvador further increased tension in the external position of the member countries. Efforts to revitalize the RIA started, but were negatively affected by external economic shocks. The oil-price rises of the 1970s and the international debt problem were the final blow to the CACM. Non-tariff barriers were reinstated, the clearing mechanism was blocked, and exchange controls spread. In the mid-1980s, a new common external tariff was put in place, coinciding with a real depreciation of the currencies of most member countries. Intra-regional trade started growing again but the general trend since then has been toward bilateralism and the disintegration of the CACM.

In contrast to the CACM, LAFTA was originally a free trade association aimed at industrial planning and at facilitating bilateral cooperation. The agreement was signed in 1960 between Argentina,

Bolivia, Brazil, Chile, Colombia, Ecuador, Mexico, Paraguay, Peru, Uruguay and Venezuela. It became effective in 1961. It focused only on preferential trading arrangements. The expansion of intra-regional trade, the main way sought to increase integration, stagnated after a promising start. As stated by Langhammer and Hiemenz (1991), the import-substitution strategy of LAFTA (implemented through regional tariff preferences and additional bilateral preferences) was viewed as a way of countering both a deterioration in the terms of trade and a dependence on imports of capital goods from industrial countries. However, a role was also played by the vested interest of the large countries in new markets for local, inward-oriented, non-competitive industries, which viewed regional preferences as substitutes for the higher costs of adjusting to other international markets. The share of intra-regional trade rose from 8 per cent in 1960 to 10 per cent in 1970 and about 14 per cent in 1980 in value terms. However, this was mostly the result of terms-of-trade changes. In fact, empirical evidence seems to point to more trade diversion than trade creation (Langhammer and Hiemenz, 1991). The failure of LAFTA moved members to establish looser forms of cooperation and intra-regional trade liberalization on a bilateral basis, resulting in the formation of LAIA in 1980. LAIA moved away from a strategy of import substitution toward the promotion of already existing bilateral trade relations, thereby increasing the differences between countries in preferential trade and in market access. Disintegration accelerated when the oil shocks and the international debt problems affected countries asymmetrically. Countries adopted different policy responses, which led to large changes in real effective exchange rates (Table 8.3). The debt crisis had a negative impact on intra-regional trade. In 1983–4, the share of intra-Latin American exports reached its lowest value since 1970. Protectionism grew in almost every country so that it was generally higher in the mid-1980s than it had been in the beginning of the decade. The share of intra-regional exports of LAIA fell to about 10 per cent in 1990, close to the level of 1970.

It is widely accepted that RIAs among industrial countries have been more successful than RIAs among developing economies (de la Torre and Kelly, 1992). A basic problem with the design of RIAs among developing countries is what Langhammer and Hiemenz (1991) call the 'fallacy of transposition', that is, in taking the EC as a model of integration. This implies forgetting that initial conditions are crucial for the success of a RIA. Those conditions include an initial high level of intra-regional trade, the capability and willingness to provide intra-regional transfer payments in case of uneven distribution of the costs of integration, the development of supranational institutions, the similarity of income and industrialization levels, and a certain congeniality of macroeconomic policy.

Table 8.3 Changes in real effective exchange rates of the LAFTA/LAIA economies (average annual percentage change), 1960 to 1991[a]

Country	Average (1)	Standard deviation (2)	Coefficient of variation (1)/(2)	Maximum	Minimum
1960–82:					
Argentina	28.7	155	5	739	−61
Bolivia	−0.7	19	−28	28	−67
Brazil	1.3	20	16	43	−52
Chile	5.2	21	4	84	−14
Colombia	0.2	10	45	21	−20
Ecuador	−1.1	11	−10	23	−34
Mexico	1.1	13	11	40	−26
Paraguay	−0.3	18	−66	49	−58
Peru	−0.3	17	−64	54	−37
Uruguay	−2.5	20	−8	38	−41
Venezuela	0.9	9	10	33	−20
1983–91:					
Argentina[b]	0.2	35	197	82	−44
Bolivia	6.4	20	3	36	−31
Brazil	−3.9	13	−3	27	−25
Chile	4.3	10	2	22	−16
Colombia	5.9	8	1	16	−8
Ecuador	7.8	19	3	47	−23
Mexico	−1.0	19	−19	38	−23
Paraguay	10.4	32	3	66	−40
Peru	−10.2	20	−2	15	−36
Uruguay	3.8	20	5	43	−33
Venezuela	11.1	29	3	55	−21

Notes: [a] Price competitiveness is calculated by deflating nominal exchange rates of each country, with respect to all its trading partners in LAFTA/LAIA, by consumer price indices.
[b] Data for Argentina are not available for 1991.

Sources: Authors' calculations based on data from the International Monetary Fund, *International Financial Statistics*, Washington, DC, various issues.

The lessons that can be drawn from the illustration provided by the RIAs discussed above encompass many different aspects of both micro- and macroeconomic policy making. In general, it is fair to say that the relative failure of CACM and LAFTA/LAIA to increase intra-regional trade on a durable basis can be traced back to the incompatibility of inward-oriented development − their import-substitution strategy − and regional liberalization. This created tension in the execution of the programs of tariff reductions, in the adoption of a common external tariff, and in the removal of constraints on labor mobility, thereby generating only transient trade liberalization.

Specifically, the failure of Latin American RIAs can be linked more or less directly to a characteristic feature of macroeconomic policy in the region: the frequent monetization of persistent fiscal imbalances as underdeveloped capital markets are unable to facilitate domestic deficit financing. As a result, inflation accelerates, which in turn generates pressures in the foreign exchange markets because it is inconsistent with the exchange rate policy inside the region, often a pegged rate. Pressure on the foreign exchanges results in a loss of international reserves. The usual policy reaction to the loss of reserves has been the imposition of exchange controls and trade restrictions.[4] As a result, the overvaluation of the domestic currency increases, black markets develop, and countries experience a further shortage of foreign exchange. At this stage, it becomes clear that the RIA cannot survive unless the source of the macroeconomic imbalance – the fiscal indiscipline – is removed.

Besides the incompatibility between the import-substitution strategy for development and the fiscal indiscipline of major Latin American countries, the experiences of the EC, the CACM and the LAFTA/LAIA suggest at least eleven additional possible explanations for the relative failure of RIAs among developing countries. They are as follows:

1. *Unbalanced distribution of the costs and benefits of adjustment.*
   LAFTA did not have a mechanism to prevent an uneven distribution of the costs and benefits from market integration among heterogeneous members. Large, more-industrialized members did not offer compensation to poorer members to the extent necessary to settle disputes over unbalanced trade. Growing inequalities in bilateral trade balances were also one of the reasons for the decline of the CACM. Regional transfers within the EC are more developed although many would argue that they are still insufficient to be compatible with the adoption of a common European currency.

2. *Losses of fiscal revenue by administrations with an inadequate taxation capacity.* One of the criteria for an FTA/CU to be growth-generating is that countries should be 'natural trading partners' prior to the agreement. If this criterion is met, the FTA/CU may result in a reduction of fiscal revenue as trade taxes on intra-regional trade disappear. This produces a tightening of the government's budget constraint, making it necessary to undertake fiscal adjustment measures elsewhere. However, even assuming that governments decide to follow a restrictive policy stance, tax collection and fiscal administration in most developing countries are underdeveloped and costly, and the alternative to international trade levies is simply not available. As fiscal stability during the creation of the FTA/CU is a necessary condition for the RIA to prosper, such arrangements among countries with very different capacities to tax the public and contract fiscal expenditure may not be feasible unless efficient transfer mechanisms are in place.

3. *Similarity in factor endowments produces large trade diversion effects and increases the need for real exchange rate adjustments.* De la Torre and Kelly (1992) argue that RIAs among developing countries have been less successful partly because of the presence of larger trade diversion effects than in industrial countries. The greater degree of trade diversion is the result of less favorable initial conditions, especially the low level of market integration prevailing in developing countries before the formation of the RIA. This has required more real exchange rate adjustments and increased the need for price and wage flexibility and factor mobility, characteristics that developing countries typically do not possess.

4. *Persistent macroeconomic imbalances result in real exchange rate overvaluation and make trade liberalization more difficult.* The experiences of CACM and LAFTA/LAIA clearly indicate that fiscal disequilibria recurrently were reflected in real exchange rate overvaluation, large variability of real exchange rates, and in balance-of-payments crises (Tables 8.3 and 8.4). They were thus

Table 8.4   Changes in real effective exchange rates of the CACM economies (average annual percentage change), 1960 to 1991[a]

Country	Average (1)	Standard deviation (2)	Coefficient of variation (1)/(2)	Maximum	Minimum
1960–75:[b]					
Costa Rica	1	5	4	15	−4.2
El Salvador	−1	5	−7	7	−17.5
Guatemala	0	3	9	7	−4.5
Honduras	−1	4	−4	9	−10.2
1976–90:					
Costa Rica	7	29	4	108	−35.1
El Salvador	−8	5	−1	−1	−21.3
Guatemala	7	12	2	40	−13.4
Honduras	−4	12	−3	15	−37.8
1976–90 (including Nicaragua):					
Costa Rica	35	128	4	492	−88.9
El Salvador	5	60	12	215	−82.2
Guatemala	23	76	3	278	−78.5
Honduras	25	122	5	472	−89.7
Nicaragua	256	968	4	3872	−88.5

Notes: [a] Price competitiveness is calculated by deflating nominal exchange rates of each country, with respect to all its trading partners in CACM, by consumer price indices. [b] Data on CPI for Nicaragua are not available for the period 1960–72.

Sources: Authors' calculations based on data from the International Monetary Fund, *International Financial Statistics*, Washington, DC, various issues, and Instituto Nacional de Estadísticas y Censos, *Anuario Estadístico de Nicaragua*, Managua, various issues.

inconsistent with the formation of stable RIAs.[5] They generated pressures to increase protection from non-members first and then, as imbalances continued, they increased the incentives for raising trade protection within the region. The former measures increase trade-diversion effects and the latter gave a final blow to the integration arrangement.

5. *High and variable inflation generates instability and stagnation of RIAs.* High inflation reduces the static and dynamic gains of market integration through several channels. First, high and variable inflation, by increasing real exchange rate variability, reduces the gains from intra-regional trade. While the average annual inflation rate in the EC oscillated between about 2 and 26 per cent between 1960 and 1990, it varied between 7 and more than 360 per cent in LAFTA/LAIA during the same period. Similarly, average annual changes in real effective exchange rates remained between − 4 and 4 per cent in the EC (Table 8.5), while they varied between − 10 and 29 per cent in LAFTA/LAIA. Second, in the long run, high rates of inflation (and the policy of restricting capital and current transactions that tends to accompany them) in Latin America largely explain the underdevelopment of capital markets there. Lack of access to domestic (and often foreign) financing hampers the process of mergers and acquisitions and thus of market integration. Finally, inflation and high international debts also affect the dynamic gains from integration to the extent that they are not conducive to a favorable investment climate. Between 1983 and 1989, according to the World Bank (1992), the total external debt of LAIA members was about two to nine times higher than their export earnings.

6. *The external economic environment may be a constraint to further market integration of developing economies, but domestic policy responses to external shocks are the key to maximizing the benefits from integration.* It is widely accepted in the literature that the formation of RIAs would, in general, be easier if it was not burdened by a hostile external economic environment such as that caused by restrictions to market access, recurrent oil shocks, or the lack of international financing. However, the presence of such factors should not be viewed as automatically condemning policies based on trade liberalization. Thus, while Brazil followed expansionary domestic policies and exchange rate overvaluation after the debt crisis of 1982, Colombia and Mexico applied macroeconomic stabilization and trade-liberalization measures. The subsequent evolution of these three economies suggests that orthodox policies may have a certain success even in a difficult external environment.

Table 8.5　Changes in real effective exchange rates of the EC-12 economies (average annual percentage change), 1961 to 1991 [a]

Country	Average (1)	Standard deviation (2)	Coefficient of variation (1)/(2)	Maximum	Minimum
1961–78:					
Belgium/Luxembourg	0.5	3.4	7.3	6.3	−7.3
Denmark	1.7	2.7	1.5	7.0	−2.4
France	−0.5	5.0	−9.8	12.0	−11.5
Germany	1.4	5.0	3.6	13.2	−11.2
Greece	−2.7	6.2	−2.3	9.4	−11.7
Ireland	−0.6	3.1	−5.4	6.5	−6.3
Italy	−1.2	4.1	−3.4	7.2	−8.3
Netherlands	2.5	2.0	0.8	6.0	−3.3
Portugal	−0.9	7.7	−8.7	15.5	−17.2
Spain	1.4	4.2	3.1	7.0	−9.0
United Kingdom	−2.4	4.7	−2.0	4.1	−14.3
1979–86:					
Belgium/Luxembourg	−2.6	4.5	−1.7	3.4	−10.1
Denmark	−1.8	4.0	−2.2	2.5	−10.7
France	−0.2	1.3	−5.9	2.1	−2.3
Germany	−0.9	4.2	−4.5	6.5	−6.1
Greece	−1.1	9.5	−8.5	11.8	−18.0
Ireland	2.3	2.8	1.2	6.5	−1.0
Italy	3.4	3.2	0.9	10.4	−0.6
Netherlands	−2.2	3.8	−1.7	4.2	−6.5
Portugal	−1.2	6.4	−5.2	11.0	−11.6
Spain	−0.5	7.0	−13.6	14.9	−10.1
United Kingdom	2.9	10.3	3.6	21.7	−12.7
1987–91:					
Belgium/Luxembourg	−1.3	1.8	−1.4	1.3	−4.4
Denmark	−0.5	3.8	−7.7	6.5	−4.7
France	−2.2	1.3	−0.6	0.0	−3.3
Germany	−1.1	2.6	−2.4	3.6	−3.5
Greece	0.3	5.4	15.4	7.6	−6.2
Ireland	−3.9	1.7	−0.4	−1.8	−6.8
Italy	2.2	1.8	0.8	4.5	0.1
Netherlands	−1.7	2.3	−1.4	2.3	−4.8
Portugal	4.3	5.0	1.2	13.5	−0.7
Spain	3.2	2.8	0.9	7.2	−0.3
United Kingdom	3.7	5.5	1.5	12.4	−3.7

Note: [a] Price competitiveness is based on unit labor costs of each country with respect to all its trading partners in the EC.

Source: Authors' calculations based on data from the Directorate-General for Economic and Financial Affairs, Commission of the European Community, Brussels.

7.　*The import-substitution policies followed by Latin American countries delayed adjustment to external shocks.* Faced with internal macroeconomic imbalances, Latin American countries were slow to correct exchange rate misalignment. The reason was that devaluation would have had contractionary effects because import-substitution policies had caused a heavy reliance on artificially cheap imports of intermediate and capital goods. However, this policy was sustainable only to the extent that export prices were high and that access to international capital markets was available. Without the latter, the flaws of the inward-oriented integration strategy of Latin America became visible.

8. *Exchange rate misalignment and the ensuing shortage of foreign exchange hampers the functioning of clearing and payments systems.* The foreign exchange shortage that affects Latin American economies results from the inconsistency between the monetary and fiscal policy mix and the exchange rate regime. To deal with this shortage, many Latin American countries have taken measures to 'save' foreign exchange. Much energy and resources have been spent in this task. According to Langhammer and Hiemenz (1991), between 1966 and 1987 the LAIA Payments System reduced the share of foreign currency transfers from 30 to 24 per cent. However, as impediments to a sustainable rise in the share of intra-regional trade lay elsewhere, member countries accumulated arrears and refused to hold large amounts of partners' non-convertible currencies. Barter and compensation arrangements prospered and the RIAs moved toward bilateralism.

9. *Lack of policy coordination reduces the gains from market integration.* The procedures contained in the CACM for the harmonization of fiscal policies did not materialize, while LAFTA/LAIA did not include any provisions for the coordination of macroeconomic policies among members. The EC efforts at integration of macroeconomic policy and convergence of major macroeconomic indicators stand as a clear example of the opposite development. As argued below, uncoordinated macroeconomic policies increase both the variability of real exchange rates and the international spill-over of domestic policies as trade liberalization proceeds. Both of these consequences may be detrimental to integration efforts.

10. *Divergent views about the degree of market decentralization and government intervention hamper policy coordination and integration.* Disputes about the level of market decentralization and the degree of government control of market forces can be fatal for a RIA. As stated by de Melo *et al.* (1992), for a RIA to be successful, there must not be large gaps between national lobbies' preferences and the level of government interference. Otherwise, it may become too costly for a government to give up part of its national autonomy, because it will suffer the full cost of a reduced ability to satisfy politically important groups. The withdrawal of

Chile from the Andean Pact in 1976 and the recent move by Bolivia to leave the Pact and become a member of the Mercosur[6] are clear examples of conflicts over the desired level of government involvement in the economy. On the other hand, the failure of LAFTA at significantly increasing intra-regional trade is largely the result of strong import-competing groups that led Latin American governments to refrain from automaticity in the implementation of trade liberalization. Alesina and Tabellini (1988) argue that policy makers in the partner countries need to have a similar policy horizon in order for the integration initiative to be successful. The reason is that the length of this horizon affects the degree of policy discipline that can be expected. The horizon is inversely related to the sensitivity of policy makers to the loss of reputation, and it is the potential loss of reputation which induces governments to pursue disciplined policies. One of the key determinants of the policy horizon of governments is the nature of their political institutions. These institutions therefore have an influence on policy discipline through the possibility they offer (or do not offer) to vote undisciplined governments out of office.

11.   *An absence of adequate institutions complicates the achievement of the RIAs' objectives.* Most RIAs among developing countries, although modeled on the EC, do not create the institutions needed to achieve their objectives. This becomes evident through inconsistent national legislation, absence of enforcement mechanisms, and ineffective dispute-settlement mechanisms. For example, failure to resolve the issue of labor mobility by CACM members is often mentioned as one of the factors that did not permit the consolidation of market integration.

8.2   Integration and the transmission of macroeconomic fluctuations

The above review of the experience of selected RIAs indicates that very large real exchange rate changes have been present in those agreements that have not functioned well. This suggests that large shocks to real exchange rates may be detrimental to regional economic integration. It also indicates that real exchange rate movements constitute an important link between macroeconomic policy and the process of integration. This link can be shown to imply both that macroeconomic policy will be influenced by the process of integration and that the process of integration will be influenced by macroeconomic policy. As countries liberalize trade in goods and services and remove obstacles to trade in assets and factors of production, a new equilibrium will almost certainly require changes in relative prices between importables and exportables on the one hand, and between tradable goods and non-tradables (that is, a change in the equilibrium real exchange rate) on the other.[7] In addition, the process may require a certain integration of economic policies, which could entail changes in taxes and government expenditures, as well as other measures which have significant influences on relative prices and therefore on the equilibrium real exchange rate. The exact way in which the equilibrium will be required to change will depend on the structure of the integrating economies and on the policy response to the integration. But whatever it turns out to be, it is bound to lead to corresponding changes in the structure of production and employment. In the presence of rigidities in factor prices and less than perfect internal mobility of factors of production, the required change in the structure of the economy is likely to lead to transitional unemployment in some sectors and regions. There are reasons to believe that this will put pressure on macroeconomic policy makers to take counter-actions.

Macroeconomic policies undertaken to achieve domestic policy objectives, on the other hand, may have important consequences for the regional integration process through their impact on the real exchange rate. This is particularly the case, as we shall see presently, if the nominal exchange rate between the countries in question is floating or when the nominal exchange rate is kept relatively stable but macroeconomic policies are not consistent with such stability. In the former case, a mismatch between the partner countries in the conduct of their monetary and fiscal policies will lead to substantial fluctuation in the bilateral real exchange rate. As a consequence, trade flows will be affected, and trade frictions may arise to the detriment of the integration process. If the authorities in one country try to fix the nominal exchange rate without adjusting macroeconomic policies accordingly, the objective of a stable real exchange rate will fail to be reached because of domestic inflation. The consequence is likely to be pressures in the foreign exchange market and recourse to various forms of trade controls to defuse them.

Although it is important, the real exchange rate is not the only channel of transmission of disturbances between countries. Thus, to illustrate how the process of economic integration influences macroeconomic interdependence between countries, it is important to examine more generally its impact on other channels of transmission of macroeconomic shocks and policies. Macroeconomic linkages result from trade in goods and in assets and from mobility of factors of production. How strong the linkages are depends on the degree of integration between the economies concerned and on the economic policies adopted by the respective governments, notably exchange rate policy. The analysis thus will proceed in a somewhat taxonomic fashion.

Consider first the case of a FTA between two countries. If this agreement succeeds in increasing bilateral trade, it will strengthen the macroeconomic interdependence between the countries through at least three well-known channels. First, as mutual trade becomes more important, aggregate demand linkages will grow, due to larger marginal propensities to import and to the larger impacts of changes in the terms of trade on real incomes and spending. Second, greater trade in intermediate goods will extend input–output linkages between the two economies and increase their interdependence via aggregate supply relationships. And third, as imported goods become increasingly more important in domestic consumption, wage settlements are likely to become more and more affected by external price developments.

In order for a FTA to deliver maximum benefits for the partner countries it is necessary that financial constraints should not hinder the expansion of trade. To take full advantage of freer trade in goods it will therefore become important to strengthen financial linkages between the two nations. This may initially take the form only of greater freedom of capital movements related to the financing of trade flows but, since funds are fungible, it is likely that the financial markets in general in the two economies will become increasingly connected. Integration of goods markets thus naturally requires some integration of financial markets. Financial integration in turn may lead to increased trade in financial services, establishment of cross-border financial intermediaries, and some harmonization of prudential rules and standardization of financial regulations.[8] This increases the degree of capital mobility and macroeconomic interdependence.

The consequence of increased financial integration for the macroeconomic performance of the countries concerned depends importantly on the exchange regime that is adopted. If the countries are linked with a fixed exchange rate, a high degree of capital mobility implies severe constraints on the monetary policies of both central banks. Attempts to follow independent policies will cause external imbalances that may induce policy makers to reimpose restrictions on trade which nullifies the benefits that trade integration was supposed to bring. Thus, a RIA that has evolved from including not only free trade in goods but also free trade in assets will be characterized by a very high degree of macroeconomic interdependence, at least as long as the countries involved are linked by fixed exchange rates.

It may be thought that the adoption of floating exchange rates insulates the economies from external shocks and allows them to pursue macroeconomic policies without regard to international constraints or feedbacks. While this view may be approximately correct when international capital mobility is very limited, it is manifestly not true in an environment of integrated financial markets. Macroeconomic interdependence continues under floating exchange rates, although it may take different forms than under fixed rates. For present purposes, two observed features of adjustment under floating rates are important to keep in mind: the relatively high degree of volatility of real and nominal exchange rates, and their tendency toward relatively prolonged deviations from purchasing power parity ('misalignments'). The volatility of nominal exchange rates stems from their character as asset prices which reflect conditions in financial markets, notably expectations of future changes in economic conditions, including future changes in economic policies. Changes in these expectations have rapid and powerful effects on current asset prices. Since prices of goods are less flexible than prices of assets, the volatility of nominal exchange rates translates into an almost identical volatility of real exchange rates.[9] The short-run stickiness of prices of goods can also explain part of the prolonged deviations from purchasing power parity that have been observed. Furthermore, the theoretical concept of 'overshooting' (that is, the notion that short-run adjustments in exchange rates are larger than long-run changes for a given disturbance) may explain why these deviations sometimes have been quite large.[10]

Disturbances in asset markets may thus lead to short-run fluctuations as well as medium-term changes in competitive positions of firms located in different currency areas. Although it is difficult to find decisive empirical evidence to support the view that volatility of exchange rates has had a significant impact on the volume of international trade, this volatility does increase the uncertainty associated with international transactions. Be that as it may, it remains true that policy makers react to exchange rate fluctuations by intervening in the foreign exchange market to smooth them. In and of themselves, such interventions lead directly to a certain degree of macroeconomic policy interdependence.[11]

Prolonged deviations from purchasing power parity are perhaps even more likely to lead to policy interdependence. The calls for policy coordination among G7 countries, for example, have often been predicated on the perceived necessity to avoid misalignments of exchange rates lest domestic protectionist pressures lead to the imposition of trade restrictions of various kinds.

If a FTA which incorporates a high degree of financial integration evolves further to include the establishment of common markets for goods, financial services, labor and capital, then the degree of macroeconomic integration described above will be reinforced. Horizontal production linkages are likely to expand, giving rise to greater interdependence of aggregate production and supply in the integrating economies. Financial linkages will be tightened, and the scope for independent policies correspondingly reduced, if exchange rates are fixed. Any remaining isolation produced by exchange rate flexibility also will disappear. In addition, if exchange rates are floating, the potentially damaging consequences of large changes in competitiveness due to currency fluctuations will lead to calls for policy coordination. The logical evolution of a CM is thus toward a full economic and monetary union (EMU) in which an independent monetary policy ceases completely to be an option for each member nation. Certain fiscal independence of subregions may still be feasible on the scale observed in current federal states like Canada, Switzerland or the United States. However, as comparisons between Europe and the United States show, the system of fiscal federalism in the latter can be a powerful shock absorber, since federal net income transfers to states vary significantly with their economic situation (Frenkel and Goldstein, 1991). In contrast, transfers between members of the EC related to temporary income short-falls are quite small. This is frequently cited as a hindrance to further EC integration, and it has been used as an argument in favor of greater integration of fiscal policy in the EC as it proceeds towards a full-fledged EU.

8.3 Market integration and macroeconomic policy discipline

Having explained how the process of market integration increases macroeconomic interdependence between the partner countries, this interdependence can be shown to require integration of their macro-economic policies as well. In showing this we stress the links between coordination and discipline in the conduct of macroeconomic policy in RIAs, and we focus not only on the final stage of integration arrange-ments but also on the intermediate phases of the process. While it is quite clear that expanding the scope of integration increases the need for coordination of macroeconomic policies, it is not necessarily true that integration per se *induces* such coordination. To understand the evolution of the integration process it is thus important to study the way it affects the incentives and objectives of macroeconomic policy makers.

When we speak of 'policy discipline' we base ourselves on widely accepted principles of monetary and fiscal policy (Lucas, 1986), and define a disciplined monetary policy as one that delivers predictable, low rates of monetary growth and low, or negative, inflation. Fiscal discipline requires the adjustment of taxation and expenditure policies so as to avoid the build-up of an unsustainable level of public debt. Excessive levels of public debt which lead to pressures to default, or to create unexpected inflation which introduces uncertainty into the future stance of policy, can only be avoided if discipline is maintained continuously.

The notion of discipline is related to the question of rules versus discretion in the conduct of macroeconomic policy (Kydland and Prescott, 1977). The issue here is the trade-off between the gains from the dynamic consistency obtained by adhering to rules and the loss of flexibility that it produces (Fischer, 1990). For instance, the adoption of a fixed exchange rate removes the possibility (and temptation) of generating an unexpected surge in domestic inflation in order to reduce the real value of the outstanding government debt or to increase output by depressing real wages. By restricting the options of the authorities in this way, it may be possible to remove an inflation premium both in domestic interest rates and in wage settlements. On the other hand, a fixed exchange rate prevents the authorities from adjusting to certain external shocks via revaluations or devaluations, and forces them instead to rely on more costly domestic adjustment measures. Which of these two options is preferable depends in part on the effectiveness of monetary and fiscal policies for stabilization and adjustment purposes. As this depends, in turn, on the degree of international integration in both goods and assets markets, the incentive to adopt rules or maintain discretion is also intimately related to the regional integration process.

Throughout the section it is assumed that integrated market areas are 'optimal' in the restricted sense that member countries satisfy a number of criteria that ensure that the wealth-increasing effects of integration offset wealth-decreasing ones. [12] This is done in order to isolate as clearly as possible the role of macroeconomic policies in the performance of the area because, if an integration area is not optimal, it is likely to stagnate and eventually dissolve regardless of the macroeconomic environment. But even an otherwise optimal RIA may fail to deliver an improvement in welfare if macroeconomic policies are inappropriately adapted. Macroeconomic discipline should thus best be thought of as a necessary enabling environment for the success of the integration process and not as a sufficient condition. As argued by Mussa (1983), the question of how to structure macroeconomic policies to achieve a degree of economic integration that maximizes some measure of social welfare can only be answered in the light of specific objectives with respect to economic integration, given the constraints within which these policies operate.

8.3.1   Interdependence and the benefits from policy integration

In Section 8.2 we noted that the process of market integration leads to increasing macroeconomic interdependence between the partner countries, as policies and disturbances originating in one country spill over more easily and readily to other members of the area. The interdependence in turn increases the benefits from coordinating macro-economic policies, and makes it more imperative to take into account the external effects of such policies. To understand the reasons for this, consider in turn the cases of two equal-sized members, of a small member, and of a large, dominating member of the area.

As two equal-sized members of an integrating area become more inter-dependent, the cross-border impact of macroeconomic policies is magnified. If each country conducts its policies without taking account of their impact on its neighbor, the resulting equilibrium is likely to be suboptimal. For example, suppose the objective of each country is to reduce an internal excess demand while at the same time maintaining external equilibrium. The concern about creating an external imbalance with the pursuit of internal deflation would prevent each country from pursuing the internal stabilization far enough. By coordinating their policies the countries would be able to pursue their internal stabilization further, since the external constraint would be removed. The result would be a more satisfactory overall outcome for the two economies. It should be kept in mind, however, that each country often has an incentive to renege on any cooperative agreement provided it can be assured that the partner continues to abide by it. To guard against this possibility, it may be necessary to design institutional mechanisms that insure compliance with mutually beneficial policy packages, a point to which we return below.

Consider next the situation of a small member of an integrating area whose policies have negligible impact on the partner countries. For such a country the external constraint on domestic policies will become greater as the process of economic integration proceeds. Unless domestic macro-economic policies are adapted to these constraints, the integration agreement is unsustainable in the medium term. As this is recognized by domestic firms and households, their behavior is likely to be such as to reduce or even eliminate the benefits of the integration and to precipitate the reversal of the integration process itself.[13] Consider, for example, a country that is following expansionary domestic policies and that is able to conserve external balance only by maintaining strict controls on international trade. If it enters a regional FTA without simultaneously taking credible steps rapidly to adjust its domestic polices, the private sector will anticipate the eventual breakdown of the FTA, increase current spending and thereby bring on a rapid depletion of international reserves which forces the reversal of trade liberalization. This behavior may be the rationale for a waiver permitting the reintroduction of trade restrictions, for balance-of-payments purposes, that FTAs and CUs of developing countries normally contemplate.[14] However, a waiver of this sort risks hampering the success of the RIA, as it reduces its credibility by removing an additional incentive for sound monetary and fiscal policies. Binding tariffs in the GATT, in contrast, would increase the cost for the government of reintroducing trade barriers, thereby increasing the credibility of the arrangement. In the context of a CM/EU, it is possible to enhance the credibility of the integration process by implementing an agreement under which net creditor countries finance transfers to net debtors. Attempts by the small member of a RIA to escape from the implied external constraint on macroeconomic policies by adopting a floating exchange rate will be less and less desirable as the integration process proceeds, if the benefits from trade integration are to be maintained. This follows from the fact that the benefits of having a fixed exchange rate increase with the degree of integration and the costs in terms of loss of seigniorage, monetary policy autonomy, and the possibility of affecting the real exchange rate through devaluations become increasingly more illusory than real.[15]

Finally, although a large, dominating member of the integrating region is not explicitly constrained in its conduct of policies, there are nevertheless limits to the extent that it can pursue its own objectives without regard for its partners. The reason is that the partners may opt out of the integration agreement altogether if the macroeconomic environment imposed by the large country becomes too unstable or otherwise undesirable.

8.3.2 RIAs and policy discipline

By our definition of the term, it is always better if national policy authorities are disciplined than if they are not, regardless of the degree of integration between their economies. The question we want to discuss here, therefore, is whether the existence of a RIA influences the social benefits from discipline, on the one hand, and whether it affects the governments' incentives to pursue disciplined policies, on the other.

Two considerations make us conclude that the need for policy discipline increases as the integration process proceeds. The first is that coordination of economic policies is more easily achieved in the presence of discipline, and the second is that real exchange rate stability is unlikely to be achieved without discipline.

We have already argued that the need for policy harmonization and coordination increases with the degree of economic integration. Harmonization in turn is easier to obtain if the countries involved follow a predictable, low-inflation monetary policy and take a conservative fiscal stance. The reason is that high inflation rates are likely also to be unstable and therefore difficult to harmonize across countries, and that significant and variable budget deficits may give rise to abrupt movements in interest rates that partner countries find difficult to accept.

Unstable policies will undoubtedly also increase the variability of real exchange rates. The clearest case is that provided by instability in monetary policy in the context of a flexible exchange rate and short-run stickiness of wages and prices. The well-known tendency for the exchange rate to overshoot its long-run equilibrium level in such circumstances implies that the real exchange rate will exhibit substantial variability. Similarly, instability and uncertainty about the stance of fiscal policy will give rise to large fluctuations in real exchange rates due to the reaction of asset markets to the financial consequences of such policies. Since we have seen in previous sections that excessive volatility of real exchange rates is detrimental to economic integration, these arguments imply an increased need for policy discipline for the process of economic integration to be successful.

That the *need* for discipline is increasing during the process of integration does not automatically mean that such discipline will actually materialize as integration and policy coordination deepens. The clearest example of this is given in Rogoff (1985), where it is shown that coordination between two central banks can actually lead to less inflation discipline than the absence of coordination. The reason is that domestic pressures to inflate in both countries will dominate when the fear of external disequilibrium is reduced as a result of the international coordination of policies. Special institutional mechanisms may thus be necessary to ensure that the policy discipline necessary for the success for the RIA will actually emerge. This is all the more so if commitments made to regional institutions can be used by a government to counteract domestic pressure groups which otherwise would block necessary changes in policies.

8.3.3 Institutional arrangements to ensure coordination and discipline

At the early stages of an integration process, when the liberalization is restricted to trade in goods and services, the necessity of creating an institutional infrastructure can be limited essentially to that which is needed to administer common commercial policies. However, to increase the chance that macroeconomic policy integration and discipline actually materialize as the integration process advances towards a CM and perhaps beyond, it may become necessary to establish certain additional institutional mechanisms. The clearest example concerns monetary policy. We have argued that the case for stable exchange rates becomes stronger as integration deepens, since increased integration implies both less need for nominal exchange rate adjustments and less effect from such adjustments on the evolution of employment and output.

Stability of exchange rates can in turn be achieved either in a decentralized fashion, whereby each individual country is responsible for maintaining stability relative to a numeraire, or in a coordinated fashion whereby adjustment rules and obligations are determined cooperatively. In both cases the stability of the entire system needs to be guaranteed by some additional arrangement. In the decentralized system the most natural such arrangement is perhaps one in which a dominating member serves as the anchor of the system as well as providing the effective numeraire. Examples of such systems are the CFA Franc Zone in West Africa, the Bretton Woods system and, according to some observers, the European Monetary System. Under the cooperative system, overall monetary stability may be pursued by the creation of an institutional mechanism which determines the overall stance of monetary policy in the region. In either case, the ability of monetary authorities in individual countries to pursue goals other than those consistent with monetary stability and discipline will have to be strictly limited. Recent theorizing based on 'political economy' arguments have concluded that the best way of doing this is to make the central bank independent of the political process in the country or region it governs, and to give it as a sole objective the pursuit of price stability. In particular, it may be necessary explicitly to prevent the central bank from monetizing government deficits. The statutes of the proposed European Central Bank can be viewed in this light (CEPR, 1991).

Institutional constraints on fiscal policy are in one sense less demanding and in another sense more so. They are less demanding in the sense that the technical viability of a system based on stable exchange rates can be assured with much less fiscal coordination than monetary coordination. As long as the monetary authorities are not required (allowed) to monetize budget deficits, and as long as governments can be assumed to respect their inter-temporal budget constraints, one might reasonably assume that a certain market discipline will prevent the build-up of excessive levels of government debt.[16] Excessive indebtedness would be sanctioned by higher interest rates, which in turn would require some fiscal correction, without the need to specify rules for such corrections in a centralized manner. The market discipline might not be maintained if some implicit or explicit region-wide guarantee on member states' solvency existed, for in this case an individual government might attempt to take advantage of such a guarantee to borrow at an interest rate which in part reflected the guarantee provided by the integration partners. To avoid the potential for such free-riding some formal limits on fiscal deficits may be required.

The institutional constraints on fiscal policy may be as demanding as those on monetary policy if the political acceptability of the integration arrangement hinges on the existence of a region-wide scheme of income redistribution, which either ensures a certain convergence of income levels among the member countries and among subregions of the member countries, or acts as a shock absorber which is supposed to attenuate significantly the effects of asymmetric disturbances on real incomes in member countries. In this case some form of region-wide fiscal authority will have to be established along the lines of those that can be found in existing federal states.

8.4   Summary and policy implications for recent integration initiatives

Macroeconomic policy is an important element in explaining the success and failure of RIAs. As market integration deepens, disturbances are transmitted via demand linkages and input–output linkages more easily within the region, increasing thereby the need for macroeconomic policy integration. Coordination of domestic fiscal and monetary policies becomes necessary, so that external imbalances do not jeopardize moves toward the liberalization of trade in goods and services and the cross-border flow of assets and factors of production. Maximization of the benefits of market integration requires thus the integration of macroeconomic policies within the region.

However, just abolishing discrimination to achieve market integration does not *automatically* bring about macroeconomic policy discipline and coordination. For instance, a FTA/CU between trading partners with traditionally undisciplined monetary authorities can result in an excessive rate of inflation, to the extent that coordination may be used to eliminate the balance of payments constraint. Similarly, in a CM in which factor mobility (especially capital mobility) is high, a certain competition in regulatory laxity may emerge as countries try to attract financial institutions (Frenkel and Goldstein, 1991). Therefore, positive actions are in some cases required to influence the incentives and objectives of national macroeconomic policies, thereby ensuring that market integration induces more discipline and coordination in policy making.

Modifying the operations of existing institutions or creating new ones may be necessary during the process of integration. For example, monetary stability in a region may require independence of the central banks and a no-bail-out clause for fiscally troubled members. In addition, to make such a clause credible and to reinforce the discipline exerted by market forces, it may be necessary to introduce restrictions on the maturity and currency denomination of public debt, as well as to introduce prudential rules and multilateral surveillance to protect financial markets from systemic risk.

An important institutional arrangement is the exchange rate regime. As openness increases when an integration arrangement moves from a FTA towards an EU, the arguments in favor of floating the exchange rates between the currencies of the member countries become less pertinent and the benefits of fixed exchange rates increase. Thus, it is more advantageous for CMs than for FTAs to have the exchange rates among member countries fixed.

What does all this tell us about macroeconomic policy making and the likelihood of the success of some recent integration initiatives in Europe and America? Consider first NAFTA, the free trade agreement between the United States, Canada and Mexico. To the extent that a certain stability of the exchange rates between the three countries is desirable, Mexican and Canadian monetary and fiscal policies will have to be coordinated with those of the dominant country in the arrangement. Attempts by Mexico, for instance, to take a more expansionary monetary stance than the United States would depreciate the domestic currency (or induce a rapid loss of international reserves). If this continued erratically it would increase real exchange rate variability. This in turn would reduce the static and dynamic gains from integration and create incentives to restrict first capital and then current transactions. In such an asymmetric RIA, a large proportion of responsibility for macroeconomic policy discipline is shifted from the 'small' member countries of the RIA to the dominant one. As in the case of the design of a stable international monetary system, the issue here becomes what set of institutions is necessary to protect the RIA from the eventual indiscipline of a dominant member.

Former socialist countries in Eastern Europe wish to integrate further their economies with the EC. There can hardly be any doubt that opening up EC markets can benefit the former socialist economies of Europe in their transition from plan to market and in the process of integrating themselves more into the world economy. Nevertheless, a prerequisite for successful integration is consistency between the monetary and fiscal policy mix and the exchange rate regime. This requires that their sizable macroeconomic imbalances be eliminated first.

Finally, the same claim can be made of the Mercosur initiative between Argentina, Brazil, Paraguay and Uruguay, which seeks to create a common market by 1995–6. However, in contrast to North America and Europe, where there is a dominant country or region that can in principle guarantee some degree of monetary and fiscal discipline, Mercosur member countries have a long tradition of frequent monetization of significant and perennial fiscal deficits, high inflation, balance-of-payments crises, large real exchange rate variability, and policy-induced shortages of international reserves. Given that macroeconomic stability is a prerequisite for the success of RIAs, some institutional means need to be found to ensure macroeconomic stability. In particular, the credibility problem associated with fiscal stabilization needs to be addressed. Otherwise, even if Mercosur succeeds in achieving its common market goal, it is likely to be an unstable agreement that will end up by stagnating or disappearing.

In the course of the preceding analysis we have raised a number of questions which clearly require additional research before they can be adequately answered. Topics that we have not had the space to treat relate to links between regional integration, macroeconomic discipline and economic growth, to the connections between the traditional criteria for optimality of membership of an integration area and the likelihood that macroeconomic policies will also be appropriate, and to the consequences of various forms of asymmetries (including size) for the evolution of macroeconomic policy discipline.

Notes

We would like to acknowledge the helpful and constructive comments that we received from Kym Anderson, Richard Blackhurst, David Henderson and Carsten Kowalczyk on the first draft of this chapter. We also thank Lidia Carlos Silvetti and Aamer Zahid for their valuable statistical assistance.
 1. An FTA implies that national policy makers give up some degree of policy freedom by relinquishing the autonomous exercise of trade policy with respect to other member countries of the region. A CU implies that they give up national trade policy completely. As the integration arrangement moves into a CM, interest rate policy and the possibility of uncoordinated exchange rate policy are surrendered. National fiscal policies also may have to be coordinated in order to avoid unnecessary real exchange rate and output variability. Finally, an EU may imply an even larger submission of fiscal policy making to a supranational authority in order, for instance, to cope more effectively with asymmetric shocks in the area.

2. Tichy (1992) discusses the criteria that have been proposed as determining the optimality of an integration agreement. An optimal FTA/CU, for example, requires a dense net of interlacing trade flows (even before integration), similar structures of production, trade and relative prices, a similar stage of development and low external tariffs. Note that, from this point of view, the *size* of the area is important only to the extent that the larger the area the more likely it is that it will be characterized by intensive trade relations among members and a minimum of competing trade relations with the rest of the world.

3. This record of successful implementation has to be qualified, however as free trade in goods was subject to less visible restrictions such as different subsidy practices among members or bilateral arrangements affecting trade in automobiles, textiles and clothing, and agriculture.

4. This may be a reason why trade liberalization attempts in some Latin American countries have not included a binding of tariffs in the GATT, which gives rise to credibility problems. Markets know that the lack of automaticity in the liberalization program of RIAs in Latin America makes it easier for member countries to backtrack in the face of a balance-of-payments crisis.

5. Edwards and Savastano (1989) argue that in the majority of 17 balance-of-payments crises in Latin America studied by them, the crisis in the form of a major devaluation was preceded by an important piling up of exchange controls and restrictions. Macroeconomic instability has been at the origin of recurrent external imbalances with concomitant negative effects on the trade regime and on the RIAs. Therefore, Latin American protectionist history has been intimately related to the region's macroeconomic instability. Our study of nine FTAs, seven CUs and two CM/EUs also suggests that successful RIAs are correlated with low nominal exchange rate variability while unsuccessful ones are associated with macroeconomic imbalances, payment restrictions, and nominal as well as real exchange rate volatility.

6. Mercosur is a regional integration agreement signed in 1991 and aiming at the formation of a CU between Argentina, Brazil, Paraguay and Uruguay by 1995–6.

7. The 'fundamental' determinants of equilibrium exchange rates include international factors such as the terms of trade and real interest rates, and domestic factors such as trade policy and restrictions on exchange and payments.

8. See Crockett (1991) on the reasons why RIAs lead to a need for capital liberalization, which in turn creates the need for closer cooperation on currency arrangements.

9. See, for example, Mussa (1986) for evidence on this point.

10. For example, the US dollar vis-à-vis the EC currencies and the yen in 1985.

11. The reason is that interventions in the foreign exchange market are not likely to have significant impacts unless they influence domestic monetary conditions, that is, unless they are of the non-sterilized variety.

12. The viewpoint adopted here is thus more limited than the one proposed by Cooper (1976), who views 'regions' as governmental jurisdictions that deliver a large number of public goods, including the functions of the government and the nature of the economic regime. That is to say, Cooper focuses beyond pure national-income considerations.

13. Froot (1988) argues this in the context of unilateral trade liberalization.
14. This waiver exists, for example, in the Chile–Mexico Free Trade Agreement signed in 1991.
15. See Nadal De Simone (1990) for an elaboration of this argument.
16. In its study, the Commission of the European Communities (1990) argues that the objective of monetary discipline in an EMU is conditional on the long-run fiscal sustainability of the union.

References

Alesina, A. and G. Tabellini (1988), 'Credibility and Politics', *European Economic Review* **32**: 542–50.

Balassa, B. (1962), *The Theory of Economic Integration*, London: Allen and Unwin.

CEPR (Centre for Economic Policy Research) (1991), *Monitoring European Integration – The Making of Monetary Union*, London: CEPR.

Commission of the European Communities (1990), 'One Market, One Money', *European Economy* **44**: October.

Cooper, R. N. (1976), 'Worldwide versus Regional Integration: Is there an Optimium Size of the Integrated Area?', in *Economic Integration: Worldwide, Regional, Sectoral*, edited by F. Machlup, London: Macmillan.

Crockett, A. D. (1991), 'Financial Market Implications of Trade and Currency Zones', in *Policy Implications of Trade and Currency Zones*, edited by the Federal Reserve Bank of Kansas, Kansas City: Federal Reserve Bank.

de la Torre, A. and M. Kelly (1992), *Regional Trade Arrangements*, IMF Occasional Paper No. 93, Washington, DC: International Monetary Fund.

de Melo, J., A. Panagariya and D. Rodrik (1992), 'Regional Integration: An Analytical and Empirical Overview', presented at a World Bank/Centre for Economic Policy Research (CEPR) conference on New Dimensions in Regional Integration, Washington, DC, April 2–3.

Edwards, D. and M. Savastano (1989), 'Latin America's Intra-Regional Trade: Evolution and Future Prospects', in Economic Aspects of *Regional Trading Arrangements*, edited by D. Greenaway, T. Hyclak and R. J. Thornton, New York: New York University Press.

Fischer, S. (1990), 'Rules vs. Discretion in Monetary Policy', in *Handbook of Monetary Economics, Vol. 2*, edited by B. M. Friedman and F. H. Hahn, Amsterdam: North-Holland.

Frenkel, J. A. and M. Goldstein (1991), 'The Macroeconomic Policy Implications of Trade and Currency Zones', in *Policy Implications of Trade and Currency Zones*, edited by the Federal Reserve Bank of Kansas, Kansas City: Federal Reserve Bank.

Froot, K. A. (1988), 'Credibility, Real Interest Rates, and the Optimal Speed of Trade Liberalization', *Journal of International Economics* **25**: 71–93.

Kydland, F. E. and E. C. Prescott (1977), 'Rules Rather than Discretion: The Inconsistency of Optimal Plans', *Journal of Political Economy* **85**: 473–91.

Langhammer, R. and V. Hiemenz (1991), 'Regional Integration Among Developing Countries', UNDP World Bank Trade Expansion Program, Occasional Paper No. 7, Washington, DC: The World Bank.

Lucas, R. E. Jr (1986), 'Principles of Fiscal and Monetary Policy', *Journal of Monetary Economics* **17**: 117–34.

Mussa, M. (1983), 'Optimal Economic Integration', in *Financial Policies and the World Capital Market*, edited by P. A. Armella, R. Dornbusch and M. Obstfeld, Chicago: University of Chicago Press.

Mussa, M. (1986), 'Nominal Exchange Rate Regimes and the Behaviour of Real Exchange Rates: Evidence and Implications', *Carnegie-Rochester Conference Series on Public Policy* **25**: 117–214.

Nadal De Simone, F. (1990), 'The Case for a Currency Area in Europe', mimeo, GATT Secretariat, December.

Pelkmans, J. (1980), 'Economic Theories of Integration Revisited', *Journal of Common Market Studies* **18**: 333–54.

Rogoff, K. (1985), 'Can International Monetary Policy Cooperation be Counterproductive?', *Journal of International Economics* **18**: 199–217.

Tichy, G. (1992), 'Theoretical and Empirical Considerations on the Dimension of an Optimum Integration Area in Europe', *Aussenwirtschaft* **47**: 107–37.

World Bank (1992), *World Debt Tables 1991–92*, Washington, DC: The World Bank.

PART 4

Political economy of integration agreements

9

Effects of international politics on regionalism in international trade

Edward D. Mansfield

One of the central debates among scholars of international political economy during the past two decades has centered on whether a single preponderant (or hegemonic) state is necessary for the existence of a liberal and stable global trading system. Hegemonic stability theorists argue that this is the case, and that periods lacking a hegemon are likely to be characterized by widespread protectionism and relatively low levels of international commerce. This view has become increasingly common among scholars and policy makers, many of whom believe that the erosion of United States hegemony bodes poorly for the stability of the global trading system and is likely to promote a series of protectionist regional integration agreements (RIAs). There have been critics of this approach, however, and the relationship between hegemony and aspects of trade remains a source of controversy. One purpose of this chapter is to examine whether the presence or absence of hegemony has been associated with the level of international trade during the nineteenth and twentieth centuries, and, if so, whether the decline and/or absence of hegemony has been associated with an increase in regionalism in international trade.

A second purpose is to analyze whether there are political incentives for states to engage in freer trade with allies than with adversaries. While political scientists have analyzed the effects of hegemony on trade in considerable depth, they have devoted far less attention to the effects of political-military alliances on trade. This chapter also considers whether alliances influence the formation of customs unions (CUs), including when customs unions form and how states choose customs union partners. A great deal of research by international trade theorists has focused on the economic incentives for customs unions to form, but few studies have analyzed the effects of alliances in this regard.

9.1   A systemic approach to international political economy

Scholars have long debated the relative importance of international (or systemic) and domestic political influences on international trade. The present analysis centers on the influence on trade policies of hegemony (as well as other aspects of the distribution of power) and political-military alliances, which are systemic factors. Systemic explanations of the international political economy posit that the constraints imposed, and the opportunities fostered, by aspects of the international system are the most salient determinants of patterns of global economic outcomes. As a result, these explanations place relatively little emphasis on domestic politics. Instead, states are usually treated as unitary, rational actors whose behavior is conditioned by the international political system (Waltz, 1979; Gilpin, 1981; Keohane, 1984a).

Systemic theories therefore stand in stark contrast to those that emphasize the effects of domestic institutions, special interest groups, and other domestic political influences on international trade (Baldwin, 1985; Katzenstein, 1986; Magee *et al.*, 1989).[1] It is clear that any comprehensive analysis of the international political economy would consider the effects of both international and domestic politics. But since this chapter focuses on the impact of hegemony and political-military alliances, a systemic approach is adopted. This is a useful research strategy because, as Keohane (1984b, p. 16) has argued:

> Without a conception of the common external problems, pressures, and challenges [that the international system exerts on states] ... we lack an analytic basis for identifying the role played by domestic interests and pressures. ... Understanding the [systemic] constraints imposed by the world political economy allows us to distinguish the effects of common international forces from those of distinctive national ones.

9.2   Hegemonic stability theory

Much research concerning the influences of international politics on trade has focused on the merits of hegemonic stability theory, which has become the most influential systemic theory of the international political economy. Although hegemonic stability theorists differ on a number of important points, they agree that the existence of a single preponderant state is a necessary (though not a sufficient) condition for the establishment and maintenance of a liberal international economic order. Many hegemonic stability theorists also agree that, because a liberal trading system takes on features of a public good, its creation and maintenance engender collective action problems. Without a state that is willing and able to act as a privileged group and unilaterally provide a liberal trading order, the establishment of this type of system is unlikely.

Hegemonic stability theorists disagree, however, on why hegemons provide a liberal trading system. According to one set of such theorists, hegemons provide public goods largely for altruistic reasons. This seems to underlie Kindleberger's (1973, 1981) argument that the Depression during the 1930s can be attributed to the absence of a benevolent 'stabilizer' to coordinate the international economy. Great Britain was unable to provide this function (as it did during the nineteenth century), and the United States was unwilling to do so. According to another set of these theorists, hegemons create and sustain a liberal international economy because they benefit disproportionately from such a system. In this vein, Gilpin (1975, 1981, 1987), Krasner (1976) and Lake (1988) maintain that the benefits that accrued to Great Britain and the United States from a liberal international economy largely explain why these states promoted open trading systems during the nineteenth and twentieth centuries.[2]

Despite the prominence of hegemonic stability theory, it has attracted a wide range of critics, some of whom have faulted it on analytical grounds. For example, small-group theorists have pointed out that the theory of collective action (Olson, 1971) does not preclude the provision of public goods by small groups. As a result, the absence of hegemony need not undermine a liberal trading order. While hegemons may ameliorate collective action problems when public goods such as a liberal trade regime are initially supplied, hegemony is not necessary for either their provision or their maintenance (McKeown, 1983; Keohane, 1984a; Snidal, 1985).

Another line of attack on hegemonic stability theorists has been based on the argument that they have mistakenly identified free trade as a public good. Because free trade is excludable, its provision is not characterized by collective action problems. A hegemon therefore need not act as a privileged group to ensure its provision (Conybeare, 1984, 1987; Russett, 1985; Snidal, 1985). It also has been argued that, contrary to the predictions of hegemonic stability theory, hegemony may actually inhibit international trade and multilateralism. Since a hegemon is likely to possess monopoly power in trade, economic factors should lead it to impose an optimal tariff, rather than promoting an open trading system (Conybeare, 1984, 1987).[3]

Hegemonic stability theory has also been criticized on empirical grounds. For example, one statistical study concluded that the relationship between hegemony and national tariff levels during the twentieth century was weak (Conybeare, 1983). Another such study found that variables related to hegemony had little impact on national import levels (as a percentage of national income) during the period from 1880 to 1987 (McKeown, 1991). Additional analyses find that, while hegemony may be associated with a relatively open trading system, the causal nature of this relationship is suspect (McKeown, 1983; Keohane, 1984a; Stein, 1984).

9.3   The distribution of power and patterns of international trade

Many of the controversies among hegemonic stability theorists and their critics arise because of disagreements over which feature of the distribution of power (typically measured by economic, demographic and military capabilities) should be emphasized in studies of the international political economy. Some emphasize the importance of the distribution of power between the most powerful state and the remaining states in the system (i.e., hegemony); others highlight the effects of power inequalities among all of the leading states in the system; and still others focus on the number of states that are needed to provide collective goods in the international political economy.

A recent study examined the effects of these aspects of the distribution of power, as well as a number of other political and economic factors, on the level of international trade (as a percentage of global production) during the period from 1850 to 1965 in order to test hegemonic stability theory and some of the alternative explanations described in the previous section (Mansfield, 1992a). That analysis of the distribution of power centered on two variables: (1) hegemony, and (2) concentration. With regard to hegemony, scholars of international relations have yet to agree on how it should be defined and measured; and there is consequently much disagreement among them regarding which periods have (and have not) been characterized by it. In order to determine the extent to which the effects of hegemony on trade were sensitive to disagreements concerning which periods were hegemonic during the nineteenth and twentieth centuries, my analysis was based on two well-known classifications of hegemony, one derived by Gilpin (1981, 1987) and the other by Wallerstein (1983). Both agree that hegemony is characterized by the political and economic preponderance of a single state, and that the United States was hegemonic during that portion of the post-World War II era that I examined. However, they differ over when British hegemony concluded: Gilpin dates its conclusion in 1914, while Wallerstein dates its conclusion in 1873.

The second variable, concentration, is generally measured by scholars of international relations with the following index (Ray and Singer, 1973):

$$CON_t = \frac{\sqrt{\sum_{i=1}^{N_t} (S_{it})^2 - 1/N_t}}{1 - 1/N_t}, \tag{9.1}$$

where S_{it} is the proportion of the aggregate capabilities (which, as pointed out above, are typically used as proxies for political power by analysts of international relations) possessed by all major powers that major power i possesses in year t,[4] and N_t is the number of major powers in the system in year t. It has been shown that CON_t can be expressed as a function of: (1) the number of major powers in the system (N_t), and (2) the relative inequality of capabilities among the major powers (V_t) in year t (Mansfield, 1992b). More specifically:

$$CON_t = \frac{V_t}{\sqrt{N_t - 1}}, \tag{9.2}$$

where V_t is the coefficient of variation (standard deviation divided by the mean) of S_{it}.

Since both hegemonic stability theorists and many of their critics have emphasized the effects of the number of major powers and the relative inequality of power among them, I have analyzed the influences of these aspects of the distribution of power, as well as their effects via concentration, on the level of international trade (Mansfield, 1992a, forthcoming). A series of regression analyses indicates that the effect of hegemony on the level of global trade (as a percentage of global production) varied considerably depending on whether Gilpin's or Wallerstein's classification of hegemony was used. The results based on Gilpin's classifications of hegemony pointed in the direction predicted by hegemony stability theorists: periods of hegemony were associated with higher levels of trade. Not only was the regression coefficient of hegemony usually statistically significant, but the level of trade also was found to be about 25 per cent greater during periods of hegemony than during periods that lacked a hegemon. The results based on Wallerstein's classifications of hegemony, however, yielded little evidence that hegemony was related to the level of global commerce. In particular, the sign of the regression coefficient of hegemony was sensitive to the specification of the model, the size of the regression coefficient of hegemony was quite small, and in no case was it statistically significant. The fact that the effects of hegemony on trade depend so heavily on which classification of hegemony is used underscores the difficulties in arriving at generalizations about the usefulness of hegemonic stability theory until scholars come to some consensus regarding how to define, measure and operationalize hegemony.

My findings also indicated that a direct relationship exists between the number of major powers in the system (N_t) and the level of international trade. Since small group theories imply that a reduction in the number of major powers enhances the likelihood that collective goods, such as the international infrastructure necessary to sustain free trade, will be provided, these results are inconsistent with predictions based on theories of this sort. Instead, the observed relationship between the number of major powers and the level of international trade suggests that the benefits from international trade may be excludable and, hence, not collective goods. This relationship may also be due to the tendency for states to worry less about how the gains from trade will be distributed as the number of major powers in the system increases (Snidal, 1991).

Finally, the results of this study indicated that a U-shaped relationship exists between concentration (CON_t) and trade, as well as between the relative inequality among the major powers (V_t) and trade. That is, the level of global trade has been greatest when concentration was both highest and lowest, and it has been lowest when concentration approached an intermediate level. (See Mansfield (1992a) for a fuller discussion of the reasons for these findings.) But both low and intermediate levels of concentration are likely to be non-hegemonic.[5] Thus, analysts who rely solely on hegemony to measure the system's structure may fail to account for potentially marked differences in the relationships between various non-hegemonic distributions of power and outcomes in the international political economy.

9.4   The concentration of capabilities and regional trade

One reason why intermediate levels of concentration (and of the relative inequality of capabilities among the major powers) were found to be associated with relatively low levels of trade may be that these distributions of capabilities are also associated with the existence of RIAs. In a seminal study, Krasner (1976) examined the relationship between the distribution of power and the extent to which the trading system was open or closed during the period from 1820 to 1970. He defined open (closed) systems as ones in which: (1) the levels of trade (as a percentage of national income) of the leading states in the system are relatively high (low); (2) the tariff levels are relatively low (high); and (3) trade is not (is) guided by RIAs.

Krasner's analysis of the determinants of openness and closure focused on the effects of three distributions of power. First, he argued that hegemonic systems were likely to be open because openness increases the power of the leading state and a hegemon possesses the ability to coerce smaller states that attempt to deviate from liberal trade policies. Second, he maintained that systems comprising many small and highly developed states are also likely to be open with respect to trade, because the opportunity costs of closure are large for each state and because trade will increase the national income of each state and its political power to roughly the same degree. Third, 'a system comprised of a few very large, but unequally developed states ... is likely to lead to a closed structure', because openness would lead to unequal rates of growth among the major powers and, hence, would alter the distribution of power among them. Under these circumstances, these ' [l] arge states, attempting to protect themselves from the vagaries of a global system, seek to maximize their interests by creating regional [trade] blocs' (Krasner, 1976, pp. 321, 324).

On the basis of Krasner's analysis, it is difficult to determine the extent to which the three distributions of power on which he focused are related to the level of concentration. But, while hegemony and concentration need not move in tandem (Mansfield, 1992a, forthcoming), it is likely that hegemonic systems will be characterized by relatively high levels of concentration, systems comprising many small states will be characterized by relatively low levels of concentration, and systems comprising a few very large states will be characterized by intermediate levels of concentration. This suggests that a U-shaped relationship might exist between the distribution of power and openness-and-closure, which is consistent with my findings concerning the relationship between the concentration of capabilities and the level of international trade. Moreover, if, as Krasner and others (for example, Gilpin, 1975, 1987) have suggested, low levels of total global trade have tended to coincide with high levels of intra-regional trade,[6] then intermediate levels of concentration may be associated with high levels of intra-regional trade.

The dearth of complete data on patterns of regional trade precludes any empirical analysis of this hypothesis for the nineteenth and twentieth centuries. But it is interesting that, given the number of major powers in the system during the 1930s, and holding constant the level of global income, the level of concentration that minimized the level of international trade as a percentage of global production from 1850 to 1965 was most closely approximated by those which obtained during the 1930s (Mansfield, 1992a). Further, Anderson and Norheim's Chapter 2 in this volume demonstrates that, based on analyses of patterns of regional trade for the period from 1928 to 1990, the worldwide propensity to trade extra-regionally was lowest during the 1930s (see their Table 2.2). There is also fairly widespread agreement that the 1930s were characterized by the development of a series of RIAs, and that, '[d]uring the 1930s the approach to PTAs [preferential trade arrangements] was not to reduce trade barriers for preferred trading partners but rather to increase trade barriers on non-preferred trade, so that instead of trade creation and trade diversion the outcome was trade destruction and trade diversion' (Pomfret, 1988, p. 56; see also Krasner, 1976). Hence, this evidence seems to be consistent with the hypothesis that intermediate levels of concentration have been associated with both low levels of total international trade and high levels of regionalism.

9.5   The dynamic time-path question

These findings concerning the relationship between concentration and trade may also bear on what Bhagwati (1992) has referred to as the dynamic time-path question. He notes that it is 'asserted often that regionalism will ... *accelerate* the multilateral process: the threat of going (unilateral and) regional will produce multilateral agreements that may be otherwise held up' (Bhagwati, 1992, pp. 13–14, emphasis in original). This argument, of which he is critical, is similar in tone to that of Kemp and Wan (1976) and Grinols (1981), who demonstrate that any subset of states *can* form a customs union that does not reduce the welfare of each member without adversely affecting the welfare of non-members, and that there are incentives for this customs union to expand until it becomes a single global customs union (i.e., for free trade to exist world-wide).

If the existence of a U-shaped relationship between the concentration of capabilities and the level of international trade bears on the issue of whether RIAs will be expansionist or protectionist, then the available evidence does not suggest that these arrangements will be outward-looking with respect to trade or that they will coagulate into a global customs union. Instead, RIAs are likely to fragment the international trading system (Bhagwati, 1992).

This position is at least partially consistent with Gilpin's (1987) observation that a series of protectionist RIAs is one likely outcome of the weakening of United States hegemony and the emergence of a system in which the United States, Japan and the EC will be the leading economic actors. Depending on the 'sizes' of the remaining states, this type of system is likely to be characterized by an intermediate level of concentration. As Gilpin has pointed out, under these circumstances, some form of 'pluralistic leadership' will be needed for the maintenance of a liberal trading system. But the collective action problems inherent in pluralistic leadership and the lack of a hegemon-in-waiting

> threaten further dissolution of the unity of the liberal international economic order. ... [Moreover, a]lthough it is highly unlikely that increased fragmentation will lead to a collapse of the global system as serious as that of the 1930s, regionalism will surely become a more prominent feature of international economic and political relations. (Gilpin, 1987, pp. 397, 407).[7]

For Gilpin and a number of other hegemonic stability theorists, the future of the current trading system and the prospects for avoiding the formation of a series of protectionist RIAs are likely to rest on the emergence of a new hegemon, a development which seems unlikely in the short run.[8] If, however, we focus on the effects of concentration, and if Gilpin's argument suggests that recent changes in the distribution of power are leading to the emergence of an intermediate level of concentration, then a further diffusion, as well as a reconcentration, of power may have the effects of promoting a liberal global trading system.

9.6   The effects of alliances on trade[9]

Related to the issue of whether the distribution of power influences trade is the issue of whether political-military alliances impact commerce. Many variants of hegemonic stability theory, as well as standard international trade theory, ignore the fact that commercial relations since the conclusion of World War II have been guided, in large measure, by the division of the global system into two political-military blocs (Gowa, 1989a, b). It is unlikely that the effects of alliances on commerce were either coincidental or unique to post-World War II trade relations. As argued below, there are reasons to expect that alliances should exert a systematic effect on international trade.

Central to the effects of alliances on trade is the anarchic nature of the international system. Because there is no central authority vested with the ability to govern international relations, each state must ensure its own security (Waltz, 1979; Gilpin, 1981). To this end, states cannot afford to neglect the effects of their behavior on their potential power relative to the remaining states in the system.

One implication of this political imperative is that states must evaluate the effects of engaging in international commerce on the distribution of power. These effects are products of the gains from trade. Since these gains generate increases in national income that can be used to augment the military power of any state that engages in trade, commercial relations are likely to influence power relations and, hence, to generate security externalities (Gowa, 1989b).

However, the political consequences of commerce are also likely to vary depending on the nature of the political relationship among the trading partners. On the one hand, trade among political allies is not expected to undermine the security of the participants. Under these conditions, the gains from trade accrue to states with common security goals. Allies therefore have little reason to view as threatening increases in the power of members that are generated by trade. In fact, the gains in efficiency that are fostered by the expansion of trade among allies should increase the aggregate income of the alliance partners and, hence, their collective political-military power. As a result, the alliance is likely to become stronger, and the alliance partners are likely to become increasingly secure, as trade flows increase among them. Alliances therefore help to internalize the security externalities associated with commerce, thereby reducing trade barriers and increasing the flow of trade among alliance members.

On the other hand, trade among actual or potential adversaries generates a security diseconomy. A state which trades freely with an adversary is likely to augment the political power of its trading partner and, hence, undermine its own security.[10] But individual traders within states are unlikely to have an incentive to take these social costs of trade with an adversarial nation into account. Under these circumstances, the private and social costs of trade diverge. The market failure that this situation gives rise to can, in principle, be remedied with recourse to a tariff or other commercial instruments.[11] As a result, unilateral free trade policies may not be optimal for states in an anarchic international system.

This argument is similar to the view that open international markets may undermine a state's defense and that governments should intervene to protect those industries that are crucial to national defense. It has been pointed out that using tariffs and other trade barriers to protect these industries is an inefficient response to this market failure, since they distort both production and consumption. However, tariffs are likely to be 'first-best' responses to market failures when the distortion resides in trade itself, rather than in suboptimal levels of production or consumption. And the distortion is likely to reside in trade itself when commerce is conducted among actual or potential adversaries.

It is clear that tariffs and other trade barriers will ameliorate the security externalities produced by trade only if they influence the real income of a trading partner. This condition will be met if the state imposing the tariff has some influence over its terms of trade. Under these conditions, the use of a tariff will increase the real income of the state using this instrument while decreasing the real income of its target.

This argument is clearly a variant of the well-known optimal tariff argument. What distinguishes it from the traditional optimal tariff argument is that the Prisoners' Dilemma structure of state preferences with respect to trade differs systematically between allies and actual and potential adversaries. In particular, allies have an easier time solving the Prisoners' Dilemma than adversaries, since cooperation in trade among allies increases the potential power of the alliance, while cooperation in trade with an adversary generates security externalities that may threaten one's security.

The relationship between alliances and trade has received little attention by empirical analysts. But a recent study examines the relationship between alliances and trade among the major powers during the twentieth century, using a standard gravity model of bilateral trade flows in order to control for the effects of certain economic factors that also would be expected to influence foreign commerce (Gowa and Mansfield, 1991). On the basis of results from a series of regressions, we found that higher levels of trade have been conducted between states which were allied than between states which were potential or actual adversaries.

The results of this study also indicate, however, that the effects of alliances on trade depend on both the type of alliance and the distribution of power. First, bilateral alliances (those comprised of only two members) have exerted more pronounced influences than multilateral alliances (those comprised of more than two members) on bilateral trade flows, although the quantitative impacts of both types of alliances on trade have been substantial. In particular, our preliminary findings indicate that, on average and holding constant a variety of other factors, the existence of a bilateral alliance more than doubles the predicted flow of trade between its members, and the existence of a multilateral alliance increases trade between its members by more than one-third.

Second, consistently with Gowa's (1989b) argument, we found that alliances have had a larger and stronger influence on bilateral trade during periods of bipolarity than during periods of multipolarity, regardless of whether they were comprised of two or more than two members. It should also be noted that these results were quite robust with respect to the sample of states analyzed, and whether or not other factors were included that might be expected to influence both alliances and trade (such as the existence of wars, military disputes or preferential trading arrangements between the trading partners, as well as whether the trading partners were democracies or not).

9.7   Alliances and customs unions

In addition to the effects that alliances have on trade, they are also likely to influence the timing of the formation of customs unions and how customs union partners are chosen. While much research has been conducted on the economics of customs union formation, it seems obvious that political factors too are likely to be important in this regard. As Bhagwati (1992, p. 28) points out,

> it is hard to imagine that the arbitrary groupings of countries that seek FTAs and CUs are dependent on economic arguments as their key determinants. Often, politics seems to drive these choices of partners, as in the case of the EC, and now in the case of FTAs throughout the Americas. This also accounts for the occasional non-regionally-proximate choice of partners in [trading] blocs.

Yet few economists or political scientists have explicitly treated the question of whether political alliances influence the choice of customs union partners and the formation of customs unions. [12]

Even a casual glance at the customs unions that have formed since the conclusion of World War II indicates that customs union partners tend to be political-military allies. All members of the European Economic Community, the Council of Mutual Economic Assistance, the Andean Common Market, the Central American Common Market, the Latin American Free Trade Association, the Central African Customs and Economics Union, the Maghreb Group, the Canada–US Free Trade Area, and the US–Israeli Free Trade Area were allies at the times when these RIAs and customs unions were formed. [13] Further, many (although not all) members of the Common Afro-Mauritian Organization, the Association of South-East Asian Nations, the East African Common Market, and the European Free Trade Association were also allied when these organizations were founded. [14]

This is not to suggest that customs unions have formed only among allies, even if we restrict our attention to the period after World War II. However, the extent to which customs unions historically have been comprised of political-military allies is striking.

9.7.1   Why are customs unions formed among allies?

The effects of alliances on trade may help to explain why customs unions often have been formed among allies. Customs unions and RIAs have the effect of reducing trade barriers among the contracting parties. In so doing, they are expected to increase the flow of trade among these states and, hence, to generate security externalities.

If adversaries form a customs union, each member must worry that the resulting increase in commerce will augment the political-military power of its foes. Thus, a customs union comprising adversaries threatens to undermine the national security of (at least some of) its members. As a result, customs unions among adversaries are likely to be rare and, in those cases when they are formed, short-lived.

Customs unions among allies pose fewer problems of this sort. At least from the standpoint of national security, the welfare of a state increases both when it gains more from trade and when its allies do. The reduction or elimination of trade barriers among a group of states is therefore likely to be far less deleterious when they are engaged in a political alliance than when they are not. Further, customs unions formed among allies are likely to enhance the reliability and predictability of trade relations. These considerations are of particular importance for the purposes of ensuring that those investments which are made in fixed assets to service a specific foreign market are not jeopardized. Since 'transaction-specific investment' is particularly susceptible to the imposition of trade barriers (Yarbrough and Yarbrough, 1987) and since, all other things being equal, trade barriers tend to be lower among allies than among adversaries, future access to the markets of customs union partners is likely to be more secure, and fixed assets in which firms invest to service these markets are therefore likely to be more profitable, when CU and RIA partners are allied than when they are not. Hence, the fact that alliances help to internalize the security externalities generated by trade, and the tendency for alliances to increase the reliability of access to the markets of trading partners, offer possible explanations for the clear tendency of states to choose allies as CU and RIA partners.

9.7.2 Alliances and the expansion of customs unions

In addition to the tendency for customs unions to form among allies, it is clear too that the expansion of customs unions has also tended to occur among allies. For example, Greece (1981), the United Kingdom (1973), Denmark (1973) and Portugal (1986) were NATO members at the times they were granted membership into the EC. And the commercial agreement between the EFTA and the EC linked NATO members and neutral states with clear pro-NATO biases (with the possible exception of Finland).

The tendency for CUs to expand among alliance partners – but not beyond the boundaries of political-military alliances – may help to explain why customs unions do not form and expand along lines consistent with Kemp and Wan's analysis. Their theorem implies that, under certain circumstances, there could be economic incentives for customs unions to 'form and enlarge ... until the world is one big customs union, that is, until world free trade persists' (Kemp and Wan, 1976, p. 96). As they point out, the absence of a global customs union may be explained by, among other factors, problems associated with choosing CU partners and the 'noneconomic' objectives of nations. National security concerns are likely to be especially salient in this regard.

In particular, the Kemp–Wan theorem calls for both setting post-union tariffs and providing a series of compensatory payments to states so that each state, regardless of whether it is or is not a CU member, would not be harmed economically by the formation of the economic union (see also Grinols, 1981). But it is obvious that, to the extent that CUs are embedded within alliances, not making *any* state outside the economic union worse off is antithetical to the political purpose of the union. Since alliances are formed primarily to bolster the security of the contracting states, it clearly makes little sense from a political stand-point to compensate, and thereby augment the political power of, adversaries.

Similarly, the expansion of a customs union, particularly one that becomes global, will certainly include both friends and foes. This engenders the problems discussed above with respect to forming customs unions that include adversaries. Thus, despite the *potential* welfare benefits from the continued expansion of a customs union, the international political costs of expanding an economic union beyond political-military allies may be substantial.

9.7.3　Alliances, trade diversion and trade creation

Finally, it is worth noting that the fact that economists often consider CUs to be trade diverting, rather than trade creating, may be attributed to the tendency for CUs to be embedded within alliances. In fact, one purpose of an alliance may be to divert trade away from states whose efficiency and, hence, their political power has been enhanced by trade. Under these conditions, trade diversion is likely to be politically beneficial for the alliance partners.

This line of argument seems to be consistent with those of Johnson (1965) and Cooper and Massell (1965a, b). As Pomfret (1988, p. 144) points out, 'if the sole aim is to replace imports from outside the union by production within the union, then trade diversion is a benefit. This is the Johnson–Cooper–Massell explanation of why customs unions are formed.' Likewise, in many cases, alliances are designed to shift production from external to internal sources for security reasons. This, in turn, may provide political benefits for those states that wish to avoid trade dependence on an adversary and the political repercussions that are likely to result from this dependence.

It is clear that the extent to which alliances divert trade depends on a host of factors that vary from alliance to alliance. But given that CUs have tended to be embedded within alliances and are trade diverting, one reason for the latter may be that trade is guided by the 'pursuit of power' as well as by the 'pursuit of plenty' (Viner, 1948).

9.8 Conclusions

This chapter has examined the effects of the distribution of power and political-military alliances on international trade. First, it is argued that both the strength and the nature of the relationship between the distribution of power and the level of international trade depend on which feature of this distribution is analyzed. When hegemony is analyzed, previous empirical research indicates that its effects vary depending on how hegemony is defined, measured and operationalized. When concentration is analyzed, there is strong evidence of a U-shaped relationship between concentration and global trade: international commerce seems to flourish both when the level of the concentration of capabilities is relatively high and when it is relatively low, while intermediate levels of concentration have been associated with low levels of trade.

Second, the effects of political-military alliances on international commerce have been examined. Central to the effect of alliances on trade are the security externalities associated with trade. These are products of the gains from trade, which can be used to augment a state's political-military power. Since alliances help to internalize these security externalities, political incentives exist for states to trade more freely with political-military allies than with adversaries. Further, given the effects of alliances on commerce, it is not surprising that, at least during the period after World War II, RIAs have tended to form and expand among allies.

It is commonly argued that the multilateral trading system and many of its attendant institutions are coming under severe strain. The arguments presented in this chapter suggest that these strains may be outgrowths of recent changes in the distribution of power and political alliances. More generally, a fuller understanding of the international political economy of trade – to which Baldwin's Chapter 18 in this volume contributes – is needed if these pressures are to be managed effectively.

Notes

The author is grateful to Kym Anderson, Jagdish Bhagwati, Richard Blackhurst, Joanne Gowa and Francisco Rivera-Batiz for helpful comments on earlier versions of this chapter.

1. See Ikenberry *et al.* (1988) for an overview of domestic political explanations of commercial policy, and a comparison of systemic and domestic approaches to the study of the international political economy.
2. A related argument is advanced by Spiro (forthcoming), who maintains that the nature of power, rather than power outcomes in the international political economy, varies as hegemons rise and decline. Spiro argues that this helps to explain why the foreign economic policies of the US have become increasingly unilateral as its relative position has declined.
3. See, however, Gilpin (1987) and especially Gowa (1989a) for rebuttals and responses to these critiques.
4. Since, as noted above, many analysts have argued that economic, demographic and military capabilities are especially important indicators of political power, these types of capabilities were used to measure concentration.
5. Indeed, even the highest observed levels of concentration may be non-hegemonic, since there need not be a particularly strong relationship between these features of the distribution of power.
6. Clearly, the level of global trade and the degree to which international commerce is characterized by inward-looking RIAs need not move in tandem. For example, Chadwick and Deutsch (1973) found that the regionalism that began during the 1930s persisted well into the 1950s, a period marked by a large expansion of trade. But see also the data compiled by Norheim, Finger and Anderson and reported in the Appendix to this volume.
7. On this point, see also Oye (1992), who agrees that the erosion of US hegemony is likely to promote commercial discrimination. He argues, however, that unlike the situation during the 1930s, 'in commercial affairs during the 1980s, economic discrimination has been an important force for liberalization' (Oye, 1992, p. 208), and that this may continue to be the case.
8. It should be noted that hegemonic stability theorists are not of a single mind on this issue. Lake (1991), for example, has argued that the conditions that have historically led non-hegemonic systems to fragment into protectionist RIAs do not seem to exist at present. Among critics of hegemonic stability theory, see McKeown (1991) and Milner (1991) for arguments that the decline of US hegemony is unlikely to usher in a period of pronounced regionalism.
9. This section is based on Gowa and Mansfield (1991).
10. Of course, if this state expects its gains from trade to exceed those of its adversary, then it might have an incentive to engage in such commerce. Under these circumstances, free trade might enhance its security vis-à-vis its adversary. However, its adversary might determine that this commercial relationship was not to its advantage because its gains from trade were less than the benefits accruing to the first state. The adversary might therefore have an incentive to limit such trade.
11. For example, in addition to tariffs, embargoes that are designed to limit the military potential of an adversary are likely to serve much the same purpose.

12. The possibility that political alliances might influence customs unions has been alluded to by a number of analysts. For example, Viner (1950, pp. 94–5) cites Gustav Schmoller (writing in 1916) in pointing out that the German Zollverein was 'the one considerable exception to the historical law that political union tends to precede commercial union', and he cites Friedrich List (writing in 1841, and not taking the Zollverein into account) as follows: 'All examples which history can show are those in which the political union has led the way, and the commercial has followed. Not a single instance can be adduced in which the latter has taken the lead, and the former has grown up from it.' Viner himself concludes that a 'generalization' can be made that 'past political unions ... preceded (or were simultaneous with) commercial union'. While the political unions to which these authors refer are primarily nation states, the argument that political union tends to precede economic union can also be applied to groupings of states and, in particular, to political-military alliances.

13. See Small and Singer (1969) for data on alliance partners. For the purposes of this discussion, I refer to defense pacts and ententes, as well as formal political-military alliances, as alliances. See Hartland-Thunberg (1980) for members of these free trade areas and customs unions.

14. Not only have customs unions tended to form among allies, but trade wars also have occurred primarily among states which were not allied. For example, Pomfret (1988, p. 17) argues that the Franco-Italian trade war that was waged from 1887 to 1898 'was the economic repercussion of Italy's decision to ally with Germany and Austria-Hungary rather than with France'. On the political dynamics of trade wars, see Conybeare (1987).

References

Baldwin, R. E. (1985), *The Political Economy of U.S. Import Policy*, Cambridge, MA: MIT Press.

Bhagwati, J. N. (1992), 'Regionalism and Multilateralism: An Overview', presented to the World Bank Centre for Economic Policy Research (CEPR) Conference on New Dimensions in Regional Integration, Washington, DC, April 2–3.

Chadwick, W. and K. W. Deutsch (1973), 'International Trade and Economic Integration: Further Developments in Trade Matrix Analysis', *Comparative Political Studies* **6**: 84–109.

Conybeare, J. A. C. (1983), 'Tariff Protection in Developed and Developing Countries: A Cross-Sectional and Longitudinal Analysis', *International Organization* **37**: 441–67.

Conybeare, J. A. C. (1984), 'Public Goods, Prisoners' Dilemmas and the International Political Economy', *International Studies Quarterly* **28**: 5–22.

Conybeare, J. A. C. (1987), *Trade Wars: The Theory and Practice of International Commercial Rivalry*, New York: Columbia University Press.

Cooper, C. A. and B. F. Massell (1965a), 'A New Look at Customs Union Theory', *Economic Journal* **75**: 742–7.

Cooper, C. A. and B. F. Massell (1965b), 'Toward a General Theory of Customs Unions for Developing Countries', *Journal of Political Economy* **73**: 461–76.

Gilpin, R. (1975), *U.S. Power and the Multinational Corporation: The Political Economy of Foreign Direct Investment*, New York: Basic Books.

Gilpin, R. (1981), *War and Change in World Politics*, New York: Cambridge University Press.

Gilpin, R. (1987), *The Political Economy of International Relations*, Princeton: Princeton University Press.

Gowa, J. (1989a), 'Rational Hegemons, Excludable Goods, and Small Groups: An Epitaph for Hegemonic Stability Theory?', *World Politics* **41**: 307–24.

Gowa, J. (1989b), 'Bipolarity, Multipolarity and Free Trade', *American Political Science Review* **83**: 1245–56.

Gowa, J. and E. D. Mansfield (1991), 'Allies, Adversaries, and International Trade', presented at the annual meeting of the American Political Science Association, Washington, DC.

Grinols, E. L. (1981), 'An Extension of the Kemp–Wan Theorem on the Formation of Customs Unions', *Journal of International Economics* **11**: 259–66.

Hartland-Thunberg, P. (1980), *Trading Blocs, U.S. Exports, and World Trade*, Boulder: Westview.

Ikenberry, G. J., D. A. Lake and M. Mastanduno (1988), 'Introduction: Approaches to Explaining American Foreign Economic Policy', *International Organization* **42**: 1–14.

Johnson, H. G. (1965), 'An Economic Theory of Protectionism, Tariff Bargaining, and the Formation of Customs Unions', *Journal of Political Economy* **73**: 256–83.

Katzenstein, P. J. (1986), *Small States in World Markets*, Ithaca: Cornell University Press.

Kemp, M. C. and H. Y. Wan (1976), 'An Elementary Proposition Concerning the Formation of Customs Unions', *Journal of International Economics* **6**: 95–7.

Keohane, R. O. (1984a), *After Hegemony: Cooperation and Discord in the World Political Economy*, Princeton: Princeton University Press.

Keohane, R. O. (1984b), 'The World Political Economy and the Crisis of Embedded Liberalism', in *Order and Conflict in Contemporary Capitalism*, edited by J. H. Goldthorpe, Oxford: Clarendon Press.

Kindleberger, C. P. (1973), *The World in Depression, 1929–1939*, Berkeley: University of California Press.

Kindleberger, C. P. (1981), 'Dominance and Leadership in the International Economy: Exploitation, Public Goods, and Free Riders', *International Studies Quarterly* **25**: 242–54.

Krasner, S. D. (1976), 'State Power and the Structure of International Trade', *World Politics* **28**: 317–47.

Lake, D. A. (1988), *Power, Protection, and Free Trade: International Sources of U.S. Commercial Strategy: 1897–1939*, Ithaca: Cornell University Press.

Lake, D. A. (1991), 'British and American Hegemony Compared: Lessons for the Current Era of Decline', in *History, the White House, and the Kremlin*, edited by M. Fry, London: Pinter.

McKeown, T. J. (1983), 'Hegemonic Stability Theory and 19th-Century Tariff Levels in Europe', *International Organization* **37**: 73–91.

McKeown, T. J. (1991), 'A Liberal Trading Order? The Long-Run Pattern of Imports to the Advanced Capitalist States', *International Studies Quarterly* **35**: 171–2.

Magee, S. P., W. A. Brock and L. Young (1989), *Black Hole Tariffs and Endogenous Policy Theory: Political Economy in General Equilibrium*, New York: Cambridge University Press.

Mansfield, E. D. (1992a), 'The Concentration of Capabilities and International Trade', *International Organization* **46**: 731–64.

Mansfield, E. D. (1992b), 'The Concentration of Capabilities and the Onset of War', *Journal of Conflict Resolution* **36**: 3–24.

Mansfield, E. D. (forthcoming), 'Concentration, Polarity, and the Distribution of Power', *International Studies Quarterly*.

Milner, H. (1991), 'A Three Bloc Trading System?', presented at the Fifteenth World Congress of the International Political Science Association, Buenos Aires.

Olson, M. (1971), *The Logic of Collective Action: Public Goods and the Theory of Groups*, Cambridge, MA: Harvard University Press.

Oye, K. A. (1992), *Economic Discrimination and Political Exchange: World Political Economy in the 1930s and 1980s*, Princeton: Princeton University Press.

Pomfret, R. (1988), *Unequal Trade: The Economics of Discriminatory International Trade Policies*, Oxford: Basil Blackwell.

Ray, J. L. and J. D. Singer (1973), 'Measuring the Concentration of Power in the International System', *Sociological Methods and Research* **1**: 403–37.

Russett, B. (1985), 'The Mysterious Case of Vanishing Hegemony', *International Organization* **39**: 207–32.

Small, M. and J. D. Singer (1969), 'Formal Alliances, 1816–1965: An Extension of the Basic Data', *Journal of Peace Research* **6**: 257–82.

Snidal, D. (1985), 'The Limits of Hegemonic Stability Theory', *International Organization* **39**: 579–614.

Snidal, D. (1991), 'Relative Gains and the Pattern of Cooperation', *American Political Science Review* **85**: 701–26.

Spiro, D. E. (forthcoming), *Hegemony Unbound: The International Political Economy of Recycling Petrodollars*, Ithaca: Cornell University Press.

Stein, A. A. (1984), 'The Hegemon's Dilemma: Great Britain, the United States, and the International Economic Order', *International Organization* **38**: 355–86.

Viner, J. (1948), 'Power versus Plenty as Objectives of Foreign Policy in the Seventeenth and Eighteenth Centuries', *World Politics* **1**: 1–29.

Viner, J. (1950), *The Customs Union Issue*, New York: Carnegie Endowment for International Peace.

Wallerstein, I. (1983), 'The Three Instances of Hegemony in the History of the Capitalist World-Economy', *International Journal of Comparative Sociology* **24**: 100–8.

Waltz, K. N. (1979), *Theory of International Politics*, Reading: Addison-Wesley.

Yarbrough, B. V. and R. M. Yarbrough (1987), 'Cooperation in the Liberalization of International Trade: After Hegemony, What?', *International Organization* **41**: 1–26.

10

Holes and loopholes in integration agreements: history and prospects

Bernard Hoekman and Michael Leidy

It often appears to be taken as self-evident that regional integration agreements (RIAs) can (and do) result in more far-reaching liberalization of intra-bloc trade than is possible if countries restrict themselves to a multilateral approach. Thus, popular assertions on the part of 'region-alists' – summarized and vigorously contested by Bhagwati (1992) – that regionalism is a quicker, more efficient, and more certain path to freer trade are based on the premise that liberalization actually occurs. This paper asks whether RIAs do in fact tend to imply or facilitate greater liberalization of trade flows *among* member countries than what has been achieved (or sought) in the multilateral GATT context. This is an issue that has received relatively little attention. The economics literature has focused instead on the welfare and external effects of RIAs, on the assumption that internal liberalization has occurred. Our underlying hypothesis is that the political-economy forces that block far-reaching liberalization in the multilateral context also remain robust and largely decisive in sculpting RIAs.

Many observers have pointed out that intra-regional trade in North America and Western Europe has grown faster than inter-regional trade in the post-World War II period. It is unclear, however, to what extent – if at all – this is due to regional integration efforts, as the incentives for this to occur may arise in any event as a result of geographical proximity, economic growth, and periodic non-discriminatory liberal-ization of trade (via the GATT) and investment (e.g., under OECD auspices). Data presented by Anderson and Norheim (Chapter 2 in this volume) reveal that since the late 1920s the intensity of intra-regional trade for the three major regions has always tended to be much higher than the intensity of extra-regional trade. Even for Europe, where intra-regional trade increased significantly over the last sixty years, Anderson and Norheim show that the index of *propensity* for extra-regional trade[1] has remained pretty much unchanged. In a setting where nondiscriminatory and preferential liberalization efforts are pursued simultaneously, trade data cannot provide an unambiguous indicator of intra-regional liberalization associated with the introduction of a RIA (Lloyd, 1992). Instead, trade data need to be complemented by policy-based indicators.

In this chapter we discuss what we call 'holes' (primarily sectoral exclusions and exemptions) and 'loopholes' (which consist of escape clauses and safeguard provisions of various kinds – including so-called unfair trade provisions – and the possibilities for using discretion to set and enforce standards and other non-tariff measures). Their prevalence in an agreement is examined to assess, albeit qualitatively, the degree to which existing RIAs involving OECD countries liberalize intra-regional trade beyond the prevailing multilateral trade policy regime. This distinguishes the analysis from related efforts which focus on the extent to which specific RIAs attain their objectives (for example, Whalley, 1992; Winters, 1992). Attention is restricted to RIAs between industrialized countries because these are the agreements that are usually considered to be of most concern for the functioning of the multilateral trading system. Moreover, these RIAs are generally considered to be relatively successful. In contrast, past Latin American or African integration efforts are generally seen as never having had significant liberalization of trade as an objective (Bhagwati, 1992). The approach is positive, not normative. Thus, welfare issues, in particular the empirical question of the magnitude of the effects associated with specific RIAs, are ignored.[2]

The chapter is structured as follows. Section 10.1 starts with a description of the major 'holes' and 'loopholes' included in the GATT, as GATT is used as a benchmark for comparison purposes. It then goes on to discuss some of the economic aspects of these holes and loopholes and their political economy rationales. The next four sections turn to existing RIAs. Section 10.2 focuses on the European Economic Community, Section 10.3 on the European Free Trade Association, and Section 10.4 on the trade agreements negotiated between the EC and other European countries. Section 10.5 turns to the Canada–U.S. Free Trade Agreement.[3] Then Section 10.6 sums up by posing two questions: (1) how much more has been achieved by these RIAs over and above multilaterally negotiated commitments; and (2) are there significant differences between alternative types of RIAs? To anticipate, the suggested answer to the first question is: not that much. It is stressed that this does not necessarily imply that the RIAs have not led to liberalization. Instead, until very recently, the rather limited progress (liberalization) that occurred over time in the regional context appears to be reflected in concurrent or subsequent efforts to achieve similar progress at the multilateral level. While this suggests that one can be rather sanguine about the historical record, certain types of RIAs appear to offer more scope – and/or imply a greater need – for holes and loopholes than others. The review of past experience of RIAs offers a number of lessons to those countries that may seek to negotiate similar agreements. These are discussed in the concluding section.

10.1 Holes and loopholes in GATT: conceptual and economic issues

10.1.1 Exceptions, exemptions and escape clauses in GATT: an overview[4]

Rather than regulating the possible spectrum of specific policies that might distort trade, the GATT relies on three fundamental principles: non-discrimination, national treatment and transparency. Non-discrimination implies that all foreign products are to be treated equally when entering the territory of a contracting party (MFN treatment). National treatment applies once a foreign product has entered the territory (that is, has satisfied whatever conditions are imposed in terms of tariffs and formalities). Attempts to ensure transparency are reflected in requirements to publish and notify trade policies and changes to GATT, in provisions to exchange information in specific circumstances, as well as in the operation of various committees and regular meetings of representatives.

The GATT applies only to merchandise trade. It does not apply to trade in services or factors of production (capital, labor). Government procurement is also formally excluded.[5] These exclusions constitute major 'holes' in the GATT. What about 'loopholes'? Provisions in the GATT that allow for the *temporary* suspension of obligations include the following:

- Article VI allows action to be taken if a product is judged to be dumped or to benefit from subsidies that affect trade and materially injure domestic industries (in which cases Article VI allows levies to be imposed to offset the effect of the dumping or subsidization).
- Articles XII and XVIII:B permit restrictions on imports to safeguard a country's external financial position and its balance of payments.
- Articles XVIII:A and XVIII:C allow trade restrictions to be imposed by developing countries in order to protect infant industries.

● Article XIX allows governments to restrict trade if imports of a product cause or threaten serious injury to domestic producers of similar products.

Contracting parties may also seek agreement from other parties to the GATT under Article XXV (Joint Action) to discontinue the application of GATT provisions for specific sectors. Such formal waivers have been accorded to contracting parties from time to time. The main sectors affected by waivers are agriculture and textiles and clothing.[6] In addition, contracting parties have also made use of informal mechanisms implying a discontinuation of GATT obligations for specific sectors. The most widely used instrument in this connection is the voluntary export restraint (VER) agreement.

Provisions of the GATT allowing for exceptions from the general obligations of the Agreement of a *continuing* nature include the following:

● Article XX (General Exceptions) and Article XXI (National Security) allow measures to be imposed to safeguard public morals, health, laws and natural resources, and national security, subject to the requirement that such measures are not applied in a manner that would constitute a means of arbitrary or unjustifiable discrimination between countries where the same conditions prevail, or act as a disguised restriction on trade.
● Article XXIV allows conditionally for the formation of free trade areas and customs unions between contracting parties.
● Article XXVIII (Modification of Schedules) gives contracting parties the option of seeking to renegotiate previously bound tariffs.

10.1.2 Economic effects of GATT holes and loopholes

Exempting specific sectors from the reach of liberalization commitments ('holes' in the terminology of this chapter) will usually distort economic incentives. Such exemptions limit the possible welfare gains associated with liberalization, especially as the sectors involved are often highly protected. Indeed, the theory of the second best illustrates that the end result of such partial liberalization may be worse than no liberalization at all.[7] While the holes in alternative trade agreements can be identified relatively easily, this is not always the case for loopholes. It is even more difficult to determine the effect of a given set of loopholes. The general consequence is that it may not be possible to determine the degree to which intra-bloc trade flows are effectively (as opposed to nominally) liberalized. Indeed, it may be that de facto internal trade does not become less restricted. This would be the case, for example, if a set of relatively low and uniform tariffs were abolished and replaced by 'free' trade within the bloc but with rules of origin that imply tariff equivalents that exceed the old tariff. As a result, exporters may prefer to continue to pay tariffs. Alternatively, internal trade could become more restrictive if markets become less competitive after the implementation of an agreement, due, for example, to common anti-dumping enforcement or a lack of adequate anti-trust enforcement.

The major problem with loopholes such as contingent protection is that a large part of their impact results from the credible threat they represent to foreign exporters and the credible prospect they represent to import-competing firms. Although the issues that arise in this connection are becoming relatively well known, a brief exposition may be useful.[8] Recent research has demonstrated that the mere existence of anti-dumping, countervailing and safeguard provisions – even if not yet exercised – may reduce competition between foreign exporters and domestic import-competing firms. Moreover, scope may exist for the 'capture' and abuse of such procedures by import-competing interests, further enhancing such threat effects. They therefore imply that the gains from whatever partial liberalization is negotiated are reduced, and perhaps even eliminated. The main conclusions of both theory and practical experience are that: (1) the mere existence of these provisions may reduce competitive pressure on domestic import-competing firms (raising prices, reducing incentives to innovate, etc.); (2) import-competing industries can be expected both to exploit substitution possibilities across instruments and to adapt their behavior so as to increase the probability of satisfying whatever necessary conditions have to be met in order to obtain protection; (3) the provisions may facilitate the negotiation and enforcement of market-sharing arrangements (frequently VERs); and (4) they are inefficient, in the sense that the costs to consumers of affected intermediate inputs and final products are invariably larger than the benefits that accrue to the protected industry.

10.1.3 Political economy of holes and loopholes in RIAs

The issue investigated in this paper is the extent to which the pressure groups that have been able to insist on the inclusion of the various holes and loopholes in the GATT are equally able to cover themselves when regional agreements are negotiated. Theory offers no clear-cut guidance. De Melo *et al.* (1992) suggest two ways through which RIAs may constrain national interest groups and thus foster more efficient outcomes. The first is the 'preference-dilution effect': because an RIA implies a larger political community, each of the politically important interest groups in member countries will have less influence on the design of common policies. The second is the 'preference-asymmetry effect': because preferences on specific issues are likely to differ across member countries, the resulting need for compromises may enhance efficiency. Olson (1982) has argued that the creation of RIAs should disrupt the formation of rent-seeking interest groups, as these have to reorganize at the regional level and establish an institutional structure that allows them to agree on a common position. It is also argued that the greater the similarity between prospective member countries the less important adjustment pressures are likely to be. This is because increased trade will be mainly of the intra-industry variety, for which there is less need for holes and loopholes. In a similar vein, a preferential agreement to liberalize trade may allow greater 'internalization' of the benefits. The implied reduction in uncertainty with respect to the outcome of liberalization may facilitate its negotiation.

It is, however, by no means certain that genuine regional liberalization will emerge. Tumlir (1983) has argued that consumer interests are harder to defend in an RIA than at the national level, whereas producer interests are more likely to be strengthened than weakened. Each national producer group may face less opposition when seeking price-increasing policies, and may indeed find support from other producer groups pursuing their own interests. The need for striking compromises may imply log-rolling among producer interests and thus result in a less liberal regulatory regime. Vaubel (1986) has argued that it may be in the interest of national politicians to let a regional organization satisfy national pressure groups, as this is less transparent for domestic voters and can be justified as being 'necessary' to maintain the agreement. Contrary to Olson's hypothesis, because national producer groups are likely to already be well organized, the marginal cost of cooperating at the regional level may be low. Peirce (1991) has noted that in the EC context, interest groups apparently found it easy – indeed, were encouraged – to relocate to Brussels. Such public choice analysts would argue that it is likely that an RIA will embody a large number of holes and loopholes, and that the final outcome may well be more restrictive than the status quo ante.

Much will also depend on the type of RIA. The foregoing arguments apply to RIAs with a common external trade policy and some reduction in national sovereignty. As pointed out by Victoria Curzon-Price,[9] a free trade area (FTA) may be much less prone to raising external trade barriers over time because import-competing firms do not have access to a centralized supply of protection services. Instead, each industry has to lobby its government leaders, who are likely to take into account the effect of protection on downstream users (assuming the products are not final consumption goods). This may be less the case in a customs union or common market than an FTA, for a variety of reasons. First, the potential pay-offs to protection of the larger market area will be higher as protection affects all members by definition: the expected pay-off for a unit of lobbying effort increases. Second, certain GATT-consistent instruments such as anti-dumping that will be available to anti-trade lobbies under the RIA make it impossible for liberal-minded governments that join a customs union to prevent protection from being sought and imposed. Thus, certain EC countries such as the Netherlands did not use or make available contingent protection before joining the EC. However, within the EC context, any Dutch firm has access to Brussels and may petition for an anti-dumping investigation, and cannot be prevented from doing so by the Dutch government.[10] Third, downstream users in the customs union may be less inclined to oppose upstream protection (assuming they are able to do so; under anti-dumping law they may have no legal standing) because the size of 'their' market has increased, thereby increasing their incentives to seek protection in turn.[11]

This issue will not be settled at the theoretical level. There is a need to examine individual agreements. As is demonstrated subsequently, while the details differ across RIAs, all embody significant holes and loopholes, largely mirroring those in the GATT.

10.2 The European Economic Community

The Treaty of Rome establishing the European Economic Community is perhaps the most far-reaching regional integration arrangement among sovereign states currently in existence. Although it might be argued that it is therefore inappropriate to compare the EC to more 'pedestrian' trade agreements, the EC is interesting precisely because its agenda goes beyond free trade in goods. It is unclear a priori what the effect will be of expanding the agenda of an international cooperation effort on the outcome for individual agenda items. Multi-dimensional efforts such as the EC may help achieve free trade by allowing implicit or explicit side-payments. Such payments may be monetary, as reflected in the creation of structural and 'cohesion' funds, or take the form of linkages across issues. Such linkages may imply that the free trade goal is sacrificed to ensure agreement on other issues deemed to be of greater importance by some participants. The impact on policies affecting internal trade is therefore uncertain in principle. What follows only looks at the performance of the EC in terms of liberalizing intra-Community merchandise trade flows.[12] For the time being we abstract from the Single European

Act (the so-called '1992' initiative, discussed above in Chapter 5 by Winters).[13]

The main objective of the EC with respect to internal trade is the realization of the four freedoms: free internal movement of goods, services, labor and capital, including the right of establishment. In order to achieve this, the Treaty of Rome calls for the gradual elimination of tariffs and quantitative restrictions (QRs) or measures with equivalent effect on intra-EC trade in industrial products and a common external trade policy. The abolition of tariffs and QRs was achieved by the end of the 1960s for the original members, and for new members by the end of whatever transitional period was applied. However, this has not led to a 'single market', as is reflected in the continued existence of often very large price differentials for identical products in different EC countries. What are some of the holes and loopholes in the Treaty of Rome that help account for this?

A number of sectors are either treated separately in the Treaty and/or excluded from its liberalization objectives. The coal-mining and iron and steel sectors are covered by the European Coal and Steel Community (ECSC), established in 1952. The ECSC provides the Community with the mandate to allocate investment and set price limits and production quotas on an EC-wide basis. In addition to ECSC regulation, national governments remain relatively free to subsidize national coal and steel industries, and have done so to varying degrees. A common policy has also been established for agriculture (the CAP), which in practice has implied a highly interventionist and convoluted system of producer subsidies and/or quantitative limits on production, price controls, licenses, etc. The agricultural dimension of the EC has been analyzed extensively (e.g., Tracy, 1989) and so will not be discussed here. Obviously, liberalization was and is not the objective.

Although in principle public procurement should be open to competition by firms originating in other EC countries, EC governments tend to source predominantly nationally. Past efforts by the Commission to open up the government procurement market have had only a limited impact at best. A Public Works Directive and a Public Supply Contracts Directive were issued during the 1970s, both of which required that contracts exceeding a certain value be published in the *Official Journal*. However, contracts relating to transport, telecommunications and public utilities were exempted. Until the Single European Act began to be implemented from 1987, the EC and GATT regimes in this regard were largely the same.[14]

The EC contains numerous safeguard-type loopholes. Articles 108 and 109 allow for measures to safeguard the balance of payments. Article 115 allows the Commission to authorize member states to take protective measures against products originating in non-member countries in cases where implementation of commercial policy measures leads to deflection of trade or economic difficulties. Article 226 allows members to apply for authorization to take protective measures if, during the transitional period after the Treaty entered into force, serious economic difficulties arose for a sector or area and were likely to persist. The balance-of-payments provision has been invoked only infrequently (e.g., by France in 1968 and Greece in 1985). As a purely temporary provision restricted to a 12-year transitional period, Article 226 became redundant for the founding member states by the end of 1969. It was invoked only 18 times in the 10-year transitional period, mostly during the early 1960s (Smit and Herzog, 1992). The industries seeking such temporary protection included agriculture, textiles and chemicals, as well as refrigerators, diodes and transistors.[15] The most frequently applied provision has been Article 115 − with over 1600 requests to the Commission between 1979 and 1986 (Sapir, 1990). However, this pertains to goods produced outside the EC. While national QRs mandated under Article 115 may also affect internal trade flows, that is not their primary purpose.

What explains the limited recourse to Articles 108−9 and 226? One possibility is that compensation schemes worked. The EC has three funds under which expenses for certain economic and social objectives can be financed. One of these pertains to agriculture and accounts for the lion's share of EC expenditure. The two major 'structural funds' − the European Social Fund and the European Regional Development Fund − provide financing for training and infrastructure respectively. They are not industry-specific. Even when doubled in size under the Single Market program, these funds are incapable of compensating fully any regions adversely affected by the completion of the internal market (Gordon, 1991).

More plausible explanations for the limited invocation of 'internal' safeguard provisions are that: (1) there was only a limited amount of adjustment pressure associated with the implementation of the agreement, given initially low trade barriers, the importance of intra-industry trade, the exclusion of major 'sensitive' sectors (agriculture, steel) and the fact that major market-segmenting policies − such as differential standards and regulations − were largely unaffected by the Treaty of Rome; and (2) that governments intervened directly to aid industries that were subjected to adjustment pressures. Rather than having recourse to formal safeguard procedures, EC governments have shown a preference for 'managed production'. In addition to the sectors for which formal institutions and procedures exist (agriculture, coal and steel), EC member states have intervened in sectors such as shipbuilding, textiles and footwear. Usually this involves subsidy policies of various kinds, often designed to satisfy Treaty constraints (e.g., they are justified as being part of a regional policy).

Articles 92 and 93 of the Treaty impose rules for state aids (subsidies). In principle, such aids are incompatible with the common market if they affect trade. The concept of a subsidy is quite wide, including, for example, equity participation on conditions that would not have been acceptable to the market. General – as opposed to sector-specific – subsidies are in principle allowed (e.g., aid of a social character). However, aid is also allowed to support regional development or to address a 'serious disturbance in the economy of a Member State'. This is no less an internal escape clause than Article 226, with the important difference that the application of these provisions is not time-bound. In practice, member states have intervened heavily in certain sectors, often with the approval of the EC Commission, which monitors such aid. Although the Commission can require a refund of subsidies that have been found to be in violation of the Treaty, it often attempts to coordinate rather than prohibit sectoral intervention.

Abstracting from direct government intervention in specific sectors, the other major barrier to internal trade has been (the non-discriminatory application of) the various regulatory provisions affecting the production and consumption of goods and services in individual countries. As is well known, it proved very difficult to eliminate non-tariff measures (NTMs) that have effects equivalent to QRs. These are in principle prohibited by Article 30 of the Treaty unless – loosely speaking – they can be shown to be necessary to meet certain non-economic objectives, do not discriminate between domestic and other sources, and are not disproportionate to achieving the objective involved (Article 36). Article 36 is analogous to GATT's Article XX on exceptions in allowing restrictions on trade flows to safeguard public policy, security or health, or to protect national treasures or commercial property. Until the late 1970s it proved to be rather ineffective in preventing NTMs from restricting internal trade flows. Following the landmark 'Cassis-de-Dijon' ruling of the European Court of Justice in 1978 – which established the principle that as long as a product was lawfully introduced into the commerce of a member state, differences in national legislation (product standards in this case) cannot be used by another member state as a ground for refusing to permit the import of the product – Article 30 became more of a binding constraint upon member states. However, the large number of Article 30 violation cases subsequently brought to the Court apparently had only a limited effect. As noted by the EC

Commission, the use of various NTMs expanded during the late 1970s and early 1980s,

> as each Member State endeavored to protect what it thought was its short term interests − not only against third countries but against fellow Member States as well. Member States also increasingly sought to protect national markets and industries through the use of public funds to aid and maintain non-viable companies. The provision of the EC Treaty that restrictions on the freedom to provide services should be progressively abolished during the transitional period not only failed to be implemented during the transitional period, but over important areas failed to be implemented at all. Disgracefully, that remains the case. (Commission of the European Communities, 1985, p. 5)

In large part this reflected successful exploitation of the holes and loopholes in the Treaty of Rome by producer groups to obtain government assistance and/or capture the regulatory process at the EC level.[16]

Summing up, how does the internal trade policy regime of the EC compare with that of the multilateral trading system? Clearly any such comparison should be made for specific points in time, as both GATT and the EC have continued to evolve. The relative importance of the tariffs and QRs affecting EC trade was rather minor to start with, so that their gradual abolition is likely to have had only a limited effect. While tariffs were by no means insignificant at the creation of the EC, external average tariffs were also periodically cut in the context of multilateral rounds of GATT negotiations so that internal and external liberalization occurred pretty much in tandem. As of the late 1980s, the unweighted average common external MFN tariff rate for industrial products is some 6 per cent (GATT, 1991). It seems fair to conclude that as far as these classical import barriers are concerned the EC has achieved greater liberalization than would be implied by the application of GATT rules and procedures to internal trade, but not very much more. In large part this is due to concurrent liberalization in the multilateral setting.

Internal trade has been restricted primarily by NTMs: the *non*-discriminatory application of standards and regulatory regimes (including tax systems), discriminatory procurement procedures, national subsidization practices, and the exclusion of certain sectors from liberalization (agriculture, steel). These non-tariff measures, and managed production and trade (VERs), have of course also emerged as the key policies with which governments have struggled in the multilateral setting. Major sectors subject to 'managed trade' in the multilateral setting, such as agriculture and steel, are subjected to 'managed production' in the EC setting. A two-pronged approach was taken in the

Treaty of Rome with respect to NTMs – application of the principles of national treatment and non-discrimination, augmented by gradual harmonization of national regulations. However, harmonization proved rather difficult to achieve and turned out to be an ineffective strategy in terms of eliminating technical barriers to trade. Indeed, to the extent that harmonization efforts allow specific industries to capture the standards-setting process, it may even constitute an inappropriate strategy to achieve liberalization. [17] As national treatment and non-discrimination are also the basic pillars of the GATT, it can be argued that prior to the Single European Act of 1986 the EC and GATT regimes were not dissimilar.

Having said that, a major difference between the EC and the GATT concerns the mechanisms for attaining (and interpreting) these norms. In many instances nationals of member states may challenge perceived violations of the Treaty of Rome before the EC Court of Justice, whose rulings are in principle binding upon member states. Intensive use has been made of this right, and member states have often been found in violation of the Treaty and required to change specific practices. Although the Court is of course restricted to the Treaty, which provides member states with an adequate number of holes and loopholes, its interpretation of Treaty provisions has at times forced member states to forgo measures that were discriminatory de facto if not de jure. An important example involves the Article 30 cases, which resulted in findings that policies applied on a non-discriminatory basis may have a discriminatory effect and therefore violate the Treaty. The Court has perhaps had its greatest impact on the structure of the EC by influencing the choice to pursue the 'mutual recognition' approach to standards and regulations in the Single European Act.

The 1992 project, if successfully implemented, clearly will lead to a significant further liberalization of intra-EC market access conditions. [18] It includes further attempts to ensure non-discriminatory sourcing in public procurement, even in those sectors that were excluded in the past (transport, telecoms, utilities) and the abolition of internal frontier controls. It defines the 'internal market', introduces majority voting in the EC Council on most matters relating to the establishment and functioning of the internal market, and introduces the concepts of minimum standards, mutual recognition and 'home country control' for regulatory regimes. Majority voting and mutual recognition of standards should reduce the influence of national interest groups that oppose greater competition (assuming that the process of establishing minimum standards is not captured by industries).

Many of the issues that figure prominently on the '1992' agenda – standards, services liberalization, procurement – also loom large on the multilateral agenda. While the 1992 project is more far-reaching than the Uruguay Round, a successful conclusion to the Round will imply that the moves towards further liberalization of EC internal policies continue to be followed by the multilateral system. But it is clear that, with the Single Market initiative, internal trade flows within the EC finally will become significantly less restricted than would have been the case if GATT rules applied.

10.3   The European Free Trade Association

EFTA was created in 1960 in reaction to the formation of the EC. Reflecting the fact that it involves European countries that did not desire to join the EC because of concerns relating to its supranational aspects, EFTA is restricted to a free trade agreement. There is therefore no common external trade policy, each country being free to maintain its external tariffs. Agricultural products and services are excluded from the liberalization provisions of the agreement ('holes', in the terminology of this paper). EFTA also has a number of loopholes, including Articles 12 and 17–20.

Articles 12 and 18 are standard 'exception' articles included in most trade agreements, allowing for policies to safeguard public morals, health and safety, and national security. All such measures are subjected to the requirement that they not be used as a means of arbitrary or unjustifiable discrimination between member states. Article 17 on dumped and subsidized imports states that EFTA countries remain free to impose anti-dumping or countervailing duties on intra-area trade, as long as such actions are consistent with GATT obligations.[19] However, the lack of dumping-related complaints in intra-EFTA trade suggests that 'unfair' trade has not been an issue (and that such procedures have not been used to harass 'internal' competitors). Article 19 allows member states to introduce quantitative restrictions for the purpose of safeguarding their balance of payments. Article 20 is the analogue of GATT's Article XIX, allowing EFTA states to restrict imports to safeguard an industry or region if authorized to do so by the EFTA Council. Article 19 has never been invoked, while Article 20 has not been invoked since the late 1960s.

As is the case in the EC, the EFTA Convention requires that government procurement be open to firms originating in any member state. Pintada *et al.* (1988) note that the import share of public purchases of EFTA governments is about 15 per cent on average. While this is much greater than for EC governments, on a sectoral basis these import shares are less than those of the private sector, indicating that procurement remains biased towards national sourcing. EFTA member states are formally constrained with respect to subsidy policies. Export subsidies are prohibited, as is any form of aid that would frustrate the benefits expected from the removal or absence of tariffs and QRs. This appears to grandfather all existing subsidy policies, however. In practice the subsidy provisions have not led to disputes as virtually no allegations have been made of aids that affect trade.

As there is no common external tariff, a system is needed to prevent trade deflection, i.e., non-member countries exporting to the EFTA country with the least restrictive policy for a specific product and subsequently shipping it to other EFTA states free of duty. EFTA countries decided to make the intra-EFTA rules of origin identical to those desired by the EC when the UK left EFTA in 1972. These rules are discussed in the next section, as they impact primarily on EC–EFTA trade. In contrast to the EC, EFTA rejected harmonization as a strategy to deal with the trade-restrictive effects of differences in standards and regulatory regimes. Instead, it accepted diversity in national standards, but sought to negotiate agreement regarding notification, international standardization, and the reciprocal or mutual recognition of tests, i.e., procedures under which exporters could have their products certified by agencies in their own country as conforming to the importing country's standard. This approach is considered to have been somewhat successful.

In conclusion, intra-EFTA trade is somewhat more liberal than if GATT rules had been applied. While under GATT their tariffs would not have been zero, there would also have been no need for rules of origin (see below). Both agreements exclude agriculture from liberalization commitments. Contingent protection remains available to import-competing firms. The approach towards NTMs is virtually identical. The Standards Code negotiated during the Tokyo Round incorporates many of the EFTA procedures and principles (see Hoekman and Stern, 1992).

10.4 EC trade agreements with non-members

The EC has negotiated a large number of preferential trade agreements with third countries. The focus here is on the EC–EFTA trade agreements and the recently negotiated agreements with East European countries. As mentioned earlier, in 1972–3 the EC negotiated 'free' trade agreements with each EFTA member. The rationale for these agreements arose from the withdrawal of the UK from EFTA and its accession to the EC, and an acceptance on the part of the EC that enlargement should not result in new barriers against intra-European trade.

The EC–EFTA agreements pertain largely to industrial products, with certain sensitive sectors excluded. However, with the familiar exception of agricultural products and steel, the holes in the agreements are rather limited (e.g., watches for Switzerland). Loopholes are also familiar, including escape clauses of various kinds, as well as instruments of contingent protection. The latter, however, seem to be relatively unimportant in practice. Thus, in the period 1987–91 EFTA countries accounted for only 3 per cent of total EC anti-dumping investigations (Commission of the European Communities, 1992). While this does not mean that contingent protection is irrelevant to EC–EFTA trade – as the threat effects may be significant – it appears that origin requirements are more important trade barriers.

The origin system used for EC–EFTA trade is based on the same principles as those of the EC and is the same as that governing other preferential trade agreements negotiated between the EC and non-member states (e.g., the ACP countries). The primary principle to determine the country of origin of a product is the 'substantial transformation' criterion. That is, wherever a product was last substantially transformed is where the product originates. The Kyoto Convention – which was adopted by the EC in 1975 – provides a number of specific criteria that signatories may employ to determine whether substantial transformation has occurred. These include: (1) a change in tariff heading in a specified nomenclature; (2) determining a list of specific processing operations which do or do not confer upon the products involved the origin of the country in which the operations were carried out; (3) requiring that the value of the materials utilized in transforming the product exceeds a specified percentage of the value of the transformed product; or (4) requiring that the percentage of value-added in the country of processing reaches a specified level. In the last two cases the precise percentage is left for national authorities to decide. Which standard is to be preferred is not specified in the EC Regulation, Kyoto Convention or GATT.[20] Authorities therefore tend to have a substantial degree of discretion when deciding whether or not a product originates in a country. As a result, origin rules/determinations may be used (abused) for protectionist purposes (as discussed by Palmeter in Chapter 15 of this volume).

The main criterion used in EC–EFTA (and intra-EFTA) trade is change in tariff heading, complemented by a large number of product-specific rules (often based on value-added criteria). Until recently, the EC did not allow an EFTA country to cumulate processing undertaken in other EFTA countries. This 'no cumulation' provision made EC–EFTA rules of origin more restrictive than intra-EFTA origin rules. Satisfying the certification requirements is often so costly that even in instances where firms meet the necessary conditions for origin they often decide that it is simpler and cheaper to pay the MFN tariff. As the average tariff on industrial goods in the EC is about 6 per cent, costs related to the demonstration of origin are clearly significant. In an empirical analysis of trade between the EC and individual EFTA countries – each of which is in principle allowed duty-free access to the EC – Herin (1986) found that the costs associated with satisfying the rules of origin imposed by the EC were high enough to induce 25 per cent of EFTA exports to enter the EC by paying the relevant MFN tariff.

EC–EFTA trade relations will change significantly once the recently negotiated European Economic Area agreement (EEA) is implemented. A major change in the status quo will be that procedures for mutual recognition of standards and EC competition rules will apply to EFTA countries. As with the EC-92 program, which in effect will also apply in large part to the EFTA countries that join the EEA, EC–EFTA trade will become significantly less restricted than if GATT rules were to be applied. Again, however, the point to be made in this connection is that up to the early 1990s, EC–EFTA trade was not much more liberal than if GATT rules and procedures had been applied.

Recent trade agreements between the EC and Poland, Hungary, and Czechoslovakia (the Europe Agreements of 1992) are also illustrative of the holes and loopholes that tend to characterize the EC's other trade agreements. Although tariffs and QRs on many industrial goods are to be abolished either immediately or gradually over a five-year period, separate arrangements are made for agriculture, steel and textiles (GATT, 1992). While there is some liberalization of market access in these sectors, it is rather limited. Moreover, there is a separate safeguard clause for agricultural liberalization which calls for consultations but explicitly allows parties to take whatever measure is deemed necessary on a unilateral basis. Anti-dumping procedures may continue to be filed by EC industries against imports originating from these countries despite the fact that the latter are obliged to adopt competition policies that are analogous to those of the EC. In addition to the sectoral 'holes' and the continued threat of anti-dumping actions, the Europe Agreements contain the standard types of loopholes: rules of origin, as well as measures to safeguard the balance of payments, specific industries or regions, public health and safety. The analogue to GATT's Article XIX is interesting in that it specifies that action may be taken on the basis of either 'serious injury to producers', 'serious disturbance to sectors' or 'serious deterioration of a region', while there is no requirement that the various disturbances be caused by liberalization under the agreements. This language implies much wider scope for action than does Article XIX of GATT. In conjunction with the anti-dumping threat, it is likely to induce a series of VERs in the coming years.[21]

10.5   The Canada–US Free Trade Agreement

The trade agreement negotiated between Canada and the United States went into effect in 1989.[22] The purported objectives of the CUSFTA include the elimination of trade barriers to goods and services, the facilitation of fair competition within the area, the liberalization of conditions for investment, and the establishment of joint mechanisms to resolve trade disputes. This agreement is similar to other RIAs in that its coverage is incomplete. It calls for the abolition of tariffs on most industrial products over a 10-year period, but contains separate arrangements for a number of sectors. The abolition of tariffs is likely to have only a limited economic impact, given that the average US tariff on Canadian exports was only 1 per cent and that almost 80 per cent of Canadian exports were eligible for duty-free entry (Whalley, 1992). Agriculture, steel, textiles, energy and services are exempted from the broad-based liberalization commitments. Agricultural liberalization is limited to the gradual elimination of tariffs and a prohibition on export subsidies. Most of the system of domestic production support in this sector remains unaffected, however. Textiles and clothing are subject to tariff quotas (listed in the chapter on rules of origin). Steel products were covered by the United States VER program when the agreement was negotiated. Tariffs on metals are to be abolished over a 10-year period starting in late 1989, but it is unclear what will happen to QR-type intervention. The recent inclusion of Canadian steel producers in a wide ranging set of AD/CVD petitions illustrates that free trade in steel products cannot be expected in the near future (*Financial Times*, 4 June, 1992). While trade in services is in principle covered by the CUSFTA – which extends the national-treatment principle to services – all existing regulations were grandfathered. A positive list approach was taken to determine the sectoral coverage of the services chapter; that is, the national treatment obligation applies only to those activities explicitly mentioned in each country's schedule.[23]

In addition to the familiar sectoral 'holes', the CUSFTA has provisions on rules of origin, standards, government procurement, services and dispute-settlement procedures. The origin rules are based on the substantial transformation criterion, defined as a change in tariff heading and/or a minimal intra-area local content of at least 50 per cent. For some products – automobiles and textiles in particular – the effective local content requirement tends to be higher. Eighteen pages are devoted to product-specific origin rules. As illustrated by a recent US Customs decision to impose tariffs on imports of certain cars produced in Canada, the application of these rules is subject to a degree of discretion and can be controversial. As was the case with EFTA, some exporters prefer to pay the (very low) MFN tariff rate rather than attempt to satisfy customs authorities that their products meet the origin requirements (Hufbauer and Schott, 1992). Little progress was made on designing procedures to reduce the trade-restricting effect of different standards. There is agreement to recognize each other's accreditation systems for testing facilities and certification bodies, exchange information regarding proposed federal standards, and attempt to make their standards-related measures more compatible. This largely duplicates the GATT Standards Code. On procurement a limited degree of liberalization occurred insofar as the threshold value of contracts to be covered by GATT's Government Procurement Code was reduced. As procurement by non-federal bodies is not covered, and not all procurement at the federal level is covered, little progress was also made in terms of going beyond multilaterally agreed disciplines in this area.

The agreement contains a number of loophole-type provisions. Articles 1101 and 1102 are safeguard provisions. These are basically the same as Article XIX of the GATT, with a few additional restrictions. Unilateral safeguard actions against products originating from the partner in the CUSFTA are allowed only during a 10-year phase-in period, can be taken only once for any product during this period, and are not to last more than three years. The CUSFTA also specifies that: (1) either partner will be excluded from a global safeguard action if its share in the other partner's market is small enough (less than 5 per cent); (2) neither partner's exports is to fall below a positive trend line; and (3) disputes relating to safeguard actions are ultimately subject to binding arbitration. Arguably, however, the liberalization implied is more apparent than real, as substitute procedures are readily accessible to import-competing industries seeking protection. Indeed, they have never been invoked. In particular, unfair trade procedures offer firms a revealed preferred path to protection (Hoekman and Leidy, 1989). Both US and Canadian producers may petition for AD/CVD. Lack of agreement on substantive disciplines on subsidies and dumping meant that AD and CVD continue to be applied to intra-area trade. Unfair trade actions by both parties have been relatively frequent and controversial. As of June 1991, 15 AD/CVD-related cases had been brought before the bilateral dispute settlement mechanism established by the agreement (Hufbauer and Schott, 1992). Although the dispute settlement panels have had some impact – in some instances overturning a finding – they are restricted to determining the consistency of the procedures followed with the legislation of the country taking an action.[24] Given the Canadian government's interest in disciplining the use of unfair trade procedures (with a stated preference for abolishing them for intra-regional trade), the fact that so little movement in this area was achieved appears to reflect the strong constituency for these trade-remedy instruments in both Canada and the United States.

10.6 Holes and loopholes: RIAs and the GATT system

How do the RIAs compare with the GATT system? In particular, to what extent has it proved possible to offset in the RIAs the resistance of producer groups to liberalization that is observed in the GATT context? This section addresses these questions first with respect to holes and then with respect to loopholes. Then in the concluding section we ask how different types of RIAs 'rank' in terms of the welfare-reducing effects of holes and loopholes.

10.6.1 Holes

The holes in RIAs are quite similar to those in GATT. Agriculture is typically excluded from liberalization. Textiles and clothing and steel also tend to be given 'special' treatment. Agriculture and textiles are the two major sectors where the multilateral system is generally regarded as having failed to induce governments to abide by GATT rules. But the RIAs illustrate that these sectors either tend to be excluded in regional agreements as well, or are subject to collective intervention (managed production *and* trade). This suggests that in the context of negotiating RIAs the industry lobbies that block genuine multilateral liberalization frequently are able to control regional liberalization initiatives as well. The original GATT treaty excluded government procurement. Procurement was brought under GATT auspices to some extent in the form of the 1979 Government Procurement Code, to which most OECD countries are a party. RIAs rarely go much beyond this code, whether in principle or in practice. In some cases, the agreement either adopts the code or imposes largely equivalent disciplines (CUSFTA, EFTA). In other instances (e.g., pre-1992 EC) the RIA goes beyond the code, but has had little impact on procurement practices.

Of course, some RIAs go beyond the GATT in that they include factor movements and/or services. However, it is only recently that such issues have appeared on the agenda of liberalization efforts, be they regional or multilateral. The main exception is the Treaty of Rome, but it is generally recognized that up to the late 1980s little effective liberalization had occurred (Hindley, 1987). The EC's Single Market program arguably signaled the first serious intent to liberalize. The CUSFTA dates from 1989, while for EFTA services only recently appeared on the agenda for the first time as part of the EEA negotiations. The GATT system proceeded pretty much in parallel with the regional efforts, with services being a major item on the agenda of the Uruguay Round. A General Agreement on Trade in Services (GATS) has been negotiated and was included as part of the draft Final Act submitted to Uruguay Round participants in December 1991 (see Hoekman, 1992).

10.6.2 Loopholes

Two types of loopholes tend to be embodied in RIAs (and in GATT also, of course). These are measures that discriminate against foreign products – including tariffs, QRs and contingent protection – and NTMs that are applied to both foreign and domestic products on a non-discriminatory basis. Most of the RIAs eliminated tariffs and QRs on much of internal trade. This cannot be said for the GATT, where tariffs remain positive (albeit small in most industrialized countries) and QRs remain important for certain products, largely in the form of VERs. However, average MFN tariffs applied by OECD countries on each other's trade are very low, and the VERs tend to be applied against third parties or involve sectors that are also excluded from RIAs (agriculture, textiles, steel). The difference between the RIAs and GATT on this front is therefore not very great.

The use that has been made of various safeguard procedures embodied in trade agreements varies across agreements, industries and time. In most instances the invocation of GATT Article XIX-type provisions has been negligible. Again, this represents a common denominator, as GATT-consistent safeguards have also been rare in the GATT setting. Instead, in the GATT context recourse is made to VERs and/or unfair trade laws, while in the RIA context, if access to unfair trade laws is eliminated, industries are obliged to lobby their governments directly for support (usually subsidies or market-sharing arrangements of some kind). If the unfair trade provisions are maintained for intra-RIA trade flows, industries have a choice between direct lobbying for assistance and invoking unfair trade actions. Even if there is no access to instruments of contingent protection, the EC experience illustrates that substitute loopholes often can be invoked.

As regards standards, it can also be argued that the effective disciplines implied by most RIAs have not gone much beyond those of the GATT, if at all. Until the Single European Act, the RIAs pursued varying degrees of harmonization complemented by notification requirements and reciprocal recognition of testing agencies, as was the case in the GATT (the Standards Code). The recent switch to mutual recognition of standards in the EC is, however, a significant departure, and is unlikely to be matched in either GATT or the North American context. Finally, with respect to subsidies, only the EC imposes stricter disciplines than the GATT. Although Articles 92 and 93 of the Treaty of Rome certainly constrain EC member states, they contain a number of loopholes. While the Commission monitors state aid, it attempts to coordinate more than prohibit. Governments have been permitted to take numerous sector-specific actions (for 'sunset' industries, such as shipbuilding, steel, textiles and footwear, as well as for 'sunrise' industries).

Summing up, the foregoing suggests that at any given point in time, some RIAs have gone further than GATT in terms of liberalizing trade, but not very much further. All of the RIAs discussed in this paper have needed renegotiation and adaptation, reflecting in part an acknowledgement of their failure to achieve the original objective of liberalizing regional trade. Thus, the EC has been augmented by the Single Market initiative, of which an explicit aim is to attain the original objectives of the Treaty of Rome. EFTA will be significantly changed as a result of the European Economic Area, while CUSFTA is likely be superseded by the NAFTA in the near future.[25] This process of gradual expansion/adaption mirrors the gradual 'deepening and widening' of the GATT, as reflected in recurring multilateral trade negotiations held under its auspices and in resulting agreements to reduce tariffs and expand the GATT's coverage (e.g., the Tokyo Round codes, and the Uruguay Round inclusion of agriculture, trade in services, rules of origin, intellectual property rights, etc.). Indeed, it appears that developments in an RIA frequently are reflected in analogous developments on the multilateral front. However, a break in this relationship is likely to have occurred with the adoption of the Single European Act. It is unlikely that the multilateral system will be able to match the degree to which intra-EC trade flows will be liberalized once the 1992 program is fully implemented. But it is clear also that the necessary conditions for such liberalization to occur are very stringent. In particular, it requires a substantial ceding of national sovereignty – as reflected in the European Court of Justice, majority voting in the EC Council on matters relating to establishing the internal market, and the adoption of the mutual recognition principle (which was a creation of the Court, not the Council or Commission). It took the EC thirty years to agree to accept the formation of the common market. It is likely that it will take longer in North America, let alone other parts of the globe. In the absence of actions to satisfy the necessary conditions for effective liberalization of trade, RIAs can be expected to continue to resemble the GATT system rather closely.

10.7 Prospects for holes and loopholes in different types of RIAs

Clearly all RIAs can be expected to embody holes and loopholes of various kinds. What does the foregoing review suggest concerning the scope for − or likelihood of − holes and loopholes in alternative types of RIAs? This is an important question, as an increasing number of countries − including the former Soviet Union − may pursue the RIA option. Two issues arise: (1) the *level* or extent of holes and loopholes embodied in an agreement when it is negotiated; and (2) the likely *change* in this level over time. There are three basic types of RIAs, assuming at least three countries are involved: a free trade area, a customs union, and a hub-and-spoke system. The first two differ from the third in that they imply non-discrimination between members of the agreement: any benefit granted to country B by country A is also available to country C. Under a hub-and-spoke system, by contrast, this is not necessarily the case, as each 'spoke' country negotiates a separate agreement with the hub and possibly also with some or all of the other 'spokes'.

A major difference between an FTA and a customs union is that the latter implies a common external trade policy. Whatever the initial level of holes and loopholes, the existence of a common external trade policy may imply an upward bias insofar as it facilitates capture of instruments of contingent protection by anti-trade lobbies (Bhagwati, 1992; see also Section 10.2 above). Contingent protection leads to less-competitive domestic markets than otherwise, due to more protection over time against outsiders (Messerlin, 1989). The scope for expansion in use and coverage of anti-dumping actions in a customs union is amply illustrated by the EC (Winters, 1992). Thus, there may be no net increase in external trade barriers at the formation of a customs union, but there can easily be an upward trend if contingent protection is maintained as an option. Moreover, the lack of similar instruments to restrict internal trade flows in a customs union implies that import-competing domestic producers need to use alternatives (subsidies, standards, procurement, regulatory regimes, etc.). In the absence of substantial ceding of national sovereignty, if there is politically powerful opposition to liberalization such instruments may be used to effectively limit liberalization of internal trade flows. For true liberalization to occur there must either be general support for opening domestic markets to greater competition, or substantial supranational authority. In the first case, a customs union is not necessary − witness the far-reaching FTA between Australia and New Zealand (Hoekman and Leidy, 1992b). In the second case, a customs union is likely to be insufficient.

The external trade policy bias toward protection that may characterize GATT-consistent customs unions that embody contingent protection vis-à-vis third parties will be weaker in a FTA: because there is no common external trade policy, FTA members compete in their external trade policies. This is because differences in trade policies will lead to arbitrage in the form of trade deflection. While rules of origin will prevent such deflection to a degree, they are unlikely to be fully effective in preventing it, especially if some processing is involved in the country of importation. More importantly, industries cannot lobby for FTA-wide protection. While import-competing firms in member countries may have an incentive to obtain such protection, each industry will have to approach its own government. The required coordination and cooperation may be more difficult to sustain than in a customs union where the centralization of trade policy requires firms to present a common front. In any particular instance, some FTA Member governments will award protection, whereas others will not. Deardorff (1992) notes that if industries in FTA member states are all competing against third suppliers, protection by one member has public good characteristics in that the industries in other member states will often benefit as well. As a result, some underprovision of protection can be expected. The foregoing political economy considerations strengthen this conclusion. Deardorff (1992) also notes that in some situations actions by one FTA member to protect its market against an outside producer may have adverse consequences for producers in another FTA member state. If so, this is likely to lead to trade friction between FTA members, again resulting in lower expected protection on net. There may therefore be significant differences between the external trade policy stance of a customs union (or common market) and a FTA.

What about a hub-and-spoke system? Essentially this consists of a set of bilateral FTAs. Because there is discrimination between members of such a system, the holes and loopholes can be expected to be greater than under a non-discriminatory FTA. Moreover, it may be more difficult to reduce the magnitude and scope of the holes and loopholes over time. As noted by Snape *et al.* (1992) and Kowalczyk and Wonnacott (1992), because a hub-and-spoke system involves separate agreements between the hub country and each spoke country there is more scope to exclude the 'sensitive' sectors from the coverage of each bilateral agreement. Each spoke is likely to have comparative advantage in a somewhat different set of such sectors. In a non-discriminatory FTA the scope for holes of this kind is likely to be less, simply because members of the FTA will have different preferences concerning the holes they are willing to live with. Similarly, the scope for loopholes also will be greater. Each country is likely to maintain the contingent protection option, and powerful import-competing industries in the hub country will have an interest in including wide-ranging safeguard clauses and stringent rules of origin. In addition to having more holes and loopholes, hub-and-spoke arrangements may be more difficult to liberalize further over time. By allowing bilateral deals on holes and loopholes, vested interests will be created that may prove more difficult to dislodge than if the agreement had been applied on a non-discriminatory basis.

Notes

This is a substantially revised version of Hoekman and Leidy (1992b). We are grateful to Kym Anderson, Victoria Curzon-Price, Carsten Kowalczyk, Peter Moser, Ernst-Ulrich Petersmann, Wouter De Ploey, André Sapir, John Whalley and participants in the GATT conference for helpful comments and suggestions. The views expressed in this paper are personal and should not be attributed to the GATT Secretariat or GATT contracting parties, nor to the International Monetary Fund.

1. Defined as the share of Western Europe's GDP that is traded with the non-West European countries, relative to the share of those other countries in global trade.
2. This is the subject of an extensive literature. See de la Torre and Kelly (1992) for reviews and analyses of some of the relevant studies. It can be argued that many of these studies failed to take into account the limited extent to which intra-bloc trade was effectively liberalized by the various RIAs.
3. Space constraints prevent a discussion of the agreements between Australia and New Zealand. See Hoekman and Leidy (1992b) for a brief treatment and Lloyd (1991) for a lengthier analysis.
4. The following discussion of GATT is by no means comprehensive. See Jackson (1989) for a detailed treatment.
5. Services and procurement may account for some 60 per cent of final consumption in most industrialized countries. Although the GATT excludes government procurement, a number of countries agreed to cover a subset of such procurement during the Tokyo Round. See Hoekman and Stern (1992) for a brief description of the Government Procurement Code.
6. A Working Party on Market Disruption was established in 1960 under the auspices of Article XXV which led to the creation of the Short Term Arrangement regarding International Trade in Cotton Textiles (GATT, 1989, pp. XXV: 8–11).
7. And, even if there appears to be scope to realize social welfare gains, the lobbying and transactions costs associated with reciprocal negotiations to liberalize trade may be such as to outweigh these potential gains. See Chapter 11 in this volume, by Leidy and Hoekman.
8. Baldwin (1992) provides a selective review of the recent literature. See also Messerlin (1989) and Leidy (1992).
9. In her comments on an earlier version of this chapter that was presented at the GATT conference in Geneva on September 4, 1992.

10. Note, incidentally, that the welfare gains to such liberal countries from joining a GATT-consistent customs union that employs contingent protection are reduced, as consumers are faced with higher expected levels of protection and do not know *ex ante* which industries will be affected.

11. As discussed in Hoekman and Leidy (1992a), under existing institutions it may benefit a downstream industry that upstream protection increases its input costs insofar as this increases the probability that it will be awarded protection in turn.

12. This is clearly an inappropriate yardstick for evaluating the performance of the EC but, as noted earlier, the goal of this chapter is to compare the internal trade policy regime implied by an RIA with that implied by the GATT.

13. For simplicity we continue to refer to the EC, although technically the discussion relates to the EEC as embodied in the Treaty of Rome.

14. See McLachlan (1985) and Pelkmans (1990). In 1980 the Public Supply Contracts Directive was amended to bring it into conformity with the GATT Government Procurement Code, negotiated during the Tokyo Round, which went beyond the initial Directive to certain respects.

15. These first three industries accounted for over three-quarters of all cases. The products involved were bread and dough, poultry, tobacco and wine; woven carding wool and silk; and citric acid, iodine, penicillin and sulphur products.

16. See Tumlir (1983) for a penetrating analysis.

17. Peirce (1991) has argued that, given the large share of the EC budget allocated to agriculture, rent-seeking producer groups will be driven to pursue this option.

18. Past history and public choice considerations suggest that the implementation of the Single Market will not eliminate all existing rents (or rent seeking).

19. Article 17 also requires a member state to accept the return, free of duty, charges or quota, of any goods exported to another member state. This provision, which is analogous to Article 91:2 of the EC's Treaty of Rome, was included so as to limit the scope for dumping or subsidizing exports by creating conditions more conducive to arbitrage. It has not seen much use, perhaps in part because re-importers may be required to demonstrate to customs authorities that the goods involved have not benefited from drawbacks (Curzon, 1974). A drawback is a restitution of indirect taxes paid on intermediates used in the production of a good when it is exported.

20. The GATT does not contain a rule of origin. However, the draft final act of the Uruguay Round contains an agreement on rules of origin.

21. See Messerlin (1992) for a similar conclusion, based upon an extensive analysis of the Europe Agreements.

22. As this chapter was finalized, negotiators had initialed the North American Free Trade Agreement (NAFTA). This section ignores the NAFTA, which is discussed by Smith in Chapter 4 of this volume. Even if adopted by all three countries, lengthy transition periods will ensure that the CUSFTA remains relevant for some years to come.

23. Transportation services, basic telecommunications, medical and legal services are among the major excluded items.

24. See Chapter 16 in this volume, by Enders, for a detailed discussion of dispute settlement procedures in the CUSFTA and a comparison with those of the GATT.

25. A similar phenomenon characterizes the evolution of trade relations between Australia and New Zealand (Hoekman and Leidy, 1992b).

References

Baldwin, R. (1992), 'Assessing the Fair Trade and Safeguards Laws in Terms of Modern Trade and Political Economy Analysis', *The World Economy* **15**: 185–202.

Bhagwati, J. N. (1992), 'Regionalism and Multilateralism: An Overview', presented at a World Bank/Centre for Economic Policy Research (CEPR) conference on New Dimensions in Regional Integration, Washington, DC, April 2–3.

Commission of the European Communities (1985), *Completing the Internal Market*, White Paper from the Commission to the European Council, Brussels, June.

Commission of the European Communities (1992), *Tenth Annual Report from the Commission to the European Parliament on the Community's Antidumping Activities*, Sec (92) 716 final, May 27, Brussels.

Curzon, V. (1974), *The Essentials of Economic Integration: Lessons of EFTA Experience*, London: Macmillan for the Trade Policy Research Centre.

Deardorff, A. (1992), 'Third-Country Effects of a Non-discriminatory Tariff', Research Forum in International Economics Discussion Paper No. 306, University of Michigan, Ann Arbor.

de la Torre, A. and M. Kelly (1992), *Regional Trade Arrangements*, Occasional Paper No. 93, Washington, DC: International Monetary Fund.

de Melo, J., A. Panagariya and D. Rodrik (1992), 'Regional Integration: An Analytical and Empirical Overview', presented at a World Bank/Centre for Economic Policy Research (CEPR) conference on New Dimensions in Regional Integration, Washington, DC, April 2–3.

GATT (1989), *Analytical Index*, Geneva: GATT Secretariat.

GATT (1991), *Trade Policy Review: The European Communities*, Geneva: GATT Secretariat.

GATT (1992), 'European Agreements Between the Czech and Slovak Federal Republic, Hungary, Poland and the European Communities', L/6992/Add.1, April 7, Geneva: GATT Secretariat.

Gordon, J. (1991), 'Structural Funds and the 1992 Program in the European Community', Working Paper No. 91/65, Washington, DC: International Monetary Fund.

Herin, J. (1986), 'Rules of Origin and Differences between Tariff Levels in EFTA and in the EC', Occasional Paper No. 13, Geneva: EFTA Secretariat.

Hindley, B. (1987), 'Trade in Services Within the European Community', in *Free Trade in the World Economy*, edited by H. Giersch, Tübingen: J. C. B. Mohr.

Hoekman, B. (1992), 'Market Access Through Multilateral Agreement: From Goods to Services', *The World Economy* **15**: 707–27.

Hoekman, B. and M. Leidy (1989), 'Dumping, Antidumping, and Emergency Protection', *Journal of World Trade* **23**: 27–44.

Hoekman, B. and M. Leidy (1992a), 'Cascading Contingent Protection', *European Economic Review* **36**: 883–92.

Hoekman, B. and M. Leidy (1992b), 'Holes and Loopholes in Regional Trading Arrangements and the Multilateral Trading System', *Aussenwirtschaft* **47**: 325–60.

Hoekman, B. and R. Stern (1992), 'An Assessment of the Tokyo Round Agreements and Arrangements', in *The Multilateral Trading System: Analysis and Options for Change*, edited by R. Stern, Ann Arbor: University of Michigan Press.

Hufbauer, G. and J. Schott (1992), *North American Free Trade: Issues and Recommendations*, Washington DC: Institute for International Economics.

Jackson, J. H. (1989), *The World Trading System: Law and Policy of International Economic Relations*, Cambridge, MA: MIT Press.

Kowalczyk, C. and R. Wonnacott (1992), 'Hubs and Spokes and Free Trade in the Americas', Working Paper No. 92-14, Dartmouth College, Hanover.

Leidy, M. (1992), 'Quid Pro Quo Restraint and Spurious Injury: Subsidies and the Prospect of CVDs', in *Analytical and Negotiating Issues in the Global Trading System*, edited by A. Deardorff and R. Stern, Ann Arbor: University of Michigan Press.

Lloyd, P. (1991), *The Future of CER: A Single Market for Australia and New Zealand*, Committee for Economic Development of Australia Monograph No. 96, Wellington: Victoria University Press.

Lloyd, P. (1992), 'Regionalization and World Trade', *OECD Economic Studies* **18**: 7–34.

McLachlan, D. L. (1985), 'Discriminatory Public Procurement, Economic Integration and the Role of Bureaucracy', *Journal of Common Market Studies* **23**: 357–72.

Messerlin, P. (1989), 'The EC Antidumping Regulations: A First Economic Appraisal, 1980–85', *Weltwirtschaftliches Archiv* **125**: 563–87.

Messerlin, P. (1992), 'The Association Agreements between the EC and Central Europe: Trade Liberalization vs. Constitutional Failure?', mimeo, Institut d'Etudes Politiques de Paris.

Olson, M. (1982), *The Rise and Decline of Nations*, New Haven: Yale University Press.

Peirce, W. (1991), 'Unanimous Decisions in a Redistributive Context: The Council of Ministers of the European Communities', in *The Political Economy of International Organizations: A Public Choice Approach*, edited by R. Vaubel and T. Willet, Boulder: Westview Press.

Pelkmans, J. (1990), 'Europe 1992: Internal and External', in *EFTA and the EC: Implications of 1992*, edited by F. Laursen, Maastricht: European Institute of Public Administration.

Pintada, X. *et al.* (1988), 'Economic Aspects of the European Economic Space', Occasional Paper No. 25, Geneva: EFTA Secretariat.

Sapir, A. (1990), 'Does 1992 come Before or After 1990? Regional versus Multilateral Integration', in *The Political Economy of International Trade*, edited by R. Jones and A. Krueger, London: Oxford University Press.

Smit, H. and P. Herzog (eds) (1992), *The Law of the European Economic Community: A Commentary*, New York: Matthew Bender Co.

Snape, R., J. Adams and D. Morgan (1992), 'Regional Trading Arrangements, Part I: Implications for Australia', mimeo, Monash University, Melbourne.

Tracy, M. (1989), *Agriculture in Western Europe, 1880–1989*, London: Harvester Wheatsheaf (third edition).

Tumlir, J. (1983), 'Strong and Weak Elements in the Concept of European Integration', in *Reflections on a Troubled World Economy*, edited by F. Machlup, G. Fels and H. Müller-Groeling, London: Macmillan.

Vaubel, R. (1986), 'A Public Choice Approach to International Organization', *Public Choice* **51**: 39–57.

Whalley, J. (1992), 'Regional Trade Arrangements in North America: CUSTA and NAFTA', presented at a World Bank/Centre for Economic Policy Research (CEPR) conference on New Dimensions in Regional Integration, Washington, DC, April 2–3.

Winters, L. A. (1992), 'The European Community: A Case of Successful Integration?', presented at a World Bank/Centre for Economic Policy Research (CEPR) conference on New Dimensions in Regional Integration, Washington, DC, April 2–3.

11

What to expect from regional and multilateral trade negotiations: a public choice perspective

Michael Leidy and Bernard Hoekman

This chapter explores the political economy of international trade negotiations using the 'public choice' approach to policy formation. The existing literature on international trade negotiations often employs a unitary actor model. That is, *nations* are the unit of analysis, and typically it is assumed that the objective of nations is to maximize social welfare.[1] Even if it is recognized that a government's negotiating position may reflect the outcome of interest group interaction in each country's domestic political 'market', the analysis of the negotiating process tends to take each government's preference ordering over possible outcomes (proposals) as given (Johnson, 1965; McMillan, 1989; Copeland, 1990). Given this ordering, the set of mutually advantageous and Pareto-efficient outcomes is identified and typically the 'solution' of the bargaining game is drawn from this set.[2] Yet it is commonly observed that international trade negotiations repeatedly *fail* to achieve outcomes that would appear to satisfy the criteria of efficiency and mutual advantage. It can be argued that this is due principally to the influence of interest groups.[3]

Some of the most important aspects of international negotiations are effectively 'black-boxed' when analysts start from a given preference ordering for negotiators. Feasible outcomes in an international negotiation should be identified as those that are mutually advantageous and efficient from the perspective of the negotiators or the principals for whom they negotiate. Only in an implausibly optimistic case of omniscient and benevolent dictators, or in a nation in which the institutional setting has somehow harnessed special interests to the public interest, might the *effective* preferences of negotiators tend to coincide with something approximating a reasonable social preference ordering. Establishing the preference ordering of negotiators over policy packages requires attention to the preferences, tactics, designs and expenditures of interest groups in each participating country. An objective of this chapter is to develop an analytical structure for thinking about the process of international trade negotiations that includes interest groups and self-interested negotiators as fundamental elements.

The plan of the chapter is as follows. Sections 11.1–11.4 bring together insights from bargaining theory and public choice to identify the essential ingredients of any international commercial policy negotiation, be it regional or multilateral. Section 11.5 simplifies this structure somewhat to consider the problem of maximizing social welfare through international negotiations. The lessons learned in these five sections help to motivate and direct the discussion of issues in Section 11.6, which examines the relationship between multilateral trade negotiations (MTNs) and regional integration agreements (RIAs). That section begins to flesh out the preceding abstract discussion by addressing the question of whether RIAs and MTNs are at odds, are substitute means to liberalization, or are complementary interacting activities. More generally, we ask: what can we reasonably expect to achieve from regional and multilateral trade negotiations? Expect just a little net liberalization and you probably will not be disappointed.

11.1 The political economy of international trade negotiations

For analytical purposes any trade negotiation can be decomposed into three stages: pre-negotiation, negotiation and post-negotiation. Interest groups play a role at each of these stages and, in general, the outcome is sensitive to the special characteristics of each stage of the process. Negotiators accommodate net lobbying pressure, subject to any personal predispositions they might have on matters of policy, in order to advance their political ambitions. Similarly, pressure groups expend resources on lobbying in order to influence political decisions in ways that stand to support member incomes.

Figure 11.1 summarizes the players and the choices occurring at various stages of the negotiation process. In the *pre-negotiation* or 'catalyst' stage there is a first mover or 'visionary'.[4] The visionary might be an interest group, but may also be a government. The implied policy 'vision' typically defines in broad terms the issues to be negotiated, placing what amount to movable constraints (movable at a cost) on the parameters of the formal negotiation that will follow. It is at the catalyst stage that an idea for negotiations is introduced and the seed of an agenda for negotiations is planted. The agenda is not set immutably, but the vision for negotiations does impose a certain amount of definition and rigidity. The vision is selected in order to maximize the expected pay-off to the visionary.

In the *negotiation stage* formal government-to-government bargaining takes place, but with interest-group participation. Subject to the implicit parameters established at the catalyst stage, negotiators are lobbied.[5] As a result, their preferences over policy packages are transformed. Negotiators then bargain over these policy packages in the post-lobbying or effective negotiation set. Ultimately, this stage produces the formal draft of an agreement with all of the detail and ambiguity contained in its clauses, articles, escape clauses, timetables, interpretive notes, annexes and the like. But the agreement that emerges from negotiations is not policy. It is a blueprint for policy.

What any trade agreement implies for a nation's trade-policy stance and the world trading system *ex post* depends on how the agreement is implemented. The final stage of interest-group/government interaction therefore occurs in the post-negotiation or *implementation* stage, which determines the kind of structure that is finally constructed from the policy blueprint. The action at the implementation stage occurs in the domestic administrative bureaucracy, the judiciary where domestic implementing legislation is interpreted, the legislature where implementing

Stage 1 Pre-negotiation	*Stage 2* Negotiation	*Stage 3* Implementation
v^k Catalyst	l^2 Bargaining	l^3 Administrative design and judicial decisions

v^k: policy vision k, broadly defining the issues to be negotiated.

l^2: lobbying activity by an interest group in stage 2.

l^3: lobbying activity by an interest group in stage 3.

Figure 11.1   Stages of decision making in international negotiations.

legislation must be passed, and the dispute-settlement regime set up as part of an agreement. The imperfect correspondence between this blueprint and the resulting administrative procedures that implement the agreement can often leave a great deal of room for flexibility. Since economic agents are generally forward-looking, the negotiation process is analyzed by starting at the end and working backward.

11.2 Stage 3: the implementation stage

An interest group's ability to affect the distribution of income through the political process depends on its ability to affect policies as implemented, not as designed. During the implementation stage all mobilized special interest groups choose their lobbying activity to maximize the expected pay-off to its members,[6] directing their efforts to influence the administrative details of the agreement.

Let x_i represent the vector of quantified characteristics for the policy package negotiated in Stage 2. As suggested above, any given policy package represents a cluster of possible outcomes due to varying degrees of administrative flexibility, autonomy, and responsiveness to lobbying pressure in the implementation stage. Thus in terms of its potential economic effects, the blueprint emerging from the negotiation stage represents a policy cluster that can be expressed as $x_i = x_i^* + \varepsilon$ where ε is a random vector with finite variance and an expected value that depends on net lobbying pressure during the implementation stage.[7] As a means of normalization, assume that the expected value of ε is zero in the absence of net lobbying pressure in Stage 3. Letting L^3 denote the vector of lobbying activity across all j groups in Stage 3, and letting L^{*3} denote those vectors of lobbying activity that imply balanced or perfectly countervailing pressure (zero net lobbying, including but not limited to $L^{*3} = 0$), we have $E(\varepsilon \mid L^{*3}) = 0$ and $E(x_i \mid L^{*3}) = x_i^*$. This amounts to a kind of 'what-you-see-is-what-you-get' assumption. More generally, $E(x_i \mid L^3) = x_i^* + E(\varepsilon \mid L^3)$.

This formulation offers a great deal of flexibility in the kind of administrative bureaucracy that can be described. It allows for the extreme case of a bureaucracy 'out of control', one that simply does what it wants unconstrained by international agreements or the domestic laws implementing these agreements. In this case x_i^* would be invariant or nearly so over i, and ε may or may not be highly responsive to lobbying pressure. Alternatively, it can also characterize an 'extremely well-behaved' bureaucracy, one that implies a different x_i^* for every possible policy cluster, reflecting the letter and intent of the negotiated package. In this case the variance for ε would be small and the expected value of ε relatively independent of net lobbying pressure.

Once the implementation stage has been reached, interest groups (foreign and domestic) choose lobbying expenditures to maximize the group's expected income by attempting to influence the administration of the negotiated policy package in their favor. The income of an interest group is a function of the random vector x_i, that is, $Y_j = Y_j(x_i^* + \varepsilon)$, whose distribution depends on net lobbying activity. Thus the conditional expected value of income for interest group j can be expressed as $E(Y_j | L^3) = [Y_j(x_i^* + \varepsilon) | L^3]$. For simplicity we can assume that income is linear in the elements of x_i so that we can write $E(Y_j | L^3) = Y_j(E[x_i^* + \varepsilon | L^3])$. The problem facing a special interest group in the implementation stage of an international negotiation can then be expressed as

$$\max_{l^3 \geqslant 0} - l_j^3 + Y_j E[x_i^* + \varepsilon | L^3], \tag{11.1}$$

where l_j^3, an element in the vector L^3, represents lobbying expenditures by group j during Stage 3. Assuming Cournot conjectures, each interest group selects lobbying expenditures such that

$$-1 + \nabla Y_j \cdot (\partial \bar{x}_i / \partial l_j^3) \leqslant 0, \tag{11.2}$$

and

$$l_j^3 \cdot [-1 + \nabla Y_j \cdot (\partial \bar{x}_i / \partial l_j^3)] = 0, \tag{11.3}$$

where $\bar{x}_i$ is shorthand for the conditional expected value of the policy vector, $\partial \bar{x} / \partial l_j^3$ is the vector of partial derivatives of $\bar{x}_i$ with respect to the jth group's lobbying expenditures, and ∇Y_j is the gradient vector of the income function Y_j. Expression (11.3) is the complementary slackness condition. A Nash equilibrium for lobbying in the implementation stage is a vector L^3 whose elements satisfy expressions (11.2) and (11.3) for each interest group j.

The solution of (11.1) yields an indirect value function for each interest group of the form

$$V_j^3 = V_j^3(x_i^*, L^3_{-ji}, \theta), \tag{11.4}$$

where θ represents parameters other than l^3 affecting the distribution of ε, and L^3_{-ji} is the set of lobbying expenditures for all lobby groups except j given policy i. Observe that the lobby's welfare in Stage 3 is a function of the parameters x_i^* and L^3_{-ji}. This indicates that when *anticipating* possible outcomes in the implementation stage (as must be done at the negotiation stage), an interest group needs a comprehensive sense of the restrictions implied by a negotiated policy package x_i, that is, of the extent of administrative autonomy under this package, of the administrative bureaucracy's responsiveness to lobbying, and of the future lobbying activity of other interest groups given this policy package. Thus when anticipating the value of a given policy package in the negotiation stage, the lobbying vector L^3_{-ji} in (11.4) must be set at some conjectural level for each possible x_i.

Several observations can be made at this point. First, in the case of an extremely well-behaved administrative bureaucracy, lobbying in the implementation stage will not pay, unless the negotiated package *intentionally* defers decisions to the bureaucracy. In this case the stakes for lobbyists at the negotiation stage increase. Second, at the other extreme, an administrative bureaucracy may have full autonomy (de facto if not de jure) regardless of the letter and intent of an agreement. Such an 'out-of-control' bureaucracy may or may not be responsive to lobbying pressure. If not, obviously lobbying in the implementation stage does not pay. Indeed, if the negotiated package in no way ties the hands of the administrative bureaucracy, lobbying at prior stages also will not arise.[8] If the bureaucracy is responsive to interest-group pressure, lobbying activity might be quite vigorous in the implementation stage. Indeed, if most of the policy action occurs in the implementation stage, lobbying resources may lie in wait during negotiations. In general, interest groups must attempt to anticipate the extent of the autonomy and malleability of the administrative bureaucracy in order to inform their lobbying decisions during the negotiation stage. The anticipated structure implied by the indirect value function in expression (11.4) becomes central to interest group behavior in earlier stages.

11.3 Stage 2: the negotiation stage

Lobbying pressure molds the effective preferences that ultimately drive negotiations. These *effective* preferences must be sharply distinguished from the *notional* preferences typically displayed for public consumption by a government. We will assume that these notional preferences represent the social welfare. That is, it is as if the political authorities would pursue social welfare as long as it cost them nothing. Lobbies, in effect, inform negotiators of the implied political costs of taking certain positions. Next, these lobbied preferences determine the set of feasible policy packages from which the negotiated solution (x_i) may be drawn. This sequence of decisions is taken as a reasonable approximation to what is clearly a repeated interactive process.

As suggested earlier, the negotiating agenda is not set during pre-negotiations. Instead, the set of possible agendas might be restricted by the pre-negotiation vision, and thus the visionary's influence and control over future negotiations comes through an ability to narrow the set of possible settlements in negotiations. Associated with the vision, v^k, therefore, there is a set, $\{x_1^k, ..., x_p^k\}$, of possible policy packages, some of which may not even be apparent to the visionary as a possible outcome. Because interest-group activity can move policy packages to and from the negotiation frontier, the agenda for negotiations is responsive to lobbying during the negotiation stage. If negotiations break down the status quo policy, x_s, occurs.

These possible policy vectors can be mapped to value space for negotiators. Let G_1 and G_2 represent the value functions for negotiators in countries 1 and 2 respectively. Figure 11.2 shows the notional ranking of the set of possible policy packages implied by the vision, v^k. The mutually advantageous and Pareto-efficient set of possible policy packages under the notional preference ordering is $\{x_1^k, x_2^k, x_4^k\}$. Since successful negotiations are assumed to produce such a package, these points constitute the feasible set of policy packages under notional preferences given the vision v^k. Lobbyists exert pressure hoping to cause a controlled migration of possible policy points in value space. In general, lobbying activity can be thought of as a contest to push certain preferred policy packages into the effective feasible set and/or to purge the feasible set of least-preferred policy packages. Some of the complexities facing interest groups in determining the optimal design of their lobbying programs are discussed below, with reference to Figure 11.2. They include indirect targeting strategies and coalition forming, issue linkages, and self-serving non-transparency.

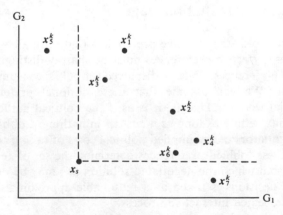

Figure 11.2   Preferences for policy packages and the feasible negotiation set.

11.3.1 Indirect targeting and coalitions

Consider a pressure group in country 2 for whom the policy package x_4^k is least preferred. Indeed, suppose x_4^k implies substantial losses for this lobby. Perhaps the lobby is the US maritime shipping industry and x_4^k contains far-reaching maritime liberalization provisions in a negotiation with a powerful maritime country like Denmark. The placement of points in Figure 11.2 shows that the US maritime industry, to continue this hypothetical case, can potentially knock x_4^k from the feasible set in several ways. First, it can lobby for the status quo at home. A small increase in the value of the status quo to negotiators in country 2 is sufficient to eliminate x_4^k from the effective feasible set. If there is a Baptist–bootlegger problem,[9] this indirect route may prove more effective per dollar spent than lobbying against x_4^k directly. As such, it may provide the least-cost means of eliminating x_4^k from consideration. Alternatively, if x_6^k does not contain the offensive provision on maritime transport liberalization, and is thus not ranked too low from the domestic maritime lobby's perspective, the US maritime industry may join with both domestic and foreign groups to lobby for package x_6^k. A reasonably strong migration of x_6^k to the northwest, produced by pro-x_6^k lobbying in countries 1 and 2, *ceteris paribus*, is sufficient to eliminate x_4^k from consideration. Finally, the industry may also choose to lobby directly against x_4^k, hoping to produce a vertical drop in its position in value space.

11.3.2 Issue linkages

Issue linkages can be thought of as replacing any two possible policy packages with one that represents a weighted average of the elements of the two. Lobbying efforts might be directed toward achieving linkage for several reasons. It is sometimes argued that issue linkage can create a region of mutual advantage where previously none existed, or can expand the set of mutually beneficial agreements.[10] Consider, for example, the set of possible policy packages $\{x_1^k, \ldots, x_4^k\}$ displayed in Figure 11.3. Let the initial placement correspond to the notional preferences of negotiators. If side-payments are not possible there is no room for agreement without issue linkage. Issue linkage serves to produce a new possible policy package whose value to negotiators, *ceteris paribus*, must fall strictly within the dashed box connecting the linked policy packages. If, for example, packages x_3^k and x_2^k were linked, the linked package might fall within the shaded region in Figure 11.3. If so, the issue linkage makes agreement possible.

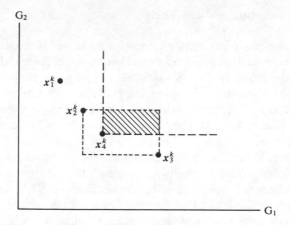

Figure 11.3   Issue linkages: creating a region of mutual advantage.

While the above linkage might be pursued directly by unlobbied governments, interest groups may also pursue issue linkage in their efforts to cause a controlled migration of policy points in (G_1, G_2) space. Interest groups might pursue such linkages strategically to move a favored set of characteristics to the negotiation frontier. Alternatively they might seek to block consideration of unfavored policies through linkage. Strong supporters of the status quo might even find it efficient to pursue issue linkages in order to empty the effective negotiation set. An example of demands for issue linkages designed to block an agreement comes from the Chicago Federation of Labor (an American Federation of Labor–Congress of Industrial Organizations affiliate). In reference to NAFTA negotiations a Federation spokesman has indicated that provisions should be included in any trade agreement to secure labor rights such as workplace standards in production, the right to organize and bargain collectively, strong workplace health and safety standards, 'appropriate' minimum wages, the elimination of child labor, stricter environmental standards and even 'some kind of debt relief' (Turner, 1992). Linking all of these provisions to any trade agreement would almost certainly ensure a breakdown of negotiations. Since the Federation's opposition to NAFTA is clear, advocacy of such linkages is best thought of in terms of a blocking strategy.

11.3.3   The value of non-transparency

The capacity of lobbying to transform the negotiation set may depend also on the transparency of political concessions in a given policy package. If negotiators are sensitive to voter preferences they may resist adopting a transparently protectionist position in favor of a more subtle approach (Krueger, 1992). By promoting policy packages that are less-transparently self-serving, they can expect the marginal return to lobbying to increase. This leads to the conclusion that the effective negotiation set will tend ultimately to contain policy elements that confer particular benefits on special interest groups, but in a non-transparent way. Well-crafted obfuscation tends to serve both protectionists and negotiators. In this regard, a well-known American businessman and would-be politician has suggested that trade agreements are typically 'squirrely'.[11] This 'squirreliness' simply reflects the value of non-transparency to both negotiators and interest groups.

11.3.4 Lobbying expenditures during the negotiation stage

These examples illustrate the potential complexities of the design of a lobbying campaign intended to affect international negotiations. Before examining the formal problem facing lobbies at the negotiation stage, it is important to mention the well-known proposition that those sectors with concentrated interests tend to be more successful in forming effective lobbies than those with diffuse interests. Liberalized trade is a public good that necessarily imposes concentrated costs on certain (import-competing) sectors of an economy. While there can also be concentrated benefits in some (export-oriented or non-tradable) sectors, consumer interests will not generally be well-represented in trade negotiations. Thus, on balance the lobbying activity that is observed tends to favor continued protection.

Consider the problem of a fully mobilized lobby at the negotiation stage. Given group j's *ex ante* beliefs about the Stage 3 (implementation) variables, $(x_i^*, L_{-ji}^3, \theta)$, its lobbying decision during the negotiation stage has the following structure:

$$\max - l_j^2 + \beta \left\{ \sum_{i=1}^{p} \rho_{ij}(L^2 \mid v^k) V_j^3(x_i^*, L_{-ji}^3, \theta) \right.$$

$$\left. + \left[1 - \sum_{i=1}^{p} \rho_{ij}(L^2 \mid v^k) \right] \cdot V_j^3(x_s, L_{-js}^3, \theta) \right\} \qquad (11.5)$$

subject to $l_j^2 \geqslant 0$, where L_{-ji}^3 is group j's conjecture about future lobbying activity should the package x_i be negotiated, $V_j^3(x_i^*, L_{-ji}^3, \theta)$ is the future value of package x_i under the conjecture L_{-ji}^3, and $\rho_{ij}(L^2 \mid v^k)$ is the jth group's perception of the relationship between the probability of a possible policy package being selected and total Stage 2 lobbying under the structure implied by the vision v^k. The term $V_j^3(x_s, L^3_{-js}, \theta)$ is the interest group's perceived income under the status quo policy package, x_s (implying negotiations breakdown) under the conjecture L^3_{-js}. The term $1 - \Sigma \ \rho_{ij}(\cdot)$ is group j's perception of a breakdown of negotiations, and β is the discount factor corresponding to the expected conclusion of the implementation stage.

Again assuming Cournot conjectures with respect to the lobbying of other groups, the necessary conditions for optimization are

$$-1 + \beta \left[\sum_{i=1}^{p} \ [V_j^3(x_i^*, L^3_{-ji}, \theta) - V_j(x_s, L_{-js}, \theta)] \right] \frac{\partial \rho_{ij}^k}{\partial l_j^2} \leqslant 0$$

(11.6)

and

$$\left\{ -1 + \beta \left[\sum_{i=1}^{p} \ [V_j^3(x_i^*, L^3_{-ji}, \theta) - V_j(x_s, L^3_{-js}, \theta)] \ \frac{\partial \rho_{ij}^k}{\partial l_j^2} \right] \right\} \cdot l_j^2 = 0.$$

(11.7)

The solution of (11.5) yields implicitly an indirect value function of the form

$$V_j^2 = V_j^2(v^k, x^*, x_s, L^2_{-j}, L^3_{-j}, \beta, \theta) \quad \forall j = 1, ..., N,$$ (11.8)

where x^* is the vector $(x_1^*, ..., x_p^*)$. This function represents the solution of (11.5) and gives the expected present value of the negotiations process to interest group j given its optimal Stage 2 lobbying expenditures. The value of the marginal product of a lobbying dollar is the discounted sum of its effect on the perceived probability of each 'possible' policy package, weighted by the conjectural value of each package relative to the status quo. Like all neoclassical models of choice, the model suggests that any group observed to be actively lobbying during negotiations chooses its total expenditures to equate the value of marginal product to marginal cost.

By abstracting from the issue of allocating lobbying expenditures to maximize lobbying productivity, the Stage 2 lobbying decision is vastly simplified. Yet it remains quite complex. The informational requirements necessary to solve expression (11.5) are extensive. In order to optimize over total expenditures, each interest group needs to assess the relationship between its expenditures and the likelihood of influencing the outcome of negotiations, given the lobbying of others and the structure imposed by the initiating vision. They must also have a good sense of where their interests lie in order to allocate these expenditures reasonably. That, in turn, requires conjectures about the lobbying fight to come at the implementation stage for each possible outcome of negotiations.

11.4   Stage 1: The catalyst stage

The vision that initiates the process of trade negotiations most often originates from a politician. In what follows we consider the 'best-case' scenario, in which the visionary is truly motivated by social concerns. The visionary attempts to formulate a catalyst for negotiations, that is, (s)he selects v_k so as to optimally modify the likely trajectory of international trade relations. What prospect is there for a public-spirited 'visionary' to achieve anything close to the objective of social-welfare maximization? Indeed, what prospect is there for achieving a social-welfare-improving outcome from trade negotiations?

The problem confronting the 'social-concerns' visionary is daunting. The simplified structure set out above suggests that, to exercise some degree of control over potential policy outcomes, the visionary needs a good sense of each of the following: (1) the relationship between the articulated vision and the implied set of possible policy packages; (2) how these packages might be ranked initially under notional preferences in value space; (3) the extent to which these policy packages might then be moved in value space by interest group activity; (4) the kinds of strategies interest groups might use to produce the desired migration of points in value space; (5) the nature of the bargaining game that selects a policy package from the effective feasible set once that set is determined; (6) the relationship between a selected policy package and the policy cluster it implies in the implementation stage; (7) the extent to which the implementation stage is subject to interest-group activity; and (8) the degree of autonomy available to bureaucratic administrators, the domestic judiciary, and dispute-settlement panels under a given policy package. Having assimilated all of this, any prospective social gains must be weighed against the anticipated resource costs of the new lobbying stimulated by the trade negotiations.

Whether *nations* are likely to lose, or simply gain less than they might have, from international trade negotiations depends both on the power of special interests in changing effective preferences and on the scope for mutual social advantage under status quo trade policies. A country that already has highly restricted trade has potentially much to gain and little to lose from trade negotiations. Once new negotiations are under way, a country that is already relatively open faces the prospect of setbacks (easier access to contingent protection, market-sharing agreements, etc.). In other words, the downside risk is low for countries starting the process with highly protective regimes, while the potential for social gain is great. The potential for social gain is small for countries with highly liberal trade regimes already in place, while the downside risk (a retreat into managed trade) is great. Thus the existence of great opportunities might suggest that relatively closed regimes may tend to stumble on social gain by pursuing a RIA, whereas a relatively liberal regime might be more likely to 'do harm'. But there are factors other than the potential for gain that affect the final disposition of the public interest. The issue of when the national interest might prevail in the presence of interest-group activity is pursued in the next section.

11.5   On bargaining power and welfare maximization

It is commonly asserted that a nation's prospects in international negotiations depend principally on its bargaining power. But this assumes negotiators pursue the national interest. As has been argued, negotiators tend to pursue their interests as modified by the expressed preferences of pressure groups. A nation with substantial bargaining power may find that its power has been captured by a pressure group or a coalition of such groups. As a consequence, in bilateral negotiations the policy package may yield a negative-sum transfer to one or more powerful interest groups in the country with great bargaining power (making the country as a whole worse off while improving the welfare of the dominant group), while actually improving social welfare in the country with relatively little bargaining power.

The potential social costs of interest-group participation and, in particular, the potential problem of 'Stiglerian capture' in international negotiations, can be examined in the Edgeworth box framework.[12] In order to simplify the exposition and discussion we concentrate exclusively on the negotiation stage. Tollison and Willet (1979) consider the case of two allied countries negotiating over how a predetermined level of defense production will be allocated across the two countries and who will be the direct provider of a predetermined level of foreign aid to a third country. They suggest the level of spending on such potential joint projects is given in the government budget of the country of each negotiator. History finds these countries at the status quo point E_0 in Figure 11.4. The indifference map specified by Tollison and Willet corresponds to the nation's 'notional' preference ordering, social preferences undistorted by pressure politics. The notional negotiation set or contract curve is given by the locus AB. This locus reflects allocations of foreign aid and defense expenditures that are mutually advantageous and Pareto-efficient from the perspective of nations.

A nation's notional preferences in a negotiation are subordinated to the effective preferences of the lobbied negotiators. It will be instructive to consider several cases of perfect capture in which negotiators find it in their interest to act exclusively on behalf of just one special interest

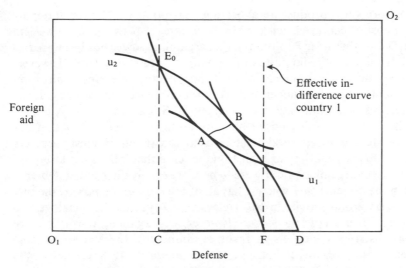

Figure 11.4   Bargaining power and the effective negotiation locus.

Notes: u_1 and u_2 are notional indifference curves
Line segment AB is the negotiation locus before lobbying
Line segment CD is the effective negotiation locus

group.[13] Suppose that the defense industry in country 1 has perfectly captured country 1's negotiator. This implies that the effective indifference map for country 1 negotiators is a series of vertical lines with the preference direction toward higher levels of domestic defense spending in 1. In the event that the effective preferences of country 2's negotiators continue to reflect social welfare, the effective negotiation locus or contract curve becomes the line segment CD in Figure 11.4. The implied dominance of the defense industry in country 1 means that the outcome of negotiations will produce an allocation along CD. Given the social indifference maps represented by u_1 and u_2, it is clear that the one-sided capture by country 1's defense industry creates pressure for negotiations to make 1's defense industry better off *at the expense of the nation as a whole*, while country 2 may be made better off. As long as the effective preferences in country 2 display *some* desire to undertake foreign aid expenditures as well as domestic defense expenditures, the outcome of negotiations will leave country 2 undertaking *all* foreign aid expenditures whenever 1's defense industry has perfectly captured 1's negotiators.

The issue of the relationship between a country's bargaining power and its expected gain from negotiations can now be clarified. In the event that country 1 has relatively great bargaining power, the outcome of negotiations will produce an allocation near point D. The social opportunity cost of capture is reflected in the difference between social welfare near D and that near B. Country 1's bargaining power has been used to directly advance the interests of its dominant pressure group. However, because the case considered displays an effective preference direction consistent with that underlying social preferences in country 1, its bargaining power mitigates the social cost of Stiglerian capture. Country 2, with little bargaining power but with an institutional setting that has apparently harnessed special interests to the public interest, achieves more from the negotiations than 1 (in the sense that it does not lose), but less than if bargaining power were to be more evenly distributed. Observe that in the extreme case where 1 has all of the bargaining power, the fact of interest group activity in 1 is irrelevant to 2, in that 2's social welfare at points B and D is the same. However, if bargaining power is more evenly distributed or falls in favor of country 2, there is an external benefit bestowed on 2 from capture in country 1. Specifically, the effective negotiation set (CD) includes attainable levels of social welfare for country 2 that would be out of reach (strictly left of F on line segment CF) were country 1 to be negotiating under its notional preferences. Thus pressure group activities at home, even when notional and effective preference directions are not in opposition, may confer benefits on one's negotiating partners. [14] That is, in the context of international negotiations social welfare consequences cannot be predicted reliably based on estimates of a nation's bargaining strength. [15]

Alternatively, suppose that each country has a dominant defense lobby. Each then has overlapping vertical effective indifference curves, implying there is no region of mutual advantage. Every point is Pareto-efficient. Thus negotiations, if they start, will break down without agreement. They will break down not because Pareto-superior allocations do not exist from a social perspective; rather, negotiations will fail because Pareto-superior allocations do not exist from the perspective of the captured negotiators. Observe that this outcome implies no social loss relative to the status quo, but a loss for both countries in terms of opportunity costs. The region of mutual social gain is non-empty but politically infeasible.

Finally, suppose that extreme Stiglerian capture exists in both countries, but it is asymmetric. Let there be a powerful lobby for foreign aid (or, equivalently, against defense spending) in country 2 while the domestic defense industry dominates the process in country 1. The dominant lobbies then form a natural coalition, each engaging in complementary lobbying. Then, as shown in Figure 11.5, the effective indifference maps appear as a set of vertical lines for country 1 and horizontal lines for country 2. The region of mutual advantage from the

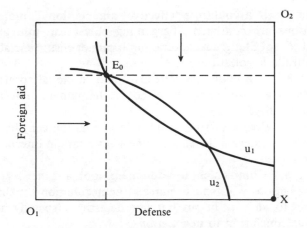

Figure 11.5   Dominant lobbies with complementary preferences.

perspective of the captured negotiators is the entire region southeast of the status quo E_0, and the negotiation locus is reduced to just a single point. Point X in Figure 11.5 is the only point within the effective region of mutual advantage that is also Pareto-efficient. This reflects a complete convergence of effective interests in the negotiations. Negotiations will produce, presumably quite expeditiously, the point at which country 1 provides all of the alliance's production of defense goods and country 2 all of its expenditures on foreign aid. Both countries have improved the well-being of their respective dominant interest groups at the expense of each nation as a whole. Notice, however, that, consistent with proposition 4 below, the strength of the anti-defense elements in country 2 confers a gain both on country 1 and on country 1's dominant lobby.

A caveat is in order regarding the application of this one-shot framework to the real world, in which negotiations typically are repeated. Lobbying activity and lobbying strength are likely to be endogenous to the distribution of income within a country. Even if a point like X in Figure 11.5 is produced from some initial negotiation, it may not be politically sustainable. The social loss implied by the movement from E_0 to X may induce a change in the balance of lobbying power. The imbalance of lobbying power that produced the extreme allocation may thus sow the seeds of its own demise.[16]

This discussion can be summarized in the following five propositions:

Proposition 1.   Relative social gains in international negotiations cannot be reliably predicted by reference to a nation's bargaining power.

Proposition 2.   If a country's 'effective' and 'notional' preference directions are consistent, bargaining power can mitigate the social cost of Stiglerian capture, but it cannot ensure social gains from trade negotiations.

Proposition 3.   If a country's 'effective' and 'notional' preference directions are diametrically opposed, bargaining power is a social liability.

Proposition 4.   Pressure-group activity in one nation can, but need not, confer external benefits on one's adversary in international negotiations.

Proposition 5.   Complementary dominant lobbying across negotiating nations will tend to narrow the negotiation set sharply, leading to an expeditious but not necessarily socially advantageous conclusion to negotiations.

11.6   Regional versus multilateral trade agreements: where do the public-choice blocks fall?

The discussion above suggests three central themes. First, trade negotiations are likely to entail a degree of *complexity* that is sufficient to guarantee that the vision initiating negotiations may in the end have very little to do with the future course of trade policy. Unless there is prior reason to believe that producer groups will engage roughly in countervailing lobbying (implying zero net lobbying), a government visionary casts his/her dart into a pressure-group maelstrom. Second, both negotiators and interest groups perceive value in *non-transparent* accommodation. A corollary of this is that in both RIAs and MTNs any liberalizing achievements will be held to the light for all to see, while protectionist concessions will be largely hidden in the esoteric details of these agreements (that is, in the 'holes and loopholes' discussed in the preceding chapter). Finally, the role of bargaining power in determining the social-welfare outcome of international trade negotiations is typically overstated or misstated. Bargaining power assists in promoting the *effective* preferences of negotiators, not necessarily in promoting the national interest. A country's bargaining power may be a liability for it while being an asset for others.

What does this public choice perspective suggest regarding the critical question as to whether RIAs and multilateral trade negotiations (MTNs) are at odds with each other in terms of advancing the goal of trade liberalization? Consider the issue of complexity first. It can be observed that RIAs often address a greater number of issues than MTNs, while the latter involve many more countries. Thus what might appear to offer increased manageability to a RIA visionary (a smaller set of negotiating countries) tends to be offset by agenda expansion that is generally beyond the visionary's control. Further, as negotiations proceed, developments can stray substantially from the visionary's original intent. A central goal for Canada in pursuing a trade agreement with the US was to eliminate the applicability of unfair trade laws between the two countries: at the least it hoped to achieve greater discipline in the use of unfair trade actions against Canadian producers (Hart, 1990). In the end, the parties agreed to a dispute settlement procedure in which a bi-national panel would decide whether existing laws were correctly applied, and to explore the prospect of supplanting anti-dumping laws with domestic competition laws. In terms of eliminating access to these laws for protectionist purposes, virtually nothing of the originally stated goal was achieved. After all, existing unfair trade laws need not be incorrectly applied to be used for protectionist purposes. Correct application does the job well enough.

In the case of MTNs, the original focus of GATT on tariff reductions promised a fair degree of control for the Bretton Woods visionaries. Still, the process that was set in motion cannot be said to have been one of unqualified success or to be in conformity with the intentions or liberal rhetoric of the 23 original contracting parties. While liberalization occurred on the tariff front, decidedly illiberal policies have been maintained or expanded under, for example, the Multifiber Arrangement (MFA), GATT Article XVIIIb (balance-of-payments exceptions), Article XIX (emergency protection), Article VI (anti-dumping and countervailing duties) and through so-called gray-area measures like voluntary export restraint agreements (VERs). It is in these exceptions that the fingerprint of protectionist special interests can be found. Moreover, even in the area of tariffs, it is well known that reductions were asymmetric, with relatively powerful import-competing industries in certain countries managing to maintain much higher tariffs than average. The ambitious expansion of the agenda for negotiations in the Uruguay Round opened the MTN process to new interest groups (both protectionist and anti-protectionist) and thus to greater uncertainty over prospective outcomes.

Next, consider the issue of the political value of non-transparency. Is there reason to believe that RIAs will be either more or less open to the non-transparent designs of protectionist interests than multilateral trade agreements? De Melo *et al.* (1992) have suggested that regional integration, should it be achieved, tends to reduce the marginal productivity of lobbying and that, as a result, we would see less of it in integrated regimes. The idea is that in a larger 'political community' each interest group becomes less politically visible and so rationally decides to play a smaller role. De Melo *et al.* call this the 'preference-dilution effect'.[17] But this begs the question of how genuine regional integration is achieved in the first place.

Applying the preference-dilution result of de Melo *et al.* to the question posed above suggests the following. If the kind of prospective trade agreement under consideration at the regional level implies the *possibility* of reduced political influence for all regional interest groups, this should enhance protectionist opposition to integration without inducing an offsetting increase in anti-protectionist forces. To the extent that multilateral trade negotiations, on the other hand, offer no real prospect of the kind of far-reaching integration needed to produce the preference-dilution effect (that is, given the nature of MTNs, advanced levels of integration are not even in the set of possible policy outcomes), protectionist interest groups will not be propelled further by the prospect of diminished future political influence to oppose multilateral liberalization. Thus the incentive to use non-transparency to block genuine liberalization/integration at the regional level may be stronger than that at the multilateral level, where genuine integration is certainly not at stake.

Still all of this is highly conjectural. Tumlir (1983), in the context of the European Community, suggests that integration will *strengthen* the influence of special interests:

> Industries, which otherwise would compete, organize for lobbying. Each national lobby is strengthened vis-à-vis its government whose executive, in turn, has less incentive to resist the pressure. If a government were to grant protection nationally, it would have to deal with the opposition of consumers or industrial users of the product in question. Presenting a decision agreed upon in Brussels, it has an argument which it could not deploy in a purely national debate, namely that its agreement to the import restrictions was a concession to European Unity.

If this is so, integration may be opposed less vigorously, or even supported, if it holds out the prospect of greater protection against the outside world. But there appears to be no compelling a priori reason for interest groups to exploit the tactic of using non-transparent details any differently in the context of regional versus multilateral trade negotiations. And as documented in the preceding chapter by Hoekman and Leidy, even the EC's Treaty of Rome – probably the most successful example of negotiated economic integration – has important holes and loopholes lurking in the agreement.

Finally, what are the prospects for achieving social-welfare-improving outcomes in regional versus multilateral trade negotiations, and what is the role of bargaining power? In both institutional settings bargaining power helps to advance the effective preferences of negotiators. Those preferences are a function of interest-group activities and thus need not represent anything like the national interest. In this regard the structure of negotiations appears to be fundamentally unmodified as we move from the regional setting (generally with few parties and many issues) to the multilateral setting (with many parties and fewer issues). This is consistent with the review of regional trade agreements in the preceding chapter, in which the protectionist holes and loopholes in several existing RIAs were found to be largely similar to those prevailing in GATT.

Even though the structure of trade negotiations is essentially the same whether regional or multilateral, the fact that they can occur simultaneously may itself have implications. Does the possibility of pursuing RIAs increase the scope for producer control by increasing the number of fora available for exercising influence? In the rhetoric of politicians, it has been suggested that regional initiatives are sometimes pursued due to their frustration with the 'lack of progress' in the multilateral setting.[18] But the rough model of the negotiation process set out here suggests there may be an alternative explanation. Regional initiatives may reflect frustration not on the part of a nation (or of the political leaders purporting to pursue the national interest), but on the part of producer groups that have been less than entirely satisfied with their ability to control the MTN process. Perhaps the perception has developed that RIAs may offer producer groups finer control of the political process, and that perception has induced a reorientation of effort in favor of regional initiatives.

One additional issue should be mentioned here. It is frequently the case that regional trade negotiations have important non-economic (often foreign policy) objectives such as reducing immigration, wanting to support the internal strength of a foreign leader, something amorphous like 'European unity', etc. When the principal objective of a visionary and/or the negotiators is nothing like trade liberalization, there is the possibility that any tendency to resist protectionist demands in trade negotiations may be reduced. That is, foreign policy gains, for example, may be seen as the quid pro quo for protectionist concessions. To the extent that such non-economic objectives are a common part of RIAs, perhaps the more economically focused MTN process, other things being equal, offers marginally more resistance to protectionist designs.

11.7 Concluding comments

The political economy of RIAs suggests that efforts to measure the net liberalization achieved in any given RIA, and indeed that achieved under GATT, must proceed with close attention to detail. There are strong incentives facing politicians to produce agreements whose profile appears distinctly liberalizing while significant protectionist character flaws tend to be buried in the esoterica. The special-interest fingerprints of protectionism (in the form of escape clauses, grandfathering, fair trade laws and the like) need to be pieced together from multiple non-transparent fragments. Unless there is an effort within nations to establish institutions that might serve to promote more balanced lobbying so that negotiator preferences will not be significantly distorted, regional and multilateral trade negotiation initiatives will produce transparent accomplishments largely offset by non-transparent exceptions, sectoral exclusions, market-sharing arrangements, unfair trade provisions, restrictive rules of origin and the like.

The standard formulation of the controversy over RIAs versus MTNs is summarized by asking whether RIAs are building blocks or stumbling blocks to the MTN process (Lawrence, 1991). That is, do regional trade initiatives help to move the process of multilateral trade liberalization forward, or do they imply greater discrimination in trade practices and thereby threaten the multilateral process? One message of this chapter is that neither position seems appropriately conceived. Both the MTN process and RIAs lead to only limited net liberalization when one considers the full trade-inhibiting effects of the esoterica of these agreements. The greatest threat to liberalization comes from a willingness/ability to accommodate special interests in the annexes, exceptions, sub-paragraphs, interpretive notes and derogations of these agreements. While we wring our hands over the 'building-or-stumbling-block' question, we might also ask how institutions can be created that will help to introduce much greater transparency in both types of agreements and thereby encourage the mobilization of diffuse consumer interests. Once that is achieved, significant progress toward liberalization – whether regional or multilateral – will become more likely.

Notes

This paper was written while Michael Leidy was with the Economic Research and Analysis Unit of the GATT Secretariat, before he moved to the IMF. We are grateful to Kym Anderson, Carsten Kowalczyk, John McMillan and other workshop participants for helpful suggestions. The views expressed in this paper are personal and should not be attributed to the GATT Secretariat, GATT contracting parties or the IMF.
   1.   See, for example, Allen (1979), Mayer (1981) or Ludema (1991). Tollison and Willett (1979) pay perfunctory attention to the role of interest groups

but then proceed as if they did not exist. However, Mayer (1985) is a notable exception, explicitly incorporating interest-group lobbying into the analysis.

2. See, for example, Brown and Whalley (1980), Chan (1985), Whalley (1985), and Baldwin and Clarke (1987). Hoekman (1992) provides a brief review of the literature on international trade negotiations.

3. See Baldwin and Clarke (1987). Baldwin (1986) also points to the inefficiency of the procedures followed in multilateral trade negotiations, which in turn reflect constraints that are endogenous to interest-group activity.

4. The pre-negotiation stage has been the focus of a good deal of recent research. See, for example, Stein (1989), Zartman (1989) and Tomlin (1989).

5. Throughout the analysis the term 'negotiators' will be used to denote the political collective responsible for negotiations. It is assumed that there are no principal-agent problems.

6. Issues pertaining to intra-interest group disputes over the distribution of pay-offs are ignored.

7. Previous lobbying activity is assumed to have no residual effect in the implementation stage. Administrative and judicial outcomes are assumed to respond only to that lobbying in the implementation period. This is a reasonable approximation since in general the bureaucracy responsible for administrative details and the courts differs from those responsible for the negotiations.

8. If this characteristic is recognized by other nations, such a regime is not likely to be an attractive partner in bilateral trade negotiations. In a multilateral context, however, it might be able to join the process as a free rider.

9. By aligning itself with other less apparently self-interested supporters of the status quo, the domestic shipping industry's intentions might be obscured for political purposes. See Yandle (1983).

10. See, e.g., Tollison and Willet (1979) and Sebenius (1983). Issue linkages are relatively rarely pursued in MTNs (Winham, 1986, 1990; Hoekman, 1992), but may be more important in RIAs (see, for example, Weber and Wiesmeth, 1991).

11. Ross Perot, *International Herald Tribune*, June 12, 1992.

12. Clearly many types of negotiations are not strictly suited to the Edgeworth box framework. Nevertheless, it serves to illustrate several fundamental characteristics of international negotiations that almost certainly generalize to trade negotiations.

13. In general, the extreme form of capture characterized by Stigler (1971) is a very special case. More typically, as Peltzman (1976) argued, government officials will find it in their interest to attempt to partially accommodate several competing groups. While extreme forms of capture are likely to occur infrequently, there is analytical value in considering such special cases.

14. In their simulations of various proposals in the Tokyo Round negotiations, Brown and Whalley (1980) found that the US, the EC and Japan each would have been better off adopting any one of the several proposals made by other countries than their own.

15. It is even possible that bargaining power is a social liability if negotiators are not sufficiently constrained by the national interest. What is required for this is that the public interest and the private interests of dominant pressure

groups are diametrically opposed. This possibility is not, of course, reflected in Figure 11.4, since social indifference curves through points near D are socially superior to those near C.

16. Indeed, to the extent that the defense industry in A anticipates the endogeneity of its lobbying power, it may choose to exercise its power with restraint and thus seek an intermediate outcome from negotiators.

17. As de Melo *et al.* (1992) point out, the idea that a larger political/economic union might imply reduced power for individual interest groups is an old idea going back at least to the Federalist papers.

18. One year before the September 1986 Punta del Este meeting that launched the Uruguay Round, President Reagan announced his intention to pursue RIAs if the multilateral process was not soon re-invigorated. He said, 'if … negotiations are not initiated or if insignificant progress is made, I have instructed my negotiators to explore regional and bilateral agreements with other nations' (quoted in Aho and Aronson, 1985, p. 131).

References

Aho, C. and J. Aronson, (1985), *Trade Talks, America Better Listen*, New York: Council on Foreign Relations.

Allen, D. L. (1979), 'Tariff Games', in *Applied Game Theory*, edited by S. J. Brams, A. Schotter and G. Schwoediauer, Wuerzburg: Physica-Verlag.

Baldwin, R. (1986), 'Toward More Efficient Procedures for Multilateral Trade Negotiations', *Aussenwirtschaft* **41**: 379–94.

Baldwin, R. E. and R. N. Clarke, (1987), 'Game Modelling the Tokyo Round of Tariff Negotiations', *Journal of Policy Modeling* **9**: 257–84.

Brown, F. and J. Whalley (1980), 'General Equilibrium Evaluations of Tariff-Cutting Proposals in the Tokyo Round and Comparisons with Extensive Liberalization of World Trade', *Economic Journal* **90**: 838–66.

Chan, K. S. (1985), 'The International Negotiation Game: Some Evidence from the Tokyo Round', *Review of Economics and Statistics* **67**: 456–64.

Copeland, B. (1990), 'Strategic Interaction Among Nations: Negotiable and Nonnegotiable Trade Barriers', *Canadian Journal of Economics* **33**: 84–108.

de Melo, J., A. Panagariya and D. Rodrik (1992), 'Regional Integration: An Analytical and Empirical Overview', presented at a World Bank/Centre for Economic Policy Research (CEPR) conference on New Dimensions in Regional Integration, Washington, DC, April 2–3.

Hart, M. (1990), 'Dumping and Free Trade Areas', in *Anti-dumping Law and Practice: A Comparative Study*, edited by J. H. Jackson and E. A. Vermulst, London: Harvester Wheatsheaf.

Hoekman, B. (1992), 'Multilateral Trade Negotiations and Coordination of Commercial Policies', in *The Multilateral Trading System: Analysis and Options for Change*, edited by R. M. Stern, Ann Arbor: University of Michigan Press.

Johnson, H. G (1965), 'An Economic Theory of Protectionism, Tariff Bargaining and Customs Unions', *Journal of Political Economy* **73**: 216–83.

Krueger, A. O. (1992), 'Government, Trade, and Economic Integration', *American Economic Review* **82**: 109–14.

Lawrence, R. Z. (1991), 'Emerging Regional Arrangements: Building Blocks or Stumbling Blocks', in *Finance and the International Economy, Vol. 5*, edited by R. O'Brien, London: Oxford University Press.

Ludema, R. (1991), 'International Trade Bargaining and the Most-Favored-Nation Clause', *Economics and Politics* **3**: 1–20.

Mayer, W. (1981), 'Theoretical Considerations on Negotiated Tariff Adjustments', *Oxford Economic Papers* **33**: 135–53.

Mayer, W. (1985), 'The Political Economy of Tariff Agreements', *Schriftes des Vereins für Socialpolitik* **148**: 423–37.

McMillan, J. (1989), 'A Game-Theoretic View of International Trade Negotiations: Implications for the Developing Countries', in *Developing Countries and the Global Trading System*, edited by J. Whalley, London: Macmillan.

Peltzman, S. (1976), 'Toward a More General Theory of Regulation', *Journal of Law and Economics* **19**: 211–40.

Sebenius, J. K. (1983), 'Negotiation Arithmetic: Adding and Subtracting Issues and Parties', *International Organization* **37**: 281–316.

Stein, J. G. (1989), 'Getting to the Table: Processes of International Pre-negotiation', *International Journal* **44**: 231–6.

Stigler, G. J. (1971), 'The Theory of Economic Regulation', *Bell Journal of Economics and Management Science* **2**: 137–46. (Reprinted in his *The Citizen and the State: Essays on Regulation*, (1975), Chicago: University of Chicago Press.)

Tollison, R. D. and T. D. Willet (1979) 'An Economic Theory of Mutually Advantageous Issue Linkages in International Negotiations', *International Organization* **33**: 425–49.

Tomlin, B. W. (1989), 'The Stages of Pre-negotiation: The Decision to Negotiate North American Free Trade', *International Journal* **44**: 254–79.

Tumlir, J. (1983), 'Strong and Weak Links in the Concept of European Integration', in *Reflections on a Troubled World Economy*, edited by F. Machlup, G. Felp and H. Mueller-Groeling, London: Macmillan.

Turner, D. (1992), 'Comments', *Journal of International Law and Business* **12**: 556–60.

Weber, S. and H. Wiesmeth (1991), 'Issue Linkage in the European Community', *Journal of Common Market Studies* **29**: 255–67.

Whalley, J. (1985), *Trade Liberalization among Major World Trading Areas*, Cambridge, MA: MIT Press.

Winham, G. (1986), *International Trade and the Tokyo Round Negotiation*, Princeton: Princeton University Press.

Winham, G. (1990), 'GATT and the International Trade Regime', *International Journal* **45**: 796–822.

Yandle, B. (1983), 'Bootleggers and Baptists: The Education of a Regulatory Economist', *Regulation* **12**: 1–16.

Zartman, I. W. (1989) 'Pre-negotiation: Phases and Functions', *International Journal* **44**: 237–53.

PART 5

Institutional and legal issues

12

History and economics of GATT's Article XXIV

Richard H. Snape

Article XXIV is an 'exceptions' article of the GATT, the exceptions being to the unconditional most-favored-nation (MFN) provision of Article I. In order to assess the economics of the exceptions which Article XXIV provides it is necessary to address the role of unconditional MFN.

Approaching trade policy in terms of maximizing income in a multi-country world, subject to the constraint of protecting some industries, has led many economists to criticize the application of the principle of MFN. Starting from the position in which a country has frontier barriers (as there have to be for a consideration of MFN), Harry Johnson argued that the theory of the second best, whether applied nationally or to the world as a whole, does not lead to the equal treatment of all foreign sources of supply. The principle of non-discrimination

> has absolutely nothing to recommend it on the grounds of either economic theory or the realities of international commercial diplomacy .... The speciousness of the principle of non-discrimination is only exceeded by the irrationality of permitting nothing less than 100 per cent discrimination in the case of customs unions and free trade areas. (Johnson, 1976, p. 30)

But he then goes on to say

> the principle has an important point and function, which can be loosely and inaccurately stated as the principle that if you pay your membership dues to a club you are entitled to decent treatment as one of the paid-up members,

and, on the basis that it is the best principle we have, argues that

> it seems the wiser course not to devise further exceptions to the principle, or re-write it, but instead to improve the framework of international economic relations within which countries receive non-discriminatory most-favoured-nation treatment. (pp. 30–1)

This chapter takes the position that it is only through the systemic and 'club' approach that one can make economic sense of the GATT principle of unconditional MFN and of the Article XXIV exceptions. Without taking into account what appear to be the motivations of governments in the implementation of their trade policies, one cannot address the question of a set of rules for a desirable co-operative outcome.

There is little evidence that national trading policies vis-à-vis other countries, jointly or severally, are related to 'optimum tariff' criteria. (OPEC may be an exception. However, a good deal of national trade activity is directed to achieving worse rather than better terms of trade, for example by persuading foreign exporters to restrain their exports.) Modeling the effects of trade blocs based on the assumption that each bloc attempts to apply the optimum tariff against the others (e.g., Krugman, 1991a) cannot be expected to shed much light on the effects of the number of trade blocs in the world on world income – as Krugman himself warns in introducing such a model. And the strategic trade literature policy propositions are so sensitive to assumptions that it would be almost impossible to apply them properly even if governments attempted to do so, although some governments' policies appear to be dressed in these clothes. Thus rather than consider the establishment of a set of rules which would just curb the tendency of each country to exercise its market power to the detriment of the system as a whole, we need to consider a framework in which national governments, unconstrained by international commitments, often take actions which appear to be contrary to their own national economic interests.

12.1   The most-favored-nation clause

Most-favored-nation (MFN) clauses apparently have at least a seven-hundred-year history in trade agreements (Jackson, 1989, p. 133), but it is in the last two hundred of these years that they have been particularly important. MFN clauses in bilateral (or plurilateral) agreements assure each party that, if the other parties to their treaty enter into any other agreements with third parties which provide more favorable treatment for the exports of those third parties, these more favorable conditions will be extended to the parties to the first agreement: that is, no other countries will be treated more favorably.

Throughout Europe in the nineteenth and early twentieth centuries MFN clauses provided that these benefits should be extended unconditionally, or were interpreted in this manner: hence unconditional MFN. The United States, on the other hand, attempted until 1922 to apply the clause conditionally. (For example, concessions judged to be equivalent to those given by Belgium to the US had to be given by France to the US for France to receive the same benefits from the US as did Belgium.) Viner (1924, p. 18) reports that conditional MFN appeared in treaties of Latin American countries and Japan, and of a number of European countries between 1820 and 1860, but that conditionality seldom appeared to have been applied in practice by countries other than the United States.[1]

Of course conditional and unconditional MFN do not sit well together. A third party which has a conditional agreement with one country and an unconditional agreement with another cannot satisfy the terms of both. The situation is made worse when a country, as did the United States in the latter nineteenth century, insists on receiving unconditional MFN treatment from its trading partners while it extends only conditional treatment to them. It is not surprising that Viner judged the conditional form to have brought to the United States:

> more variations in construction, more international ill-feeling, more
> conflict between international obligations and municipal law, and between
> judicial interpretation and executive practice, more confusion and
> uncertainty of operation, than have developed under all the unconditional
> most-favored-nation pledges of all the other countries combined. (Viner,
> 1924, p. 25.)

While nineteenth-century Europe saw a great number of bilateral trade treaties which incorporated MFN provisions, Viner (1950, p. 14) argues that it was the MFN *principle* rather than MFN *pledges* 'that constituted the important barrier to preferential tariff arrangements in the past'. In other words, it was the interpretation of the clauses that mattered.

Following the Cobden-Chevalier Treaty in 1860, liberalizing bilateral trade agreements with unconditional MFN at their cores spread throughout Europe (United States Tariff Commission, 1919, p. 395; Irwin, 1992). While there was some retreat from liberality after 1870, it is difficult to believe that such liberal trading conditions could have spread in continental Europe under conditional rather than unconditional MFN clauses – and certainly they could not have done so under a hub-and-spoke system of trade agreements with no provisions for relating the benefits of one agreement to those of others, even if Britain had been at the hub. Intent on discriminating against Germany in particular, France embraced conditional MFN in 1922, but reverted to unconditional MFN so as to obtain access to German markets in 1927 (Tumlir, 1985, p. 24; Pomfret, 1988, p. 23).

Accepting the recommendations of its Tariff Commission (United States Tariff Commission, 1919), in 1922 the US abandoned the conditional interpretation. Following the passage of the Smoot-Hawley tariff in 1930 and then the Reciprocal Trade Negotiations Act of 1934, the US concluded bilateral trade pacts with 28 countries over the decade from the mid-1930s. (League of Nations, 1945, p. 18). These treaties incorporated unconditional MFN clauses, but were negotiated with careful selection of product coverage, so as to minimize free riding. Since the inception of the GATT no bilateral treaty negotiated by the US has incorporated a MFN clause, conditional or unconditional.

The major innovation of the GATT was to incorporate unconditional MFN into a multilateral framework. Article I requires that no contracting party can treat the trade of any other *country*[2] (whether it is or is not a contracting party to the GATT) more favorably than any other GATT contracting party: any concession which is given to any country must be passed on immediately and unconditionally to all contracting parties. The obverse of this multilateral unconditional MFN rule is that there can be no discrimination *against* any contracting party to the GATT by any other contracting party, though of course there can be discrimination against countries which are not contracting parties. The fundamental rule is one of equal treatment of members, though not of course of equal treatment of all the products traded by the members. This guarantee against discrimination has been critical in preventing discriminatory application of Article XIX safeguard actions against 'fair' trade, and provides an incentive for joining the GATT.

Multilateral unconditional MFN under GATT has not driven unconditional MFN completely out of bilateral trade agreements. Thus the bilateral Closer Economic Relations Agreement between Australia and New Zealand provides that neither country can have tariffs against the other in excess of those applied to any other country (except for developing country preferences) and that each accords the other MFN treatment with respect to services trade (Article 4.9 and 4.10 of the 1983 Agreement and Article 6 of the Protocol on Trade in Services of 1988). On the other hand, there is no such clause in the Canada–United States Free Trade Agreement, or in the free trade agreement between the United States and Israel. With respect to the Canada–US negotiations, Wonnacott (1991, p. 81) reports that Canada sought to ensure that Canada would 'automatically receive any benefits that the United States might extend to any other country such as Mexico'. The US refused. The draft North American Free Trade Agreement (NAFTA) circulated in September 1992 contains no MFN provision for goods but does for services 'in like circumstances', a term which perhaps could take a conditional MFN interpretation. Of course a truly free trade agreement would provide no opportunity for additional benefits to be extended to non-member countries.

The advantages and disadvantages of unconditional MFN have been examined many times. Prior to World War II, the question of conditional and unconditional MFN was argued largely in the context of bilateral treaties. Since the formation of the GATT it has moved much more into a plurilateral or multilateral context. In asking whether it has outlived its usefulness, Hufbauer (1986) groups the arguments for unconditional MFN into political (international), preservation of the balance of the bargain, economic efficiency, and guardian of multilateral trade. The first of these, the international political aspect, lay behind the incorporation of unconditional MFN in Woodrow Wilson's Fourteen Points for peace and post-war international order, enunciated in 1918, and was much emphasized by Cordell Hull and his followers.

Regarding maintenance of the balance of the bargain, the incorporation of an unconditional MFN clause into trade treaties provides an insurance against the erosion of benefits which have been paid for by so-called concessions. These concessions can be regarded as 'paying' not just for immediate benefits but for benefits in the future, including the unconditional receipt of favors which trading partners extend to others. A classic statement of the other side of this position – that is, against securing greater benefit than has been paid for – is that of John Jay in 1787 (cited in Viner, 1924, p. 19):

> It would certainly be inconsistent with the most obvious principles of justice and fair construction, that because France purchases, at a great price, a privilege of the United States, that therefore the Dutch shall immediately insist, not on having the like privileges at the like price, but without any price at all.

Hufbauer (1986, pp. 37–8) suggests that, in a world in which competitive conditions are changing rapidly, preservation of the bargain considerations are downgraded in comparing conditional and unconditional MFN. It is difficult to press this very far; many countries were concerned with discrimination implicit in the Canada–US Trade Free Agreement, and desire to preserve its bargain in that agreement drove Canada to join in the negotiations with the US and Mexico for the North America Free Trade Agreement.

As regards efficiency, the quote from Harry Johnson at the beginning of this chapter warns us to tread carefully. The income-maximizing structure of tariffs, subject to the constraint of retaining protective tariffs, will depend on the objectives of the protection, the extent to which terms of trade with each trading partner can be affected, and the negotiating bargains which can be secured with each country. It is unlikely that equality of tariff (and other trade measures) treatment for each trade partner would be the most efficient outcome from this calculus.

But there are at least two other ingredients in considering efficiency. One is that the form of protection and the ability to discriminate between trading partners is likely to affect the supply of and demand for protection in the country imposing the protection; that is, the supposed objectives of governments with respect to trade policy are endogenous. The possibility of discrimination may lead to the selective raising, rather than lowering, of trade barriers. Second, and not independent of the first point, is the effect on other countries' policies, whether these policies are discriminatory or not, and whether or not the policies are retaliatory. The efficiency question thus leads inevitably to the fourth category listed by Hufbauer: guardian of multilateral trade. Thus we consider the two together.

There are basically two opposing views of discrimination in the context of multilateral liberalization. Both are set in the context of domestic protectionist pressures on governments. One is that preferential discrimination permits countries to liberalize further than otherwise, by engaging in reciprocal reduction of barriers in agreement with like-minded countries. The other is that discrimination permits governments to raise, selectively, barriers against 'troublesome' exporting countries – and thus to bow to domestic protectionist pressures – in a manner in which they could not if the barriers had to be raised against all exporters, friends as well as foes.

A leading advocate of the latter view was Jan Tumlir. Tumlir (1985) argued strongly that unconditional MFN provides a firm constraint on protection. He saw the possibility of discrimination among sources as weakening a government's resolve to resist protectionist pressures, and pointed out that some forms of protection which have been growing even as tariffs have been falling over the last two or three decades (for example, country-specific import quotas and voluntary export restraints) could not be imposed in a system that was really non-discriminatory. Strong implementation of unconditional MFN would have prevented them.

On the other hand, Irwin (1992, pp. 23–4) emphasizes the futility and perhaps counter-productivity[3] of the various international conferences, many under the auspices of the League of Nations, which attempted to reinstate unconditional MFN multilaterally in Europe in the inter-war period, when economic (and political) instability had led to direct controls of international trade. Those who negotiated the post-World War II international economic institutions took economic stabilization as a sine qua non of trade liberalization, and subsequent events suggest they were correct. Unconditional MFN is only likely to constrain protectionist forces if the underlying economic conditions are relatively stable.

While it is often argued against Tumlir's position that unconditional MFN does not guarantee the development of a liberal, multilateral trading system, unconditional MFN does ensure that any liberalization is spread to other countries, providing the environment is appropriate. The liberal system in Europe started to be eroded from the early 1870s, despite unconditional MFN. French protectionists were able to claim that the Cobden-Chevalier Treaty, with its unconditional MFN provisions, was initially imposed undemocratically (by Napoleon III) and that the same provision was later part of a peace treaty imposed on them by Prussian victors in 1871 (Tumlir, 1985, p. 23). If governments wish to circumvent the constraints of unconditional MFN they can do so by multiplying tariff classifications, by not renewing bilateral treaties as they expire, or by providing notice of withdrawal under the terms of the treaties (Pomfret, 1988, p. 18). But all these actions have costs; unconditional MFN can impose a constraint.

A position opposed to that of Tumlir is presented by those who argue that unconditional MFN is a drag on trade liberalization by encouraging free riding and foot-dragging. The possibility of free riding, it is argued, discourages negotiation and curbs the selection of products to be covered. Foot-dragging from those who already benefit from unconditional MFN provisions, and who hope to secure benefits without paying the price, causes some countries not to negotiate at all, when conditionality could have brought them to the table. Conditional MFN and the discrimination implied by it then could facilitate more rapid liberalization.

It appears to me that comments on free riding and foot-dragging frequently tend to focus on the proximate and ignore the whole. It is difficult to envisage a world of criss-crossing, bilaterally negotiated, conditional MFN agreements, each designed to discourage free riding and foot-dragging and each therefore with limited coverage, leading to a stable and harmonious trading system, or even one with the degree of harmony and stability produced by that which we have. We return to this question in Section 12.4 below.

12.2 MFN and customs unions

Under the bilateral trade agreements which proliferated in Europe and elsewhere in the nineteenth and early twentieth centuries, exceptions to the unconditional MFN rule and practice were allowed for customs unions, imperial preferences and limited 'regional' agreements. While Britain maintained that an explicit exception was required to exempt customs unions from MFN legitimately (Viner, 1950, p. 12), other countries were not so demanding. What was generally required, however, was that the customs unions be 'complete', on which more later. Imperial preferences within a common sovereignty were generally accepted, but preferences between autonomous countries of the British Commonwealth were not regarded (except by the participants) as reasonable exceptions (Viner, 1950, p. 16). US hostility to these British preferences in the negotiations which led to the GATT was intense (Gardner, 1980).

Bilateral agreements frequently provided for exemptions from MFN for countries which had close affinity or which were contiguous, but these exemptions were minor in practice, at least until after World War I. The British government, having participated in the substantial extension of preferences at the Ottawa Conference in 1932 and justified such exemption from unconditional MFN on the basis of historical association, then argued that preferential arrangements based on any other criterion were unacceptable (Viner, 1950, pp. 19–21).

The conditions which Viner saw as necessary for a perfect or complete customs union were complete elimination of tariffs between partners, a common external tariff schedule, and the sharing of customs revenue according to an agreed formula (Viner, 1950, p. 5). These criteria in fact were specified by Cavour[4] in arguing the case for Sardinia against Austria: both Prussia (on behalf of the Zollverein) and Sardinia objected to an 1857 treaty between Austria and Modena in that it compromised MFN without being a 'complete' customs union (Viner, 1950, pp. 7–9). Customs unions were acceptable because a unified customs jurisdiction was being formed;[5] such unions always had political implications and on some occasions (for example, the Zollverein) led to political union.

It is most unlikely that the formation of a federation, or the political integration of two previously separate countries, would be objected to on the basis that the new trade 'bloc' would infringe unconditional MFN or inhibit the flow of international trade. It is in the light of an extension of a unified customs jurisdiction and the systemic implications of this that the traditional 'exception' for a customs union can be viewed.

There is a clear distinction here between a customs union and, say, a free trade area. A free trade area does not involve the loss of an autonomous customs territory. But we should note the importance of the customs union being 'complete': without this the systemic effect of losing one or more customs territories essentially does not apply.

12.3 Customs unions and Article XXIV

With this background one can readily see why in multilateralizing unconditional MFN in the GATT, customs unions were proposed as exceptions and why, until the last moment, free trade areas were not.[6] It may be noted that Article XXIV throughout refers to customs territories and that each 'customs territory shall, exclusively for the purpose of this Agreement, be treated as though it were a contracting party' (Article XXIV,1),[7] and that a customs territory shall be understood to mean 'any territory with respect to which separate tariffs ... [etc.] are maintained for a substantial part of the trade of such territory with other territories' (Article XXIV,2).

On the other hand, the form in which the customs union exception is expressed and the inclusion of free trade areas indicate that the traditional concept and basis for excepting customs unions were significantly bent by the time the form of the GATT was agreed. That is, the formation of a single customs territory was no longer the major criterion for exemption from unconditional MFN. We may note that Article XXIV would not exist but for MFN being unconditional in Article I; conditional MFN would not have led to the demand for such exceptions, as preferences would have been unconstrained.

The dispute between the US and Britain regarding preferences when the GATT was being negotiated is well known, as is its resolution: existing preferences were grandfathered and beyond them Article XXIV applies. Preferences were opposed, but customs unions were favored by the United States, and the American Proposals for the Charter for the International Trade Organization (ITO) provided for customs unions (Wilcox, 1949, pp. 70–1). It was only at Havana that the Article was extended to embrace free trade areas, curiously on the motion of Lebanon and Syria.[8] It appears that the title 'free trade area' as a technical name for the trade agreement with which we associate the term may have been invented in the Havana negotiations.

It can be maintained that 'if any one person can be described as the originator of the movement for an International Trade Organization it is James Meade' (Penrose, 1953, pp. 89–90). Meade's 1942 proposal for a Commercial Union generally followed the non-discriminatory prescription of Article VII of the Mutual Aid Agreement, finally agreed earlier that year after eight months of negotiations. However, Meade did provide for an exception to unconditional MFN, not for customs unions or free trade areas but for 'preferences up to a maximum of, say, 10 per cent to the produce of another state with which it formed a special recognised geographical or political union' (Meade, 1942, para. 13). He did not address the question of 'complete' customs unions, though in view of the history of such unions as exceptions he possibly took them for granted. Meade's modest exception did not see its way through to the US Proposals which formed the basis of negotiations for the ITO.

Comparing the original US Proposals of September 1946 for an ITO, as they related to customs unions, etc., with the provisions which were finally settled in the Charter negotiated in Havana between November 1947 and March 1948, there were the following significant differences (Viner, 1950, pp. 111 ff):

1. There was no preamble regarding desirability. (In the Havana Charter this appeared as 'Members recognize the desirability of increasing freedom of trade by the development, through voluntary agreements, of closer integration between the economies of the countries parties to such agreements'.)[9]
2. Free trade areas were not mentioned.
3. There was no provision for interim arrangements leading to customs unions.
4. In defining the external barrier structure of a customs union, the words 'average level' rather than 'general incidence' were used for the level, which 'shall not be higher or more restrictive' after the union than before.
5. Trade barriers had to be reduced on substantially all trade between all constituent territories; in the Havana Charter the words 'or at least with respect to substantially all the trade in products originating in the constituent territories' were added.
6. There were no provisions for retaining barriers between participants for balance of payments, agricultural stabilization, health and similar purposes.
7. There were no specific provisions for waiving the constraints on the formation of customs unions. At Havana, provision for such waiving of the main requirements was introduced 'provided that the proposals lead to the formation of a customs union or free-trade area in the sense of this Article [Article XXIV of GATT], and if approved by two-thirds of the members of the ITO.
8. Unlike the initial US Proposals, the Havana Charter allowed for preferential arrangements (limited to not more than 15 years) in special circumstances[10] between territories which were contiguous or in the same economic region. The approval of two-thirds of the members of the ITO was required. The agreements had to be open to other 'qualifying' parties.

With the exception of (8) in the above list, all the additions were carried from the Havana Charter into the GATT.

Generally regretting the concessions to discrimination, Viner (1950, p. 127) writes:

> The provisions of the Charter with respect to customs unions, free-trade areas and new regional agreements, *taken by themselves*, do constitute what is on paper at least an appreciable removal of pre-existing barriers to official discrimination in trade barriers, and it is significant that many of these provisions are written in terms of hearty encouragement rather than of regrettable departure from an ideal made necessary by special circumstances or by the less-than-universal acceptance of the ideal.

Earlier on the same page he refers to the 'odor of sanctity' given to practices which, 'whether widely practiced or not, were hitherto not in good repute'. But immediately he says:

> It should be conceded, however, that much can be said in support of the preferability of a code, even if imperfect, enforced by international sanction to an even better code enforced only by the possibility of unilateral national retaliation.

12.4 The economics of Article XXIV

The general thrust thus had been shifted from customs unions being an exception allowed by the territorial application of common customs legislation, to the modes by which liberal trade might be facilitated within a multilateral agreement. Much of the economic analysis of customs unions and free trade areas has been in terms of the resource allocation implications of specific preferential arrangements – Viner's trade creation, diversion and suppression frequently being the starting point. But for the multilateral process of liberalization for which the founders of the GATT hoped, and which to a significant extent has been achieved, the main economic consequences are to be found in the economics of the process as a whole rather than in the resource allocation effects of any particular agreement. Of course if each agreement has beneficial resource allocation effects as well as contributing to a beneficial process, so much the better. As suggested at the outset of the chapter, to illuminate the process element, a brief consideration of the economics of clubs is helpful.[11]

Clubs are formed between those who wish to share in the benefits of impure or excludable public goods, recognizing that a voluntary cooperative arrangement in the area of interest will be superior to unilateral action. In some cases the club will be formed to reinforce resolve to do what one knows is good for oneself (Alcoholics Anonymous). The

GATT club comprises members who recognize that by making commitments to each other they constrain the actions of others against them and also constrain their own actions, and create a system that itself yields benefits – a public good. The entrance fee is the constraint on one's own actions, a fee that in itself may be regarded as a political cost but an economic benefit in many countries.

In clubs the questions arise as to how broad the coverage of the rules should be, whether there should be special provisions for certain classes of members, whether higher fees can purchase additional benefits, whether the membership is open or closed and, if open, whether new members will be admitted on the same conditions as the old, how much the basic rules should be bent in order to retain members (particularly important ones), how to enforce the rules, and whether there might be a network of clubs with similar but differentiated purposes with partially overlapping membership. All these questions arise with respect to the GATT club.

The objectives of GATT as stated in the Preamble to the Agreement are the raising of income, ensuring full employment, developing full use of resources, and increasing the production and exchange of goods; the means are the liberalization of trade and elimination of discrimination. Equality of treatment of members thus was regarded as a key element of club membership and the natural complement to liberalization.

As noted above, GATT club membership is defined in terms of customs territories rather than countries, so complete customs unions are not to be considered 'exceptions' from equality of treatment. The main relevant exceptions to the basic non-discrimination rule of the club then are incomplete customs unions, all free trade areas, and interim arrangements leading to customs unions and free trade areas. Were these exceptions necessary to create a club membership large or important enough to generate the public good associated with the establishment of the club? Do they damage the real purpose of the club and reduce the production of the public good significantly?

The answer to the first of these questions probably is yes. The GATT is not of course just an economic agreement – it is 'an international legal document whose primary purpose is to promote or protect certain political goals of nation-states' (Baldwin, 1980, p. 138). Even before the negotiation of the ITO there were those who looked to some form of European economic integration as a political (rather than economic)[12] necessity. While the Treaty of Rome rode fairly roughshod over Article XXIV (see Dam, 1970, Chapter 16; Jackson, 1969, Chapter 24), had the Article provided only for 'complete' customs union and for no (or short) phasing-in, the Treaty would have done even more harm: it is doubtful that the GATT had much influence on the form of the Treaty. If there had been an effective enforcement mechanism in the GATT so that Article XXIV had been applied strictly, the EC-6 almost certainly would have left GATT, probably with the support of the US. Thus the exceptions (and slack enforcement) protected the club.

The second of these questions – whether the exceptions damage the real purpose of the club and reduce the production of the public good significantly – addresses the question of how important non-discrimination really is for the achievement of liberalization. It was introduced in Section 12.1 above in outlining the two sides of the unconditional/conditional MFN debate. On the one side there is the view expressed forcefully by Tumlir and others that allowing discrimination (conditional MFN or preferences) facilitates the raising of trade barriers; on the other side is the view that allowing discrimination permits negotiation of more barrier reduction.[13]

The exceptions in practice extend well beyond reasonable interpretations of Article XXIV. The Director General of GATT reports that the Working Party established to examine the Canada–US Free Trade Agreement, which was not able to reach a unanimous conclusion as to the consistency of this agreement with the provisions of Article XXIV, 'was the latest in a series of more than fifty working parties on . . . customs unions or free trade areas which have not reached definitive conclusions on the compatibility of these agreements with the GATT' (GATT, 1992, p. 20). Furthermore, under the Enabling Clause[14] negotiated in the Tokyo Round of multilateral trade negotiations, developing countries can do more or less whatever they want to do with respect to preferences for each other, unconstrained by Articles I and XXIV.

What Article XXIV still does, however, is to constrain the granting of preferences (apart from those between and for developing countries) to what at least purport to be free trade areas or customs unions, and this does appear to have a restraining influence. One might note the recent attempt by the countries of the Mercosur agreement (Argentina, Brazil, Paraguay and Uruguay) to bring this agreement to GATT under the Enabling Clause, and the insistence by the US in particular that it be examined under the provisions of Article XXIV (*Financial Times*, July 14, 1992; GATT, 1992, p. 20). Governments also do appear generally to adhere to the provisions restricting the increase in trade barriers upon the formation of preferential arrangements, though the methods by which average trade barriers are to be calculated have been much in dispute.[15]

Does (or would) Tumlir's point that discrimination is the enemy of progressive liberalization still apply when the raising of barriers against third parties is proscribed and that proscription is generally adhered to? It is difficult to sustain his argument when it is interpreted narrowly, though he does make a telling point that discriminatory non-tariff barriers have flourished even as (non-discriminatory) tariffs have been reduced. But his argument gains more substance when it is considered in the context of the development of a system. The main worry is that the less demanding are the constraints on preferences, the more preferential arrangements will develop. Each agreement on its own may satisfy Vinerian-type criteria for improved resource allocation, but each can lead to resistance by governments to further liberalization as existing preferences are defended,[16] each tends to make further negotiation with other parties more difficult, each tends to lead to new rules of origin[17] and dispute-settlement procedures, and each is likely to lessen the system's resistance to further implicit discrimination against some countries – a development that can easily lead to explicit discrimination. Krugman (1991b, p. 56) makes the point sharply: 'the great political advantage [to Europeans and North Americans] of regional pacts is that they can exclude Japan'.

Viewed from this perspective, the economics of Article XXIV really concerns the public good produced by the club and the damage which discrimination can do to its production. The rules of Article XXIV attempt to limit discrimination by imposing a high (political) cost on it: strictly interpreted, they would only allow it when the parties are really serious about favoring each other (free trade among the partners for most products) and when external barriers are not raised. The high political cost of establishing such preferential arrangements acts as a deterrent to their formation. However, interpretation of Article XXIV has lowered this cost for all countries, while the Enabling Clause has reduced the cost for developing countries even further. The plethora of pseudo-free trade agreements now being implemented or proposed, and the threat which they provide to an efficient, liberalizing, multilateral system, suggest that the cost may now be too low.

To help to ensure that clubs within the GATT club were facilitating the achievement of GATT's overall objectives, one could suggest an accession clause requiring openness to new members on conditions similar to those required of the existing members (Bhagwati, 1991, p. 77; Snape *et al.*, 1992, Chapter 6).[18] But *pace* Tumlir and Krugman, if a purpose of at least some of the actual or proposed discriminatory trading arrangements of some of the major trading powers is to discriminate against particular countries, this suggestion is not likely to gain much favor where it matters.

Until one of the major trading groups of the world decides to press for adherence to the existing rules, the utility of introducing additional constraints into Article XXIV appears limited. There was no provision for accession in the Canada–US Free Trade Agreement, and the accession clause in the proposed NAFTA is very tight. Thus, the scope for a binding 'openness' requirement for preferential arrangements under the GATT appears remote.

12.5 Summary

While non-discrimination among countries, or unconditional MFN, does not guarantee a liberal multilateral trading system, it still appears to be the best general principle on which to build a plurilateral or multilateral trading framework. In the nineteenth century in Europe, bilateral treaties with unconditional MFN clauses brought an era of widespread trade liberalization. Again, in the decade following 1934, and on the initiative of the US, bilateral treaties with a similar clause helped reverse the wholesale raising of trade barriers associated with the Great Depression. From the introduction of GATT in 1947, unconditional MFN within the GATT club was at the heart of the multilateral liberalization of international trade which occurred in the following decades.

A traditional exception to unconditional MFN has been for 'complete' customs unions, and effectively GATT's rules are written for customs territories rather than countries. While the initial US Proposals which led to the formation of the GATT allowed only for this exception, by the time the GATT was implemented in 1947 the relevant exceptions article (Article XXIV) had grown to include 'incomplete' customs unions and free trade areas, and interim arrangements designed to lead to free trade areas and customs unions. The enforcement of the rules constraining these exceptions has been very lax, while preferences for and among developing countries have been virtually removed from constraints.

The economics of Article XXIV are best looked at in terms of a process of developing a liberalizing trading system, or club, rather than in terms of the resource allocation implications of particular preferential agreements considered on their own. The objective of the GATT club is to provide, through cooperation, a more desirable outcome than is achievable by each country acting independently. The exceptions to non-discrimination allowed in Article XXIV are provided to attract and retain some members that might not otherwise remain in the club. But at the same time the exceptions may adversely affect the degree of liberalization among the club members. The exception rules were constructed so as to discourage all preference schemes less than (almost) full preferences, so as to discourage the proliferation of preferential agreements: the political cost of negotiating preferences thus was deliberately made high. It is argued that an abundance of partial preferential agreements is more likely to damage the development and maintenance of a liberal, multilateral trading system than is a small number of almost complete preferential agreements.

Erosion of the constraints of Article XXIV, together with forms of discrimination which evade or ignore unconditional MFN, is in fact yielding a plethora of regional integration agreements and proposals which threaten the foundations and successes of the GATT. Requiring a liberal accessions clause in free trade area and customs union agreements, as put forward in the GATT-Plus proposals (see Baldwin's Chapter 18 in this volume), would ensure that these clubs within the GATT club would further, rather than threaten, the aims of the GATT itself. But this is not likely to find favor among countries which are using the existing arrangements to discriminate implicitly or explicitly against some other countries.

Notes

Research by the author into the economics of the GATT has been supported, in part, by the Australian Research Council.

1. See also United States Tariff Commission (1919, pp. 393ff). The attitude of the United States in practice is shown in the following quotation from p. 41 of the US Tariff Commission Report:

   The experience of the United States in meeting the claim of Switzerland in 1898 affords an excellent example of the impossibility of the practice of entering into reciprocity agreements with the giving of unconditional most-favored-nation pledges. ... [In] the negotiation of the treaty of 1850 with Switzerland, the American plenipotentiary had pledged the United States to unconditional most-favored-nation treatment. The Government stood by the pledge. Switzerland was therefore given, without compensation, the benefit of concessions made to France ... [in a treaty in 1897]. Other States at once claimed the right to the same treatment, and it became necessary [sic] to denounce the favored-nation provision in the Swiss treaty.

2. As noted below, 'country' in fact is interpreted as 'customs territory'.
3. Irwin argues that the Ouchy Convention, which was signed in 1932 between the Benelux countries but was open to others, and which agreed to staged tariff reductions of 50 per cent, could have formed the basis for more general trade liberalization. But Britain and other countries insisted that without unconditional MFN extension of the tariff reductions, the convention was unacceptable. 'In the inter-war period ... progressive bilateralism – the sole hope for freer trade – was extinguished in the misplaced desire to restore unconditional MFN treatment first' (Irwin, 1992, p. 27).
4. Cavour was Prime Minister of Sardinia and leader with Garibaldi in the unification of Italy. Sardinia, with France, went to war against Austria in 1859.
5. This view is expressed also by Haight (1972, p. 392), a member of the secretariat of the Geneva and Havana conferences which negotiated the charter for the ITO, and of the secretariat of the GATT from 1948 to 1970.

6. We may recall that while we are now accustomed to thinking of a customs union as a possible precursor to and facilitator of closer political association (as in the German Zollverein and the European Economic Community), or at least for the two to occur at the same time (as in the Australian Federation), in earlier days political union tended to precede customs union. Viner writes that 'it was almost a general rule until comparatively recently that the area of political unification was greater than the area of tariff unification' (1950, p. 95). From 1997 it is likely that Hong Kong, Macao and mainland China will provide new examples of the older tradition.

7. This paragraph refers to the 'metropolitan customs territories' of contracting parties and to any other customs territories on behalf of which the Agreement has been signed.

8. The proposal envisaged that the free trade area be between countries of the same region, but this restriction was removed by the relevant subcommittee (Haight, 1972, p. 393).

9. Haight (1972, pp. 395–7) writes that this sentence originated from a proposal by France to write into the objectives of the ITO in Article I of the Havana Charter,

> to facilitate the progressive freeing of trade in increasingly extensive economic zones by promoting ... between neighbouring countries, or countries which are closely related economically owing to the complementary nature of their economic systems, of economic units wider in character than those resulting from political frontiers.

Against objections by the French the wording was changed to that in the text and the sentence was moved to the customs union Article, its location in that Article being determined by a desire not to change the existing paragraph numbering. As Haight says: 'Thus did the word "integration" creep into the GATT, and the desirability of closer economic integration was inscribed – more by accident than design – as the philosophical basis for the formation of customs unions [and free trade areas]'.

10. Not necessarily confined to reconstruction and development, though the conditions appear in an Article under this heading.

11. The book by Cornes and Sandler (1986) is a very useful reference on the theory of clubs.

12. Late in the nineteenth century there were many Europeans who saw it as necessary to counter the economic might and threat of the US.

13. This is the process which (taking their position at its face value) the French appeared to be envisaging in seeking to encourage preferential arrangements at the Havana negotiations (see note 9 above). It is also the process envisaged by Kemp and Wan (1976) in their well-known paper.

14. This clause (termed 'Differential and More Favourable Treatment Reciprocity and Fuller Participation of Developing Countries') provides that 'Notwithstanding Article I of the General Agreement, contracting parties may accord differential and more favourable treatment to developing countries, without according such treatment to other countries.' As well as applying to preferences granted by developed countries to developing countries under the generalized system of preferences, they also apply (*inter alia*) to 'regional or global' arrangements among developing countries.

15. The Draft Final Act of the Uruguay Round of multilateral trade negotiations, placed on the table by the Director General of the GATT on December 20, 1991 (the 'Dunkel Draft'), provides that in calculating the before and after incidence of tariffs upon the formation of customs unions in order to judge that the general incidence against outsiders has not been increased, a weighted average of applied tariffs is to be calculated by the GATT Secretariat. This appears to be a very useful specification. John McMillan (in Chapter 13 of this volume) makes an interesting proposal regarding the calculation of common tariffs, consistent with Kemp and Wan (1976).

16. There have been several cases in which developing countries have objected to proposed reductions of MFN tariffs by developed countries on the grounds that the reductions would erode existing preferences for developing countries.

17. There are 193 pages of rules of origin in the draft NAFTA circulated in September 1992.

18. GATT-Plus proposals, as referred to by Baldwin in Chapter 18 of this volume, have this characteristic and further the liberal, multilateral objectives of the GATT.

References

Baldwin, R. E. (1980), 'The Economics of the GATT', in *Issues in International Economics*, edited by P. Oppenheimer, London: Oriel Press. (Reprinted in Baldwin's *Trade Policy in a Changing World Economy*, London: Harvester Wheatsheaf; page references are to the reprinted version.)

Bhagwati, J. N (1991), *The World Trading System at Risk*, London: Harvester Wheatsheaf.

Cornes, R. and T. Sandler (1986), *The Theory of Externalities, Public Goods and Club Goods*, Cambridge: Cambridge University Press.

Dam, K. W. (1970), *The GATT: Law and International Economic Organization*, Chicago: University of Chicago Press.

Gardner, R. N. (1980), *Sterling–Dollar Diplomacy in Current Perspective: The Origins and Prospects of Our International Economic Order*, New York: Columbia University Press, revised edition.

GATT (1992), *International Trade and the Trading System: Report by the Director General, 1991–1992*, Geneva: GATT Secretariat, May.

Haight, F. A. (1972), 'Customs Unions and Free-Trade Areas under GATT: A Reappraisal', *Journal of World Trade Law* 6: 391–404.

Hufbauer, G. C. (1986), 'Should Unconditional MFN be Revived, Retired or Recast?', in *Issues in World Trade Policy: GATT at the Crossroads*, edited by R. H. Snape, London: Macmillan, and New York: St Martins Press.

Irwin, D. A. (1992), 'Multilateral and Bilateral Trade Policies in the World Trading System: An Historical Perspective', presented at the World Bank/Centre for Economic Policy Research (CEPR) Conference on New Dimensions to Regional Integration, Washington, DC, April 2–3.

Jackson, J. H. (1969), *World Trade and the Law of GATT*, Charlottesville: Michie.

Jackson, J. H. (1989), *The World Trading System: Law and Policy of International Economic Relations*, Cambridge, MA: MIT Press.

Johnson, H. G. (1976), *Trade Negotiations and the New International Monetary System*, Leiden: A. W. Sijthoff, for the Graduate Institute of International Studies, Geneva, and the Trade Policy Research Centre, London.

Kemp, M. C. and H. Y. Wan (1976), 'An Elementary Proposition Concerning the Formation of Customs Unions', *Journal of International Economics* **6**: 95–7.

Krugman, P. R. (1991a), 'Is Bilateralism Bad?', in *International Trade and Trade Policy*, edited by E. Helpman and A. Razin, Cambridge, MA: MIT Press.

Krugman, P. R. (1991b), 'Regional Trade Blocs: The Good, the Bad and the Ugly', *The International Economy* **5**: 54–6.

League of Nations (1945), *Commercial Policy in the Post-War World*, Report of the Economic and Financial Committees, C.31.M.31.1945.II.A, Geneva: League of Nations.

Meade, J. E. (1942), 'A Proposal for an International Commercial Union', published as an addendum to J. Culbert, 'War-time Anglo-American Talks and the Making of the GATT', *The World Economy* **10**: 381–407, December 1987. (Meade's proposal is dated July 25, 1942.)

Penrose, E. F. (1953), *Economic Planning for Peace*, Princeton: Princeton University Press.

Pomfret, R. (1988), *Unequal Trade: The Economics of Discriminatory Trade Policies*, Oxford: Basil Blackwell.

Snape, R. H., J. Adams and D. Morgan (1992), *Regional Trade Agreements, Part I: Implications for Australia* (Report to the Australian Government's Department of Foreign Affairs and Trade), Monash University, Melbourne, June.

Tumlir, J. (1985), *Protectionism: Trade Policy in Democratic Societies*, Washington, DC: American Enterprise Institute.

United States Tariff Commission (1919), *Reciprocity and Commercial Treaties*, Washington, DC: Government Printing Office.

Viner, J. (1924), 'The Most-Favored-Nation Clause in American Commercial Treaties', *Journal of Political Economy* **32**: 101–29. (Reprinted in his *International Economics*, Glencoe: The Free Press, 1951; page references are to the reprinted version.)

Viner, J. (1950), *The Customs Union Issue*, New York: Carnegie Endowment for International Peace. (Reprinted by Anderson Kramer Associates, Washington, DC, 1961.)

Wilcox, C. (1949), *A Charter for World Trade*, New York: Macmillan.

Wonnacott, P. and M. Lutz (1989), 'Is there a Case for Free Trade Areas?', in *Free Trade Areas and U.S. Trade Policy*, edited by J. J. Schott, Washington, DC: Institute for International Economics.

Wonnacott, R. J. (1991), 'Canada's Role in the US–Mexican Free Trade Negotiations', *The World Economy* **14**: 79–86.

13

Does regional integration foster open trade? Economic theory and GATT's Article XXIV

John McMillan

Over 40 per cent of world trade currently occurs within regional integration agreements like the European Community and the Canada–US free trade area, and new or expanded agreements continue to be negotiated. Yet it is widely argued that the GATT's rules on regional integration agreements are inadequate. This chapter proposes a test for the acceptability of regional integration agreements that is both better grounded in economic theory and, I argue, simpler than the current GATT rules.

GATT's rules say, among other things, that barriers on trade with the rest of the world must not be raised following the signing of a regional integration agreement (Article XXIV). Measuring the height of trade barriers, however, is difficult. Most empirical researchers investigate the effects of regional integration agreements (RIAs) by estimating their effects not just on trade barriers, but on trade volumes. Focusing on trade volumes is not only the most direct way of measuring the effects of regional integration; it also has a deep justification in economic theory.

Theory says that it is always possible for a RIA to be structured in such a way as to create gains for the member countries without harming any non-members: it can do this by keeping trade volumes with the rest of the world at their pre-integration levels. This suggests the appropriateness of a rule requiring that external trade volumes not be lowered as a result of forming a RIA, *ceteris paribus*.

If any enlargement of an existing RIA, by adding new member countries, is required to be done in such a way as to keep external trade volumes at least at their previous levels, then the theory further says that it is in the interest of any RIA to continue to admit new members. Given conformity to the rule that external trade volumes not be lowered, therefore, RIAs are unambiguously a step toward open trade on a global scale.

13.1 Admissible regional integration agreements

An old question has been reopened by the trend toward RIAs: should regional integration be regarded as a step toward global free trade? Jacob Viner addressed this question in 1950; but his answer was indecisive. A RIA represents freer trade to the extent that it results in trade creation: the shifting of the production of some goods from a less efficient member country to a more efficient member country. It represents more-restricted trade to the extent that it results in trade diversion: the shifting of production from an efficient non-member country to a less efficient member country. Whether, in any particular case, trade creation outweighs trade diversion is a purely empirical question. The huge amount of modeling that built on Viner's insight only added further complications to this theoretical inconclusiveness. Of all areas of economic analysis, the theory of RIAs has been especially susceptible to Herbert Hoover's plea for a one-armed economist ('so we will not always hear, "On the other hand…"').[1]

The theory was tidied up by Kemp (1964), Vanek (1965), Ohyama (1972), and Kemp and Wan (1976). They looked at regional integration from a different angle from Viner and offered a theorem that, in clarifying the sense in which RIAs are unambigously a good thing, is one of the most elegant and important of all contributions to the theory of customs unions: *It is always possible for a regional integration agreement, formed among an arbitrary group of countries, to structure itself in such a way as to make the member countries better off without making any of the non-member countries worse off.*[2]

This result is elementary, as Kemp and Wan said, but it nevertheless is fundamental for understanding the potentialities of RIAs. The logic goes as follows. Let us, temporarily, hypothetically freeze the imports and exports between members and outsider countries at their pre-integration levels. Next, we reduce or eliminate any pre-existing barriers to trade among the member countries and let internal prices adjust freely so as to equate supply and demand of each item, including in the supply-and-demand accounting the amounts being traded with the rest of the world. By the classical gains-from-trade argument, this reallocation makes the member countries better off (though compensatory payments may be needed from one member country to another).[3] Finally, we compute what common external tariffs the newly formed RIA would have to set so that, in the liberalized economy that the RIA now represents, import demands and export supplies will be exactly at the levels at which we froze them (that is, their pre-integration levels). These tariffs equal the difference between the new internal market-clearing prices and world prices. (This will mean lowering some tariffs and possibly raising others.) If the RIA's tariffs are set at these levels, then in the new trading equilibrium there is the same amount of trade with the rest of the world as before integration: the member countries gain from the RIA, and the rest of the world has the same level of welfare as it had before the agreement. This ends the proof of the theorem.

Does this piece of theory have any relevance for real RIAs? The fact that it is possible for regional agreements to avoid harm to outsiders while improving their own welfare does not mean that they do not actually harm outsiders. Interest groups within the member countries might be influential enough to cause external trade restrictions to be tightened, as with agriculture in the EC.[4] Also, if the members among themselves produce a large fraction of the world's supply of some goods, the RIA might restrict external trade in order to exploit its new-found monopoly power in world trade. The Kemp–Vanek model is, therefore, probably not a good description of how integration occurs in practice. (Its authors did not claim it was.)

I suggest, however, that this theorem has normative significance for evaluating RIAs. Let us define a RIA to be Kemp–Vanek admissible if, for each item traded, the volume of imports into the RIA is *at least as high* as the net volume imported from the rest of the world by the member countries before integration. The RIA envisaged in the theorem is on the very edge of Kemp–Vanek admissibility, in that the volume of imports is exactly the same before and after union. It is always possible, as we have seen, for any RIA to structure itself in such a way as to be Kemp–Vanek admissible while still providing gains for its members.

Can RIAs foster open trade? An implication of the Kemp–Vanek theorem is that, as Kemp and Wan put it, 'an incentive to form and enlarge customs unions persists until the world is one big customs union, that is, until world free trade prevails' (1976, p.96). This is because the theorem applies to any grouping of countries. Thus it is always possible to add a country to an existing RIA in such a way as to improve the welfare of the members of the expanded RIA without causing harm to those who remain outside. If it could somehow be ensured that RIAs be Kemp–Vanek admissible, they would not be an impediment to global free trade.

The Kemp–Vanek approach therefore sidesteps the second-best, on-the-one-hand, on-the-other-hand indecisiveness of most of customs-union theory. Any change in trade policy produces gainers and losers. The classical gains-from-trade theorem says that freer trade results in a larger pie; but it is silent about how the pie is to be distributed. It says there exists a potential Pareto-improvement, but it does not show how to realize it. For the gains from trade to be spread around the population, some of the gains must be redistributed to those who would otherwise suffer from the policy change. Within a RIA there exists a range of instruments for achieving these redistributions, either in the form of trade-adjustment assistance for laid-off workers and reinvestment subsidies for affected regions and industries, or by log-rolling, linking different issues during internal negotiations. Between the RIA and outside countries, there is much less scope for redistribution. To ensure that the potential gains from trade liberalization are as close as possible to realized Pareto-gains, it helps if such redistribution between member and non-member countries is unnecessary. This is ensured if the integration agreement is Kemp–Vanek admissible.

Trade theorists have usually evaluated RIAs either from the point of view of the world as a whole (asking whether the trade creation outweighs the trade diversion) or from the point of view of the members (asking how to maximize the gains from trade creation). I suggest that, for the rules of international trade, the size of any trade creation among member countries is irrelevant. In practice it is possible that some member countries will not benefit from a RIA. But it seems reasonable to have a hierarchy of concerns: to put preventing harm to third countries ahead of preventing members from harming themselves. The draft Uruguay Round agreement of December 1991 says of RIAs: 'the parties to them should to the greatest possible extent avoid creating adverse effects on the trade of other contracting parties.' GATT Director-General Arthur Dunkel said recently that GATT's rules are 'designed to ensure above all that regional trading integration should not be at the expense of third parties.'[5] If an integration agreement is to be evaluated by its external effects – by whether it causes harm to non-participating countries – then the best test for this, I suggest, is that it be Kemp–Vanek admissible.

Given that what matters from a global perspective is the RIA's impact on non-member countries, the focus is put onto trade diversion: the switching of demand for a given import from an outsider to a fellow member country. But textbook trade diversion is not all that is encompassed by the admissibility test. It is possible that increased efficiencies within the member countries' industries following integration – generated, for example, by economies of scale or heightened inter-firm competition – might increase the demand for imports from non-member countries, partially offsetting any trade-diversion effects. Estimates of the effects of the EC's '1992' liberalization predict significant gains (adding two or more percentage points to national income) from economies of scale and increased competition (Emerson *et al.*, 1988; Jacquemin and Sapir, 1991; Winters, 1992). Estimates of the gains from Canada–United States free trade and Australia–New Zealand Closer Economic Relations also find gains from economies of scale, rationalization, and competition effects (Harris and Cox, 1983; Bollard and Thompson, 1987). Furthermore, the dynamic gains from trade liberalization, due to increased physical and human capital formation, can be large (Baldwin, 1992). The trade gains envisaged by trade theory, and in particular by the Kemp–Vanek theorem, arise from improvements in the allocation of resources across sectors. Adding the economies of scale and competition gains, as well as increased capital accumulation, strengthens the empirical force of the theorem, since it increases the total gains from integration and therefore increases the potential for avoiding harm to non-members.

The common external tariffs that leave trade with the rest of the world unchanged are computed, in the proof of the theorem, as the difference between world prices and market-clearing prices within the liberalized internal economy (with external trade held constant). These internal equilibrium prices are difficult to compute, even within reasonably simple models, because of the complex interactions in supplies and demands that are possible among the different goods. Thus computing the common external tariffs that would leave external trade exactly unchanged, as in the theorem, is a tall order. Kemp–Vanek admissibility is, however, a much less stringent criterion than that used in the theorem; all that is required is that the common external tariffs be such that external trade is no lower than before.

Requiring specified levels of imports has a certain managed-trade flavor: it sounds like a quantitative trade restraint. There is a crucial difference, however: a quantitative restraint specifies a maximum level of imports, whereas admissibility specifies a minimum level of imports. Quantitative restraints, according to standard theory, reduce social welfare whereas admissibility, according to the Kemp–Vanek theorem, guarantees a welfare improvement.

Kemp–Vanek admissibility requires that there be no reduction in any of the RIA's imports and exports. This would be difficult to check in practice, as it would be necessary to check thousands of commodity classifications. Moreover, if a RIA were required to satisfy this criterion, it would be driven toward extremely detailed management of its import and export quantities. For a less stringent requirement, let us define a RIA to be admissible if the volume of trade between members and the rest of the world, measured at some specified level of aggregation, is no lower after integration. The simplest definition of admissibility is in terms of the total volume of external trade. A more satisfactory but still implementable definition is in terms of broad product categories: for example, trade volumes might be broken down into agricultural products, industrial products and services.

The value of Kemp–Vanek admissibility is that it ensures that the amounts available for consumption of each traded item in each outsider country are no smaller after integration; thus no outsider country is harmed. With any aggregative measure of admissibility, we cannot be sure that there are no losers among outsider countries. Hence the aggregative measures of admissibility fall short of the theoretical ideal; but they still provide a yardstick of the agreement's impact. If the RIA is admissible just in terms of total trade volume, then the income the rest of the world earns by selling to the member countries is not lowered following integration. Admissibility in aggregative terms is a necessary condition for Kemp–Vanek admissibility; thus if a RIA fails an aggregative admissibility test, we can conclude that there are likely to be some losses in the rest of the world. Aggregative measures of admissibility, then, are useful; but less aggregative measures are to be preferred to more aggregative measures, for they are closer to the theoretically ideal (Kemp–Vanek) measure. Measuring total trade volumes is less satisfactory than, say, measuring agricultural, industrial and services trade separately; and this is less satisfactory than a still finer classification of traded items. In choosing the appropriately aggregative definition of admissibility, these considerations must be weighed against the costs of implementation, for finer classifications involve more data collection.[6] Kemp–Vanek admissibility is ideal but unimplementable; aggregative admissibility is implementable but blunt.

13.2   The shortcomings of GATT's Article XXIV

Regional integration agreements are covered by Article XXIV of the General Agreement on Tariffs and Trade. Article XXIV is, however, often criticized; and many have advocated making it stricter and more precise. According to an eminent study group appointed by the Director-General of GATT, many existing RIAs

> fall far short of the requirements [of Article XXIV] ... The exceptions and ambiguities which have thus been permitted have seriously weakened the trade rules, and make it very difficult to resolve disputes to which Article XXIV is relevant. They have set a dangerous precedent for further special deals, fragmentation of the trading system, and damage to the trade interests of non-participants ... GATT rules on customs unions and free-trade areas should be examined, redefined so as to avoid ambiguity, and more strictly applied. (Leutwiler *et al.*, 1985, p. 41).

A former Deputy Director-General of GATT said:

> Of all the GATT articles, this is one of the most abused, and those abuses are among the least noted. Unfortunately, therefore, those framing any new [free trade area] need have little fear that they will be embarrassed by some GATT body finding them in violation of their international obligations and commitments and recommending that they abandon or alter what they are about to do. (Patterson, 1989, p. 361)

A 1991 report on the Canada–United States Free Trade Agreement by a GATT working party was unable to reach a conclusion as to whether the agreement was consistent with GATT rules. The chairman of the working party, Ambassador David Hawes, said the inconclusiveness was to be expected: 'Over fifty previous working parties on individual customs unions or free-trade areas had been unable to reach unanimous conclusions as to the GATT consistency of these agreements. On the other hand, no such agreement has been disapproved explicitly.' Commenting on this report, the Indian delegate said that 'the lack of definitive conclusions in reports of Article XXIV working parties posed the danger of giving carte blanche to participants in regional trade arrrangements.'[7]

As various scholars have noted, GATT's rules have had little impact on the way RIAs have been structured:

> The effort to attain precision and to force future arrangements into Article XXIV's mold proved to be ... a failure, if not a fiasco. The RIAs that came before the GATT did not conform to the tests of Article XXIV, and in the face of the conflict, the GATT and not the regional groupings yielded. (Dam, 1970, p. 275)

> Only a small proportion of the [free trade areas] that have evolved in the post-war years, and have been notified to the GATT, have been found to be compatible with Article XXIV by the working parties established at the time. The typical working party ... reports are generally inconclusive with regard to GATT compatibility. (Whalley, 1989, p. 366)

Article XXIV's 'design is inadequate to today's tasks. Its redesign must clearly get on to the ongoing agenda of revitalizing and refashioning the GATT' (Bhagwati, 1991, p. 78).

One of the requirements that Article XXIV imposes on a newly forming or an enlarging RIA is that the tariffs and other regulations that the agreement sets on trade with the rest of the world must be no higher than the average level of pre-existing tariff equivalents in the joining countries.[8] This rule can be criticized on two grounds.

First, it focuses on the wrong variable. Tariffs do not directly affect people's well-being; they affect it only indirectly, via their impact on trade volumes and thereby on people's consumption. The volume of trade more directly affects welfare, and so it makes more sense to look at the RIA's effects on trade volumes. Even if tariffs were held at their average pre-union level, integration could result in considerable trade diversion. This is illustrated, following Kemp (1969, Chapter 4), by considering three countries, A, B and C. Suppose countries B and C are identical, but different from country A. If A and B formed a customs union and set their common external tariffs at the average of the pre-union levels, then there would be considerable trade diversion against the rest of the world, C. The agreement between A and B would be, in our terms, admissible, and harm to C avoided, only if the external tariffs on the potentially trade-diverted goods were drastically lowered.

Extrapolating from this example, we can conclude that outside countries that have an economic structure similar to one of the integrating countries are likely to be harmed. Even if Article XXIV's current provisions against raising external tariffs are fully met, Caribbean countries, for example, are likely to be harmed by the North American Free Trade Agreement, as their textile and agricultural sales to the United States are lost to Mexico. Avoiding harm to the rest of the world might require a newly forming RIA to lower its external tariffs on some items. It is possible for a RIA to be consistent with Article XXIV in not raising average external tariffs, but to be harmful to the rest of the world.

The second criticism of the rule against raising average external tariffs is that, as it is written, it is vague. Paragraph 5(a) of Article XXIV states that external trade barriers 'shall not on the whole be higher or more restrictive than the general incidence of the duties and regulations of commerce applicable in the constituent territories prior to the formation of such union' (GATT, 1986, p. 42). But nowhere is it specified how the 'general incidence' of a set of tariffs is to be measured. Are before and after tariffs to be compared item by item, or are average tariffs to be compared? If the latter, is it a simple average, or a weighted average with trade volumes as weights? When a RIA sets its common external tariffs, some countries' tariffs on some goods fall, and others rise. Paragraph 6 says that non-member countries are entitled to compensation for any increases in tariffs that occur in the process of creating a common external tariff; but 'due account shall be taken' of the benefits to outsiders of any tariff reductions in that process (GATT, 1986, p. 42). But it is not specified how tariff increases are to be weighed against tariff reductions. 'Article XXIV gives no guidance at all', according to Dam (1970, p. 278), on how to calculate whether in net terms the integration has increased the barriers to external trade.

The Uruguay Round negotiators have attempted to tighten Article XXIV by making the wording more precise; but the focus has remained on tariff rates. The draft of the Uruguay Round agreement of December 1991 (the 'Dunkel Draft') said that future evaluations of Paragraph 5 of Article XXIV would

> be based on an overall assessment of weighted average tariff rates and of customs duties collected. This assessment shall be based on import statistics for a previous representative period to be supplied by the customs union, on a tariff-line basis and in values and quantities, broken down by GATT country of origin. The GATT Secretariat shall compute the weighted average tariff rates and customs duties collected in accordance with the methodology used in the assessment of tariff offers in the Uruguay Round. (GATT, 1991, p. U.2.)

This revised formulation of Article XXIV addresses the second of the above criticisms, in being precise. But it does not overcome the first of the above criticisms: it does not succeed in protecting outside countries from harm, in that an integration agreement that conformed to these requirements, in not raising its average external tariffs, could, nevertheless, generate considerable trade diversion.

13.3 A proposal for the revision of Article XXIV

Article XXIV could be made more workable by phrasing its requirements not in terms of the height of tariffs but in terms of trade volumes; that is, by looking at the trade consequences of the restrictions rather than trying to measure their effect on domestic prices. Article XXIV's statement that duties 'shall not on the whole be higher or more restrictive than the general incidence of the duties ... prior to the formation of such union' should, in this view, be interpreted to mean that external tariffs be such that the union passes the test of admissibility. A proposed RIA, in order to get GATT's imprimatur, would have to promise not to introduce policies that result in external trade volumes being lowered. And, if after some years the RIA is seen to have reduced its imports from the rest of the world, it would be required to adjust its trade restrictions so as to reverse this fall in imports.[9]

Admissibility is not itself defined until the level of aggregation is specified. As noted earlier, the finer the degree of aggregation the better, subject to limitations on data collection. Admissibility defined in terms of the total volume of trade is probably inadequate to ensure the absence of harm to outsider countries. The level of aggregation should admit some sector-by-sector differentiation.

Measuring the height of trade barriers, as contrasted with measuring trade volumes, is made still more problematic by the trend away from tariffs toward less transparent forms of protection like import licenses, anti-dumping procedures and voluntary export restraints. In the biggest RIA of all, the EC, 13 per cent of imports from industrial countries and 23 per cent of imports from less-developed countries in 1986 were subject to non-tariff barriers with significant restrictive effects. The use of anti-dumping, countervailing and safeguard procedures by the EC has increased markedly: there were 9 of these actions between 1971 and 1975, 102 between 1976 and 1980, and 127 between 1981 and 1985 (Secchi, 1990, pp. 52–4). It would seem to be more reliable to measure the effect of such procedures on trade volumes than to try to compute their tariff equivalents.

A further distortion that RIAs may cause that is difficult to measure is in misdirecting investment flows. Foreign direct investment can be motivated by the need to get inside a tariff wall. There are important reasons, however, why foreign direct investment can be efficient: as well as standard comparative-advantage effects, often there are advantages to locating plants close to customers or suppliers or sources of new technology. It is difficult to measure how much of, say, Japan's investment in the EC is driven by fears of 'Fortress Europe' and how much by genuine efficiency considerations. Measuring the height of trade barriers in this case requires estimation of the protective effect of local-content rules. But if the above admissibility criterion is used, there is no need to make the distinction betweeen efficient and protectionism-driven foreign investment, since the latter will show up in smaller trade flows.

Any law that is rarely complied with is a bad law. That Article XXIV is ineffective is explainable, at least in part, by the fact that it is subject to a wide range of interpretations. A rule that was, on the other hand, simple and perceived to be fair would have a reasonable chance of being obeyed by GATT contracting parties. Nations do often obey GATT rulings in other areas, even when they perceive them to be against their immediate interests. And GATT has one ultimate enforcement mechanism that it can invoke if its laws are clearly breached: contracting parties breaking its rules can be subjected to retaliatory trade restrictions imposed on their exports by other contracting parties (McMillan, 1989, 1992, Chapter 7).

Evaluating a RIA by checking its effect on trade flows is, of course, a straightforward test, and it has long been used by empirical economists. Krause (1968), for example, used it in studying the original formation of the EC. (He estimated that the total loss of US export sales over the period 1958–70 was, in 1958 dollars, $2.2 billion, most of which came from agriculture but with a small loss also in industrial products.) The point of the present chapter is that this straightforward criterion has more advantages than just its simplicity – although simplicity is itself an important attribute of international rules, for complicated rules are likely to be unworkable. The other appealing attribute of the above admissibility criterion is that it is validated by economic theory. By contrast, the current GATT rule is both more complicated and unsupported by economic theory.

13.4 Testing for admissibility

In a static world, it would be easy to check whether a given RIA passes the test of admissibility: it would simply be a matter of comparing trade volumes before and after integration. In the real world, things are obviously not so simple. A vast multiplicity of factors can and do cause trade volumes to change: long-term economic growth, short-term macro-economic fluctuations, changes in technology, in input prices, in consumers' tastes and so on. In testing whether a RIA is admissible, these extraneous sources of change must somehow be filtered out of the data. The question is: are external trade volumes lower than they would have been in the absence of the RIA? There exist well-developed econometric techniques for testing whether any observed change in trade volumes is caused by policy or by extraneous influences. But there exists no uniquely correct way of doing this. In applying the admissibility test, a judgment must be made as to where the weight of evidence lies.

Since a major cause of change in trade volumes is changes in national income, a quick adjustment of the data can be done using gross domestic product (GDP). The adjusted admissibility test is: does trade volume divided by total member countries' GDP fall following integration? Another easy method is to compute the average rate of growth of imports over the, say, four years before integration, extrapolate that trend, and compare the import volume so predicted with the actual import volume.[10] An alternative method is to use statistical time-series techniques to remove any underlying trends from the data, inserting a dummy variable to represent the integration, and then to test the hypothesis that integration did not significantly lower the volume of trade with the rest of the world. Still another source of information relevant to admissibility is evidence on specific practices adopted by the RIA that have the effect of either opening or closing external trade, linked to data on trade volumes in the affected sectors. The estimated trade-volume effects of integration will differ depending on the estimation technique. In testing for admissibility, however, all that is needed is the direction, not the magnitude, of any change in trade volumes; and it is not unlikely that different estimation methods will agree about the sign of the change, even if they disagree about its size.[11]

The enlargement of the EC in 1973, when the United Kingdom, Ireland and Denmark were admitted, illustrates the possibility for disputes over changes in tariff levels. On joining, the three new members adjusted their external tariffs to equal the existing EC tariffs. This meant raising their tariffs on agricultural products and lowering them on industrial products. Initially the EC argued that the more open industrial markets far outweighed the heightened restrictions in agriculture. The United States disagreed, and lengthy negotiations ensued. Eventually the EC agreed to increase market access for a miscellaneous list of items. (The list was notably diverse: it included tobacco, oranges, kraft paper, photographic film, non-agricultural tractors, excavating machinery, diesel and marine engines, engine additives, measuring instruments, pumps and plywood – see Jackson and Davey (1986, pp. 408–9).)

The US–EC dispute was repeated in 1986 when Spain and Portugal joined the EC. Grain purchases by Spain and Portugal were diverted from the United States to the EC; the United States claimed this would result in $400 million in lost revenue for US exporters. As before, the EC argued GATT's rules were being met because Spain's and Portugal's lowering of industrial tariffs compensated for their higher agricultural tariffs. The United States threatened to retaliate by raising its tariffs on some food imports from the EC; the EC threatened to counter-retaliate by raising its tariffs on some US agricultural products. The United States took the position that Article XXIV's rules about tariffs being no more restrictive should be applied product-by-product rather than by total trade. After a year of acrimonious negotiations an agreement was reached under which the United States could sell to Spain and Portugal about $300 million worth of grain each year for four years (Sawyer and Sprinkle, 1988).

In the US–EC disputes about the enlargement of the EC, the disagreement was essentially about whether, in my terminology, the EC was an admissible RIA. The EC claimed that the lowering of industrial tariffs by the newly admitted countries more than outweighed the raising of agricultural tariffs; thus it was implicitly arguing that the appropriate criterion was admissibility defined in terms of the total volume of trade. The United States argued that the EC enlargement should not reduce agricultural imports into the former EC plus Spain and Portugal; thus the United States was implicitly proposing sector-by-sector admissibility.

The EC–US disputes show that admissibility is already implicitly used in practice as a criterion for evaluating RIAs. My suggestion is that this criterion should be made explicit; that the rules governing integration be written in terms of the agreement's effects on trade volumes rather than, as is now the case, in terms – necessarily vaguely worded – of average levels of tariffs. The rules should, furthermore, require that both sides to a dispute about whether a RIA restricts trade should be required to base their arguments on thoroughly documented statistical estimates of the effects of the agreement on trade volumes.

GATT is regularly called upon to make decisions that are at least as difficult as deciding whether an observed change in trade volume is attributable to integration. GATT refers disputes on GATT legal issues to panels of experts. As described by an authority on international law,

> Normally, panels consist of three to five experienced GATT delegates from countries not involved in the legal dispute. Delegates act in their personal capacity, not under instruction from their countries. GATT panels function like appellate tribunals. The parties to the dispute present written and oral legal arguments, usually at two meetings about a month apart. The panel then meets in closed session, where, assisted by the staff of the GATT Secretariat, it prepares a written report stating and explaining its ruling. The report is referred to the GATT membership, which alone has the power to rule. (Hudec, 1987, p. 214)

A decision on whether or not a RIA has violated admissibility could perhaps be made similarly, with the panel evaluating testimony from both sides.

In the disputes about the enlargement of the EC, neither the EC nor the United States backed up their positions with rigorous, detailed empirical studies. The EC asserted that the United States' gains in industrial exports would completely offset its losses in agricultural exports from the southern enlargement of the EC, but offered no data to support this quantitative claim. The United States refused to admit that any of its exports could increase following the enlargement (Sawyer and Sprinkle, 1988, pp. 94–5). Each side simply insisted on the self-evident truth of its own case. A more fruitful way to adjudicate disputes about RIAs would be for a GATT panel to hear expert testimony about the predicted or observed effects of the agreement on trade volumes. Such proceedings would be similar to a US anti-trust court case over, say, a proposed merger, in which expert witnesses testify as to the likely effects of the merger on the degree of competition in the industry. The effects of a merger on competition are no less complex than the effects of tariff changes on trade volumes. That it is feasible to do *ex ante* empirical studies predicting the effect of a proposed RIA on trade volumes is illustrated by the analysis of the addition of Spain and Portugal to the EC by Sawyer and Sprinkle (1988). The United States would lose, by its own estimate, $100 million worth of agricultural exports (after the EC concession mentioned above). US non-agricultural exports to Spain and Portugal could be expected to rise because of lowered tariffs, according to the Sawyer–Sprinkle model, by $277 million. Thus the predicted net increase in US exports was $177 million. There is no uniquely correct way to estimate trade responses. The simplifying assumptions underlying any such calculation are open to question; different assumptions would yield different estimates of the volume-of-trade effects.[12] The GATT panel would have to make a judgment, after hearing testimony from both sides, about where the weight of the evidence lay. Disputes about the computational details of careful quantitative studies must be more fruitful, however, than disputes that are uninformed by the data.

GATT's judgments about admissibility could be made both *ex ante* and *ex post*. The likely trade-volume effects of a new RIA could be assessed at its inception. Then, perhaps four or five years later, the agreement could be retrospectively assessed, and required to lower some of its external trade barriers if integration were judged to have caused external trade volumes to have fallen.

The choice of the level of aggregation of trade volumes in the definition of admissibility is not a mere technical question: as the US–EC disputes show, it is itself a highly charged issue. Should admissibility be defined in terms of the total volume of trade, or more disaggregatively, sector by sector? With the less aggregative definition, both the original formation and the successive enlargements of the EC would probably fail the test of admissibility, because of the lowering of agricultural imports. But in terms of total volume of trade, the EC might well have passed the admissibility test, because of the increase in industrial imports. (According to the Sawyer–Sprinkle model, as noted, the enlargement of the EC by the addition of Spain and Portugal did satisfy admissibility by total trade volume, at least for trade with the United States.) The issue of aggregation has been the subject of dispute in the Uruguay Round negotiations, with non-EC countries arguing for examination of the effects of RIAs on specific countries and products, and the EC arguing that 'compensation' be possible – that is, integration-induced increases in protection be permissible if there are decreases in protection elsewhere (Devuyst, 1992).

The Kemp–Vanek analysis suggests that disaggregated trade-volume statistics are more reliable measures of integration's impact on the rest of the world than aggregated statistics. The Dunkel Draft of the Uruguay Round agreement is consistent with this in recognizing that a disaggregative approach to assessing RIAs is necessary: 'For the purpose of the overall assessment of the incidence of other regulations of commerce for which quantification and aggregation are difficult, the examination of individual measures, regulations, products covered and trade flows affected may be required' (GATT, 1991, p. U.2).

A decision on whether a RIA had caused undue harm would involve not only judgments about facts, such as whether trade volumes changed as a result of the integration; it would also involve value judgments, weighing competing claims. How much, say, would the United States have to gain in industrial exports in order to compensate for its losses in agricultural trade? How are one outsider country's gains to be compared with another outsider country's losses? To what extent should any harm to developing countries be given extra consideration? [13]

These difficulties are, however, not unique to the volume-of-trade criterion. They arise also under the current GATT rules, for any serious attempt to judge whether a RIA had restricted trade would have to face questions such as these. The volume-of-trade criterion in fact makes these problems less severe, because it is precise: it reduces the amount of subjectivity involved in the decision, by shifting the debate, in large part, to an argument about numbers.

13.5 Conclusion

Regardless of what economists think of them, RIAs are here to stay. Regional integration can foster global trade; but it can also impede it. The relevant issue is not whether RIAs are a good thing per se, but how to design international laws that ensure they are structured so as to avoid harming the global economy.

I have suggested that the best test for judging whether a RIA is harmful is the simplest possible: does the agreement result in less trade between member countries and outsider countries? If the answer to this question is no, then the RIA is consistent with open trade, as the Kemp–Vanek theorem shows: the agreement makes its member countries better off without making the outsider countries worse off; and the member countries have an incentive to continue extending the integration by adding new members.

Notes

I thank Kym Anderson, Jagdish Bhagwati, Richard Blackhurst, Joseph Grunwald, Chalmers Johnson, Murray Kemp, Carsten Kowalczyk, Lawrence Krause, Rodney Ludema, Michael Rothschild and the participants in the GATT conference for useful comments.
1. James (1984, p. 64) attributes this to Hoover. Harry Johnson's outburst on the pitfalls of second-best analysis applies to customs-union theory:

> The fundamental problem is that, as with all second-best arguments, determination of the conditions under which a second-best policy actually leads to an improvement of social welfare requires detailed theoretical and empirical investigation by a first-best economist. Unfortunately policy is

generally formulated by fourth-best economists and administered by third-best economists; it is therefore very unlikely that a second-best welfare optimum will result from policies based on second-best arguments. (Johnson, 1970, p. 101)

Theory that is to be useful for policy must come to a conclusion that can be stated simply.

2. The first statement of the proposition was given independently by Kemp (1964, p. 176) and Vanek (1965). Formal proofs came later, by Ohyama (1972) and Kemp and Wan (1976). Subsequent work includes Grinols (1981) and Bliss (1990). (I am grateful to Murray Kemp for pointing out the origins of the idea, and in particular Vanek's contribution.) I shall refer to it as the Kemp–Vanek theorem, in recognition of its initial formulation. A model that is related, in looking at the trade-volume effects of regional integration, is that by Kowalczyk and Wonnacott (1992).

3. That the gains from the removal of internal trade barriers can be large is indicated by estimates of the effects of the EC's 1992 internal liberalization. An EC study has predicted that the EC's gross domestic product will increase, after an initial transitional period, by between 4.5 and 7 per cent as a result of the '1992' initiative (Emerson *et al.*, 1988).

4. Of all the GATT lawsuits between 1960 and 1985, nearly one-third (25 out of 80) were brought against EC agricultural-trade barriers (Hudec, 1988, p. 22).

5. The quotations are respectively from GATT (1991, p. U.1) and the *Financial Times*, August 22, 1992, p. 2.

6. An early precedent for a disaggregated sector-by-sector study of the effects of a RIA is the 1958 study by a GATT working party of the effects of the EC's preferential trade with certain historically related countries on the exports of the countries that did not receive these preferences. Trade studies were prepared for 12 commodities (cocoa, coffee, tea, bananas, sugar, tobacco, oilseeds, cotton, hard fibers, wood, aluminum and lead), which amounted to 80 per cent of the trade with the countries covered by the preferences (Curzon, 1966, pp. 276–82).

7. *GATT Focus*, Nov.–Dec. 1991, p. 5.

8. A further requirement imposed by Article XXIV is that any trade restrictions between the countries forming the RIA must be not merely lowered, but eliminated. This, also, is not in general in the interests of either the member countries or the rest of the world. A zero intra-union tariff usually causes unnecessarily large amounts of trade diversion, as Meade (1955) showed. Given that the RIA retains restrictions on trade with outsiders then, from standard second-best analysis, an intra-union tariff that is best from the members' point of view is typically non-zero. It is zero if and only if what is imported from a partner country is, in consumption, independent of (that is, neither a complement of nor a substitute for) what is imported from the rest of the world (McMillan and McCann, 1981). However, as argued by Snape in Chapter 12 of the present volume, there are broad systemic reasons for requiring that intra-union tariffs be reduced to zero.

9. A possible disadvantage of focusing on trade volumes instead of tariff levels is that, in principle, tariff levels can be observed in advance, whereas trade volumes can be measured only after the RIA has been in existence for a few years. The implications of a new trading arrangement for trade volumes can, however, be predicted using an economic model. And a new agreement

could be monitored over time and required to adjust its external trade restrictions on specific items should it turn out to be failing the admissibility test.

10. This is the method used, for example, by Balassa (1989) to estimate the effect of the EC's formation on its imports from other countries.

11. On estimating the trade-volume effects of RIAs, see Chapters 2 and 3 in this volume by Anderson and Norheim and by Srinivasan, Whalley and Wooton. While the various studies surveyed by Srinivasan, Whalley and Wooton (see their Table 3.4) come to differing conclusions about the *size* of integration-induced changes in trade volumes, they are mostly consistent with each other in their estimates of the *direction* of these changes, which, as noted above, is all that is needed to assess admissibility.

12. Quantitative estimates of the effects on trade of the enlargement of the EC are surveyed by Winters (1987).

13. Putting the burden of proof on the country that is claiming to have been harmed by the RIA might help resolve such issues as how fine the appropriate classification of items should be. The complainant country would be required to present a case for its chosen definition of trade flows.

References

Balassa, B. (1989), 'Trade Creation and Trade Diversion in the European Common Market', in his *Comparative Advantage, Trade Policy, and Economic Development*, London: Harvester Wheatsheaf.

Baldwin, R. (1992), 'Measurable Dynamic Gains from Trade', *Journal of Political Economy* **100**: 162–174.

Bhagwati, J. N. (1991), *The World Trading System at Risk*, Princeton: Princeton University Press.

Bliss, C. (1990), 'The Optimal External Tariff in an Enlarging Customs Union', Discussion Paper No. 368, London: Centre for Economic Policy Research.

Bollard, A. and M. A. Thompson (1987), *Trans-Tasman Trade and Investment: The Effects of CER*, Wellington: New Zealand Institute of Economic Research.

Curzon, G. (1966), *Multilateral Commercial Diplomacy*, New York: Praeger.

Dam, K. W. (1970), *The GATT: Law and the International Economic Organization*, Chicago: University of Chicago Press.

Devuyst, Y. (1992), 'GATT Customs Union Provisions and the Uruguay Round: The European Community Experience', *Journal of World Trade* **26**: 15–34.

Emerson, M. *et al.* (1988), *The Economics of 1992*, London: Oxford University Press.

GATT (1986), *The Text of the General Agreement on Tariffs and Trade*, Geneva: GATT Secretariat.

GATT (1991), *Draft Final Act Embodying the Results of Uruguay Round of Multilateral Trade Negotiations*, mimeo, Geneva: GATT Secretariat, December 20.

Grinols, E. L. (1981), 'An Extension of the Kemp–Wan Theorem on the Formation of Customs Unions', *Journal of International Economics* **11**: 259–66.

Harris, R. G. and D. Cox (1983), *Trade, Industrial Policy, and Canadian Manufacturing*, Toronto: Ontario Economic Council.

Hudec, R. E. (1987), 'Transcending the Ostensible': Some Reflections on the Nature of Litigation Between Governments', *Minnesota Law Review* **72**: 211–26.

Hudec, R. E. (1988), 'Legal Issues in US–EC Trade Policy: GATT Litigation 1960–1985', in *Issues in US–EC Trade Relations*, edited by R. E. Baldwin, C. Hamilton and A. Sapir, Chicago: University of Chicago Press.

Jackson, J. H. and W. J. Davey (1986), *Legal Problems of International Economic Relations*, St Paul: West Publishing Co.

Jacquemin, A. and A. Sapir (1991), 'Europe Post-1992: Internal and External Liberalization', *American Economic Review* **81**: 166–70.

James, S. (1984), *A Dictionary of Economic Quotations*, Totowa, NJ: Rowman and Allanheld, 2nd edition.

Johnson, H. G. (1970), 'The Efficiency and Welfare Implications of the International Corporation', in *Studies in International Economics*, edited by I. A. McDougall and R. H. Snape, Amsterdam: North-Holland.

Kemp, M. C. (1964), *The Pure Theory of International Trade*, Englewood Cliffs: Prentice-Hall.

Kemp, M. C. (1969), *A Contribution to the General Equilibrium Theory of Preferential Trading*, Amsterdam: North-Holland.

Kemp, M. C. and H. Y. Wan (1976), 'An Elementary Proposition Concerning the Formation of Customs Unions', *Journal of International Economics* **6**: 95–7.

Kowalkzyk, C. and R. Wonnacott (1992), 'Hubs and Spokes, and Free Trade in the Americas', Working Paper No. 92-14, Dartmouth College, Hanover.

Krause, L. B. (1968), *European Economic Integration and the United States*, Washington, DC: The Brookings Institution.

Leutwiler, F. *et al.* (1985), *Trade Policies for a Better Future*, Geneva: GATT Secretariat.

McMillan, J. (1989), 'A Game-Theoretic View of International Trade Negotiations: Implications for the Developing Countries', in *Developing Countries and the Global Trading System, Vol. 1*, edited by J. Whalley, London: Macmillan.

McMillan, J. (1992), *Games, Strategies, and Managers*, New York and London: Oxford University Press.

McMillan, J. and E. McCann (1981), 'Welfare Effects in Customs Unions', *Economic Journal* **91**: 697–703.

Meade, J. (1955), *The Theory of Customs Unions*, Amsterdam: North-Holland.

Ohyama, M. (1972), 'Trade and Welfare in General Equilibrium', *Keio Economic Studies* **9**: 37–73.

Patterson, G. (1989), 'Implications for the GATT and the World Trading System', in *Free Trade Areas and U.S. Trade Policy*, edited by J. J. Schott, Washington, DC: Institute for International Economics.

Sapir, A. (1992), 'Europe 1992: The External Trade Implications', *International Economic Journal* **6**: 1–15.

Sawyer, W. C. and R. L. Sprinkle (1988), 'EC Enlargement and U.S. Exports: An Analysis of the Trade Effects', *Journal of World Trade* **22**: 89–96.

Secchi, C. (1990), 'Protectionism, Internal Market Completion, and the Advantages of a Unified Market', in *The New Protectionist Wave*, edited by E. Grilli and E. Sassoon, London: Macmillan.

Vanek, J. (1965), *General Equilibrium of International Discrimination: The Case of Customs Unions*, Cambridge, MA: Harvard University Press.

Viner, J. (1950), *The Customs Union Issue*, New York: Carnegie Endowment for International Peace.

Whalley, J. (1989), 'Comments', in *Free Trade Areas and U.S. Trade Policy*, edited by J. J. Schott, Washington, DC: Institute for International Economics.

Winters, L. A. (1987), 'Britain in Europe: A Survey of Quantitative Trade Studies', *Journal of Common Market Studies* **25**: 315–35.

Winters, L. A. (1992), 'The Welfare and Policy Implications of the International Trade Consequences of "1992"', *American Economic Review* **82**: 104–8.

14

The relationship between regional integration agreements and the multilateral trade order

Frieder Roessler

The multilateral trade order established in 1947 by the General Agreement on Tariffs and Trade (GATT) permits the formation of customs unions and free trade areas provided that 'the duties and other restrictive regulations of commerce are eliminated on substantially all trade between the constituent territories in products originating in such territories' (Article XXIV). Economists have questioned the requirement that an agreement establishing a customs union or free trade area (hereinafter referred to as regional integration agreements or RIAs) cover substantially all trade, suggesting instead that the relevant criterion should be whether or not the preferences granted in the framework of a RIA create trade. Others have argued that the current spread of RIAs is undermining the principle of most-favored-nation (MFN) treatment of the GATT and that the GATT, as the portion of trade effectively covered by its rules declines, is losing its relevance. The GATT has also been criticized for not effectively enforcing its requirements for RIAs, in particular by failing to reach decisions interpreting the provisions on regional agreements. The purpose of this chapter is to examine these common assertions and to present an alternative perspective on the relationship between RIAs and the GATT.

The focus of the analysis will be regional agreements involving developed countries, because under GATT rules developing countries may accord each other preferences within the framework of regional and global arrangements that need not conform to Article XXIV.[1] The references to RIAs in this chapter should be understood to exclude the EC unless otherwise indicated. The rules of the GATT essentially apply to trade between the customs territories of its contracting parties, which can be either a sovereign state or 'a separate customs territory possessing full autonomy in the conduct of its external commercial relations and of the other matters provided for in this Agreement' (Article XXXIII). The EC, possessing this autonomy, could theoretically accede to the GATT, in which case its existence would no longer require justification under Article XXIV. It would also be open to become a member of the proposed Multilateral Trade Organization. Many of the observations on regional agreements falling under Article XXIV that are made in this chapter can therefore not be meaningfully extended to the EC.

14.1   The economic and political significance of GATT's 'substantially-all-trade' requirement

Economists − following Viner's (1950) theory of customs unions − have analyzed RIAs primarily by comparing the relative efficiency of preferential and multilateral trade liberalization, their standard conclusion being that tariff preferences may or may not increase welfare depending on whether they divert or create trade. From that perspective the substantially-all-trade criterion makes little sense, because it obliges contracting parties to include in their RIAs preferences that divert trade from more efficient producers in third countries to less efficient producers in the preference-receiving country, thereby reducing world welfare. Dam (1970, p. 289) writes that 'certainly it is strange to state, as Article XXIV effectively does, that discrimination is forbidden unless it is 100 per cent effective'. Rather than requiring that the discrimination in favor of the regional partners be complete, so he and others argue, the GATT should insist that RIAs do not divert trade or at least do not divert more trade than they create.

This proposal does not take into account that most RIAs have their origin mainly in political considerations. The partners to these agreements generally wish to create closer economic ties in order to create greater political cohesion between them. The EC's Treaty of Rome is the most obvious example: according to its preamble its purpose was to establish 'the foundations of an ever-closer union among the European peoples' and 'to strengthen the safeguards of peace and liberty'. The establishment of a European common market was a means to these ends. One of the purposes of the ASEAN Preferential Trading Arrangements was to 'contribute to political and economic stability in the region'.[2] The Australia−New Zealand Closer Economic Relations Trade Agreement (ANZCERTA) emphasizes in its preamble that the close historic, political, economic and geographic relations between Australia and New Zealand would be further strengthened by an expansion of trade between them. To propose that regional agreements be examined in the GATT solely in the light of economic efficiency considerations is thus to ignore the fact that most RIAs are not concluded solely for those reasons and that the main function of the GATT rules governing such agreements is to permit contracting parties to pursue regional trade liberalization for non-economic purposes.

The proposal to judge RIAs in the light of economic efficiency considerations (as discussed, for example, in the previous chapter of this volume by McMillan) cannot easily be transformed into a rule of conduct capable of influencing the behavior of governments negotiating a regional agreement. An international rule of trade policy conduct must distinguish between legal and illegal behavior on the basis of factors which governments can control or foresee. Whether a regional agreement covers substantially all trade can be determined by the governments when they negotiate it. The economic impact of a tariff preference included in a regional agreement can, however, normally not be determined in advance with precision, *inter alia* because such a determination would require a quantitative general equilibrium analysis in which critical parameter values have to be assumed. It would in particular require information about elasticities of supply and demand that is generally not available. Moreover, that impact can change as market conditions and the economic policies of third countries change. Also, foreign direct investments related to the formation of the customs union or free trade area can substantially modify the impact of the preferences on trade. A preference that diverts trade today may for these reasons create trade tomorrow and vice versa, and this as a result of factors which the parties to the RIA do not control or foresee. For these reasons, the idea that RIAs should be permitted by the GATT only if they create trade or if they create more trade than they divert cannot be transformed into a rule of conduct capable of guiding the behavior of governments negotiating RIAs.

The GATT's experience with rules that make the legal status of a measure dependent on its economic consequences has not been favorable. For example, the rule according to which subsidies on the export of agricultural products shall not be applied by a contracting party in a manner 'which *results* in that contracting party having more than an equitable share of world export trade in that product' (Article XVI:4) has been inoperative largely because of the difficulty of determining the causal link between subsidies and changes in global market shares.[3] A rule according to which the legal status of a regional agreement would have to be determined in the light of its results on trade flows would encounter the same difficulties. Moreover, while the amount of subsidies granted to the export of a particular agricultural product can perhaps be readily adjusted in the light of the trade consequences of previous subsidies, the scope of RIAs cannot be constantly changed with the aim of bringing about prescribed trade effects. After all, RIAs are intended to generate predictability and legal security in trade relations for decades to come so as to permit long-term investment planning. A rule according to which the scope of RIAs would have to be constantly modified to ensure that they achieve prescribed results in changing market conditions would be incompatible with the need to ensure legal stability. As Röpke (1954, p. 212) rightly points out, the basis of international trade is not merely the law of comparative advantage but above all the law of nations.

What purposes does the substantially-all-trade requirement then serve? It serves first of all a useful domestic policy function. Domestic protectionist pressures will tend to favor trade diversion over trade creation, and governments negotiating RIAs will therefore be under pressure to avoid preferences in those sectors in which they are likely to increase imports. If the GATT were to permit governments to accord preferences selectively for certain products only, trade-diverting preferences would tend to prevail. The substantially-all-trade requirement can therefore be seen as a means to contain the moral hazard that would result from this possibility.

The requirement also helps reduce the number of RIAs. It can reasonably be assumed that the political forces behind RIAs that cover substantially all trade are such that a quasi-universal organization such as the GATT must permit them lest it lose its members. RIAs covering a small portion of trade are unlikely to have as strong a political support. The substantially-all-trade requirement can therefore be seen as a requirement that helps differentiate between politically unavoidable and containable deviations from the most-favored-nation principle, as a requirement which determines the point where trade policy is allowed to give way to foreign policy. In Chapter 12 of this volume, Snape has cast this thought in economic terms.

14.2 RIAs in zero-tariff world

Most authors who examine the relationship between RIAs and the GATT concentrate on the effects of regional agreements on the realization of GATT's MFN principle. However, a number of developments since the creation of the GATT suggest that the impact of RIAs on the realization of the MFN principle no longer deserves to be the sole focus of the analysis of this relationship.

In the early years of the GATT, tariffs were high and the economic impact of tariff preferences was therefore substantial. Today, the import tariffs imposed by the developed countries are low: the average tariff of the EC is roughly 5 per cent, as is that of the United States, while Japan's average tariff is less than 3 per cent.[4] These tariffs would be reduced further as a result of a Uruguay Round agreement. Under these circumstances, tariff preferences accorded by developed countries in the framework of RIAs can generate only limited benefits for the beneficiary countries.

A further erosion of the preferential benefits that RIAs generate can result from a shift in the protection of industries from import tariffs and other trade restrictions to production subsidies. The latter form of protection cannot be applied in a manner discriminating between trading partners: a production subsidy necessarily grants the domestic industry an advantage relative to its competitors in all other countries. This applies to any form of assistance directly granted to enterprises. Therefore, as governments replace border measures by internal measures assisting domestic industries, the relevance of trade preferences under RIAs declines even if the overall level of industry assistance is retained.

Import protection has remained high in the field of agricultural products. Trade preferences could therefore still generate significant benefits for agricultural exporters. However, most RIAs do not cover agricultural trade at all or only to a very limited extent. One of the aims of the Uruguay Round is to commit GATT contracting parties to transform import restrictions on agricultural products into import tariffs, to lower these tariffs over time, to reduce trade-distorting domestic support of agricultural production and to transform such support into income support decoupled from the production of agricultural products.[5] To the extent that these goals are realized, the import measures from which individual regional partners can be exempted would be replaced by internal measures that cannot be applied in a manner favoring certain trading partners.

High levels of protection are often accorded through anti-dumping and countervailing duties as well as price and volume undertakings negotiated in the framework of anti-dumping or countervailing duty proceedings. However, under most RIAs, the constituent countries do not exempt each other from their anti-dumping and countervailing duty laws. The member states of the EC may not apply anti-dumping and countervailing duties against each other, but the EC has reserved its right to do so under the RIAs it has concluded with third countries.[6] Canada and the United States have retained the right to apply their anti-dumping or countervailing duty laws against each other's trade under the CUSFTA; they accorded each other merely the privilege of having certain decisions under their anti-dumping and countervailing duty laws reviewed by binational panels of experts.[7]

The above analysis suggests that, in a world of declining border protection, even if partly offset through contingency protection and production subsidies, the market access rights which most RIAs involving developed countries can still generate, in addition to those already generated by the multilateral trade order, have become increasingly limited and could become largely insignificant as a result of the Uruguay Round. It is of course true that the preferences exchanged in the framework of RIAs undermine the MFN principle, but it is equally true that the multilateral market access commitments exchanged in the framework of the GATT have undermined these regional preferences. In a zero-tariff world – a utopia as yet, but one towards which the eight GATT negotiating rounds have been moving – the MFN principle would automatically re-establish itself.

Some of the more recent RIAs extend into fields of domestic policy not covered by the present or post-Uruguay Round legal system of the GATT. Thus, the CUSFTA, going beyond the GATT Agreement on Technical Barriers to Trade, establishes a framework for reaching agreement on technical regulations and standards. It also provides for the accreditation of test facilities, guarantees national treatment to investors, and limits the parties' right to expropriate them.[8] The negotiations on the NAFTA have covered subject matters outside the current and post-Uruguay Round realm of the GATT, such as specific environmental programs and the facilitation of road transportation. The Agreement on the European Economic Area (EEA) between the EC and EFTA Member States provides for only a few preferential market access opportunities for goods in addition to those already available to the EFTA countries; one of the most important consequences of the EEA for trade in products would be the mutual recognition of internal product standards and the international harmonization of production regulations within the EEA.

Given the declining impact of the preferences exchanged in RIAs and the rising importance of efforts to harmonize domestic regulations and to coordinate domestic policies in the framework of RIAs, future research on the relationship between those regional agreements and the multilateral trade order should perhaps not focus on the well-explored subject of preferences but rather on the question of whether harmonization and coordination efforts should be undertaken regionally or multilaterally. It seems that a stage has been reached at which this relationship is more fruitfully explored in the light of theories related to the territorial distribution of powers, such as the theories of federalism, policy assignments and optimal integration areas, rather than in the light of Viner's venerable theory of customs unions.

14.3 How to avoid losing GATT rights through a RIA

RIAs can undermine the basic aims of the multilateral trade order not only by *adding* preferential market access rights to the market access rights accorded multilaterally but also by *eliminating*, in the relations between the regional partners, market access rights and other rights negotiated under the GATT. In the long run, the preferential additions may be less of a problem than the discriminatory eliminations because, as further GATT rounds reduce trade barriers multilaterally, the impact of the preferential additions would necessarily decline while the discriminatory eliminations could not but widen the gap between multilateral commitments and regional practices.

The elimination of rights under the GATT through regional agreements can take many different forms. The parties to a RIA may explicitly agree to eliminate certain GATT rights in their relations with one another or to replace GATT rules by other rules imposing fewer constraints, such as rules on safeguard actions that establish fewer conditions than those of the GATT.[9] In most RIAs basic rules contained in the GATT are replaced by similarly worded clauses. Such an incorporation of GATT rules into a regional agreement does not result in a substantive change of rights, but it does change the treaty on which they are based and therefore implies a loss of access to the GATT procedures for the settlement of disputes concerning the interpretation of these rules (unless, of course, the right to resort to the GATT procedures is explicitly retained, which – with the two exceptions discussed below – has so far not been done). A regional agreement narrower in scope than the GATT legal system may also be conceived by its parties as an agreement regulating comprehensively their trade relations and therefore as an agreement replacing the GATT legal system as a whole, notwithstanding its narrower scope. A de facto elimination of GATT rights through a regional agreement may result from an understanding among regional partners to resolve in the regional fora rather than the multilateral fora of the GATT.

In practice, the parties to RIAs have used the GATT to settle differences between them only in rare instances. During the past decade the EC has been involved in 22 GATT panel proceedings. The other party to these disputes was the United States in 16 cases, Japan in three, Canada in two and Chile in one. The other party in the disputes was thus in all cases a country with which the EC had not concluded a preferential trade agreement. The only dispute during the past decade between the EC and a trading partner enjoying preferences under a RIA concerned a complaint by Austria related to restrictions on the circulation of Austrian lorries imposed by Germany.[10] The choice of the GATT procedures was probably due to the fact that the RIA between the EC and Austria − unlike the GATT − does not contain provisions guaranteeing freedom of transit. Whether legal considerations, informal understandings or political restraints were the cause, in practice RIAs have traditionally operated as agreements eliminating the regional partners' access to GATT fora and procedures.

There is one important exception. The CUSFTA gives the United States and Canada explicitly the right to choose between the fora of the CUSFTA and the GATT for disputes on matters covered by both agreements. [11] A similar right has been included in the draft agreement establishing the North American Free Trade Area. [12] Canada and the United States have made ample use of their right under CUSFTA to resort to the dispute settlement procedures under the GATT. Of the twelve panels established by the GATT in 1991, four concerned disputes between Canada and the United States. This demonstrates that the retention of GATT rights under a regional agreement can be of great practical importance.

There are several reasons why other contracting parties may find it in their interest to follow the examples of the CUSFTA and NAFTA. With the exception of the EC, no RIA has so far established a regulatory framework for trade relations as comprehensive and detailed as that of the GATT legal system. This gap would widen further with the adoption of the Uruguay Round results. Many RIAs exempt agricultural products from all liberalization commitments, contain safeguards provisions more generous than those of the GATT, permit − unlike the GATT − the imposition of restrictions for balance-of-payments purposes without the supervision of the International Monetary Fund, and contain general exceptions more broadly worded than those of the GATT. [13] The parties to RIAs have thus often embedded their preferential tariff reductions in a legal framework much less rigorous than that of the GATT. The decision to export a product or to invest in export-oriented production depends not only on the tariff levied on the product but also (and, given today's low tariffs, perhaps above all) on the predictability of the importing country's trade-policy measures. A zero-tariff commitment incorporated in a regional agreement leaving broad scope for the unilateral imposition of other import controls, or providing for no effective dispute settlement procedures, may therefore generate less trade than a tariff binding at a moderate level under the GATT.

No RIA, again with the exception of the EC, benefits from dispute-settlement procedures as developed and as predictable as those of the GATT; in fact, many RIAs do not provide for third-party adjudication of disputes at all, thus leaving it to each party to impose its interpretation of its rights under the agreement through threats of retaliation. For instance, the agreements concluded between the EFTA member states, on the one hand, and the EC, certain East European countries and Israel, on the other, permit any party which considers that another party has failed to fulfil its obligations to take unilaterally 'appropriate measures' if no commonly acceptable solution could be found in bilateral consultations or in an examination by a Joint Committee. The submission of the dispute to independent experts is not foreseen in these agreements.

In the early days of the GATT, the subject matters covered by RIAs and those covered by the GATT largely overlapped. Essentially, both RIAs and the GATT provided for the reduction of tariffs and the elimination of restrictions on the importation of products and for national treatment of imported products; the principal difference was the level of the tariff reductions and the number of treaty partners benefiting from them. At that time it may have been natural to conceive RIAs as legal instruments replacing the whole of the GATT in the relations between the regional partners. More recently, however, the GATT legal system has expanded into areas not covered by those of RIAs. The rules established under the GATT in the field of subsidies, procedures for countervailing measures and anti-dumping duties, technical standards and regulations, government procurement and customs valuation methods are much more extensive and detailed than those provided for under most regional agreements. The conclusion of the Uruguay Round would extend the GATT legal system, *inter alia*, into the areas of intellectual property rights, trade in services and pre-shipment inspection as well as sanitary and phyto-sanitary measures – all areas not covered in most RIAs. The Uruguay Round's results in the field of agriculture also go much further than those attained in RIAs. With the exception of the EC, no regional agreement covers all the subject matters that would be covered by the legal system resulting from the Uruguay Round. Under these circumstances, it no longer seems justified to conceive all RIAs as legal instruments designed to replace the whole of the GATT legal system in the relations between the parties. Given the legal complexities that now arise from the coexistence of RIAs and the GATT legal system and the many disputes that can result from these complexities, it also seems more and more necessary to regulate in RIAs expressly their relation with the GATT legal system.

For these reasons, regional agreements less comprehensive than the GATT should ideally contain a clause which expressly preserves all substantive and procedural rights under the GATT. Such a clause (which will be referred to hereinafter as 'GATT *acquis* clause') has numerous advantages both from the perspective of the parties to the RIA and from that of the multilateral trade order. First, a GATT *acquis* clause anchors the market-access rights of the parties in two legal systems and thereby provides an assurance against procedural or substantive breakdowns in either system. RIAs are often seen as safeguards against the risk of breakdowns in the GATT but, as Enders notes in Chapter 16 of this volume, it should not be forgotten that the GATT can also constitute a safeguard against operational difficulties in RIAs. Without a GATT *acquis* clause the partners to a regional agreement may merely be shifting their eggs from one basket to another; with such a clause the RIA can truly provide additional legal security. RIAs among developing countries have frequently run into difficulties. The study on RIAs by de la Torre and Kelly (1992) concludes that these schemes failed to increase intra-regional trade in part because so little of the intended integration was actually implemented. This experience suggests that developing countries should be particularly careful not to abandon their GATT rights in return for preferential market access rights under a regional agreement.

Secondly, a GATT *acquis* clause provides an assurance against an unanticipated erosion of market access rights through the operation of the RIA (for instance, through an unexpectedly frequent resort to its safeguards provisions by the regional partner). A clause permitting the parties to invoke alternatively their rights under the RIA and those under the GATT ensures that each party can resort to the rules which serve its export interests best, and that consequently the more liberal of the solutions found regionally and multilaterally can prevail.

Thirdly, a GATT *acquis* clause can help avoid disputes between the parties to the RIA on the question of whether the agreement or the GATT applies to a given subject matter. For instance, if the RIA applies only to industrial and not to agricultural products, the question could arise whether the agreement modifies, in the relation between the parties, all rules of the GATT, including those applicable to agricultural products, or whether it modifies them only in respect of industrial products. A GATT *acquis* clause would clearly settle such issues.

Fourthly, a GATT *acquis* clause would permit the parties to the RIA to choose between two sets of dispute settlement procedures in all instances in which the commitments under the RIA and those under the GATT legal system overlap. As pointed out above, the dispute settlement procedures under RIAs are sometimes rudimentary and in many instances do not provide for a third-party adjudication of disputes. To the extent that these agreements supersede the GATT, they prevent their parties from resorting to the GATT dispute-settlement procedures, which entitle the parties to disputes to an examination by independent experts and prohibit unilateral enforcement measures. A GATT *acquis* clause would permit the complaining party to allow the more effective of the two procedures to prevail.[14]

A GATT *acquis* clause also would have substantial advantages from the perspective of the GATT. It can help avoid that regional trade liberalization in certain sectors is achieved at the expense of liberalization commitments already made under the GATT, and ensure that the overall impact of the RIA on trade – tariff reductions and the actual operation of the legal framework into which they are imbedded, taken together – is not such so as to impair the trade liberalization achieved in the GATT.

14.4 GATT's enforcement of RIA admissibility criteria

It follows from the above that the GATT should focus on two issues when examining RIAs. The first is the traditional question of whether the preferences accorded under the RIA apply to substantially all trade. The second is the question of whether the RIA preserves the legal *acquis* of the GATT either by incorporating the preferences into a legal framework equivalent in depth and scope to that of the GATT or by expressly preserving the regional partners' rights under the GATT.

Do the current procedures of the GATT lend themselves to a review of RIAs from these perspectives? The record under the current procedures is not encouraging. During the past three decades about 50 working parties have been established to examine RIAs. None of them was able to reach a unanimous conclusion on the GATT-consistency of the agreements examined, mainly because the parties to the agreement disagreed with third contracting parties on the question of whether the RIA covered substantially all trade (GATT, 1989, p. XXIV-22). For instance, EFTA was considered by some to be covering less than substantially all trade because it excludes agricultural trade;[15] and the agreements which the EC has concluded with developing countries were criticized for not providing reciprocal market-access opportunities for the EC in those countries.[16] The legal status of all of these agreements has therefore remained undetermined.

This is essentially due to the fact that GATT working parties take their decisions by consensus. In the absence of unanimous views, they can therefore only report on the opinions expressed and not propose a decision. If a GATT contracting party, faced with a lack of consensus in the working party, nevertheless wishes to challenge the GATT-consistency of a regional agreement, it can resort to the GATT dispute-settlement procedures. However, in spite of the fact that the conformity of all RIAs examined in the GATT was put into question by at least one contracting party, none has so far used the GATT dispute-settlement procedures for the purpose of obtaining a ruling on that conformity. Neither the working party procedure nor the dispute-settlement process of the GATT has therefore led to a formal decision on the conformity of a RIA with the provisions of the GATT.

There is for these reasons no decision of the GATT CONTRACTING PARTIES interpreting any of the conditions set out in Article XXIV for regional agreements. There is in particular no decision clarifying the meaning of 'substantially all trade', determining within which time period this requirement has to be met, [17] or settling the question of whether the partners to a regional agreement may exempt each other from safeguard actions, such as measures taken under the GATT's balance-of-payments exception. The lack of interpretative decisions that could exert a normative influence on governments considering the formation of customs unions or free trade areas has often been regretted by the GATT contracting parties, most recently by the Chairman of the Working Party which examined the Canada–United States Free Trade Agreement (CUSFTA) without reaching a conclusion on its GATT-consistency. He noted at the November 1991 GATT Council meeting that,

> in the following year or two, the Council would be asked to examine the many new customs unions or free trade areas that were currently being negotiated or envisaged in various parts of the world. While contracting parties engaged in such negotiations would make efforts to reach GATT-consistent agreements, only limited guidance would unfortunately be available to them from past reports of GATT working parties on such agreements. One might therefore question what point was there in establishing a working party if no-one expected it to reach consensus findings in respect of specific provisions of such agreements, or to recommend to the participants how to meet certain benchmarks. ... As further agreements came along, there might be a risk that they would be treated increasingly superficially and that contracting parties would lose – if they had not already done so – the ability to distinguish between agreements of greater or lesser GATT-consistency. [18]

The problem identified by the Chairman of the Working Party has arisen mainly because the GATT relies for the enforcement of its rules solely on the initiative of individual contracting parties pursuing their export interests. However, individual contracting parties are generally not interested in enforcing the substantially-all-trade requirement. A contracting party not meeting this requirement has two options: either to abandon the regional agreement altogether or to expand its coverage. The former is usually not a politically realistic alternative. For a third party to insist that a regional agreement meet the substantially-all-trade requirement means therefore in practice to insist that the countries forming a customs union or free trade area extend it to substantially all trade, which in turn means that the third party asks that the discrimination against it be broadened. For instance, the United States' export interests would not be served if it were to insist that Tunisia, under its regional agreement with the EC, reduce its tariffs on products originating from the EC, because this could not but worsen the competitive position of United States products in the Tunisian market. It is for these reasons not surprising that third countries have so far shown no interest in resorting to legal proceedings to enforce the substantially-all-trade requirement.

Individual contracting parties have so far also shown no interest in the maintenance of the legal *acquis* of the GATT in the relations between other contracting parties. Voluntary export restraint agreements are the most common form of eliminating this *acquis* by mutual consent. These agreements clearly run counter to the objectives of the GATT, and the measures through which they are implemented – generally discriminatory export restrictions – are inconsistent with the provisions of the GATT. Nevertheless, no contracting party has so far brought a complaint under the GATT dispute settlement procedures against measures under such agreements because, in most circumstances, third parties have no interest in preventing measures that reduce competition for them.

An effective control of RIAs by the GATT would for these reasons require the creation of a review body that could act independently of the initiative of individual contracting parties. To adopt new substantive norms for RIAs without such a body would serve little purpose, because it is unlikely that the existing enforcement mechanisms of the GATT would in practice be applied to them. So far, however, the GATT contracting parties have shown little willingness to transfer the right to initiate enforcement procedures to an independent body. A first step in the direction of a more effective GATT review of RIAs might be to submit such agreements to scrutiny under GATT's Trade Policy Review Mechanism, a procedural framework now used to review periodically the trade policies of individual contracting parties, albeit not directly for rule-enforcement purposes.[19]

14.5 Conclusions

The basic conclusions resulting from the above analysis are the following. Firstly, the GATT's substantially-all-trade rule for RIAs could not be replaced by a requirement that such agreements increase world welfare because such a requirement would be at odds with the political nature of the GATT provisions on RIAs and could – given the unpredictability of the welfare effects of RIAs – not be transformed into a rule of conduct.

Secondly, given the declining importance of border measures restricting trade, and the more and more frequent references to domestic policy measures in RIAs, the question of the proper distribution of roles between RIAs and the multilateral trade order is no longer merely one of whether regional or multilateral trade liberalization is more efficient, but raises above all the question of whether the international harmonization of domestic regulations or coordination of domestic policies is best achieved regionally or multilaterally.

Thirdly, RIAs not only provide for the *creation* of market access rights not available under the GATT; they frequently also lead – de jure or de facto – to the *elimination* of rights guaranteed under the GATT legal system. As the depth and scope of the commitments assumed multilaterally under the GATT increase, the creation of market access rights accorded under regional agreements loses importance, while the elimination of GATT rights through the operation of those RIAs becomes more significant. The GATT, in reviewing RIAs, should therefore shift its focus of attention from the preferential creation of rights to the discriminatory elimination of rights under such agreements.

Fourthly, with the exception of the EC, no regional agreement now covers all the subject matters covered by the GATT legal system, and it is therefore no longer justified to treat a regional agreement as a complete substitute for the GATT legal system in the trade relations between the regional partners. The parties to RIAs should explicitly retain all their rights under the GATT legal system, including their rights under the GATT dispute settlement procedures. This would ensure that the regional and multilateral approaches to trade liberalization are fully complementary.

Finally, the GATT could enhance its influence in respect of RIAs by revising its procedures for the review of such agreements, in particular by making the procedures independent of the initiative of individual contracting parties pursuing their export interests.

Notes

Thanks are due for helpful comments and suggestions to Alice Enders, John Croome, Bernard Hoekman, Carsten Kowalczyk and Ernst-Ulrich Petersmann.
 1. See the so-called Enabling Clause adopted by the GATT CONTRACTING PARTIES in 1979. See the 26th Suppl., p. 203, of GATT's *Basic Instruments and Selected Documents* (hereinafter referred to as *BISD*).
 2. See the report of the GATT Working Party on the Agreement on ASEAN Preferential Trading Arrangements, in *BISD*, 26th Suppl., p. 322.
 3. See, for example, the conclusions of the GATT Panel on 'European Communities – Refunds on Exports of Sugar' in *BISD*, 26th Suppl., p. 319.

4. GATT documents C/RM/10A, p. 66; C/RM/S/23A, p. 45; and C/RM/S/8A, p. 32.
5. GATT documents MTN.TNC/W/FA, pp. L.2–34.
6. See, for example, Articles 25 and 26 of the free trade agreements between the European Communities and the EFTA countries.
7. Chapter 19 and Article 1904 of the CUSFTA.
8. See Chapter 16 in this volume, by Enders.
9. For other examples see Chapter 10 in this volume, by Hoekman and Leidy.
10. GATT document DS14/1.
11. Article 1801:2 of the CUSFTA.
12. Chapter 20 of the draft NAFTA agreement dated September 6, 1992.
13. See Chapter 10 in this volume, by Hoekman and Leidy.
14. For a detailed analysis of the relative advantages of the GATT and the CUSFTA dispute settlement procedures, see Chapter 16 in this volume, by Enders.
15. See *BISD*, 9th Suppl., p. 83.
16. See the discussion on the Lomé Convention in *BISD*, 23rd Suppl., p. 54.
17. According to a proposed Understanding on the Interpretation of Article XXIV of the General Agreement on Tariffs and Trade, included in the Draft Final Act Embodying the Results of the Uruguay Round, this period 'should exceed ten years only in exceptional cases' (GATT document MTN.TNC/W/FA, p. 17. U.2).
18. GATT document C/M/253, p. 25.
19. See the 1989 decision of the GATT CONTRACTING PARTIES on the functioning of the GATT system in *BISD*, 36th Suppl., p. 403. Arthur Dunkel, Director-General of the GATT, said in a recent speech on regional integration:

> Implementation is ... the key factor in assessing the compatibility of regional agreements with the GATT. Closer surveillance of regional agreements, through an extension of GATT's new Trade Policy Review Mechanism, might be useful in this respect: at present the European Community is the only regional grouping reviewed under the TPRM exercise. (See GATT document GATT/1551, p. 7)

References

Dam, K. (1970), *The GATT: Law and International Organization*, Chicago: University of Chicago Press.

de la Torre, A. and M. Kelly (1992), *Regional Trading Arrangements*, IMF Occasional Paper No. 94, Washington, DC: International Monetary Fund.

GATT (1989), *Analytical Index*, Geneva: GATT Secretariat.

Röpke, W. (1954), 'Economic Order and International Law', *Recueil des Cours* 2.

Viner, J. (1950), *The Customs Union Issue*, New York: Carnegie Endowment for International Peace.

15

Rules of origin in customs unions and free trade areas

David Palmeter

By definition, customs unions (CUs) and free trade areas (FTAs) offer tariff preferences to the importation of goods from member countries. Rules are required to determine when goods are entitled to these preferences, hence the need for rules of origin generally. This chapter briefly surveys rules of origin, distinguishing between rules of origin per se and rules of preference, which are not always the same. It then assesses the merits of the major methods employed for determining origin – substantial transformation, change in tariff heading, value-added and specified process, concluding that the selection of any of these methods amounts to the selection of a 'lesser evil'. Change in tariff heading increasingly is the favored rule of origin and this is discussed with particular reference to CUs and FTAs.

The chapter then gives examples of the rules of origin used in some of the more important CUs and FTAs, and surveys attempts that have been made at achieving international harmonization of rules of origin. Some of the issues presented by rules of origin are discussed, noting that they are more likely to raise questions with FTAs than with CUs and that they further the 'hub-and-spoke' pattern into which regional integration agreements may develop. Next, the chapter discusses whether there is a need for harmonization of rules of origin, concluding that harmonization would be highly beneficial. Finally, current negotiations toward harmonization are considered, and I argue that it is possible that rules of origin may not be as susceptible to 'capture' by industries interested in trade restriction when they are negotiated and adopted multilaterally as when they are negotiated and adopted in smaller, regional contexts.

15.1 Rules of origin generally

Customs unions (CUs) and free trade areas (FTAs), permitted by Article XXIV of the General Agreement on Tariffs and Trade, are inherently discriminatory.[1] They exist for the purpose of granting trade preferences to the products of their members. Rules of origin are needed to determine what products, for purposes of the CU or FTA, are entitled to the trade preference; that is, what products 'originate' in the territory of one of its members. If countries A and B have established a CU or FTA, an article produced in country C will not be given duty-free treatment by A simply because it has been trans-shipped to A through B. Something must be done in B to make the article a product of B. Rules of origin are used to establish the extent of this 'something'.

Rules of origin have other purposes as well. When used in conjunction with a country-of-origin marking requirement they may be thought of as a form of consumer notification, permitting those who so wish to obtain or avoid the products of certain countries.[2] They are necessary whenever discrimination, apart from that permitted by Article XXIV, occurs in international trade. For example, if a country does not grant most-favored-nation (MFN) treatment to the world at large, rules of origin are needed to determine whether goods are from a country or territory entitled to MFN treatment.[3] Similarly, if goods are subject to country-specific import quotas, rules of origin are needed to determine quota eligibility.[4] Rules of origin therefore are required to administer the current international trading system. They are a legal necessity, but they are an economic impediment. As Hindley (1990, p. 21) has observed:

> From an economic standpoint, taking the economic welfare of the world at large as the criterion, the best rule of origin would be that which allowed every trader to choose the origin that suits him best. That would typically be origin in the importing country, and would be tantamount to global free trade.

15.2 Rules of origin versus rules of preference

When discriminatory trade preferences are extended, rules of origin are employed to determine eligibility. Preference eligibility, however, sometimes is granted only on an 'origin plus' basis. For example, in the United States the 'substantial transformation' test historically has been used to determine origin. While that test also is used to determine origin under most US preference programs, those programs usually contain additional criteria before preference eligibility is conferred. The generalized system of preferences and the Caribbean Basin Initiative require not only that the goods 'originate' in the beneficiary developing country under the criteria of the substantial transformation test; they also require that a specified minimum value be added there. The rules of the United States–Israel Free Trade Area are comparable. If, as in situations like these, one rule of origin is used for 'ordinary' purposes and another rule for preferential purposes, including CUs and FTAs, it is possible for an article to 'originate' in a country for 'ordinary' purposes, such as marking or quotas, but not for preferences.

15.3 Assessment of different methods for determining origin

Different methods have been used to determine origin, but none has proved totally satisfactory, and none is likely to do so. Adoption of a particular rule amounts in significant part to acceptance of one set of shortcomings rather than another.

15.3.1 Substantial transformation

This is the general rule of origin that is used in the United States. An article that combines materials or processes from two or more countries will be deemed the product of the country in which it last underwent a substantial transformation. A transformation is 'substantial' when it yields an article which is 'new and different' from the article that entered the transforming process, one that has a new name, a new character and new use.[5]

Substantial transformation is determined on a case-by-case basis, and is a methodology congenial to common-law legal systems. Its advantages are those of that system: the slow, incremental development of the rule built upon its application to specific factual situations, reasoning from case to case. As explained by Levi (1949, pp. 1–2):

> It is a three-step process described by the doctrine of precedent in which a proposition descriptive of the first case is made into a rule of law and then applied to a next similar situation. The steps are these: similarity is seen between cases; next the rule of law inherent in the first case is announced; then the rule of law is made applicable to the second case.

By building upon precedent, reasoning by analogy, and taking one step at a time, such a system can establish sound, predictable rules. Critics, however, do not see the substantial transformation system in that way. They see the test as inherently imprecise and subjective. What is a substantial transformation to one administrator or court may be an insubstantial one to another. This, so the argument goes, can lead to inconsistency and confusion (Simpson, 1988).

Regardless of whether substantial transformation works well within a particular national legal system, it would be difficult to use as an international standard. Most of the world does not use the case-oriented common-law system and, even if it did, the system works only if there is, at its top, a body charged ultimately with deciding appealed cases, thereby creating the law. No such international body exists, nor is one contemplated. This responsibility would be far beyond the role of a panel convened to resolve a dispute under any likely international rules of origin code.

15.3.2 Change in tariff heading

The perceived shortcomings of the substantial transformation test have led to increased focus on change in tariff heading (CTH) as a rule for determining origin. CTH appears to be the wave of the future. It is the basis of the US proposal to GATT for an international code on rules of origin (Palmeter, 1990) and has largely been accepted in the Uruguay Round negotiations (Navarro, 1992).

Under CTH, an article completed in one country from materials originating in another will be deemed to originate in the second country if the processing there was sufficient to change the tariff classification of the imported materials. The use of a specific tariff schedule to measure change, rather than the use of a general term such as 'substantial transformation', can be more transparent, more predictable and less subjective.

But CTH is not without its shortcomings. One problem is that existing tariff schedules were not designed with origin determinations in mind. The most widely used tariff schedule, the Harmonized Commodity Description and Coding System (the 'Harmonized System'), classifies articles at a two-digit chapter level, a four-digit heading level, a six-digit subheading level and an eight-digit statistical level. The Canada–US FTA, which uses CTH as its basic rule of origin, employs changes at all of these levels to determine origin, depending upon the product. No ascertainable rule or principle was employed in determining what level of change would be required for any particular product. With a tariff schedule not designed to facilitate origin determinations, perhaps no single rule or principle is possible.

The absence of a general rule or principle in CTH points to another of its shortcomings: its susceptibility to capture by industries interested in minimizing their exposure to competition. Tariff schedules are lengthy, complex, tedious documents. Generally a section of a tariff schedule dealing with a particular industry will be comprehensible only to those familiar in detail with the products and processes of that industry. Rules providing that, for one industry or product, change at the two-digit level will suffice, while for others four-, six- or eight-digit change will be required are, superficially, comprehensible to all. But their rationale usually is not. What is it about the operations of one industry that dictate a two-digit change rather than a four-, six-, or eight-digit one? What is it that will require several of these levels of change within a single industry? Rarely will anyone not directly connected with the industry know.

The major shortcoming of CTH, as manifested in the Canada–US FTA and the pending North American Free Trade Agreement (NAFTA) among Canada, Mexico and the US, is the absence of any general principle underlining the selection of which specific tariff change is chosen to confer origin on particular articles. In the substantial transformation system, administrators and judges have some concept of what is meant by 'substantial'. They are able to look at other applications of the rule and reason by analogy to the problem before them. The concept of 'substantial' ideally, therefore, is the same regardless of the nature of the products involved. Certainly the process is not an exact one, and certainly, too, administrators and judges at times have missed even the inexact goals set for them by the system. But substantial transformation is a rule-based system, a system under which informed generalists can make intelligent assessments as to the correctness of particular decisions. This is difficult if not impossible under CTH.

The inherent obscurity of CTH provides an opportunity for industries to formulate rules specifically tailored to advance their private interests. For example, one CTH rule of origin that is comprehensible to the non-specialist is the rule in the Canada–US FTA which provides that the production of aged cheese from fresh milk does not confer origin on the country where the cheese was made if it is different from the country where the milk was produced.[6] The rule suggests that elements of the Canadian and US dairy industries agreed to stay on their own sides of the border, hardly a trade-creating stance. The hundreds of pages and thousands of lines of a tariff schedule offer many opportunities for similar, less obvious, rules – rules that may amount to covenants not to compete. This appears to be happening in the pending North American Free Trade Agreement. As Davis (1992) notes,

NAFTA contains a catalog of special-interest measures. It is a free-trade agreement, perhaps, but one full of protectionism for certain companies.

Through special domestic-content regulations known as rules of origin, for instance, General Motors Corp. would get a leg up on Honda Motor Co. in Mexico. US textile makers would be able to shut out India's. Zenith would be able to use changes in tariff rules to check incursions by low-cost Korean imports.

The NAFTA rules as initially drawn for computers using flat panel screens were so restrictive that International Business Machines Corp., a major buyer, found it necessary to lobby in Mexico City, Ottawa and Washington to have them dropped. An IBM spokesman was quoted as saying, 'To use the rule of origin as an instrument of industrial policy for flat panels is a misuse of the rules' (Davis 1992). This concern is echoed by Aho (1992):

Adoption of stringent rules of origin for some industries will be emulated in other blocs and lobbied for by other industries. The trading system could fragment into competing blocs because such discriminatory agreements cannot combine to form a globally consistent, stable system of national trade policies.

All of these characterizations refer to proposed CTH rules of origin. CTH also presumes that origin can be determined by a quick glance at the tariff schedules where the rule, presumably, is spelled out plainly for all to see. Very often this indeed will be the case, but very often too it will not. Customs classification disputes are frequent; they have been a mainstay of the practice of customs lawyers for generations. Whether an article is properly classified in one tariff heading or another can be a difficult question. At times such questions have become just as political, and the decisions presumably just as 'subjective', as the decisions of administrators applying the substantial transformation test.[7] Another problem with CTH is its tendency to become outdated if the underlying tariff schedule is not kept up to date. When dealing with a particular product area, tariff schedules usually list the major products within the area, and then provide a 'basket' heading for all other related products. In rapidly developing product areas, there is a tendency for the trade to move into the basket category as new products are developed and replace those listed in the schedule. This problem can be remedied by keeping the tariff schedule up to date, but if the tariff schedule involved requires international negotiation, this may not always be easy. What industries in one country may see as 'updating', industries in another may see as a threat. It seems unlikely that any significant change would be made in any tariff schedule without the concurrence of the industries concerned, effectively giving a veto to those who believe they would face increased competition as a result of the change.

Finally, CTH can be burdensome and expensive. Producers who, for example, wish to take advantage of the free trade agreements between the EC and the individual EFTA countries, which are based on CTH, must maintain records establishing the tariff classification not only of the finished product but also of all raw and intermediate materials imported from third countries. The cost of the border formalities alone needed to administer this system has been estimated to amount to at least 3 per cent of the value of the goods concerned, while the total economic cost has been estimated to amount to at least 5 per cent of that value. This burden is enough to lead exporters of up to 25 per cent of presumably eligible trade to forgo the preference and simply pay the normal duty (Herin, 1986).

15.3.3 Value-added

The requirement that a minimum value be added to imported materials to confer origin for the finished product on the importing country may be employed as a separate rule of origin or in conjunction with another rule. Because processing and assembly operations often do not result in meaningful tariff changes when parts and components are assembled into a final product, value-added generally supplements CTH. Like CTH, value-added has the advantage of being a rule that may be stated plainly and unambiguously. But also, like CTH, value-added may be more certain in its statement than in its application.

Calculation of value-added frequently depends upon resolution of complex or controversial accounting issues, which can raise considerable uncertainty. The need for resolution of accounting issues points up a further disadvantage of a value-added rule: the need for lengthy and costly audits to verify value-added claims. These are an inherent part of any value-added system, imposing a continuing administrative cost well beyond that which prevails with other rules of origin. Uncertainty is heightened under a value-added system because origin is never finally determined until audits are completed – a process that can take years. If the auditors disagree with the calculations of the parties, enormous, unexpected demands for payment of duties may result (Palmeter, 1992a). Whatever else value-added as a rule of origin may be, certain and efficient it is not.

Further, under a value-added rule, origin may change in unpredictable or unusual ways. The same operations in the same facility may confer origin one day but not the next because of fluctuations in exchange rates or material costs. Operations that will confer origin in one country may not do so in another because of different labor costs. Thus, in the proposed North American Free Trade Area, origin and preference eligibility will be conferred more easily under value-added on higher-wage Canadian and US operations than on lower-wage Mexican operations. In this way, a rule may distort economic efficiencies and divert investment from where it might otherwise occur.

15.3.4 Specified process

Under a specified-process system, rules are drawn in terms of concrete industrial operations. The system shares with CTH the apparent advantages of transparency, predictability, and less subjectivity than the substantial transformation system. However, it also shares with CTH the problem of obsolescence, as technical developments may tend to overtake the texts of specific rules; and, more important, it shares a susceptibility to capture by those industries that do not always view trade creation as a worthy goal. When governments base rules on the details of industrial processes, the industries concerned are likely to have a major influence in their formulation. Since 1984, for example, the US has used a specified-process system for its textile rules of origin. These rules are widely perceived as having been driven by the protectionist interests of the domestic textile industry (Giesse and Lewin, 1987, p. 129 ff; Palmeter, 1987, p. 26).

For a more recent example, consider a rule specifying that origin will be conferred on finished garments only if all operations from the yarn forward are performed in the CU or FTA. This rule could be stated in terms of either CTH or specified process. Under such a rule, it would not be enough to make a finished garment from imported fabric, nor would it be enough to make a finished garment from fabric woven in the CU or FTA from imported yarn. Under such a rule, only if the yarn itself is spun in the CU or FTA would origin be conferred on the garment. This rule has been proposed for the North American Free Trade Area (Bovard, 1992).[8]

Moreover, the task of drafting a comprehensive specified-process rule on which an entire system of origin is based may well be beyond human capability. Any rule of origin must apply to any product that conceivably could be traded internationally, from shoes to ships to sealing wax, to say nothing of semiconductors. Who could possibly draft rules encompassing even the major processes involved in the production of every article that exists now, let alone any article that will exist in the future?

Drafters of tariff schedules face the same problem, but they are able to use 'basket' categories. This simply means that any article that is not included by name is subject to the rate of duty applicable to an 'all other' or basket category. It is not clear just what inclusion in a basket category of a specified process rule would mean. At best, it could seem to mean that origin is or is not conferred by such categorization.[9] As an overall rule of origin, therefore, specified process has serious limitations; however, as a limited supplement to other systems, particularly CTH, it may prove useful.

15.4 Examples of rules of origin in customs unions and free trade areas

By way of illustration, consider the following six integration agreements:

1. *ASEAN Free Trade Area.* The 1992 Agreement on the Common Effective Preferential Tariff scheme for the ASEAN Free Trade Area provides that a product shall be deemed to be originating from ASEAN Member States if at least 40 per cent of its content originates from any member state.[10]

2. *Australia–New Zealand CER.* The 1983 Australia–New Zealand Closer Economic Relations Agreement relies on a 50 per cent value-added standard. It also requires that the last process performed in the manufacture of the goods involved be performed in the territory of the exporting member state (Steele and Moulis, 1992).

3. *Canada–US FTA.* The Free Trade Agreement between Canada and the United States, as mentioned above, rests primarily on CTH, supplemented by a 50 per cent value-added standard (Palmeter, 1992b).

4. *EC Association Accords.* The EC has a variety of preferential trade arrangements which may be considered regional, such as the agreements with the countries of the European Free Trade Association (Austria, Finland, Iceland, Norway, Sweden and Switzerland), the African, Caribbean and Pacific (ACP) countries, the Mashreq countries (Egypt, Jordan, Lebanon and Syria), and the Magreb countries (Algeria, Morocco and Tunisia). The rules of origin vary slightly from agreement to agreement, but in general they are based on CTH supplemented by specified processing and, in some cases, value added (Waer, 1992).

5. *Israel–US FTA.* The 1985 Free Trade Agreement between Israel and the United States uses substantial transformation plus value-added as the origin criterion. The value-added requirement is 35 per cent. For purposes of calculating whether 35 per cent value has been added by the exporting party, the value of products of the other party may be counted for as much as 15 per cent of the final value,

thereby reducing the value-added requirement to as low as 20 per cent. [11]

6. *Mercosur*. The Treaty of Asuncion, establishing the Mercado Comun del Sur (Mercosur), a free trade area among Argentina, Brazil, Paraguay and Uruguay, provides basically for change in tariff heading based upon the nomenclature of the Latin American Integration Association, supplemented with a 50 per cent value-added test for processing operations. [12]

15.5 Attempts at harmonization

A number of attempts have been made over the years at harmonizing rules of origin, but virtually no progress has been made. In 1976, the Organization for Economic Cooperation and Development (OECD) produced a compendium of rules of origin used by OECD countries. This compendium was followed by the United Nations Conference on Trade and Development (UNCTAD) in preparing a 1982 compendium dealing with rules of origin applicable to developing countries under different preference arrangements. In 1982 the Customs Cooperation Council (CCC) produced a comparative study of rules of origin (US International Trade Commission, 1985).

Earlier, in 1973, the CCC approved the Kyoto Convention, which was designed to simplify and harmonize customs procedures generally, including rules of origin. However, the Convention merely describes origin systems in use and does not set forth mandatory requirements. It uses the term 'substantial transformation' and suggests that CTH be used to determine whether substantial transformation has occurred. The GATT Secretariat prepared a note on rules of origin in 1981 and, in November 1982, ministers agreed to study the rules of origin used by GATT's contracting parties (US International Trade Commission, 1985).

Not much more was heard of rules of origin internationally until well into the Uruguay Round negotiations, but in the late 1980s, developments in three important areas served to focus more attention on the problems posed by rules of origin: (1) increased use of preferential trading arrangements, including regional arrangements, with their various rules of origin; (2) an increased number of origin disputes growing out of quota arrangements, such as the Multifiber Arrangement and the 'voluntary' steel export restraints applicable to the United States; and (3) increased use of anti-dumping laws, particularly by the EC and the US, and subsequent claims of 'circumvention' of anti-dumping restraints through use of third country facilities.

In September 1989, the United States submitted a comprehensive proposal concerning rules of origin to the GATT (Palmeter, 1990). The US called for a two-step program leading to eventual harmonization. In Step 1, the Customs Cooperation Council would be requested to provide three reports to the GATT. The first would identify where change within the Harmonized System Tariff Nomenclature would result in the transformation of a product sufficient to confer origin, and where change in tariff nomenclature alone might not be an adequate basis for origin. The second report would identify product areas which typically are subject to a variety of rules of origin, or rules different from the 'primary rule of origin' used by various countries. The third report would identify non-MFN policies and programs (such as preferences) that are subject to special rules of origin. In Step 2, the GATT contracting parties – using the three studies – would, within a year, negotiate an international agreement harmonizing rules of origin.

Negotiations have proceeded in the Uruguay Round along the lines suggested by the US. There appears to be no significant disagreement on the subject thus far. Just how much all of this will apply to regional blocs and their internal rules of origin, however, is unclear, because the draft agreement reportedly states that it does not apply to tariff preferences 'going beyond the application of Article I:1 of the General Agreement' (Navarro, 1992).

15.6 Issues

Gardner (1980, p. 14) has observed that regionalism 'will probably do more to give the participating countries sheltered markets against the outside world than it does to stimulate vigorous competition between them'. Rules of origin are a major weapon in the arsenal of those who wish to shelter regional markets against the outside world. They may be used to change what might otherwise be a trade-creating CU or FTA into a trade-diverting one, and they may be used to exacerbate the trade-diverting effects of CUs and FTAs to which that characterization already applies.

15.6.1 Customs unions versus free trade areas

Rules of origin are more important to FTAs than to CUs because members of FTAs, unlike members of CUs, maintain their own external tariffs. All other things being equal, processing operations involving materials and components from outside the FTA would tend to locate in the country with the lowest external tariff. Restrictive rules of origin could limit this trade deflection.

15.6.2 'Hubs and spokes'

The proliferation of FTAs could create trade patterns which would resemble the 'hub-and-spoke' pattern of airlines operations. The United States, for example, presently has FTAs with Canada and Israel, and is negotiating with Mexico. Other countries, particularly in Latin America, may be waiting in the wings. If all of these countries do not have comparable FTAs with each other – that is, if they do not comprise a single free trade area – then the common denominator will be the United States. The desire to avoid being just such a spoke with the US as hub is a major reason why Canada joined the Mexico–US free trade area negotiations.

Because they maintain a common external tariff, CUs would seem not to be as susceptible to this phenomenon. The United States, to continue with the example, may enter into a free trade arrangement with Chile without directly affecting its existing arrangements, but the European Communities would not permit an FTA between Chile and one of its members. Member states of the EC are required to maintain the EC's common external tariff and may not, therefore, participate separately as hubs or spokes – but, of course, the EC itself can and does.

This 'hub-and-spoke' phenomenon may be characteristic of free trade areas generally, but it can be greatly exacerbated and complicated by rules of origin. To return to the US example, the existing free trade arrangements the US maintains with Canada and Israel have different rules of origin. If additional FTAs are made by the US with other countries, and if these FTAs, too, involve separate rules of origin, the result could be the erection of complex discriminatory arrangements that make tariff discrimination look simple, if not benign, by comparison.

15.6.3 The need for harmonization of rules of origin

Do we need to harmonize rules of origin to have freer trade? No, but it would help. A significant reduction in tariffs and the elimination of quotas would lead to freer trade regardless of rules of origin. But the proliferation of rules of origin adds complexity to the trading system, and complexity serves only to add cost and inhibit trade. The question, therefore, is not whether multiple rules of origin inhibit freer trade, for they most certainly do; the question is how much do they inhibit freer trade. A related question is whether there is any sound policy reason for maintaining a system with multiple rules of origin with its consequent trade-restrictive effects.

This complexity exists both at the national and at the international level. Internationally, of course, different countries maintain widely different rules of origin. This is what the attempts at harmonization are all about. But within nations and CUs, different rules of origin frequently apply for different purposes. The EC maintains a wide variety of differing preferential rules of origin. The US maintains one 'regular' rule, its substantial transformation standard, but employs different or additional rules for most of its preference programs: there is one rule in the FTA with Canada; there is another rule in the FTA with Israel; there is still a different rule for the generalized system of preferences; and there is yet another for the Caribbean Basin Initiative. The US employs still different rules of origin for government procurement and an even different rule for determining whether circumvention of anti-dumping or countervailing duty orders has occurred.

This complexity would be eliminated if each jurisdiction adopted a single, universally accepted rule. However, adoption of a single rule in place of the current multiplicity may well mean adoption of a more restrictive rule – restrictive in the sense that more must be done in order to confer origin on a country involved in the assembly or processing of imported components or materials. A reasonable rule might hold, for example, that the production of a garment from imported fabric confers origin on the country where the garment is produced. A more restrictive rule would require both production of the garment and production of the fabric in order to confer origin on the garment, otherwise origin would remain in the country where the fabric was produced. A still more restrictive rule might require production of the garment, production of the fabric and production of the yarn.

What is restrictive about such a rule is not that in any particular instance it denies origin to the last country in the chain. What is restrictive is that the consequences which flow from this result, because of tariff discrimination and quotas, are restrictive. That is the reason industries lobby for and governments adopt these rules.

Origin matters only if it results in differential treatment. The way to ameliorate the effect of rules of origin is to eliminate, or reduce, the differential. The way to do that is to eliminate, or reduce, tariffs and quotas. In a world of no tariffs and no quotas – in a world of free trade – origin, apart from consumer preferences, would not matter. But in a world far from free trade, rules of origin are used to enforce and enhance discriminatory regimes. Whether these regimes are permitted by GATT, such as CUs and FTAs under Article XXIV or perhaps textile and apparel quotas under the Multifiber Arrangement, or whether they are not, they nevertheless are discriminatory and in most instances probably are trade diverting. In this imperfect world, these regimes may have to be tolerated, but their effects can be reduced if tariffs are reduced and if quotas, whether GATT-sanctioned or 'gray-area', are eliminated.

15.6.4 Negotiating an international code

Rules of origin are not one of the important stumbling blocks in the Uruguay Round – perhaps because, thus far, the hard issues have not been addressed. If all goes well with the Round, the Customs Cooperation Council (CCC) will face the hard issues and report to GATT, whose members in turn will face them.

For lack of an alternative, the CCC probably will propose a code based on CTH, supplemented by value-added, despite the shortcomings of these systems. The common-law substantial transformation system prevailing in the United States is not practically transferable to an international agreement. A specified process rule would not overcome most shortcomings of CTH and would add a few of its own, not the least of which would be the absence of an agreed starting point such as the Harmonized Tariff Schedule.

It probably is far easier for industries to control the adoption of CTH-based origin rules in bilateral or trilateral regional negotiations than in a multilateral forum. Multilaterally, the strength of a particular national industry may be diluted by the larger number of interests likely to be competing for its government's attention; opportunities for cozy 'you-stay-in-your-market, we'll-stay-in-ours' agreements between industries may not be as readily available. If the CCC performs its CTH exercise with some consistent internal view as to just how 'substantial' a tariff heading change must be, and if a completed document is presented to the negotiating group, individual industries might have difficulty in forcing significant change. Governments could be expected to resist significant change lest the entire package unravel.

This is an optimistic view of how CTH in multilateral negotiations might overcome one of its major shortcomings, even though there is little ground for optimism for its use in CUs and FTAs. A pessimist, however, might note that even if the CCC produces an ideal code (whatever that might be), industries unable to control the content of the code nevertheless may be in a position to block its acceptance by their governments. A pessimist might note further that, in so far as the use (or abuse) of rules of origin in regional agreements is concerned, a code may be irrelevant since it may not apply to preferential arrangements, including CUs and FTAs (Navarro, 1992). If it applies only to questions of marking and eligibility for MFN treatment, then a code would be of limited importance. Finally on a pessimistic note, there is a danger that restrictive rules of origin contained in regional agreements could become the starting point for negotiation of a multilateral code, with demands from industries that the regional rules not be 'weakened' multilaterally.

15.7   Summary and conclusion

Rules of origin have achieved an importance among trade issues in recent years largely in response to the growing importance of preferential – that is, discriminatory – import tariff arrangements and the increased use of import quotas on manufactured articles. Exporters seek to avoid quotas and obtain lower duties by shifting production from one country to another. Their protection-seeking competitors look for ways to stop them. To be sure, tariff preferences and quotas are not new to the world trade scene. No doubt such phenomena as the development of the multinational corporation, cheaper and more rapid transportation and communication, and the expansion of international trade generally have had much to do with the increased importance of rules of origin. It is far easier to move production operations, as well as parts and components, around the world than it was formerly, and in many cases economic factors – other than trade impediments – increasingly encourage multi-country production. But the intersecting of all of these factors is making issues of origin ever-more significant.

Every rule of origin has its shortcomings, and, consequently, selection of any particular rule is in many ways the selection of a 'lesser evil'. Change in tariff heading, supplemented by value-added, seems to be the most widely favored rule in recent years. Use of this system in CUs and FTAs seems particularly susceptible to capture by industries whose interests lie in trade-diverting rather than in trade-enhancing regional agreements. The trade-diverting effects of rules of origin in CUs and FTAs can be reduced or eliminated in the same way that other trade-diverting aspects of CUs and FTAs can be reduced or eliminated: by multilateral tariff reduction and quota elimination. The lower the MFN trade barriers, the lower the importance of rules of origin.

Notes

Thanks are due to Bernard Hoekman for his helpful comments on an earlier version of this paper.

1. The difference between a customs union and a free trade area is that members of the former adopt a common external tariff; members of the latter do not.
2. Marks of origin are treated in GATT Article IX.
3. GATT, of course, requires MFN treatment only for GATT contracting parties and, even then, discrimination apart from Article XXIV is permitted in a variety of instances. See GATT Article I.
4. In allocating quotas among contracting party countries, GATT contracting parties are required to approach as closely as possible the shares which those countries might be expected to obtain in the absence of quotas. See GATT Article XIII:2.
5. *Anheuser-Busch Assn.* v. *United States*, 207 US 556 (1907).
6. Canada–United States Free Trade Agreement, 27, *International Legal Materials*, 281, Annex 301.2. Section I of Annex 301.2 requires a change at the chapter level of the Harmonized System to confer origin; changes within chapters will not suffice. All dairy products are included within a single chapter, Chapter 4, of the Harmonized Tariff Schedule. Consequently, the origin of manufactured dairy products such as cheese will always be the country in which the milk was produced, regardless of where the cheese is made. Indeed, as the rule is written, fresh milk would not be considered substantially transformed for FTA purposes even if a Merlin could change it into birds' eggs or natural honey, since these, too, are included within Chapter 4.
7. See, for example, 'Canadian Sugar Refiners Voice Opposition to US Customs Tariff Change on Sweeteners', *International Trade Reporter* (BNA) **6**: 176 (February 8, 1989) and *Tariff Classification of Wire Rope With Becket Attachments*, Federal Register 53:49117 (December 6, 1989). Perhaps the best example is the ongoing dispute of whether vans should be classified as automobiles at a 2.5 per cent duty or as trucks at a 25 per cent duty. See 'When is a Truck?', *Washington Post*, February 22, 1989, p. A16, col. 1; 'If It Quacks Like a Truck, It is a Truck', *Washington Tariff and Trade Letter*, February 20, 1989, p. 3; 'Bill Would Increase Tariffs on Multipurpose Vehicle Imports', *International Trade Reporter* (BNA) **9**: 1126 (July 1, 1992).
8. After noting that 'the key protectionist danger in NAFTA lies in its new rules of origin', Bovard (1992) addresses the proposed 'yarn forward' rule as follows: 'The intent of this "yarn forward" rule is to oblige Mexican and Canadian apparel makers to buy yarn and fabrics from American textile mills before being allowed to sell clothing to US consumers. This makes as much sense as forcing Belgian companies to use American sugar for their chocolate exports'. The reason Bovard says Mexican and Canadian apparel makers would be obliged to use US yarn and fabrics is that their apparel industries – Canada's in particular – traditionally have been supplied with imported yarns and fabrics. The rule would tend to divert trade from their traditional Asian and European suppliers to US yarn spinners and fabric mills. Indeed, the rule might halt their trade altogether. The Canadian apparel industry enjoys a distinct US market niche for its garments made from European fabric. It might not be worthwhile, or even possible, for the Canadian apparel industry to substitute US yarn and fabric.
9. Whether a rule is stated positively or negatively can make a difference, particularly in a specified-process system. For example, a rule that states

positively that processes A, B and C confer origin may hold, under the legal doctrine of the 'implied negative', that all other processes do not. Conversely, a rule that states that processes A, B and C do not confer origin strongly implies that all other processes would do so. N. J. Singer, 1A, *Sutherland Statutory Construction* §§24.01–24.04 (4th edition, 1985).

10. 'Fourth ACP–EEC Convention, Protocol 1 Concerning the Definition of the Concept of "Originating Products" and Methods of Administrative Cooperation', EC *Official Journal*, L84/8, 1990.

11. 'Israel–United States: Free Trade Agreement', *International Legal Materials* **24**: 653, Annex 3:5.

12. 'Argentina–Brazil–Paraguay–Uruguay: Treaty Establishing a Common Market', *International Legal Materials* **31**: 1041, Annex II.

References

Aho, C. M. (1992), 'After NAFTA: Troubles Aplenty', *Journal of Commerce*, July 22, p. 6A, col. 2.

Bovard, J. (1992), 'NAFTA's Protectionist Bent', *Wall Street Journal*, July 31, p. A12, col. 4.

Davis, R. (1992), 'Sweetheart Deals – Pending Trade Pact with Mexico, Canada Has a Protectionist Air', *Wall Street Journal*, July 22, p. 1, col. 6.

Gardner, R. N. (1980), *Sterling–Dollar Diplomacy in Current Perspective*, New York: Columbia University Press.

Giesse, C. R. and M. J. Lewin (1987), 'The Multifiber Arrangement: "Temporary" Protection Run Amuck', *Law and Policy in International Business* **19**: 51–170.

Herin, J. (1986), 'Rules of Origin and Differences Between Tariff Levels in EFTA and in the EC', Occasional Paper No. 13, Geneva: EFTA Secretariat.

Hindley, B. (1990), *Foreign Direct Investment: The Effects of Rules of Origin*, Discussion Paper No. 30, London: Royal Institute of International Affairs.

Levi, E. H. (1949), *An Introduction to Legal Reasoning*, Chicago: University of Chicago Press.

Navarro, E. (1992), 'Rules of Origin in GATT', in *Rules of Origin in International Trade: A Comparative Study*, edited by J. Bourgeois, E. Vermulst and P. Waer, Ann Arbor: University of Michigan Press.

Palmeter, N. D. (1987), 'Rules of Origin or Rules of Restriction? A Commentary on a New Form of Protectionism', *Fordham International Law Journal* **11**: 1–50.

Palmeter, N. D. (1990), 'The US Rules of Origin Proposal to GATT: Monotheism or Polytheism?', *Journal of World Trade* **24**: 25–36.

Palmeter, N. D. (1992a), 'The Honda Decision: Rules of Origin Turned Upside Down', *Free Trade Observer* 32A, June.

Palmeter, N. D. (1992b), 'Rules of Origin in the United States', in *Rules of Origin in International Trade: A Comparative Study*, edited by J. Bourgeois, E. Vermulst and P. Waer, Ann Arbor: University of Michigan Press.

Simpson, J. P. (1988), 'Reforming Rules of Origin', *Journal of Commerce*, October 4, p. 12A, col. 2.

Steele, K. and D. Moulis (1992), 'Country of Origin: The Australian Experience', in *Rules of Origin in International Trade: A Comparative Study*, edited by J. Bourgeois, E. Vermulst and P. Waer, Ann Arbor: University of Michigan Press.

US International Trade Commission (USITC) (1985), *The Impact of Rules of Origin on US Imports and Exports*, Publication No. 1695, Washington, DC: USITC.

Waer, P. (1992), 'EC Rules of Origin', in *Rules of Origin in International Trade: A Comparative Study*, edited by J. Bourgeois, E. Vermulst and P. Waer, Ann Arbor: University of Michigan Press.

16

Dispute settlement in regional and multilateral trade agreements

Alice Enders

Insofar as regional integration agreements (RIAs) in the past were conceived as agreements comprehensively regulating the trade among member states, they were a substitute for the GATT legal system for managing intra-regional trade relations.[1] Canada and the United States, by contrast, followed an alternative approach in their 1988 Free Trade Agreement (CUSFTA), in that each country explicitly retained its GATT rights. This chapter considers the implications of this alternative approach for the settlement of trade disputes between member states of a RIA, drawing on the CUSFTA experience with its own and GATT dispute-settlement procedures.

The chapter begins by describing, by way of background, the layers of commitments that Canada and the US have made on bilateral trade issues under both CUSFTA and the GATT. It then examines the dispute-settlement provisions of both CUSFTA and GATT, first pointing out their similarities and differences, then analyzing the experience in dispute settlement between Canada and the United States under CUSFTA Chapter 18 since 1989, and finally drawing out the implications of CUSFTA dispute settlement for future RIAs. In the third section a review of Canadian–US bilateral disputes regarding trade remedy laws is provided, before the chapter concludes by summarizing the lessons learnt from CUSFTA's experience to date in dispute settlement.

16.1 The layers of commitments by CUSFTA parties

The first layer of commitments in CUSFTA involves those provisions which are wholly separate from GATT. In this group are found the departures from GATT principles permitted by Article XXIV, such as regional preferences, and the provisions designed to contain the benefits of the RIA to the two parties. Also found in this group are the 'new' commitments of CUSFTA in areas not covered by GATT, such as the steps to liberalize services, direct investment and the temporary movement of business persons. These commitments are enforced within CUSFTA by several dispute-settlement procedures (DSP) and are not considered further.

The second layer of commitments, and the principal concern of this chapter, consists of the provisions of the GATT and Tokyo Round Agreements incorporated in CUSFTA. National treatment is a commitment of CUSFTA parties, with an exemption for several Canadian measures affecting the internal sale and distribution of wine and distilled spirits, and for US and Canadian practices relating to beer and malt-containing beverages. The general prohibition of quantitative restrictions (QRs) is also incorporated, but exemptions include controls on US and Canadian exports of logs, 'process-in-Canada' requirements for fish under six Maritime provincial statutes, and agricultural products. QRs may, however, be applied to bilateral trade under the cover of the GATT's balance-of-payments provision, the exceptions clause, or the national security clause under more narrowly defined circumstances.[2] Non-discriminatory practices by state monopolies are also mandatory, on the basis of GATT Article XVII. With respect to the Tokyo Round Agreements, the standards code applies to industrial products but, for agricultural products, the CUSFTA goes beyond the code by establishing a framework for reaching agreement on technical regulations and standards. The government procurement code is also incorporated in CUSFTA, but the threshold for purchases by entities covered by the code open to competition from Canadian and US suppliers is lower, unless procurements are reserved for small business or excluded for reasons of national security.

For disputes regarding this second layer of commitments, the CUSFTA and GATT were conceived as *alternative* fora, with the choice left to the complaining party. Early critics such as Steger (1988) and Parker (1989) asserted that CUSFTA Chapter 18 procedures were superior to the DSP of the GATT. The case is made below that the impartiality of judgments, the weight of the GATT Council behind rulings, and emphasis on the peaceful settlement of trade disputes gives multilateral DSP inherent advantages over regional DSP.

A final group of bilateral commitments consists of GATT obligations not incorporated in CUSFTA, apart from those which do not apply to parties in a RIA (such as the MFN principle). These include areas in which the parties could not agree a substitute bilateral regime, such as agriculture and disciplines on anti-dumping and countervailing duty practices and subsidies – matters taken up in the Uruguay Round – as well as areas where the parties were content with the pre-existing regimes (such as the Agreement on Import Licensing Procedures, the International Dairy Arrangement, the Arrangement Regarding Bovine Meat, and the Agreement on Trade in Civil Aircraft). Also included in this group are several basic GATT provisions, such as the obligations to grant freedom of transit and to administer trade regulations in a transparent manner, whose importance was apparently overlooked by the CUSFTA negotiators. Finally, a truce was declared in the long-running battle over market access for beer in CUSFTA by the exemption for the obligation to grant national treatment to alcoholic beverages. For this group of commitments the parties to CUSFTA explicitly retained their multilateral rights under the GATT, including recourse to GATT dispute settlement.

16.2   Dispute-settlement provisions of CUSFTA and GATT

In CUSFTA, disputes regarding domestic anti-dumping and countervailing law are dealt with under Chapter 19 (see Section 16.3 below), while other disputes regarding the CUSFTA provisions for trade in goods fall under the dispute-settlement provisions of Chapter 18. Matters arising under the GATT are dealt with under Articles XXII and XXIII and disputes on issues covered by the six Tokyo Round Agreements fall under their respective dispute settlement provisions, with procedures codified in the 1979 Understanding Regarding Notification, Consultation, Dispute Settlement and Surveillance. Dispute settlement under the GATT has been further enhanced by the 1989 Improvements to the GATT Dispute Settlement Rules and Procedures. The CUSFTA DSP is modeled on that 1979 Understanding, with several modifications which became part of the 1989 Improvements.[3]

16.2.1   Similarities and differences between CUSFTA and GATT DSP

One important difference between GATT and CUSFTA is that the CUSFTA DSP covers proposed measures, while GATT DSP covers only measures in place. This additional scope of CUSFTA DSP has the advantage that potential disputes can be settled before the complaining party has suffered trade damage from a measure – damage which could be difficult to remove subsequently.

When the dispute concerns a measure within the scope of both CUSFTA and GATT, the forum for dispute settlement is chosen by the complaining party, and must be used to the exclusion of the other to prevent a duplication of procedures. There are numerous considerations which determine the choice of forum for each dispute and some of these can be seen by first examining the similarities and differences between CUSFTA and GATT with respect to the overseeing body, the panel procedures, and the implementation of panel reports.

Overseeing body

Bilateral consultations are a preferred method of resolving disputes in both CUSFTA and GATT, but no party is required to respond to the request for consultations. When the parties have failed to satisfactorily resolve a dispute, the complaining party may refer the matter for further action to the overseeing body – the Commission in CUSFTA and the Council in the GATT. Each of these generally takes decisions by consensus. Disputes concerning safeguard actions are mandatorily settled by arbitration under CUSFTA when consultations have failed, but there is no such requirement in GATT. For all other disputes, a complaining party may request the establishment of a panel, or binding arbitration if the respondent party agrees.

Panel procedures

Both CUSFTA and GATT DSP recognize an 'automatic' right to panel procedures. The maximum lag for the establishment of a panel from the date when a request for consultations is notified to the overseeing body is 70 days in CUSFTA and generally no more than three months in GATT.

GATT panels are composed of three members agreed by the parties to the dispute (five is an option by mutual agreement), selected from a large group of governmental representatives and a roster of non-governmental panelists. Nationals of the parties to the dispute generally do not serve as panelists. Should there fail to be an agreement by the parties on the panelists within 20 days of the establishment of a panel, the Director-General of GATT decides. In contrast, CUSFTA Chapter 18 panels are composed of five panelists, two selected by each party from a roster of citizens of their country unaffiliated with their government, with the fifth chosen by consensus by the Commission or, failing agreement at that level, by the four panelists.[4] The composition of the panel must be finalized after not more than 30 days in both CUSFTA and GATT from the date of the establishment of the panel.

The issue the CUSFTA Chapter 18 panel is instructed to examine – the terms of reference – is agreed by both parties to the dispute. In contrast, GATT panels have standard terms of reference unless both parties agree otherwise. GATT panels are instructed to examine the measure in the light of the relevant provisions of the GATT, described by the applicant party in its notification requesting the establishment of a panel to the Council, and to propose recommendations or rulings.

An initial report under Chapter 18 procedures is issued within 90 days after the panel composition is agreed, containing its conclusions on the issue before it. Parties have the opportunity to make written statements within 14 days, statements which the panel may consider in issuing its final report 30 days after the initial report. The facts and findings of the CUSFTA Chapter 18 panel are published unless the Commission (that is, the two parties to the dispute) decides otherwise. GATT panels take longer to complete their deliberations (normally six months), and procedural provisions for written statements by the parties are absent. Decisions are circulated to other contracting parties.

When the legal questions arising from the measure in dispute require analysis difficult to deliver within the foreseen deadlines, the parties can agree under CUSFTA procedures, as under GATT DSP, to a delay in the delivery of the final report. On the whole, CUSFTA and GATT panel procedures are similar, but the CUSFTA procedures are more expeditious due to shorter time periods allotted to consultations and the issuance of a final report, adding up to a three-month time advantage for CUSFTA.

Implementation of panel reports

After the GATT panel releases its report to the parties to the dispute, the complaining party generally requests adoption by the Council. Adoption occurs unless the respondent party blocks consensus, and is facilitated by continuing Council oversight of the matter. Once the respondent party has agreed to adoption – establishing the legal basis of the panel's rulings or recommendations – the second step is the time schedule for implementation. A 'reasonable period of time' is foreseen but lengthy delays have recently appeared (and, in one case each, the EC, Japan, Canada and the US have linked implementation to the conclusion of the Uruguay Round).

Under GATT DSP, measures taken by the respondent party to settle the dispute must be consistent with the GATT to protect the rights of other contracting parties. The final recourse of a complaining party dissatisfied with the implementation of a panel ruling is to propose retaliatory measures and request the authorization to proceed to the contracting parties (Article XXIII:2). The past two instances of proposed retaliatory measures (the Netherlands against the US in 1952 and the EC against the US in 1989) involved measures of equivalent effect, but there is no presumption to this effect in Article XXIII:2.

A similar first step is required under CUSFTA following release of the panel report. The Commission – the two parties to the dispute – agrees on 'the resolution to the dispute, which normally shall conform with the recommendation of the panel. Whenever possible, the resolution shall be non-implementation or removal of a measure not conforming ... or, failing such resolution, compensation' (Article 1807:8). The resolution of the dispute continues therefore to require agreement between the two parties to the dispute as in the GATT DSP. But unlike GATT DSP, removal or modification of the non-conforming measure is not the sole option of the respondent party, and measures announced or taken by the respondent party to settle the dispute need not be consistent with other CUSFTA obligations. After 30 days, the applicant party can proceed to suspend benefits of 'equivalent effect' without securing the approval of the Commission, which, in any case, would make little sense in a bilateral mechanism.

16.2.2 Experience with Canadian–US dispute settlement since 1989 under CUSFTA's Chapter 18

In light of the above features of the two alternative dispute-settlement procedures available under CUSFTA's Chapter 18, how have Canada and the US in fact acted? In the two bilateral disputes regarding measures within the scope of both GATT and CUSFTA since 1989, the applicant party chose CUSFTA DSP, an experience which has revealed certain features of Chapter 18 DSP.[5]

The first case, 'Canada's Landing Requirement for Pacific Coast Salmon and Herring' (CUSFTA, 1989), involved a complaint by the US regarding the consistency with CUSFTA of Canada's landing requirement for 100 per cent of the herring and salmon caught commercially in Canadian waters. The landing requirement replaced the export restrictions which had been the subject of a complaint brought successfully by the US to the GATT. In the bilateral consultations that followed, the US sought to secure a quota of fish exempted from the landing requirement to permit its processing in the northwest of the US, but Canada did not agree until after the Chapter 18 panel had rendered its report. In the conclusions, the panel argued that exempting 10 to 20 per cent of the catch from the landing requirement would bring the measure into conformity with the requirement of GATT Article XX(g) that it be 'primarily aimed at' conservation, a decision without legal precedent in GATT jurisprudence. As it happens, the upper limit of the suggested exemption coincided with the quota the US desired and subsequently received.

In 'Lobsters from Canada' (CUSFTA, 1990),[6] the second case to be examined by a Chapter 18 panel, the parties agreed to instruct the panel to examine only whether the measure was a QR, and not whether it was inconsistent with CUSFTA obligations as such. The majority found the measure to be an internal and not a border measure. The panel had not been instructed to consider the consistency of the measure with national treatment; for example, whether the treatment for Canadian small-size lobsters was at least as favorable as the best treatment granted to US small-size lobsters in intra-state commerce, bearing in mind the shorter carapace length minimums in New Jersey and Delaware. There the matter has rested, presumably because further proceedings on the same measure are precluded under CUSFTA.

The final report of the Lobsters panel is notorious as a decision split along national lines. The three US panelists endorsed their government's position that the measure was an internal measure falling within the scope of the national treatment clause, while the two Canadian panelists reiterated their government's position that the measure was a GATT-illegal import restriction. When issued, the final report raised the prospect of future decisions also split along national lines, calling into question the judicial impartiality of all proceedings.

Has recourse to CUSFTA dispute settlement for matters within the scope of GATT impaired the rights of other GATT contracting parties?[7] At least with respect to the two such cases processed under CUSFTA DSP, their settlement was consistent with the GATT tradition of viewing disputes between parties as self-contained matters. No third parties identified themselves in the GATT panel established to consider the Canadian measures which led to the first CUSFTA Chapter 18 panel, and the second Chapter 18 panel concerned a US measure affecting the export interests only of Canadian lobster producers. Should third party interests be affected in future proceedings, there is no obstacle to a complaint being initiated in the GATT by a concerned contracting party.

16.2.3   Implications of CUSFTA dispute settlement for future RIAs

Role of the Commission

Parker (1985) and Steger (1988) argue that the two parties of the CUSFTA Commission can achieve consensus more easily than in the

GATT Council, where fifty or so governments are regularly represented. At least with respect to dispute settlement, this reasoning is flawed. First, consensus-but-one is the practice of both the GATT Council and the CUSFTA Commission in responding to requests to establish panels. Second, adoption of the panel report and resolution of the dispute require an agreement between the complaining and respondent parties in both dispute settlement fora. Consensus therefore has the same role in both the CUSFTA and GATT DSP; that is, the complaining party cannot prevent the respondent party from blocking the procedures at any of the points where a decision of the overseeing body is required.

Panel procedures

The CUSFTA DSP demonstrates that it is possible to design a speedier procedure in a RIA, although the difference between it and GATT's procedure is not great. Another advantage of the CUSFTA process is the opportunity for parties to comment on the preliminary report of the panel, which may remove possible sources of confusion from the final report.

On the other hand, a disadvantage of the CUSFTA DSP is that terms of reference are not standard, as in GATT DSP, but must be agreed by the respondent party. Because successive procedures on the same measure are precluded under CUSFTA, the respondent party has an interest in the narrowest possible definition of the issue before the panel; for example, consistency of a measure with a particular clause of the CUSFTA rather than the CUSFTA itself. It is also in the interest of the respondent party to prevent the panel from issuing a recommendation or ruling, and defer this element to the Commission, where its agreement is required. In contrast, the terms of reference of GATT panels do not require the agreement of the respondent party, and recommendations or rulings are part of the terms of reference unless both parties agree otherwise. Future RIAs would do well to adopt the GATT practice of standard terms of reference for panels.

Horlick (1992) argues that the composition of a panel in CUSFTA from citizens of the interested parties has the disadvantage that one party – either the complaining or respondent party – always has a majority of its citizens on the panel, which raises the prospect of decisions being made along national lines. More generally, a dispute-settlement mechanism which relies on panel review by nationals of the parties to the RIA will raise questions of judicial impartiality, however detached and competent the panelists may be known to be. Only when judicial review is independent, as in the EC, or not conducted by citizens of interested parties, as in the GATT, is the issue of potential partiality set aside.

Implementation

Recognizing the significant domestic resistance to removing or altering existing measures found to be inconsistent with the GATT, Horlick (1992, p. 9) asserts that 'you would rather have a GATT panel report which at least has the moral force of all the Contracting Parties of the GATT behind it than a binational panel whose only moral force is your own country'. Combined with the judicial impartiality which third-party adjudication affords, the weight of the Council behind rulings is the most powerful element of the GATT DSP.

Is the greater number of options for the respondent party in CUSFTA with respect to a non-conforming measure an advantage over GATT DSP? Permitting other options increases the chance of settling the dispute for those instances where it is not possible for the government to overcome domestic resistance to removal of the inconsistent measure. Its disadvantage is that the respondent party may select an option which is second best to the complaining party. Under GATT, the complaining party and other contracting parties are secure in the knowledge that the sole option is the removal or modification of the inconsistent measure; only in 'non-violation' cases is compensation in the form of trade concessions an option to settle the dispute.

Is the unilateral retaliation of CUSFTA, independent of Commission oversight, an advantage? Davey (1992) asserts that retaliation is not a viable option in GATT because the respondent party will always block the consensus required for Council decisions. In this regard, it may be recalled that the US did not block consensus in the retaliation of the Netherlands agreed by GATT contracting parties in 1952 (GATT, 1952, p. 4). Furthermore, instances of retaliation have taken place between GATT contracting parties outside the supervision of the Council, and it is unsupervised retaliation that seems to be the greatest concern of trade partners. In this respect, CUSFTA offers no improvement.

Finally, it is worth emphasizing that retaliation is costly to the complaining party: not only does it close the door to a possible removal of the non-conforming measure, but domestic consumers pay additionally in the form of higher prices for products. In recognition of this cost, the GATT has numerous mechanisms, such as good offices, conciliation and mediation, as well as the influence of the Council, which use the efforts of third parties to promote a settlement to the dispute. These mechanisms play no role, understandably, in a bilateral RIA such as CUSFTA, but may play a role in a trilateral RIA such as NAFTA.

16.3 Disputes regarding trade remedy laws

Prior to the CUSFTA negotiations, both Canada and the US frequently applied trade remedy laws on products imported from the other.[8] Canada gave the issue top priority as a result of the perception that access to the US market was less secure through the increasingly arbitrary application of trade remedy laws, and because it was understood that the benefits of future tariff-free access to the US market for Canadian exporters could be eroded by anti-dumping duties on imported products. While Canada hoped to obtain a complete exemption from the application of US anti-dumping law for its exports by harmonizing competition law, no agreement was possible.[9] Instead, a Working Group was established to develop bilateral rules and disciplines on subsidies and countervailing duties and on the use of anti-dumping measures. (It has not met since 1989.)

The pre-existing commitments of Canada and the US under GATT Articles VI and XVI and the Subsidies and Anti-Dumping Codes therefore continue to apply. Trade remedy statutes — Canada's 1988 Special Import Measures Act (SIMA) and the United States' 1988 Omnibus Trade and Competitiveness Act — are 'nested' within the obligations of the GATT and those of the more specific Codes.[10] Every aspect of the domestic use of trade remedy laws, from the statute itself to administrative practice, is subject to the disciplines of the GATT. Dispute settlement is conducted by the Committee of a Code, and the review of GATT panels encompasses only the consistency of actions of the respondent party with GATT obligations.

In this context, the CUSFTA offered one important change with respect to the status quo ante. Scrutiny by an Article 1903 panel of the GATT-consistency of *changes to* statutes, but not the GATT-consistency of current statutes, may be requested (although there have been no such changes since the CUSFTA came into effect). Should an Article 1903 panel be requested, severe sanctions are foreseen if modifications to statutes are recommended but none are made within a set time period: the complaining party may either take comparable legislative or equivalent executive action, or terminate the CUSFTA within 60 days.[11]

Another change of CUSFTA was the option of binding arbitration for reviews of final anti-dumping and countervailing duty determinations by an Article 1904 panel. In both countries, judicial review of actions taken by domestic agencies may be requested by an interested party: in the US, at the Court of International Trade (CIT), and in Canada, at the Canadian International Trade Tribunal (CITT). Under CUSFTA

Chapter 19, a government, or, through their government, parties entitled to commence domestic procedures for judicial review of a final anti-dumping or countervailing duty determination, may now select the option of Chapter 19 review over the domestic court procedure. The Article 1904 panel review is limited to an assessment of 'whether such determination was in accordance with the anti-dumping and counter-vailing duty law of the importing party' (Article 1904:2), and the panel applies the standard of review and general legal principles that a court of the importing party otherwise would apply to a review of a deter-mination of the competent investigating authority. While Canadian commentators have argued that the CIT did not apply US trade laws objectively in the past, the identical standard of review of binational panels implies that the major advance for Canadian parties is a more rapid appeal process with a clear deadline (Cannon, 1991). On the other hand, the recurring recourse to binational panel review for the same cases is a feature of the Chapter 19 process to date which bears reflection concerning its overall effectiveness at defusing these disputes.

On the whole, this review of the dispute settlement regime for disputes concerning trade remedy laws reveals only one substantial change for Canada and the US in the CUSFTA relative to the status quo ante: a GATT-inconsistent change in a trade remedy statute is subject to severe sanctions. Actions by Canada or the US directed at altering the current trade remedy statutes or practices of the other party to CUSFTA have consequently continued to be brought to the GATT; the GATT's DSP was the forum for Canada's complaint against the US in the infamous pork case, and five proceedings concerning anti-dumping and counter-vailing duty measures were subject to DSP under the Codes. In several instances, the Chapter 1904 panels and GATT DSP have been used as complementary proceedings: the first procedure reviews whether the agency has erred in its application of domestic law, and the second proce-dure examines the consistency of the practice or the statute with GATT obligations.

Unfortunately, dispute settlement under the Codes has been stymied since its inception. In the Subsidies Code, the first instance of adoption of a panel report occurred in March 1992 (Canada was the respondent party), leaving five outstanding unadopted panel reports. The narrow interests represented on the Committee compared to the overall interests of those of Council members may be one explanatory factor. In view of the number of the disputes involving Canada and the US, non-adoption may also be related to the continuing differences between the two regarding subsidies and trade remedy laws.

16.4 CUSFTA, NAFTA and other RIAs in the 1990s

The major advantage of retaining GATT rights for subject matters not covered by the RIA is that there is no loss in substantial or procedural rights. For example, Canada and the US exempted each other from the obligation to grant national treatment in each other's market for beer, but each sought subsequently to secure this treatment through DSP under the GATT. At the same time, the DSP of a RIA is necessary to protect or clarify the scope of regional preferences, as the third CUSFTA Chapter 18 panel demonstrates. If GATT rights are retained in a RIA, as is the case of both CUSFTA and the recently concluded North American Free Trade Agreement (NAFTA), it is complementary to the GATT with respect to the level of obligation, and its DSP is a complement to that of GATT for matters only within the scope of each agreement.

In CUSFTA and NAFTA, agreement on norms governing trade remedy laws proved elusive. Even when international norms have been agreed, as is the case of signatories to the Subsidies and Anti-Dumping Codes, a blocked dispute settlement process reflects the different interpretations of their application. It may be that a solution will be found by the Uruguay Round negotiators.

With respect to matters within the scope of both CUSFTA and GATT, or more generally within the scope of both a RIA and GATT, retaining an avenue to GATT DSP preserves all DSP options. It is worth recalling that at least one reason why Canada and the US sought an alternative forum for dispute settlement was the fear of blockage in the GATT process, of which there had been several episodes in the 1980s. [12] Blockage, however, is not the exclusive preserve of GATT and can occur in the RIA. Retaining all DSP options is an 'insurance policy' in the event of a substantive breakdown in the bilateral or multilateral system, and in the preservation of rights, both present and future, secured in the GATT.

Provided the multilateral process avoids blockage, the more effective DSP available multilaterally – impartiality of judgments, weight of the Council behind rulings, options to promote the peaceful settlement of disputes – is a powerful counter-argument to those who argue that regional trade liberalization is an alternative to the multilateral process. [13] At the same time as the enthusiasm for regional integration agreements among GATT members seems unprecedented, commitments enforced by multilateral DSP offer greater security to those enforced by regional DSP in addition to the greater market access resulting from multilateral commitments.

Notes

1. See Chapter 14 in this volume, by Roessler.
2. No mention is made of the voluntary export restraint applied by Canada to exports of steel to the US, which expired March 31, 1992.
3. Canada and the US played leading roles in the elaboration of the Montreal procedures in the Uruguay Round negotiations.
4. Apparently, the Chairman of a panel is selected by the panelists of the side having won the toss of a coin.
5. The third Chapter 18 proceeding, 'Article 304 and the Definition of Direct Cost of Processing or Direct Cost of Assembling' (1992), concerned a dispute regarding rules of origin within the scope of CUSFTA alone.
6. Brought by Canada, the case concerned a 1989 amendment to the Magnuson Fishery Conservation and Management Act. By that amendment, lobsters originating in foreign countries or in states having minimum lobster-size requirements smaller than the minimum limits imposed by US federal law are prohibited from entering into inter-state or foreign commerce for sale within or from the US.
7. See the views expressed in GATT (1991).
8. Canada initiated 21 cases involving the US between 1984 and 1988 (out of a total of 51 cases); the US initiated 23 cases involving Canada between July 1980 and July 1989 (out of a total of 381 cases).
9. See Hart (1990) for a discussion of the relation between anti-dumping and competition laws in free trade areas.
10. As Koulen (1990, p. 367) argues with respect to the GATT Anti-Dumping Code, '[it] operates as a broad framework law within which the chief users of anti-dumping measures (Australia, Canada, the EC and the United States) apply statutory rules and/or administrative regulations which are far more precise and detailed than the provisions of the Code.' He further notes that the substantial differences between parties with respect to implementation of certain Code provisions do not, however, necessarily imply inconsistency with Code commitments.
11. Panel procedures are similar to those under CUSFTA Chapter 18, and panels consequently have the same potentiality for decisions split along national lines.
12. Hudec (1991) states that adoption was blocked in 16 out of 57 cases in the period between 1975 and 1989. Of the 16 cases, five were eventually adopted after some delay, three were rejected by the Council, and the remainder remained blocked. Extensive delays have largely been eliminated since 1989, but adoption remains a lengthy and cumbersome process in GATT.
13. Panel procedures are similar to those under Chapter 18 of CUSFTA, and panels have the same potentiality for decisions split along national lines.

References

Cannon, J. R., Jr (1991), 'Binational Panel Dispute Settlement under Article 1904 of the U.S.–Canada Free Trade Agreement: A Procedural Comparison with the United States Court of International Trade', *Law and Policy in International Business* 22: 689–720.

CUSFTA (1989), *Final Report of the Panel, 'Canada's Landing Requirement for Pacific Coast Salmon and Herring'*, Ottawa: CUSFTA Commission, October 16.

CUSFTA (1990), *Final Report of the Panel, 'Lobsters from Canada'*, Ottawa: CUSFTA Commission, May 25.

Davey, W. J. (1992), 'The GATT Dispute Settlement System: Proposals for Reform in the Uruguay Round', presented to the Workshop on the Multilateral Trade Negotiations of GATT: Issues and Policy Implications for Taiwan, Taipei, March 19.

GATT (1952), *Contracting Parties, 7th Session (Summary Record SR 7/16)*, Geneva, GATT Secretariat, November.

GATT (1991), *Working Party on the Free-Trade Agreement between Canada and the United States: Report*, Geneva: GATT Secretariat, October 31.

Hart, M. (1990), 'Dumping and Free Trade Areas', in *Antidumping Law and Practice: A Comparative Study*, edited by J. Jackson and E. Vermulst, London: Harvester Wheatsheaf.

Horlick, G. N. (1992), 'The U.S.–Canada FTA and GATT Dispute Settlement Procedures', *Journal of World Trade* 26(9): 5–16.

Hudec, R. E. (1991), 'The Uruguay Round Negotiations on Dispute Settlement: the Story to Date', in *Uruguay Round Trade Negotiations: Where Do We Go From Here?*, Washington, DC: American Bar Association.

Koulen, M. (1990), 'Implementation of the GATT Antidumping Code', in *Antidumping Law and Practice: A Comparative Study*, edited by J. Jackson and E. Vermulst, London: Harvester Wheatsheaf.

Parker, R. P. (1989), 'Dispute Settlement in the GATT and the Canada–U.S. Free Trade Agreement', *Journal of World Trade* 23(3): 83–92.

Steger, D. P. (1988), 'The Dispute Settlement Mechanism of the Canada–U.S. Free Trade Agreement: Comparison with the Existing System', presented at the University of Ottawa Law Faculty Conference on the Canada–U.S. Free Trade Agreement: Analysis of the Text, Ottawa, January 21.

17

Guarantees of market access and regionalism

Brian Hindley and Patrick Messerlin

Regionalism is a current focus for concern among liberally inclined observers of trade policy. Sometimes, though, the concern is expressed in a way that makes it sound like just one more of those vague anxieties that afflict people when they see a gap between reality and the way they thought the world was or should be. But for thought about regionalism to be useful, the issue needs defining. What problems are raised by regionalism?

Trade liberals – including ourselves – have in recent years often drawn pictures of an unpleasant world divided into three trading blocs, mutually hostile to one another. That display is usually designed to suggest to governments – especially those of the US and the EC – that their trade-policy activities and inactivities should be assessed in wider terms than they seem willing to adopt. It is not mere rhetoric, though. Taking a view over the next one or two decades, the possibility of such a world is real.

But if that is the possibility that gives rise to concern, why discuss it under the rubric of 'regionalism'? That rubric covers, for example, the Australia–New Zealand free trade area and the Mercosur pact between Argentina, Brazil, Uruguay and Paraguay. Such agreements raise many interesting economic, political and legal issues. But one would be hard pressed to argue that they threaten the structure of the world as we know it, which is the level of concern often signaled by those bemoaning regionalism.

Of course, in a world of genuine free trade, much in regional integration agreements (RIAs) such as these would be otiose, and they might take different forms or not come about at all. Such agreements therefore point to the failure of the GATT contracting parties to create a world of free trade. But that failure is not in itself blameworthy, for who expected GATT to create a world of genuine free trade? And it is not news. In any case, if the lack of completeness of the GATT is the issue, why sidle up to it via regionalism?

A better guess at the roots of concern about regionalism, it seems to us, is that they are basically concerns about the European Community; that they are primarily political, not economic; and that the 'regionalism' rubric is a device to avoid what is judged to be a counter-productive focus on the EC per se. A first concern is with the emergence of a trading bloc of similar weight and importance in world trade to the United States, but without the traditional regard of the US for the multilateral trading system (a tradition that may itself be wearing thin − see the next chapter, by Baldwin), and perhaps with a perceived interest in working outside the multilateral system. A second concern is that the US, tired of inconclusive tussling with the EC, will shift its trade-diplomatic energies away from the GATT and concentrate instead on bilateral relations with the rest of the Americas, and perhaps with countries on the other side of the Pacific. A third concern is that under these circumstances, the GATT will either cease to exist, or, more likely, will become a mere talking shop − a venue for US–EC bilateral discussions. In neither case will the GATT provide much protection to countries that are not associated with the US or the EC; and the fundamental idea underlying the GATT, that international law not national power should control international economic relations, will have been decisively rejected.

To run a global trading system along GATT lines when that system is dominated by one giant may be possible − particularly if the giant has some concern for principle and takes some account of global welfare. Is it possible to run a global trading system along GATT lines, though, if a second giant appears, larger than the first in some dimensions, and with interests that it defines rather narrowly? Some might doubt it. A natural response for a doubting policy maker is to seek alliances − possibly but not necessarily with one of the giants − that might add to national comfort in a giant-dominated and effectively GATT-less world.

These are genuine grounds for concern. It is not clear, though, what can be done about them. The EC will continue to expand if it wishes to do so (see Chapter 5 in this volume, by Winters), as will the RIAs of the US. In trade terms, we live in a world of two giants, each of which has a de facto veto on GATT activities.[1]

Whether or not our guess correctly identifies the substance behind concerns with regionalism, the EC and its expansion are clearly a topic within the general subject of regionalism, and a very important one. In what follows, we shall concentrate on that topic.

17.1   A hypothesis about regionalism

The previous section suggests the hypothesis that countries or governments are driven to join RIAs by a fear of the consequences of being 'left out in the cold' in a GATT-less world. The hypothesis has two aspects. One is that governments anticipate a world that is GATT-less – it makes no difference whether de facto or de jure – and are responding to that anticipation by taking out, via regionalism, insurance policies against an uncertain and possibly threatening future. The other is that many parts of the international trading system are essentially GATT-less *now*, and that regionalism is an adjustment to that awkward fact.

We suggest that country A will pay more (in the form of the conditions it accepts for a RIA) for guaranteed access to the markets of country B, the wider the gap between the access to B's markets currently enjoyed by A and the access guaranteed by the GATT, the more dependent is the prosperity of country A on the access to B's markets that it currently enjoys, and the higher the probability (as perceived by country A) that the government of country B will limit access to its markets in the future.

Clearly, this is at best only a partial explanation of RIAs. It does not, for example, address the question of the price that country B will accept for accepting a RIA with country A. Moreover, we do not want to suggest that lack of security of market access is the *sole* incentive for countries to enter RIAs, only that it is *an* incentive. Countries may have many positive reasons for wishing to form RIAs. A wish that France and Germany should live in future peace and harmony, for example, was a major motive for the Treaty of Rome (and the 1951 Paris Treaty, establishing the European Coal and Steel Community), and is still regarded as central to the structure of the EC by some commentators and policy makers.

There is, though, distinguished academic support for the importance of the insurance motive. Dornbusch *et al.* (1989, p. 36), for example, comment that:

> the increasing interference with trade by application of the US trade laws raises the costs of and uncertainty of exporting to the US market.
> Individual developing countries would therefore find it of interest to strike a bargain where unimpeded access to the US market is the *quid pro quo* for a privileged opening to the US of their own markets.

If that is true for the US, it is also true for the EC. Nor is it necessary to restrict the comment to developing countries. Freedom from US anti-dumping and countervailing duty action was a major Canadian objective in the negotiations leading to the Canada–US FTA, though not an objective that was fully attained.[2] Freedom from EC anti-dumping action was a major objective of at least some EFTA countries in the negotiations with the EC leading to the EEA (European Economic Area) agreement, and in that case was achieved (by means discussed below).

The area in which the GATT fails to provide the level of security that may be obtained through a RIA, however, is much broader than that defined by 'fair trade' laws. The EC, for example, is moving toward genuine free trade between its member states. But much more is involved than free trade in goods. The titles of Part Two of the Treaty of Rome tell the story: Title I: *Free movement of goods* (Chapter 2 of which mandates the elimination of quantitative restrictions and 'measures having equivalent effect'); Title III: *Free movement of persons, services and capital* (including Chapter 2, which provides for freedom of establishment to enterprises incorporated in a member state, regardless of the nationality of ownership, so that enterprises owned outside of the EC may, by establishing a subsidiary in a member state, enjoy the freedom of the single market); and Title IV: *Transport* (including civil aviation). In addition, Title I of Part Three of the Treaty provides for common rules, most relevantly, in the present context, of competition policy, including rules on 'Aids granted by States'.

This is the content that many would like to see, but few have high hopes of seeing, in the GATT. But in the absence of similar GATT coverage, consider the position of a non-member country of the EC whose residents engage in many transactions with residents of the EC. The prosperity of such a country is likely to depend – at least in the medium term – upon its continued access to the EC market. But in the absence of special arrangements with the EC, all that guarantees access is *EC* law and policy. Such a country therefore has an incentive to seek a treaty with the EC that provides a more secure basis for relying on access in the future. We believe the EEA agreement illustrates this.

17.2 The EEA agreement

The EEA agreement, signed in a redrafted version on May 2, 1992, covers the 12 EC member states and the 7 EFTA member states (Austria, Switzerland, Finland, Iceland, Norway, Liechtenstein and Sweden).[3] Within that area, there will be free movement of persons, services, capital and goods (other than agricultural products). The EEA has a population of 380 million and, treating trade between EEA members as international trade, it accounts for close to 50 per cent of world trade.

The Agreement requires EFTA countries to accept without modification a large body of existing Community legislation (the *acquis communitaire*) relating to the single market. More striking, EFTA countries must in practice accept relevant *future* EC legislation, even though they will have no control over its drafting or its acceptance by the EC.[4] In addition, EFTA countries will adopt EC competition law, and mergers within the EEA will be subject to the provisions of the EC Merger Control Regulation. The EFTA countries also agree to accept EC law in such matters as the environment, social and consumer policy and company law. The provisions of the EEA will be interpreted in accordance with EC law and precedent.

This arrangement might seem rather one-sided. To obtain it, though, the EFTA states made further concessions. They accepted an obligation to contribute to the EC Cohesion Fund for aiding poorer EC member states, and partially opened EFTA fisheries to EC vessels.

What did they get in exchange? In discussions of what the EFTA countries wanted from the EEA agreement, the phrase 'assured access to the EC market' occurs again and again.[5] Why, though, did the EFTA countries perceive their access to be threatened? In 1972, recall, they entered a free trade agreement with the EC. Thus, there was free movement in goods other than agricultural products in the EEA area prior to the EEA treaty. Under Article 58 of the Treaty of Rome, EFTA service providers can establish EC subsidiaries having full access to the single market. EFTA governments are free to unilaterally approximate EC legislation relating to services. And EFTA governments can establish free capital mobility by removing their own restrictions: the EC currently has none.

Some things that the EFTA countries obtain through the EEA they could not have obtained through unilateral action. They could not, for example, unilaterally establish free movement of persons between EFTA and the EC; and they could not unilaterally obtain cabotage rights for their airlines in the EC. And if EFTA service providers operate in the EC via Article 58, they will be under the regulatory control of the EC country in which they are established, not that of their EFTA base country. But on at least some of these issues (movement of persons and cabotage rights, for example), it is likely that the EFTA countries could have made arrangements with the EC covering the specific sectors, rather than accepting the very extensive loss of national decision-making power entailed by the EEA agreement.

The EFTA countries paid a high price for the EEA. We conjecture that much of what made that price acceptable to them is the acquisition of a right by Treaty to things that prior to the EEA agreement they had only through the benevolence of the EC.[6] It is true, for example, that each EFTA country has a free trade agreement with the EC. But under those agreements, goods from EFTA are subject to EC anti-dumping action, which, as some EFTA countries were very much aware, could be used by the EC to unilaterally gut the rest of the agreement. Virtually the only tangible concession made by the EC to EFTA in the EEA agreement is that anti-dumping action between the EC and EFTA will be done away with. That concession is conditional upon EFTA acceptance of EC competition law, which permits 'dumping' to be dealt with under that body of law, as it is between the member states, rather than under anti-dumping law.

The EEA agreement illustrates, it seems to us, the enormous drawing power of the EC single market and the high price that the EC can extract from its neighbors for guarantees of future access to that market. The price its neighbors will pay, moreover, depends on EC actions. The more restrictive the trade policies of the EC, the higher the probability its neighbors may place upon it withdrawing their access to the EC market, and the higher the price they will be prepared to pay for guarantees of access.

If the EC wants to expand further, it can do so. Several EFTA countries (Austria, Sweden, Finland and Switzerland) have formally applied for EC membership. Others are likely to do so – having accepted the EEA, an EFTA country might reasonably reflect that it might as well become a full EC member and get a voice and a vote on the form of EC legislation that it will anyway have to accept.[7] Poland, Czechoslovakia and Hungary have made clear their wish to become full EC members, as have Cyprus, Malta, Turkey and Morocco. When a formerly independent country joins the EC, of course, it gives up its vote and independent voice in the GATT.

17.3 'Fair trade' laws and security of market access

To illustrate the proposition that GATT does not offer secure market access, even in areas that it nominally controls, we concentrate below on 'fair trade' laws. For the EC, that means anti-dumping action.

A wish to be less exposed to US fair trade laws was an important motive for Canadian acceptance of the Canada–US FTA; and a similar wish with respect to the EC is an important motive for acceptance of the EEA by at least some EFTA countries (most notably Sweden). We do not want to suggest, however, that misuse of anti-dumping action is always the primary contingency against which insurance is demanded. For other EFTA countries, a guarantee of access to the EC service sector may have been more important.

There are currently no GATT guarantees of access to the service sector, so that our general point about the weakness of GATT guarantees applies a fortiori. We believe that it will continue to apply even if the Uruguay Round is completed, and some GATT-type disciplines apply to international trade in services. Anti-dumping (AD) action, though, has been a responsibility of the GATT throughout its existence. The GATT appears to control AD action, and should control it, but in fact GATT provides only a rather loose constraint on the use of AD for protectionist purposes by national governments. The failure to control misuse of AD action was the most significant breakdown of GATT guarantees during the 1980s. The central problem raised by AD laws lies in the ability of anti-dumping authorities to bias their calculations so as to find dumping and injury where there has in fact been no dumping or injury. They thereby provide themselves with a rationale for the application of trade-reducing 'remedies' where no dumping and no injury have occurred.

17.3.1 The economic impact of anti-dumping action

A first question, though, is whether AD action constitutes a threat of sufficient magnitude to provide the incentive to form regional associations that we hypothesize. That question is sometimes answered with estimates of the trade flows subject to contingent protection.[8] That indicator, however, is systematically biased downward. Imports subject to AD measures will typically fall. If AD measures are severe enough, no products subject to AD duties will be imported at all, and calculation of the import coverage of AD measures will yield the absurd result that the measures have had no effect.

It has been suggested that contingent protection is a marginal phenomenon because it affects only 3 per cent of total EC imports. But roughly 70 per cent of the EC's AD actions have led to high trade barriers and, on average, these have halved imports in the five years after their initiation. Moreover, the remaining quarter of their AD actions that are terminated by findings of 'no dumping' or 'no injury' exhibit a similar impact on imports. A crude adjustment based on these facts suggests that a better estimate of the import coverage of EC anti-dumping measures is 8 or 9 per cent. The 3 per cent of imports that remain after the application of the measures should be multiplied by two (to take account of the decline in imports following AD measures), and the resulting 6 per cent by one and one-third (to take into account the trade affected by 'no measures'). That figure, however, is still likely to substantially underestimate the overall effect of AD measures. It takes no account of the role of AD measures in creating voluntary export restraints (VERs), nor of the effects on trade flows of efforts by traders to avoid AD action and its effects.

17.3.2 Anti-dumping action as a 'manager' of VERs

During the 1980s, AD actions became the principal means of introducing new VERs or of maintaining existing VERs and other 'gray-area' measures. Importing countries – especially the EC and the US – offered VERs to exporting countries as a means of settling disputes based upon allegations of dumping.

The first large-scale use of AD cases for imposing and monitoring VERs came in the late 1970s, with almost 75 EC anti-dumping cases in the steel industry. From 1977 to March 1992, EC steel trade with Central and East European countries was regulated by a web of quantitative restrictions (the so-called Europe Agreements) with the explicit statement that these exporters would not be subject to AD actions if they fulfilled their obligations under the Agreements. In 1982, the US steel industry launched more than 110 AD cases for the same purpose. The EC's 1982 AD case on Japanese video casette recorders prepared the way for the quotas on these, and the 1985 US anti-dumping case on chips aimed, in effect, at cartelization of world markets. The late 1980s and early 1990s are witnessing a similar evolution in the textiles and apparel sectors, where the slow erosion of the MFA quota system is closely matched by an increase in the number of AD actions.

Table 17.1 provides more systematic information on the employment of AD action in obtaining VERs. According to the list of VERs provided by the GATT (document NG9/W/2/Rev1), 82 per cent of US VERs on manufactured goods in 1988 had been 'installed' by earlier or ongoing AD actions. Two-thirds of VERs enforced at the Community level were 'installed' by AD actions. The proportion is lower for VERs imposed by EC member states, as might be expected, since AD actions are now usually ruled by Community law and enforced at the level of the Community. Nevertheless, only one important group of VERs is not yet

Table 17.1 Anti-dumping actions as 'manager' of VERs

| | European Community | | | | |
	At EC level	Member states	USA	Canada	Total
All VERs, total number of AD actions:					
All sectors	46	17	40	5	108
Manufacturing	29	17	40	5	91
AD-related VERS – total number of AD actions as a percentage of all VERs:	19	4	33	0	56
All sectors	41	24	83	0	52
Manufacturing	66	24	83	0	62

Sources: Compiled by the authors using information from GATT (NG/W/2/Rev.1), the US International Trade Commission, and the EC *Official Journal*.

managed through AD action, namely, those imposed on Japanese exports of cars (though US anti-dumping actions on mini-vans could signal the end of this special situation).

17.3.3 Anticipation effects

Even when the effect of identifiable VERs is taken into account, however, the full effect of AD actions on trade flows still has not been captured. Traders do not want to get involved in AD actions. Whatever the outcome of the case, involvement is expensive and commercially disruptive. A trader selling a product that has not been the target of an AD action, but who thinks that in the future it might be, has an incentive to act in such a way as to avoid that event, or to reduce its costs should it occur. S(he) can hope to avoid AD action (and also to reduce the probability that, if his/her product *is* targeted, s(he) will be found to have injured the import-competing industry) by easing the commercial pressure s(he) brings to bear on local competitors – by pulling his/her competitive punches. S(he) can reduce the probability that s(he) will be found to dump, or the size of the dumping margin that will be attributed to him/her, by raising the price of the product in the export market. These actions will reduce his/her sales in that market.

Traders can work these tactics out for themselves. But, should their competitive practices still have too hard an edge for the liking of members of the local import-competing industry, current AD practices will lend a considerable force to any warnings or representations they care to make to the traders. The mere threat of AD action can produce many of the effects of a VER without any formal VER being in place. Proper calculation of the effect of AD action on trade flows will take account of that effect.

17.3.4 Undermining the GATT guarantee

During the past four decades, the GATT has successfully implemented two principles: tariffs that are (1) non-discriminatory and (2) bound. Table 17.2 provides evidence that the enforcement of contingent protection has significantly eroded these two pillars.

On average, an AD action leads to four different rates of duties where there was previously only one tariff – a large increase in discrimination. In some cases, AD action has led to the existence of 10–15 different AD duties (as GATT rules allow different AD duties for different firms). Table 17.2 suggests that the erosion of the non-discrimination rule is

Table 17.2 Indicators of undermining of the GATT guarantee[a]

Trading partners	MFN tariff rates[b] (%)	Anti-dumping duties[c] (%)	Ratio of MFN to AD duties	Average number of AD duty rates[d] (%)
Industrial countries	6.8	18.7	3.1	6.7
Less-developed countries	7.1	28.2	4.3	3.2
Newly industrialized countries	6.7	25.5	3.9	1.0
Non-market economies	8.0	47.8	5.8	1.0
All countries	7.1	28.5	4.1	3.9

Notes: [a] These results are based on a sample of 30 EC anti-dumping cases initiated between 1980 and 1987, and terminated by *ad valorem* or specific duties.
[b] GATT 'bound' tariff rates.
[c] *Ad valorem* equivalent of anti-dumping duties.
[d] Anti-dumping duty rates by exporter (country and firm).

Sources: Authors' calculations based on the EC *Official Journal* and the World Bank's SMART data base.

most accentuated in trade between industrial countries, that is, precisely where the GATT has been perceived to be the most successful. Moreover, the *ad valorem* equivalents of AD measures are on average three to four times higher than the corresponding most-favored-nation tariffs.

17.3.5   EFTA and EC anti-dumping action

The EFTA countries have not been a particular target of formal EC anti-dumping action. Between 1980 and 1989, 17 out of roughly three hundred and fifty EC anti-dumping cases were against products from EFTA countries. The cases involved exporters from all EFTA countries, though exporters from Austria, Sweden and Norway were the most frequent defendants. They cover a wide range of industries, though chemicals and steel are prominent among them (and wood and paper if case reviews initiated in the 1970s are considered).

Comparing the period 1985–9 with 1980–4, EFTA's share of EC anti-dumping actions against OECD countries increased from 8 to 14 per cent. Cases terminated by AD measures grew from 57 to 67 per cent of all cases initiated against EFTA countries. These figures suggest the possibility of a shift in EC policy that is adverse to the interests of the EFTA countries. Nevertheless, on the face of it, EFTA countries have not been too seriously affected by EC anti-dumping action.

Yet there is no reason to doubt that removal of the EC's threat of AD action provided a principal motive for at least some EFTA countries to subscribe to the EEA, and ultimately to apply for entry into the EC. One possible explanation of the seeming discrepancy is that EFTA concerns with EC anti-dumping action were based on anticipation: the EFTA countries recognized that they *could* be targeted by the EC, and wished to remove their vulnerability. Another possible explanation is that, for the reasons discussed above, EFTA exporters felt more constrained in their tactics in the EC market than the number of formal actions suggests, so that the number of formal EC actions understates the true effect of EC anti-dumping action on EFTA exporters to the EC.

17.4   RIAs and anti-dumping

The 'insurance' hypothesis raises two questions that might be answered by looking at the available evidence. One is whether countries that have severely suffered from RIA anti-dumping actions before their accession (and thus have a clear motive to join the RIA) have used them against more efficient competitors left outside. The second is whether RIAs have triggered 'mimicking' of AD actions – introducing a dynamic aspect in our proposition.

17.4.1 'Changing sides': RIAs, anti-dumping and trade diversion

Bhagwati (1992) has suggested that 'trade creation can degenerate rapidly into trade diversion when anti-dumping actions are freely used.' For instance, the EC hard-board industry would rapidly eliminate the (let us assume) inefficient Spanish producers as soon as Spain joins the EC. This would illustrate a trade-creating effect of the RIA – a positive effect, though second best if Austria, left outside the EC, is a more efficient producer than the EC. Spanish producers, though, could initiate an AD action against Austria aimed at slowing the decline of the Spanish industry. Is there any evidence to support the proposition that RIAs have been used by new members to reduce outside competition?

The EC, together with its latest members – Spain and Portugal – offers an excellent field of observation for three reasons. First, EC anti-dumping cases against these two countries *before* their accession provide information about the relative efficiency of Portuguese and Spanish firms. Second, there are roughly twenty EC anti-dumping cases in which Portuguese and/or Spanish firms were complainants *after* these two countries joined the EC. These two sets of cases can be compared to see whether there is any correlation between inefficiency before accession and AD actions after accession. Finally, EC anti-dumping law and enforcement were relatively stable during the 1980s, so that changes in these factors do not distort comparison of the two sets of cases.

Two broad observations provide preliminary support for the trade diversion proposition. First, Spanish firms have been very active in EC anti-dumping actions since Spanish accession. Spanish firms represent 13 per cent of all EC firms mentioned as complainants (though Spanish GDP is less than 7 per cent of EC GDP). Second, Table 17.3 presents all cases initiated between 1980 and 1992 in which Portuguese or Spanish firms were mentioned as defendants (before the accession) or as complainants (after the accession). Cases involving Portuguese and Spanish firms in the *same industry* (defined at a four-digit level of disaggregation) before and after their accession have occurred in four industries: pulp and paper, industrial chemicals, synthetic products (synthetic textile fibers) and cement. These cases represent between 55 and 65 per cent of all cases.

Table 17.3 EC anti-dumping cases involving Portugal and Spain (number of cases) before and after their accession to the EC in 1986

ISIC industry	Before accession, 1980–6[a]		After accession, 1987–92[b]	
	Portugal	Spain	Portugal	Spain
Cases by industry:				
3211 Spinning and weaving			2	3
3311 Sawmills	1	1	1	1
3240 Footwear			1	1
3411 Pulp, paper		1		6
3511 Industrial chemicals		9		1
3512 Fertilizers		1		2
3513 Synthetic products		1		
3610 Pottery and china		1		1
3692 Cement		1		
3699 Non-metallics (nec[c])	1	1		
3710 Iron and steel		2		
3829 Machinery (nec)		1		2
3831 Radios and TVs				1
3909 Other manufacturing				
All cases	2	18	4	18
Common cases (before and after accession)	0	12	1	10
Common cases as a percentage of all cases	0	67	25	56

Notes: [a] EC cases (excluding reviews) against Portugal and Spain.
[b] EC cases in which Portuguese or Spanish firms are among EC complainants.
[c] Not elsewhere classified.

Source: Authors' computations based on data in the EC *Offical Journal,* various issues.

More refined evidence is needed, though, to make sure that exactly the same products and firms are involved. Table 17.4 presents all cases where Portuguese or Spanish firms were defendants, and also the EC anti-dumping cases (covering exactly the same product) initiated after the accession of Portugal and Spain to the EC. The cases presented in Table 17.4 can be divided into four groups.

First, six pre-accession cases were directed at Spanish producers only. In all of these cases, dumping was found (though in one case it was *de minimis*). These cases are likely to be instances where Spanish firms were (and still are) relatively efficient and eager to compete (hence, the AD measures). We conjecture that in such cases, no matching AD case will be observed after accession – efficient and competition-oriented firms will neither need nor demand protection. And, indeed, only one of this group was followed by a case initiated after 1986, and it concerns a steel product, for which EC protection covered many countries other than Spain.

Second, four pre-accession cases were terminated by no dumping (and consequently no measures) against Portuguese or Spanish firms and firms from other countries. That the EC Commission found no dumping suggests that the Portuguese or Spanish firms were relatively efficient. However, the presence of other foreign firms in the complaints opens the possibility that the Portuguese or Spanish firms involved were induced to be competitive merely in order to meet foreign competition in the EC markets. As a result, they may support AD actions after accession in order to enjoy rents in the enlarged EC markets. In fact, Portuguese and Spanish firms have been active complainants in three (out of four) cases. In the oxalic acid and copper sulphate cases, the proceedings of the EC pre-accession cases make clear reference to the fact that Spanish markets were highly concentrated and protected – leading to the conclusion that rent-seeking is a plausible motive for post-accession cases. Definitive conclusions are difficult to reach in the corundum case (because the determination of Spanish dumping was made on the basis of Yugoslav domestic prices) and in the hard-board case (because there is no public information on the reasons the case was terminated under Article 380:1 of the Act of Accession).

Third, four pre-accession cases were initiated against Portuguese or Spanish firms and firms from other countries and terminated by dumping but no measures against Portuguese or Spanish firms. These cases are likely to involve Portuguese or Spanish firms too small to have an impact on the EC markets involved. We conjecture that these firms are unlikely to be part of the 'major proportion of the industry' or to be involved as a complainant in post-accession cases. And in fact, no post-accession case is observed.

Table 17.4 EC anti-dumping where Spanish or Portuguese firms have been defendants before and/or complainants after their accession to the EC in 1986

	Years of initiation		Margins of dumping		Anti-dumping measures against Portugal or Spain	Years of expiry	Cases after accession		
							Initiation of cases	Portuguese or Spanish complainants[a]	Countries involved
	Portugal	Spain	Portugal or Spain	Lowest other					
A. Pre-1986 cases in which Spain was the only country involved									
Steel, beams		1982	9.9	—	Undertaking	b			
Tiles, ceramic		1983	0.5	—	None: *de minimis*	1984			
Steel, reinforced bars		1983	12.4	—	Undertaking	b	1990	n.a.	Turkey
Paraformaldehyde		1984	17.4	—	Undertaking	1989 c			
Polystyrene sheets		1984	25.6	—	*Ad valorem* duty				
Plasterboard		1984	7.0	—	Undertaking	1990			
B. Pre-1986 cases terminated by no dumping and no measures									
Corundum		1983	0.0	6.3	(See text)	1984	1990	S	Brazil, Yugoslavia
							1990	n.a.	Poland, China Czechoslovakia, Hungary, Soviet Union
Oxalic acid		1984	0.0	15.2	(See text)	1984	1987	P + S	Korea, Taiwan
							1987	S	China, CSFR
							1989	S	Brazil
							1990	P + S	India
							1990	n.a.	China
Copper, sulphate		1984	0.0	18.0	(See text)	1984	1986	Neither	CSFR, Poland, USSR, Hungary
Board, hard	1985		n.a.	34.7	None e	1986	1988	S	Bulgaria, USSR

C. Pre-1986 cases terminated by dumping but no measures

Product									
Furfural		1980	n.a.	n.a.	None: no injury	1981			
Fridge compressors		1980	0.2	0.2	None: *de minimis*	1981			
Board, particule		1984	n.a.	n.a.	None: no injury	1985			
Steel, wire rod	1985		49.0	0.3	None: no injury	1985			

D. Pre-1986 cases terminated by dumping and measures

Product									
Trichlorethylene		1981	61.0	13.0	Undertaking	1987			
Board, hard		1981	18.8	1.4	Undertaking	1986	1988	S	Brazil, Sweden, USSR, CSFR, Poland, Romania
							1989	S	Finland, Argentina, Switzerland, Yugoslavia
Perchlorethylene		1982	82.6	67.9	Undertaking	1987	1986	n.a.	USSR, Finland, Sweden, Austria, Canada, USA
Pentaerythritol		1983	6.2	3.6	Undertaking	1989	1987	P + S	Brazil, South Africa
Kraftliner	1982[c]	1984	10.6	2.5	Undertaking	1989	1991	n.a.	USSR, Poland, China, Norway
Silicon, carbide		1984	n.a.	4.3	Yes[d]	1986			
Cement, Portland		1985	n.a.	25.0	Yes[d]	1986	1989	Neither	Yugoslavia, Turkey, Romania, Tunisia
							1992	S	

Notes: [a] The presence of Portuguese or Spanish firms as complainants is marked by P or S.
[b] Under steel arrangements with the ECSC or special provisions of the Treaty of Accession.
[c] Under review in 1986.
[d] No measure under Article 380:1 and yes under Article 380:3 of the Act of Accession.

Sources: EC *Official Journal*, various issues.

Lastly, seven pre-accession cases were initiated against firms from Portugal, Spain and other countries, and terminated by measures against Portuguese or Spanish firms. If we assume that dumping margins mirror efficiency rankings (so that high margins imply low efficiency), we conjecture that the pre-accession cases where Portuguese and Spanish producers have higher margins of dumping than other exporters involved in these cases will be followed by matching post-accession cases. This is observed in four out of the seven cases, and is best illustrated by the kraftliner case.

In 1987, an AD case against kraftliner from Brazil and South Africa was initiated by three EC firms – La Cellulose du Pin (France), INPACSA (Spain) and Portucel (Portugal). This case is the exact counterpart of a 1982 pre-accession review of a case against Portugal (among other exporters of kraftliner) and a 1984 pre-accession case against Spain where La Cellulose du Pin (France) was the only EC complainant, Portucel the only Portuguese producer, and INPACSA one of two Spanish producers accused of dumping. The 1982 and 1984 cases provide crucial information: the margins of dumping of Portucel and INPACSA were in the upper end of the range (9 to 12 per cent, whereas eight of the 14 non-EC firms had dumping margins lower than 9 per cent). If dumping margins mirror efficiency rankings, this information supports our hypothesis about the use of the EC anti-dumping procedure by relatively inefficient producers after accession. Moreover, La Cellulose was mentioned as the 'sole Community producer',[9] and the case was terminated by undertakings (said to eliminate injury) by the two Spanish firms. The 1987 case was terminated without measures. The Commission observed, however, that while there had been dumping at the beginning of the period of investigation, prices charged by Brazilian and South African firms increased during the rest of the investigation period so that no dumping was found during this second period. Such price behavior clearly may reflect price alignment by exporters from Brazil and South Africa (which were not caught in previous EC anti-dumping cases on kraftliner).

17.4.2 'Fatal attraction': RIAs, anti-dumping and mimicking

What is the impact of AD actions by a RIA on crucial trading partners outside the RIA? Is there a domino effect – do RIA anti-dumping actions disturb the markets of trading partners which then feel entitled to react by introducing AD rules and actions of their own?

A pure illustration of this situation is the EC and Turkey (whose accession to the EC has been postponed for a substantial number of

Table 17.5 EC anti-dumping cases against Turkey and Turkish anti-dumping cases

		EC anti-dumping cases involving Turkey				Turkish anti-dumping cases				
		EC measures against Turkey				Countries common to EC and Turkish cases				
						EC cases		Turkish cases		
Year	Products involved	Types^a	Level^b (%)	Year	Countries	Types^a	Level^b (%)	Types^a	Level^b (%)	Other countries involved
1982	Ferro-silicon	Undert.								
1983	Acrylic fibers	Mixed								
1985	Glass	Undert.		1990	Romania	Undert.		Duty	100	
				1990	Romania	Undert.		Duty	100	
1985	Acrylic fibers	Mixed		1990	Romania	Undert.		None		
1986	Polyester fibers	None								
1987	Polyester fibers	Duty	9	1989	Taiwan	Duty	9	Duty	20	Korea
				1989	Romania	Duty	23	Duty	20	Italy
				1989	Romania			Duty	15	
1987	Polyester yarn	Duty		1991						Italy
1987	Steel sections	Mixed	8							
1989	Denim	None								
1989	Steel, tubes, welded	Mixed								
1990	Towels, cotton	None								
1990	Asbestos, pipes	n.a.								
1990	Cotton yarn	Duty^c	10	1990	Egypt	None		None		Pakistan
				1990	India	None		None		
1990	Polyester yarn	Duty^c	52							
1990	Steel, bars, alloy	n.a.								Brazil
1990	Steel, semis	Mixed	16							

Notes: ^a Undert.', undertaking; 'mixed': mixed outcome (duty and undertaking or no measures):
^b *Ad valorem* amount for duty (no official estimates are available for other measures).
^c Provisional duty.

Sources: Authors' calculations based on the EC *Official Journal* and the Turkish *Official Gazette*, various issues.

years). This situation can also be illustrated by countries which pertain to the same RIAs, however, if these RIAs permit AD actions between their member states, as in the case of the Canada–US Free Trade Agreement. From this point of view, relations between the US and Mexico from 1986 to 1992 represent a shift from a situation very similar to the EC–Turkey situation to a situation similar to the Canada–US FTA.

A quick look at the list of AD cases shows that there are many common AD cases in EC and Turkish enforcement, and in US and Mexican enforcement (until, that is, the start of the NAFTA negotiations in 1989). However, to count the number of common cases says little about the real extent of the intricacies between the AD cases of the RIA and its trading 'satellites'.

Table 17.5 provides more refined information by focusing on EC anti-dumping cases against Turkey and Turkish AD cases dealing with the same products. The first Turkish AD case was initiated in December 1989, but already one-fourth of EC anti-dumping cases against Turkey (four out of 16) is 'mimicked' – in terms of both products and countries – by Turkish AD cases.

It might be argued that such mimicking merely reflects the fact that 'dumpers' dump all over the world. A detailed examination of cases, though, reveals their close relationship. For instance, following an EC case on glass, initiated to protect a Greek producer from imports (including imports from Turkey), the Turkish authorities took AD action against Romanian glass. The Turkish authorities, however, used the factory price of the only Greek producer (which was subject to a price fixed by the Greek government) as a basis for their reference price.

17.5 Anti-dumping in the Uruguay Round

Article VI of the GATT prevents *totally* arbitrary use of AD action. But, as currently formulated and applied, it fails to prevent many actions that are too arbitrary for the health of the GATT. The GATT is weakened by this, and contracting parties are provided with an incentive to seek remedies outside of the GATT – most importantly, in the present context, through RIAs.

The Uruguay Round presented a clear opportunity to improve this situation. What in fact has been achieved? Abuse of AD legislation is hidden in the technical details of dumping calculations – the saying 'the devil is in the detail' might have been invented to describe AD law. Exposure of abuse involves discussion of those technical details (see, for example, Hindley, 1988; Palmeter, 1989). To avoid technicality as much as possible, we provide here three examples of specific EC practices which, it seems clear, satisfactory GATT action on AD action would tackle. Our focus on the EC is due merely to the fact that we are more familiar with its procedures than with those of other jurisdictions; we do not intend to imply that the EC is the worst offender (although it is certainly possible that it is).

17.5.1 Averaging methods

Products are not typically sold at a single price, but at prices that vary with market conditions at the time of the sale and the characteristics of the sale (for example, whether it involves a large or small volume). To obtain a dumping margin, however, AD authorities must subtract 'the' price in the export market from 'the' price in the home market of the exporter. A natural solution to the problem of obtaining 'a' price is to take an average. The EC does that, but it does not take simple averages.

First, in calculating the price in the exporter's home market (often referred to as the 'reference' price), the EC Commission is likely to throw out low-priced sales in the home market of the exporter on the basis that they are unprofitable. In that event, the reference price calculated by the Commission will be higher than the simple weighted average of prices in the exporter's home market.

Second, EC methodology treats all export sales made at a price above the reference price *as if they had been made at the reference price*. Thus, the 'export price', as calculated by the EC, is an average of the prices of export sales that are *less* than the reference price, and the reference price itself. That is, it is a figure that cannot be higher than the reference price, and that will typically be lower. Hence, if *any* export sales have been made at a price lower than the artificially increased reference price, the Commission will find dumping.

Article 2(6) of the existing Code gives general strictures as to what AD authorities must do 'in order to effect a fair comparison between the export price and the domestic price in the exporting country'. Arguably, a complaint in the GATT against the averaging procedures described above could have been supported on the basis that they were unfair – but the question has not been tested. Article 2.4.2 of the Dunkel Draft final Act of the Uruguay Round (GATT, 1991), however, expressly authorizes these procedures:

> [A] normal value established on a weighted average basis may be compared to prices of individual transactions if the authorities find a pattern of export prices which differ substantially among different

purchasers, regions or time periods and if an explanation is provided why such differences cannot be taken into account appropriately by the use of a weighted average-to-weighted average or transaction-to-transaction comparison.

The requirement that authorities must provide an explanation if they use the EC method of averaging may restrict the use of that method. The severity of the restriction obviously depends upon the quality of explanation that is required.

Article 2.2.2 of the Dunkel Draft requires that 'the amounts for administrative selling and any other costs and for profits shall be based on actual data pertaining to production and sales in the ordinary course of trade'. The EC's rationale for rejecting sales 'made at a loss' is that such sales cannot be 'in the ordinary course of trade'. The Dunkel Draft leaves this rationale intact. Hence, it appears to allow the EC (and other AD authorities) to pick and choose among transactions, and thus to raise the calculated reference price. It also allows the Commission to inflate the profit margins on domestic sales of exporters to the EC. In EC methodology, that translates directly into an increase in calculated dumping margins (Hindley, 1988).

17.5.2 Measuring costs

Products are often sold through marketing companies associated with the manufacturer. That raises a genuine problem – the GATT recommends ex-factory prices for comparisons, but the ex-factory price of a transaction between associated companies is not necessarily the true transaction price. There are reasonable grounds on which to reject transactions between associated companies and to take instead the price of the first arm's-length sale. To obtain an ex-factory price from that first arm's-length sale, however, requires deduction of costs incurred between the factory and that sale.

The EC, though, does not give allowances for the overheads or advertising expenses of a related sales company on the home market of the exporter. The Commission deducts such expenses on the export side of its calculation, but not in its calculation of the home-market reference price. Clearly, this makes it much easier for the Commission to discover large dumping margins on the exports of such companies.

The Dunkel Draft, rather than merely stating how a fair comparison should be made, as does the Tokyo Round Code, requires (Article 2.4) that 'a fair comparison *shall* be made between the export price and the normal value' (emphasis added). It also requires that

> due allowances shall be made in each case, on its merits, for differences which affect price comparability including differences in conditions and terms of sale, taxation, levels of trade, quantities, physical characteristics, and *any other differences which are also demonstrated to affect price comparability.* [emphasis added]

This expands on Article 2.6 of the existing Code, which reads 'Due allowance shall be made in each case, on its merits, for differences in conditions and terms of sale, differences in taxation, and for the other differences affecting price comparability'. When the export price has been constructed, the new text also requires that 'if ... price comparability has been affected, the authorities shall establish the normal value at a level of trade equivalent to the level of trade of the constructed export price, *or make due allowance as warranted under this paragraph*' (emphasis added). The existing Code requires merely that allowances should be made 'for costs, including duties and taxes, incurred between importation and resale, and for profits accruing'.

Perhaps this language increases the probability that a GATT panel will find against practices such as those of the EC. On the other hand, those practices are so gross that it seems likely (to a non-lawyer observer) that they would have been caught by the existing language if anybody had complained about them.

17.5.3 Refund of anti-dumping duties: duty as a cost

Under the GATT, anti-dumping duties are corrective, not punitive, and should be refundable if the dumping has ceased. EC regulations provide for refunds. In practice, however, it is difficult to obtain them, and there are long delays in payment.[10]

The Tokyo Round Code requires that if 'the duty so collected exceeds the actual dumping margin, the amount in excess of the margin shall be reimbursed as quickly as possible'. Article 9.3.2 of the Dunkel Draft calls for the 'prompt refund, upon request, of any duty paid in excess of the margin of dumping. A refund of any such duty ... shall normally take place within twelve months, and in no case more than 18 months, after the date on which a request for a refund, duly supported by evidence, has been made by an importer'. The phrase 'duly supported by evidence' is pregnant with possibilities of delay. The Dunkel Draft does not require payment of interest on delayed reimbursements of dumping duties.

Obtaining a refund from the EC is especially difficult for marketing companies associated by ownership with the manufacturer of the product. The problem arises because the EC Regulations direct the Commission, when calculating the margin of dumping, to deduct from the export price 'any anti-dumping duties'. Thus, product X is found to have a dumping margin in the EC of 20 per cent, and an AD duty of 20 per cent is imposed upon it. The importer raises the price of X by 20 per cent. Has s(he) stopped dumping X? EC methodology says not. When the Commission constructs the export price after the AD duty, it will deduct 20 per cent (the AD duty) that it did not deduct before; and, despite the price increase, it will find an unchanged export price, and an unchanged dumping margin. The Commission says that in this case, 'a reimbursement will be granted if the resale price [to an independent buyer] has been increased by an amount equivalent to the margin of dumping *and* the amount of duty paid' (emphasis added).[11]

In this context, Article 9.3.3 of the Dunkel Draft is a masterpiece of drafting:

> In determining whether and to what extent a reimbursement should be made when the export price is constructed in accordance with Article 2.3, authorities should take account of any change in normal value, any change of costs incurred between importation and resale, and any movement in the resale price which is duly reflected in subsequent selling prices, and should calculate the export price with no deduction for the amount of anti-dumping duties paid when conclusive evidence of the above is provided.

Alternatively stated, the authorities *may* calculate the export price with a deduction for the amount of anti-dumping duties paid when the importer fails to provide *conclusive* proof of the above. 'The above', however, includes 'any movement in the resale price which is duly reflected in subsequent selling prices'. One interpretation of this, it seems, is that the importers must conclusively prove, not only that *their* price has increased by the amount of the dumping duty, but that the price charged *by those to whom they sell* has increased by that amount. To put the matter gently, importers may have difficulty in conclusively proving this to skeptical authorities. If they fail, however, it seems that their export price may be calculated with deduction of dumping duties, as is current EC practice.

17.5.4 Assessment of injury

The GATT does not condemn dumping per se. The preamble of the

Anti-Dumping Code says that: '*anti-dumping practices* should not constitute an unjustifiable impediment to international trade' (emphasis added). Only after identification of *that* threat does the preamble go on to say that 'anti-dumping duties may be applied against dumping *only* if such dumping causes or threatens material injury to an established industry in the territory of a contracting party or materially retards the establishment of an industry' (emphasis added).

'Determination of Injury' is the subject of Article 3 of both the existing Code and the Dunkel Draft. A curious addition to the list of factors to be examined in determining injury in Article 3.3 ('no one or several of [which] can necessarily give decisive guidance') is the 'magnitude of the margin of dumping'. Consider two import-competing industries, A and B, which have the same symptoms of injury. Industry A, however, faces imports on which a high 'dumping margin' has been found, while B faces imports with a lower dumping margin. If B is not injured, can A be found to be injured merely because of the higher dumping margin? Given the elasticity in calculations of dumping margins, it will not be difficult for AD authorities to find high dumping margins where there is no other evident injury, if a high dumping margin will fill the gap.

Article 3.4 of the Dunkel Draft now includes, rather than merely an exhortation to take account of unspecified factors other than dumping that might have caused injury, a list of factors 'which may be relevant'.

17.5.5 Conclusion on the Dunkel Draft

The EC practices that we have discussed are not banned by the Dunkel Draft. The relevant question is whether the Draft provides a firmer basis for complaints about those practices in the GATT. The language of the Draft is in some instances clearer and firmer than that of the existing Code: perhaps it will provide a better basis for complaints and for GATT panel findings against the EC and other abusers of AD law.

But put the point another way. If you were the government of an EFTA country and you thought it possible – just possible – that at some time in the future the EC might target your country's exports for AD action, would you regard the Dunkel Draft Anti-Dumping Code as a good substitute for the EEA?

17.4 Conclusions

The defects or absence of GATT guarantees of market access, relative to those that can be obtained through RIAs, provide an 'insurance' motive for RIAs. The specific defect that we have used as an illustration here is that created by misuse of AD action. Our examination of the proposed Uruguay Round Anti-Dumping Code suggests that the GATT has failed to narrow the gap in that area. We conjecture that the position is not markedly different in other areas – for example, services. If that is so, however, the strength of the insurance motive for RIAs is unlikely to diminish in the foreseeable future.

What this implies for the future of the GATT is unclear. That future depends largely on the behavior of the EC and the US. It is possible to visualize a happy world in which neither is distracted from the demands of the multilateral trading system by its regional ties, or a less happy world in which one or both neglect the multilateral system, or reject it outright, causing its demise.

The insurance hypothesis, however, has an unpleasant implication. The worse the behavior of the EC and the US in the context of the multilateral system, the more probable will appear the collapse of that system, and the more valuable will be association with the EC or the US. Either one, therefore, by threatening the multilateral system, may generate signals that it can interpret as applause for itself and its policies. It is far from evident that that position is stable.

Notes

We thank David Henderson, Bernard Hoekman, Ernst-Ulrich Petersmann and Per Magnus Wikjman for their helpful comments on an earlier draft. None of them, however, are implicated in our analysis or conclusions.

1. The presence of a third giant – Japan – complicates matters further. So far, however, Japan has shown little interest in formal regional trading arrangements and has been rather passive in the GATT. To describe the current situation as one of domination by two giants does not do great violence to reality in the present context.
2. See Krueger (1992) for a discussion of the political economy of NAFTA in terms consistent with the argument in this paper.
3. The original Treaty was scheduled for signing on November 18, 1991. Postponement and redrafting were required by the objections of the European Court of Justice to the position in which the original draft would have placed it.
4. The agreement calls for 'close consultation' between the EC and EFTA countries in drawing up future EC legislation. EFTA countries will have no formal control over the adoption of legislation by the EC, however. An EEA Joint Committee will take the final decision on whether such legislation will apply in EFTA countries. If the Committee rejects EC legislation, however, Article 102(5) of the Treaty says that 'the affected part [of the agreement] ... is regarded as provisionally suspended.'

5. The surge of EFTA investment in the EC since 1985 suggests the possibility that EFTA companies thought that their access to the EC market was dependent on a physical presence in the EC.

6. Winters, in his Chapter 5 in this volume, suggests another possibility. It is that the EFTA countries wanted to 'lock in' domestic liberalization through association with the EC (as Mexico appears to want to do via NAFTA). We do not dispute that possibility: Winters' suggested motivation could coexist with the demand for 'insurance'.

    Even in the light of either or both of these motives, though, EFTA gains from the EEA agreement might still seem small in comparison with the apparently large concessions of EFTA national power in the various areas covered by the Treaty. It is certainly possible, however, to take a gloomy view of the EC's future potential for damaging and arbitrary action in the area of administrative protection, which would justify a high price in terms of the insurance motive.

    Moreover, the EFTA countries may have given up less than appears at first sight. The EFTA countries are small economies on the periphery of a much larger economy. Many transactions of their residents are naturally with EC residents, and the EC rules for such transactions therefore have a substantial influence on the rules adopted by an EFTA country. If the EC adopts particular minimum standards for a product, an EFTA government will be under heavy pressure to adopt standards that take account of that minimum. If the EC banking and insurance system requires a certain minimum regulatory standard, subsidiaries of EFTA banks and insurance companies operating in the EC will be required to conform to that minimum, and are likely to press for similar regulations in their home country. It could be argued, therefore, that the EFTA countries were merely giving up de jure what they had already lost de facto.

7. This is an oversimplification. Several EFTA countries are neutral, for example, and are therefore concerned about EC plans for a unified defence and foreign policy.

8. From an economic perspective, it would be better to look at the impact of contingent protection on the *production* of the country imposing such measures, rather than the impact on trade. Trade flows are merely the result of the 'mismatch' between domestic production and consumption, so looking at the impact of contingent protection on domestic production would provide a more accurate estimate of the magnitude of this impact – and of its costs.

    Correct estimation of the production coverage of AD measures, however, is very difficult. First, information on production (at the product level used in AD actions) is hard to obtain. Second, correct assessment of the production effect of an act of contingent protection requires an extensive knowledge of the technological and economic relations between the products involved in AD cases and other goods produced by the domestic economy. For instance, protecting a product may have a substantial impact on production of a complementary good or on that of a good requiring the protected product as an input.

9. See the EC *Official Journal*, L224/31, recital 16, August 21, 1984.

10.

    Until recently, even the fastest [refund] procedures took over two years, and some applications have taken up to four years to be decided. Such a lethargic approach is objectionable in itself for the loss and uncertainty it causes those making claims ... The delays accompanying refund payments have been so great that importers must regard them as windfalls. (McGovern, 1990, p. 45)

11. 'Ball Bearings Originating in Singapore (Refunds)' in the EC *Official Journal*, L148, 1988.

References

Bhagwati, J. N. (1992), 'Regionalism and Multilateralism: An Overview', presented to the World Bank/Centre for Economic Research (CEPR) Conference on New Dimensions in Regional Integration, Washington, DC, April 2–3.

Dornbusch, R., P. Krugman and Y. C. Park (1989), *Meeting World Challenges: U.S. Manufacturing in the 1990s*, Rochester, NY: Eastman Kodak.

GATT (1991), *Draft Final Act Embodying the Results of the Uruguay Round of Multilateral Trade Negotiations*, mimeo, GATT Secretariat, Geneva, December 20.

Hindley, B. (1988), 'Dumping and the Far East Trade of the European Community', *The World Economy* 11: 445–63.

Krueger, A. O. (1992), 'Government, Trade, and Economic Integration', *American Economic Review* 82: 109–14.

McGovern, E. (1990), *The Anti-Dumping Report*, London: Globefield Press.

Messerlin, P. A. (1990), 'Anti-dumping Regulations or Pro-cartel Law? The EC Chemical Cases', *The World Economy* 13: 465–92.

Palmeter, N. D. (1989), 'The Capture of the Anti-dumping Law', *Yale Journal of International Law* 14: 182–9.

PART 6
Looking to the future

18

Adapting the GATT to a more regionalized world: a political economy perspective

Robert E. Baldwin

International economic organizations such as the General Agreement on Tariffs and Trade (GATT) or the International Monetary Fund (IMF) generally are formed or significantly changed only during, or shortly after, periods of international crisis. It is then that political pressures from vested interests for the maintenance of the status quo can most easily be overcome and significant new institutional arrangements established. The GATT and IMF were created, for example, after the chaotic period of the 1930s when competitive exchange rate and tariff changes were commonplace and after a major world-wide war in which governmental structures were profoundly altered. It was then possible through international cooperation to break out of the Prisoners' Dilemma situation of the 1930s, which was characterized by a sub-optimal level of world economic welfare.

As writers from Karl Marx (1906) to Mancur Olson (1982) have pointed out, basic economic conditions continue to change after major institutional reforms, sometimes facilitated by the new institutions and sometimes impeded by these institutions. However, some international institutions eventually seem to become impediments to the optimal development of changing economic conditions and, in reaction to the constraints of these institutions, individual countries or groups of countries adopt policies that increase their own economic welfare but may reduce the collective welfare of the international community. Such actions also tend to weaken the established institutions and make them less relevant for serving their intended purposes. Unless these institutions can be changed, the world economy may be pushed into increasingly sub-optimal welfare conditions.

Trade-policy developments in the 1980s suggest that this scenario may be applicable to the GATT. The increase in the number of regional integration agreements, the greater use of aggressive bilateral negotiations to achieve trade-policy goals, and the increased willingness to take unilateral actions against so-called unfair trade practices all indicate that the GATT may no longer be facilitating increases in world trading welfare to the extent it did in the period from the late 1950s through the 1970s. While these policies are not illegal under the GATT, they weaken a central principle of the agreement, namely, that multilateral procedures should be the main means for resolving trade disputes and achieving trade-policy goals. Furthermore, it is significant that the prime country behind the establishment of the GATT and its major supporter prior to the 1980s, the United States, is leading the movement toward the greater use of these non-multilateral policies.

Two key questions come to mind. First, exactly why has there been a shift away from the multilateral approach and what changes in basic economic conditions and relationships have occurred to turn certain countries away from multilateralism? Second, what, if any, changes can be made in the GATT to restore its earlier effective role in promoting the multilateral liberalization of world trade?

This chapter investigates these two questions. Section 18.1 examines the reasons for the success of the GATT system in its early years, and how this success helped to change the underlying structure of economic power relationships among countries. Section 18.2 discusses various weaknesses and drawbacks of the GATT that became apparent under these new international economic relationships, while Section 18.3 suggests changes in the GATT system aimed at correcting these weaknesses and strengthening the GATT's facilitator role in liberalizing world trade. Finally Section 18.4 summarizes the analysis and proposals.

18.1   The role of the GATT in facilitating world trade to the mid-1960s

During the period from the late 1950s to the mid-1960s, the GATT was highly successful in promoting increases in world trading welfare and in resolving trading disputes. Two factors seem particularly important in accounting for this success. First, the GATT negotiating mechanism proved to be especially well suited for achieving general welfare gains from increased trade. Secondly, the hegemonic role played by the United States increased the economic welfare of most non-communist nations and served to minimize the adverse effects of certain flaws in the GATT. However, after tariffs in the industrial countries had been cut to low levels and the economic dominance of the United States had declined significantly, as Japan, the European Community and a growing number of newly industrializing developing countries gained economic prominence, these flaws acted as increasingly important impediments to the continued rise in world welfare through expanded international trade. The remainder of this section elaborates these various points.

18.1.1 Tariff-cutting techniques

Free and open world trade suffered a significant setback in the early 1930s when a wave of protectionism swept through the major trading nations, fanned by the beggar-thy-neighbor mentality that tends to arise during a major world-wide depression. Tariff levels in the United States and other industrial countries reached historical highs as a Prisoners' Dilemma game played itself out. However, by the mid-1930s there was a growing collective desire to break out of this unsatisfactory situation. Among the various attempts to do so, one successful effort was the enactment of the US Trade Agreement Act of 1934. This law gave the President the power to reduce US tariffs by up to 50 per cent through reciprocal negotiations with other countries.

The technique devised was to conduct bilateral tariff-reducing negotiations with other countries on those products for which each country tended to be the principal (or, at least, a major) supplier of the products to each other. This principal-supplier rule reduced the free riding of non-participating countries due to the most-favored-nation (MFN) duty cuts made by the United States and the country with which it conducted a trade-liberalizing negotiation. The item-by-item approach also helped to control the objections of sensitive import-competing industries to reductions in protection, since these industries knew that a specific decision was required to cut duties in their sectors and that the government had pledged not to cause serious injury to any sector as a result of duty reductions.

The negotiating process proved to be very successful, with 30 separate agreements with some 25 countries being concluded by the early 1940s. The average US tariff level fell from about 60 per cent after the Smoot-Hawley Tariff Act of 1930 to about 45 per cent in 1945.

The founders of the GATT adopted this negotiating technique as part of their efforts to reduce world tariff levels further. However, instead of conducting bilateral exercises, multilateral tariff-cutting negotiations were held. In effect, the negotiations took the form of a series of simultaneous bilateral negotiations, but efforts in a particular bilateral negotiation to take account of the results of other country negotiations helped to overcome the balancing limitations imposed by the old bilateral reciprocity approach, as well as the free-rider problem.

This multilateral approach achieved a significant degree of trade liberalization, with the initial negotiation producing an average duty cut of about 25 per cent. Several factors contributed to the success of the duty-cutting process. First, many tariffs had been raised in the 1930s to levels that sharply curtailed all but the most inelastic types of demand. Countries found they could reduce these duties without running into very much opposition from domestic import-competing interests. Furthermore, in many countries producers had not expanded domestic capacity in response to the increased duties of the early 1930s. During the 1930s the world-wide depression kept demand and thus capacity down, while supply disruptions prevented expansion during World War II. Consequently, the vested interests created by increased protectionism were weak in these countries. In the United States, where capacity increases had taken place during the war and the fear of a post-war recession was widespread, there was considerable opposition to permitting further deep tariff cuts, but foreign policy considerations related to creating peaceful and prosperous conditions in the rest of the world were given greater weight by policy makers.

Tariffs, unlike many non-tariff measures, can be measured readily as the ratio of duties collected to the value of imports. Of course, the trade or employment impact of equal cuts in products with similar tariff levels and import volumes can be quite different. But, fortunately, negotiators did not quibble excessively over such matters as differences in demand and supply elasticities in determining whether reciprocity had been achieved. Duty reductions on roughly the same volume of trade was accepted as reciprocity early on. Later, equivalent reductions in tariff revenue based on the initial volume of imports was used as a reciprocity measure.

As successive negotiations were undertaken in the late 1940s and 1950s, it became increasingly apparent that the item-by-item, principal-supplier approach had definite limitations as a technique for continuing the process of tariff liberalization. The difference in the volume of principal-supplier trade between any two countries limits the opportunities for reciprocal cuts between these countries. The multilateral approach can theoretically overcome this problem, but in practice it became too difficult to try to take account of all the trade effects resulting from other country negotiations in determining reciprocity. Consequently, the average level of cuts achieved in these later negotiations was disappointingly low.

Again GATT negotiators demonstrated their innovative skills and commitment to continued liberalization by agreeing to follow a tariff-cutting formula approach. In the Kennedy Round a 50 per cent duty-cutting formula was applied, with exceptions taking the form of less-than-50 per cent cuts or no reduction at all. An average cut of about 35 per cent for manufactured goods was achieved in this Round. To meet the objection of the EC that this type of formula produced insufficient decreases in the dispersion of tariff rates, a formula was agreed on in the Tokyo Round that produced greater percentage cuts for high-duty items. The resulting duty cuts of about 30 per cent reduced average manufacturing duties in the industrial countries to less than 5 per cent.

18.1.2 US hegemony

Despite the ingenuity and commitment of the trade negotiators, the deep levels of duty cuts achieved during the early years never would have been possible without the hegemonic actions of the United States. The industrial capacity of the continental nations of Europe and of Japan had been reduced far below pre-war levels as a consequence of World War II, and the United Kingdom was heavily in debt to other members of the Commonwealth. All of these countries were forced to impose exchange controls to ration their limited supplies of foreign exchange. Consequently, the tariff cuts they made in the early post-war years were not very meaningful in terms of increasing imports; the binding constraints on imports of goods were the exchange controls rather than the tariffs on the goods.

US officials were well aware that cuts in foreign tariffs had little effect in themselves in increasing US exports, while cuts in US tariffs increased US imports. However, they also knew that the demand for American goods would be high, since the United States was the only country with the industrial capacity to supply the goods needed to rebuild the war-damaged economies of Europe and Japan. Furthermore, US political leaders placed a high priority on the goal of rebuilding these economies as a means of promoting peaceful relationships and, after the expansionary behavior of the Soviet Union, of strengthening the so-called free world economically so the leaders of the countries in this group could better resist the threat of being absorbed into the communist group of nations. Significantly reducing US tariffs and providing large amounts of foreign aid were important means of implementing these objectives. The United States was so strong economically that it was politically feasible domestically both to give away some of its output and to not require immediate reciprocity for its tariff cuts. US behavior with regard to international monetary matters and, of course, in the military sphere was also consistent with this hegemonic role.

18.1.3 The changing structure of world trade

US international policies were highly successful in accomplishing their objectives. By the late 1950s most countries whose productive capacities had been significantly reduced by World War II had regained their pre-war production levels and shares in world export markets, and these countries removed exchange controls. Communist expansion had also been largely contained. However, one consequence of these successes was a reduction in the relative economic power of the United States. For example, the US export share in the markets of the industrial countries declined from 35.2 per cent in 1952 to 29.9 per cent by 1960 (Baldwin, 1962). (This figure was still higher than the 1938 share of 25.6 per cent.) The situation with respect to manufactured products alone was much the same. The US world export share decreased sharply from 29.4 per cent in 1953 to 18.7 per cent in 1959, while the shares of Western Europe and Japan rose from 49.0 per cent to 53.7 per cent and from 2.8 per cent to 4.2 per cent respectively (Branson, 1980). The export market share of Western Europe remained unchanged in the 1960s but the Japanese share continued to rise and reached 10.0 per cent in 1971. The US share of world exports of manufactured goods fell to 13.4 per cent by 1971.

Not only was there a sharp decline in the world export share of the United States, but the absence of significant import pressures in major industries ended. Stiff competition from the Japanese in the cotton textile industry was evident by the late 1950s, and the United States initiated the formation of a trade-restricting international cotton textile agreement in 1962. A broad group of other industries also began to face significant import competition in the late 1960s. The products affected included footwear, radios and television sets, motor vehicles and trucks, tyres and inner tubes, semiconductors, hand tools, earthenware table and kitchen articles, jewelry, and some steel items.

The US share of world exports of manufactures continued to decline in the 1970s and 1980s, but at a much reduced rate. The US export share was 13.3 per cent in 1980 and 11.4 per cent in 1988. However, as a consequence of the combination of tight US monetary policies and a very large budget deficit, there was a sharp appreciation of the US dollar in the early 1980s, with the result that the merchandise trade deficit rose from $25 billion in 1980 to $160 billion by 1987. The share of world exports of manufactured goods for Japan rose to 11.2 per cent in 1980 and 12.7 per cent in 1988, while the share for developing countries increased from 9.5 per cent in 1980 to 15.1 per cent in 1988.

By the 1970s the economic adjustments required among nations by the significantly changed distribution of international economic power began to reveal various weaknesses of the GATT as an institution capable of adapting to changing times. These weaknesses became apparent not only to the United States and the nations of Europe, whose relative influence in the world trading system was declining, but to Japan and the developing nations, which had the ability to increase their market shares.[1]

18.2 Weaknesses of the GATT as an institution facilitating the new economic changes

18.2.1 Opening the markets of newly industrializing countries

From the outset of the GATT, developing countries have been subject to less stringent rules on trade liberalization than developed countries, and on several occasions in the last forty-five years these rules were eased further. Article XVIII included infant-industry exceptions for tariffs and quantitative restrictions and, as a consequence of the 1954–5 Review Session, amendments were made to this Article permitting quantitative restrictions on balance-of-payments grounds, and urging developed countries not to insist on full reciprocity from developing countries in trade-liberalizing multilateral negotiations.

An entire new section (Part IV) was added to the GATT in the 1960s. It re-emphasized the need for special treatment for developing countries, and in 1971 a waiver was adopted permitting tariff preferences toward developing countries. In 1979 the so-called Enabling Clause was included in the Framework Agreements of the Tokyo Round, which gave permanent legal authorization for tariff preferences for developing countries, preferences in trade among these countries, more favorable treatment with regard to rules dealing with non-tariff matters, and specially favorable treatment for the least developed countries. Furthermore, the Framework Agreements broadened the exceptions on infant-industry grounds and restated the non-reciprocity principle, although they also stated that developing countries would make further trade concessions as they reached higher levels of development. The effect of these various GATT provisions, according to Hudec (1987, p. 132), is that 'developing countries have effectively been excused from legal obligations regarding their own trade policy measures; developed countries have accepted several formal texts obliging them, in principle, to grant concessions without reciprocity.'

During the early years of the GATT, when most developing countries were mainly primary-product exporters, the developed countries were quite willing to grant these special privileges for equity and foreign policy reasons. But, as some developing countries became important exporters of manufactured goods in the 1970s and 1980s, the United States and the industrial countries of Europe, which were losing market shares to these countries and Japan, began to press for an opening of the markets of the developing countries as a means of slowing this erosion of market position. However, it has proved to be very difficult to modify GATT rules to open up these markets as rapidly as the developed countries believe is justified.

This inability to gain the desired access to developing country markets has been an important source of dissatisfaction with the GATT by the advanced industrial countries, especially the United States. It has provided a rationale for these countries to impose restrictions outside of the GATT framework, such as 'voluntary' export restraints. Furthermore, this issue has been a factor in causing some countries, such as the United States, to adopt an aggressive bilateral and unilateral approach toward the opening of foreign markets, through the use of such policies as Section 301 of the US 1974 Trade Act.

18.2.2 Opening the markets of advanced industrial countries

The developing countries have also been frustrated by the difficulties of gaining access to the domestic markets of the advanced industrial countries. They have long complained about the tariff escalation that discourages exports of more-processed primary products, but they have been especially concerned by the unwillingness of the developed countries to cut back on the production of many simply produced manufactures that the developing countries can now produce more efficiently. The Multifibre Arrangement covering textiles and apparel is the most obvious manifestation of this unwillingness by the developed countries to open some of their domestic markets, but quantitative import restrictions also have been imposed by these countries on such products as footwear, steel and consumer electronics.

The basic problem is the lack of a clear GATT rule requiring countries to eliminate all import barriers on a particular product within an explicitly stated time period. Article XIX permits protection in response to increased imports that cause or threaten serious injury 'to the extent and for such time as may be necessary to prevent or remedy such injury'. In the United States the period can be up to eight years and a new petition for protection can be initiated again after only three more years.

The escape clause is also basically flawed due to the time consistency problem. Factors employed in an industry in which the government reduces the tariff or quota protecting the industry in a trade-liberalizing negotiation are aware that the government also uses tariffs and quotas for income redistribution purposes under Article XIX. In particular, they realize that, if they do not move out of the industry after its protective tariff is cut and they thereby become seriously injured or become so threatened, the government will remedy this injury by increasing the degree of protection again. Consequently, the incentive to adjust is less pressing than if income distribution concerns were dealt with by wage vouchers or an insurance mechanism that became effective when workers moved to another industry. (See Baldwin (1992) for further discussion of this issue.) This helps account for the modest reduction in protection for some products over the years. However, the fact that trade policy, unlike such matters as monetary and exchange rate policies, is highly politicized, so that large (in voting terms) and/or financially powerful import-competing industries can often block liberalization, also has played an important part in determining the pattern of US protection.

Even in sectors in which tariffs and quotas have been reduced significantly, it has been possible to obtain protection against imports by utilizing the unfair trade laws, mainly the anti-dumping and countervailing duty laws. The GATT has been unable to prevent the United States, the European Community and certain other industrial countries from making it easier to obtain protection via this route. (See Boltuck and Litan (1991) for an analysis of developments in the United States.)

Just as the perception on the part of developed countries that the GATT system has failed to open sufficiently developing-country markets has made developed countries more willing to engage in protectionist activities themselves, so too has the perception of inadequate market access in developed nations on the part of developing countries encouraged protectionism in these latter countries. Moreover, this view has led developing countries to pursue various means for getting around the adverse effects of developed-country protection, such as quality upgrading in the case of quantitative restrictions, changing the nature of the product slightly in response to quantitative restrictions and anti-dumping duties, and shifting production facilities to other countries to avoid country-specific import controls. Some developing countries have also reacted by adopting industrial policies encouraging the production of more complex manufactured goods. These efforts have often increased the tension between the two groups of countries.

The perception of inadequate market access on the part of both developed and developing countries also has been a factor in accounting for the greater reliance on regional integration agreements. Many developing and small industrial countries want to participate in regional integration agreements with the United States and the Community because of their belief that this will result in a more limited use of US and EC anti-dumping and countervailing-duty laws against them, as well as in an easing of the various 'voluntary' export restraints forced on them by these large trading blocs. At the same time, the US and the EC recognize that, through regional integration agreements, they gain access to markets that otherwise would be denied to them and can also negotiate rules on unfair trade issues more to their liking than through the GATT multilateral process.

18.2.3 Absence of rules covering business practices and government procurement policies

One of the reasons for the rejection of the ITO Charter by the United States was the inclusion of a chapter on restrictive business practices. Yet it is clear that a major reason for the current trade frictions between the United States and Japan is the lack of GATT rules covering competition policies. Many Japanese firms are members of an industrial group or keiretsu and are interconnected through such means as the cross-holding of shares, intra-group financing, use of a common trading arm, and joint participation in research projects, and these firms often prefer to purchase from group members than from foreign suppliers, despite lower bids by the foreign firms. This may be for such reasons as the joint sharing of profits, the greater supply reliability of member firms, or perhaps for non-economic factors such as personal friendships.

Whatever the reasons for the preferences given to group members by other members, such actions constitute anti-competitive behavior that is inconsistent with an efficient allocation of world resources. These practices are usually outlawed under the domestic competition policies of most industrial countries, but the absence of GATT rules in this area prevents countries that are hurt by those practices from attempting, through the GATT dispute settlement process, to prevent such injury.

The United States and other industrial countries have responded to these Japanese business practices by such unilateral means as bringing 301- and Super-301-type actions. These methods are very time-consuming and often the concessions made by Japan are not extended to all countries. The Japanese, for their part, resent what they consider to be unwarranted 'Japan-bashing', and they seem to drag out negotiations on these matters deliberately. The result is a worsening of economic relations between Japan and other industrial countries and a strengthening of the view by all participants that the GATT is not working properly.

The failure to include rules aimed at eliminating preferential treatment for domestic suppliers by government agencies has been another deficiency of the GATT (and the ITO) that has helped bring about greater reliance on unilateral, bilateral and regional means to achieve trade policy objectives. As political economy theory indicates, government agencies, which generally are less concerned than privately owned firms in maximizing profits, but who do take into consideration political support considerations, tend to favor domestic over foreign suppliers. The code on government purchasing practices negotiated in the Tokyo Round has not had much effect in curtailing government purchasing procedures favoring domestic suppliers.

The greater proportion of economic activity undertaken by state enterprises in Europe, Japan and the developing countries than by state enterprises in the United States makes the absence of adequate international rules on government procurement practices especially burdensome for the United States. While US negotiators in the Uruguay Round have not made the further strengthening of the existing code a priority objective, due in part to the desire to maintain some of the country's own preferential practices, it does seem that the absence of effective rules in this area is a significant element in the disillusionment of many US export-oriented industries with the GATT system.

18.2.4 The failure to liberalize agricultural trade

Probably the most frustrating feature of the international trading system at the present time for the United States and a number of other developed and developing countries is the existence of both high import barriers and large export subsidies on agricultural goods in many developed and developing countries. The high levels of import protection and export subsidization by the EC and the protectionist policies of Japan for such commodities as rice, beef and various fruits have been the main targets of criticism by agricultural-exporting nations, but many other countries also extensively protect their domestic agriculture.

Ironically, it was the United States that was instrumental in excluding agriculture from GATT rules when it obtained a GATT waiver in 1955 for import restrictions applied under its domestic legislation. Other countries now claim the same waiver right for similar import restrictions on grounds of fairness. Now, however, the United States is pressing for substantial agricultural liberalization on the part of the EC as a condition for signing the Uruguay Round Agreement. The divergent views on agriculture, especially between the EC and the United States, have been the major obstacle to the successful conclusion of the Round for the last two or three years.

18.2.5 Disagreements on 'fair trade' rules

Differences among countries over the rules covering dumping and government subsidization are another cause of the weakening of support for the GATT system. In this case the United States and the EC want the rules to be tightened, while Japan, Canada and the industrializing developing countries want them loosened. In particular, US and EC negotiators want stricter rules to prevent the evasion of anti-dumping and countervailing duties by such means as producing slightly different products for upstream or downstream production or channeling exports through countries not subject to these duties. In contrast, the other group of countries claim that the US and the EC are using the fair trade rules to protect domestic industries facing increasing import competition that is based on 'fair' changes in comparative cost conditions, and to prevent them from moving into high-technology sectors. These other countries are especially concerned about the use of the cost-of-production criterion in dumping cases. They argue that, in industries with significant scale economies and learning-by-doing effects, selling below average costs in the early part of a product's life cycle is both a normal and a necessary business practice.

18.2.6 Problems with pursuing new issues

The incident that seemed to serve as 'the straw that broke the camel's back', in the sense of causing the United States to pursue unilateral and plurilateral routes much more actively, was the rejection by other GATT members at the 1982 Ministerial Meeting of the US proposal for a new round to negotiate rules on such new subjects as trade in services and intellectual property rights. This rejection solidified the US view that the GATT multilateral mechanisms had become too cumbersome and that desirable initiatives could be too easily blocked by a few unduly self-oriented countries.

This perception by the United States and other countries of the inability of the GATT to reach reasonable decisions in a timely manner extends to other activities of the organization. One is the dispute-settlement process. Many countries are frustrated by the ability of a member against which a case has been brought before a GATT panel to block the acceptance of the panel's findings by the members as a whole. This frustration is further increased by the practice on the part of some countries of modifying actions found to be GATT-illegal only after a long period of time.

18.3 Adapting the GATT to changing world trading conditions

18.3.1 Earlier multilateral trade negotiations

The existence of various weaknesses in the GATT has long been recognized by those involved in trade matters in their roles as government officials, representatives of private businesses, and scholars. These individuals have been responsible for ensuring that recent multilateral trade negotiations have not been devoted just to reducing existing trade barriers but to formulating new rules covering both old and new commercial policy issues. The Tokyo Round Agreement, for example, included new codes of behavior covering such topics as dumping, subsidies, government purchasing policies, standards, and custom valuation procedures.

Unfortunately, however, the Tokyo Round codes have done little to prevent the increase in non-tariff protection that has occurred in the 1980s through the use of such measures as voluntary export restraints nor in restraining such government actions as subsidizing particular sectors or granting substantial preferences to domestic suppliers of goods and services purchased by governments. Also, few governments are satisfied with the way the dumping code has worked out. Part of the problem has been that many countries, especially developing countries, have not signed the key Tokyo Round codes. But, more fundamentally, the codes had to be so general to gain acceptance by member countries that they are basically ineffective in changing existing practices.

The draft agreements embodying the results of the Uruguay Round negotiations definitely represent an improvement over the Tokyo Round codes. For example, they cover important new areas such as textiles and clothing, agriculture, safeguards, trade in services, and trade-related intellectual property issues. The new articles are also more precise and internally consistent. However, while the tentative Uruguay Round agreement represents an important step in the right direction, in my view it will not be sufficient to prevent the continued erosion of the multilateral approach to trade policy and to restore the GATT to its earlier, more effective role in promoting the multilateral liberalization of world trade.

The rules are, for example, still not tight enough to ensure the opening of the internal markets of developing countries at a sufficiently rapid pace to turn the developed countries away from their increased use of unilateral and regional measures as a means of gaining access to these markets. Developing countries still have great latitude in maintaining import restrictions for balance-of-payments reasons, and the special provisions applying to developing countries in such key areas as sub-sidies, technical barriers to trade, safeguards, trade-related investment measures and intellectual property rights can also be used to delay market-opening actions for long periods.

Similarly, the commitment to market opening on the part of the developed countries in the new agreements is too weak to strengthen significantly the support of the developing countries for the GATT system. For example, while the agreement on textiles and clothing calls for the gradual integration of these sectors into the GATT, the postpone-ment of most of the liberalization until the year 2003 and the inclusion of a transitional safeguard clause raises considerable doubts about how much integration will actually occur. The new safeguards agreement, though a definite improvement over the vague language of Article XIX, still does not address the basic time inconsistency problem discussed earlier. Furthermore, the new anti-dumping code does little to reassure developing countries that the anti-dumping laws of some countries will not continue to be used for protectionist purposes.

The Uruguay Round has also failed to achieve the progress that is needed in certain important fields. For example, the one-page agreement on government procurement merely invites interested parties to parti-cipate in the Tokyo Round agreement, while the agreement on trade-related investment measures goes little beyond existing GATT rules in eliminating trade distortions arising from controls over the activities of foreign investors. Furthermore, no attempt to negotiate an agreement covering restrictive business practices was made in the Uruguay Round, and the failure so far to reach agreement on integrating agriculture into the GATT threatens the successful conclusion of the Round. Although a commendable effort has been made to increase the likelihood that panel decisions in dispute-settlement cases will be implemented and that countries will not ignore GATT procedures in seeking to redress alleged GATT violations, it is by no means clear that the new agreements covering these matters will improve on the existing situation to any considerable extent.

One especially important feature of the December 1991 draft text of the Uruguay Round results is the requirement that members of the new Multilateral Trade Organization (MTO) to replace the GATT must accept all of the various agreements and arrangements negotiated in the Uruguay and Tokyo Rounds. This provision represented a significant strengthening of the organization.

18.3.2 An agreement with new responsibilities and privileges

In discussing possible changes in the GATT beyond those proposed in the draft Uruguay Round agreements, it is crucial to recognize that adapting the GATT to increased regionalism is, by itself, insufficient for making the system viable under the new set of world trading conditions. The shift toward regionalism is just one manifestation of the fundamental problems discussed in the last section, and to deal with the regionalism issue adequately requires confronting these basic problems and their other manifestations.

The ideal solution to GATT's problems is to amend its rules to correct the deficiencies already outlined. This would involve, for example, changing the articles dealing with developing countries so that their preferential treatment does not continue after they successfully begin the industrialization process, promptly bringing agriculture and such products as textiles and apparel within the GATT framework, reforming the safeguard provisions, significantly reducing the degree of preferences given domestic suppliers in the area of government procurement, introducing an effective set of rules covering trade-distorting business practices, and changing the fair trade laws to prevent their misuse to thwart legitimate competition, but also to prevent firms from avoiding the legitimate purpose for which they were intended. Anticipating future GATT problems with environmental issues (see Anderson and Blackhurst, 1992), new rules covering these matters also should be put in place.

Realistically, the chances of getting the entire membership of the organization to agree on such changes is remote. The Uruguay Round negotiations have demonstrated once again how divergent the views of many members are and the unwillingness of many to compromise. At the same time, however, it is clear from the current negotiations that a number of key countries agree on the need for significant changes in various negotiating areas. For example, most of the developed countries have agreed that it is necessary to bring textiles and apparel gradually under the GATT rules that apply to most other sectors. At the same time, a number of important developing countries are willing to accept stricter intellectual property standards and seem to be ready to accept a stricter schedule of giving up special and differential treatment as they industrialize. Considerably more progress in opening up bidding by foreigners for government contracts and in further liberalizing trade in services seems feasible. Reforms aimed at making the organization more responsive to new initiatives and limiting the ability of one or two members from blocking generally accepted decisions also seem possible. Whether key developed and developing countries are ready to accept such reforms as bringing agriculture under the GATT framework, adding a restrictive business practices code, revising the fair trade laws to prevent their misuse and avoidance, and limiting trade-restricting investment policies is less certain.

The lack of consensus for sweeping GATT changes, yet the willingness of a number of key members to make substantial changes in several areas, raises a crucial question for the organization. Should it continue along the traditional path of trying to adapt to changing conditions by holding periodic multilateral negotiations aimed at developing codes of behavior in new fields, or should a less comprehensive group within the GATT accept a new level of responsibilities and privileges along the lines of the GATT-Plus proposed several years ago? In view of the likelihood that the draft Uruguay Round agreements, even if accepted without further modifications, will not reverse the decline in the role of the GATT in world trade, it seems to me that we should seriously explore this last course of action.

The additional responsibilities and privileges would apply only to those countries that signed the new agreement, much in the way that such Tokyo Round codes as the government procurement code apply only to signatories and that non-GATT members do not enjoy the privileges of the GATT. Any GATT member would be free to join the agreement when it first goes into effect or at a later time. Furthermore, new responsibilities and privileges would be added to the agreement, if the initial effort were successful.

The new agreement not only would pledge the members to follow stricter rules, to substantially reduce quantitative restrictions such as those on textiles and apparel, to significantly reduce the preferences given to domestic bidders on government contracts, and to accept stricter intellectual property rules. It would as well set up negotiating mechanisms and schedules for implementing the objectives set forth in the agreement. These negotiations could be either bilateral or multilateral, and they could be driven by the threat of retaliation if satisfactory results were not achieved. However, the negotiations would need to be monitored by the GATT Secretariat for the purpose of preventing outcomes that resulted in increased discrimination against some members or led to GATT-illegal retaliatory action.

In getting members to accept the greater responsibilities and privileges of the GATT-Plus agreement, the GATT would rely on the same motivations that have driven countries toward greater regionalism. Some large industrial countries like the United States want new rules covering areas such as intellectual property rights, trade in services, special and differential treatment for developing countries, foreign investment opportunities, and dumping and subsidization, and, in return, are prepared to open further certain important domestic markets and to act in a less-aggressive unilateral manner. Many developing countries and small industrial nations are attracted by the export possibilities associated with this market-opening and to the prospects of less-arbitrary unilateral actions by the large industrial countries. In turn, they are willing to make some of the changes sought by the large industrial countries. Mutually beneficial gains can also be achieved among developed countries as well as among developing countries.

With the GATT playing the initiating role, such a new agreement would be attractive to most developed and developing countries and could slow down the trend toward exclusive trading blocs, while still furthering the trade liberalization being achieved in the current regional movement. It is important that the three main industrial trading groups (the US, the EC and Japan) be participants in the agreement and that a substantial number of developing countries, especially those who are industrializing, also be signatories. If these countries supported the new agreement, most other countries would be likely to join quickly. Consequently, the net effect would be the creation of a comprehensive international organization whose strengthened trading rules would significantly increase the chances that multilateralism would remain the centerpiece of the world trading system.

Some argue that the difficulty the United States, the European Community and Japan have had in resolving disputes among themselves in recent years dooms any chance that these countries could be part of the cornerstone of a GATT-Plus agreement. However, in my view, such a conclusion is not warranted. Except in the case of agriculture, the disputes between the US and the EC have been mainly over interpretations of particular GATT rules rather than over the basic objectives of trading rules.[2] Many disputes between the US and Japan also have been over the interpretation of existing GATT rules, but the absence of rules covering restrictive business practices has been an important reason for disagreements between these countries on trade issues.

The acceptance by the three countries of all of the Tokyo Round codes demonstrates their agreement on trading objectives. The many liberalizing measures being adopted by the EC in its effort to complete its internal market by the end of 1992 is a further indication of the similarity of views on basic issues of international trade between the Community and the United States. These measures range from eliminating all remaining border restrictions within the EC and preventing differences in technical regulations from acting as intra-EC trade barriers to eliminating preferential arrangements for home-country suppliers of goods and services sold to governments and strengthening the rules encouraging competition. Although the EC is not prepared to extend immediately this degree of liberalization to non-member countries, any more than the United States is prepared to extend the trading benefits enjoyed by any one state to all countries, the Community's '1992' initiative does indicate the type of world trading system this bloc of countries is prepared to accept.

Japan also appreciates the importance of a liberal trading system to ensure its continued prosperity, as this country's early Uruguay Round proposal to free world trade in all manufactured goods shows. Japan has been slow to remove import barriers on certain agricultural products and various internal impediments in services trade, but this reluctance seems to be due more to sectional political pressures and the lack of adequate adjustment assistance mechanisms than to basic philosophical differences on the nature of the desired world trading system. A number of the more advanced, industrializing developing countries are similar to Japan in this regard.

Trade-policy disagreements between the advanced industrial countries and most developing countries are the major cause of erosion of support for the GATT system. The developing countries are reluctant to open many of their internal markets for manufactured goods of export interest to the advanced industrial countries, partly because they believe they deserve special consideration on income-distribution grounds and partly because they observe the failure of the developed countries to open their markets for primary and manufactured products of export interest to them. Similarly, the developed countries are unwilling to remove import barriers on goods of export interest to the developing countries because these latter countries keep out many products of export interest to them. The best opportunity for raising trade and income levels in the world significantly and restoring confidence in the GATT system is to increase the extent of access to the rapidly expanding markets in developing countries and to open more fully the markets for simply produced manufactured goods in developed countries.

It is possible, of course, that the number of negotiating areas in which agreements on greater responsibilities and privileges could be reached would be too small to warrant a GATT-Plus agreement. Furthermore, even if an agreement along the lines described is negotiated, it may not be sufficient to halt the decline in the effectiveness of the GATT. But the disastrous outcome that is possible, if the erosion of a rule-based, multilateral system of international trade continues, makes a serious effort to negotiate a GATT-Plus type agreement very much worthwhile.

18.4 Summary

This chapter considers two questions: why was the GATT so successful in facilitating trade liberalization in its early years, and what changes can now be made in the trading system to halt the recent decline in the effectiveness of the GATT in carrying out this liberalization objective? It is argued that the organization was highly successful in its early period both because the negotiating mechanisms used were especially well suited for reducing the high tariffs levels existing at the end of World War II and because the hegemonic behavior of the United States in its international economic relations served to minimize the adverse effects of certain flaws in the GATT.

The principal-supplier rule adopted in the negotiations helped to control the free-riding problem associated with MFN tariff reductions, and the item-by-item technique helped to reduce the objections of import-sensitive industries to trade liberalization by requiring a specific decision to reduce tariffs in a particular sector. These two negotiating procedures also made it relatively easy for governments to determine whether they had achieved reciprocity in the negotiations. As the mutual benefits from trade liberalization became more apparent and fears of its disruptive effects moderated, negotiators switched to a formula-cutting approach to increase the depth of duty reductions. The early post-war negotiations would not have been successful, however, without the hegemonic behavior of the United States in conducting its international economic relations. Because of its dominant economic position, the United States was able to pursue its goal of strengthening the non-communist nations economically not only by forgoing reciprocity in its tariff negotiations during the period when most other countries were forced to impose exchange controls but also by providing a substantial volume of foreign aid to these nations.

These US international economic policies were highly successful in helping to promote economic recovery throughout the so-called free world. However, one consequence of this success was a significant restructuring in the distribution of economic power as comparative cost conditions changed. The United States lost its hegemonic position, while Western Europe and especially Japan and the newly industrializing countries of East Asia became important international competitors.

The economic adjustments necessitated by these changes in world trading patterns revealed various weaknesses in the GATT system that had been clouded over during the US hegemonic period. These include the difficulty of opening the domestic markets of developing countries as these countries begin to export industrial products successfully; the difficulty faced by developing countries in gaining access to the markets in developed countries for such manufactures as textiles and apparel, steel, and consumer electronic products; the absence of GATT rules covering restrictive business practices and the existence of only ineffective rules in the area of government purchasing policies; the inability to reach agreement between the more-advanced developed countries and most other countries on rules governing so-called unfair trade; the failure so far to bring agriculture under GATT discipline; and the inability of

GATT members to reach decisions in a timely fashion on matters ranging from trade disputes to rules in new areas of negotiations.

The traditional means followed by the GATT in dealing with perceived weaknesses has been to undertake rule-making negotiations among all members, such as those conducted in the Tokyo and Uruguay Rounds. While the Tokyo Round codes have done little to stem the erosion of the multilateral approach to reducing trade barriers, due to their vagueness and lack of internal consistency, the draft agreements resulting from the Uruguay Round are much better in these regards and represent a definite improvement over the Tokyo Round codes. Unfortunately, the draft agreements reached to date in the Uruguay Round and the ineffectiveness of the Tokyo Round codes do not make one very optimistic about the extent of reform that can be achieved through this mechanism. While they are a step in the right direction, the draft Uruguay Round agreements, even if approved as they now stand, will not be sufficient in my view to halt the erosion in the multilateral approach to dealing with issues of international trade.

An alternative approach, which is suggested here, is to seek agreement among a subset of GATT members to accept a higher level of GATT discipline and responsibilities along the lines of the GATT-Plus proposed several years ago. This initiative could take advantage of the desire to establish stricter trading rules that is leading some countries to pursue regional agreements with other like-minded countries. The organization would be open to all GATT members at any time and would involve both greater responsibilities (e.g., an increased willingness to open domestic markets and accept GATT panel decisions) and additional privileges (e.g., greater access to the markets of signatories and better safeguards against unilateral retaliation).

There seems to be sufficient agreement among the United States, the EC, Japan and a number of developing nations on several key issues to make the effort to establish such an organization worthwhile. If these countries can agree on a set of strengthened trading rules, most other countries are also likely to sign the agreements. The net result would be a significant strengthening of the multilateral approach to the liberalization of world trade. There are, of course, risks that such an endeavor will not succeed. However, the outlook for the world trading system if the erosion of the multilateral approach continues makes the effort very much worthwhile.

Notes

1. In contrast to the views of the proponents of the theory of hegemonic stability (see Kindleberger, 1981; Gilpin, 1987), most economists and

political scientists do not believe that widespread protectionism is inevitable, once there is no longer a hegemon. Both repeated game theory and the theory of collective action indicate that a liberal international economic regime can continue by means of cooperative actions through such organizations as the GATT (see Keohane, 1984).

2. The EC has now recognized that basic reforms are needed in its agricultural policy and is planning to implement major changes. It has also expressed a willingness to liberalize its international policies in this field, but the United States is pressing for a greater liberalization commitment than the Community has offered thus far.

References

Anderson, K. and R. Blackhurst (eds) (1992), *The Greening of World Trade Issues*, London: Harvester Wheatsheaf, and Ann Arbor: University of Michigan Press.

Baldwin, R. E. (1962), 'The Commodity Composition of Trade: Selected Industrial Countries', in *Factors Affecting the United States Balance of Payments, Part I*, Washington, DC: Joint Economic Committee, 87th Congress, 2nd Session.

Baldwin, R. E. (1992), 'Assessing the Fair Trade and Safeguard Laws in Terms of Modern Trade and Political Economy Analysis', *World Economy* **15**: 185–202.

Branson, W. (1980), 'Trends in International Trade and Investment Since World War II', in *The American Economy in Transition*, edited by M. Feldstein, Chicago: University of Chicago Press.

Boltuck, R. and R. E. Litan (1991), *Down in the Dumps: Administration of the Unfair Trade Laws*, Washington, DC: Brookings Institution.

Gilpin, R. (1987), *The Political Economy of International Relations*, Princeton: Princeton University Press.

Hudec, R. E. (1987), *Developing Countries in the GATT Legal System*, Aldershot: Gower.

Keohane, R. O. (1984), *After Hegemony: Cooperation or Discord in World Political Economy*, Princeton: Princeton University Press.

Kindleberger, C. P. (1981), 'Dominance and Leadership in the International Economy: Exploitation, Public Goods, and Free Rides', *International Studies Quarterly* **25**: 242–53.

Marx, K. (1906), *Capital: A Critique of Political Economy*, New York: Charles Kerr.

Olson, M. (1982), *The Rise and Decline of Nations: Economic Growth, Stagflation, and Social Rigidities*, New Haven: Yale University Press.

19

Regional integration agreements, world integration and the GATT

Richard Blackhurst and David Henderson

Regional integration agreements form one aspect, not always or necessarily an important one, of the more general phenomenon of cross-border economic integration. Current and prospective agreements therefore need to be viewed in relation to other developments across the world which have affected, or could well affect, the economic significance of political boundaries. This chapter addresses the question of how far regional integration agreements (RIAs) make for closer economic integration in the international system generally, both directly and through their interaction with the multilateral trading system as embodied in the GATT.

Closer economic integration may result from one or both of two influences, which themselves may interact. The first influence is technological change, including in particular new or improved means of long-distance transport and communication, which cause the costs associated with cross-border transactions to decline relative to the costs of transactions within geographic regions or national states. The second influence is official policies. When governments act in such a way as to make cross-border transactions freer and less discriminatory, the extent of international economic integration is increased: liberalization and closer integration march together. RIAs are one path to liberalization which governments may choose to take, but governments can also act unilaterally or through broader, multilateral agreements. They may also decide, whether unilaterally or in conjunction with others, to move away from liberalism and toward interventionism. The question of how RIAs affect the extent of world economic integration can thus be rephrased, so as to ask how far they are likely to further the cause of liberalizing economic exchange in the world as a whole.

In the analysis that follows, we review the likely effects of RIAs on the economies of the participating countries, on the economies of countries which are not parties to the agreements in question, and on the extent of integration within the world economy generally. Next, we look at the interactions of such agreements with the GATT-based multilateral trading system. In the final section we summarize our main conclusions.

19.1 Regional agreements and world economic integration

Under this heading we proceed in three stages. We first examine the significance of RIAs, then look historically at international integration and disintegration within the world economy, and finally consider the current situation and possible future developments.

19.1.1 The significance of regional integration agreements

The wider effects of a particular RIA depend on three interrelated factors: the original motives that gave rise to its formation, the form that it takes, and the way in which it changes over time. In reviewing the possibilities, it is easiest to start with what may be termed the purest example, in which the sole object is to bring about closer economic integration within the region concerned. This is a case in which the RIA's provisions are limited to reducing or abolishing cross-border obstacles to trade, investment, capital flows and (possibly) labor movements within the area concerned; and this liberalization of intra-regional transactions is undertaken for the sake of its expected consequences within the region – for example, its effects in widening the market and increasing the extent of competition. Such a RIA is viewed by the participating states as a program of internal reform.

This is how the issues are normally seen in relation to closer integration within an existing national sovereign state. It is not difficult to find present-day examples of national economies within which barriers to integration persist and are a matter of concern. In a 1988 economic survey of Canada, for example, the OECD Secretariat made the point that:

> Paradoxically, while the Free Trade Agreement liberalizes trade between
> [Canada and the United States], significant trade barriers between
> Canadian provinces remain. Provincial procurement policies are a major
> barrier ... Other restrictions include transport regulations, marketing

boards, agricultural policies, product standards and liquor board policies.
(OECD, 1988, p. 75.)

Similarly, a survey of Australia referred to 'the web of inconsistent
regulations and controls' that impedes the free inter-state movement of
goods, services and labor. It also noted the view of Australia's Industry
Commission that when the Single Market has been established within the
European Community, 'trade between the member states of the
EC... [would] be less restrictive than between the States and Territories
of Australia' (OECD, 1992, p. 77).

Suppose that in a federal state, such as Canada or Australia, action
is taken to bring down the barriers that restrict transactions between the
constituent provinces or states. The end result of such a process would
be very close to what the twelve member countries of the European
Community are planning to achieve by 1993. In both Canada and
Australia, there would be a single market. But it would not normally be
said, nor would it make sense to say, that by acting in this way the
Canadian provinces or the Australian states, in conjunction with their
respective federal governments, were creating a 'trade bloc' where no
such thing existed before. Provided that in each case the external trade
and investment regime was unaffected, no new element of international
disintegration would have been created. In fact, closer integration within
each country would have broadly positive effects on economies in the rest
of the world. Insofar as integration gave a stimulus to internal efficiency
and growth, the result would be to widen the market for imports and
stimulate international trade. Moreover, the benefits accruing from the
freer internal market would be shared by all businesses operating within
Canada or Australia, including those that were foreign-owned.

The same argument applies in the case of an agreed program for closer
integration between two or more national states – as between the US and
Canada, or the twelve member states of the EC. Economic integration
within an area comprising several countries is not a qualitatively different
process from integration within a single sovereign state. In both
instances, closer regional integration *in itself* does not cause the region
to become less integrated with the rest of the world, while the benefits
that are generated within the region by internal liberalization give rise to
new opportunities for countries located outside it.

This is not the end of the matter, of course, since there is no guarantee
that the external regime will remain unaffected by the process of regional
integration. For one thing, integration across national boundaries may
well entail establishing a common external regime where this did not exist
before. Such has been the case, in a number of areas, even with respect
to the EC's Single Market program, and it is inevitable when two or more

countries enter into a customs union. In these situations, it may be difficult to judge whether the new joint external regime is on balance more or less liberal than the set of country-specific measures that it has replaced.

There is also the question of the way in which the creation of a RIA affects the prospects for future multilateral trade liberalization. It may cause participants or third countries to reassess the importance they attach to multilateral liberalization. Depending on the extent of its conformity with GATT's rules, a RIA may also enhance or reduce the credibility of the multilateral rules and disciplines.

Much depends on the relative strength of different economic motives and rationales for concluding a regional agreement, and on the ways in which the balance of arguments, pressures and incentives develops as integration goes ahead. Both within and between national states, regional integration may be pursued for reasons which go beyond the efficient working of internal markets. It can be viewed by the governments concerned as one element of a dual strategy, in which the second element is to create a larger and more protected internal market, and thus to promote greater national or regional self-sufficiency and reduce dependence on the rest of the world. Even if this is not the official view to start with, those who hold it, or who would benefit from its adoption, may prove able to influence regional policies more effectively than they could the previous national policies. More generally, however, to the extent that RIAs incorporate, and afterwards maintain, pre-existing forms of discrimination and protection against countries outside the region, these illiberal elements may well owe their existence not to integration as such, but to the protectionist momentum carried over from the previous national trade regimes.

Insofar as mercantilist thinking enters into the establishment of a regional agreement or gains ground as a result of it, closer integration may well go together with a more protectionist trade and investment regime for the region as a whole. This would in itself be a force for disintegration within the world economy, and in addition might provoke retaliatory protectionist measures on the part of countries outside the region. However, there is nothing inevitable about such a development. It is also possible, and even likely, that regional integration will open up new avenues, and create new incentives for external liberalization. The direction of trade and investment policies in every country is the outcome of conflicting influences — liberal and interventionist — and both of these respond to new events and situations. In so far as policies of the participating countries are affected by RIAs the effects may well be of both kinds, liberal and illiberal. But it is quite possible that on balance closer regional integration will cause barriers against the rest of the world to be reduced rather than raised. [1]

One reason for this is that a RIA can affect the balance between pro-liberalization and pro-protection forces in third countries.[2] Faced with increased discrimination against their exports to the member countries, it is not surprising that third countries have an incentive to push to reduce the degree of discrimination via multilateral reductions in barriers – especially if the member countries account for an important share of world trade. Perhaps the best-known example of this is the reaction of other countries, led by the US, to the creation of the EC. It is widely accepted that the signing of the Treaty of Rome was the major stimulus behind the decision to launch and successfully conclude the Dillon Round (1960–2) and the Kennedy Round (1964–7) of multilateral trade negotiations.[3] The subsequent enlargement of the EC was a key factor behind the launching of the Tokyo Round (1973–9), and the inclusion of financial and other services in the EC's Single Market program helped propel the negotiations on services in the Uruguay Round. The pace of post-1960 trade liberalization, and of the extension of the GATT into new areas such as services, might have been a good deal slower in the absence of the 'commercial challenge' posed by the evolution of the EC.

There is in fact no reason to think of RIAs as either inherently favorable or inherently unfavorable to the cause of external liberalization in the world as a whole. Whether or not a particular RIA contributes to liberalization more broadly, and hence to closer integration in the world economy generally, will depend to a large degree on the specific provisions of the agreement and the way in which official policies in the participating countries – and in third countries – evolve as a consequence of it. Integration as such is a liberalizing process. Only insofar as it is accompanied by a shift toward protectionism, which though possible is not at all inevitable, does it become at the same time a source of disintegration on the wider international scene. That part of the current debate which portrays regionalism on the one hand, and liberalism or multilateralism on the other, as warring or contradictory principles is therefore misplaced. The true antithesis, both within regions and in the world economy at large, is between liberalism and interventionism.

19.1.2 Integration and disintegration within the world economy

For almost half a century now, since the end of World War II, there has been a clear and continuing trend toward closer international economic integration – as indeed there had been during the century which ended with World War I. Some of the evidence that bears on this is given in Table 19.1, which compares growth rates for world output and

Table 19.1 Growth in the volumes of world GDP and merchandise exports (annual average percentage rates of change), 1870 to 1987

	(1870–1900)	1900–13	1913–50	1950–73	1973–87
GDP	(2.9)	2.5	2.0	4.8	3.3
Merchandise exports	(3.8)	4.3	0.6	7.6	4.5

Note: For the period 1870–1900, the figures relate to 14 out of the 16 current OECD countries for which information is available, including the seven largest economies. From 1900 onwards, the figures relate to 32 countries, comprising 16 current OECD countries, including the seven largest economies; the former Soviet Union; and 15 countries from Asia and Latin America including China, India, Argentina and Brazil.

Sources: Maddison (1989, 1991).

merchandise exports (both in real terms) for five periods over the years 1870 to 1987. In four out of the five periods shown the growth rate of exports exceeded the growth of output, so that in this respect national economies were becoming more integrated. The exception is the period 1913–50, which is clearly unrepresentative since it includes two world wars and a devastating international depression. The most striking feature in the table is the contrast between that period and the 1950–73 years, in which world output grew faster than ever before while world exports increased at an average annual rate more than ten times the estimated rate for 1913–50.

Many factors contributed to this extraordinary break in trends, but it is clear that one important influence, over the quarter-century to the early 1970s, was a far-reaching liberalization of the trade and payments regimes of the OECD countries. The measures taken included very substantial reductions in tariffs, the removal of most of the pre-war and wartime quantitative restrictions in Western Europe, a partial freeing of capital movements including in particular foreign direct investment flows, and the establishment of an effective system of multilateral exchange and payments with full convertibility of the major currencies. Liberalization was achieved via all three available routes – unilateral, regional and multilateral. Outside Western Europe, however, RIAs were scarcely involved, while within Europe they were only one of the paths that countries took.

From the early 1970s to the late 1980s the OECD member countries took further substantial steps towards external liberalization, though these were not for the most part related to merchandise trade. An outstanding development of the 1980s, to which technological factors helped to lend impetus, was the far-reaching liberalization of financial markets and international capital flows. At the same time, restrictions and obstacles to private direct investment were greatly reduced, and the regulations that bear on it relaxed. As a result of both these initiatives, the world economy has become more closely integrated. Indeed it is sometimes now suggested, quite misleadingly, that an economically borderless world has been achieved or is a near-term prospect.

This, however, is not the whole OECD story. In most of the member countries of this group, and most conspicuously in the two largest trading entities, the US and the EC, there has been an obvious tendency toward greater reliance on forms of trade intervention which are clearly discriminatory. The measures chiefly involved are voluntary export restraints, anti-dumping actions, and other unilateral actions to influence specified market outcomes. Under all these headings, the evolution of policies has been gradual and undramatic, but the cumulative effect over the years has been considerable: managed trade has become an integral feature of economic policies in the OECD area and an obvious element of disintegration within the world economy.

Thus over this period there were conflicting tendencies within the OECD area, though despite the protectionist aspects just noted the balance has remained tilted toward liberalization and closer integration. But these various developments, whether liberal or interventionist, were alike in that they were almost entirely the result of decisions taken by governments either unilaterally or through multilateral processes – due allowance being made for the stimulus to multilateral efforts from ongoing developments in the EC. In the sequence of recent events outlined above, RIAs *as such* played only a small part, which, as in the earlier period, was largely confined to Western Europe.

In this respect – the relatively minor influence of regional agreements – the same can be said of the way in which policies evolved over four decades or so in the developing countries, though in other respects both the actual policies and the trends in policies were very different. Within this group of countries, there has been and is considerable diversity with respect to external economic policies. But from the early postwar years onward there was a clear tendency in most developing countries, by contrast with OECD member states, to move in the direction of greater trade protectionism and closer control over international transactions in general. In this, however, governments acted almost entirely on their own. While various attempts were made to set up RIAs among developing countries, some of these did not survive and none had more than limited effects. In the developing world, even more than in the OECD area, those policy initiatives which actually influenced events were, with few exceptions, unilaterally framed and carried out.

Since about the mid-1980s, a remarkable change has taken place in the trade regimes of a growing number of developing countries – as also, more recently, in certain countries of Central and Eastern Europe.

Substantial liberalization of trade has taken place and is still in progress, while a parallel and equally striking development has been the change in attitudes toward, and in the regulations affecting, private foreign direct investment. In both these areas of policy, non-OECD countries have been consciously moving toward closer integration with the world economy. Once again, however, the actions taken were very largely unilateral. It is only recently that RIAs have emerged as a possible significant factor.

From this brief account of the course of events over forty years or more, it can be seen that external policy regimes across the world were subject to diverse and substantial changes, and that on balance these changes brought the world economy appreciably closer to – or perhaps one should say less far from – full integration. In this process the main impetus came from official policies relating to international trade and investment, and while as usual these policies included both liberal and interventionist elements, it was the former that broadly prevailed. As compared with other channels of policy, both unilateral and multilateral, RIAs were not a major factor. With one important exception, namely the creation and enlargement of the European Community – which, as was noted above, influenced attitudes toward liberalization not only in the member countries, but also in third countries – RIAs had little influence on the extent or direction of liberalization. Outside Europe the story of integration and disintegration within the world economy can be told almost without reference to them.

This conclusion is confirmed by statistics on post-war trade flows. Chapter 2 above by Anderson and Norheim, and Chapter 3 by Srinivasan, Whalley and Wooton, find that the evolution of trade flows outside Western Europe gives little evidence of a 'regionalization' of world trade. While there has been some tendency for intra-regional trade to increase in relation to total trade, the statistics – even those for the second half of the 1980s – do not reveal an inexorable march toward a more regionalized world economy. Rather, it is the increase in international trade in general, relative to the rise in world output, which is the striking feature of the past forty years. As Anderson and Norheim show, that increase has been large enough to permit both an increase in the relative importance of intra-regional trade *and* an increase in the share of countries' GDP that is traded extra-regionally.[4]

It is apparent, moreover, that there have been market-related influences, independent of policy, working to raise the share of intra-regional trade in the world total. In East Asia, for example, the rising share owes nothing to formal RIAs, and even in Europe the same impersonal factors have undoubtedly been at work alongside official integration programs. Thus in relation to changes in actual trade flows, as well as in the record of policy initiatives, RIAs seem to have played an unimportant role on every stage but that of Western Europe.

It is possible, but far from certain, that this situation is now changing. We turn next to consider the possible implications for the world economy of recent and prospective moves toward closer integration within specific regions.

19.1.3 Regional agreements and world liberalization: current and prospective developments

Two sets of events in particular, one in Europe and the other in North America, have given rise to the notion that the world economy is now in the process of being transformed into three increasingly distinct, and possibly increasingly separate, economic regions. Within Europe, the EC is in the course of completing the Single Market. It is scheduled to be joined by most of the EFTA countries in 1993 to form the European Economic Area (EEA); the five largest EFTA countries – Austria, Finland, Norway, Sweden and Switzerland – have applied for membership of the EC and all but Switzerland are expected to join in the mid-1990s, and the EC has signed association accords (the 'Europe Agreements') with Hungary, Poland and the Czech and Slovak Federal Republic, while similar links with other countries in Eastern Europe are likely in due course to be established. Looking further ahead, there are possibilities of still wider membership, while within the existing member states, together with those about to join, there may well be further moves toward deeper economic and monetary union. In North America, the Canada–US Free Trade Agreement was signed in 1988, and with the addition of Mexico has evolved into the draft North American Free Trade Agreement. It is possible that at some later stage other countries in Latin America may join the NAFTA or sign a RIA with one or two of the NAFTA countries.

Outside these two areas, the Closer Economic Relations Trade Agreement between Australia and New Zealand has now created what is in effect a common market (except that there is no unified external trade policy regime), while various possibilities of closer regional association are currently under review in Latin America, East Asia, South Asia and Africa. But it is the developments in Europe and North America that are of particular importance, because of the size of the economies involved (the EEA and NAFTA countries together currently account for almost two-thirds of world output and trade) and the extent to which closer integration has in fact been taken or is in prospect. Indeed, it is partly in response to these events that the issue of closer regional links is being pursued elsewhere.

It is often now suggested or assumed that these developments have created, or are in the course of creating, three well-defined 'trade blocs' – in Europe, North America, and either East Asia or (if Australia and New Zealand are counted in) the Western Pacific region. This is not so. There are fundamental differences between these three areas with respect to both the cross-border relationships that now exist and the prospects for deepening those relationships.

In the Western Pacific only the Australia–New Zealand Closer Economic Relations Trade Agreement goes at all far towards integration. None of the five leading traders in Asia is a member of a RIA, and it is not easy at present to imagine an agreement which would include, for example, China, Japan and Taiwan. Aside from some coordination of policy positions among the members of ASEAN, the countries in the region do not act together when it comes to trade negotiations. It is true that intra-regional trade has been growing fast in Asia but, as noted in Chapter 5 above, this has not been due to official integration agreements and it does not make such agreements inevitable or even probable.

By contrast, the NAFTA does represent a clear move toward regional integration, which may over time embrace more countries. Here again, however, the three countries do not concert their actions in relation to trade matters, and they have not acted together in the Uruguay Round negotiations. Certainly there is no talk of a joint parliament, a common currency or anything approaching a 'United States of North America'. It is only in Western Europe that there is a common policy for external economic relations, which in this case forms one element of a broader and explicit attempt to move towards closer economic and political union.

In short, the world economy is not now, and is not in the process of becoming, an aggregation of trade blocs. Nor is it 'tripolar'. And on present evidence the recent and prospective developments which are bringing closer integration in both Europe and North America will not necessarily, nor even probably, have the effect of systematically raising trade or investment barriers either between these two areas or between each of them individually and the countries that are not parties to the agreements.

It is true that in both cases some aspects of these agreements may prove illiberal. While concerns about 'Fortress Europe' are overdone, they respond to both a strand of thinking and a set of well-articulated pressures which have long been influential within the EC, and which are referred to in a number of the earlier chapters in this volume. It is possible that in the coming years the mercantilist elements in EC policies will gain ground in relation to the more liberal ones; and if so, this may be in part the result of shifts in opinion which closer integration has brought, or because enlargement of the EC has made it easier for protectionist measures to win acceptance.[5] But this is not bound to happen, and the evidence so far concerning the effects of completing the Single Market does not point toward it. Admittedly, the agreement that was eventually reached as part of the Single Market process on a common trade regime for automobiles could hardly be described as a victory for liberal ideas. On the other hand, the governments of the twelve EC member states have explicitly stated their intention that EC markets should remain open to the rest of the world, and in the case of the second banking directive the EC has shown itself responsive to the concerns expressed that its original proposals were discriminatory and protectionist.

With the NAFTA also there are likely to be conflicting trends and influences, even though a 'Fortress North America' has not been widely viewed as a threat. In Chapter 4 above, Smith takes the view that while the final shape of NAFTA depends in part on the outcome of the Uruguay Round, the Agreement on the whole represents a step toward freer trade. One reason for holding this view is that participation in NAFTA should help to ensure that liberalization in Mexico is secured and extended.

It may well prove that, as in the past, new RIAs will not be a strong influence on the balance between liberalism and interventionism in the international arena. If policies within RIAs were to evolve in such a way that they became a force for disintegration rather than integration within the world economy, it is very likely that this would not be due to regional integration as such. Rather, it would be an extension of already established illiberal features of the trade regimes of the member countries that might well have been apparent even in the absence of a regional agreement.

Since the drift to managed trade in many OECD countries over the past decade or more is not attributable to regional integration, the current talk about 'trade blocs' is doubly misguided, for it is both alarmist and complacent. It conjures up a picture of a global trading system which is now reasonably well knit together and in good shape, within which, however, a new and powerful impulse toward disintegration has come upon the scene. Both elements in this picture are distorted. First the new RIAs are not bound, or even likely, to have clearly disintegrating effects. Second, the global trading system is not at all in good shape: as the previous two chapters suggest, pressures for disintegration are endemic within the system, for reasons which are not new and have little or no connection with RIAs.[6]

Insofar as current and prospective RIAs exert an influence of their own on the extent of integration in the world economy generally, this influence in our view is likely to be positive. There are grounds for thinking that both in Europe and in North America the various agreements that are now under way or in prospect will tilt the balance somewhat further toward liberalization. This is partly because of what the governments concerned have said about their intentions; but even more, it is because of what the agreements actually provide – the illiberal aspects are more than balanced by features that extend liberalization among the members beyond what is currently called for by GATT rules. Examples from the NAFTA are cited in Chapter 4 above. In the case of the EEA, there are the provisions for the mutual recognition of product standards, the harmonization of production regulations, and common competition policies among the members. And, of course, the EC's Single Market program commits its members to an even wider range of liberalizing policy changes.

It is also important not to overlook the influence of ideas. As was noted earlier, it is now generally accepted that integration brings benefits through lower transactions costs, wider markets and more effective competition. If these gains result from liberalization within a region, they can be expected likewise, and by the same logic, to result from extending integration still further so as to include other countries as well. The chief economic argument for regional integration is equally an argument for taking integration beyond the boundaries of the region. A growing awareness that this is so may help to ensure that RIAs go together with a more general reduction in impediments to cross-border transactions.

How far such a liberalizing effect will materialize depends to a large extent, as we have noted, on both the actual content of the RIAs and the way in which they are interpreted and administered over time. These can be affected by the GATT-based multilateral rules which bear on such agreements, to which we now turn.

19.2 Regional agreements and the GATT system

Although there were no major examples of FTAs or CUs in place 45 years ago, the drafters of the General Agreement anticipated the need for multilateral rules to guide the creation of RIAs. GATT's principal rules for FTAs and CUs are contained in Article XXIV. Simplifying somewhat, they are that barriers to trade among the participants are completely eliminated (no partial preferences) on substantially all the trade among the members, and that there is, on the whole, no increase in the duties and other regulations of commerce affecting imports from third countries. In addition, the 1979 Enabling Clause permits developing countries to extend preferences to one another within the framework of regional or global arrangements that need not conform to Article XXIV.

The result is an institutional framework and set of rules through which GATT's contracting parties can influence RIAs (in particular those covered by Article XXIV) to help ensure that they are compatible with – indeed, contribute to – a progressively more open world trading system. The main purpose of this section is to consider (1) the experience to date with the operation of those rules and (2) possible reforms to enhance their future effectiveness. First, however, it is instructive to briefly consider how the GATT can help RIAs achieve *their* goals of increased competition and closer integration among the economies of the participating countries.

19.2.1 How GATT helps regional integration agreements

There clearly exists a close link between the pursuit of liberal, outward-oriented trade policies by the participating countries and the likelihood of a particular RIA being successful. The efforts at regional integration in Latin America in the 1960s and 1970s, for example, failed because they were based on the same premises as the national policies of the participating countries, in particular a misguided confidence in the ability of high trade barriers and extensive direct controls on domestic economic activity to promote industrialization and economic growth. The authors of a recent study of current integration efforts in Latin America stress the positive role which liberal trade policies can play: 'Unilateral trade reforms have such a critical role in this integration process that they cannot be sufficiently overemphasized.' Both authors were 'convinced that it will be the political commitment to a liberal multilateral trading system that will determine the outcome of this process [of integration] and, ultimately, the economic prospects of Latin America'.[7] Through its rules, accession requirements and periodic multilateral negotiations, the GATT promotes the pursuit of liberal trade policies, thus creating conditions which increase the likelihood that RIAs will be successful.

Second, the officials who draft RIAs can draw on the General Agreement. GATT's rules and procedures often provide a model for corresponding parts of a RIA. Certain parts of the GATT can be taken over *in toto* when they fully meet the parties' needs or when the parties are unable to agree on new rules for those particular parts of the RIA. A number of examples from the CUSFTA are noted by Smith and Enders in Chapters 4 and 16 above. Both the CUSFTA and draft NAFTA give the participants the right to choose between the FTA or

GATT dispute settlement procedures on matters covered by both agreements. As the recent Agreement between the EFTA states and the Czech and Slovak Federal Republic demonstrates, another option is for the parties to a RIA to include in the agreement an explicit preservation of their rights and obligations under the GATT.[8] In Chapter 14 in this volume Roessler has called this a 'GATT *acquis* clause'.

RIAs typically group countries of varying sizes (as measured by GDP, trade or population). By setting limits on what the larger countries can demand during the drafting stage, Article XXIV helps to protect small and medium-sized participants from the excessive use of economic and political muscle by the larger participants. The inclusion of a GATT *acquis* clause would extend the protection to the interpretation and administration of the RIA as it evolves over time.

Finally, GATT facilitates RIAs by providing an internationally sanctioned framework within which countries can pursue regional integration without fear of jeopardizing relations with third countries.

It is evident from these brief comments that GATT's rules are not exclusively, or even primarily, a straitjacket for RIAs. True, they place limits on what the participating countries can agree to among themselves. But the rules, whose purpose is to ensure that RIAs are consistent with the goal of promoting external liberalization in the world as a whole, also make important contributions to the success of RIAs themselves. From the viewpoint of RIAs the GATT multilateral system is a supportive rather than competing approach to organizing countries' trading relations.

If the GATT helps RIAs, is it also true that RIAs help the GATT? RIAs affect the GATT in two ways, one general and one specific. To the extent that they make a net positive contribution to freer trade and increased predictability of border and trade-related 'domestic' policies − that is, increased predictability of future market access − RIAs support the GATT system by contributing to the achievement of GATT's primary goal. The analysis in the first part of this chapter suggests that, at a minimum, post-war RIAs have not interfered with the pursuit of international economic integration more broadly, and that in all likelihood they have on balance made a positive contribution. As we saw, there is nothing inherently liberal or illiberal about RIAs, they appear so far to have had relatively little impact on trade flows outside Western Europe, and the integration efforts in Western Europe may well have provided a stimulus to multilateral liberalization − mainly via their impact on the desire of third countries to pursue further MFN reductions in barriers − as well as to regional trade liberalization.

When it comes to the question of whether post-war RIAs have supported the multilateral trading system by conforming to the rules and procedures laid down in the GATT, the record is less favorable. This is cause for concern, first because it increases the risk that particular RIAs will contain features that work directly against the goal of increased international integration, and second because the disregard of multi-lateral rules in one area affects the credibility of the entire system of rules and thus its ability to promote international integration.

19.2.2   Experience with GATT rules and procedures affecting RIAs

Opinions vary on the extent to which agreements involving OECD countries have met the substantive requirements laid down in GATT's Article XXIV.[9] There is little doubt, however, that the procedural aspects are not working as well as the drafters of the GATT intended.

The Leutwiler Report, presented to GATT's Director General in 1985, singled out the full range of issues surrounding Article XXIV as a priority area for attention.[10] More recently, the Chairman of the Working Party on the Canada–United States Free Trade Agreement concluded his report[11] to the GATT Council in November 1991 by observing that:

> Over fifty previous working parties on individual customs unions or free-trade areas had been unable to reach unanimous conclusions as to the GATT consistency of those agreements. On the other hand, no such agreements had been disapproved explicitly ... One might ... question what point was there in establishing a working party if no-one expected it to reach consensus findings in respect of specific provisions of such agreements, or to recommend to the participants how to meet certain benchmarks. It might not be irrelevant that the Working Party on the Agreement under consideration commenced work only after a delay of more than two years. As further agreements came along, there might be a risk that they would be treated increasingly superficially and that contracting parties would lose – if they had not already done so – the ability to distinguish between agreements of greater or lesser GATT-consistency.

The Council adopted the Working Party's report and agreed to revert at a future meeting to the issue raised by the Chairman. As of the end of 1992, no further discussion had taken place.

Under any circumstances, such a record would be a source of concern for a rules-based agreement. As was noted above, actions which call into question the authority of the rules in one area affect the credibility of all GATT's rules. Moreover even if it is true, as we believe it is, that post-war RIAs have advanced the cause of multilateral liberalization, there is no guarantee that this will be the case with future agreements nor, for that matter, with the evolution of current agreements. Effective surveillance of RIAs is and will continue to be one of the GATT's most important responsibilities.

This is not the place for an in-depth discussion of options or recommendations for reforming GATT's RIA-related provisions. The purpose of the remainder of this section, rather, is to call attention to some of the issues and suggestions for dealing with those issues that are likely to arise in the course of any future attempt at reform.

19.2.3 Aspects of possible reforms in the GATT rules

When considering reforms, it is important to distinguish between the issue of rules, and the issue of compliance with the rules. If compliance is a problem, and many would argue that it is, then strengthening of the rules without any change in the incentives for compliance would risk creating an even larger gap between obligations and performance.

A number of analysts believe that the criteria in Article XXIV are not the best available for ensuring that a particular agreement will not create problems, either for third countries or for the global trading system. The focus of the criticism is not on the 'substantially-all-trade' requirement, which virtually all impartial trade specialists accept as the key to avoiding a mass of protectionist-oriented agreements that exclude broad ranges of 'sensitive' sectors (see, for example, Chapters 12 and 14 above). Rather, the focus is on alternatives to the 'no-increase-in-protection' requirement.

One suggestion is to require that the formation of a CU or FTA include a reduction in barriers to goods from third countries, a goal which could be achieved in the case of a CU by specifying that the lowest pre-union tariff among the participants on a particular item become the common external tariff (Bhagwati, 1993). Another, which McMillan proposes in Chapter 13 above, would alter the rules to define a RIA as GATT-conforming as long as it did not reduce the volume of trade between member countries and outside countries.[12]

The diminishing importance of tariffs in the industrial countries, coupled with the growing use of administered protection in the form of anti-dumping and countervailing duties and safeguard provisions, is also raising important issues. To the extent that such measures continue to be used by members of a RIA against one another (the EC is the only current RIA which rules out such actions among member states), questions could be raised regarding the fulfilment of the requirement that duties and other restrictive regulations of commerce between the participants be eliminated. There is also a risk that the intensified competition between members of a RIA will increase the use of administered protection against third countries (Bhagwati, 1993). Because the problems created by administered protection are not limited to RIAs, efforts to curb RIA-related abuses are likely to be more effective if they take place not in the context of reforming Article XXIV, but rather as part of a GATT-wide effort to rein in administered protection.

Another issue which is attracting increasing attention, and could easily find its way into a reform effort, concerns whether some types of RIAs pose a greater inherent risk to further global integration than others. It has been argued, for example, that because 'rules of origin ... extend the protection accorded by each country to producers in other FTA member countries ... they can constitute a source of bias toward economic inefficiency in FTAs in a way they cannot do with customs unions' (Krueger, 1992, p. 3). Note that the argument is not that rules of origin are inherently protectionist, but rather that they are an easy target for protectionists. This suggests a strengthening of multilateral rules regarding rules of origin. [13]

A variation on the traditional FTA is an arrangement which has been christened a 'hub-and-spoke system'. [14] This occurs, for example in the case of three countries, when country A enters into individual FTA agreements with countries B and C, but there is no FTA between B and C. When this option – which would have been realized in North America if Canada had not joined the Mexico–United States FTA negotiations, and which continues to arise in discussions of possible future agreements with NAFTA and other countries – is compared to the alternative of a free trade agreement encompassing all three countries, analysts typically stress the possibility that the hub-and-spoke option would be less liberalizing/more protectionist. Reasons include the reduced scope for gains in efficiency, and the increased scope for tailoring the individual agreements in response to protectionist pressures.

Another criticism of hub-and-spoke agreements concerns their distorting impact on the patterns of foreign direct investment (relative to a conventional FTA), as firms face an incentive to put their production facilities in the hub country (Baldwin, forthcoming). Higher administrative and transport costs, as well as increased incentives for lobbying activities, would result in a waste of resources under hub-and-spoke agreements (Kowalczyk and Wonnacott, 1992). Noting that the FTAs which the US has with Canada and Israel have different rules of origin, Palmeter (in Chapter 15 above) adds 'If additional FTAs are made by the US with other countries, and if these FTAs, too, involve separate rules of origin, the result could be the erection of complex discriminatory arrangements that make tariff discrimination look simple, if not benign, by comparison.' Finally, because the expected income gains in the participating countries are smaller under the hub-and-spoke option, the willingness of their member states to pursue further multilateral trade liberalization is likely to be smaller.[15]

One way of reducing concern about hub-and-spoke agreements would be to exercise some multilateral discipline over the nature of accession clauses in FTAs. An accession clause that guaranteed the automatic entry of any country willing to meet the same entry conditions as the founding members would be a check on many of the possible negative effects of hub-and-spoke agreements. Of course, multilateral rules would not necessarily go that far, but there is a case for the international trading community exercising some influence over RIA accession provisions (see Chapter 12 above, and Bhagwati, 1991).

Liberal, rule-oriented (minimum-of-discretion) accession clauses would also help deal with a problem which has to date received relatively little attention, namely the plight of small countries which risk being left out of RIAs involving their key export markets. A current example is the acute concern of a number of small Caribbean countries over recent regional developments, in particular the draft NAFTA agreement. Liberal accession clauses would also discourage the formation of a FTA or CU based on the illiberal goal of excluding certain countries from a move toward freer trade. If the world trading community were to adopt multilateral guidelines or rules for RIA accession clauses, it presumably would be necessary to make allowances for RIAs which involve much more than free trade among the participants. As Winters notes above in Chapter 5, 'in schemes as far-ranging as the EC, an open door is frankly inconceivable. Existing members are affected by accession not only through their trade, but also via factors such as budgetary transfers and shifts in the balance of political power.'

Yet another issue concerns the GATT rights of participants in a RIA. As Roessler notes in Chapter 14, RIAs can eliminate, in the relations between the participants, market access rights and other rights negotiated under the GATT. Examples drawn from existing agreements include an explicit agreement to replace GATT rules by other rules imposing fewer constraints (for example, on safeguard actions) and the loss of access to GATT dispute-settlement procedures, either formally or as a result of an understanding among the participants to resolve all disputes *en famille*. This could be changing, however. As was noted above, the recent agreement between the EFTA countries and the Czech and Slovak Federal Republic explicitly maintains the full GATT rights of all the participants, and similar (but more limited) provisions can be found in the CUSFTA and the NAFTA (see Chapters 4, 14 and 16 above). With an eye to protecting in particular the rights of smaller participating countries, future reforms of Article XXIV might include incentives for RIAs to include a 'GATT *acquis* clause', exceptions being allowed when the participants can demonstrate that one or more of the rights in question is protected at least as well under the RIA as it is under the GATT (as is the case, for example, with the availability of the European Court of Justice to resolve disputes among the twelve EC member countries).

Another aspect of GATT's rules on RIAs which is likely to arise in any future comprehensive look at possible reforms is the provision in the 1979 Enabling Clause which, in effect, exempts RIAs between developing countries from the requirements laid down in Article XXIV (GATT, 1986). There are still staunch defenders of this provision among GATT's contracting parties: witness, for example, the debate in the GATT Council (still unresolved as of the end of 1992) between Argentina, Brazil and Uruguay on the one hand, and many developed countries on the other, as to whether the Mercosur agreement should be notified to the GATT under Article XXIV or under the Enabling Clause.[16] Nevertheless, it seems likely that there has been a change in sentiment on this issue, as more developing countries have come to accept the export-led growth model of trade and development. Indeed, to the extent that one of the key interests of many developing countries in joining a current or proposed RIA is to lock in recent trade policy reforms, they could become advocates of the greatest possible compliance with Article XXIV (Hudec, 1993). While not everyone is prepared to endorse Finger's (1993) observation that 'if the GATT reviews developing countries' regional arrangements of the 1990s against the same standard as was applied to those of the past, then GATT will continue to be a vehicle for developing countries to avoid policy reform, not a vehicle to advance that reform', the thinking behind it finds a wider audience among developing countries today than it would have a decade ago.

19.2.4 Improving compliance

A good starting point for a discussion of how to improve countries' compliance with GATT's rules and procedures on RIAs is a review of the explanations that have been put forward to explain what many observers have judged to be the poor record to date.

One of the most contentious issues concerns the extent to which the 'substantially-all-trade' requirement has been met. Yet as Roessler notes in Chapter 14, a country which lodges a specific complaint that the requirement has not been met is asking, in effect, for the discrimination against its exports to be broadened. This may be why no third country has ever taken the issue beyond the general complaint stage and exercised its right to challenge the GATT consistency of a RIA under GATT's dispute-settlement procedures.

A second explanation centers on the fact that the RIA working parties – like all GATT working parties – take their decisions by consensus. In a setting in which (1) the participants in the RIA being examined are full members of the working party, (2) the FTA or CU – laboriously negotiated among the member countries and approved by the national legislatures – is already in place (the working party examination is always *ex post*), and (3) not all criteria are rigorously precise (how much is 'substantially all'?), it is perhaps not surprising that no working party has ever rejected or required changes in a RIA.

A third factor which undoubtedly influences the priority given to compliance is the presence of overriding political goals among the participants in a RIA, especially when those political goals find support among third countries. The leading example obviously is the Treaty of Rome and the creation of the EC, but non-trade considerations are present to varying degrees in other RIAs.[17] Generally speaking, it appears that the less important the purely trade objectives in the overall agreement, the less inclined will be third parties to mount a serious challenge in the GATT.[18]

Together these three explanations do not paint a rosy picture of the prospects for improving substantially on the past record of compliance with GATT's rules and procedures for RIAs. It is possible to think of institutional reforms that would help overcome the first two, but they would be major and there is no evidence that such reforms would find widespread support among GATT contracting parties at any time in the near future. Indeed, the unwillingness of third countries to take advantage of their existing right to use the dispute-settlement procedures to challenge questionable parts of RIAs is telling in this regard. As for the third explanation, no options come to mind for altering the outcome when Article XXIV runs up against overriding political goals.

This is not the whole story, however. The enforcement of GATT rules occurs not only in the working parties, but also in the process of national decision making prior to the adoption of measures. As Hudec (1993) has observed:

> Although GATT itself never intervenes at this [prior] stage, GATT rules often do exert a major influence on shaping the measure ... There is plenty of anecdotal evidence testifying that the diplomats negotiating each of these agreements [EC, EFTA, EC–EFTA and CUSFTA] were operating under instructions to make maximum efforts to comply with GATT rules, and the actual results of these negotiations testify that a quite important degree of GATT compliance was achieved.

The principal motivation behind those negotiating instructions is 'peer pressure' and the strong aversion of contracting parties to being accused of openly ignoring or violating GATT rules.[19] But this means, in turn, that *ex post* surveillance plays a more important role than might appear at first glance. That is, while experience indicates that *ex post* surveillance is unlikely to bring about changes in an established FTA or CU, knowledge that there will be such surveillance is very likely to have an a priori impact on the contents of the agreement.[20] Furthermore, an important part of any RIA is the interpretation and administration of the contents of the agreement, activities in which *ex post* surveillance can, additionally, influence the evolution of RIAs in a liberal direction.

One step that could be taken to improve on current surveillance efforts would be to revive the practice of regular examinations of developments under regional agreements.[21] In 1971, the contracting parties directed the GATT Council to carry out such examinations – an ongoing activity, as distinct from the one-time working party reports – based on reports submitted every two years by the parties to the agreements. However, the absence of specific reporting requirements substantially reduced the usefulness of these exercises, and they were allowed to lapse in 1987. A decision to revive them is unlikely to noticeably strengthen GATT's surveillance of RIAs unless it includes substantive terms of reference and detailed reporting requirements.

An alternative would be for the contracting parties to agree to extend the coverage of GATT's Trade Policy Review Mechanism (TPRM) to cover RIAs.[22] While the current TPRM reviews touch on RIAs in the course of reviewing the overall trade regimes of countries which are participants in such agreements, a separate TPRM review which focused exclusively on the RIA would provide a much more thorough examination. Such reviews would be limited by the fact that the TPRM is explicitly not intended to serve as a basis for the enforcement of specific GATT obligations, but that would not preclude them from making a general contribution to transparency and to peer pressure to follow policies consistent with multilateral obligations. By examining aspects of RIAs which may arise in possible future efforts to reform Article XXIV, the reviews could also provide experience to draw on in designing reforms. This could include, among other things, the impact on the trade of third countries, the use of administered protection, rules of origin, the operation of hub-and-spoke FTAs, accession clauses, and the loss of GATT rights by participants.

Implementation of the reforms to Article XXIV included in the draft Uruguay Round agreement would represent a modest but clear improvement over the present situation. There are guidelines for calculating the incidence of tariffs and other measures before and after the formation of a CU, as well as for making compensatory adjustments in response to changes in bound rates resulting from the introduction of a common external tariff. Responding to concerns about excessively long transition periods, the conditions for interim agreements are made more explicit by stating that they 'should exceed ten years only in exceptional cases', requiring that a full explanation be provided in exceptional cases, and requiring the working party to recommend a plan and a schedule in its report if the parties to such an agreement fail to include them in its notification. Finally, the availability of GATT's dispute-settlement provisions for resolving conflicts over the application of Article XXIV is confirmed, and there is a preambular reference to the diminished value of agreements which exclude any major sector of trade.

In the area of new rules, the draft General Agreement on Trade in Services (GATS) contains criteria, modeled for the most part on Article XXIV of the GATT, which a RIA must meet to be in conformity with the GATS rules. This is particularly important because in the absence of multilateral rules (the current situation of services), the scope for including protectionist-oriented policies in a RIA often is limited only by the economic and political power of concerned third countries.

A successful Uruguay Round also would contribute in a more general way to the goal of ensuring that RIAs are consistent with the pursuit of increased international economic integration. The reductions in tariffs and other barriers would reduce the degree of discrimination between participants and third countries, while the revised and extended rules would strengthen the parameters within which RIAs among GATT's member countries must operate.

19.3 Conclusions

We draw six principal conclusions from the preceding analysis of the impact of regional agreements on the pace of international economic integration. First, because economic integration within an area comprising several countries is not a qualitatively different process from integration within a single sovereign state, RIAs do not pose an inherent threat to efforts to promote continued integration on a world-wide basis. More generally, RIAs are neither inherently liberal nor illiberal, but rather depend for their orientation on (1) their detailed provisions (2) the way in which they evolve, and (3) their influence on the trade policies of third countries.

Second, RIAs are only one of several factors that led to the substantial growth of cross-border integration from the mid-1940s to the late 1980s. Outside of Western Europe, the story of post-war economic integration (and, at certain times and in some respects, disintegration) can be told with little or no reference to RIAs.

Third, we believe the integration efforts currently under way in Western Europe and North America are likely to have a net positive impact on the pace of international economic integration. Whether or not this belief turns out to be correct, the world is *not* witnessing the creation of three well-developed and inward-oriented 'trading blocs'. Not only does extra-regional trade continue to be very important for Europe, North America and Asia, but the differences between what is occurring in each of these three areas are fundamental, with respect to both existing cross-border relationships and their prospective evolution. [23]

Fourth, peer pressure is a key 'enforcement mechanism' in the GATT and countries generally try to forestall future conflicts by keeping their multilateral obligations in mind when drafting and administering RIAs. As a consequence, *ex post* evaluation and surveillance can have a greater impact on compliance with the rules than is implied by the virtual absence of *ex post* revisions to agreements. Implementation of the provisions in the draft Uruguay Round agreement would improve certain aspects of the multilateral surveillance process and, more importantly, provide for the first time multilateral rules for the services-related parts of RIAs.

Fifth, while post-war RIAs among OECD countries almost certainly have made a net positive contribution to broader international economic integration, the record to date is less favorable when it comes to the careful observance of the multilateral rules in Article XXIV and the efficient functioning of multilateral surveillance procedures. This record is a cause for concern because (1) in the absence of improved compliance (and probably some reforms in the rules), we cannot be confident that RIAs will continue to play a supportive role, and (2) the perceived neglect of the rules and procedures for RIAs not only sets questionable precedents, but also has an adverse effect on the credibility of GATT's rules and procedures in other areas.

Sixth, efforts to improve compliance with GATT principles and rules face two challenges: (1) how to improve compliance in the case of FTAs and CUs which are driven primarily by economic goals, and (2) how to improve compliance when the trade provisions are only a part of a larger agreement driven by the pursuit of political goals. Although the second challenge is a good deal less tractable than the first, the issue of rule credibility makes it important to seek an accommodation that improves on the current practice of tacitly looking the other way when Article XXIV runs up against overriding political goals.

Notes

The analysis and conclusions in this paper are those of the authors and do not necessarily reflect the views of the GATT Secretariat or the member countries of the GATT.

1. By creating a larger internal market, the establishment of a free trade area or customs union (FTA or CU) may reduce the pressure to continue pursuing multilateral liberalization, as some firms or industries find that the enlarged internal market offers sufficient opportunities to capture economies of scale. For similar reasons, if an industry in a small country comes under competitive pressure, the prevailing view is likely to be that there is no choice but to adjust. But if that small country gains unrestricted access to a larger market by joining a FTA or CU, future demands for increased protection to reduce pressures for structural adjustment (coming from outside the area) may receive a more sympathetic hearing. See Chapter 5 of this volume and Winters (1993) for additional reasons as to why RIAs may increase the level of protection.

   One of the factors which offset these negative effects, to a greater or lesser degree, is the impact of competition *within* the larger market on the level of efficiency in the participating countries. As intra-area competition weeds out the least-efficient firms and stimulates increased efficiency in the surviving firms, resistance to further multilateral trade liberalization is likely to decline in the participating countries.

2. This is not the only way in which a RIA can influence the pace of global integration. As is evident from the experience of the EC, a RIA is virtually certain to create pressure within the union for reductions in non-tariff measures which distort trade among the participating countries, such as production subsidies and arbitrary product standards. In the case of non-tariff distortions which cannot be reduced on a preferential basis, trade with third countries will also benefit from the reductions.

3. See, for example, Preeg (1970, p. 26), Jackson and Davey (1986, p. 407) and Hudec (1990, p. 214).

4. This has also been true for important sub-periods of the EC's history. For example, the analyses of Jacquemin and Sapir (1988), and Neven and Röller (1990), covering the years 1973–83 and 1975–85 respectively, arrive at this conclusion, both adding that the only major exception was farm productions (which is not surprising, considering the extent of protection under the Common Agricultural Policy).

5. One source of concern has been flagged by Dornbusch (1989, pp. 354–5) and Curzon Price (1991). They note that the various social policies included in the Single Market program – in particular, the harmonization of policies on such matters as job security, minimum wages and social security benefits – could reduce international competitiveness (especially in those member countries with below average labor productivity), thereby leading to calls for increased protection at the border and for subsidies.

6. See also Tumlir (1977), Jackson (1978), Leutwiler *et al.* (1985), and Henderson (1991).

7. As quoted in the *IMF Survey* of April 27, 1992. The study in question is by Nogués and Quintanila (1993).

8. In Chapter 14 above Roessler notes that the preamble to the agreement states that 'no provision of this Agreement may be interpreted as exempting

the States Parties to this Agreement from their obligations under other international agreements, especially the General Agreement on Tariffs and Trade'.

9. Hudec (1990) has observed that 'Except for agriculture ... and ... the EC's relationship with former colonies, the four developed country agreements delivered to GATT [EC, EFTA, EC–EFTA and CUSFTA] were essentially GATT-conforming.' As noted below, however, other observers – including ones with first-hand experience of the working party review process – have taken a different view.

10. Noting that the EC and the EFTA essentially meet the requirements in Article XXIV, the report continues as follows:

> However, many other agreements presented under the rules, including some agreements between the European Community and its associates, fall far short of the requirements. The exceptions and ambiguities which have thus been permitted have seriously weakened the trade rules, and make it very difficult to resolve disputes to which Article XXIV is relevant.

The seventh on their list of 15 proposals for action reads 'The Rules permitting customs unions and free-trade areas have been distorted and abused. To prevent further erosion of the multilateral trading system, they need to be clarified and tightened up' (Leutwiler *et al.*, 1985).

11. See GATT document C/M/253, p. 25.

12. See, however, Chapter 14 in this volume for Roessler's critique of proposals that involve making the legal status of a measure (such as a RIA) dependent on its economic consequences.

13. As proposed by Palmeter in Chapter 15 in this volume. In contrast, it has been charged by others that a CU is more likely than a FTA to tilt the balance in favor of pro-protection forces because it centralizes trade policy making, thereby reducing the cost of protectionist lobbying. However, for the same reason it also reduces the cost of pro-liberalization lobbying. If, as the political economy literature suggests, protectionist groups generally have an easier time marshalling lobbying resources than do groups advocating freer trade, reductions in lobbying costs may well favor the latter groups. See Hoekman and Leidy's Chapter 10 above for further details.

14. There are a number of variations on the hub-and-spoke theme, including the present arrangement in which the United States has one FTA agreement with Israel and another joint (draft) FTA agreement with Canada and Mexico.

15. The flavor of life for the spoke countries in a hub-and-spoke system is captured nicely in the following quotation from Kowalczyk and Wonnacott (1992, p. 15):

> This conclusion can very simply be illustrated by considering the limiting case in which all countries in the [American] hemisphere are included in an FTA. Then Canada would look out on a hemisphere in which it would enjoy tariff-free trade in all directions, with the expected gains from trade this implies. Compare this to a hemisphere-wide hub-and-spoke system [centered on the United States], in which Canada would see free trade as it looks to the United States, but face a Byzantine maze of discriminatory trade restrictions as it looks towards other hemispheric countries.

16. Paraguay, which will also participate in the Mercosur, is not yet a GATT contracting party (its application to join is currently being considered by a working party).

17. See Cairncross *et al.* (1974, Chapter 1) for a clear and authoritative description of the motivations behind the formation of the EC. Each of the four key motivations they describe is either political or strategic, and they observe that 'The primary aim of European unity was therefore overwhelmingly political' (p. 2).
18. A similar explanation has been offered for the reluctance of GATT's members to be strict about the Article XXIV conformity of RIAs involving developing countries. In this instance, the overriding factors were an acceptance of the infant-industry/import-substitution approach to development, coupled with a view that the developed countries should not make unreasonable demands on developing countries (Hudec, 1987; Finger, 1993).
19. See Blackhurst (1991) regarding the role of peer pressure in GATT's surveillance activities.
20. A presumption that GATT is destined to influence RIAs primarily (only) during the drafting stage is one of the principal criticisms of proposals to revise Article XXIV to include criteria that depend on the *ex post* economic effects of a RIA (see Roessler's Chapter 14 in this volume).
21. This was proposed in March 1992 in the Director General's annual report to the GATT Council (GATT, 1992b).
22. The Director General of GATT mentioned this possibility in a recent talk in Brazil. See GATT Press Release GATT/1551, August 21, 1992.
23. Regarding the continued importance of extra-regional trade, see Lawrence (1991), Frankel (1991) and GATT (1990, pp. 26–8; 1992a, pp. 9–10), as well as Chapters 2, 3 and 6 in this volume. Lawrence's essay takes a generally optimistic view of the implications of RIAs for international economic integration.

References

Baldwin, R. (forthcoming), *An Eastern Enlargement of EFTA: Why the East Europeans Should Join and the EFTAns Should Want Them*, Centre for Economic Policy Research (CEPR) Occasional Paper, London: CEPR.

Bhagwati, J. (1991), *The World Trading System at Risk*, London: Harvester Wheatsheaf.

Bhagwati, J. (1993), 'Regionalism and Multilateralism: An Overview', in *New Dimensions in Regional Integration*, edited by J. de Melo and A. Panagariya, Cambridge: Cambridge University Press (forthcoming).

Blackhurst, R. (1991), 'Strengthening GATT Surveillance of Trade-Related Policies', in *The New GATT Round of Multilateral Trade Negotiations: Legal and Economic Aspects*, edited by M. Hilf and E.-U. Petersmann, Deventer: Kluwer, 2nd edition.

Cairncross, A., H. Giersch, A. Lampfalussy, G. Petrilli and P. Uri (1974), *Economic Policy for the European Community: The Way Forward*, London: Macmillan.

Curzon Price, V. (1991), 'The Threat of "Fortress Europe" from the Development of Social and Industrial Policies at a European Level', *Aussenwirtschaft* **46**: 119–38.

Dornbusch, R. (1989), 'Europe 1992: Macroeconomic Implications', *Brookings Papers on Economic Activity* 2: 341–62.

Finger, J. M. (1993), 'GATT's Influence on Regional Arrangements', in *New Dimensions in Regional Integration*, edited by J. de Melo and A. Panagariya, Cambridge: Cambridge University Press (forthcoming).

Frankel, J. A. (1991), 'Is a Yen Bloc Forming in Pacific Asia?', in *Finance and the International Economy vol. 5*, edited by R. O'Brien, London: Oxford University Press.

GATT (1986), *The Text of the Tokyo Round Agreements*, Geneva: GATT Secretariat.

GATT (1990), *International Trade 1989–90*, Geneva: GATT Secretariat.

GATT (1992a), *International Trade 1990–91*, Geneva: GATT Secretariat.

GATT (1992b), *International Trade and the Trading System: Report by the Director-General 1991–1992*, Geneva: GATT Secretariat.

Henderson, P. D. (1991), 'The world trading system' in *Economic Policies for the 1990s*, edited by J. Llewellyn and S. Potter (Oxford: Blackwell).

Hudec, R. (1987), *Developing Countries in the GATT Legal System*, Thames Essay No. 50, London: Gower, for the Trade Policy Research Centre.

Hudec, R. (1990), *The GATT Legal System and World Trade Diplomacy*, Salem: Butterworth, 2nd edition.

Hudec, R. (1993), 'Comments on GATT's Influence on Regional Arrangements', in *New Dimensions in Regional Integration*, edited by J. de Melo and A. Panagariya, Cambridge: Cambridge University Press (forthcoming).

Jackson, J. and W. Davey (1986), *Legal Problems of International Economic Relations*, St Paul: West Publishing Co., 2nd edition.

Jackson, J. H. (1978), 'The Crumbling Institutions of the World Trade System', *Journal of World Trade Law* 12: 93–106.

Jacquemin, A. and A. Sapir (1988), 'European Integration or World Integration', *Weltwirtschaftliches Archiv* 124: 127–39.

Kowalczyk, C. and R. J. Wonnacott (1992), 'Hubs and Spokes, and Free Trade in the Americas', Working Paper No. 92-14, Dartmouth College, Hanover, July.

Krueger, A. O. (1992), 'Free Trade Agreements as Protectionist Devises: Rules of Origin', mimeo, Duke University, Durham, September.

Lawrence, R. Z. (1991), 'Emerging Regional Arrangements: Building Blocks or Stumbling Blocks?', in *Finance and the International Economy, vol. 5*, edited by R. O'Brien, London: Oxford University Press.

Leutwiler, F. *et al.* (1985), *Trade Policies for a Better Future*, Geneva: GATT Secretariat.

Maddison, A. (1989), *The World Economy in the 20th Century*, Paris: OECD.

Maddison, A. (1991), *Dynamic Forces in Capitalist Development*, New York: Oxford University Press.

Neven, D. J. and L.-H. Röller (1990), 'European Integration and Trade Flows', Discussion Paper No. 367, London: Centre for Economic Policy Research, February.

Nogués, J. and R. Quintanilla (1993), 'Latin America's Integration and the Multilateral Trading System', in *New Dimensions in Regional Integration*, edited by J. de Melo and A. Panagariya, Cambridge: Cambridge University Press (forthcoming).

OECD (1988), *Economic Survey: Canada*, Paris: OECD.

OECD (1992), *Economic Survey: Australia*, Paris: OECD.

Preeg, E. (1970), *Traders and Diplomats*, Washington, DC: The Brookings Institution.

Tumlir, J., (1977), 'Can the International Economic Order Be Saved?', *The World Economy* **1**: 3–20.

Winters, L. A. (1993), 'The EC: A Case of Successful Integration', in *New Dimensions in Regional Integration*, edited by J. de Melo and A. Panagariya, Cambridge: Cambridge University Press (forthcoming).

Appendix

Trends in the regionalization of world trade, 1928 to 1990

Hege Norheim, Karl-Michael Finger and Kym Anderson

This appendix documents the trade and GDP data base used in Chapter 2 in this volume by Anderson and Norheim, for the period 1928 to 1990. It defines the geographic regions adopted, the shares and indexes calculated from the raw data that serve as indicators of regionalization, and the sources of those raw data. Because comprehensive data on the direction of international trade in services are not available, only merchandise trade is included.

Geographic regions

There is no perfect way to divide the world into geographic regions for the purpose of examining the changing extent of regionalization of international trade. National boundaries alter through time; those currently changing in Eastern Europe and the former Soviet Union are but the most recent. Membership of a significant preferential trading agreement might seem a useful criterion, but that also keeps changing, and in any case such agreements are not always regionally based. Perhaps the most notable changes of relevance to the present study are the demise of British Commonwealth preferences and the changing compositions of the European Community (EC) and the European Free Trade Association (EFTA). For this study the availability of data over a long period is important, and meant that it was most efficient to settle on using the regional breakdown adopted by the GATT Secretariat's statisticians.

The seven basic regions used by the GATT Secretariat (and the abbreviations used to indicate them in the column headings of the tables) are as follows:

1. *Western Europe (WE)*, which in addition to the EC and EFTA is defined to include Turkey and the former Yugoslavia. Since the United Kingdom (*UK*) was such an important trader earlier this century, and had significant preferential trading agreements with non-European countries, it and continental Western Europe (*CWE*) are also shown separately.
2. *Eastern Europe and the former Soviet Union (EESU)*, or the European members of the former Comecon grouping including the former East Germany. Trade between the former Soviet republics is considered to be intra-national trade and so is ignored.
3. *North America (NA)*, involving Canada and the United States but not Mexico, although a separate entry is shown for these three countries combined as well (*NA* + *M*).
4. *Latin America (LA)*, which includes Mexico, Central America, South America and the Carribean (non-Spanish as well as Spanish speaking), although a separate entry is shown for Latin America excluding Mexico (*LA* − *M*) as well.
5. *Asia (AS)*, which involves all countries from Afghanistan east that are also south of Russia. That is, the Southwest Pacific islands are included in this region. Because Japan (*JA*) is so dominant it is shown separately, as is Australasia (Australia plus New Zealand (*ANZ*), between which there is a Closer Economic Relations agreement). The developing economies of Asia and the Southwest Pacific (*DA*) comprise the remainder of this region.
6. *Africa (AF)*, which includes South Africa.
7. *Middle East (ME)*, the region south of Turkey, east of Egypt and west of Afghanistan.

The current US dollar values of international merchandise trade within these regions and sub-regions, and between each of them and the world as an aggregate, are shown in Table A1 for selected years between 1928 and 1990 (10-year intervals to 1958, 5-year intervals thereafter, except that 1979 is used instead of 1978 simply because data for the former were more readily available). Aggregates are also shown for all of Europe and all of the Americas, as well as for the world. These data relate to exports; for the purpose of calculating the parameters mentioned below, it is assumed that A's imports from B equal B's exports to A.

Indicators of regionalization

Having settled on a way to group the world's trading nations into regions, there are various indicators available for summarizing the extent to which international trade is conducted within rather than between those regions. The most commonly used indicator is the share of a region's trade that is intra-regional (or extra-regional). The intra-regional shares are shown in percentages in Table A2. To conserve space, just the simple average for exports and imports is shown. The shares for Europe and the Americas (each aggregates of two of the seven GATT regions) refer to the super-region, rather than being an average for the two regions within each super-region, whereas the world shares refer to the weighted average for the seven GATT regions, the weights being the share of each region in global trade in the relevant year, given in Table A3.

As discussed in Chapter 2 by Anderson and Norheim above, intra-regional trade shares are expected to change as the importance of regions in global trade alters. For that reason it is helpful to net out this effect on regional trade by calculating the indexes of intensity of intra- and extra-regional trade. These are defined formally following equation (2.1) in Chapter 2 above. Roughly, the intra-regional trade intensity index is the share of a region's trade that is with other countries in the region divided by the share of that region in world trade, and conversely for the extra-regional trade intensity index. These indexes therefore take a positive number that may be more or less than one, but would equal one if there were no geographic bias in the region's trade, *ceteris paribus*. Table A4 shows the simple average of these export and import indexes. Again, the values for total Europe and for the Americas are as if they were each a single region, whereas those for the world are the weighted average for the seven GATT regions, using the region's shares of world trade (from Table A3) as weights.

It may be that even if the share or intensity of a region's trade with other regions has declined, the region nonetheless has become more open over time to intra-regional or even extra-regional trade. A useful indicator of that aspect of international economic integration is the percentage of gross domestic product (GDP) that is traded internationally (although see the qualifications mentioned in Chapter 2 above). This indicator is shown in Table A5 for total merchandise trade, in Table A6 for intra-regional trade, and in Table A7 for extra-regional trade. Unfortunately, reliable GDP data for some developing countries are not available for all earlier years. For the purpose of generating regional and global aggregates, however, 'guesstimates' have been made of the total trade-to-GDP ratios for those missing years, based on available data for a subset of countries within each region in question. These guesstimates, which appear in Table A5, are limited to years prior to 1958 for Africa, Latin America and Developing Asia, to years prior to 1963 for the Middle East, and to years prior to 1990 for Eastern Europe and the former Soviet Union. With these assumed values and the value of trade data in Table A1, plus actual GDP data for other countries and years, it is possible to estimate both the shares of each region in global GDP (Table A8) and an index of 'relative openness', defined as a region's total trade-to-GDP ratio divided by the international trade-to-GDP ratio for the world as a whole (Table A9). The latter is of course equivalent to the ratio of the region's share of world trade to the region's share of world GDP.

Like the shares of a region's trade that are intra- or extra-regional, the intra- and extra-regional trade-to-GDP ratios in Tables A6 and A7 could have changed through time partly because of changes in the importance of different regions in world trade. To net out this effect, Anderson and Norheim in Chapter 2 suggest using an index of what they call the propensity to trade intra- (or extra-)regionally, defined in their equation (2.4). It is roughly the intra- (or extra-)regional trade-to-GDP ratio divided by the share of the partner region in world trade, and is equivalent to the product of the trade intensity index and the total trade-to-GDP ratio. These propensity to trade indexes are shown in Table A10.

Data sources

The basic source for the current US dollar value of merchandise trade from 1963 is the GATT Secretariat's annual report, *International Trade* (Geneva: GATT, 1987, 1990, 1992). The 1938, 1948 and 1958 trade data are from the United Nations' *Yearbook of International Trade Statistics* (New York: United Nations, 1964). And the 1928 trade data are from the League of Nations' *The Network of World Trade* (Geneva: League of Nations, 1942), supplemented from Japanese sources (kindly supplied by Ippie Yamazawa) in order to add intra-Japanese empire trade.

GDP data in current US dollars from 1968 are from the World Bank's *World Tables* diskettes (Washington, DC: The World Bank, 1988, 1992). For earlier years they are from the United Nations' *Statistical Yearbook* (New York: United Nations, particularly 1954, 1969). For some developing countries, however, data were not available for some earlier years. As mentioned above, the missing values were 'guesstimated' by examining the trade-to-GDP ratios for a subset of countries in each of those regions, guesstimating from economic policy history as to what the ratio was for the whole region, and then dividing the value of the region's trade by that ratio to get an estimated value for GDP. Rough though this method is, these regions at those times represented a sufficiently small share of global GDP for the parameter values calculated for the major regions that are dependent on those GDP numbers to be insignificantly different from their true values. An appropriate degree of caution is required in interpreting GDP-based indicators for the developing country regions involved, though; these are Africa, Latin America and Developing Asia prior to 1958, the Middle East prior to 1963, and Eastern Europe and the former Soviet Union prior to 1990.

(Tables A1 to A10 follow, pp. 441–86)

Table A1 Values of intra-regional and total merchandise trade, various country groups, 1928 to 1990 (current US$ million)

1928	WE	UK	CWE	EESU	TEU	NA	NA+M	LA	LA–M	TAM	TASIA	JAP	ANZ	DAS	AF	ME	World
Western Europe	7738	1835	5903	943	8681												13721
United Kingdom	1078		1078	83	1161												3871
Continental Western Europe	6660	1835	4825	860	7520												9850
Eastern Europe and Soviet Union	1270	197	1073	313	1583												1782
Europe, total	9008	2032	6976	1256	10264												15503
North America						1434	1553	964	845	2398							6534
North America + Mexico						1603	1722	978	859	2581							6777
Latin America						1114	1128	313	299	1427							3192
Latin America – Mexico						945	959	299	285	1244							2949
America, total						2548	2681	1277	1144	3825							9726
Asia											2668	846	144	1678			6232
Japan											604		22	582			1113
Australasia											148	60	31	57			912
Developing Asia											1916	786	91	1039			4207
Africa															150		1353
Middle East																12	259
World, total	16815	5168	11647	1524	18339	5039	5282	2407	2164	7446	5533	1178	870	3485	1558	225	32641

(continued)

Table A1 *(continued)*

1938	WE	UK	CWE	EESU	TEU	NA	NA+M	LA	LA–M	TAM	TASIA	JAP	ANZ	DAS	AF	ME	World
Western Europe	5120	935	4185	600	5720												9415
United Kingdom	705		705	105	810												2420
Continental Western Europe	4415	935	3480	495	4910												6995
Eastern Europe and Soviet Union	1340	410	930	198	1538												1960
Europe, total	6460	1345	5115	798	7258												11375
North America						745	809	592	528	1337							3974
North America + Mexico						795	859	596	532	1391							4084
Latin America						580	584	326	322	906							2010
Latin America – Mexico						530	534	322	318	723							1900
America, total						1325	1393	918	850	2243							5984
Asia											2269	678	136	1455			4584
Japan											843		28	815			1123
Australasia											93	26	37	30			852
Developing Asia											1333	652	71	610			2609
Africa															110		1058
Middle East																10	302
World, total	11580	3744	7836	1050	12630	2799	3014	1701	1486	4500	4232	1110	620	2502	1438	251	23430

(continued)

Table A1 (*continued*)

1948	WE	UK	CWE	EESU	TEU	NA	NA+M	LA	LA−M	TAM	TASIA	JAP	ANZ	DAS	AF	ME	World
Western Europe	8690	1215	7475	890	9580												17970
United Kingdom	1870		1870	87	1957												6300
Continental Western Europe	6820	1215	5605	803	7623												11670
Eastern Europe and Soviet Union	1180	243	937	1405	2585												3170
Europe, total	9870	1458	8412	2295	12165												21140
North America						3440		3490		6930							15650
North America + Mexico							4514		2416	6930							16115
Latin America						2716		1363		4079							7210
Latin America − Mexico							1642		2437	4079							6745
America, total						6156	6156	4853	4853	11009							22860
Asia											3241	445	229	2567			8270
Japan											127	12	4	123			260
Australasia											267	433	75	180			2093
Developing Asia											2847		150	2264			5917
Africa															325		3550
Middle East																282	1310
World, total	23657	7396	16261	2869	26526	9375	9888	6514	6001	15889	8441	626	1436	6379	4209	1445	57130

(*continued*)

Table A1 *(continued)*

1958	WE	UK	CWE	EESU	TEU	NA	NA+M	LA	LA−M	TAM	TASIA	JAP	ANZ	DAS	AF	ME	World
Western Europe	22440	2875	19565	1515	23955												41770
United Kingdom	2650		2650	125	2775												8890
Continental Western Europe	19790	2875	16915	1390	21180												32880
Eastern Europe and Soviet Union	1810	210	1600	6060	7870												10110
Europe, total	24250	3085	21165	7575	31825												51880
North America						6460	7397	4375	3438	10835							22810
North America + Mexico						7020	7957	4397	3460	11417							23532
Latin America						4345	4367	1620	1598	5965							9640
Latin America − Mexico						3785	3807	1598	1576	5383							8918
America, total						10805	11764	5995	5036	16800							32450
Asia											5938	1005	612	4321			13589
Japan											995		70	925			2880
Australasia											578	220	155	203			2359
Developing Asia											4365	785	387	3193			8350
Africa															515		5580
Middle East																419	3995
World, total	43207	9350	33857	9737	52944	17963	18694	9571	8840	27534	15405	2635	2420	10350	7347	2970	107455

(continued)

Table A1 *(continued)*

1963	WE	UK	CWE	EESU	TEU	NA	NA+M	LA	LA–M	TAM	TASIA	JAP	ANZ	DAS	AF	ME	World
Western Europe	40865	4605	36260	2605	43470												64150
United Kingdom	4730		4730	380	5110												11415
Continental Western Europe	36135	4605	31530	2225	38360												52735
Eastern Europe and Soviet Union	1750	250	1500	6870	8620												9730
Europe, total	42615	4855	37760	9475	52090												73880
North America						7880	8710	3800	2970	11680							29630
North America + Mexico						8480	9316	3841	3011	12327							30614
Latin America						4330	4371	1720	1679	6050							11320
Latin America – Mexico						3724	3765	1679	1638	5403							10336
America, total						12210	13081	5520	4649	17730							40950
Asia											8923	1615	855	6453			17539
Japan											1878		341	1537			5450
Australasia											1265	610	220	435			3699
Developing Asia											5780	1005	294	4481			8390
Africa															968		11440
Middle East																390	5310
World, total	69515	13462	56053	9540	79055	22675	23915	9835	8595	32510	20458	5720	3388	11350	13204	3770	154100

(continued)

Table A1 (*continued*)

1968	WE	UK	CWE	EESU	TEU	NA	NA+M	LA	LA−M	TAM	TASIA	JAP	ANZ	DAS	AF	ME	World
Western Europe	65105	6520	58585	4642	69747												101510
United Kingdom	6120		6120	540	6660												30534
Continental Western Europe	58985	6520	52465	4102	63087												70976
Eastern Europe and Soviet Union	4860	375	4485	15220	20080												24900
Europe, total	69965	6895	63070	19862	89827												126410
North America						16460	17840	5745	4365	22205							46510
North America + Mexico						17195	18575	5846	4466	23041							47795
Latin America						5355	5456	2420	2319	7775							13860
Latin America − Mexico						4620	4721	2319	2218	6939							12575
America, total						21815	23296	8165	6684	29980							60370
Asia											11642	4840	1067	5735			30550
Japan											2405		485	1920			12970
Australasia											1620	880	230	510			4300
Developing Asia											7617	3960	352	3305			13280
Africa															1070		11930
Middle East																610	8770
World, total	105250	16850	88400	23020	128270	42980	44942	12160	10198	55140	33190	10870	4310	18010	11470	6220	239140

(*continued*)

Table A1 *(continued)*

1973	WE	UK	CWE	EESU	TEU	NA	NA+M	LA	LA−M	TAM	TASIA	JAP	ANZ	DAS	AF	ME	World
Western Europe	179030	17458	161572	11647	190677												259455
United Kingdom	15090	15090		770	15860												30535
Continental Western Europe	163940	17458	146482	10877	174817												228920
Eastern Europe and Soviet Union	11810	530	11280	30070	41880												52000
Europe, total	190840	17988	172852	41717	232557												311455
North America						33560	36570	10810	7800	44370							98890
North America + Mexico						35278	38288	11073	8063	46351							101341
Latin America						11035	11298	5025	4762	16060							29510
Latin America − Mexico						9317	9580	4762	4499	14079							27059
America, total						44595	47868	15835	12562	60430							128400
Asia											36279	11499	3408	21372			87670
Japan											11472		1501	9971			36930
Australasia											5745	3453	769	1523			12170
Developing Asia											19062	8046	1138	9878			38570
Africa															1900		26980
Middle East																1310	27510
World, total	269530	38843	230687	50530	320060	92375	96521	31220	27074	123595	86455	34250	9827	42378	23295	15745	582015

(continued)

Table A1 *(continued)*

1979	WE	UK	CWE	EESU	TEU	NA	NA+M	LA	LA–M	TAM	TASIA	JAP	ANZ	DAS	AF	ME	World
Western Europe	478570	61458	417112	30605	509175												703445
United Kingdom	52620		52620	2050	54670												90485
Continental Western Europe	425950	61458	364492	28555	454505												612960
Eastern Europe and Soviet Union	36970	1197	35773	71140	108110												135615
Europe, total	515540	62656	452884	101745	617285												839060
North America						76145	86210	31050	20985	107195							244820
North America + Mexico						82472	92537	31665	21600	114137							253803
Latin America						34815	35503	18655	17967	53470							88750
Latin America – Mexico						28488	29176	18655	17967	47143							79767
America, total						110960	121713	49705	38952	160665							333570
Asia											104395	31541	9486	63368			255200
Japan											28883	5826	3168	25715			103030
Australasia											12145		1506	4813			23372
Developing Asia											63367	25715	4812	32840			128798
Africa															4455		85255
Middle East																7310	148000
World, total	742075	102413	639662	127590	869665	263235	277889	94935	80281	358170	253450	95435	20618	137397	71355	78295	1661125

(continued)

Table A1 (*continued*)

1983	WE	UK	CWE	EESU	TEU	NA	NA+M	LA	LA−M	TAM	TASIA	JAP	ANZ	DAS	AF	ME	World
Western Europe	464805	61217	403588	30060	494865												709540
United Kingdom	51214	61217	51214	763	51977												91650
Continental Western Europe	413591	61217	352374	29297	442888												617890
Eastern Europe and Soviet Union	45640	864	44776	96235	141875												18005
Europe, total	510445	62081	448364	126295	636740												889545
North America						93835	99548	27110	21397	120945							272140
North America + Mexico						107305	113018	28856	23143	136161							297699
Latin America						46200	46513	17460	17147	63660							109200
Latin America − Mexico						32730	33043	15714	15401	48444							83641
America, total						140035	146061	44570	38544	184605							381340
Asia											146281	37804	14897	93580			357790
Japan											47592		8194	39398			146800
Australasia											13190	5872	1501	5817			26054
Developing Asia											85499	31932	5202	48365			184936
Africa															3375		77540
Middle East																9265	123000
World, total	727400	100075	627325	156020	883420	321875	332771	87800	76904	409675	323020	126437	26791	169792	79160	112380	1844605

(*continued*)

Table A1 *(continued)*

1990	WE	UK	CWE	EESU	TEU	NA	NA+M	LA	LA–M	TAM	TASIA	JAP	ANZ	DAS	AF	ME	World
Western Europe	1164150	146000	1018150	45410	1209560												1612750
United Kingdom	115000		115000	2000	117000												185160
Continental Western Europe	1049150	146000	903150	43410	1092560												1427590
Eastern Europe and Soviet Union	62290	3000	59290	76920	139210												181650
Europe, total	1226440	149000	1077440	122330	1348770												179440
North America						177950	211575	55750	22125	233700							525260
North America + Mexico						211000	244625	58000	24375	269000							566264
Latin America						68600	70600	19800	17800	88400							148000
Latin America – Mexico						36000	38000	18000	16000	54000							106996
America, total						246550	282175	75550	39925	322100							673260
Asia											358000	85000	22000	251000			791000
Japan											98000		9000	89000			287581
Australasia											29000	12000	3000	14000			49325
Developing Asia											231000	73000	10000	148000			454094
Africa															5900		93650
Middle East																6970	132000
World, total	1618200	222777	1395423	157100	1775300	619710	661348	136280	94642	755990	703000	235368	51533	416099	90500	92360	3485000

Table A2 Shares of intra-regional trade in total merchandise trade, various country groups, 1928 to 1990 (per cent, average for exports and imports)

1928	WE	UK	CWE	EESU	TEU	NA	NA+M	LA	LA–M	TAM	TASIA	JAP	ANZ	DAS	AF	ME	World
Western Europe	51	10	41	7	58												
United Kingdom	32		32	3	35												
Continental Western Europe	59	14	45	9	68												
Eastern Europe and Soviet Union	67	8	58	19	86												
Europe, total	53	10	43	8	61												
North America						25		18		44							
North America + Mexico							29		15	44							
Latin America						37		11		49							
Latin America – Mexico							36		11	48							
America, total						29	31	16	14	45							
Asia											46	12	02	31			
Japan											63		4	60			
Australasia											16	5	3	8			
Developing Asia											47	18	2	27			
Africa															10		
Middle East																5	
World, total																	39

(continued)

Table A2 *(continued)*

1938	WE	UK	CWE	EESU	TEU	NA	NA+M	LA	LA−M	TAM	TASIA	JAP	ANZ	DAS	AF	ME	World
Western Europe	49	8	41	9	58												
United Kingdom	27		27	8	35												
Continental Western Europe	58	11	47	9	68												
Eastern Europe and Soviet Union	63	15	47	14	77												
Europe, total	51	9	42	10	61												
North America						23		18		40							
North America + Mexico							25		15	40							
Latin America						32		18		50							
Latin America − Mexico							32		19	48							
America, total						26	27	18	15	44							
Asia											75	26	4	45			
Japan											88		3	84			
Australasia											55	12	16	28			
Developing Asia											76	41	2	33			
Africa															9		
Middle East																4	
World, total																	37

(continued)

Table A2 *(continued)*

1948	WE	UK	CWE	EESU	TEU	NA	NA + M	LA	LA – M	TAM	TASIA	JAP	ANZ	DAS	AF	ME	World
Western Europe	43	7	35	5	48												
United Kingdom	23		23	2	25												
Continental Western Europe	52	11	41	6	59												
Eastern Europe and Soviet Union	34	5	29	47	81												
Europe, total	41	7	34	10	52												
North America						29		26		55							
North America + Mexico							37		16	53							
Latin America						46		20		66							
Latin America – Mexico							32		38	71							
America, total						35	35	23	23	59							
Asia											39	3	3	32			
Japan											60	0	2	58			
Australasia											14		4	10			
Developing Asia											44	5	3	37			
Africa															8		
Middle East																21	
World, total																	33

(continued)

Table A2 (*continued*)

1958	WE	UK	CWE	EESU	TEU	NA	NA+M	LA	LA−M	TAM	TASIA	JAP	ANZ	DAS	AF	ME	World
Western Europe	53	7	46	4	57												
United Kingdom	30		30	2	32												
Continental Western Europe	59	8	51	4	63												
Eastern Europe and Soviet Union	17	2	15	61	78												
Europe, total	46	6	40	15	61												
North America						32		22		54							
North America + Mexico							38		18	56							
Latin America						45		17		62							
Latin America − Mexico							41		18	59							
America, total						36	39	20	18	56							
Asia											41	7	4	30			
Japan											36		5	31			
Australasia											25	6	6	12			
Developing Asia											47	9	3	35			
Africa															8	3	
Middle East															5	12	
World, total																	40

(*continued*)

Table A2 (continued)

1963	WE	UK	CWE	EESU	TEU	NA	NA+M	LA	LA-M	TAM	TASIA	JAP	ANZ	DAS	AF	ME	World
Western Europe	61	7	54	3	65												
United Kingdom	38		38	3	40												
Continental Western Europe	67	9	58	3	70												
Eastern Europe and Soviet Union	23	3	19	71	94												
Europe, total	56	7	50	12	68												
North America						31		16		47							
North America + Mexico							35		13	47							
Latin America						38		16		55							
Latin America – Mexico							36		17	53							
America, total						33	35	16	14	49							
Asia											47	9	6	33			
Japan											31		8	23			
Australasia											30	13	6	10			
Developing Asia											63	13	4	46			
Africa															8		
Middle East																9	
World, total																	44

(continued)

Table A2 *(continued)*

1968	WE	UK	CWE	EESU	TEU	NA	NA+M	LA	LA–M	TAM	TASIA	JAP	ANZ	DAS	AF	ME	World
Western Europe	63	06	57	05	68												
United Kingdom	29		29	02	31												
Continental Western Europe	75	08	67	05	80												
Eastern Europe and Soviet Union	20	02	18	64	83												
Europe, total	55	05	50	16	71												
North America						37		12		49							
North America + Mexico							40		10	50							
Latin America						43		19		62							
Latin America – Mexico							41		20	60							
America, total						38	40	14	12	52							
Asia											37	12	4	21			
Japan											32		6	26			
Australasia											31	16	5	10			
Developing Asia											45	20	3	22			
Africa															9	3	
Middle East															4	8	
World, total																	47

(continued)

Table A2 *(continued)*

1973	WE	UK	CWE	EESU	TEU	NA	NA+M	LA	LA–M	TAM	TASIA	JAP	ANZ	DAS	AF	ME	World
Western Europe	68	6	62	4	72												
United Kingdom	47		47	2	49												
Continental Western Europe	71	7	64	5	76												
Eastern Europe and Soviet Union	23	1	22	59	82												
Europe, total	60	5	55	13	74												
North America						35		11		47							
North America + Mexico							39		9	48							
Latin America						36		17		53							
Latin America – Mexico							33		17	49							
America, total						35	37	13	11	48							
Asia											42	13	5	23			
Japan											32		7	25			
Australasia											41	22	7	12			
Developing Asia											50	22	3	24			
Africa															8		
Middle East																7	
World, total																	49

(continued)

Table A2   *(continued)*

1979	WE	UK	CWE	EESU	TEU	NA	NA+M	LA	LA–M	TAM	TASIA	JAP	ANZ	DAS	AF	ME	World
Western Europe	66	8	58	05	71												
United Kingdom	59		59	02	61												
Continental Western Europe	67	9	58	05	72												
Eastern Europe and Soviet Union	26	1	24	54	80												
Europe, total	60	7	53	12	72												
North America						30		13		43							
North America + Mexico							35		10	44							
Latin America						36		20		56							
Latin America – Mexico							32		22	54							
America, total						32	34	15	12	47							
Asia											41	12	4	25			
Japan											31		5	26			
Australasia											49	20	7	22			
Developing Asia											48	19	4	25			
Africa															6		
Middle East																7	
World, total																	46

(continued)

Table A2 (*continued*)

1983	WE	UK	CWE	EESU	TEU	NA	NA+M	LA	LA-M	TAM	TASIA	JAP	ANZ	DAS	AF	ME	World
Western Europe	65	8	57	5	70												
United Kingdom	59	9	59	1	59												
Continental Western Europe	66		57	6	72												
Eastern Europe and Soviet Union	22	0	22	58	80												
Europe, total	57	06	50	15	72												
North America						32		12		44							
North America + Mexico							36		9	45							
Latin America						37		18		55							
Latin America – Mexico							35		19	54							
America, total						33	36	14	11	47							
Asia											43	13	4	26			
Japan											31		5	26			
Australasia											53	27	6	21			
Developing Asia											51	20	3	27			
Africa															4	2	
Middle East															2	8	
World, total																	45

(*continued*)

Table A2 (*continued*)

1990	WE	UK	CWE	EESU	TEU	NA	NA+M	LA	LA–M	TAM	TASIA	JAP	ANZ	DAS	AF	ME	World
Western Europe	72	8	64	3	75												
United Kingdom	64		64	1	65												
Continental Western Europe	73	9	64	4	77												
Eastern Europe and Soviet Union	32	1	30	46	77												
Europe, total	68	7	61	7	76												
North America						31		11		42							
North America + Mexico							40		5	45							
Latin America						44		14		58							
Latin America – Mexico							31		16	46							
America, total						34	39	11	07	45							
Asia											48	12	3	32			
Japan											35		4	31			
Australasia											51	21	6	24			
Developing Asia											56	19	3	34			
Africa															6	3	
Middle East															2	6	
World, total																	52

Table A3 Shares of world merchandise trade, various country groups, 1928 to 1990 (per cent, average for exports and imports)

	1928	1938	1948	1958	1963	1968	1973	1979	1983	1990
Western Europe	46.8	44.8	36.4	39.5	43.4	43.2	45.4	43.5	39.0	46.4
United Kingdom	13.9	13.2	12.0	8.5	8.0	9.9	6.0	5.8	5.2	5.9
Continental Western Europe	32.9	31.7	24.5	31.1	35.3	33.3	39.5	37.7	33.8	40.5
Eastern Europe and Soviet Union	5.1	6.4	5.3	9.2	6.3	10.0	8.8	7.9	9.1	4.9
Europe, total	51.8	51.2	41.7	48.8	49.6	53.3	54.3	51.4	48.1	51.2
North America	17.7	14.5	21.9	19.0	17.0	18.7	16.4	15.3	16.1	16.4
North America + Mexico	18.5	15.2	22.8	19.7	17.7	19.4	17.0	16.0	17.1	17.6
Latin America	8.6	7.9	12.0	8.9	6.9	5.4	5.2	5.5	5.3	4.1
Latin America – Mexico	7.8	7.2	11.2	8.3	6.1	4.8	4.7	4.8	4.4	2.9
America, total	26.3	22.4	33.9	27.9	23.8	24.2	21.7	20.8	21.4	20.5
Asia	18.0	14.6	14.6	13.5	12.3	13.3	15.0	15.3	18.5	21.4
Japan	3.6	4.8	0.8	2.6	3.6	5.0	6.1	6.0	7.4	7.5
Australasia	2.7	2.1	3.1	2.2	2.3	1.8	1.9	1.3	1.4	1.5
Developing Asia	11.8	8.7	10.8	8.7	6.4	6.5	7.0	8.0	9.6	12.5
Africa	4.5	5.3	6.8	6.0	8.0	4.9	4.3	4.7	4.3	2.6
Middle East	0.7	1.2	2.4	3.2	3.0	3.1	3.7	6.8	6.4	3.2
World, total	100.0	100.0	100.0	100.0	100.0	100.0	100.0	100.0	100.0	100.0

Table A4   Indexes of intensity of intra- and extra-regional merchandise trade, various country groups, 1928 to 1990 (average for exports and imports; extra-regional trade refers to trade with all off-diagonal country groups, except those in parentheses where the relevant region is Western Europe or Asia)

1928	WE	UK	CWE	EESU	TEU	NA	NA+M	LA	LA–M	TAM	TASIA	JAP	ANZ	DAS	AF	ME	World	Extra-regional
Western Europe	1.13		1.23	1.39	1.13													0.89
United Kingdom	0.85	0.68	0.85	0.50	0.80													(1.17)
Continental Western Europe	1.23	0.96	1.43	1.74	1.28													(0.64)
Eastern Europe and Soviet Union	1.42	0.57	1.77	4.36	1.66													0.85
Europe, total	1.10	0.67	1.28	1.62	1.20													0.79
North America						2.59		1.94		2.27								0.83
North America + Mexico							2.21		1.84	2.07								0.80
Latin America						2.12		1.37		1.89								0.97
Latin America – Mexico							1.96		1.51	1.83								0.96
America, total						1.65	1.68	1.70	1.70	1.76								0.73
Asia											2.61	3.46	0.91	2.55				0.66
Japan											4.17		1.24	4.86				(0.41)
Australasia											0.97	1.26	2.52	0.69				(1.01)
Developing Asia											2.66	5.01	0.70	2.40				(0.64)
Africa															2.37			0.94
Middle East																7.56		0.96
World, total																	1.85	0.86

(continued)

Table A4 (continued)

1938	WE	UK	CWE	EESU	TEU	NA	NA+M	LA	LA–M	TAM	TASIA	JAP	ANZ	DAS	AF	ME	World	Extra-regional
Western Europe	1.14																	0.89
United Kingdom	0.74	0.59	1.27	1.37	1.14													(1.20)
Continental Western Europe	1.28	0.84	1.55	1.47	1.30													(0.65)
Eastern Europe and Soviet Union	1.39	1.13	1.49	2.61	1.51													0.91
Europe, total	1.11	0.67	1.30	1.48	1.21													0.79
North America						2.91		2.07		2.47								0.84
North America + Mexico							2.33		2.01	2.20								0.83
Latin America						2.23		2.30		2.25								0.89
Latin America – Mexico							2.11		2.73	2.13								0.87
America, total						1.80	1.79	2.07	2.00	2.00								0.72
Asia											2.83		0.86	2.82				0.28
Japan											4.65	3.62	0.76	5.75				(0.13)
Australasia											0.93	0.78	3.23	0.67				(0.49)
Developing Asia											2.96	6.01	0.68	2.27				(0.27)
Africa															1.73			0.96
Middle East																3.47		0.97
World, total																	2.16	0.75

(continued)

Table A4 *(continued)*

1948	WE	UK	CWE	EESU	TEU	NA	NA+M	LA	LA–M	TAM	TASIA	JAP	ANZ	DAS	AF	ME	World	Extra-regional
Western Europe	1.21		1.41	0.92	1.14													0.88
United Kingdom	0.81	0.61	0.81	0.38	0.63													(1.12)
Continental Western Europe	1.42	0.91	1.77	1.19	1.38													(0.70)
Eastern Europe and Soviet Union	0.94	0.43	1.20	10.22	1.96													0.56
Europe, total	1.12	0.59	1.38	1.92	1.27													0.81
North America						2.39		1.89		2.11								0.80
North America + Mexico							2.24		1.31	1.84								0.74
Latin America						2.12		1.71		1.96								0.91
Latin America – Mexico							1.41		3.55	2.11								0.69
America, total						1.61	1.55	1.73	1.94	1.77								0.61
Asia											2.74		0.98	2.98				0.71
Japan											4.29	4.09	0.56	5.42				(0.44)
Australasia											1.08	0.56	2.81	0.88				(0.99)
Developing Asia											3.10	5.43	0.89	3.56				(0.65)
Africa															1.27			0.98
Middle East																9.55		0.81
World, total																	2.43	0.83

(continued)

Table A4 *(continued)*

1958	WE	UK	CWE	EESU	TEU	NA	NA+M	LA	LA−M	TAM	TASIA	JAP	ANZ	DAS	AF	ME	World	Extra-regional
Western Europe	1.38	0.75	1.46	0.41	1.16													0.76
United Kingdom	0.89		0.89	0.18	0.67													(1.09)
Continental Western Europe	1.46	0.96	1.70	0.48	1.28													(0.70)
Eastern Europe and Soviet Union	0.42	0.19	0.48	7.62	1.60													0.42
Europe, total	1.14	0.65	1.27	1.56	1.27													0.75
North America						3.07		2.19		2.63								0.76
North America + Mexico							2.72		1.98	2.43								0.70
Latin America						2.42		1.95		2.26								0.91
Latin America − Mexico							2.11		2.22	2.14								0.89
America, total						1.92	1.93	2.03	1.98	2.07								0.60
Asia											3.15	2.70	1.85	3.42				0.68
Japan											3.28		2.38	3.49				(0.68)
Australasia											2.00	2.41	5.77	1.46				(0.86)
Developing Asia											3.56	3.57	1.47	4.13				(0.61)
Africa															1.38			0.98
Middle East																4.25		0.90
World, total																	2.65	0.75

(continued)

Table A4 *(continued)*

1963	WE	UK	CWE	EESU	TEU	NA	NA+M	LA	LA–M	TAM	TASIA	JAP	ANZ	DAS	AF	ME	World	Extra-regional
Western Europe	1.46	0.85	1.50	0.51	1.30												0.67	
United Kingdom	0.98	1.05	0.98	0.38	0.81													(1.04)
Continental Western Europe	1.50		1.71	0.54	1.38													(0.58)
Eastern Europe and Soviet Union	0.52	0.41	0.55	13.19	1.90												0.30	
Europe, total	1.27	0.80	1.38	1.86	1.40												0.62	
North America						3.31		2.11		2.76							0.76	
North America + Mexico							2.77		1.93	2.48							0.73	
Latin America						2.30		2.46		2.34							0.90	
Latin America – Mexico							2.05		2.94	2.27							0.88	
America, total						1.94	1.98	2.12	2.12	2.10							0.66	
Asia											3.96	2.53	2.39	4.99			0.60	
Japan											3.47		3.51	3.40				(0.72)
Australasia											2.61	3.60	5.35	1.58				(0.80)
Developing Asia											5.19	3.52	1.59	7.55				(0.42)
Africa															1.01		1.00	
Middle East																3.37	0.94	
World, total																	2.84	0.68

(continued)

Table A4   *(continued)*

1968	WE	UK	CWE	EESU	TEU	NA	NA+M	LA	LA−M	TAM	TASIA	JAP	ANZ	DAS	AF	ME	World	Extra-regional
Western Europe	1.51	0.67	1.68	0.45	1.27													0.64
United Kingdom	0.82		0.82	0.18	0.63													(1.18)
Continental Western Europe	1.69	0.90	2.08	0.53	1.47													(0.41)
Eastern Europe and Soviet Union	0.45	0.20	0.54	7.30	1.56													0.40
Europe, total	1.24	0.58	1.47	1.53	1.35													0.62
North America						3.57		2.08		3.02								0.70
North America + Mexico							2.90		1.96	2.65								0.68
Latin America						2.29	2.09	3.55		2.56								0.86
Latin America − Mexico							2.09		4.28	2.51								0.84
America, total						2.04	2.07	2.31	2.33	2.21								0.63
Asia											2.84	2.40	2.32	3.24				0.73
Japan											3.81		3.12	4.04				(0.73)
Australasia											2.47	3.26	5.88	1.51				(0.79)
Developing Asia											3.37	4.25	1.52	3.44				(0.64)
Africa															1.91			0.95
Middle East																3.00		0.94
World, total																	2.81	0.67

(continued)

Table A4 (*continued*)

1973	WE	UK	CWE	EESU	TEU	NA	NA+M	LA	LA−M	TAM	TASIA	JAP	ANZ	DAS	AF	ME	World	Extra-regional
Western Europe	1.54	1.01	1.52	0.49	1.33													0.58
United Kingdom	1.12	1.12	1.12	0.21	0.90													(0.92)
Continental Western Europe	1.52	1.17	1.68	0.53	1.36													(0.52)
Eastern Europe and Soviet Union	0.50	0.22	0.54	7.67	1.50													0.45
Europe, total	1.30	0.89	1.36	1.47	1.38													0.56
North America						3.93		2.02		3.18								0.71
North America + Mexico							3.22		1.81	2.81								0.69
Latin America						2.19		3.28		2.45								0.88
Latin America − Mexico							1.92		3.70	2.29								0.87
America, total						2.15	2.20	2.23	2.15	2.27								0.66
Asia											2.88	2.15	2.73	3.25				0.68
Japan											3.43		3.39	3.40				(0.71)
Australasia											2.89	3.58	7.41	1.72				(0.69)
Developing Asia											3.39	3.62	1.73	3.66				(0.59)
Africa															1.80			0.96
Middle East																1.97		0.97
World, total																	2.62	0.64

(*continued*)

Table A4 *(continued)*

1979	WE	UK	CWE	EESU	TEU	NA	NA+M	LA	LA–M	TAM	TASIA	JAP	ANZ	DAS	AF	ME	World	Extra-regional
Western Europe	1.57	1.33	1.51	0.57	1.38													0.58
United Kingdom	1.48		1.48	0.21	1.18													(0.69)
Continental Western Europe	1.51	1.53	1.60	0.63	1.38													(0.55)
Eastern Europe and Soviet Union	0.58	0.22	0.64	7.88	1.55													0.49
Europe, total	1.35	1.16	1.38	1.52	1.43													0.56
North America						3.63		2.17		3.01								0.76
North America + Mexico							3.09		1.87	2.71								0.72
Latin America						2.34		3.80		2.72								0.84
Latin America – Mexico							1.97		4.82	2.59								0.81
America, total						2.06	2.13	2.49	2.44	2.29								0.67
Asia											2.77	1.99	3.18	3.04				0.69
Japan											3.08		3.20	3.05				(0.73)
Australasia											3.32	3.39	10.31	2.73				(0.60)
Developing Asia											3.17	3.24	2.74	3.21				(0.62)
Africa															1.24	0.29		0.99
Middle East															0.29	1.17		0.99
World, total																	2.64	0.68

(continued)

Table A4 *(continued)*

1983	WE	UK	CWE	EESU	TEU	NA	NA+M	LA	LA−M	TAM	TASIA	JAP	ANZ	DAS	AF	ME	World	Extra-regional
Western Europe	1.72	1.47	1.65	0.56	1.46													0.57
United Kingdom	1.64		1.64	0.09	1.24													(0.65)
Continental Western Europe	1.65	1.70	1.75	0.63	1.46													(0.54)
Eastern Europe and Soviet Union	0.56	0.09	0.64	7.28	1.66													0.46
Europe, total	1.43	1.21	1.46	1.63	1.53													0.53
North America						3.63		2.08		3.02								0.75
North America + Mexico							2.98		1.91	2.68								0.72
Latin America						2.25		3.47		2.56								0.87
Latin America − Mexico							2.02		4.57	2.53								0.84
America, total						2.05	2.09	2.34	2.37	2.23								0.67
Asia											2.41	1.69	2.86	2.66				0.69
Japan											2.62		3.30	2.52				(0.73)
Australasia											2.97	3.54	7.88	2.17				(0.57)
Developing Asia											2.79	2.71	2.17	2.95				(0.60)
Africa															1.03			1.00
Middle East																1.38		0.98
World, total																	2.68	0.66

(continued)

Table A4 *(continued)*

1990	WE	UK	CWE	EESU	TEU	NA	NA+M	LA	LA–M	TAM	TASIA	JAP	ANZ	DAS	AF	ME	World	Extra-regional
Western Europe	1.60	1.34	1.54	0.66	1.47													0.51
United Kingdom	1.48		1.48	0.23	1.27													(0.64)
Continental Western Europe	1.54	1.54	1.64	0.73	1.47													(0.46)
Eastern Europe and Soviet Union	0.68	0.25	0.74	10.88	1.51													0.57
Europe, total	1.44	1.24	1.47	1.48	1.51													0.49
North America						3.50		2.44		3.14								0.75
North America + Mexico							3.21		1.63	2.90								0.67
Latin America						2.66		3.53		2.83								0.90
Latin America – Mexico							1.73		5.70	2.26								0.86
America, total						2.05	2.20	2.58	2.12	2.26								0.68
Asia											2.31	1.63	2.38	2.51				0.66
Japan											2.33		2.64	2.30				(0.70)
Australasia											2.47	2.84	8.17	1.92				(0.62)
Developing Asia											2.64	2.47	1.92	2.83				(0.56)
Africa															2.48			0.96
Middle East																2.23		0.96
World, total																	2.62	0.62

Table A5 Total trade as a share of GDP, various country groups, 1928 to 1990 (total merchandise exports plus imports as a percentage of GDP)

	1928	1938	1948	1958	1963	1968	1973	1979	1983	1990
Western Europe	33.5	24.0	35.4	33.5	31.4	33.8	42.7	47.5	43.3	45.8
United Kingdom	44.3	27.2	33.2	32.4	29.3	46.6	38.3	46.9	36.9	41.8
Continental Western Europe	30.4	22.9	36.6	33.8	31.9	31.2	43.5	47.6	44.4	46.5
Eastern Europe and Soviet Union	30.0	25.0	25.0	25.0	30.0	40.0	40.0	40.0	40.0	41.5
Europe, total	33.1	24.1	33.6	31.5	31.2	34.8	42.3	46.2	42.6	45.4
North America	10.4	7.5	10.7	9.2	8.2	9.5	13.0	19.4	16.1	19.2
North America + Mexico	10.7	7.8	10.9	9.3	8.4	9.6	13.0	19.3	16.3	19.8
Latin America	45.0	30.0	30.0	29.8	24.6	21.4	24.7	26.7	25.4	27.5
Latin America – Mexico	45.7	30.3	31.1	32.5	26.9	24.0	28.6	28.9	27.2	25.4
America, total	13.9	10.2	13.9	11.8	10.2	10.9	14.7	20.9	17.7	20.4
Asia	31.9	24.1	24.6	26.3	21.5	21.2	23.3	27.3	26.9	29.2
Japan	35.0	23.6	8.0	18.6	16.4	16.6	20.4	19.9	22.2	17.8
Australasia	38.1	21.7	46.6	31.0	28.9	24.5	28.9	29.2	23.8	29.8
Developing Asia	30.0	25.0	25.0	28.7	23.5	25.8	25.0	37.3	33.0	47.2
Africa	60.0	50.0	50.0	45.8	56.3	38.3	40.8	48.2	36.6	48.8
Middle East	60.0	50.0	50.0	58.0	36.8	37.2	47.5	56.1	50.9	53.2
World, total	24.3	19.8	22.4	21.7	21.1	21.8	27.9	34.6	30.6	33.5

Table A6 Intra-regional trade as a share of GDP, various country groups, 1928 to 1990 (intra-regional (as defined in Table A4) merchandise exports plus imports as a percentage of GDP)

	1928	1938	1948	1958	1963	1968	1973	1979	1983	1990
Western Europe	17.0	11.7	14.8	17.7	19.2	21.3	28.9	31.5	28.0	33.0
United Kingdom	(14.3)	(7.2)	(7.5)	(9.8)	(11.0)	(12.4)	(18.0)	(27.7)	(21.6)	(26.8)
Continental Western Europe	(13.6)	(10.8)	(14.7)	(17.1)	(18.5)	(20.5)	(27.7)	(27.7)	(25.2)	(29.7)
Eastern Europe and Soviet Union	5.7	3.3	11.6	15.3	21.4	25.4	23.5	21.6	22.9	18.8
Europe, total	20.1	14.6	17.2	19.1	21.3	24.5	31.1	33.4	30.6	34.3
North America	2.6	1.7	2.9	2.9	2.5	3.5	4.6	5.8	5.1	6.0
North America + Mexico	3.1	1.9	3.8	3.5	2.9	3.9	5.0	6.7	5.8	7.9
Latin America	5.0	5.3	6.0	5.0	4.0	4.0	4.1	5.4	4.5	3.8
Latin America – Mexico	5.1	5.7	11.9	5.8	4.7	4.7	4.8	6.5	5.2	4.0
America, total	6.2	4.4	7.9	6.6	4.9	5.7	7.1	9.7	8.3	9.2
Asia	14.5	16.0	9.6	10.8	10.1	7.8	9.7	11.2	11.6	14.0
Japan	(22.2)	(19.9)	(5.2)	(6.7)	(5.1)	(5.0)	(6.6)	(6.1)	(6.9)	(6.2)
Australasia	(6.2)	(5.0)	(6.6)	(7.7)	(8.6)	(7.7)	(12.0)	(14.3)	(12.6)	(15.0)
Developing Asia	(14.0)	(17.2)	(11.0)	(13.3)	(14.6)	(11.0)	(12.5)	(17.8)	(16.7)	(26.2)
Africa	6.2	4.4	4.2	3.7	4.4	3.5	3.1	2.7	1.6	3.1
Middle East	3.0	1.8	10.2	7.0	3.2	3.0	2.9	3.6	4.0	3.3
World, total	9.4	7.4	7.3	8.8	9.3	10.3	13.8	15.9	13.8	17.4

Table A7 Extra-regional trade as a share of GDP, various country groups, 1928 to 1990 (extra-regional (as defined in Table A4) merchandise exports plus imports as a percentage of GDP)

	1928	1938	1948	1958	1963	1968	1973	1979	1983	1990
Western Europe	16.5	12.3	20.6	15.8	12.2	12.5	13.8	16.1	15.3	12.8
United Kingdom	(30.0)	(19.9)	(25.7)	(22.6)	(18.3)	(34.1)	(20.3)	(19.1)	(15.2)	(15.1)
Continental Western Europe	(16.7)	(12.2)	(21.9)	(16.7)	(13.4)	(10.7)	(25.8)	(19.9)	(19.3)	(16.7)
Eastern Europe and Soviet Union	24.3	21.7	13.4	9.7	8.6	14.6	16.5	18.4	17.1	22.7
Europe, total	13.0	9.5	16.5	12.4	10.0	10.2	11.1	12.8	12.0	11.1
North America	7.8	5.9	7.8	6.3	5.7	6.0	8.5	13.6	11.0	13.2
North America + Mexico	7.7	5.9	7.1	5.8	5.5	5.8	8.0	12.6	10.5	11.9
Latin America	40.0	24.7	24.0	24.8	20.6	17.4	10.6	21.3	20.9	23.7
Latin America – Mexico	40.6	24.6	19.2	26.8	22.2	19.4	23.8	22.4	22.0	21.4
America, total	7.7	5.9	6.0	5.2	6.3	5.2	7.7	11.2	9.5	11.2
Asia	17.4	8.1	15.1	15.5	11.4	13.5	13.6	16.1	15.4	15.2
Japan	(23.9)	(3.7)	(2.8)	(11.8)	(11.3)	(11.5)	(13.8)	(13.8)	(15.3)	(11.6)
Australasia	(36.8)	(20.0)	(44.7)	(29.0)	(27.1)	(23.2)	(26.9)	(27.2)	(22.4)	(28.0)
Developing Asia	(22.0)	(17.5)	(15.8)	(18.9)	(12.9)	(20.4)	(18.9)	(28.1)	(24.0)	(31.2)
Africa	53.8	45.6	45.8	42.2	51.9	34.8	37.7	45.5	35.0	45.6
Middle East	57.0	48.2	40.0	51.0	33.6	34.2	44.6	52.5	46.9	50.0
World, total	14.9	12.4	14.9	12.9	11.8	11.6	14.2	18.8	17.4	16.1

Table A8 Shares of world GDP, various country groups, 1928 to 1990 (per cent, based on current US dollars)

	1928	1938	1948	1958	1963	1968	1973	1979	1983	1990
Western Europe	34.0	36.9	23.0	25.6	29.2	27.9	29.7	31.7	27.6	33.9
United Kingdom	7.6	9.6	8.1	5.7	5.8	4.6	4.4	4.3	4.3	4.7
Continental Western Europe	26.4	27.3	15.0	19.9	23.4	23.3	25.3	27.4	23.3	29.2
Eastern Europe and Soviet Union	4.1	5.1	4.7	8.0	4.4	5.5	6.2	6.9	7.0	3.9
Europe, total	38.1	42.0	27.8	33.6	33.6	33.4	35.8	38.6	34.6	37.9
North America	41.4	38.1	45.9	44.7	43.7	42.8	35.2	27.3	30.6	28.7
North America + Mexico	41.9	38.6	46.8	45.7	44.8	44.0	36.5	28.7	32.1	29.8
Latin America	4.6	5.2	9.0	6.5	5.9	5.6	5.9	7.2	6.4	5.0
Latin America – Mexico	4.2	4.7	8.0	5.5	4.8	4.3	4.6	5.8	4.9	3.8
America, total	46.1	43.4	54.8	51.2	49.6	48.3	41.1	34.5	37.0	33.7
Asia	13.7	12.0	13.3	11.1	12.1	13.7	18.0	19.4	21.0	24.7
Japan	2.4	3.2	2.2	3.0	4.7	6.6	8.4	10.4	10.2	14.2
Australasia	1.7	1.9	1.5	1.55	1.7	1.6	1.8	1.6	1.9	1.6
Developing Asia	9.6	6.9	9.6	6.6	5.8	5.5	7.8	7.4	8.9	8.9
Africa	1.8	2.1	3.0	2.8	3.0	2.8	3.0	3.4	3.6	1.8
Middle East	0.3	0.5	1.1	1.2	1.7	1.8	2.2	4.2	3.8	2.0
World, total	100.0	100.0	100.0	100.0	100.0	100.0	100.0	100.0	100.0	100.0

Table A9 Index of 'relative openness', various country groups, 1928 to 1990 (group total trade-to-GDP ratio divided by the global trade-to-GDP ratio of Table A5)

	1928	1938	1948	1958	1963	1968	1973	1979	1983	1990
Western Europe	1.38	1.21	1.58	1.54	1.49	1.55	1.53	1.37	1.41	1.37
United Kingdom	1.82	1.37	1.48	1.50	1.39	2.14	1.37	1.35	1.20	1.25
Continental Western Europe	1.25	0.94	1.50	1.39	1.31	1.28	1.79	1.96	1.83	1.91
Eastern Europe and Soviet Union	1.23	1.26	1.12	1.15	1.42	1.84	1.43	1.16	1.31	1.24
Europe, total	1.36	1.22	1.50	1.45	1.48	1.60	1.51	1.33	1.39	1.35
North America	0.43	0.38	0.48	0.42	0.39	0.44	0.47	0.56	0.53	0.57
North America + Mexico	0.44	0.39	0.49	0.43	0.40	0.44	0.47	0.56	0.53	0.59
Latin America	1.85	1.51	1.34	1.38	1.16	0.98	0.88	0.77	0.83	0.82
Latin America – Mexico	1.88	1.53	1.39	1.50	1.27	1.10	1.02	0.83	0.89	0.76
America, total	0.57	0.52	0.62	0.55	0.48	0.50	0.53	0.60	0.58	0.61
Asia	1.31	1.22	1.10	1.21	1.02	0.97	0.83	0.79	0.88	0.87
Japan	1.44	1.19	0.36	0.86	0.78	0.76	0.73	0.57	0.72	0.53
Australasia	1.57	1.09	2.08	1.43	1.37	1.13	1.04	0.84	0.78	0.89
Developing Asia	1.23	1.26	1.12	1.32	1.11	1.18	0.90	1.08	1.08	1.41
Africa	2.47	2.52	2.53	2.11	2.66	1.76	1.46	1.39	1.19	1.45
Middle East	2.47	2.52	2.23	2.68	1.74	1.71	1.70	1.62	1.66	1.59
World, total	1.00	1.00	1.00	1.00	1.00	1.00	1.00	1.00	1.00	1.00

Table A10 Indexes of propensity to trade intra- and extra-regionally, various country groups, 1928 to 1990 (average for merchandise exports and imports)

1928	WE	UK	CWE	EESU	TEU	NA	NA+M	LA	LA–M	TAM	TASIA	JAP	ANZ	DAS	AF	ME	World	Extra-regional
Western Europe	0.38	0.28	0.39	0.48	0.39													0.30
United Kingdom	0.29		0.29	0.17	0.28													(0.52)
Continental Western Europe	0.39	0.35	0.43	0.56	0.40													(0.19)
Eastern Europe and Soviet Union	0.41	0.21	0.50	1.31	0.48													0.25
Europe, total	0.36	0.27	0.41	0.56	0.40													0.26
North America						0.27		0.19		0.23								0.09
North America + Mexico							0.24		0.19	0.22								0.09
Latin America						1.01		0.62		0.89								0.43
Latin America – Mexico							0.92		0.69	0.85								0.44
America, total						0.24	0.24	0.23	0.23	0.25								0.10
Asia											0.83	1.19	0.28	0.79				0.21
Japan											1.37		0.25	1.65				(0.14)
Australasia											0.39	0.69	0.96	0.22				(0.38)
Developing Asia											0.82	1.55	0.24	0.72				(0.19)
Africa															1.42			0.56
Middle East																4.53		0.57
World, total																	0.45	0.21

(continued)

Table A10 *(continued)*

1938	WE	UK	CWE	EESU	TEU	NA	NA+M	LA	LA–M	TAM	TASIA	JAP	ANZ	DAS	AF	ME	World	Extra-regional
Western Europe	0.27		0.31	0.33	0.28													0.21
United Kingdom	0.20	0.15	0.20	0.22	0.14													(0.33)
Continental Western Europe	0.29	0.19	0.36	0.35	0.28													(0.15)
Eastern Europe and Soviet Union	0.34	0.32	0.35	0.65	0.37													0.23
Europe, total	0.27	0.18	0.32	0.37	0.29													0.19
North America						0.22		0.14		0.18								0.06
North America + Mexico							0.18		0.15	0.17								0.06
Latin America						0.72		0.69		0.71								0.27
Latin America – Mexico							0.66		0.83	0.61								0.26
America, total						0.19	0.18	0.20	0.22	0.20								0.07
Asia											1.27	1.23	1.23	1.22				0.07
Japan											2.53		0.98	2.68				(0.03)
Australasia											0.25	0.23	3.23	0.12				(0.11)
Developing Asia											1.35	2.15	1.17	0.98				(0.07)
Africa															0.86			0.48
Middle East																1.74		0.49
World, total																	0.43	0.15

(continued)

Table A10 (continued)

1948	WE	UK	CWE	EESU	TEU	NA	NA+M	LA	LA−M	TAM	TASIA	JAP	ANZ	DAS	AF	ME	World	Extra-regional
Western Europe	0.43	0.18	0.51	0.34	0.42													0.31
United Kingdom	0.30		0.30	0.08	0.19													(0.37)
Continental Western Europe	0.51	0.29	0.65	0.49	0.51													(0.25)
Eastern Europe and Soviet Union	0.22	0.15	0.26	2.56	0.44													0.14
Europe, total	0.37	0.18	0.46	0.71	0.43													0.27
North America						0.26		0.19		0.22								0.09
North America + Mexico							0.25		0.15	0.20								0.08
Latin America						0.69		0.51		0.62								0.27
Latin America − Mexico							0.44		1.10	0.68								0.21
America, total						0.23	0.21	0.24	0.26	0.25								0.08
Asia											0.67	1.20	0.27	0.68				0.18
Japan											0.28		0.05	0.34				(0.04)
Australasia											0.43	0.24	1.31	0.35				(0.46)
Developing Asia											0.84	1.66	0.25	0.89				(0.16)
Africa															0.63			0.49
Middle East																4.77		0.41
World, total																	0.54	0.19

(continued)

Table A10 (continued)

1958	WE	UK	CWE	EESU	TEU	NA	NA+M	LA	LA−M	TAM	TASIA	JAP	ANZ	DAS	AF	ME	World	Extra-regional
Western Europe	0.46	0.26	0.49	0.13	0.40													0.26
United Kingdom	0.28		0.28	0.05	0.19													(0.35)
Continental Western Europe	0.50	0.33	0.58	0.15	0.43													(0.24)
Eastern Europe and Soviet Union	0.11	0.06	0.12	1.90	0.40													0.11
Europe, total	0.36	0.21	0.40	0.50	0.40													0.24
North America						0.29		0.18		0.23								0.07
North America + Mexico							0.26		0.16	0.21								0.07
Latin America						0.80		0.58		0.73								0.27
Latin America − Mexico							0.80		0.72	0.77								0.29
America, total						0.23	0.25	0.22	0.21	0.24								0.07
Asia											0.83		0.52	0.85				0.18
Japan											0.53	0.79	0.20	0.60				(0.13)
Australasia											0.57	1.17	1.79	0.27				(0.27)
Developing Asia											1.07	1.10	0.59	1.18				(0.17)
Africa															0.63			0.45
Middle East																2.47		0.52
World, total																	0.57	0.16

(continued)

Table A10 *(continued)*

1963	WE	UK	CWE	EESU	TEU	NA	NA−M	LA	LA−M	TAM	TASIA	JAP	ANZ	DAS	AF	ME	World	Extra-regional
Western Europe	0.46	0.25	0.48	0.20	0.43													0.21
United Kingdom	0.30		0.30	0.14	0.23													(0.30)
Continental Western Europe	0.47	0.31	0.55	0.21	0.44													(0.19)
Eastern Europe and Soviet Union	0.12	0.09	0.13	3.96	0.52													0.09
Europe, total	0.39	0.23	0.43	0.63	0.44													0.19
North America						0.27		0.15		0.22								0.06
North America + Mexico							0.23		0.14	0.20								0.06
Latin America						0.64		0.60		0.63								0.22
Latin America − Mexico							0.63		0.79	0.67								0.24
America, total						0.21	0.21	0.20	0.20	0.21								0.07
Asia											0.85		0.47	1.05				0.13
Japan											0.57	0.53	0.45	0.60				(0.12)
Australasia											0.80	1.27	1.55	0.46				(0.23)
Developing Asia											1.24	0.76	0.37	1.77				(0.10)
Africa															0.57			0.56
Middle East																1.24		0.34
World, total																	0.60	0.14

(continued)

Table A10 *(continued)*

1968	WE	UK	CWE	EESU	TEU	NA	NA+M	LA	LA–M	TAM	TASIA	JAP	ANZ	DAS	AF	ME	World	Extra-regional
Western Europe	0.51		0.51	0.16	0.44													0.21
United Kingdom	0.23	0.30	0.23	0.08	0.18													(0.55)
Continental Western Europe	0.58	0.40	0.65	0.18	0.51													(0.13)
Eastern Europe and Soviet Union	0.17	0.08	0.19	2.92	0.61													0.16
Europe, total	0.43	0.26	0.46	0.55	0.47													0.21
North America						0.34		0.21		0.29								0.07
North America + Mexico							0.28		0.20	0.26								0.07
Latin America						0.46		0.76		0.52								0.18
Latin America – Mexico							0.48		1.03	0.58								0.20
America, total						0.22	0.22	0.26	0.27	0.24								0.07
Asia											0.60	0.74	0.41	0.52				0.15
Japan											0.31		0.33	0.31				(0.12)
Australasia											0.71	1.09	1.44	0.38				(0.19)
Developing Asia											1.09	1.69	0.38	0.89				(0.16)
Africa															0.73			0.37
Middle East																1.12		0.35
World, total																	0.61	0.15

(continued)

Table A10 *(continued)*

1973	WE	UK	CWE	EESU	TEU	NA	NA+M	LA	LA−M	TAM	TASIA	JAP	ANZ	DAS	AF	ME	World	Extra-regional
Western Europe	0.66	0.42	0.65	0.22	0.58													0.25
United Kingdom	0.45		0.45	0.10	0.34													0.35
Continental Western Europe	0.66	0.49	0.73	0.23	0.59													(0.23)
Eastern Europe and Soviet Union	0.19	0.06	0.22	3.07	0.59													0.18
Europe, total	0.55	0.36	0.58	0.64	0.58													0.24
North America						0.51		0.24		0.40								0.09
North America + Mexico							0.42		0.21	0.36								0.09
Latin America						0.58		0.81		0.64								0.22
Latin America − Mexico							0.61		1.06	0.70								0.25
America, total						0.32	0.33	0.31	0.29	0.33								0.10
Asia											0.67	0.52	0.53	0.76				0.16
Japan											0.66		0.46	0.71				(0.15)
Australasia											0.97	1.38	2.15	0.49				(0.20)
Developing Asia											0.85	0.88	0.44	0.91				(0.15)
Africa															0.73			0.39
Middle East																0.94		0.46
World, total																	0.73	0.18

(continued)

Table A10 (*continued*)

1979	WE	UK	CWE	EESU	TEU	NA	NA+M	LA	LA–M	TAM	TASIA	JAP	ANZ	DAS	AF	ME	World	Extra-regional
Western Europe	0.75	0.66	0.71	0.26	0.67													0.28
United Kingdom	0.66	0.66	0.66	0.13	0.51													(0.32)
Continental Western Europe	0.72	0.76	0.76	0.28	0.66													(0.26)
Eastern Europe and Soviet Union	0.24	0.06	0.27	3.15	0.62													0.20
Europe, total	0.62	0.55	0.63	0.71	0.66													0.26
North America						0.70		0.40		0.57								0.15
North America + Mexico							0.60		0.32	0.51								0.14
Latin America						0.66		1.01		0.75								0.22
Latin America – Mexico							0.63		1.39	0.80								0.24
America, total						0.44	0.46	0.50	0.48	0.48								0.14
Asia											0.76	0.59	0.81	0.80				0.19
Japan											0.55		0.46	0.57				(0.15)
Australasia											1.03	1.26	3.01	0.72				(0.17)
Developing Asia											1.23	1.29	1.12	1.20				(0.23)
Africa															0.60			0.48
Middle East																0.66		0.56
World, total																	0.91	0.23

(*continued*)

Table A10 (continued)

1983	WE	UK	CWE	EESU	TEU	NA	NA+M	LA	LA-M	TAM	TASIA	JAP	ANZ	DAS	AF	ME	World	Extra-regional
Western Europe	0.74	0.67	0.71	0.21	0.65													0.24
United Kingdom	0.57		0.57	0.03	0.41													(0.24)
Continental Western Europe	0.74	0.80	0.78	0.24	0.65													(0.24)
Eastern Europe and Soviet Union	0.25	0.03	0.29	2.91	0.67													0.18
Europe, total	0.61	0.54	0.62	0.70	0.65													0.23
North America						0.58		0.31		0.48								0.12
North America + Mexico							0.48		0.29	0.43								0.12
Latin America						0.62		0.88		0.67								0.22
Latin America – Mexico							0.59		1.24	0.71								0.23
America, total						0.37	0.38	0.40	0.40	0.40								0.12
Asia											0.65	0.41	0.77	0.74				0.19
Japan											0.63		0.79	0.60				(0.16)
Australasia											0.71	0.78	1.87	0.57				(0.23)
Developing Asia											0.89	0.83	0.64	0.97				(0.20)
Africa															0.38			0.37
Middle East																0.70		0.50
World, total																	0.82	0.20

(continued)

Table A10 *(continued)*

1990	WE	UK	CWE	EESU	TEU	NA	NA+M	LA	LA−M	TAM	TASIA	JAP	ANZ	DAS	AF	ME	World	Extra-regional
Western Europe	0.73	0.63	0.70	0.28	0.69													0.23
United Kingdom	0.61		0.61	0.09	0.49													(0.27)
Continental Western Europe	0.72	0.73	0.76	0.31	0.68													(0.26)
Eastern Europe and Soviet Union	0.30	0.11	0.34	4.52	0.63													0.24
Europe, total	0.65	0.58	0.67	0.67	0.68													0.22
North America						0.67		0.47		0.61								0.14
North America + Mexico							0.63		0.29	0.57								0.13
Latin America						0.72		0.97		0.76								0.25
Latin America − Mexico							0.47		1.45	0.59								0.22
America, total						0.42	0.45	0.53	0.42	0.46								0.14
Asia											0.67	0.46	0.54	0.75				0.19
Japan											0.42		0.35	0.43				(0.13)
Australasia											0.89	1.06	2.43	0.70				(0.19)
Developing Asia											1.21	1.12	0.70	1.34				(0.26)
Africa															1.21			0.47
Middle East																1.19		0.51
World, total																	0.88	0.21

Index